Real-World Programming for OS/2® 2.11

Second Edition

Derrel R. Blain

Kurt R. Delimon

William Jeffrey English

201 West 103rd Street, Indianapolis, IN 46290

This book is dedicated to our wives, Laurie, Beth, and September, each of whom is a professional in her own right. Thanks for enabling us to take the time out of our lives and the general business of living to spend even more time glued to our computers.

SECOND EDITION

International Standard Book Number: 0-672-30563-1

Library of Congress Catalog Card Number: 94-66647

97 96 95 94 5 4 3 2

Interpretation of the printing code: the rightmost double-digit number is the year of the book's printing; the rightmost single-digit, the number of the book's printing. For example, a printing code of 94-2 shows that the second printing of the book occurred in 1994.

Composed in AGaramond and MCPdigital by Macmillan Computer Publishing

Printed in the United States of America

Trademarks

Screen reproductions in this book were created by means of the program Collage Plus from Inner Media, Inc., Hollis, NH.

Publisher
Richard K. Swadley

Associate Publisher
Jordan Gold

Acquisitions Manager
Stacy Hiquet

Managing Editor
Cindy Morrow

Acquisitions Editor
Gregory S. Croy

Development Editor
Brad Jones

Software Development Specialist
Wayne Blankenbeckler

Production Editor
James Grass

Editor
Joe Williams

Editorial Coordinator
Bill Whitmer

Editorial Assistants
Carol Ackerman
Sharon Cox
Lynette Quinn

Technical Reviewer
Scott Kliger

Marketing Manager
Gregg Bushyeager

Cover Designer
Tim Amrhein

Book Designer
Michele Laseau
Alyssa Yesh

Director of Production and Manufacturing
Jeff Valler

Imprint Manager
Juli Cook

Manufacturing Coordinator
Paul Gilchrist

Production Analysts
Dennis Clay Hager
Mary Beth Wakefield

Graphics Image Specialists
Tim Montgomery
Dennis Sheehan
Susan VandeWalle

Production
Katy Bodenmiller, Elaine Brush,
Ayrika Bryant, Carol O. Bowers,
Cheryl Cameron, Elaine Crabtree,
Steph Davis, Carol Johantges
Ayanna Lacey, Shelly Palma,
Chad Poole, Sharon Provart,
Kim Scott, Marc Shecter,
Susan Shepard, SA Springer,
Scott Tullis, Michelle Worthington

Indexer
Bront Davis

Overview

Contents

Foreword

In our six years of publishing for OS/2 application developers, we have learned what programmers need: real-life, function-filled, practical programming examples. Both new and intermediate developers seem to learn best from good source code samples. Often, they will cut-and-paste, building a new application on a working base, learning as they go.

Real-World Programming for OS/2 2.11, Second Edition, understands and meets that need. This book is filled with practical, meaty tips and techniques about OS/2 programming. The authors deliver their considerable experience in the form of useful sample programs and narrative. They have tested their code on four popular OS/2 compilers, and they have provided it on a diskette for the convenience of their readers.

This book sets a new standard in practical programming. The authors are to be congratulated!

Dick Conklin
Editor
OS/2 Developer Magazine

Chapter 1

Programming for OS/2

The Nature of This Book

More than likely you bought this book because you have a programming problem to solve. That's the reason we wrote it. We know from experience that the way to start programming on a new platform and the way to solve many programming tasks is not to stand back theorizing for a couple of weeks about how it should be done. Instead, you get a good example to work from, then tear into it with your own additions and changes. Now, more than likely, your first efforts will serve only as a stepping stone for later development, but you need that initial experience to build on.

Trouble is, many times the software development kits do not have the room to provide examples for you to work with, and the last thing the world needs is another programming book showing you how to write another "Hello, World" program, only for OS/2. This book covers areas of programming that are largely ignored or poorly exemplified in software development kits and documentation. It is aimed at intermediate level programmers. This does not mean you must be an intermediate level programmer for OS/2, only that you should have the habit of analysis and be familiar with coding concepts that come with programming experience.

Again, the emphasis is on developing code and techniques directly applicable to your programming efforts. Each sample application in this book is designed as a framework on which you can base your efforts. General areas of knowledge covered are message-based architecture, working with OS/2 windows, working with fonts, working with printers, creating Dynamic Link Libraries (DLLs), interprocess coordination, menus, and drawing. Although you can work from the front to the back, it is not necessary to follow only that path. We suggest that you first work through Chapter 2, "OS/2 Application Window Fundamentals," Chapter 3, "Window Management," and Chapter 4, "Common Dialogs," consecutively. After that, you should be able to dive into the chapters that apply to your particular need.

The sample applications in this book are longer than usual, but we felt this was necessary to provide you with a useful framework. As a result, there is not a line-by-line discussion of each sample; otherwise, the book would have been huge! We suggest you first read the discussion about the concepts and important API entries at the beginning of each chapter. After that, load the working executable from the companion disk and spend some time working with it. This will help familiarize you with the general issues involved. Then, you can begin working through the code to see how the general concepts and behavior of the application have been realized.

The applications in this book use the graphical user interface facilities provided by the Presentation Manager API of OS/2. This continues to be an area in which many programmers need some assistance. Don't forget that OS/2 still allows character-based applications to run perfectly well in a window or full-screen session. These types of applications just aren't the focus of this book.

This is a book designed to help you solve some of the more difficult issues involved in creating a nontrivial program for OS/2. We have tried to address the issues that programmers frequently face—like how to open a file by using the common file dialogs and how to use multithreading.

That's what this book is, but we should also say a word about what the book is not. This is not a programming manual about how to program in C. There simply isn't room. This book also is not simply a recapitulation of the OS/2 Technical Library. We have tried to distill the essential elements. We have tried to bring together things that are sometimes located all over the documentation in several different manuals; and we hope this helps; but really this book is a collection of applications that shows how to get something done—something usually fairly complicated. We tried to go far beyond the examples you will see both in the documentation for OS/2 and for the compiler that you will be using.

You are welcome to build applications on the code that we supply with the book. We, however, do insist that you do not redistribute the software or the code from this book without substantial modification and addition on your part.

If you have not built an application for OS/2 yet with your compiler, we certainly recommend working through one of the smaller examples supplied with the compiler before tackling one of the applications in this book. This will ensure that your environment is set up correctly and will save you a considerable amount of frustration.

Each application on the disk that accompanies the book has a number of files associated with it. There is a compiled executable, along with a command file, a make file, and the C, DEF, RC, ICO, DLG, and all the other files necessary to build the application. To begin understanding the applications, we suggest you first use the compiled versions that are shipped on the disk.

Compilers Used

We wrote the sample applications for this book to be compatible with the major C compilers in the OS/2 environment. These are the Watcom, Borland, and IBM C Set/2 compilers. Each has its own characteristics, which may make one more desirable than another.

We have included MAKE files, so you may use these as models if you are still using older compilers. Believe it or not, you can still created a valid OS/2 object file using Microsoft's C6.00.

Building the Applications

The fact that a suite of applications could actually be made compatible across all these compilers says volumes about the stability of the platform and the tools developed for it. Each application has been provided with a make file that can be used to build the application for each of the compiler products. This process is described in greater detail in this chapter in the section "Building a Sample Application." You can, of course, use the integrated development environments provided with the compilers. Merely follow their instructions about where to place particular modules, switches, and so forth.

We have not focused on explaining the integrated environments for each compiler, because really these are features of the compiler, and our purpose here is showing how to program for OS/2. Programming is complicated. Integrated environments are even more complicated, with all their options for library placement, instruction set generation, and so forth. So make sure your compiler is set up, using the samples included with that product, before tackling the large projects here.

Installing Your Compiler

Each of the compilers installs in a different way. You must follow the instructions for the compiler you plan to use. Further, we suggest that you practice with some of the smaller examples provided with your compiler. This will ensure that your development environment is set up correctly before you take on some of the larger projects that accompany this book. We strongly suggest you ensure that the `PATH`, `INCLUDE`, and `LIBPATH` environment variables are set correctly.

Installing the Software

We have provided an installation program with the software. This installation program will copy the software from the companion distribution disk to your hard drive. It will also ensure that the proper directory structure to contain the software is set up on your hard drive.

To use the installation program, start an OS/2 session, either full screen or in a window. Change to the drive containing the distribution disk. Then, type this command:

```
INSTALL
```

First, the installation program will present you with the screen shown in Figure 1.1.

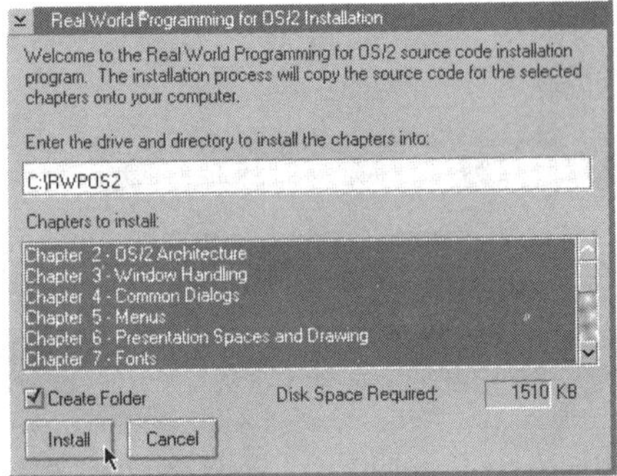

Figure 1.1.
Opening screen shot file.

You may choose which chapters to install. You may also select a checkbox to cause the installation program to place all the programs automatically in a folder on the desktop. You may also change the root directory under which the software will be installed. If you do not make a change to the default directory name, the software will be installed in a directory structure by chapter under a directory named \RWPOS2.

Once the installation has begun, you will be presented with the dialog box shown in Figure 1.2.

This dialog box will change to show the progression of the installation.

Building a Sample Application

Before building any of the samples, we suggest practicing with the sample .EXE that was installed. After your compiler is installed on your system and the sample software is installed, you are almost ready to build the samples. Notice that executable versions of the samples are shipped for each chapter. You do not have to run the make utility to use the programs. We included the make files, however, because more than likely you will want to make additions and changes to the samples.

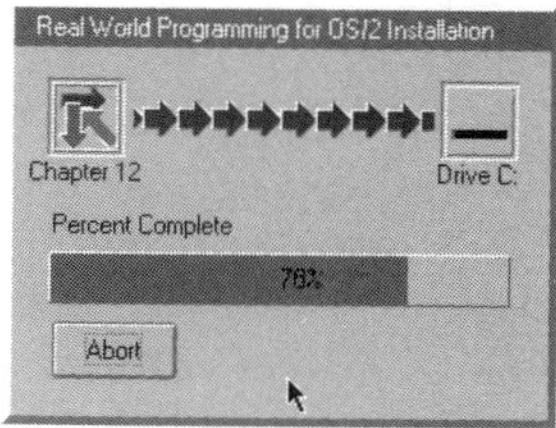

Figure 1.2.
Dialog box file.

First, before building any of the applications, you need to indicate which of the compilers you will be using to create the application. This is done by setting an environment variable for the compiler. This environment variable is used in the command file to determine which of the compilers to use to build the application for the GO command file.

To set up the environment variable use this command:

```
SET COMPILER=
```

You may choose from these:

```
BORLAND
WATCOM
IBMC
ZORTECH
CL386
```

For example, if you are using the Watcom compiler, enter this command:

```
SET COMPILER=WATCOM
```

To make it even easier, we suggest making this line a part of your CONFIG.SYS file.

There is a file common to all the applications. This is the About box. Before you can build any of the applications, this needs to be created with the compiler that you will be using. After you have set the environment variable, therefore, change to the \COMMON directory and enter the `GO` command. You are now ready to begin building the samples.

Each sample is built by using the following:

- The modules that make up the application code. These include C code modules, resources, and include files.
- The "About" dialog box from the \COMMON directory.
- A file that is a list of dependencies for each sample. This file will have the extension .DEP.
- A make file for each of the compilers.
- An OS/2 command file that starts the make process.

The SKELETON application, for example, will have these files in its installed directory:

SKELETON.DEP
SKELETON.H
SKELETON.DEF
GO.CMD
SKELETON.C
SKELETON.RC
SKELETON.OBJ
SKELETON.RES
SKELETON.MAP
SKELETON.ICO
SKELETON.EXE

To build this sample, change to the directory that contains these files and enter the following commands:

CHAP2

GO

CHAP2 is a self-extracting executable which will expand into the C, include files, and so forth. GO will cause the command file to start the build for the SKELETON application. The actual lines in the command file are as follows:

```
@ECHO -------------------------
@ECHO ¦ Skeleton Application                        ¦
@ECHO ¦ Real-World Programming for OS/2             ¦
@ECHO ¦ Copyright (c) 1994 Blain, Delimon, and English ¦
@ECHO -------------------------
@if "%COMPILER%"==""    goto nocompiler
@if %COMPILER%==CL386   set MAKECMD=nmake
@if %COMPILER%==cl386   set MAKECMD=nmake
@if %COMPILER%==BORLAND set MAKECMD=make
@if %COMPILER%==borland set MAKECMD=make
@if %COMPILER%==IBMC    set MAKECMD=nmake
@if %COMPILER%==ibmc    set MAKECMD=nmake
@if %COMPILER%==WATCOM  set MAKECMD=wmake
@if %COMPILER%==watcom  set MAKECMD=wmake
@if %COMPILER%==ZORTECH set MAKECMD=make
@if %COMPILER%==zortech set MAKECMD=make
%MAKECMD% -f ..\%COMPILER%.mak MAKEFILE=skeleton.dep
@goto done
:nocompiler
@ECHO
@ECHO »»» COMPILER environment variable must be set to compiler name
@ECHO
:done
```

The make file follows the usual structure. There is a make file for each of the compilers supported. Each of these is in the root directory where you installed the distributed files. Let's say you are using the Borland compiler. The make file for this compiler has these lines:

```
#=====================================================================
# Borland C++ for OS/2
# Compiler Definition File
# Real-World Programming for OS/2
# Copyright (c) 1994 Blain, Delimon, and English
#=====================================================================

#=====================================================================
# Inference rules
#=====================================================================

BORLANDEXEOPTS  = -m -aa -Toe -L$(LIB)
BORLANDDLLOPTS  = -m -Tod -L$(LIB)
ABOUT           = ..\common\about.obj

.c.obj :
    @echo »»»
    @echo «« Compiling $*.c using Borland options »»»
    @echo »»»
    bcc -c -K -w -D__BORLAND__ $(BORLANDOPTS) $*.c > $*.err
    type $*.err

.asm.obj :
    @echo »»»
    @echo «« Assembling $*.asm using MASM386 options »»»
    @echo »»»
    tasm -ml -mx -d__TASM__ -oi -w2 $*.asm,$*.obj;

.rc.res :
    @echo »»»
    @echo «« Running resource compiler on $*.rc »»»
    @echo »»»
    rc -r $*.rc

.def.lib :
    @echo »»»
    @echo «« Creating import library from $*.def »»»
    @echo »»»
    implib $*.lib $*.def

.obj.exe :
    @echo »»»
    @echo «« Building $*.exe using Borland options »»»
    @echo »»»
    tlink $(BORLANDEXEOPTS) c02 $(OBJS) $(ABOUT),$*.exe,$*.map ,$(LIBS)
c2 os2386,$*.def

    rc $*.res $*.exe

.obj.dll :
```

```
    @echo »»»
    @echo «« Building $*.dll using Borland options »»»
    @echo »»»
    tlink $(BORLANDDLLOPTS) $(OBJS) $(BORLANDINITOBJ),$*.dll,$*.map,$(LIBS) os2386,$*.def

    rc $*.res $*.dll

!include $(MAKEFILE)

# MEMINST.OBJ must be built this way to force the _INSTANCEDATA segment
# to be placed in a separate segment from the _DATA segment
# The -oi option of tasm creates the correct kind of object record
# for the linker
meminst.obj : meminst.c
    bcc -c -K -w -S -D__BORLAND__ -zR_INSTANCEDATA -zTFAR_DATA $(BORLANDOPTS) $*.c >
$*.err
    tasm -ml -mx -d__TASM__ -oi -w2 $*.asm,$*.obj;
    del $*.asm
```

This file, in turn, depends on a file that lists the dependencies for the particular sample being made. There is a dependency file for each sample. In the SKELETON application in Chapter 2, the dependency file is named SKELETON.DEP. It contains these lines:

```
#======================================================================
# Skeleton Dependencies Make File
# Real-World Programming for OS/2
# Copyright (c) 1994 Blain, Delimon, and English
#======================================================================

#======================================================================
# Dependencies and Build Items
#======================================================================

OBJS = skeleton.obj

all: skeleton.exe

skeleton.obj: skeleton.c skeleton.h

skeleton.res: skeleton.rc skeleton.ico

skeleton.exe: $(OBJS) skeleton.res skeleton.def
```

Heading Out on Your Own

After you have built a few of the applications just as they are installed, you can begin to modify them to suit your own purposes. We suggest making small changes at first. This will keep you from getting too far off the track.

In the first edition, we said to write if you got some work, and many of you did, so we were glad about that. We hope this new edition serves you as well.

Chapter 2

OS/2 Application Window Fundamentals

Windows

OS/2 Presentation Manager applications are organized around the concept of windows. Windows in PM applications are not simply rectangular areas on the video screen. They are sets of structures, queues, data, and characteristics that define how the application, the user, and the operating system will interact. The windows of an application are the means by which the application and the user communicate.

The operating system also communicates with the application by sending messages to the application's windows. Your application code associated with the window is responsible for responding to or processing these messages. These messages can contain input from the keyboard, or even notification from the operating system that a window should destroy itself. This interaction, the posting and processing of messages, can be complex.

Fortunately, when your application creates a window, much of the behavior of that window is defined automatically. You are then able to add code that concentrates on the particular messages and behavior that are the focus of your application.

The sample application, SKELETON, detailed in subsequent text, illustrates the creation and destruction of a simple window. However, before you can begin a line-by-line analysis of that code, you must understand some basic concepts. First to examine are the relationships that may exist among the various windows that may be on the Presentation Manager desktop. There are two fundamental relationships with which you must be concerned. One is a parent-child relationship; the other is ownership. These are independent relationships and must be understood separately.

Parent-Child Relationship

The windows open during a Presentation Manager (PM) session are organized in a hierarchy. At the top of the hierarchy is the desktop window. OS/2 creates the desktop window when PM is started. Windows created by applications running under PM make up the next level. These windows are called main windows or top-level windows. These main windows may, in turn, have other windows that belong to them. You may think of these in terms of a parent-child relationship.

For example, if you start OS/2 on your computer and then open an application, the computer's video screen will display something like Figure 2.1. One main window is open that also has a child window open. The desktop window is the parent of Draw for OS/2's main window, which is in turn the parent of the Page window.

All windows, except the desktop window, have a parent window. (There is another type of window without a parent. It is the desktop-object window, which we will return to much later.) An application designates the parent to a window when it is created. A window can have only a single parent window, but it may have any number of child windows. The operating system uses this relationship between the parent and child windows to determine several important things described later.

The rules governing parent-child window relationships apply to all windows at all times. These cannot be modified. Location and arrangement of the windows also is governed by this parent-child relationship. You can see that all main windows are siblings because they all share the common parent of the desktop window. Sibling windows may overlap. Users may arrange these sibling windows in whatever order desired. The parent window, however, will always be at the bottom of the stack. The desktop window, therefore, will always be behind all the main windows, and all the child windows of an application's main window will be in front of that main window. Figure 2.2 shows the parental hierarchy of the desktop, application windows, and a dialog window or dialog box.

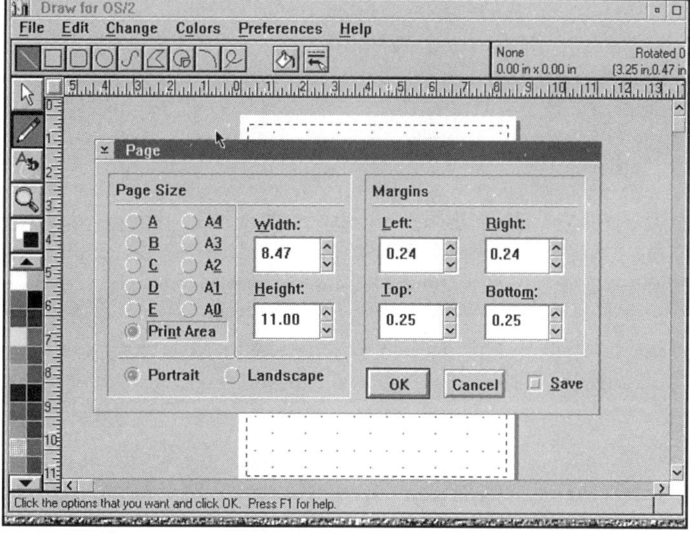

Figure 2.1.
A typical desktop.

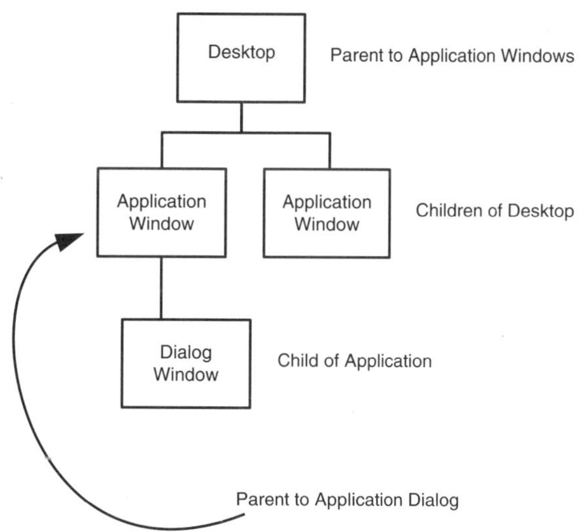

Figure 2.2.
Window parental hierarchy.

The child window is drawn relative to its parent. A main window is drawn relative to the lower-left corner of the desktop window. The child window of an application is drawn relative to the lower-left corner of its main window. A child window is never drawn outside the region of its parent window. Any part of the child window that extends outside the borders of its parent window is not drawn.

Strangely, an application may change the parent of a child window at any time using the `WinSetParent` function. When the parent window is changed, the child window is immediately redrawn inside the region of its new parent. It also takes on the styles that belong to the new parent.

The parent-child relationship also governs what happens when windows are hidden, minimized, or destroyed. When an application is terminated, every child window is destroyed before its parent. The child windows are destroyed at the lowest level of descendency up to the main parent window. When a parent window is minimized, the parent window is actually hidden. Because the parent is now hidden, none of its children are visible. The actual activity of the operating system is slightly different than IBM's official documentation implies. The operating system does not step through minimizing all the child windows. The child window takes on some of the attributes of its parent; if the parent window's visibility state changes to not visible, none of its children are visible.

When it determines a window must be redrawn, the operating system makes the determination that because none of the parents are visible, none of the descendants are visible. The `WS_VISIBLE` flag of the children's window style, however, is unchanged. Likewise, if a parent window is disabled, none of its children are enabled. The child windows are not physically changed in any way, but because of the hierarchical relationship, their display characteristics are changed in practice.

Ownership

Ownership is a relationship among windows that is independent of the parent-child relationship. Any window can have an owner window. A window may have a parent and an owner; these are not necessarily the same window. Ownership is a linkage established between windows so that they may perform tasks in a coordinated manner. Windows that are owned notify their owners of significant events, such as when the window is dragged to a new location. In another example, the `WM_MENUSELECT` message is sent from a menu window to its owner when a menu item is selected. Usually, ownership is a relationship established between a main window and its associated control windows. These control windows are such things as the titlebar, the min-max buttons, and the menu bar. In this case, `WM_CONTROL` messages are sent from a control window to its owner.

With the parent-child and ownership concepts established, you can now understand something that is often surprising to programmers new to the Presentation Manager architecture. The object that appears on the desktop that is normally thought of as the application's window is not a single entity. It is not a single window with special areas for titlebars, min-max buttons, and other controls. Instead, it is a group of windows that are related to each other by ownership.

In fact, the client area, the area in which an application may draw or display information, is actually a child window of the frame window to which it belongs. Essentially, the frame window is the border window, or the root window, where all the other control windows are attached.

Ownership is established when the window is created. `WinCreateWindow` specifies both a parent and an owner. Ownership can be changed through the `WinSetOwner` API entry. Menu windows have their ownership set based on their submenu hierarchy.

The preregistered window classes are the following:

```
WC_FRAME
WC_MENU
WC_COMBOBOX
WC_BUTTON
WC_STATIC
WC_ENTRYFIELD
WC_LISTBOX
WC_SCROLLBAR
WC_TITLEBAR
WC_MLE
WC_SPINBUTTON
WC_CONTAINER
WC_SLIDER
WC_VALUESET
WC_NOTEBOOK
```

Windows related to each other by ownership must be created within the same thread. This means they must also have the same message queue. Owner relationships are not permitted between windows created by different threads.

Messages

OS/2 is a true multitasking operating system. Because an application must share the keyboard and mouse with other applications running simultaneously on a particular system, individual applications cannot have total control of these resources. Some means is necessary to share these system resources. Further, because several applications will often be running simultaneously, some means must be provided for the operating system to communicate with them. Messages and message queues provide this means.

Messages are necessary to enable the concurrent running of applications and the sharing of the system devices. Messages are the means by which the various windows, the operating system, and the user notify each other of events. Remember, events are usually such things as keys being pressed or the mouse being clicked. Usually a message is sent to tell an application a certain event has occurred. Sometimes, the application may need to respond to this event, other times not.

Messages have a structure defined in the include file PMWIN.H, which is included by the file OS2.H. The message structure is listed in the following code. You can see that it is not difficult to understand. A message is a collection of bytes defining a handle, a message index, parameters passed with the message, and the time and mouse position when the message was generated.

The actual code that defines the message structure is as follows:

```
typedef struct _QMSG     /* qmsg */
{
```

```
   HWND     hwnd;
   ULONG    msg;
   MPARAM   mp1;
   MPARAM   mp2;
   ULONG    time;
   POINTL   ptl;
   ULONG    reserved;
} QMSG;
```

With a little thought, you can easily think of the possible sources of events that cause messages to be sent to applications. Mouse and keyboard events, such as clicking a titlebar or pressing and releasing keys, cause the operating system to send messages to the appropriate application's window. The operating system may also send messages to an application when, for example, the application needs to repaint the client area. As another example, a `WM_TIMER` message will be sent at regular intervals when a timer has been set by an application. Applications may communicate by sending messages to each other. An application may even define its own set of messages, in addition to those defined by the system, which it can use to communicate about events between its own windows.

This list of possible sources can be used to formalize the types of messages. "User-initiated messages" are created when the user presses a key, makes a menu choice, or performs some similar action. "Application-initiated messages" are generated by a window of an application when it must send a message to another window about an event or some necessary action. "System-initiated messages" occur as the result of a system event.

A message is information, a request for information, or a request for an action to be carried out by an application. If all messages had to be acted on immediately by every application, efficient coordination among applications and system resources would be nearly impossible. The message queue provides a means for messages to be posted to applications for later processing.

Every application that will be receiving and responding to messages must create a message queue. This is performed with a call to `WinCreateMsgQueue`. You do not need to know the details about the actual structure of a message queue. A message queue is a place the operating system uses to store the messages directed to an application. As you might guess, this involves a block of memory big enough to hold a certain number of messages. This size is set at the `WinCreateMsgQueue` call. The queue also has a priority system so that some messages are reordered to make their processing by the application more efficient. For example, `WM_PAINT` messages come after `WM_SIZE` messages, because you would not want to paint a window, resize it, and then paint it again.

The application is responsible for retrieving messages from its message queue. In most applications, this task is performed in a loop. Each message is retrieved, then passed to the appropriate window within the application. In the following application, this is performed with these lines:

```
while (WinGetMsg (hab, &qmsg, 0, 0, 0))
    WinDispatchMsg (hab, &qmsg);
```

The `while` loop continues until a `WM_QUIT` message is received. Each message is retrieved as a structure from the queue and then dispatched to the window. When each of these messages is retrieved, WinGetMsg returns a value of TRUE. When a WM_QUIT message is received, WinGetMsg returns a value of FALSE, and the loop exits.

An application may use the line

```
WinPeekMsg (hab, &qmsg, 0, 0, PM_NOREMOVE)
```

to check whether a message is in the queue, although we do not use that call in our sample application here. This function call returns immediately without waiting for a message. This can be used during long processing times to ensure that message response time is not being delayed by time consuming calculations. The pseudocode for something like this would read as follows:

```
while (not done doing very long spreadsheet recalculation)
{
  do recalculate the next column
  while (WinPeekMsg (hab, &qmsg, 0, 0, PM_REMOVE))
    WinDispatchMsg (hab, &qmsg)
}
```

If the message queue is empty, the operating system will cause processing for the message loop to cease until a new message appears in the queue. This allows more efficient use of the processor and its facilities.

An application may have several windows, but only one message queue is needed. Each message retrieved from the queue is a structure as defined previously that contains, among other things, the handle to the window to which the message belongs.

Messages are generally posted to the queue and processed in a first-in and first-out order. An application, though, may search for specific messages in the queue and at other times ignore whole classes of messages. This enables you to give your application considerable flexibility in responding to the messages posted to it.

The Window Procedure

The last thing you must understand before we can get to the sample code is the operation of the window procedure. The window procedure is a function that receives and processes the messages for an application. A basic application will often have only a single window procedure, although some more complex applications will have many.

Windows are defined in terms of window classes. Each window class has its own window procedure. Every instance of a window of that class will use that window procedure to process its messages. In our following SKELETON example, the window class is CLIENT, and its associated window procedure is the function ClientWndProc. This association is made with the function call WinRegisterClass. The call appears as follows:

```
WinRegisterClass (hab, szClientClass, ClientWndProc, 0, 0);
```

Notice that two of the parameters are the name of the class and the name of a window procedure. Here, we have registered a private window class. Messages that this private window class receives will always be processed by the window procedure ClientWndProc. Now, take a look at the code for the window procedure ClientWndProc. Looking at the code, it appears that ClientWndProc responds to only two messages, WM_PAINT and WM_ERASEBACKGROUND. A window procedure, however, cannot ignore any message sent to it. This, however, does not mean an application must define a response for every message it may receive. Look again at the "switch" statement in the window procedure. Besides the WM_PAINT and WM_ERASEBACKGROUND cases, it also has a default case. This default case sets a variable signifying the message was not processed. Outside the switch statement are these lines:

```
if (!bHandled)
    mReturn = WinDefWindowProc (hWnd,msg,mp1,mp2);
```

The function WinDefWindowProc passes the message back to the operating system for processing. This call must be made for every message for which the window procedure does not provide its own processing. WinDefWindowProc performs all default processing for the window.

Window Procedures Return Values

Every message processed must return the proper value defined for it. For instance, in the window procedure ClientWndProc, the processing for the message to erase the background is performed with these lines:

```
case WM_ERASEBACKGROUND:
    mReturn = MRFROMLONG(1L);
    break;
```

This causes the window procedure to return the long integer value of 1 every time it receives a WM_ERASEBACKGROUND message. This causes the area inside the frame to be repainted. If a zero is returned, the system will not repaint the area.

Later, after you have successfully compiled and executed the application, you might try deliberately returning an incorrect value. For example, try changing the return value to 0. Notice that the background is never repainted. The portion of the screen within the frame when it was first created remains there even when the window is moved.

SKELETON Application

We wrote the SKELETON application to do two things. One is to illustrate the basic components of a PM application. The other is to provide you a framework with which you can begin building your applications. If you have never written applications for the OS/2 PM environment, we suggest you spend some time studying each of these component files. The thorough knowledge you gain with these will save you much guesswork later. First, we will describe the components of the SKELETON application; then, we will work through the process of building the application.

Component Files

Many programming languages and environments have a scheme in which multiple modules are linked. OS/2 PM applications also follow that model. The components that make up a PM application, though, are more than additional code modules. Some are compiled programming code, but others are files that contain instructions for the disposition of the code in memory at runtime. Still others are bitmaps that define the appearance of the application's icon. These different components require different compilers and linkers for them to be fitted together as a working executable file. Each of these components is eventually bound into a single executable file, but this is not a linear process. It requires a number of different steps.

For example, the component files for the SKELETON application are as follows:

```
SKELETON.C
SKELETON.H
SKELETON.RC
SKELETON.DEF
SKELETON.ICO
```

Each of the readable files is listed and discussed in the following sections.

SKELETON.C

This file contains the application code to create and destroy the window that appears on the user's desktop. Here, we have used only a single C module for all the code for our application. Complex OS/2 programs may have many dozens of modules. This C file also defines the "window procedure" for the SKELETON application. This window procedure, in turn, defines the messages to which the application will process internally. The behavior of this code is described in detail as follows:

```
/* ------------------------------
Skeleton Program
Real-World Programming for OS/2
Copyright (c) 1994 Blain, Delimon, and English
------------------------------ */

#define INCL WIN
#define INCL_GPI
#include <os2.h>
#include "skeleton.h"
#include "..\common\about.h"

MRESULT EXPENTRY ClientWndProc (HWND,ULONG,MPARAM,MPARAM);

HAB   hab;
HWND  hWndFrame,
      hWndClient;
CHAR  szTitle[64];

int main()
{
```

```
  HMQ    hmq;
  QMSG   qmsg;
  ULONG flFrameFlags    = FCF_TITLEBAR ¦ FCF_SYSMENU ¦ FCF_ICON ¦ FCF_SIZEBORDER ¦
                          FCF_MINMAX ¦ FCF_MENU ¦
FCF_SHELLPOSITION ¦ FCF_TASKLIST;
  CHAR   szClientClass[] = "CLIENT";

  hab = WinInitialize (0);
  hmq = WinCreateMsgQueue (hab, 0);

  WinRegisterClass (hab, szClientClass, (PFNWP)ClientWndProc, 0, 0);
  WinLoadString (hab, 0, ID_APPNAME, sizeof(szTitle), szTitle);

  hWndFrame = WinCreateStdWindow (HWND_DESKTOP, WS_VISIBLE,
      &flFrameFlags, szClientClass, szTitle, 0, 0,
      ID_APPNAME, & hWndClient);

  while (WinGetMsg (hab, &qmsg, 0, 0, 0))
    WinDispatchMsg (hab, &qmsg);

  WinDestroyWindow (hWndFrame);
  WinDestroyMsgQueue (hmq);
  WinTerminate (hab);
  return (0);
}

MRESULT EXPENTRY ClientWndProc (HWND hWnd, ULONG msg, MPARAM mp1,
                                MPARAM mp2)
{
  HPS     hps;
  BOOL    bHandled = TRUE;
  MRESULT mReturn  = 0;

  switch (msg)
  {
    case WM_PAINT:
      hps = WinBeginPaint (hWnd,0,0);
      WinEndPaint (hps);
      break;

    case WM_ERASEBACKGROUND:
      mReturn = MRFROMLONG(1L);
      break;

    case WM_COMMAND:
      switch (LOUSHORT(mp1))
      {
        case IDM_ABOUT:
          DisplayAbout (hWnd, szTitle);
          break;
      }

    default:
      bHandled = FALSE;
      break;
```

```
   }

   if (!bHandled)
   mReturn = WinDefWindowProc (hWnd,msg,mp1,mp2);

   return (mReturn);
}
```

Understanding the Application Code

Two files together make up the applications code: the C code file SKELETON.C and its associated include file SKELETON.H.

The application must also include OS2.H. Look at the first lines of code in SKELETON.C to see the preprocessor commands, as follows:

```
#define INCL_WIN
#define INCL_GPI
#include <os2.h>
```

OS2.H is the standard highest level OS2 SDK file that includes all the other header files required. Because we don't want all the possible header files included, we use `INCL_WIN` and `INCL_GPI` to include only the Win... and Gpi... header files. This practice is used to decrease the number of header files, which speeds compile time. We could have made this even more efficient in our example by specifically saying which parts of Win... and Gpi... API we wanted. For example, `INCL_GPIREGIONS` includes only the API entry points concerned with Gpi region functions.

We suggest you take a look at the text for the OS2.H header file. This file is reproduced here so that you can see how it is organized. It's important to immediately get under the hood of OS/2 and any other system you are working with. Looking at any available information about internal code will help you better understand and program for the operating system. A table of the define statements you can use to include only certain parts of the header files is listed at the end of this section.

```
/****************************** Module Header *******************/
*                                                               *
* Copyright (c) 1987  - 1992 IBM Corporation                    *
*                                                               *
* Module Name: OS2.H                                            *
*                                                               *
* This is the top level include file that includes all          *
* the files necessary for writing an OS/2 application.          *
/***************************************************************/

#ifdef __IBMC__
#pragma checkout( suspend )
   #ifndef __CHKHDR__
      #pragma checkout( suspend )
   #endif
#pragma checkout( resume )
```

```
#endif

#ifndef __OS2_H__
#define __OS2_H__

#define OS2_INCLUDED

/* Common definitions */
#include <os2def.h>

/* OS/2 Base Include File */
#ifndef INCL_NOBASEAPI
   #include <bse.h>
#endif /* INCL_NOBASEAPI */

/* OS/2 Presentation Manager Include File */
#ifndef INCL_NOPMAPI
   #include <pm.h>
#endif /* INCL_NOPMAPI */

#endif /* __OS2__ */

#ifdef __IBMC__
#pragma checkout( suspend )
   #ifndef __CHKHDR__
      #pragma checkout( resume )
   #endif
#pragma checkout( resume )
#endif
```

You can see little that's mysterious about this file. It makes certain defines and includes a number of other include files. We suggest you use a text editor to open up some of the other important system include files. While on the subject of windows, look inside the file PMWIN.H. If you have a compiler or development kit for OS/2 installed on your system, PMWIN.H should be located in a directory with other include files for OS/2.

Includes

Use the following defines within your code to include only certain portions of the OS/2 header files.

Atom manager	INCL_WINATOM
Button controls	INCL_WINBUTTONS
Clipboard manager	INCL_WINCLIPBOARD
Country support	INCL_WINCOUNTRY
DBCS window manager definition	INCL_NLS
Desktop API	INCL_WINDESKTOP
Dialog boxes	INCL_WINDIALOGS
Entry Fields	INCL_WINENTRYFIELDS
Error code definitions	INCL_WINERRORS

Frame controls	INCL_WINFRAMECTLS
Frame manager	INCL_WINFRAMEMGR
General window management	INCL_WINWINDOWMGR
Heap manager	INCL_WINHEAP
Help manager definitions	INCL_WINHELP
Hook manager	INCL_WINHOOKS
Keyboard accelerators	INCL_WINACCELERATORS
Listbox controls	INCL_WINLISTBOXES
Load/Delete Library/Procedure	INCL_WINLOAD
Menu controls	INCL_WINMENUS
Message management	INCL_WINMESSAGEMGR
Mouse and keyboard input	INCL_WININPUT
Mouse pointers	INCL_WINPOINTERS
Multiple line entry fields	INCL_WINMLE
Rectangle routines	INCL_WINRECTANGLES
Scroll bar controls	INCL_WINSCROLLBARS
Set error info API	INCL_WINSEI
Shell data	INCL_WINSHELLDATA
Shell program list API	INCL_WINPROGRAMLIST
Shell switch list API	INCL_WINSWITCHLIST
Static controls	INCL_WINSTATICS
System values (and colors)	INCL_WINSYS
Text cursors	INCL_WINCURSORS
Thunk procedure API	INCL_WINTHUNKAPI
Timer routines	INCL_WINTIMER
WinTrackRect() function	INCL_WINTRACKRECT

The Main Procedure

The Main Procedure for most PM applications will be similar to that listed here for the SKELETON application. In general, the main procedure for OS/2 applications performs three tasks in the following order:

1. Creates a window and message queue for the application.
2. Processes messages destined for the window in a loop.
3. Destroys the window and message queue when the loop ends, then exits.

Creating the Application Window

The SKELETON application window is created when the function `WinCreateStdWindow` is called. You can see from inspecting the code that some other things are performed before this function is called. These prepare for the creation of the window.

Two things must always be done before the application's window can be created: obtain a handle to an anchor block and create a message queue.

`WinInitialize` must be the first Presentation Manager call made by any thread that uses the Presentation Manager facilities. If you are reading closely, the word "thread" may seem odd. You may have expected the word "application" instead. Most applications have a single thread, a single line of execution. OS/2, however, allows applications to have many simultaneous lines of execution. These are called threads. Each of these threads must establish their own anchor block if they will be using facilities within Presentation Manager. It is possible one of the threads in your application may have no need of PM services. Multiple threaded applications are discussed in greater detail in Chapter 14, "Threads and Semaphores."

SKELETON calls `WinInitialize` immediately after declaring some variables and before any other processing.

```
hab = WinInitialize (0);
```

`WinInitialize` takes a single parameter that must always be 0. This parameter indicates that all the messages for the window will initially be available for processing by the application. `WinInitialize` returns a handle to an anchor block.

You can think of the function `WinTerminate` as the function that corresponds to `WinInitialize`. Notice that SKELETON makes a call to `WinTerminate` as the last call in the code to a Presentation Manager API entry. `WinTerminate` ends an application's use of Presentation Manager facilities and releases all the associated resources. Notice also that SKELETON destroys all the windows and message queues before calling `WinTerminate`. If the services of PM are terminated before all these things are released, return values from the call to `WinTerminate` and those of subsequent calls are indeterminate.

Message Queues

The message queue is created for the application when it calls the function `WinCreateMsgQueue`. This is done with the following line:

```
hmq = WinCreateMsgQueue (hab, 0);
```

The input parameters for our example are the handle to the anchor block returned by `WinInitialize` and a size for the message queue. This call must be made after the call to `WinInitialize`, but before any other Presentation Manager functions are called. One message queue serves all the windows in a thread. In this example, we have only one window and one thread, so this is easy to sort out.

The function `WinCreateMsgQueue` returns a handle that can be used by `WinGetMsg` to retrieve messages from the queue. In SKELETON, this handle is assigned to the variable `hmq`. Notice, however, the call that SKELETON makes to function `WinGetMsg` uses the handle to the anchor block.

The size of the message queue can be specified by the application. The second parameter in the call to `WinCreateMsgQueue` in our SKELETON application is `0`. This does not specify a queue of length zero; it causes a queue of the default size to be created. The system default queue size has a length that allows for 10 messages.

As the application runs, the operating system receives all the input from the mouse and keyboard into its own message queue. It then converts these input events into messages and posts them to the proper application message queues. The application, during its processing, retrieves the messages from its queue and processes them. For the SKELETON example, the messages are processed for only one window with the `ClientWndProc` window procedure. Several windows, however, may be assigned to one message queue, though we have not done that here.

You should also know that if messages within the queue would be redundant, the operating system may update the message queue to shorten it. Adding messages to a message queue is called *posting a message.* The operating system does not post messages to a queue and then ignore them. For example, if posting a new message would place more than one `WM_PAINT` message in the queue, the operating system will combine the regions described by the paint messages into a single region. It then posts a `WM_PAINT` message with that larger region to the queue.

Before an application terminates, its message queues must be destroyed. This is accomplished by calling the function `WinDestroyMsgQueue`. The input parameter is the handle to the message queue returned by `WinCreateMsgQueue` at the start of the program.

Registering a Class

After getting a handle to an anchor block and creating a message queue, the SKELETON application registers a private window class for CLIENT. We have used the name CLIENT, and this is completely arbitrary. The name CLIENT is associated in the SKELETON code with the window procedure `ClientWndProc`. All windows created with the class name of CLIENT in SKELETON would use the `ClientWndProc` window procedure.

Loading a String

`WinLoadString` loads a string resource. In SKELETON.C, this function is called with this line:

```
WinLoadString (hab, 0, ID_APPNAME, sizeof(szTitle), szTitle);
```

The parameter `ID_APPNAME` identifies the string resource to be loaded. This string resource is defined in the resource file SKELETON.RC with this line:

```
ID_APPNAME        "Skeleton"
```

Take a quick look at the resource file for comparison.

This resource string is loaded into the buffer `szTitle` that is defined at the beginning of the code as 64 characters. The maximum length of this buffer is indicated with the call `sizeof(szTitle)` used as one of `WinLoadString`'s parameters. `WinLoadString` will append a terminating 0 character to the string.

You could hard code this string value into the application rather than retrieve it as a string resource. This is usually a bad practice. Placing titles, button names, and other similar strings in the resource file gives you several advantages. It saves redundantly hard coding the same values in many places in your application. It keeps these string values grouped together, making them easier to revise and compare. If your application should ever have to be translated to another language, it makes it far easier for your application to be localized.

SKELETON.H

Only a single define statement is used in this example. Some examples listed later in the book, however, have large header files.

```
/* ----------------------------------
Skeleton Header File
---------------------------------- */

#define ID_APPNAME 1
#define IDM_ABOUT 2
```

This include file does no more than define the constant `ID_APPNAME`. This constant is used both in the SKELETON.C code file and in the SKELETON.RC resource file.

SKELETON.RC

The resource script file for this application defines the application name, associates it with the skeleton icon, and defines some other characteristics described in more detail in subsequent text. Like the application code, it is an ASCII text file. It can be created by using any ASCII text editor.

The resource script file does have many syntactic similarities to C code, for instance the use of #include statements, but it is not C code. The resource file requires its own resource compiler to make the file useful in the application's executable code. A resource compiler is provided with the IBM Developer's Toolkit for OS/2. Resource compilers are also often provided with other vendors' development toolkits.

After a syntactically correct resource script file has been created, it is used as input to the resource compiler. The output from that compiler will be a file with the extension RES. This file is not readable by humans. It will be bound into the application's executable. The resources it defines, such as strings and dialog box definitions, are then available for the application to use when it is running.

Many application elements may be defined in an application's resource file, including the following:

Fonts	Fonts may be edited and created with the Font Editor, which comes as a part of the OS/2 development toolkit.
Icons	These include mouse pointers and bitmaps, as well as window icons. These may be created and edited by using the Icon Editor, which also comes with the toolkit.
Menus	Menus are also defined in the resource file.
String Tables	Tables of text strings can be defined for the application's use.
Accelerator Tables	Accelerator keys enable your users to access an action or menu choice without clicking each menu choice, for example, using Alt+H to cause general help to pop up. Tables to define these keys are created in the resource file.
Dialog Templates	Dialog boxes are frequently created in the form of templates. These may be created using the Dialog Box Editor, which comes with the OS/2 development toolkit. Often these dialog box templates are included in the resource file using the #include keyword.
Window Templates	Window templates may also be created using the dialog editor and made available to the application through the resource file.

The resource file for the SKELETON example defines only an icon and a string table. Other examples, later in the book, define considerably more.

Notice that our sample resource file also begins with the following statement:

```
#include <os2.h>
```

This is frequently necessary because many of the symbolic names used in resource script files may actually be defined in the C include file. This may seem odd—mixing of file types—so do not be confused. Although it is generally associated with C code, the include file is often processed by a preprocessor before the compiler even looks at it. That is the case here for the resource compiler as well. The include file OS2.H is also processed by a preprocessor for use in the resource file before the resource compiler begins working with the resource file.

Notice also that our sample file also uses another C include file, SKELETON.H. This is a file that is also used by the application code. It defines `ID_APPNAME` to have the value of `1`. Again, this is another arbitrary value. The next line in the file is as follows:

```
ICON ID_APPNAME SKELETON.ICO
```

The `ICON` keyword designates the resource identifier `ID_APPNAME`—which follows `ICON`—as an icon resource. In every case, the symbolic name that follows the keyword must be defined as an integer constant. This definition for our sample here is accomplished in the include file SKELETON.H.

```
/* --------------------------------
Skeleton Resource File
Real-World Programming for OS/2
Copyright (c) 1994 Blain, Delimon, and English
-------------------------------- */

#include <os2.h>
#include "skeleton.h"

ICON ID_APPNAME SKELETON.ICO

STRINGTABLE LOADONCALL MOVEABLE
BEGIN
    ID_APPNAME      "Skeleton Application"
END

MENU ID_APPNAME
{
    MENUITEM "~About", IDM_ABOUT
}

rcinclude ..\common\about.dlg
```

After the icon definition, a string table is defined. This is signaled by the keyword `STRINGTABLE`. String tables are used to incorporate text into the application's executable. This text is then available for use in many different ways including menu bars, error messages, and so forth.

The string table for the SKELETON application has only a single entry. The string "Skeleton" is associated with the identifier `ID_APPNAME` that was defined in the include file SKELETON.H. Notice, the string table is delimited by the keywords `BEGIN` and `END`. By the way, the curly brackets { and } can be substituted for `BEGIN` and `END`.

Compiling SKELETON.RC

The resource file must be compiled before it can be bound to the executable file. This compilation is accomplished with the resource compiler. A resource compiler is provided with the OS/2 toolkit. Resource compilers may also be provided by a third-party compiler vendor.

If you are using an integrated development environment, like that supplied by Borland, this compilation may be handled automatically. Although you do not generally compile the resource file by hand, take the time to do that now to get some practice. For example, be sure the resource compiler is in the same directory as SKELETON.RC, or that it is in a directory that's in your path statement. Then, on the command line at an OS/2 prompt, enter this command:

```
RC -h
```

The output you see should be similar to this:

```
Operating System/2  Resource Compiler
```

```
Version 2.01.000 Feb 09 1993
(C) Copyright IBM Corporation 1988-1993
(C) Copyright Microsoft Corp. 1985-1993
All rights reserved.


Creating binary resource file skeleton.RES
RC:  RCPP -E -D RC_INVOKED -f skeleton.rc -ef d:\os2\RCPP.ERR
-I E:\ibmcpp\include -I D:\TOOLKT21\C\OS2H -I D:\TOOLKT21\C\OS2H\VDD
-I D:\TOOLKT21\ASM\OS2INC -I d:\toolkt21\os2bin
Error opening file ..\common\about.dlg
```

You can see that using the `-h` option causes the resource compiler to write out the options available to you. Now, enter this command:

```
RC SKELETON.RC
```

Because no executable name is provided, the resource script file will be converted to its compiled .RES version. Your output should look similar to this:

```
Operating System/2  Resource Compiler
Version 2.01.000 Feb 09 1993
(C) Copyright IBM Corporation 1988-1993
(C) Copyright Microsoft Corp. 1985-1993
All rights reserved.


Creating binary resource file skeleton.RES
RC:  RCPP -E -D RC_INVOKED -f skeleton.rc -ef d:\os2\RCPP.ERR
-I E:\ibmcpp\include -I D:\TOOLKT21\C\OS2H -I D:\TOOLKT21\C\OS2H\VDD
-I D:\TOOLKT21\ASM\OS2INC -I d:\toolkt21\os2bin

skeleton.rc....
Writing resources to OS/2 v2.0 Linear .EXE file
Writing 1 DEMAND resource object(s)
  Writing:  1680 bytes in 1 page(s)
    1.1 (1010 bytes)
    1.3 (23 bytes)
    10000.4 (586 bytes)
    1.5 (54 bytes)
Writing Extended Attributes:  Default Icon
Writing Extended Attributes:  Checksum
```

Look in the directory that contained the resource script file. You should see a file with an .RES extension with a recent file creation time. This .RES file contains the compiled resource that would be bound to the application's executable file.

SKELETON.DEF

Presentation Manager applications need a module definition file. This file is used for creating application programs and for creating Dynamic Link Libraries (DLLs). For our example, we are

interested in the file's use for creating PM programs. This file is utilized at the linking stage when building your application to define some specifics about the disposition of your code when it is run.

This file is an ASCII text file with the extension .DEF. It can be created by using any text editor. The syntax for module definition files contains a limited number of keywords. Before we list all those, take a look at the module definition file for the SKELETON sample. It contains these lines:

```
NAME           SKELETON   WINDOWAPI
DESCRIPTION    'Skeleton Program  Blain, Delimon, & English, 1994'
STACKSIZE      32768
EXPORTS        ClientWndProc
               AboutDlgProc
```

You can see at a glance that each line begins with a keyword followed by a value or a string. The first line, which begins with the keyword `NAME`, assigns the module the name SKELETON. This is followed by the keyword `WINDOWAPI`, which designates this application is a full Presentation Manager application. It does not simply run in a text window or full-screen session.

The next line begins with the keyword `DESCRIPTION`. The string that follows it becomes a part of the application's executable. You can take a look at this string's location in the actual executable file by using a HEX editor.

The line

```
STACKSIZE      32768
```

indicates that 32KB of memory are to be set aside for use as the application's stack. The recommended minimum stack size for Presentation Manager applications is 8KB. Recall that the stack is the area in which local variables along with passed parameters are kept.

The last line in our sample module definition file begins with the keyword `EXPORTS`. This keyword is not needed here because we are generating an executable file. OS/2 is able to find `ClientWndProc` because its address was given during the call to `WinRegisterClass`. The function does not need to be exported as it needed to be in prior versions of OS/2. The `EXPORT` keyword is now used to allow functions in DLLs to be resolved by the loader when the DLL is loaded. As a result, it is necessary for DLLs, but it is not required for executables. The string that follows `EXPORTS` is the name of the windows procedure used by SKELETON. Look in the code SKELETON.C to see where `ClientWndProc` is defined. Notice that no function header is in SKELETON.C. `ClientWndProc` is called by the operating system with the messages that it should process for its associated window.

SKELETON.ICO

This is a bitmap which is used as the application's icon. It was created by ICONEDIT. ICONEDIT is provided with OS/2, but there are many different third-party resource editors

you could use. Notice that we refer to the icon as a "resource." This is the customary terminology. Icons, bitmaps, and cursors are frequently referred to as resources for the application. Do not confuse this with the resource file that has an entirely separate use. Icons, cursors, and bitmaps are, of course, displayed. Resource files are used to provide things such as string tables, accelerator tables, and more to the executable code.

Using the Skeleton Application

Double-click the SKELETON icon to start the application. The application window for the SKELETON application should appear as in Figure 2.3.

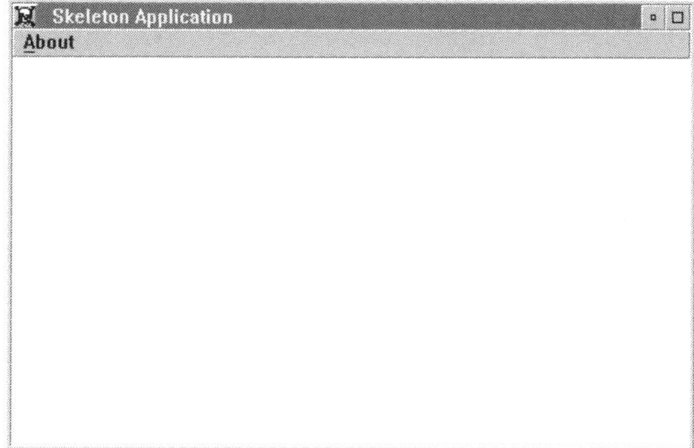

Figure 2.3.
The SKELETON application window.

Beyond adding the SKELETON application to a window and double-clicking to open its main window, there is little more that can be done with it. It is important, however, as a basis for learning. Consider each of the features that are a part of the main window, such things as the titlebar, the system menu, and others. Compare these features with that part of the code that caused them to be included with the frame window. You may even try adding some additional capability. For example, you might include the frame control flag for a vertical scroll bar and then rebuild the application's executable file.

You may want to use the code for the SKELETON application as a basis for further experimentation. Spend some time adding features or changing window styles to familiarize yourself with programming for OS/2.

Useful Window Reference Material

Some of the common functions, flags, and identifiers used in conjunction with windows under Presentation Manager are listed in the following text. This is not an exhaustive list by any means, because you can quickly see that the OS/2 technical documentation is much larger—so much larger, in fact, that it is sometimes difficult for a programmer new to OS/2 to know where to begin. Therefore, we have listed some of the more common items of interest here. Familiarizing yourself with these will help you with future application development.

Common Window Functions

The following is a list of commonly useful window functions. These are grouped by their general area of use and each is followed by a short description. For a detailed reference about each function, please refer to either the paper documentation or the online help for the OS/2 programming toolkit.

Creation and Destruction of Windows

WinCreateWindow

Use this function to create a window. It has a more general form than `WinCreateStdWindow`.

WinCreateStdWindow

Use this function to create one of OS/2's standard windows.

WinDestroyWindow

Destroys a window. All the window's child windows are also destroyed. Resources used by the windows are also freed.

Visibility of Windows

WinIsWindowShowing

Use this function to find out whether any part of a window is currently displayed. This function returns `TRUE` only if part of the window is physically displayed, not if the window is simply marked visible by the operating system.

WinShowWindow

Use this function to change the state of visibility for a window.

Sizing and Positioning of Windows

WinSetWindowPos

Use this function to position a window on the display. The window is positioned in terms of its parent's lower-left corner. This function also has a number of options for such things as hiding, maximizing, deactivating, and other similar operations.

WinQueryWindowPos

Use this function to get the size and position of a particular window.

WinGetMinPosition

Use this function in conjunction with `WinSetWindowPos`. `WinGetMinPosition` returns the available spot to which a window may be minimized. Then use `WinSetWindowPos` to minimize the window.

WinSetMultWindowPos

Use this function to change the position of several windows with a single function call. All windows to be repositioned with this call must have the same parent.

WinQueryWindowRect

Use this function to obtain the coordinates of a window rectangle. These are measured in terms of the window itself. The lower-left has the value pair 0,0. The upper-right is measured in terms of window coordinates. This effectively yields the window coordinates.

WinMapWindowPoints

Call this function to obtain the coordinates of a window mapped relative to the coordinates of another window.

Relationships Among Windows

WinSetParent

Use this function to change the parent window of a window. The descendent of a window cannot be made the parent of that same window.

WinQueryWindow

Use this function to return the handle to a window that has one of the following relationships to the input window handle:

Next window in the z-order
Previous window in the z-order
Top child window
Bottom child window
Window owner
Window parent

Z-order is simply the relative layer in which windows lie on the desktop. Window handles with other more complicated relationships may also be obtained with this function.

WinSetOwner

Use this function to change the owner of a window. You may use the input constant `NULLHANDLE` to mark a window as "disowned."

WinBeginEnumWindows

Use this function to enumerate the child windows for a window. Use in conjunction with `WinGetNextWindow` call to obtain the handles to the child windows in z-order.

WinGetNextWindow

See `WinBeginEnumWindows` in preceding text.

WinEndEnumWindows

Ends the child window enumeration process.

WinIsChild

Use this function to determine if one window is the child of another.

WinQueryDesktopWindow

Use this function to obtain the handle to the desktop window. You may also use the constant `HWND_DESKTOP` as input for many window functions, rather than explicitly obtaining this handle.

WinQueryObjectWindow

Use this function to obtain the handle to the desktop object window.

WinWindowFromID

Use this screen function to get the handle of a child window using a specific ID, which was assigned at creation.

WinWindowFromPoint

Use this function to get the handle of a window that is below a specific point and a descendent window of the input window handle.

WinMultWindowFromIDs

Use this function to obtain an array of handles to all the child windows of a specified window.

Window Input Functions

WinQueryActiveWindow

Use this function to obtain the handle to the active window.

WinSetActiveWindow

Use this function to make a frame window the active window.

WinQueryFocus

Use this function to obtain the handle to the window that has the focus.

WinSetFocus

Use this function to give the specified window the input focus.

WinQuerySysModalWindow

Use this function to obtain the handle to the current system modal window. Modal windows force the user to complete processing within that window before continuing.

WinSetSysModalWindow

Use this function to make a window a system-modal window. Other windows are not alerted when the system-modal state is entered. You may also use this function to end the system-modal state. A system modal window prevents interaction with other windows on the desktop.

WinStartApp

Use this function to start another application from within a window. A handle to the application started is returned to the window. The message `WM_APPTERMINATENOTIFY` is posted to the window's message queue when the application terminates.

WinTerminate

When a thread within your application has finished processing, use this function to terminate its use of Presentation Manager's facilities. All windows and message queues created by the thread must be destroyed first, before calling `WinTerminate`.

WinTerminateApp

Use this function to terminate an application that was started from within a window using the `WinStartApp` function. This function must be called from within the same process that called `WinStartApp`.

Window Word Data

WinQueryWindowUShort

Use this function in conjunction with an input index to obtain a specific value from the window word's memory of a window. You may obtain such things as the y coordinate to which the window is minimized, or the window's ID.

WinSetWindowUShort

This function is similar to `WinQueryWindowUShort`, except it is used to set a value within the window word's memory.

WinQueryWindowULong

This function is similar to `WinQueryWindowUShort` in use. Use it to obtain values for such things as window style or default push button for a dialog.

WinSetWindowULong

This function is similar to `WinQueryWindowULong`, except it is used to set a value within the window word's memory.

WinQueryWindowPtr

Use this function to obtain a pointer value from the window word's memory.

WinSetWindowBits

Use this function to set individual bits within a window word's memory. This function can also set bits in the form of a mask.

Standard Window Classes

Window classes may be public or private. Public window classes have a re-entrant window procedure that resides in a DLL. Public window classes may be used by any process to create windows. OS/2 provides a number of public window classes, listed in the following text. Private window classes are registered by individual applications for their own use. The window procedure resides either in the application code or in a DLL of the application.

The standard window classes are as follows:

WC_BUTTON	Defines buttons and boxes for the user to click with the mouse.
WC_CONTAINER	Groups objects in a logical manner.
WC_ENTRYFIELD	Single line of text, editable by the user.
WC_FRAME	Window class that generally contains child windows of the other classes listed here.
WC_LISTBOX	Contains a list of text items from which the user may make a selection.
WC_MENU	Presents a list of items to be used as a menu. Generally provides a command interface for the user to utilize with the application.
WC_NOTEBOOK	Presents a control displayed as a stack of pages.
WC_SCROLLBAR	Enables the user to scroll the contents of another window associated with the scroll bar.
WC_SLIDER	Presents a control that the user may utilize to select among a range of values.
WC_SPINBUTTON	Presents the user with a spinner control.
WC_STATIC	Window class that displays items with which no interaction is needed.
WC_TITLEBAR	Presents the user with a title or caption. It also enables the user to move its owner.
WC_VALUESET	Presents a set of mutually exclusive values the user may select. It is similar to a radio button control.

Class Styles

Every window class may have one or more class styles. These indicate to the system which characteristics the window will have when created. Class styles for private window classes are set when the class is registered. After a class is registered, the application cannot change its style. Notice that these characteristics apply to a "class" of windows. Characteristics, within some limitations, may be set for individual windows using the window styles, listed in a following section.

CS_CLIPCHILDREN	Prevents a window from painting over its children. This is useful in working with dialogs.
CS_CLIPSIBLINGS	Use this to prevent sibling windows from painting over each other.
CS_FRAME	Use this to designate the window as a frame window.
CS_HITTEST	The window will receive HITTEST messages whenever the mouse is moved in the window.

`CS_MOVENOTIFY`	The window will receive `WM_MOVE` messages whenever the window is moved.
`CS_PARENTCLIP`	Prevents child window from painting on its parent window.
`CS_SAVEBITS`	This causes the system to save the area under the window as a bitmap. When the window is hidden or moved, the image is replaced from memory, rather than repainted by the application. This can improve performance, at the expense of memory.
`CS_SIZEREDRAW`	This causes the window to be invalidated and to receive a `WM_PAINT` message when it is resized. This forces the whole area to be redrawn, rather than only a part.
`CS_SYNCPAINT`	This forces `WM_PAINT` messages to be sent to the window any time part of the window becomes invalid. Otherwise, the window would receive `WM_PAINT` messages only when no other messages are waiting to be processed.

Standard Window Styles

Windows may have a number of different styles. Whereas class styles apply to every window of a particular class, window styles apply to individual windows. The OS/2 operating system has a number of styles that it provides for windows. The more common styles are listed here:

`WS_CLIPCHILDREN`	The child windows descended from the window will not be painted over.
`WS_CLIPSIBLINGS`	Sibling windows of the window will not be painted over.
`WS_DISABLED`	This causes a window to reject input.
`WS_MAXIMIZED`	The window is enlarged to its maximum size.
`WS_MINIMIZED`	The window is reduced to the size of an icon.
`WS_PARENTCLIP`	The clip region of a window is extended to include the area of the parent window.
`WS_SAVEBITS`	This causes the system to save the area under the window as a bitmap. When the window is hidden or moved, the image is replaced from memory, rather than repainted by the application. This can speed performance, again at the expense of memory.
`WS_SYNCPAINT`	This causes `WM_PAINT` messages to be sent to the window immediately after any part of it becomes invalid.
`WS_VISIBLE`	This causes the window to be made visible. The window will be displayed if it can be.

Dialog Manager Styles

WS_GROUP	In the case when the user may move from control to control in a dialog box by using the arrow keys, this value designates which control is the first control.
WS_TABSTOP	Each control that has WS_TABSTOP as a style will receive keyboard focus in turn as the user presses Tab.

Frame Control Flags

FCF_ACCELTABLE	An accelerator table from the resource file will be loaded for this window; therefore, of course, one must be made available.
FCF_AUTOICON	This optimizes performance. When the operating system redraws iconized frames, the icon will be redrawn, but no WM_PAINT message will be sent to the application.
FCF_BORDER	The window is drawn with a thin border.
FCF_DLGBORDER	The window is drawn with a standard border.
FCF_HIDEBUTTON	This includes a hide button as one of the frame controls.
FCF_HIDEMAX	This includes hide and maximize buttons with the frame controls.
FCF_HORZSCROLL	A horizontal scroll bar is created with the window.
FCF_ICON	This causes an icon to be associated with the window. This is the icon displayed when the window is minimized.
FCF_MAXBUTTON	A maximize button is created with the window.
FCF_MENU	An application menu is created with the window.
FCF_MINBUTTON	A minimize button is created with the window.
FCF_MINMAX	Minimize and maximize buttons are created with the window.
FCF_NOBYTEALIGN	When this flag is NOT set, optimizations such as moving the window in 8 pel increments are performed. Setting the flag causes the optimizations not to be performed.
FCF_NOMOVEWITHOWNER	The window that has this flag set will not be moved when its owner is moved.

`FCF_SHELLPOSITION`	When the window is created, its size and position will be determined by the OS/2 shell. The application does not have to explicitly state these size and position values.
`FCF_SIZEBORDER`	A sizing border is created with the window.

`FCF_STANDARD`	This frame control flag is the equivalent of a number of the other frame control `OR`ed together. As its name implies, this is the single frame control flag that will be used most often. It is the equivalent of the following flags all `OR`ed together:
	`FCF_ACCELTABLE`
	`FCF_ICON`
	`FCF_MAXBUTTON`
	`FCF_MENU`
	`FCF_MINBUTTON`
	`FCF_SHELLPOSITION`
	`FCF_SIZEBORDER`
	`FCF_SYSMENU`
	`FCF_SYSMODAL`
	`FCF_TASKLIST`
	`FCF_TITLEBAR`

`FCF_SYSMENU`	A system menu is created with the window.
`FCF_TASKLIST`	The flag causes the program title and the frame window text to be concatenated. This concatenated text is used as the window title and in the task list.
`FCF_TITLEBAR`	A titlebar is created with the window.
`FCF_VERTSCROLL`	A vertical scroll bar is created with the window.

Frame Control Identifiers

These are the system defined identifiers given to control windows:

`FID_CLIENT`	Client window.
`FID_HORZSCROLL`	Horizontal scroll bar.
`FID_MENU`	Menu.
`FID_MINMAX`	Minimize and maximize buttons.
`FID_SYSMENU`	System menu.
`FID_TITLEBAR`	Titlebar.
`FID_VERTSCROLL`	Vertical scroll bar.

Predefined Window Handles

Certain window handles must be accessed often within Presentation Manager code. A number of constants for specific windows are in the following list. The handles could be explicitly obtained by making a function call, but using these constants is more convenient.

`HWND_DESKTOP`	Desktop window.
`HWND_OBJECT`	Desktop object window.
`HWND_TOP`	Extreme top window.
`HWND_BOTTOM`	Extreme bottom window.

Chapter 3

Window Management

Introduction

The first window created by OS/2 at start-up is the window known as the *desktop object window*. The desktop object window serves as a base window for applications and system usage, but is never displayed. Because it can never become visible, none of its descendants can be visible. This object window, referred to as HWND_OBJECT, can be used as the parent and/or owner of any window that acts as a "server" window or that must be temporarily disconnected from its window family tree without being destroyed. The identifier HWND_OBJECT can be used whenever the object window is used, or you can query the actual object window handle by using the WinQueryObjectWindow API:

```
HWND hWndObjectWindow = WinQueryObjectWindow (HWND_DESKTOP);
```

The second window created by PM at start-up is the window known as the *desktop window*. This window is also known as the "workplace" window. This window serves as the base window for applications and is always visible. It is responsible for painting the screen background and serves as the parent of all top-level windows. The desktop window, referred to as HWND_DESKTOP, can be used as the parent and/or owner of any window. The identifier HWND_DESKTOP can be used when the desktop window is used, or you can query the actual desktop window handle by using the WinQueryDesktopWindow API:

```
HWND hWndDesktopWindow = WinQueryDesktopWindow (hAB, NULL);
```

Windows created as children of HWND_OBJECT are called *object windows.* Windows created as children of HWND_DESKTOP are called *top-level windows.* All windows that your application creates are descendants of one of these two windows.

The Family Tree

All windows have both a parent and an owner window. These relationships establish how the window is drawn and how the window interacts with other windows. The most important relationship in determining the appearance of a window is the parent-child relationship. A child can never draw outside the boundary of its parent. Its coordinates are specified relative to the parent's lower-left corner. All children with the same parent are called siblings. For example, the top-level window of all applications are children of the desktop window; therefore, all these top-level windows are also siblings of each other.

Because it is possible for windows to overlap one another, there must be some defined order for how and when windows are drawn. Parent windows are always drawn before their children. Sibling windows are drawn based on what is called the z-order of the windows. The z-order is an ordering, or stacking, of the sibling windows. You can imagine the z-order by picturing the windows from the side of the screen and seeing the sibling windows as being stacked from bottom to top. The top half of Figure 3.1 shows four overlapping sibling windows. The bottom half of the figure shows how they might appear from the side. The windows are drawn from bottom to top based on the z-order.

All windows created by an application define both a parent window and an owner window. The owner window can be NULL. After the windows have been created, it is possible to query the handle of the parent:

```
HWND hWndParent = WinQueryWindow (hWndChild, QW_PARENT);
```

the handle of the owner:

```
HWND hWndOwner = WinQueryWindow (hWndOwnee, QW_OWNER);
```

or the handle of any child with a given identifier (for example ID_CHILD):

```
HWND hWndChild = WinWindowFromID (hWndParent, ID_CHILD);
```

You can also query the sibling windows in a sequence based on their z-order. The extreme top child window can be queried:

```
HWND hWndTopMostChild = WinQueryWindow (hWndParent, QW_TOP);
```

or the extreme bottom child window can be queried:

```
HWND hWndBottomMostChild = WinQueryWindow (hWndParent, QW_BOTTOM);
```

Starting with the extreme top child window, you can query the child window below that window (in z-order):

```
HWND hWndNextChildBelow = WinQueryWindow (hWndChild, QW_NEXT);
```

You can continue using the `QW_NEXT` parameter until the `WinQueryWindow` call returns zero, which indicates the extreme bottom window has been reached. Likewise, if you start with the extreme bottom child window, you can query the child window above that window (in z-order):

```
HWND hWndNextChildAbove = WinQueryWindow (hWndChild, QW_PREV);
```

You can continue using the `QW_PREV` parameter until the `WinQueryWindow` call returns zero, which indicates the extreme top window has been reached.

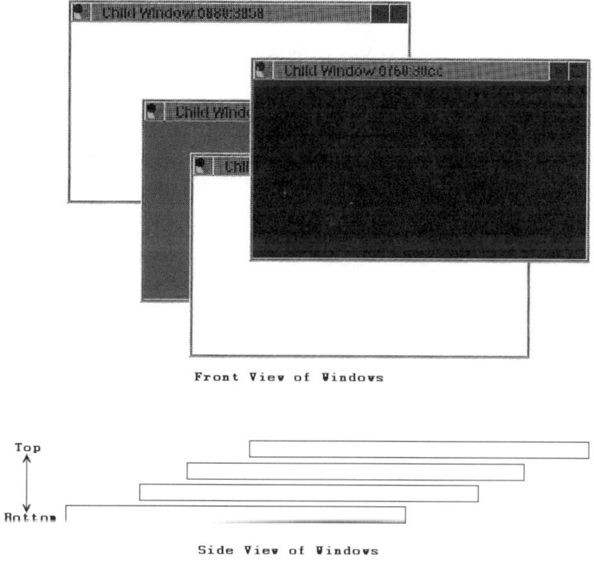

Figure 3.1.
Z-order relationship of sibling windows.

It is also possible to enumerate all the siblings of a window one at a time within what is called a window enumeration loop. To start window enumeration, use the `WinBeginEnumWindows` function. This function will take a "snapshot" of the list of child windows for the specified window handle. Then use `WinGetNextWindow` to retrieve each child window. When you are through enumerating, call `WinEndEnumWIndows` to release the list of child windows. This method enumerates the windows in z-order from extreme top to extreme bottom.

The following function can be used to enumerate all the descendants of a window:

```
VOID EnumerateDescendants (HWND hWndParent)
{
    HENUM hEnum;
    HWND  hWndChild;

    hEnum = WinBeginEnumWindows (hWndParent);

    while ((hWndChild = WinGetNextWindow (hEnum)) != 0)
    {
        ...
        EnumerateDescendants (hWndChild);
    }

    WinEndEnumWindows (hEnum);

    return;
}
```

To enumerate all windows in the system, call this function with `HWND_DESKTOP`:

```
EnumerateDescendants (HWND_DESKTOP);
```

To move a window in front of another sibling, you must change its z-order. The z-order of windows can be modified by calling `WinSetWindowPos` and by using the `SWP_ZORDER` flag:

```
WinSetWindowPos (hWnd, hWndAfter, 0L, 0L, 0L, 0L, SWP_ZORDER);
```

The window `hWnd` is positioned below `hWndAfter`. The predefined constants `HWND_TOP` and `HWND_BOTTOM` can be used to specify that the window be positioned at the top of the z-order or the bottom of the z-order.

The parent and owner of a window are defined when a window is created. Both of these, however, can be changed at any time with the `WinSetParent` and `WinSetOwner` functions. Changing the parent causes the window's position to change relative to the new parent. The `WinSetParent` API is used to change the parent of a particular window:

```
BOOL bRedraw = TRUE;
WinSetParent (hWndChild, hWndNewParent, bRedraw);
```

This will change the parent of `hWndChild` to be `hWndNewParent`. The `bRedraw` para-meter tells PM whether it should redraw the child window when the parent window is changed. You should set the `bRedraw` parameter to `FALSE` if the functions immediately following will cause either further changes in the window or the window to be painted. Changing the owner of a window changes the window that receives the notification messages from the child. The `WinSetOwner` API is used to change the owner of a particular window:

```
WinSetOwner (hWndChild, hWndNewOwner);
```

This will change the owner of hWndChild to be hWndNewOwner. All notification messages sent from hWndChild will then be sent to hWndNewOwner.

If you have the window handle and want to determine whether that window is a descendant of a particular parent window, use the WinIsChild API:

```
BOOL bChild = WinIsChild (hWndChild, hWndParent)
```

The WinIsChild function will return TRUE if hWndChild is a descendant of hWndParent or is equal to hWndParent (a window can be a child of itself). A window handle can be validated with the WinIsWindow API:

```
HAB hab;
BOOL WinIsWindow (hab, hWnd);
```

The WinIsWindow function will return FALSE if the window handle is no longer a valid window and TRUE if the window handle is valid.

A Look at the Frame Window

Most applications will create at least one window that serves as the main window for the application. This window is usually a frame window and in most cases serves as the central coordinator for the application. (See Figure 3.2.) To properly manipulate and coordinate the window activity, it's important to understand the relationship of the frame window to all its frame control windows. The window class WC_FRAME is defined by PM. Windows created with class WC_FRAME are responsible for sizing, positioning, and coordinating all the frame controls. A frame window is created with a call to WinCreateStdWindow. The frame control flags tell PM what frame controls to create as children of this frame window.

Figure 3.2.
A frame window and control window identifiers.

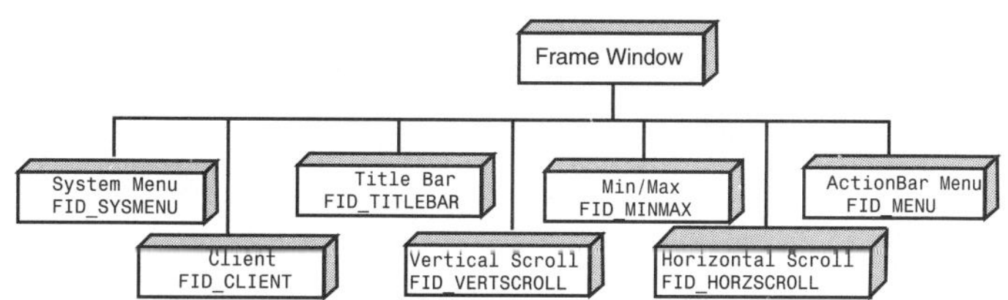

Each of these control windows has a window class predefined by PM except for the client window that is defined by your application. The sizing and positioning of these controls is handled by the frame window and notification messages are sent to each window to tell them the specifics. It is possible to alter the behavior, position, and appearance of these controls by processing some of the messages sent to the frame window, but we will discuss that later in this chapter.

In Chapter 2, "OS/2 Application Window Fundamentals," we showed how to create a frame window and its controls with the WinCreateStdWindow call:

```
ULONG flFrameFlags     = FCF_TITLEBAR ¦ FCF_SYSMENU ¦ FCF_SIZEBORDER ¦
                         FCF_MINMAX   ¦ FCF_SHELLPOSITION ¦
                         FCF_TASKLIST ¦ FCF_ICON;
HWND  hWndClient;

hWndFrame = WinCreateStdWindow (HWND_DESKTOP, WS_VISIBLE,
    &flFrameFlags, "CLIENT", "Test App", 0, NULL, 100, &hWndClient);
```

This creates a frame window with the following frame control windows: titlebar, system menu, minmax, and client. Alternately, you can use the WinCreateWindow API to create a window of class WC_FRAME. When you do this, you must pass a pointer to a FRAMECDATA structure for the class-specific data in the WinCreateWindow call. The FRAMECDATA is defined as follows:

```
typedef struct _FRAMECDATA {
   USHORT  cb;
   ULONG   flCreateFlags;
   HMODULE hmodResources;
   USHORT  idResources;
} FRAMECDATA;

cb              size of the FRAMECDATA structure
flCreateFlags   frame control flags
hmodResources   module handle for resources
idResources     identifier of resources
```

To create a frame window in this way, you first fill in the FRAMECDATA fields and pass this information to WinCreateWindow:

```
FRAMECDATA FrameData;
FrameData.cb = sizeof(FRAMECDATA);
FrameData.flCreateFlags = FCF_TITLEBAR ¦ FCF_SYSMENU ¦ FCF_SIZEBORDER ¦
                          FCF_MINMAX   ¦ FCF_SHELLPOSITION ¦
                          FCF_TASKLIST ¦ FCF_ICON;
FrameData.hmodResources = NULL;
FrameData.idResources   = 100;

hWndFrame = WinCreateWindow (hWndParent, WC_FRAME, "Frame Title",
    0L, 0, 0, 0, 0, NULL, HWND_TOP, 100,
    (PVOID)(PFRAMECDATA)&FrameData, NULL);
```

This creates the frame window and the specified control windows. It does not create a client window. With the frame window created, you then create the client window for this frame by using the client window's class and an identifier of FID_CLIENT:

```
hWndClient = WinCreateWindow (hWndFrame, "CLIENT", NULL,
    0L, 0, 0, 0, 0, NULL, HWND_BOTTOM, FID_CLIENT, NULL, NULL);
```

To prevent unnecessary repainting and resizing during the creation process, the frame window is created without the WS_VISIBLE style bit. After the window and all its children have been created, call WinShowWindow to make it visible:

```
WinShowWindow (hWndFrame, TRUE);
```

The window handles of the frame control windows can be queried by using the `WinWindowFromID` API and the predefined frame control IDs:

```
HWND hWndTitleBar = WinWindowFromID (hWndFrame, FID_TITLEBAR);
HWND hWndSysMenu  = WinWindowFromID (hWndFrame, FID_SYSMENU);
HWND hWndMenu     = WinWindowFromID (hWndFrame, FID_MENU);
HWND hWndMinMax   = WinWindowFromID (hWndFrame, FID_MINMAX);
HWND hWndClient   = WinWindowFromID (hWndFrame, FID_CLIENT);
HWND hWndVScroll  = WinWindowFromID (hWndFrame, FID_VERTSCROLL);
HWND hWndHScroll  = WinWindowFromID (hWndFrame, FID_HORZSCROLL);
```

A more practical and efficient way of querying the window handles of a range of window IDs is to use the `WinMultWindowFromIDs` function. This function fills in an array with the handles of the child windows that fall within the specified range of identifiers. After the call, the individual window handles can be indexed by subtracting the identifier from the base identifier of the range. For example, to retrieve all the frame control window handles:

```
HWND hWndFrameControls[FID_CLIENT - FID_SYSMENU + 1];
LONG lCount;
lCount = WinMultWindowFromIDs (hWndFrame, hWndFrameControls,
    FID_SYSMENU, FID_CLIENT);
```

`lCount` tells how many window handles were found in the range `FID_SYSMENU` to `FID_CLIENT`. Each entry in the array `hWndFrameControls` is filled with a window handle or `NULL` if no window with the identifier exists. You can now reference a specific window handle by subtracting the identifier from the base identifier of the array (`FID_SYSMENU`) in this case.

```
HWND hWndTitleBar = hWndFrameControls[FID_TITLEBAR - FID_SYSMENU];
HWND hWndSysMenu  = hWndFrameControls[FID_SYSMENU - FID_SYSMENU];
HWND hWndMenu     = hWndFrameControls[FID_MENU - FID_SYSMENU];
HWND hWndMinMax   = hWndFrameControls[FID_MINMAX - FID_SYSMENU];
HWND hWndClient   = hWndFrameControls[FID_CLIENT - FID_SYSMENU];
HWND hWndVScroll  = hWndFrameControls[FID_VERTSCROLL - FID_SYSMENU];
HWND hWndHScroll  = hWndFrameControls[FID_HORZSCROLL - FID_SYSMENU];
```

`WinMultWindowFromIDs` can be used with any parent window to query any range of child window identifiers.

Window Characteristics

Each window is defined by many characteristics including its position, size, parent, owner, style, and others. All these characteristics can be queried and changed at any time.

For a window to be seen on the screen, it must be visible. If a window is not visible, none of its children are visible either. When a window is created, one of the flags you can use is the `WS_VISIBLE` flag. This flag is part of the window style and can be changed in various ways. For example, when a window is minimized and an icon is defined for the window, the frame

window is made invisible (hidden); thus, none of its child windows are visible. The WinShowWindow or WinSetWindowPos functions can be used to change the visibility state of a window. For instance, to hide a window, use this line of code:

```
WinShowWindow (hWnd, FALSE)
```

or use this line of code:

```
WinSetWindowPos (hWnd, 0L, 0L, 0L, 0L, 0L, SWP_HIDE);
```

To show a window, use this line of code:

```
WinShowWindow (hWnd, TRUE);
```

or use this line of code:

```
WinSetWindowPos (hWnd, 0L, 0L, 0L, 0L, 0L, SWP_SHOW);
```

It is more efficient to use the WinSetWindowPos call because WinShowWindow calls WinSetWindowPos with the proper flag. This function sets or clears the WS_VISIBLE flag in the window style. It does not enumerate the children and set or clear the WS_VISIBLE flag for each one; however, it does keep track of whether the children are currently visible. The WinIsWindowVisible API can be used to query the current visibility state of a window:

```
BOOL bVisible = WinIsWindowVisible (hWnd);
```

It is important to notice a particular nuance of the visibility state of minimized windows. The visibility state of the frame window of a minimized window is TRUE, whereas that of its frame controls and client window is false. Keep this in mind when checking the visibility state of the window in which you are interested.

A window can be enabled or disabled. When a window is enabled, it can receive user input, including being selected by the user clicking the window with the mouse. A disabled window cannot receive user input and cannot be clicked with the mouse. The purpose of disabling a window is to prevent unwanted input while another activity is occurring or to prevent a window from being selected when it doesn't make sense for that particular input to occur. For example, if your application displays a dialog box, the owner window is disabled so that only the controls in the dialog box can be selected. Clicking the owner window is not allowed. A window can be enabled or disabled with the WinEnableWindow API:

```
BOOL bEnable = FALSE;
WinEnableWindow (hWnd, bEnable);
```

This will disable the window hWnd and all its child windows. The window can be reenabled by calling WinEnableWindow with bEnable set to TRUE. A window can also be initially created in the disabled state by using the WS_DISABLED flag for the window style. It is usually a good practice to reset the enabled state of a window to its previous state when you no longer need the window to be in the disabled state. If the window is already disabled when you disable it, you may not want to arbitrarily set it to the enabled state when your function completes. The WinIsWindowEnabled API can be used to retrieve the current enabled state of a window:

```
BOOL bPrevEnabled = WinIsWindowEnabled (hWnd);
WinEnableWindow(hWnd, FALSE);

... perform operations ...

WinEnableWindow (hWnd, bPrevEnabled);
```

A maximized window is one that is enlarged to fill the entire area of its parent window. A window can be maximized in one of three ways. The user can click the maximize button of the window; the `WS_MAXIMIZED` style can be specified when the window is created; or `WinSetWindowPos` can be called with the `SWP_MAXIMIZE` flag:

```
WinSetWindowPos (hWnd, 0L, 0L, 0L, 0L, 0L, SWP_MAXIMIZE);
```

A minimized window is one that has been reduced to the size of an icon in its parent window. Like maximizing, a window can be minimized in one of three ways. The user can click the minimize button of the window; the `WS_MINIMIZED` style can be specified when the window is created; or the `WinSetWindowPos` can be called with the `SWP_MINIMIZE` flag:

```
WinSetWindowPos (hWnd, 0L, 0L, 0L, 0L, 0L, SWP_MINIMIZE);
```

A maximized or minimized window can be restored in one of two ways. The user can click the restore button of the window, or the `SWP_RESTORE` flag can be used with the `WinSetWindowPos` call:

```
WinSetWindowPos (hWnd, 0L, 0L, 0L, 0L, 0L, SWP_RESTORE);
```

The current minimized or maximized state can be retrieved in two ways. A call to `WinQueryWindowPos` retrieves the current size and position of the window. In addition, `WinQueryWindowPos` supplies the `SWP` flags indicating its current state:

```
SWP Swp;
BOOL bMinimized;
BOOL bMaximized;

WinQueryWindowPos (hWnd, &Swp);
bMinimized = Swp.fl & SWP_MINIMIZE;
bMaximized = Swp.fl & SWP_MAXIMIZE;
```

A second and easier way is to query the current window. The resulting style can be checked with the `WS_MINIMIZED` and `WS_MAXIMIZED` flags, `WS_MINIMIZED` and `WS_MAXIMIZED`.

```
    ULONG ulStyle;
    ulStyle = WinQueryWindowULong (hWnd, QWL_STYLE);
    bMinimized = ulStyle & WS_MINIMIZED;
    bMaximized = ulStyle & WS_MAXIMIZED;
```

Window Data

When a window is created, a data structure is allocated to contain the information pertaining to the particular class of window. An application has access to several fields of the window data.

You have already looked at the window style by using the `WinQueryWindowULong` API and the `QWL_STYLE` parameter. The size of the data structure allocated varies depending on the class of the window. An application can define a number of bytes to be allocated in addition to the system-defined data structure size, and can use these bytes to maintain any application-specific data for the window. The number of additional bytes to allocate is specified when the window class is registered. In the following example, a class called `"CLIENT"` is registered, specifying that 8 extra bytes should be allocated for each window created of this class:

```
WinRegisterClass (hab, "CLIENT", ClientWndProc, 0L, 8L);
```

This application-defined data can be accessed by an offset starting at offset zero. Using our example, if you want to store 2 `ULONG` values with the window, the first `ULONG` is at offset 0 and the second `ULONG` is at offset 4. It is recommended that you do not hard code sizes, but use the sizeof directive to accumulate the sizes of the values you want to maintain.

There are six different APIs available to access or modify the window-extra data. Each one requires a window handle and an offset into the data structure. The size and type of the value retrieved or set is determined by the API used:

`WinSetWindowUShort` and `WinQueryWindowUShort` access `USHORT` values:

```
USHORT usValue;
ULONG  ulOffset;

WinSetWindowUShort (hWnd, ulOffset, usValue);
usValue = WinQueryWindowUShort (hWnd, ulOffset);
```

`WinSetWindowULong` and `WinQueryWindowULong` access `ULONG` values:

```
ULONG  ulValue;
ULONG  ulOffset;

WinSetWindowULong (hWnd, ulOffset, ulValue);
ulValue = WinQueryWindowULong (hWnd, ulOffset);
```

`WinSetWindowPtr` and `WinQueryWindowPtr` access pointer values:

```
PVOID  pData;
ULONG  ulOffset;

WinSetWindowPtr (hWnd, ulOffset, pData);
pData = WinQueryWindowPtr (hWnd, ulOffset);
```

The data within the predefined PM window data structure is accessed with predefined identifiers. Notice that whereas application-defined data is referenced with positive value offsets, the PM window data is referenced by negative values. These negative values are not offsets by any means, but are predefined identifiers that enable PM to know which field to return. The prefix of the identifier defines the size of the field.

`QWS_`	Value is a short.
`QWL_`	Value is a long.
`QWP_`	Value is a pointer.

Identifier	*Value*	*Description*
QWS_ID	(-1)	Window identifier.
QWL_STYLE	(-2)	Window style.
QWP_PFNWP	(-3)	Window procedure.
QWL_HMQ	(-4)	Message queue for window.

For example, to retrieve the identifier for a window:

```
USHORT usID = WinQueryWindowUShort (hWnd, QWS_ID);
```

or to retrieve the message queue for a window:

```
HMQ hMQ = (HMQ)WinQueryWindowULong (hWnd, QWL_HMQ);
```

Because a frame window is registered as its own class, it also defines some window extra data when the `WC_FRAME` class is registered. The frame-specific data can be set and queried just as application-defined data. Notice that the frame window-specific values are actual offsets into the window extra bytes allocated for the frame window.

Identifier	*Value*	*Description*
QWS_USER	0	Start of application data.
QWL_USER	0	Start of application data.
QWL_HHEAP	0x0004	Handle to heap.
QWS_FLAGS	0x0008	Window flags.
QWS_RESULT	0x000a	Dialog result value.
QWS_XRESTORE	0x000c	X position for restored window.
QWS_YRESTORE	0x000e	Y position for restored window.
QWS_CXRESTORE	0x0010	Width of restored window.
QWS_CYRESTORE	0x0012	Height of restored window.
QWS_XMINIMIZE	0x0014	X position of minimized window.
QWS_YMINIMIZE	0x0016	Y position of minimized window.
QWL_HWNDFOCUSSAVE	0x0018	Descendant window to receive focus when this window receives the focus.

Window Sizing and Positioning

The position of a window is always specified relative to its parent window. The initial size and position of a window is specified when the window is created, but can be changed at any time by the application. You may have noticed by now that the call to `WinCreateStdWindow` does not have parameters for specifying an initial size or position. If the `FCF_SHELLPOSITION` is specified, PM will calculate a default size and position for the window. PM does this internally by calling `WinQueryTaskSizePos` as shown here:

```
SWP Swp;
Swp.hwndInsertBehind = HWND_TOP;
SWP.fl = (SWP_ACTIVATE ¦ SWP_SIZE ¦ SWP_MOVE);
```

```
Swp.x  = 20;
Swp.y  = 20;
Swp.cx = 600;
Swp.cy = 310;
WinQueryTaskSizePos (hab, 0, &Swp);
```

The SWP structure returned describes an initial X and Y position and width and height for the first window created by an application. The WinQueryWindowPos function calculates this information for a frame window having the FCF_STANDARD flag. If the FCF_SHELLPOSITION is not specified, the application is responsible for setting the position and size of the window after it is created.

When creating child windows or other top-level frame windows, the FCF_SHELLPOSITION is normally not specified. When using the WinCreateWindow API to create a window, you have parameters for specifying the window's initial position and size.

A window's current size and position can be retrieved with the WinQueryWindowPos API:

```
SWP Swp;
WinQueryWindowPos (hWnd, &Swp);
```

This function fills in the SWP structure with the window's current size, position, and current state:

```
typedef struct _SWP {
   ULONG   fl;
   SHORT   cy;
   SHORT   cx;
   SHORT   y;
   SHORT   x;
   HWND    hwndInsertBehind;
   HWND    hwnd;
   ULONG   ulReserved1;
   ULONG   ulReserved2;
} SWP;
```

For the WinQueryWindowPos call, these fields take on the following meaning:

```
fl      - Current window state
             SWP_MINIMIZE    Window is currently minimized
             SWP_MAXIMIZE    Window is currently maximized
             Otherwise       Window is neither minimized or maximized
cx      - Window width
cy      - Window height
x       - Window X position (relative to lower-left corner of parent)
y       - Window Y position (relative to lower-left corner of parent)
```

The other fields are used when setting a window's position.

It is also possible to query the window's position and size with the WinQueryWindowRect API:

```
RECTL Rectl;
WinQueryWindowRect (hWnd, &Rectl);
```

This function fills in a RECTL structure with the window's current size:

```
typedef struct _RECTL {
   LONG  xLeft;
   LONG  yBottom;
   LONG  xRight;
   LONG  yTop;
} RECTL;
```

For this call, however, the xLeft and yBottom fields will always be zero. The xRight and yTop fields define the width and height of the window. Essentially, this function returns the window's position relative to itself. Given that you have the position of any window relative to another window, it is always possible to calculate the window's position relative to still another window. This is accomplished with the WinMapWindowPoints API:

```
POINTL Ptl;
Ptl.x = 0L
Ptl.y = 0L;
WinMapWindowPoints (hWndFrom, hWndTo, &Ptl, 1L);
```

This function takes the points in Ptl (which are specified relative to hWndFrom) and converts them to points relative to hWndTo. Using the earlier call to WinQueryWindowRect, you can convert the window's position from (0,0) to coordinates relative to its parent window.

```
RECTL Rectl;
WinQueryWindowRect (hWnd, &Rectl);
WinMapWindowPoints (hWnd, WinQueryWindow (hWnd, QW_PARENT),
    (PPOINTL)&Rectl, 2L);
```

The window size is now calculated by subtracting xLeft from xRight and yBottom from yTop because both the lower-left and upper-right points were converted.

To convert a window's position from or to screen coordinates, you can specify HWND_DESKTOP for the from- or to-window handle.

A window's size and position can be set with the WinSetWindowPos API. If you want to move a window to position (10,10), you use:

```
WinSetWindowPos (hWnd, 0L, 10L, 10L, 0L, 0L, SWP_MOVE);
```

To change the size to 75 pels by 50 pels, you use:

```
WinSetWindowPos (hWnd, 0L, 0L, 0L, 75L, 50L, SWP_SIZE);
```

It is possible to move and size a window with a single call by combining the SWP flags:

```
WinSetWindowPos (hWnd, 0L, 10L, 10L, 75L, 50L, SWP_MOVE | SWP_SIZE);
```

If you have more than one window to move or size, it is more efficient to make a single call to WinSetMultWindowPos. This reduces the amount of repainting that occurs when individual calls to WinSetWindowPos are made. To use WinSetMultWindowPos, it is necessary to create an array of SWP structures, one for each window to move or size. Using the earlier example, set the position and size of one window to (10, 10) with a size of 75 pels by 50 pels. You'll also position a second window to (100,100):

```
SWP Swp[2];
Swp[0].fl   = SWP_SIZE ¦ SWP_MOVE;
Swp[0].x    = 10L;
Swp[0].y    = 10L;
Swp[0].cx   = 75L;
Swp[0].cy   = 50L;
Swp[0].hwnd = hWndOne;
Swp[1].fl   = SWP_MOVE;
Swp[1].x    = 100L;
Swp[1].y    = 100L;
Swp[1].hwnd = hWndTwo;
WinSetMultWindowPos (hab, Swp, 2L);
```

When a window's size or position is changed, PM will usually send the window procedure for the window a WM_ADJUSTWINDOWPOS message. The mp1 parameter contains a pointer to a SWP structure that specifies the window's size and position, which allows the window procedure to modify the final size or position of the window. The fl field of the SWP structure must be examined to determine whether the window is being sized or moved or both. If you do not have to process the WM_ADJUSTWINDOWPOS message, you can prevent this message from being sent to the window procedure by specifying the SWP_NOADJUST flag in the fl field.

After a window's size has changed, the window procedure for the window is sent a WM_SIZE message. This message specifies both the old and new window size:

```
WM_SIZE
   SHORT1FROMMP (mp1) - Old width
   SHORT2FROMMP (mp1) - Old height
   SHORT1FROMMP (mp2) - New width
   SHORT2FROMMP (mp2) - New height
```

If the window has the CS_MOVENOTIFY class style, the window procedure will also be sent a WM_MOVE message whenever the window's position changes. The new position of the window must be queried as described previously.

Whenever a window is moved, any children of that window are also moved an equivalent distance to maintain their position relative to the parent. Frame windows, however, can be forced to maintain their current position whenever their owner window moves.

The FCF_NOMOVEWITHOWNER flag can be used to tell PM that a particular frame window should not be moved when its owner moves. In many circumstances, an application may be interested in a window's new size only when the window is minimized or maximized. This is especially important when writing a Multiple Document Interface (MDI) application. Rather than query the system every time a WM_SIZE message is received, you can use the WM_MINMAXFRAME message sent when a frame window is minimized, maximized, or restored. The mp1 parameter contains a pointer to a SWP structure defining the action that is about to occur. At the time the WM_MINMAXFRAME message is received, the window's size has not been changed. To have PM perform the default action, do nothing to the SWP structure and return FALSE. If you want to perform your own minimizing, maximizing, or restoring, return TRUE, and PM will perform no action. It's also possible to do a little of both by modifying the SWP structure and returning FALSE. Because the SWP structure passed is the same one that PM will use when FALSE is returned, changes you make will be used by PM. You will see an example of using the WM_MINMAXFRAME message in the example program.

Window Focus and Activation

All keyboard input is sent to the window that currently has the focus. The focus window is then responsible for processing the keyboard messages it receives. Focus can be changed by calling WinSetFocus. When a window receives or loses the focus, it is sent a WM_SETFOCUS message.

When a window is receiving the focus, the parameters are set to the following:

```
mp1 - Handle of window losing the focus
mp2 - TRUE
```

When a window is losing the focus, the parameters are set to the following:

```
mp1 - Handle of window gaining the focus
mp2 - FALSE
```

PM does not allow an application to change the focus while focus is in the process of changing. Calls to WinSetFocus during the WM_SETFOCUS message will fail.

Actually, the call to WinSetFocus results in a call to WinFocusChange with the flFocusChange flags set to zero. The WinFocusChange function can be used to change the focus without having it generate certain messages. For example, to prevent the WM_SETFOCUS message from being sent to the window losing the focus or to the window gaining the focus, use the following call:

```
WinFocusChange (HWND_DESKTOP, hWndNewFocus,
                FC_NOSETFOCUS | FC_NOLOSEFOCUS);
```

The WinQueryFocus function can be used at any time to query the window that currently has the focus:

```
HWND hWndFocus = WinQueryFocus (HWND_DESKTOP);
```

It is not possible to set the focus to a disabled window. Disabling a window that currently has the focus causes that window to lose the focus.

All frame windows that are ancestors of the window with the focus are considered to be active windows. An active frame window is usually identified by a border and/or titlebar drawn in a highlighted state. When a frame window becomes active, the client window receives a WM_ACTIVATE message. If a frame window is becoming active, the mp1 parameter is TRUE, and mp2 is the handle of the frame window becoming active. If a frame window is losing activation, the mp1 parameter is FALSE, and mp2 is the handle of the frame window losing activation.

Application Activation

A window receives a WM_ACTIVATE message when it is activated or deactivated. The first parameter of the message is TRUE if gaining activation, and FALSE if losing activation. If a window is active, all its ancestors are active. When a frame window receives the WM_ACTIVATE message, it responds by setting or clearing the FF_ACTIVE bit of the frame flags (QWS_FLAGS), sending the TBM_SETHILITE message to the FID_TITLEBAR window, and redrawing the frame in either the highlighted or unhighlighted state. The frame window then passes this message to the client window.

This message, however, gives no indication whether the application is gaining activation or losing activation. This would be useful if certain events should be active only while the application is the active application. For example, an application that is a clipboard viewer should set itself as the clipboard viewer only when the application is active and then release itself as the viewer when not active. Because the window activation can change to another window in the same application (a message box being displayed), looking for the WM_ACTIVATE message does not sufficiently show the activation state of the application. You would need to know the identity of the other window receiving or losing activation to know whether that window is in another application.

One way to attempt this is to set or clear a global flag whenever one of the windows receives the WM_ACTIVATE message. If the flag was not set when you received a TRUE WM_ACTIVATE message, the application is gaining activation from another application. If the flag was set when you received a FALSE WM_ACTIVATE message, the application is losing activation to another application. The problem with this is that if the activation is changing to another window within the same application, the final state of the flag would be FALSE. This is because the TRUE WM_ACTIVATE message is sent before the FALSE WM_ACTIVATE message. The flag would be set to FALSE by the second WM_ACTIVATE message.

You can take advantage of another message used when focus is changing from one window to another. The WM_FOCUSCHANGE message is sent whenever the focus is changing from one window to another. It is a notification message that is passed up the owner chain telling each side of the focus process who is losing the focus and who is gaining the focus. If Window A is gaining the focus and Window B is losing the focus, a WM_FOCUSCHANGE message is sent to both Window A and Window B.

Window	*Message*	*mp1*	*SHORT1FROMMP(mp2)*
Window A	WM_FOCUSCHANGE	Window B	TRUE
Window B	WM_FOCUSCHANGE	Window A	FALSE

Notice that each window receives the identity of the window on the other side of the focus change. If you check the message queue handles of each window and they are the same, focus is changing to another window in the same application. If the message queues are different, focus and activation are changing between applications. Because the WM_FOCUSCHANGE message is passed along the owner chain, you can check this message in the window procedure for the top-level window of the application.

```
case WM_FOCUSCHANGE:
    if ( WinQueryWindowULong (hWnd, QWL_HMQ) !=
         WinQueryWindowULong ((HWND)mp1, QWL_HMQ) )
    {
        if (SHORT1FROMMP(mp2))
           /* Application is gaining activation */
           bAppIsActive = TRUE;
        else
           /* Application is losing activation */
           bAppIsActive = FALSE;
    }
    mReturn = WinDefWindowProc (hWnd, ulMsg, mp1, mp2);
    break;
```

When the WM_FOCUSCHANGE is received, you check the message queue handles. If they are the same, there is nothing to do. If they are different, you are changing application activation. If SHORT1FROMMP(mp2) is TRUE, the application is gaining activation; otherwise, the application is losing activation. Passing the WM_FOCUSCHANGE message to WinDefWindowProc simply causes the message to be passed to the frame window's owner window.

Window Subclassing

When a class is registered, a window procedure is specified. This window procedure receives and processes all messages associated with windows of that class. When a window is created, a block of memory is allocated to maintain information for the window. The window's current position, owner window, parent window, and current style are examples of this type of information. (See Figure 3.3.) In addition, the window procedure for the class is copied to this block of memory and is called when a message is to be processed for the window.

When you want to alter the behavior of a window, you can subclass the window so that a different window procedure is called. Subclassing is performed only on the specified window. To subclass a window, use the WinSubclassWindow function specifying a new window procedure.

```
PFNWP OldWndProc;
OldWndProc = WinSubclassWindow (hWnd, MyNewWndProc);
```

The return value from WinSubclassWindow is the previous window procedure. It is important to save this value and pass messages that your new window procedure does not process to the previous window procedure. When you are done subclassing the window, the window procedure can be reset by calling WinSubclassWindow again:

```
WinSubclassWindow (hWnd, OldWndProc);
```

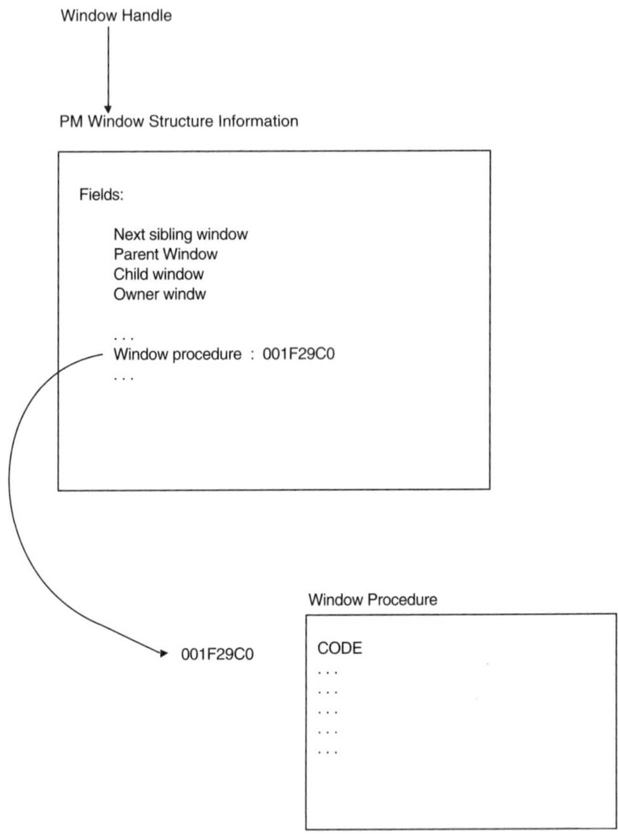

Figure 3.3.
PM window structure information.

All the predefined PM window classes use window procedures defined in PM. Your application, thus, never receives or processes messages for the frame or its controls unless the frame passes the message to the client window. By subclassing the frame or its controls, you can change the default behavior of these windows. In the following sections, you will look at various things that can be done by subclassing the frame window or the frame controls. We will do this principally by subclassing the frame window:

```
PFNWP pfnFrameProc;
pfnFrameProc = WinSubclassWindow (hWndFrame, FrameSubclassProc);
```

When OS/2 sends a message to a subclassed window procedure, the subclassed window procedure may or may not process the message. For messages you are not interested in or for those cases where you process the message, but still want PM to do something, call the default window procedure for the frame window:

```
mReturn = (*pfnFrameProc) (hWnd, msg, mp1, mp2);
```

Titlebar Painting

During the normal course of operation, your application has control only of how the client window is painted; however, it is possible to do your own painting of the frame window and its controls by intercepting the WM_PAINT messages. As an example, suppose you are writing a game program and want to use the titlebar area to display a bitmap showing the number of children that exist. You start by creating the frame window without the WS_VISIBLE flag. This enables you to subclass the titlebar before its first paint message. Next, subclass the titlebar window:

```
MRESULT EXPENTRY TitleBarSubclassProc (HWND,ULONG,MPARAM,MPARAM);
PFNWP pfnTitleBarProc;


hWndFrame = WinCreateStdWindow (HWND_DESKTOP, 0L,
    &flFrameFlags, szClientClass, szTitle, 0, NULL,
    ID_APPNAME, &hWndClient);

pfnTitleBarProc = WinSubclassWindow (
  WinWindowFromID (hWndFrame, FID_TITLEBAR), TitleBarSubclassProc);

WinShowWindow (hWndFrame, TRUE);
```

In this example, you will draw a heart-shaped image in the titlebar window. You will do something a little differently here. You will use a pointer rather than a bitmap because the color of the titlebar can be controlled by the desktop settings. Because you don't know in advance what that color will be, you must draw the image in the window and leave the background color alone wherever the images background bits appear. This can be done through several steps by using various ROP (raster operation) codes and the GpiBitBlt API, but you can take advantage of the fact pointers and icons are drawn in exactly this manner (that is, transparent bitblt). The function WinDrawPointer enables you to draw a pointer or icon at a specified location, leaving the background bits alone wherever the pointer or icon bits specify transparency.

You load the pointer during the WM_CREATE message for the client window and destroy it during the WM_DESTROY message:

```
HPOINTER hPtrHeart2  = NULL;
ULONG    NumChildren = 0L;

MRESULT EXPENTRY ClientWndProc (HWND hWnd, ULONG msg, MPARAM mp1,
                                MPARAM mp2)
{
   BOOL     bHandled = TRUE;
   MRESULT mReturn  = 0;
   HPS      hps;

   switch (msg)
   {
      case WM_CREATE:

          hPtrHeart2 = WinLoadPointer (HWND_DESKTOP,0L,IDPTR_HEART2);break;
```

```
        case WM_DESTROY:

            WinDestroyPointer (hPtrHeart2);break;
...

    }

    return (mReturn);
}
```

Next, we define the window procedure for the titlebar window subclass. For the titlebar, you must process three different messages. The titlebar window maintains an internal state value indicating its current highlighted state. Because you don't have direct access to that field, you can use the fact that the `WC_TITLEBAR` class is defined with window extra words, including a long for the `QWL_USER` field. You can use this field to keep track of the current state. You will set the low bit to 1 if the titlebar window is currently in the highlighted state:

```
#define IS_HIGHLIGHTED 0x0001L

MRESULT EXPENTRY TitleBarSubclassProc (HWND hWnd, ULONG msg,
                                       MPARAM mp1, MPARAM mp2)

{
    MRESULT mReturn = 0L;
    ULONG   ulCurState,
    ulNewState;
    HPS     hps;

    switch (msg)
    {
      case WM_MOUSEMOVE:
        WinSetPointer (HWND_DESKTOP, hPtrTitleBar);
        break;

      case TBM_QUERYHILITE:
        mReturn =(MRESULT)(WinQueryWindowULong(hWnd,QWL_USER)
                          & IS_HIGHLIGHTED);
        break;

      case TBM_SETHILITE:
        mReturn = (MRESULT)TRUE;
        ulCurState = ulNewState = WinQueryWindowULong (hWnd,QWL_USER);
        if (LOUSHORT(mp1))
          ulNewState |= IS_HIGHLIGHTED;
        else
          ulNewState &= ~IS_HIGHLIGHTED;

        /* Only need to update if the state is changing */
        if (ulCurState == ulNewState)
          break;
        WinSetWindowULong (hWnd,QWL_USER,ulNewState);

        hps = WinGetPS (hWnd);
        PaintTitleBar (hWnd,hps);
        WinReleasePS (hps);
        break;
```

```
      case WM_PAINT:
        hps = WinBeginPaint (hWnd,0,0);
        PaintTitleBar (hWnd,hps);
        WinEndPaint (hps);
        break;

      default:
        mReturn = (*pfnTitleBarProc) (hWnd, msg, mp1, mp2);
        break;
    }

    return (mReturn);
}
```

The TBM_QUERYHILITE message requests the current highlighted state of the titlebar. The TBM_SETHILITE message says to set the current highlighted state to that in LOUSHORT(mp1). You query the current state and compare it with the new state. If there is no change, there is nothing to do. Otherwise, set the new state and repaint the titlebar window in its new state. When you get the WM_PAINT message, you merely repaint the titlebar window. For all other messages, you pass the message on to the default titlebar window procedure.

For the painting of the titlebar window, you define the function PaintTitleBar:

```
#define DB_RAISED         0x0400
#define DB_CORNERBORDER   0x8000
#define IS_HIGHLIGHTED    0X0001L

VOID PaintTitleBar (HWND hWnd, HPS hps)
{
  RECTL Rectl;
  BOOL  bActive;
  SHORT Scale,
        X;
  ULONG inx;

  /* If window is not visible then nothing to paint */
  if (!WinIsWindowVisible (hWnd))
     return;

  /* Get the current active state of the titlebar */
  bActive = (BOOL)(WinQueryWindowULong (hWnd, QWL_USER)
                  & IS_HIGHLIGHTED);

  /* Draw the correct border for the titlebar */
  WinQueryWindowRect (hWnd, &Rectl);
  WinDrawBorder (hps, &Rectl, bActive ? 0L : 1L, 1L,
       SYSCLR_TITLEBOTTOM,
       bActive ? SYSCLR_ACTIVETITLE : SYSCLR_INACTIVETITLE,
       DB_RAISED ¦ DB_CORNERBORDER ¦ DB_STANDARD ¦ DB_INTERIOR);

  /* Draw a heart for each child window that exists. Since the WC_TITLEBAR class is not
CS_CLIPSIBLINGS it is possible to write over the minmax window.  Only output as many
hearts as will fit in the titlebar window. Use the WinDrawPointer  API so we get a
transparent bitblt.*/
```

```
    Scale = (SHORT)(Rectl.yTop - Rectl.yBottom - 2 -
            2 * WinQuerySysValue (HWND_DESKTOP, SV_CYBORDER));

    if (bAppIsActive)
    {
      if ((inx = ulNumChildren) != 0)
      {
        X = (SHORT)(WinQuerySysValue (HWND_DESKTOP, SV_CXBORDER) + 1);
        while ( inx && ((LONG)(X + Scale) < Rectl.xRight) )
        {

          WinDrawPointer (hps, X, 2, hPtrHeart2, DP_NORMAL);
          inx--;
          X += (SHORT)(Scale + 2);
        }
      }
      else
      {
        POINTL Ptl;
        Ptl.x = WinQuerySysValue (HWND_DESKTOP, SV_CXBORDER) + 1;
        Ptl.y = 2;
        GpiCharStringAt (hps, &Ptl, 21L, (PSZ)"MiniMDI - No children");
      }
    }
    else
    {
      POINTL Ptl;
      Ptl.x = WinQuerySysValue (HWND_DESKTOP, SV_CXBORDER) + 1;
      Ptl.y = 2;
      GpiCharStringAt (hps, &Ptl, 20L, (PSZ)"MiniMDI - Not Active");
    }

    return;
}
```

If the window is not visible, there is nothing to paint. Otherwise, query the current state and use the `WinDrawBorder` function to draw the border around the window and fill its interior. Finally, you draw a heart in the window for each child. Because the `WC_TITLEBAR` class does not include the `CS_CLIPSIBLINGS` flag, it is possible to draw outside the titlebar window and over sibling windows. For that reason, you do not want to draw a heart that might extend past the end of the titlebar window rectangle. Because the titlebar is drawn with a raised border, subtract the height of the border and then subtract 2 to provide a separation between the border and the heart.

Mouse Pointer

The mouse pointer displays the current position of the mouse. The pointer that is used is set by the application whenever a `WM_MOUSEMOVE` message is received or when time-consuming processing is about to begin. Typically, the mouse pointer is set to display a pointer that represents the type of operation performed in a window. The default pointer used, if no setting of the pointer is done by the application, is the arrow pointer.

To control the pointer in your client window, set the pointer when the application receives the WM_MOUSEMOVE message:

```
case WM_MOUSEMOVE:
    WinSetPointer (HWND_DESKTOP, hPtrNew);
    break;
```

When the mouse is positioned over a control window, the control will send a WM_CONTROLPOINTER message to its owner:

```
WM_CONTROLPOINTER
    SHORT1FROMMP(mp1) = identifier of control window
    mp2               = handle of pointer to use
```

The return value for this message is the handle of the pointer to display. Passing this message to WinDefWindowProc will return the handle contained in mp2. The owner can change the pointer by returning a different pointer handle. This example sets a different pointer if the pointer is over the window with identifier ID_TOOLBAR:

```
case WM_CONTROLPOINTER:
    if (SHORT1FROMMP(mp1) == ID_TOOLBAR)
        mReturn = hPtrHeart;
    else
        mReturn = mp2;
    break;
```

It is possible to set the pointer for the frame window and its controls by subclassing the frame window. The frame window will receive the WM_CONTROLPOINTER for the system menu, actionbar menu, minmax menu, and the frame. No WM_CONTROLPOINTER message will be received from the titlebar window because it does not send one to its owner. The titlebar merely sets it to the arrow pointer; however, if you subclass the titlebar, you can set the pointer by processing the WM_MOUSEMOVE message. In the sample application, you will set the pointer to represent the frame control that the mouse is over. In addition, you will use a feature of the mouse WM_HITTEST result to indicate exactly what part of the frame window the mouse is over.

You begin by subclassing the frame window, titlebar window, system menu, and actionbar menu:

```
pfnFrameProc    = WinSubclassWindow (hWndFrame,FrameSubclassProc);
pfnTitleBarProc = WinSubclassWindow (
  WinWindowFromID (hWndFrame, FID_TITLEBAR), TitleBarSubclassProc);
pfnSysMenuProc = WinSubclassWindow (
  WinWindowFromID (hWndFrame, FID_SYSMENU), SysMenuSubclassProc);
pfnMenuProc = WinSubclassWindow (
  WinWindowFromID (hWndFrame, FID_MENU), MenuSubclassProc);
```

While the WM_CONTROLPOINTER for the system menu and actionbar menu is passed to the frame window, you have no way of knowing if the mouse is over a pull-down menu. By subclassing these two windows, you know that the WM_CONTROLPOINTER received is for a pull-down or cascaded menu owned by the top-level menu. You don't subclass the minmax menu because it does not have a pull-down menu. In FrameSubclassProc, you will process both the WM_CONTROLPOINTER and WM_MOUSEMOVE messages:

For the client window, you will set the pointer when the WM_MOUSEMOVE message is received:

```
case WM_MOUSEMOVE:
    WinSetPointer (HWND_DESKTOP, hPtrClient);
    break;
```

All the pointers are loaded during the WM_CREATE message and destroyed during the WM_DESTROY message in ClientWndProc:

```
case WM_CREATE:
    hPtrHeart       = WinLoadPointer (HWND_DESKTOP, 0L, IDPTR_HEART);
    hPtrClient      = WinLoadPointer (HWND_DESKTOP, 0L, IDPTR_CLIENT);
    hPtrSysMenu     = WinLoadPointer (HWND_DESKTOP, 0L, IDPTR_SYSMENU);
    hPtrMenu        = WinLoadPointer (HWND_DESKTOP, 0L, IDPTR_MENU);
    hPtrMinMax      = WinLoadPointer (HWND_DESKTOP, 0L, IDPTR_MINMAX);
    hPtrLeft        = WinLoadPointer (HWND_DESKTOP, 0L, IDPTR_LEFT);
    hPtrTop         = WinLoadPointer (HWND_DESKTOP, 0L, IDPTR_TOP);
    hPtrLeftTop     = WinLoadPointer (HWND_DESKTOP, 0L, IDPTR_LEFTTOP);
    hPtrRightTop    = WinLoadPointer (HWND_DESKTOP, 0L, IDPTR_RIGHTTOP);
    hPtrTitleBar    = WinLoadPointer (HWND_DESKTOP, 0L, IDPTR_TITLEBAR);
    hPtrPopupMenu   = WinLoadPointer (HWND_DESKTOP, 0L, IDPTR_POPUPMENU);
    break;

case WM_DESTROY:
    WinDestroyPointer (hPtrHeart);
    WinDestroyPointer (hPtrClient);
    WinDestroyPointer (hPtrSysMenu);
    WinDestroyPointer (hPtrMenu);
    WinDestroyPointer (hPtrMinMax);
    WinDestroyPointer (hPtrLeft);
    WinDestroyPointer (hPtrTop);
    WinDestroyPointer (hPtrLeftTop);
    WinDestroyPointer (hPtrRightTop);
    WinDestroyPointer (hPtrTitleBar);
    WinDestroyPointer (hPtrPopupMenu);
    break;
```

Figure 3.4 displays the image of each of these declared PTR values.

Figure 3.4.
Image of each sample PTR.

Preventing Window Tracking

The size of a window can be changed with the mouse by pressing and holding the mouse button while positioned on the border of the frame. In addition, a window can be moved with the mouse by pressing and holding the mouse button while positioned on the titlebar window. This process is referred to as "tracking" the window. When this process starts, the frame window receives a WM_TRACKFRAME message.

```
WM_TRACKFRAME
    SHORT1FROMMP(mp1) = Frame tracking flags
```

The frame tracking flags can be a combination of the following:

TF_LEFT	0x0001
TF_TOP	0x0002
TF_RIGHT	0x0004
TF_BOTTOM	0x0008
TF_MOVE	0x000F

The frame tracking flags indicate the operation that is about to start. To prevent a particular tracking operation from occurring, intercept the WM_TRACKFRAME message and do not pass it to the frame's window procedure. It is necessary to subclass the frame window to intercept this message. To prevent the window from being moved, you do the following:

```
MRESULT EXPENTRY FrameSubclassProc (HWND hWnd, ULONG msg, MPARAM mp1,
                                    MPARAM mp2)
{
   MRESULT mReturn;

   switch (msg)
   {
      ...
      case WM_TRACKFRAME:
         if ((SHORT1FROMMP(mp1) & TF_MOVE) == TF_MOVE)
            mReturn = 0L;
         else
            mReturn = (*pfnFrameProc) (hWnd, msg, mp1, mp2);
         break;
...
   }

   return (mReturn);
}
```

To prevent the window from being sized to the right or moved by the mouse, you check for the following:

```
case WM_TRACKFRAME:
   switch (SHORT1FROMMP(mp1) &TF_MOVE)
   {
      case TF_MOVE:
      case TF_RIGHT:
```

```
        case TF_RIGHT | TF_BOTTOM:
        case TF_RIGHT | TF_TOP:
            mReturn = 0L;
        break;
        default:
            mReturn = (*pfnFrameProc) (hWnd, msg, mp1, mp2);
    }
    break;
```

Restricting a Window's Size

When the frame window receives the `WM_TRACKFRAME` message, the frame window immediately sends a `WM_QUERYTRACKINFO` message to itself. The frame window fills in the `TRACKINFO` structure with the data that specifies the minimum and maximum size of the tracking rectangle:

```
WM_QUERYTRACKINFO
   SHORT1FROMMP(mp1) = Tracking flags
   mp2               = Pointer to TRACKINFO structure
```

To restrict the size of a window being resized by the mouse, intercept the `WM_QUERYTRACKINFO` message and set the `ptlMinTrackSize` and `ptlMaxTrackSize` fields of the `TRACKINFO` structure. To restrict the movement of the window within a particular area, set the `rclBoundary` field. It is necessary to subclass the frame window to intercept this message.

In the sample application, you use the `WM_QUERYTRACKINFO` to restrict the minimum size to 75 pels by 50 pels. Also, you restrict the maximum size to be 40 pels wider and higher than the current width and height. Although you do not restrict the boundary in which the window can be moved, you could do that by specifying a rectangle in coordinates relative to the parent window in the `rclBoundary` field.

The child window is subclassed when the "Move" or "Track" checkboxes are checked:

```
WinSubclassWindow (WinQueryWindow (hWndActiveChild, QW_PARENT),
     ChildSubclassProc);
```

Because you subclassed another frame window earlier in the application, we have the address to PM's frame window procedure in `pfnFrameProc`.

When the `WM_QUERYTRACKINFO` message is received by `ChildSubclassProc`, you first pass the message to the default frame window procedure. This allows the `TRACKINFO` structure to be initialized by PM. Afterwards, you can update the structure with our restrictions on the window sizing and positioning:

```
MRESULT EXPENTRY ChildSubclassProc (HWND hWnd, ULONG msg, MPARAM mp1,
                                    MPARAM mp2)
{
   BOOL    bHandled = FALSE;
   MRESULT mReturn = 0L;

   switch (msg)
```

```
    {
       ...
       case WM_QUERYTRACKINFO:
           if (WinQueryWindowULong (
               WinWindowFromID (hWnd, FID_CLIENT), QWL_TRACKING))
           {
              PTRACKINFO pti;
              RECTL      Rectl;

              /* Let the PM frame window function initialize TRACKINFO */
              mReturn = (*pfnFrameProc) (hWnd, msg, mp1, mp2);

              WinQueryWindowRect (hWnd, &Rectl);
              pti                     = (PTRACKINFO)mp2;
              pti->ptlMinTrackSize.x = 75L;
              pti->ptlMinTrackSize.y = 50L;
              pti->ptlMaxTrackSize.x = Rectl.xRight + 40;
              pti->ptlMaxTrackSize.y = Rectl.yTop   + 40;
              bHandled = TRUE;
           }
    }

    if (!bHandled)
       mReturn = (*pfnFrameProc) (hWnd, msg, mp1, mp2);

    return (mReturn);
}
```

All coordinates specified are relative to the parent window.

Window Icons

The icon that is used when a window is minimized is stored with the window information for each frame window. This icon can be defined when the window is created, or the icon can be set later with the WM_SETICON message. To define an icon when the window is created, use the FCF_ICON frame control flag. The identifier of the icon that will be loaded is the same as the identifier of the frame window. The icon resource is loaded from the module specified by the module handle field of the WinCreateStdWindow call. This example creates a frame window with an icon having identifier ID_APPNAME.

Here is the resource file:

```
ICON ID_APPNAME HEART.ICO
```

Here is the header file:

```
#define ID_APPNAME   1
```

Here is the source file:

```
HMQ    hmq;
```

```
ULONG flFrameFlags     = FCF_TITLEBAR ¦ FCF_SYSMENU ¦ FCF_SIZEBORDER ¦
                         FCF_MINMAX   ¦ FCF_SHELLPOSITION ¦ FCF_TASKLIST ¦
                         FCF_ICON;
CHAR  szClientClass[] = "CLIENT";

hab = WinInitialize (NULL);
hmq = WinCreateMsgQueue (hab, NULL);

WinRegisterClass (hab, szClientClass, ClientWndProc, 0, 0);
WinLoadString (hab, NULL, ID_APPNAME, sizeof(szTitle), szTitle);

hWndFrame = WinCreateStdWindow (HWND_DESKTOP, 0L,
    &flFrameFlags, szClientClass, szTitle, 0, NULL, ID_APPNAME,
    &hWndClient);
```

You might think the icon with identifier `ID_APPNAME` is automatically used in this example. There is, however, one slight variation that PM adds to this scenario. If the identifier of the icon is "1," PM will attempt to look for an icon-extended attribute. If PM finds one, it will use that icon regardless of the icon specified in the `WinCreateStdWindow` call. Here is an outline of the logic used to determine which icon is set for a frame window during the creation of the frame window:

```
hIcon = NULL;
if the FCF_ICON flag is specified
{
    if the resource identifier is equal to 1
       hIcon = Search for icon extended attribute using
                  the module handle
    if (!hIcon)
    {
       hIcon = WinLoadPointer (HWND_DESKTOP, module handle, resource id);
       if (!hIcon)
          return (FALSE);
    }
    WinSendMsg(hWndFrame, WM_SETICON, hIcon, 0L);
}
```

If you specify the `FCF_ICON` flag, but forget to include the icon in the resource file, the window creation will fail. The icon used for a frame can be changed at any time by sending the `WM_SETICON` message to the frame window:

```
HPOINTER hIcon = WinLoadPointer (HWND_DESKTOP, 0L, 100);
WinSendMsg (hWndFrame, WM_SETICON, hIcon, 0L);
```

The current icon handle can be retrieved by using the `WM_QUERYICON` message:

```
HPOINTER hIcon = WinSendMsg (hWndFrame, WM_QUERYICON, 0L, 0L);
```

If there is no icon defined for a frame window, when the window is minimized, no icon is displayed and the application is sent a `WM_PAINT` message to draw in the minimized window area.

Message Processing

As discussed in Chapter 2, messages are the primary means of communicating between windows and are at the heart of any windowing system. Messages are communicated to an application window in two manners: sent or posted. Messages that are sent are directed *immediately* to the window procedure for a window. If the window that is to receive the message belongs to another process, OS/2 performs the necessary steps to switch tasks and returns to the sending task when the message has been processed. Examples of sent messages are notification messages such as `WM_CONTROL`, and `WM_ACTIVATE`. Messages are sent by using `WinSendMsg`:

```
MRESULT APIENTRY WinSendMsg (HWND hWnd, ULONG msg, MPARAM mp1, MPARAM mp2);
```

When `WinSendMsg` is used, the call does not return until the message is processed by the receiving window. (See Figure 3.5.)

Figure 3.5. Diagram of `WinSendMsg` *message flow.*

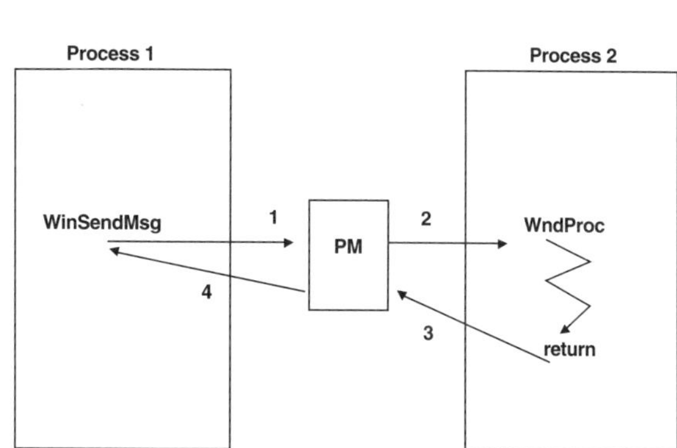

Posted messages are those placed in the message queue of the process that created the window and are processed when the receiving application retrieves the message from its message queue. Examples of posted messages are `WM_SIZE` and `WM_MOVE`. Messages are posted by using `WinPostMsg`:

```
MRESULT APIENTRY WinPostMsg (HWND hWnd, ULONG msg, MPARAM mp1, MPARAM mp2);
```

When `WinPostMsg` is used, the call returns immediately after placing the message in the appropriate message queue. (See Figure 3.6.)

It is also possible to post a message to a particular message queue. Messages posted to a message queue do not contain a window handle. Applications processing these types of messages must explicitly look for a message with no window handle, as these messages are not dispatched to any window procedure. Messages are posted to a message queue by using `WinPostQueueMsg`:

```
BOOL APIENTRY WinPostQueueMsg (HMQ hmq, ULONG msg, MPARAM mp1, MPARAM mp2);
```

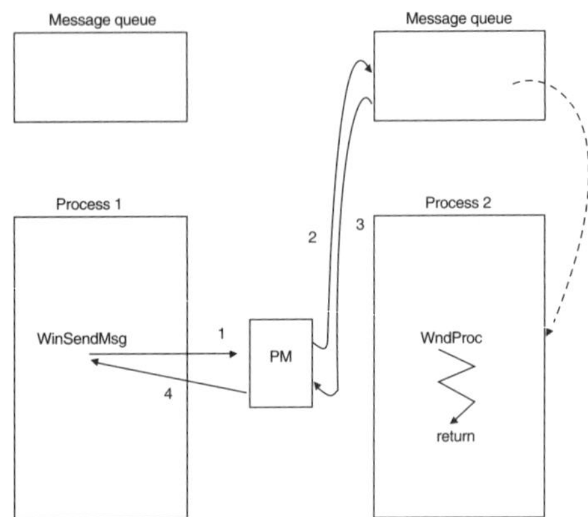

Figure 3.6.
Diagram of `WinPostMsg` *message flow.*

When you want to send or post a message to all child windows of a particular window, you can use the `WinBroadcastMsg` function. This function will either post or send a message to all immediate child windows. Broadcasting messages is typically used to notify all children that a system-wide or application-wide attribute has changed (see Figure 3.7):

```
BOOL APIENTRY WinBroadcastMsg (HWND hWnd, ULONG msg, MPARAM mp1, MPARAM mp2, ULONG rgf);
```

The `rgf` parameter can contain the following mutually exclusive flags:

`BMSG_POST`	Message is posted to the windows.
`BMSG_SEND`	Message is sent to the windows.
`BMSG_POSTQUEUE`	Message is posted to the message queue of all threads.
`BMSG_DESCENDANTS`	Broadcast message to all descendants of `hWnd`.
`BMSG_FRAMEONLY`	Only frame windows receive the message.

Applications retrieve messages from their message queue by calling either `WinGetMsg` or `WinPeekMsg`. After a message has been removed from a message queue, it is dispatched to the window's window procedure by calling `WinDispatchMsg`. There are a couple of subtle differences between `WinGetMsg` and `WinPeekMsg`. First, look at their definitions:

```
BOOL APIENTRY WinGetMsg (HAB hab, PQMSG pqmsg, HWND hwndFilter,
                ULONG msgFilterFirst, ULONG msgFilterLast);

BOOL APIENTRY WinPeekMsg (HAB hab, PQMSG pqmsg, HWND hwndFilter,
                ULONG msgFilterFirst, ULONG msgFilterLast, ULONG fl);
```

Both of these functions are passed a pointer to a `QMSG` structure. The `hWndFilter`, `msgFilterFirst`, and `msgFilterLast` parameters are used for message filtering that you will look at in a minute. The main difference is the `fl` parameter for `WinPeekMsg`. Calls to `WinGetMsg` do not return until a message is placed in the message queue. When a message is placed in the queue, `WinGetMsg` returns after removing the message from the message queue. (See Figure 3.8.)

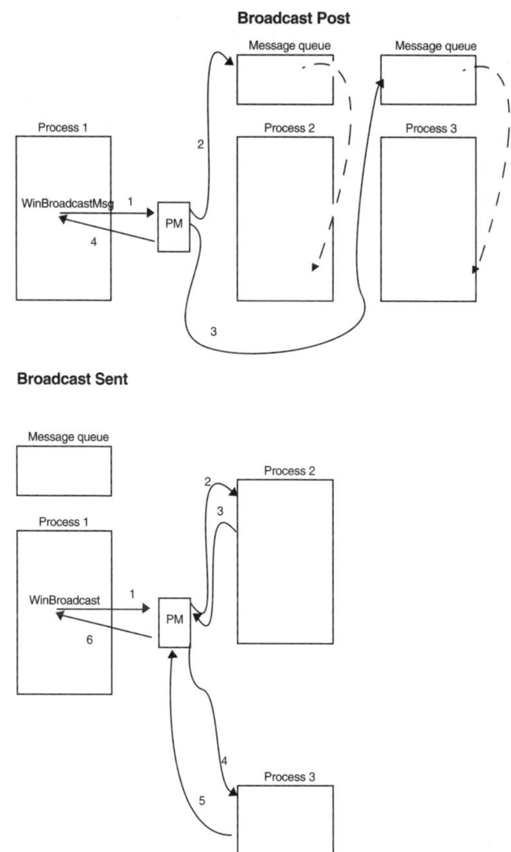

Figure 3.7.
Diagram of `WinBroadcastMsg` *message flow.*

`WinPeekMsg`, however, always returns immediately with its return value that indicates whether a message was found in the queue. `WinPeekMsg` is typically used to look into the queue and see whether messages are waiting to be processed so that processing can continue if no messages need to be processed. The `fl` parameter specifies what to do with the message if one is found in the queue.

`PM_REMOVE`	Remove the message from the queue.
`PM_NOREMOVE`	Do not remove the message from the queue.

Figure 3.9 shows that a call to `WinPeekMsg` returns immediately with a return value of `FALSE` when no messages are present in the message queue.

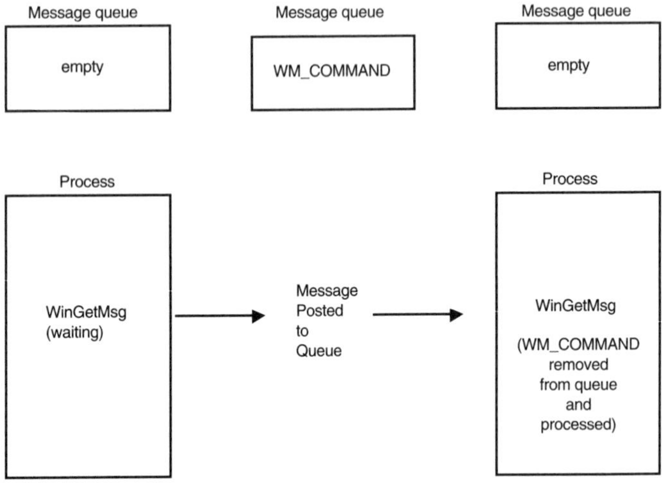

Figure 3.8.
Message flow for `WinGetMsg`.

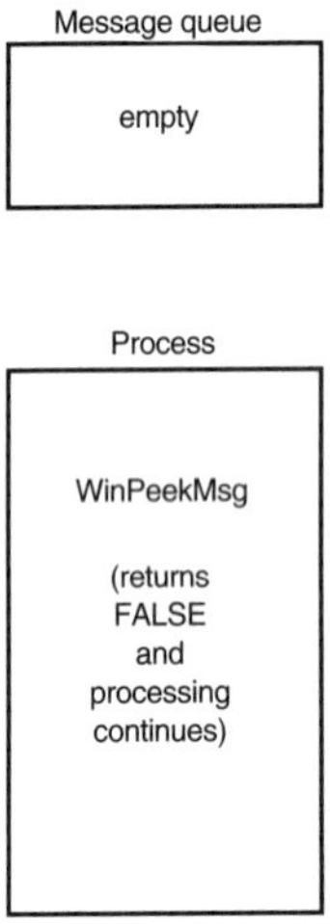

Figure 3.9.
Message flow for `WinPeekMsg`.

One important difference between `WinGetMsg` and `WinPeekMsg` is the handling of the `WM_QUIT` message. `WinGetMsg` always returns `TRUE` unless the message removed from the queue is the `WM_QUIT` message, in which case `WinGetMsg` returns `FALSE`. `WinPeekMsg` returns `TRUE` if a message-even if it is the `WM_QUIT` message-is in the queue.

After a message has been removed from the queue, `WinDispatchMsg` is called to send it to the window procedure:

```
MRESULT APIENTRY WinDispatchMsg (HAB hab, PQMSG pqmsg);
```

The process of dispatching a message is shown in Figure 3.10. A message is removed from the queue by calling `WinGetMsg`. `WinDispatchMsg` is called to send the message to the window procedure for the window to which the message belongs.

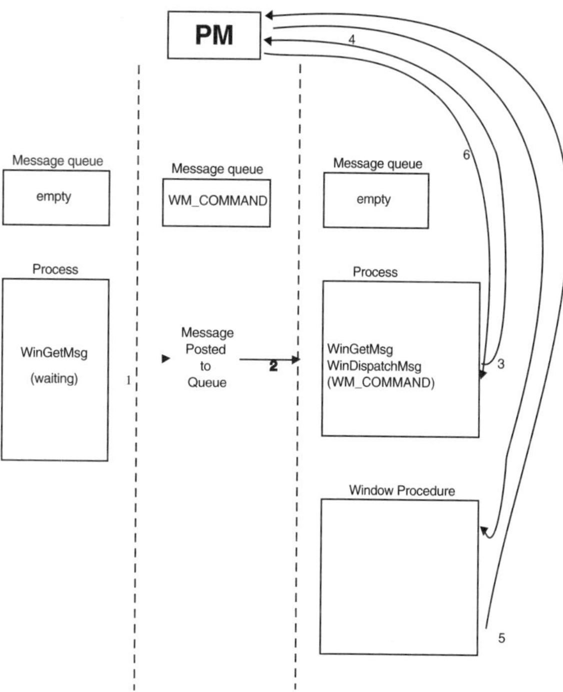

Figure 3.10.
`WinDispatchMsg` processing.

The code for a normal message loop for an application looks something like this:

```
QMSG qmsg;

while (WinGetMsg (hab, &qmsg, 0L, 0L, 0L))
    WinDispatchMsg (hab, &qmsg);
```

You can also implement the exact same loop by using `WinPeekMsg` and the `WinWaitMsg` functions.

```
QMSG qmsg;
while (WinWaitMsg (hab, 0L, 0L))
{
   while ( WinPeekMsg (hab, &qmsg, 0L, 0L, 0L, PM_REMOVE) &&
           (qmsg.msg != WM_QUIT) )
      WinDispatchMsg (hab, &qmsg);

   if (qmsg.msg == WM_QUIT)
      break;
}
```

The WinWaitMsg function does not return until a message is placed in the message queue. WinGetMsg can be used to wait for a particular message if your application is waiting for a particular event to occur. One of the more common uses of the WinPeekMsg call is to continue to process messages while a long process is occurring. For example, if a long drawing sequence is being performed, you do not want to halt the processing of messages in the system while the drawing is being performed. WinPeekMsg, thus, is used to process all the messages in the queue, and the drawing is performed only when no messages are in the queue.

```
QMSG qmsg;

while ( long process is not complete &&
        (qmsg.msg != WM_QUIT) )
{
   while ( WinPeekMsg (hab, &qmsg, 0L, 0L, 0L, PM_REMOVE) &&
           (qmsg.msg != WM_QUIT) )
      WinDispatchMsg (hab, &qmsg);

   if (qmsg.msg == WM_QUIT)
      continue;

   /* Perform long drawing */
}
```

This loop enables the user to switch to another process or perform other actions while the long drawing process is occurring. Another option is to perform the long drawing operation in a separate thread. This is discussed in Chapter 14, "Threads and Semaphores."

Message filtering is a feature of WinPeekMsg, WinGetmsg, and WinWaitMsg that allows an application to select a specific range of messages or messages destined for a particular window. When a message filter is used, only those messages that satisfy the criteria specified are returned. Message filtering is frequently used to look ahead in the message queue or to remove a certain type of message. The message range is specified by the msgFilterFirst and msgFilterLast parameters. If hwndFilter is specified, only those messages posted to hwndFilter or its descendants are retrieved. For example, to filter for all mouse messages for any window, you can use the following:

```
if (WinPeekMsg (hab, &qmsg, 0L, WM_MOUSEFIRST, WM_MOUSELAST,
     PM_NOREMOVE))
```

Care must be taken when using message filtering with WinGetMsg or WinWaitMsg. You must be certain that a message satisfying the criteria can be placed in the queue or else these functions will never return. If you are interested only in determining whether a particular type of message is in the queue, a method more efficient than message filtering is to use the WinQueryQueueStatus function:

```
ULONG APIENTRY WinQueryQueueStatus(HWND hwndDesktop);
```

The return value from WinQueryQueueStatus contains flags indicating the types of messages that are currently in the queue. The following flags are used:

QS_KEY	WM_CHAR message(s).
QS_MOUSEBUTTON	Mouse button message(s).
QS_MOUSEMOVE	WM_MOUSEMOVE message(s).
QS_MOUSE	Mouse button or WM_MOUSEMOVE message(s).
QS_TIMER	WM_TIMER message(s).
QS_PAINT	WM_PAINT message(s).
QS_POSTMSG	Message posted by the WinPostMsg function.
QS_SEM1	WM_SEM1 message(s).
QS_SEM2	WM_SEM2 message(s).
QS_SEM3	WM_SEM3 message(s).
QS_SEM4	WM_SEM4 message(s).
QS_SENDMSG	Message sent from another application.

To check quickly whether there are any mouse button messages, you use the following:

```
if (WinQueryQueueStatus (HWND_DESKTOP) & QS_MOUSEBUTTON)
```

At this point, if you are interested in retrieving mouse button messages, you can call WinPeekMsg or WinGetMsg with a mouse button filter (WM_BUTTON1DOWN, WM_BUTTONLAST), knowing that a mouse button message will be returned.

Messages are retrieved from the message queue based on a predefined priority. Messages of a higher priority are returned before messages with a lower priority.

Priority	*Message*
1	WM_SEM1.
2	Messages posted with WinPostMsg.
3	Keyboard and mouse messages.
4	WM_SEM2.
5	WM_PAINT.
6	WM_SEM3.
7	WM_TIMER.
8	WM_SEM4.

Looking at the priorities, you will always retrieve input messages before WM_PAINT messages, and you will always retrieve WM_PAINT messages before WM_TIMER messages. Notice that messages posted with WinPostMsg are assigned a priority of 2 even if the message your application posts is WM_TIMER.

WM_USER Messages

Your application is not restricted to using only the messages defined by PM. You can define your own application messages. The predefined message identifier WM_USER has been set aside

for you to define your own messages. You should not define messages with a value less than WM_USER (0x1000), but are free to define messages above this value. Typically, this is done by adding values to WM_USER as shown here:

```
#define WM_USER_POSITION      WM_USER+1
#define WM_USER_CHILDACTIVATE WM_USER+2
```

Multiple Document Interface Application

Now, you put all this information to use by creating a sample application. The sample application will be a basic Multiple Document Interface (MDI) application with a floating toolbar. MDI applications are a main application window that contains multiple child windows, all managed by the main window. The main window handles the creation, arrangement, activation, and destruction of the child windows. Figure 3.11 illustrates the MDI window for the sample application. It contains two MDI child windows and a floating toolbar window.

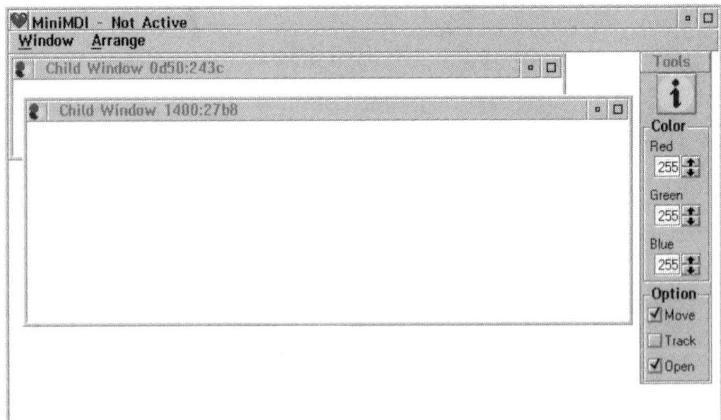

Figure 3.11.
Multiple Document Interface application windows.

The sample will use most of the concepts discussed in this chapter including window enumeration, z-order maintenance, frame window subclassing, window data, window sizing and positioning, application and window activation, and window tracking.

We begin by defining the resources that will be used. The resource file MINIMDI.RC contains the definitions for the icons, pointers, stringtable, menus, and dialogs.

MINIMDI.RC

```
/* --------------------------------
MiniMDI Resource File
Real-World Programming for OS/2
Copyright (c) 1993, 1994 Blain, Delimon, and English
-------------------------------- */
```

```
#include <os2.h>
#include "minimdi.h"

/* Icons    */
ICON    ID_APPNAME          MINIMDI.ICO
ICON    ID_CHILDWINDOW      CHILD.ICO
ICON    IDC_WININFO         WININFO.ICO

/* Pointers */
POINTER IDPTR_HEART         HEART.PTR
POINTER IDPTR_CLIENT        CLIENT.PTR
POINTER IDPTR_SYSMENU       SYSMENU.PTR
POINTER IDPTR_MENU          MENU.PTR
POINTER IDPTR_MINMAX        MINMAX.PTR
POINTER IDPTR_LEFT          LEFT.PTR
POINTER IDPTR_TOP           TOP.PTR
POINTER IDPTR_LEFTTOP       LTOP.PTR
POINTER IDPTR_RIGHTTOP      RTOP.PTR
POINTER IDPTR_TITLEBAR      TITLEBAR.PTR
POINTER IDPTR_POPUPMENU     POPUP.PTR
POINTER IDPTR_HEART2        HEART2.PTR

STRINGTABLE LOADONCALL MOVEABLE
BEGIN
   ID_APPNAME       "MiniMDI Application"
END

MENU ID_APPNAME
{
   SUBMENU "~Window",          IDM_WINDOW
   {
      MENUITEM "~New Child",     IDM_NEWCHILD
      MENUITEM "Ne~xt Child",    IDM_NEXTCHILD
      MENUITEM "",               -1,              MIS_SEPARATOR
      MENUITEM "~Close All",     IDM_CLOSEALL
      MENUITEM "",               -1,              MIS_SEPARATOR
      MENUITEM "~About",         IDM_ABOUT
   }
   SUBMENU "~Arrange",          IDM_ARRANGEMENU
   {
      MENUITEM "~Tile",          IDM_TILE
      MENUITEM "~Cascade",       IDM_CASCADE
      MENUITEM "~Arrange Icons", IDM_ARRANGE
   }
}

rcinclude toolbar.dlg
rcinclude wininfo.dlg
rcinclude ..\common\about.dlg
```

You use two dialogs in this application. One is used to display the toolbar window and the other is used to display the window information.

TOOLBAR.DLG

```
/* ------------------------------
MiniMDI Toolbar Dialog
Real-World Programming for OS/2
Copyright (c) 1993, 1994 Blain, Delimon, and English
------------------------------ */

DLGTEMPLATE IDD_TOOLBAR LOADONCALL MOVEABLE DISCARDABLE
BEGIN
  DIALOG  "Tools", IDD_TOOLBAR, 0, 0, 41, 133, NOT FS_DLGBORDER
          | FS_BORDER,
          FCF_TITLEBAR | FCF_NOBYTEALIGN | FCF_NOMOVEWITHOWNER
  BEGIN
    PUSHBUTTON    "#200", IDC_WININFO, 9, 115, 24, 18, WS_GROUP |
                  WS_TABSTOP | BS_ICON
    GROUPBOX      "Color",   -1, 1, 43, 40, 71
    LTEXT         "Red",     -1, 5, 97, 20, 8
    PRESPARAMS PP_FONTNAMESIZE, "8.Helv"
    CONTROL       "", IDC_RED, 8, 88, 27, 12, WC_SPINBUTTON,
                  SPBS_READONLY | SPBS_NUMERICONLY | SPBS_MASTER |
                  SPBS_JUSTRIGHT | SPBS_FASTSPIN |
                  WS_GROUP | WS_TABSTOP | WS_VISIBLE
                  PRESPARAMS PP_FONTNAMESIZE, "8.Helv"
    LTEXT         "Green",   -1, 5, 76, 28, 8
                  PRESPARAMS PP_FONTNAMESIZE, "8.Helv"
    CONTROL       "", IDC_GREEN, 8, 67, 27, 12, WC_SPINBUTTON,
                  SPBS_READONLY | SPBS_NUMERICONLY | SPBS_MASTER |
                  SPBS_JUSTRIGHT | SPBS_FASTSPIN |
                  WS_GROUP | WS_TABSTOP | WS_VISIBLE
                  PRESPARAMS PP_FONTNAMESIZE, "8.Helv"
    LTEXT         "Blue",    -1, 5, 55, 22, 8
                  PRESPARAMS PP_FONTNAMESIZE, "8.Helv"
    CONTROL       "", IDC_BLUE, 8, 46, 27, 12, WC_SPINBUTTON,
                  SPBS_READONLY | SPBS_NUMERICONLY | SPBS_MASTER |
                  SPBS_JUSTRIGHT | SPBS_FASTSPIN |
                  WS_GROUP | WS_TABSTOP | WS_VISIBLE
                  PRESPARAMS PP_FONTNAMESIZE, "8.Helv"
    GROUPBOX      "Option", -1, 1, 0, 40, 42
    AUTOCHECKBOX "Move",  IDC_MOVE,  4, 24, 35, 10, WS_GROUP
                  | WS_TABSTOP PRESPARAMS PP_FONTNAMESIZE, "8.Helv"
    AUTOCHECKBOX "Track", IDC_TRACK, 4, 13, 35, 10, WS_GROUP
                  | WS_TABSTOP PRESPARAMS PP_FONTNAMESIZE, "8.Helv"
    AUTOCHECKBOX "Open",  IDC_OPEN,  4,  2, 36, 10, WS_GROUP
                  | WS_TABSTOP PRESPARAMS PP_FONTNAMESIZE, "8.Helv"
  END
END
```

The Toolbar dialog was created by using the dialog editor that comes with the OS/2 toolkit with some changes made to the file. You want the toolbar to be capable of moving freely about the screen without much control from its owner. The FCF flags define the style for this dialog:

```
DIALOG  "Tools", IDD_TOOLBAR, 0, 0, 41, 133, NOT FS_DLGBORDER | FS_BORDER,
        FCF_TITLEBAR | FCF_NOBYTEALIGN | FCF_NOMOVEWITHOWNER
```

The only frame control you want for the toolbar is the titlebar. You use the FCF_NOMOVEWITHOWNER flag mentioned earlier so that the toolbar window remains in its current position when its owner window is moved around the screen. The first control is a push button control; however, you use a button style of BS_ICON. This defines a push button as usual except that an icon, rather than text, is drawn on the button face. The icon to use is defined by the text in the format "#iconID". The iconID is the numeric identifier associated with the icon to use. In this case, it is the WININFO.ICO identified with id 200 (IDC_WININFO). The toolbar also contains a set of RGB controls to define the color mix for the child window. The Red, Green, and Blue values are enclosed in a group box with each color specified by a spinner. (See Figure 3.12.) For each control within the group box, you use a slightly smaller font, so we have defined a PRESPARAMS for each. The PRESPARAMS attribute enables you to define many presentation parameter styles for the control:

```
PRESPARAMS PP_FONTNAMESIZE, "8.Helv"
```

This says that we want to use the Helv 8 point font for this control. Finally, we have three checkboxes enclosed in another group box. These checkboxes are used to set the three options that we have defined. (See Figure 3.12.)

Figure 3.12.
Toolbar dialog using spinners and checkboxes.

WININFO.DLG

```
/* ------------------------------
MiniMDI WinInfo Dialog
Real World Programming for OS/2
Copyright (c) 1993, 1994 Blain, Delimon, and English
------------------------------ */

DLGTEMPLATE IDD_WININFO LOADONCALL MOVEABLE DISCARDABLE
BEGIN
  DIALOG  "Window Information", IDD_WININFO, 67, 62, 192, 51, WS_VISIBLE, FCF_SYSMENU |
FCF_TITLEBAR

  BEGIN
    LTEXT      "Title:",    -1,         6, 39,  22,   8
    GROUPBOX   "Position", -1,         3,  4, 111,  30
```

```
    LTEXT       "X:",        -1,       11, 17,  20,   8
    LTEXT       "Y:",        -1,       11,  7,  20,   8
    LTEXT       "Width:",    -1,       49, 17,  32,   8
    LTEXT       "Height:",   -1,       49,  7,  32,   8
    GROUPBOX    "State",     -1,      125, 18,  57,  16
    ENTRYFIELD "",        IDC_TITLE,  31, 38, 150, 8, ES_MARGIN ¦
                WS_GROUP ¦ WS_TABSTOP
    PUSHBUTTON "OK",      DID_OK,    124,  3,  40, 13,
WS_GROUP ¦ WS_TABSTOP
    RTEXT       "0000",   IDC_XPOS,   22, 17,  23, 8
    RTEXT       "0000",   IDC_YPOS,   22,  7,  23, 8
    RTEXT       "0000",   IDC_WIDTH,  81, 17,  25, 8
    RTEXT       "0000",   IDC_HEIGHT, 81,  7,  25, 8
    LTEXT       "Normal", IDC_STATE, 128, 19,  51, 8
  END
END
```

The Window Information dialog was also created using the dialog editor. The FCF flags define the styles for this dialog:

```
DIALOG  "Window Information", IDD_WININFO, 67, 62, 192, 51, WS_VISIBLE,
        FCF_SYSMENU ¦ FCF_TITLEBAR
```

This dialog is defined to contain a system menu and a titlebar. This dialog consists of several static control fields, an edit window, and a push button. The edit window is used to display the child window text, and the push button is used to accept the changes to the window text. We move now to the application code.

MINIMDI.C

```
/* ---------------------------------
MiniMDI Program
Real-World Programming for OS/2
Copyright (c) 1993, 1994 Blain, Delimon, and English
------------------------------- */

#define INCL_WIN
#define INCL_GPI

#include <os2.h>
#include <stdio.h>
#include "minimdi.h"
#include "..\common\about.h"

/* Window and Dialog Functions        */
MRESULT EXPENTRY ClientWndProc  (HWND,ULONG,MPARAM,MPARAM);
MRESULT EXPENTRY ChildWndProc   (HWND,ULONG,MPARAM,MPARAM);
MRESULT EXPENTRY ToolBarDlgProc (HWND,ULONG,MPARAM,MPARAM);
MRESULT EXPENTRY WinInfoDlgProc (HWND,ULONG,MPARAM,MPARAM);

/* Window Subclass Functions          */
MRESULT EXPENTRY ChildSubclassProc    (HWND,ULONG,MPARAM,MPARAM);
MRESULT EXPENTRY FrameSubclassProc    (HWND,ULONG,MPARAM,MPARAM);
```

```
MRESULT EXPENTRY MenuSubclassProc      (HWND,ULONG,MPARAM,MPARAM);
MRESULT EXPENTRY SysMenuSubclassProc   (HWND,ULONG,MPARAM,MPARAM);
MRESULT EXPENTRY TitleBarSubclassProc  (HWND,ULONG,MPARAM,MPARAM);

/* Local Functions                     */
VOID ArrangeIcons (HWND);
VOID CascadeChildWindows (HWND);
VOID CenterWindow (HWND);
VOID CloseAllChildWindows (HWND);
VOID CreateChildWindow (HWND);
VOID GetNextWindowPos (ULONG, PSWP);
VOID InitializeAppWindow (HWND);
BOOL IsWindowMaximized (HWND);
BOOL IsWindowMinimized (HWND);
VOID PaintTitleBar (HWND, HPS);
VOID SwitchToNextChildWindow (VOID);
VOID TileChildWindows (HWND);


/* Undocumented WinDrawBorder Flags */
#define DB_RAISED        0x0400
#define DB_CORNERBORDER  0x8000

/* User-Defined messages               */
#define WM_USER_POSITION      WM_USER+1
#define WM_USER_CHILDACTIVATE WM_USER+2

/* User-Defined Window Extra Words  */
#define QWL_COLOR_RGB  QWL_USER                              /* ULONG  */
#define QWL_MOVE       QWL_COLOR_RGB + sizeof(ULONG)   /* BOOL   */
#define QWL_TRACKING   QWL_MOVE      + sizeof(BOOL)    /* BOOL   */
#define QWL_OPEN       QWL_TRACKING  + sizeof(BOOL)    /* BOOL   */
#define QWL_EXTRA      QWL_OPEN      + sizeof(BOOL)

/* Global Variables                    */
HAB        hab;
HWND       hWndFrame,
           hWndClient,
           hWndToolBar,
           hWndActiveChild;
CHAR       szTitle[64];
BOOL       bAppIsActive     = FALSE;
ULONG      ulNumChildren    = 0L;
ULONG      ulNumMinChildren = 0L;

/* Pointer Handles                     */
HPOINTER hPtrHeart        = 0;
HPOINTER hPtrClient       = 0;
HPOINTER hPtrSysMenu      = 0;
HPOINTER hPtrMenu         = 0;
HPOINTER hPtrMinMax       = 0;
HPOINTER hPtrLeft         = 0;
HPOINTER hPtrTop          = 0;
HPOINTER hPtrLeftTop      = 0;
HPOINTER hPtrRightTop     = 0;
```

```
HPOINTER hPtrTitleBar      = 0;
HPOINTER hPtrPopupMenu     = 0;
HPOINTER hPtrHeart2        = 0;

/* Subclassed PM Window Callbacks   */
PFNWP     pfnFrameProc;                 /* Frame Window       */
PFNWP     pfnTitleBarProc;              /* TitleBar Window    */
PFNWP     pfnSysMenuProc;               /* System Menu Window */
PFNWP     pfnMenuProc;                  /* Menu Window        */

int main()
{
  HMQ   hmq;
  QMSG  qmsg;
  ULONG flFrameFlags    = FCF_TITLEBAR ¦ FCF_SYSMENU ¦ FCF_ICON ¦
                          FCF_SIZEBORDER ¦ FCF_MINMAX ¦ FCF_MENU ¦
                          FCF_SHELLPOSITION ¦ FCF_TASKLIST;
  CHAR  szClientClass[] = "CLIENT";

  hab = WinInitialize (0);
  hmq = WinCreateMsgQueue (hab, 0);

  WinRegisterClass (hab, szClientClass, ClientWndProc, 0, 0);
  WinLoadString (hab, 0, ID_APPNAME, sizeof(szTitle), szTitle);

  /* Create the main application window */
  hWndFrame = WinCreateStdWindow (HWND_DESKTOP, 0,
              &flFrameFlags, szClientClass, szTitle, 0, 0, ID_APPNAME,
              &hWndClient);

  /* Subclass the frame control windows */
  pfnFrameProc     = WinSubclassWindow (hWndFrame,
                         (PFNWP)FrameSubclassProc);
  pfnTitleBarProc = WinSubclassWindow (
     WinWindowFromID (hWndFrame, FID_TITLEBAR),
         (PFNWP)TitleBarSubclassProc);
  pfnSysMenuProc   = WinSubclassWindow (
     WinWindowFromID (hWndFrame, FID_SYSMENU),
         (PFNWP)SysMenuSubclassProc);
  pfnMenuProc      = WinSubclassWindow (
     WinWindowFromID (hWndFrame, FID_MENU),
         (PFNWP)MenuSubclassProc);

  InitializeAppWindow (hWndClient);

  WinShowWindow (hWndFrame, TRUE);

  while (WinGetMsg (hab, &qmsg, 0, 0, 0))
    WinDispatchMsg (hab, &qmsg);

  WinDestroyWindow (hWndFrame);
  WinDestroyMsgQueue (hmq);
  WinTerminate (hab);
  return (0);
}
```

```
/* ---------- Local Functions ---------- */

VOID ArrangeIcons (HWND hWnd)
{
  PSWP  pSwp;

  /* Allocate memory to hold the SWP structures */
  if (!DosAllocMem ((PPVOID)&pSwp, sizeof(SWP) * ulNumMinChildren,
      fALLOC))
  {
    HWND  hWndChild;
    ULONG ulChildCnt;
    HENUM hEnum;

    ulChildCnt  = 0;

    /* Begin child window enumeration */
    hEnum = WinBeginEnumWindows (hWnd);

    /* Get handle to each child frame window */
    while ((hWndChild = WinGetNextWindow (hEnum)) != 0)
    {
      if ( IsWindowMinimized (hWndChild) )
      {
        pSwp[ulChildCnt].fl      = SWP_MOVE | SWP_FOCUSDEACTIVATE;
        pSwp[ulChildCnt].x       =
        pSwp[ulChildCnt].y       = 0;
        pSwp[ulChildCnt++].hwnd = hWndChild;
        /* Destroy the current minimize position - a little
PM trick */
        WinSetWindowUShort (hWndChild,QWS_XMINIMIZE,(USHORT)-1);
        WinSetWindowUShort (hWndChild,QWS_YMINIMIZE,(USHORT)-1);
      }
    }

    /* End child window enumeration */
    WinEndEnumWindows (hEnum);

    /* Arrange the iconic windows   */
    WinSetMultWindowPos (hab, pSwp, ulChildCnt);

    /* Free the allocated memory    */
    DosFreeMem ((PVOID)pSwp);
  }

  return;
}

VOID CascadeChildWindows (HWND hWnd)
{
  PSWP  pSwp;
  ULONG ulChildCnt = (ulNumChildren - ulNumMinChildren);

  /* Allocate memory to hold the SWP structures */
```

```
  if (!DosAllocMem ((PPVOID)&pSwp, sizeof(SWP) * ulChildCnt, fALLOC))
  {
    HWND  hWndChild;

    ulChildCnt = 0L;

    /* Query the bottommost child frame window in the z-order */
    hWndChild  = WinQueryWindow (hWnd, QW_BOTTOM);

    while (hWndChild)
    {
      /* Skip ICONTEXT windows and minimized windows */
      if ( WinQueryWindowUShort (hWndChild, QWS_ID) &&
           !IsWindowMinimized (hWndChild) )
      {
        GetNextWindowPos (ulChildCnt, &pSwp[ulChildCnt]);
        pSwp[ulChildCnt].fl = SWP_MOVE ¦ SWP_SIZE ¦ SWP_SHOW;

        /* If child is maximized then restore it */
        if (IsWindowMaximized (hWndChild))
            pSwp[ulChildCnt].fl ¦= SWP_RESTORE;

        pSwp[ulChildCnt++].hwnd = hWndChild;
      }

      /* Query the previous child frame window in the z-order */
      hWndChild = WinQueryWindow (hWndChild, QW_PREV);
    }

    /* Arrange the cascaded windows */
    WinSetMultWindowPos (hab, pSwp, ulChildCnt);

    /* Free the allocated memory    */
    DosFreeMem ((PVOID)pSwp);
  }

  return;
}

VOID CenterWindow (HWND hWnd)
{
  ULONG ulScrWidth, ulScrHeight;
  RECTL Rectl;

  ulScrWidth  = WinQuerySysValue (HWND_DESKTOP, SV_CXSCREEN);
  ulScrHeight = WinQuerySysValue (HWND_DESKTOP, SV_CYSCREEN);
  WinQueryWindowRect (hWnd,&Rectl);
  WinSetWindowPos (hWnd, HWND_TOP, (ulScrWidth -Rectl.xRight)/2,
      (ulScrHeight-Rectl.yTop)/2, 0, 0, SWP_MOVE ¦ SWP_ACTIVATE);
  return;
}

VOID CloseAllChildWindows (HWND hWnd)
{
```

```
  HWND  hWndChild;
  HENUM hEnum;

  /* Begin child window enumeration */
  hEnum = WinBeginEnumWindows (hWnd);

  /* Get handle to each child frame window */
  while ((hWndChild = WinGetNextWindow (hEnum)) != 0)
    WinDestroyWindow (hWndChild);

  /* End child window enumeration */
  WinEndEnumWindows (hEnum);

  return;
}

VOID CreateChildWindow (HWND hWnd)
{
  HWND  hWndChild;
  HWND  hWndChildFrame;
  CHAR  szTitle[23];
  ULONG flChildFrameFlags  = FCF_TITLEBAR ¦ FCF_SYSMENU ¦ FCF_ICON ¦
                             FCF_SIZEBORDER ¦ FCF_MINMAX ¦
                             FCF_NOBYTEALIGN;

  if ((hWndChildFrame = WinCreateStdWindow (hWnd, 0L,
        &flChildFrameFlags,
        "CHILD", "", 0L, 0L, ID_CHILDWINDOW, &hWndChild)) != 0)
  {
    SWP Swp;

    /* If the currently active child is maximized restore it */
    if (hWndActiveChild && IsWindowMaximized (hWndActiveChild))
      WinSetWindowPos (WinQueryWindow (hWndActiveChild, QW_PARENT),
          0L, 0L, 0L, 0L, 0L, SWP_RESTORE);

    WinSetOwner (hWndChild, hWndChildFrame);

    sprintf (szTitle, "Child Window %04x:%04x",
          HIUSHORT(hWndChildFrame), LOUSHORT(hWndChildFrame));
    WinSetWindowText  (hWndChildFrame, szTitle);

    GetNextWindowPos (ulNumChildren - 1L, &Swp);
    WinSetWindowPos (hWndChildFrame, 0L, Swp.x, Swp.y, Swp.cx, Swp.cy,
        SWP_MOVE ¦ SWP_SIZE ¦ SWP_SHOW ¦ SWP_ACTIVATE);

    /* Force a repaint of the titlebar window */
    WinInvalidateRect (WinWindowFromID(hWndFrame,FID_TITLEBAR),
        NULL, FALSE);
  }

  return;
}
```

```
VOID GetNextWindowPos (ULONG ulCnt, PSWP pSwp)
{
  RECTL Rectl;
  ULONG ulXDiff,
  ulYDiff,
  ulWindowsPerStack;

  WinQueryWindowRect (hWndClient, &Rectl);
  if (ulNumMinChildren)
    Rectl.yBottom += WinQuerySysValue (HWND_DESKTOP, SV_CYICON) * 2;

  ulXDiff  = WinQuerySysValue (HWND_DESKTOP, SV_CXSIZEBORDER) +
        WinQuerySysValue (HWND_DESKTOP, SV_CXMINMAXBUTTON) / 2;
  ulYDiff  =  WinQuerySysValue (HWND_DESKTOP, SV_CYSIZEBORDER) +
        WinQuerySysValue (HWND_DESKTOP, SV_CYMINMAXBUTTON);

  ulWindowsPerStack  = (Rectl.yTop - Rectl.yBottom) / (3 * ulYDiff);
  pSwp->cx = Rectl.xRight - (ulWindowsPerStack * ulXDiff);
  pSwp->cy = (Rectl.yTop - Rectl.yBottom) -
             (ulWindowsPerStack * ulYDiff);
  ulWindowsPerStack++;
  pSwp->x  = (ulCnt % ulWindowsPerStack) * ulXDiff;
  pSwp->y  = Rectl.yTop - pSwp->cy -
             ((ulCnt % ulWindowsPerStack) * ulYDiff);

  return;
}

VOID InitializeAppWindow (HWND hWnd)
{
  WinRegisterClass (hab, "CHILD", ChildWndProc, 0, QWL_EXTRA);

  hWndToolBar = WinLoadDlg (HWND_DESKTOP, hWnd, ToolBarDlgProc,
       0L, IDD_TOOLBAR, NULL);

  /* Create three children initially */
  CreateChildWindow (hWnd);
  CreateChildWindow (hWnd);
  CreateChildWindow (hWnd);

  WinPostMsg (hWndToolBar, WM_USER_POSITION, 0L, 0L);
  WinPostMsg (hWnd, WM_COMMAND, (MPARAM)IDM_TILE, 0L);
  return;
}

BOOL IsWindowMaximized (HWND hWnd)
{
  /* If hWnd is the client window, query the frame window
(ie. the parent) */
  if (WinQueryWindowUShort (hWnd, QWS_ID) == FID_CLIENT)
    hWnd = WinQueryWindow (hWnd, QW_PARENT);
  return (WinQueryWindowULong (hWnd, QWL_STYLE) & WS_MAXIMIZED);
}

BOOL IsWindowMinimized (HWND hWnd)
{
```

```
  if (WinQueryWindowUShort (hWnd, QWS_ID) == FID_CLIENT)
    hWnd = WinQueryWindow (hWnd, QW_PARENT);
  return (WinQueryWindowULong (hWnd, QWL_STYLE) & WS_MINIMIZED);
}

VOID PaintTitleBar (HWND hWnd, HPS hps)
{
  RECTL Rectl;
  BOOL  bActive;
  SHORT Scale,
        X;
  ULONG inx;

  /* If window is not visible then nothing to paint */
  if (!WinIsWindowVisible (hWnd))
      return;

  /* Get the current active state of the titlebar */
  bActive = (BOOL)(WinQueryWindowULong (hWnd, QWL_USER) & 1);

  /* Draw the correct border for the titlebar */
  WinQueryWindowRect (hWnd, &Rectl);
  WinDrawBorder (hps, &Rectl, bActive ? 0L : 1L, 1L,
      SYSCLR_TITLEBOTTOM,
      bActive ? SYSCLR_ACTIVETITLE : SYSCLR_INACTIVETITLE,
      DB_RAISED ¦ DB_CORNERBORDER ¦ DB_STANDARD ¦ DB_INTERIOR);

  /* Draw a heart for each child window that exists.
  Since the WC_TITLEBAR class is not CS_CLIPSIBLINGS, it is
possible to write over the minmax window.  Only output as many
  hearts as will fit in the titlebar window.
  Use the WinDrawPointer API so we get a transparent bitblt.*/

  Scale = (SHORT)(Rectl.yTop - Rectl.yBottom - 2 -
          2 * WinQuerySysValue (HWND_DESKTOP, SV_CYBORDER));

  if (bAppIsActive)
  {
    if ((inx = ulNumChildren) != 0)
    {
      X = (SHORT)(WinQuerySysValue (HWND_DESKTOP, SV_CXBORDER) + 1);
      while ( inx && ((LONG)(X + Scale) < Rectl.xRight) )
      {

        WinDrawPointer (hps, X, 2, hPtrHeart2, DP_NORMAL);
        inx--;
        X += (SHORT)(Scale + 2);
      }
    }
    else
    {
      POINTL Ptl;
      Ptl.x = WinQuerySysValue (HWND_DESKTOP, SV_CXBORDER) + 1;
      Ptl.y = 2;
      GpiCharStringAt (hps, &Ptl, 21L, (PSZ)"MiniMDI - No children");
    }
```

```
  }
  else
  {
    POINTL Ptl;
    Ptl.x = WinQuerySysValue (HWND_DESKTOP, SV_CXBORDER) + 1;
    Ptl.y = 2;
    GpiCharStringAt (hps, &Ptl, 20L, (PSZ)"MiniMDI - Not Active");
  }

  return;
}

VOID SwitchToNextChildWindow ()
{
  HWND hWndNext,
  hWndActiveFrame;

  hWndNext        =
  hWndActiveFrame = WinQueryWindow (hWndActiveChild, QW_PARENT);

  /* We need to query the next until we find a
non-WC_ICONTEXT window */
  while ( ((hWndNext = WinQueryWindow (hWndNext, QW_NEXT)) != 0) &&
          !WinQueryWindowUShort (hWndNext, QWS_ID))
  {
    /* Do Nothing */
  }
  if (hWndNext)
  {
    /* If current active child is maximized then restore it */
    WinSetWindowPos (hWndNext, HWND_TOP, 0, 0, 0, 0,
        SWP_ZORDER | SWP_ACTIVATE);
    WinSetWindowPos (hWndActiveFrame, HWND_BOTTOM, 0, 0, 0, 0,
        IsWindowMaximized (hWndActiveFrame) ?
            SWP_RESTORE | SWP_ZORDER : SWP_ZORDER);
  }

  return;
}

VOID TileChildWindows (HWND hWnd)
{
  PSWP  pSwp;
  ULONG ulChildCnt = (ulNumChildren - ulNumMinChildren);

  /* Allocate memory to hold the SWP structures */
  if (!DosAllocMem ((PPVOID)&pSwp, sizeof(SWP) * ulChildCnt, fALLOC))
  {
    ULONG ulSquare,
          ulNumRows,
          ulNumCols,
          ulExtraCols,
          ulWidth,
          ulHeight;
```

```
RECTL Rectl;
HWND  hWndChild;

for (ulSquare = 2; ulSquare * ulSquare <= ulChildCnt; ulSquare++);

{}

ulNumCols   = ulSquare - 1;
ulNumRows   = ulChildCnt / ulNumCols;
ulExtraCols = ulChildCnt % ulNumCols;

WinQueryWindowRect (hWnd, &Rectl);
if (ulNumMinChildren)
    Rectl.yBottom += WinQuerySysValue (HWND_DESKTOP, SV_CYICON) * 2;
if (Rectl.xRight > 0L && (Rectl.yBottom < Rectl.yTop))
{
  HENUM hEnum;

  /* Begin child window enumeration */
  hEnum = WinBeginEnumWindows (hWnd);

  /* Get handle to each child frame window */
  if ((hWndChild = WinGetNextWindow (hEnum)) != 0)
  {
    ULONG ulCurRow,
          ulCurCol;

    ulChildCnt = 0L;
    ulHeight   = (Rectl.yTop - Rectl.yBottom) / ulNumRows;

    for (ulCurRow = 0; ulCurRow < ulNumRows; ulCurRow++)
    {
      if ((ulNumRows - ulCurRow) <= ulExtraCols)
          ulNumCols++;
      for (ulCurCol = 0; ulCurCol < ulNumCols; ulCurCol++)
      {
        ulWidth = Rectl.xRight / ulNumCols;

        /* Skip ICONTEXT windows and minimized windows */
        while ( hWndChild &&
                ( !WinQueryWindowUShort (hWndChild, QWS_ID) ||
                  IsWindowMinimized (hWndChild) ) )
           hWndChild = WinGetNextWindow (hEnum);

        if (hWndChild)
        {
          pSwp[ulChildCnt].fl     =
              SWP_MOVE | SWP_SIZE | SWP_SHOW;

          /* If child is maximized, then restore it */
          if (IsWindowMaximized (hWndChild))
             pSwp[ulChildCnt].fl |= SWP_RESTORE;

          pSwp[ulChildCnt].x      = ulWidth * ulCurCol;
```

```
            pSwp[ulChildCnt].y      = Rectl.yTop - (ulHeight * (ulCurRow + 1));
            pSwp[ulChildCnt].cx     = ulWidth;
            pSwp[ulChildCnt].cy     = ulHeight;
            pSwp[ulChildCnt++].hwnd = hWndChild;

            /* Get handle to next child frame window */
            hWndChild = WinGetNextWindow (hEnum);
          }
        }
        if ((ulNumRows - ulCurRow) <= ulExtraCols)
        {
          ulNumCols--;
          ulExtraCols--;
        }
      }
    }

    /* End child window enumeration */
    WinEndEnumWindows (hEnum);
  }

  /* Arrange the tiled windwos */
  WinSetMultWindowPos (hab, pSwp, ulChildCnt);

  /* Free the allocated memory    */
  DosFreeMem ((PVOID)pSwp);
}

return;
}

/* -------- Window and Dialog Functions -------- */

MRESULT EXPENTRY ClientWndProc (HWND hWnd, ULONG msg, MPARAM mp1,
                                MPARAM mp2)
{
  BOOL    bHandled = TRUE;
  MRESULT mReturn  = 0;
  RECTL   Rectl;
  HPS     hps;

  switch (msg)
  {
    case WM_CREATE:
      hPtrHeart     = WinLoadPointer(HWND_DESKTOP,0L,IDPTR_HEART);
      hPtrClient    = WinLoadPointer(HWND_DESKTOP,0L,IDPTR_CLIENT);
      hPtrSysMenu   = WinLoadPointer(HWND_DESKTOP,0L,IDPTR_SYSMENU);
      hPtrMenu      = WinLoadPointer(HWND_DESKTOP,0L,IDPTR_MENU);
      hPtrMinMax    = WinLoadPointer(HWND_DESKTOP,0L,IDPTR_MINMAX);
      hPtrLeft      = WinLoadPointer(HWND_DESKTOP,0L,IDPTR_LEFT);
      hPtrTop       = WinLoadPointer(HWND_DESKTOP,0L,IDPTR_TOP);
      hPtrLeftTop   = WinLoadPointer(HWND_DESKTOP,0L,IDPTR_LEFTTOP);
      hPtrRightTop  = WinLoadPointer(HWND_DESKTOP,0L,IDPTR_RIGHTTOP);
```

```
  hPtrTitleBar  = WinLoadPointer(HWND_DESKTOP,0L,IDPTR_TITLEBAR);
  hPtrPopupMenu = WinLoadPointer(HWND_DESKTOP,0L,IDPTR_POPUPMENU);
  hPtrHeart2    = WinLoadPointer(HWND_DESKTOP,0L,IDPTR_HEART2);
  break;

case WM_MOUSEMOVE:
  WinSetPointer (HWND_DESKTOP, hPtrClient);
  break;

case WM_PAINT:
  hps = WinBeginPaint (hWnd,0,0);
  WinQueryWindowRect (hWnd, &Rectl);
  WinFillRect (hps, &Rectl, CLR_WHITE);
  WinEndPaint (hps);
  mReturn = 0L;
  break;

case WM_FOCUSCHANGE:
  if ( WinQueryWindowULong (hWnd, QWL_HMQ) !=
       WinQueryWindowULong ((HWND)mp1, QWL_HMQ) )
  {
    if (SHORT1FROMMP(mp2))
      /* Application is gaining activation */
      bAppIsActive = TRUE;
    else
      /* Application is losing activation */
      bAppIsActive = FALSE;

    /* Force a repaint of the titlebar window */
    WinInvalidateRect (WinWindowFromID(hWndFrame,FID_TITLEBAR),
        NULL, FALSE);
  }
  bHandled = FALSE;
  break;

case WM_INITMENU:
  if (SHORT1FROMMP(mp1) == IDM_ARRANGEMENU)
  {
    BOOL bEnable = (ulNumChildren != ulNumMinChildren);
    WinEnableMenuItem ((HWND)mp2, IDM_TILE,    bEnable);
    WinEnableMenuItem ((HWND)mp2, IDM_CASCADE, bEnable);
    WinEnableMenuItem ((HWND)mp2, IDM_ARRANGE, ulNumMinChildren);
  }
  else if (SHORT1FROMMP(mp1) == IDM_WINDOW)
  {
    WinEnableMenuItem ((HWND)mp2, IDM_NEXTCHILD,
        ulNumChildren > 1);
    WinEnableMenuItem ((HWND)mp2, IDM_CLOSEALL,
        ulNumChildren);
  }
  break;

case WM_COMMAND:
  switch (LOUSHORT(mp1))
  {
```

```
        case IDM_NEWCHILD:
          CreateChildWindow (hWnd);
          break;

        case IDM_NEXTCHILD:
          if (hWndActiveChild)
             SwitchToNextChildWindow ();
          break;

        case IDM_TILE:
          TileChildWindows (hWnd);
          break;

        case IDM_CASCADE:
          CascadeChildWindows (hWnd);
          break;

        case IDM_ARRANGE:
          ArrangeIcons (hWnd);
          break;

        case IDM_CLOSEALL:
          CloseAllChildWindows (hWnd);
          break;

        case IDM_ABOUT:
          DisplayAbout (hWnd, szTitle);
          break;
      }
      break;

    case WM_DESTROY:
      WinDestroyPointer (hPtrHeart);
      WinDestroyPointer (hPtrClient);
      WinDestroyPointer (hPtrSysMenu);
      WinDestroyPointer (hPtrMenu);
      WinDestroyPointer (hPtrMinMax);
      WinDestroyPointer (hPtrLeft);
      WinDestroyPointer (hPtrTop);
      WinDestroyPointer (hPtrLeftTop);
      WinDestroyPointer (hPtrRightTop);
      WinDestroyPointer (hPtrTitleBar);
      WinDestroyPointer (hPtrPopupMenu);
      WinDestroyPointer (hPtrHeart2);
      break;

    default:
      bHandled = FALSE;
      break;
  }

  if (!bHandled)
     mReturn = WinDefWindowProc (hWnd,msg,mp1,mp2);

  return (mReturn);
```

```
}

MRESULT EXPENTRY ChildWndProc (HWND hWnd, ULONG msg, MPARAM mp1,
                               MPARAM mp2)
{
  MRESULT mReturn = 0L;
  ULONG   ulColorRGB;
  PSWP    pSwp;
  RECTL   Rectl;
  HPS     hps;

  switch (msg)
  {
    case WM_CREATE:
      /* Initialize window extra words */
      WinSetWindowULong (hWnd, QWL_COLOR_RGB, 0x00FFFFFF);
      WinSetWindowULong (hWnd, QWL_MOVE,      TRUE);
      WinSetWindowULong (hWnd, QWL_TRACKING,  FALSE);
      WinSetWindowULong (hWnd, QWL_OPEN,      TRUE);
      ulNumChildren++;

      /* If this is first child window, then enable the toolbar */
      if (ulNumChildren == 1)
         WinEnableWindow (hWndToolBar, TRUE);
      break;

    case WM_PAINT:
      hps = WinBeginPaint (hWnd,0,0);
      WinQueryWindowRect (hWnd, &Rectl);
      /* Set color state in the hps to RGB mode */
      GpiCreateLogColorTable (hps, LCOL_RESET, LCOLF_RGB, 0L, 0L,
          NULL);
      ulColorRGB = WinQueryWindowULong (hWnd, QWL_COLOR_RGB);
      WinFillRect (hps, &Rectl, ulColorRGB);
      WinEndPaint (hps);
      break;

    case WM_MINMAXFRAME:
      pSwp = (PSWP)mp1;

      /* Are we becoming minimized? */
      if (pSwp->fl & SWP_MINIMIZE)
         ulNumMinChildren++;
      else
      {
        /* hWnd is the client window handle - use the frame */
        HWND hWndFrame = WinQueryWindow (hWnd, QW_PARENT);

        if (IsWindowMinimized (hWndFrame))
        {
          /* Is the child window allowed to restore itself? */
          if (WinQueryWindowULong (hWnd, QWL_OPEN))
          {
            ulNumMinChildren--;
            WinSetWindowUShort (hWndFrame, QWS_XMINIMIZE, (USHORT)-1);
```

```
            WinSetWindowUShort (hWndFrame, QWS_YMINIMIZE, (USHORT)-1);
          }
          else
          {
            /* Don't allow the window to restore itself.
               Reset the window position */
            WinQueryWindowPos (hWndFrame, pSwp);
            mReturn = (MRESULT)TRUE;
          }
        }
      }
      break;

    case WM_ACTIVATE:
      if (SHORT1FROMMP(mp1))
      {
        hWndActiveChild = hWnd;

        /* Notify toolbar of new active child window */
        WinSendMsg (hWndToolBar, WM_USER_CHILDACTIVATE, 0L, 0L);
      }
      break;

    case WM_CLOSE:
      /* Don't let the WM_CLOSE go to WinDefWindowProc.  The default
         processing for this is to post a WM_QUIT message to the
         application.  Since this is a child closing we don't want
         that to occur - just destroy the window. */
      WinDestroyWindow (WinQueryWindow (hWnd, QW_PARENT));
      break;

    case WM_DESTROY:
      if (IsWindowMinimized (hWnd))
         ulNumMinChildren--;
      ulNumChildren--;

      /* If there are no children left then disable the toolbar */
      if (ulNumChildren == 0)
         WinEnableWindow (hWndToolBar, FALSE);

      /* Force a repaint of the titlebar window */
      WinInvalidateRect (WinWindowFromID(hWndFrame,FID_TITLEBAR),
          NULL, FALSE);
      break;

    default:
      mReturn = WinDefWindowProc (hWnd,msg,mp1,mp2);
      break;
  }

  return (mReturn);
}

MRESULT EXPENTRY ToolBarDlgProc (HWND hWnd, ULONG msg, MPARAM mp1,
                                 MPARAM mp2)
{
```

```
MRESULT mReturn  = 0L;
BOOL    bHandled = TRUE;
HWND    hWndOwner;
RECTL   Rectl;

switch (msg)
{
  case WM_INITDLG:
    WinSendDlgItemMsg (hWnd, IDC_RED, SPBM_SETTEXTLIMIT,
        (MPARAM)3, (MPARAM)0);
    WinSendDlgItemMsg (hWnd, IDC_RED, SPBM_SETLIMITS,
        (MPARAM)255L, (MPARAM)0L);
    WinSendDlgItemMsg (hWnd, IDC_BLUE, SPBM_SETTEXTLIMIT,
        (MPARAM)3, (MPARAM)0);
    WinSendDlgItemMsg (hWnd, IDC_BLUE, SPBM_SETLIMITS,
        (MPARAM)255L, (MPARAM)0L);
    WinSendDlgItemMsg (hWnd, IDC_GREEN, SPBM_SETTEXTLIMIT,
        (MPARAM)3, (MPARAM)0);
    WinSendDlgItemMsg (hWnd, IDC_GREEN, SPBM_SETLIMITS,
        (MPARAM)255L, (MPARAM)0L);
    WinSetFocus (HWND_DESKTOP, WinWindowFromID (hWnd, IDC_WININFO));
    break;

  case WM_USER_POSITION:
    /* Position the toolbar in the lower-left corner of the owner */
    hWndOwner = WinQueryWindow (hWnd, QW_OWNER);
    WinQueryWindowRect (hWndOwner, &Rectl);
    WinMapWindowPoints (hWndOwner, HWND_DESKTOP,
        (PPOINTL)&Rectl, 1L);
    WinSetWindowPos (hWnd, 0, Rectl.xLeft, Rectl.yBottom, 0L, 0L,
        SWP_MOVE | SWP_SHOW);
    break;

  case WM_USER_CHILDACTIVATE:
  {
    ULONG ulRGB = WinQueryWindowULong (hWndActiveChild,
                    QWL_COLOR_RGB);
    WinCheckButton (hWnd, IDC_MOVE,
        (USHORT)WinQueryWindowULong (hWndActiveChild,
                    QWL_MOVE));
    WinCheckButton (hWnd, IDC_TRACK,
        (USHORT)WinQueryWindowULong (hWndActiveChild,
                    QWL_TRACKING));
    WinCheckButton (hWnd, IDC_OPEN,
        (USHORT)WinQueryWindowULong (hWndActiveChild,
                    QWL_OPEN));
    WinSendDlgItemMsg (hWnd, IDC_RED,   SPBM_SETCURRENTVALUE,
        (MPARAM)((ulRGB & 0x00FF0000) >> 16), (MPARAM)0L);
    WinSendDlgItemMsg (hWnd, IDC_GREEN, SPBM_SETCURRENTVALUE,
        (MPARAM)((ulRGB & 0x0000FF00) >>  8), (MPARAM)0L);
    WinSendDlgItemMsg (hWnd, IDC_BLUE, SPBM_SETCURRENTVALUE,
        (MPARAM)(ulRGB & 0x000000FF), (MPARAM)0L);
  }
  break;

case WM_CONTROL:
```

```
if (hWndActiveChild)
{
  BOOL bChecked;
  switch (SHORT1FROMMP(mp1))
  {
    case IDC_MOVE:
      if (SHORT2FROMMP(mp1) == BN_CLICKED)
      {
        bChecked = WinQueryButtonCheckstate (hWnd, IDC_MOVE);
        WinSetWindowULong (hWndActiveChild, QWL_MOVE, bChecked);
        WinSubclassWindow (
            WinQueryWindow (hWndActiveChild, QW_PARENT),
            (PFNWP)ChildSubclassProc);
      }
      break;

    case IDC_TRACK:
      if (SHORT2FROMMP(mp1) == BN_CLICKED)
      {
        bChecked = WinQueryButtonCheckstate (hWnd, IDC_TRACK);
        WinSetWindowULong (hWndActiveChild, QWL_TRACKING,
            bChecked);
        WinSubclassWindow (
            WinQueryWindow (hWndActiveChild, QW_PARENT),
            (PFNWP)ChildSubclassProc);
      }
      break;

    case IDC_OPEN:
      if (SHORT2FROMMP(mp1) == BN_CLICKED)
      {
        bChecked = WinQueryButtonCheckstate (hWnd, IDC_OPEN);
        WinSetWindowULong (hWndActiveChild, QWL_OPEN, bChecked);
      }
      break;

    case IDC_RED:
    case IDC_GREEN:
    case IDC_BLUE:
      if (SHORT2FROMMP(mp1) == SPBN_ENDSPIN)
      {
        ULONG ulRed,
              ulGreen,
              ulBlue;

        WinSendDlgItemMsg (hWnd, IDC_RED,
            SPBM_QUERYVALUE, (MPARAM)&ulRed, 0L);
        WinSendDlgItemMsg (hWnd, IDC_GREEN,
            SPBM_QUERYVALUE, (MPARAM)&ulGreen, 0L);
        WinSendDlgItemMsg (hWnd, IDC_BLUE,
            SPBM_QUERYVALUE, (MPARAM)&ulBlue, 0L);
        WinSetWindowULong (hWndActiveChild, QWL_COLOR_RGB,
            (ulRed << 16) | (ulGreen << 8) | ulBlue);

        /* Force the child to repaint NOW */
        WinInvalidateRect (hWndActiveChild, NULL,   FALSE);
```

```
          WinUpdateWindow (hWndActiveChild);
        }
        break;
      }
    }
    break;

  case WM_COMMAND:
    switch (LOUSHORT(mp1))
    {
      case IDC_WININFO:
        if (hWndActiveChild)
        {
          WinEnableWindow (hWndFrame, FALSE);
          WinDlgBox (HWND_DESKTOP, hWnd, WinInfoDlgProc,
                     0L, IDD_WININFO, NULL);
          WinEnableWindow (hWndFrame, TRUE);
        }
        break;
    }
    break;

  default:
      bHandled = FALSE;
      break;
  }

  if (!bHandled)
    mReturn = WinDefDlgProc (hWnd, msg, mp1, mp2);

  return (mReturn);
}

MRESULT EXPENTRY WinInfoDlgProc (HWND hWnd, ULONG msg, MPARAM mp1,
                                 MPARAM mp2)
{
  MRESULT mReturn  = 0;
  BOOL    bHandled = TRUE;
  CHAR    szTitle[40];
  HWND    hWndActiveFrame;
  POINTL  Ptl;
  SWP     Swp;

  switch (msg)
  {
    case WM_INITDLG:
      CenterWindow (hWnd);
      hWndActiveFrame = WinQueryWindow (hWndActiveChild, QW_PARENT);
      WinQueryWindowText (hWndActiveFrame, sizeof(szTitle), szTitle);
      WinQueryWindowPos (hWndActiveFrame, &Swp);
      Ptl.x = Swp.x;
      Ptl.y = Swp.y;
      WinMapWindowPoints (hWndActiveFrame, hWndFrame, &Ptl, 1L);

      WinSendDlgItemMsg  (hWnd, IDC_TITLE, EM_SETTEXTLIMIT,
                          (MPARAM)sizeof(szTitle), 0L);
```

```
      WinSetDlgItemText  (hWnd, IDC_TITLE, szTitle);
      WinSetDlgItemShort (hWnd, IDC_XPOS,   (SHORT)Ptl.x,   TRUE);
      WinSetDlgItemShort (hWnd, IDC_YPOS,   (SHORT)Ptl.y,   TRUE);
      WinSetDlgItemShort (hWnd, IDC_WIDTH,  (USHORT)Swp.cx, FALSE);
      WinSetDlgItemShort (hWnd, IDC_HEIGHT, (USHORT)Swp.cy, FALSE);
      if (Swp.fl & SWP_MINIMIZE)
         WinSetDlgItemText (hWnd, IDC_STATE, "Minimized");
      else if (Swp.fl & SWP_MAXIMIZE)
         WinSetDlgItemText (hWnd, IDC_STATE, "Maximized");
      else
         WinSetDlgItemText (hWnd, IDC_STATE, "Normal");
      WinSetFocus (HWND_DESKTOP, WinWindowFromID (hWnd, IDC_TITLE));
      break;

    case WM_COMMAND:
      switch (LOUSHORT(mp1))
      {
        case DID_OK:
          WinQueryDlgItemText (hWnd, IDC_TITLE, sizeof(szTitle),
               szTitle);
          WinSetWindowText (
          WinQueryWindow (hWndActiveChild, QW_PARENT), szTitle);
          WinDismissDlg (hWnd, DID_OK);
          break;
      }
      break;

    default:
      bHandled = FALSE;
      break;
  }

  if (!bHandled)
     mReturn = WinDefDlgProc (hWnd, msg, mp1, mp2);

  return (mReturn);
}

/* -------- Window Subclass Functions -------- */

MRESULT EXPENTRY ChildSubclassProc (HWND hWnd, ULONG msg, MPARAM mp1,
                                    MPARAM mp2)
{
  BOOL     bHandled = FALSE;
  MRESULT mReturn = 0L;

  switch (msg)
  {
    case WM_TRACKFRAME:
      if ( ((SHORT1FROMMP(mp1) & TF_MOVE) == TF_MOVE) &&
             !WinQueryWindowULong (
                 WinWindowFromID (hWnd, FID_CLIENT), QWL_MOVE))
        bHandled = TRUE;
      break;

    case WM_QUERYTRACKINFO:
```

```
        if (WinQueryWindowULong (
              WinWindowFromID (hWnd, FID_CLIENT), QWL_TRACKING))
        {
          PTRACKINFO pti;
          RECTL      Rectl;

          /* Let the PM frame window function initialize TRACKINFO */
          mReturn = (*pfnFrameProc) (hWnd, msg, mp1, mp2);

          WinQueryWindowRect (hWnd, &Rectl);
          pti                     = (PTRACKINFO)mp2;
          pti->ptlMinTrackSize.x = 75L;
          pti->ptlMinTrackSize.y = 50L;
          pti->ptlMaxTrackSize.x = Rectl.xRight + 40;
          pti->ptlMaxTrackSize.y = Rectl.yTop   + 40;
          bHandled = TRUE;
        }
    }

    if (!bHandled)
      mReturn = (*pfnFrameProc) (hWnd, msg, mp1, mp2);

    return (mReturn);
}

MRESULT EXPENTRY FrameSubclassProc (HWND hWnd, ULONG msg, MPARAM mp1,
                                    MPARAM mp2)
{
  MRESULT  mReturn = 0L;
  HPOINTER hPtr;

  switch (msg)
  {
    case WM_CONTROLPOINTER:
      switch (SHORT1FROMMP(mp1))
      {
        case FID_SYSMENU:
          mReturn = (MRESULT)hPtrSysMenu;
          break;

        case FID_MENU:
          mReturn = (MRESULT)hPtrMenu;
          break;

        case FID_MINMAX:
          mReturn = (MRESULT)hPtrMinMax;
          break;

        default:
          mReturn = mp2;    /* Use the default pointer */
      }
      break;

    case WM_MOUSEMOVE:
      switch (SHORT1FROMMP(mp2))
      {
        case TF_LEFT:
```

```
        case TF_RIGHT:
          hPtr = hPtrLeft;
          break;

        case TF_TOP:
        case TF_BOTTOM:
          hPtr = hPtrTop;
          break;

        case TF_LEFT | TF_TOP:
        case TF_RIGHT | TF_BOTTOM:
          hPtr = hPtrLeftTop;
          break;

        case TF_RIGHT | TF_TOP:
        case TF_LEFT | TF_BOTTOM:
          hPtr = hPtrRightTop;
          break;

        default:
           hPtr = 0;
      }
      if (hPtr)
         WinSetPointer (HWND_DESKTOP, hPtr);
      else
         mReturn = (*pfnFrameProc) (hWnd, msg, mp1, mp2);
      break;

    default:
       mReturn = (*pfnFrameProc) (hWnd, msg, mp1, mp2);
    break;
  }

  return (mReturn);
}

MRESULT EXPENTRY MenuSubclassProc (HWND hWnd, ULONG msg, MPARAM mp1,
                                    MPARAM mp2)
{
  if (msg == WM_CONTROLPOINTER)
     return ((MRESULT)hPtrPopupMenu);
  else
     return (*pfnMenuProc) (hWnd, msg, mp1, mp2);
}

MRESULT EXPENTRY SysMenuSubclassProc (HWND hWnd, ULONG msg,
                                       MPARAM mp1, MPARAM mp2)
{
  if (msg == WM_CONTROLPOINTER)
     return ((MRESULT)hPtrPopupMenu);
  else
     return (*pfnSysMenuProc) (hWnd, msg, mp1, mp2);
}

MRESULT EXPENTRY TitleBarSubclassProc (HWND hWnd, ULONG msg,
                                        MPARAM mp1, MPARAM mp2)
```

```
{
  MRESULT mReturn = 0L;
  ULONG   ulCurState,
          ulNewState;
  HPS     hps;

  switch (msg)
  {
    case WM_MOUSEMOVE:
      WinSetPointer (HWND_DESKTOP, hPtrTitleBar);
      break;

    case TBM_QUERYHILITE:
      mReturn =(MRESULT)(WinQueryWindowULong(hWnd,QWL_USER) & 0x0001);
      break;

    case TBM_SETHILITE:
      mReturn = (MRESULT)TRUE;
      ulCurState = ulNewState = WinQueryWindowULong (hWnd,QWL_USER);
      if (LOUSHORT(mp1))
          ulNewState |= 1;
      else
          ulNewState &= ~1;

      /* Only need to update if the state is changing */
      if (ulCurState == ulNewState)
         break;
      WinSetWindowULong (hWnd,QWL_USER,ulNewState);

      hps = WinGetPS (hWnd);
      PaintTitleBar (hWnd,hps);
      WinReleasePS (hps);
      break;

    case WM_PAINT:
      hps = WinBeginPaint (hWnd,0,0);
      PaintTitleBar (hWnd,hps);
      WinEndPaint (hps);
      break;

    default:
      mReturn = (*pfnTitleBarProc) (hWnd, msg, mp1, mp2);
      break;
  }

  return (mReturn);
}
```

MINIMDI.H

```
/* ------------------------------
MiniMDI Header File
Real-World Programming for OS/2
Copyright (c) 1993, 1994 Blain, Delimon, and English
------------------------------ */
```

```
#define ID_APPNAME          1
#define IDD_TOOLBAR         2
#define IDD_WININFO         3

#define ID_CHILDWINDOW      11

#define IDPTR_HEART         20
#define IDPTR_CLIENT        21
#define IDPTR_SYSMENU       22
#define IDPTR_MENU          23
#define IDPTR_MINMAX        24
#define IDPTR_LEFT          25
#define IDPTR_TOP           26
#define IDPTR_LEFTTOP       27
#define IDPTR_RIGHTTOP      28
#define IDPTR_TITLEBAR      29
#define IDPTR_POPUPMENU     30
#define IDPTR_HEART2        31

#define IDM_WINDOW         100
#define IDM_NEWCHILD       101
#define IDM_NEXTCHILD      102
#define IDM_CLOSEALL       103
#define IDM_ABOUT          104

#define IDM_ARRANGEMENU    110
#define IDM_TILE           111
#define IDM_CASCADE        112
#define IDM_ARRANGE        113

#define IDC_WININFO        200
#define IDC_RED            201
#define IDC_GREEN          202
#define IDC_BLUE           203
#define IDC_MOVE           204
#define IDC_TRACK          205
#define IDC_OPEN           206

#define IDC_TITLE          300
#define IDC_XPOS           301
#define IDC_YPOS           302
#define IDC_WIDTH          303
#define IDC_HEIGHT         304
#define IDC_STATE          305
```

MINIMDI.DEF

```
NAME           MINIMDI   WINDOWAPI
DESCRIPTION    'MiniMDI Program (c) Blain, Delimon, & English, 1993, 1994'
PROTMODE
HEAPSIZE       4096
STACKSIZE      32768
EXPORTS        ClientWndProc
               ChildWndProc
               ToolBarDlgProc
```

```
WinInfoDlgProc
FrameSubclassProc
TitleBarSubclassProc
SysMenuSubclassProc
MenuSubclassProc
ChildSubclassProc
AboutDlgProc
```

How MINIMDI Works

This application will do several things. The main window will have all its frame controls subclassed as well as the frame window itself. This will enable you to set the pointer to various pointer shapes as the mouse is moved over the various frame control windows. In addition, the frame window of a child window may be subclassed if the Move option is disabled or the Track option is enabled. To perform the subclassing, you define a subclass window function for each window class:

```
/* Window Subclass Functions        */
MRESULT EXPENTRY ChildSubclassProc    (HWND,ULONG,MPARAM,MPARAM);
MRESULT EXPENTRY FrameSubclassProc    (HWND,ULONG,MPARAM,MPARAM);
MRESULT EXPENTRY MenuSubclassProc     (HWND,ULONG,MPARAM,MPARAM);
MRESULT EXPENTRY SysMenuSubclassProc  (HWND,ULONG,MPARAM,MPARAM);
MRESULT EXPENTRY TitleBarSubclassProc (HWND,ULONG,MPARAM,MPARAM);
```

We are using two application-defined messages:

```
#define WM_USER_POSITION      WM_USER+1
#define WM_USER_CHILDACTIVATE WM_USER+2
```

`WM_USER_POSITION` is a message we will post to the toolbar dialog window after it is created. The `WM_USER_CHILDACTIVATE` message will be posted to the toolbar dialog when a child window becomes active.

In addition, each child window will use application-defined window data:

```
/* User-Defined Window Extra Words  */
#define QWL_COLOR_RGB  QWL_USER                          /* ULONG  */
#define QWL_MOVE       QWL_COLOR_RGB + sizeof(ULONG)     /* BOOL   */
#define QWL_TRACKING   QWL_MOVE      + sizeof(BOOL)      /* BOOL   */
#define QWL_OPEN       QWL_TRACKING  + sizeof(BOOL)      /* BOOL   */
#define QWL_EXTRA      QWL_OPEN      + sizeof(BOOL)
```

The offset of each item will be identified by an application-defined `QWL_` definition. Each offset is defined in reference to the previous offset plus the size of the previous data item. The total number of bytes that must be allocated for each window of the child class is `QWL_EXTRA`, which is the sum of all the items.

Processing begins by creating the main application window and then subclassing all the frame control windows except the `FID_MINMAX` frame control:

```
   /* Create the main application window */
   hWndFrame = WinCreateStdWindow (HWND_DESKTOP, 0L,
      &flFrameFlags, szClientClass, szTitle, 0, NULL, ID_APPNAME,
      &hWndClient);
```

```
   /* Subclass the frame control windows */
   pfnFrameProc    = WinSubclassWindow (hWndFrame, FrameSubclassProc);
   pfnTitleBarProc = WinSubclassWindow (
WinWindowFromID (hWndFrame, FID_TITLEBAR), TitleBarSubclassProc);
   pfnSysMenuProc  = WinSubclassWindow (
WinWindowFromID (hWndFrame, FID_SYSMENU), SysMenuSubclassProc);
   pfnMenuProc     = WinSubclassWindow (
WinWindowFromID (hWndFrame, FID_MENU), MenuSubclassProc);

   InitializeAppWindow (hWndClient);

   WinShowWindow (hWndFrame, TRUE);
```

The main window is created with the `WS_VISIBLE` flag turned off. This enables you to complete the initialization and create the child windows before any painting is done. The call to `InitializeAppWindow` takes care of initialization:

```
VOID InitializeAppWindow (HWND hWnd)
{
   WinRegisterClass (hab, "CHILD", ChildWndProc, 0, QWL_EXTRA);

   hWndToolBar = WinLoadDlg (HWND_DESKTOP, hWnd, ToolBarDlgProc,
         0L, IDD_TOOLBAR, NULL);

   /* Create three children initially */
   CreateChildWindow (hWnd);
   CreateChildWindow (hWnd);
   CreateChildWindow (hWnd);

   WinPostMsg (hWndToolBar, WM_USER_POSITION, 0L, 0L);
   WinPostMsg (hWnd, WM_COMMAND, (MPARAM)IDM_TILE, 0L);
   return;
}
```

The registration of the child window class `"CHILD"` specifies that `QWL_EXTRA` bytes are to be allocated for window data. The toolbar dialog window is loaded with a call to `WinLoadDlg`. This creates a modeless dialog window that uses the dialog template identified by `IDD_TOOLBAR`. Because you want the dialog to be capable of moving freely about the screen without restriction to the boundary of the application window, you use a parent of `HWND_DESKTOP`. The main application window will serve as the owner window for the dialog. You arbitrarily create three child windows to begin the application. Next, post the `WM_USER_POSITION` message to `hWndToolBar`. Because you have not entered the `WinGetMsg` loop, the `WM_SIZE` message for the main application window has not been retrieved from the message queue. You want to position the toolbar initially at the lower-left corner of the application window; however, because the application window has not been sized yet, you post this message so that it is retrieved and processed after the `WM_SIZE` message. You then post a `WM_COMMAND` message with the command identifier of `IDM_TILE` so that the three child windows will be arranged in a tiled manner.

The `ArrangeIcons` function is used to neatly arrange the minimized child windows at the bottom of the client window. You will use the `WinSetMultWindowPos` to make a single call to arrange all the minimized windows. Here, you use the window enumeration functions to retrieve the child windows one at a time in z-order from top to bottom. A call to `IsWindowMinimized` will tell whether the window is an iconic window; if so, you fill in the `SWP` structure for the current minimized window. Here is where you need to perform a little PM trick:

```
if ( IsWindowMinimized (hWndChild) )
{
   pSwp[ulChildCnt].fl     = SWP_MOVE ¦ SWP_FOCUSDEACTIVATE;
   pSwp[ulChildCnt].x      =
   pSwp[ulChildCnt].y      = 0;
   pSwp[ulChildCnt++].hwnd = hWndChild;
   /* Destroy the current minimize position - a little
      PM trick */
   WinSetWindowUShort (hWndChild,QWS_XMINIMIZE,(USHORT)-1);
   WinSetWindowUShort (hWndChild,QWS_YMINIMIZE,(USHORT)-1);
}
```

Every frame window has the X and Y position from its last minimization in its window data. These values are referenced with the `WinQueryWindowUShort` function and the `QWS_XMINIMIZE` and `QWS_YMINIMIZE` offsets. When a window is minimized, PM will try to calculate a position for the icon. OS/2 will skip positions that are currently in use by another iconic window. OS/2 does this by examining the `QWS_XMINIMIZE` and `QWS_YMINIMIZE` values of all sibling windows. Because we are rearranging the icons, we don't want an iconic window to have an existing position because OS/2 will skip that position. Setting these values to -1 indicates to PM that the icon has no previous minimized position. When `WinSetMultWindowPos` is called and an iconic window has the `SWP_MOVE` flag set, PM will arrange each icon in order along the bottom of the window. (See Figure 3.13.) This eliminates the need to come up with any algorithm for spacing and positioning iconic windows.

Figure 3.13.
Diagram of iconic windows neatly arranged.

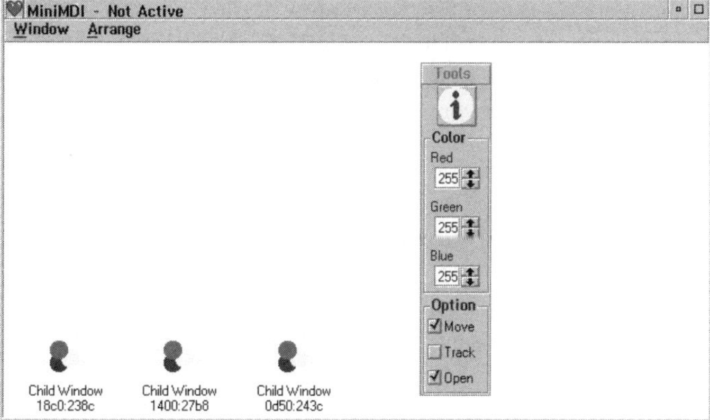

The `CascadeChildWindows` function is used to arrange the nonminimized windows in a cascaded fashion. (See Figure 3.14.)

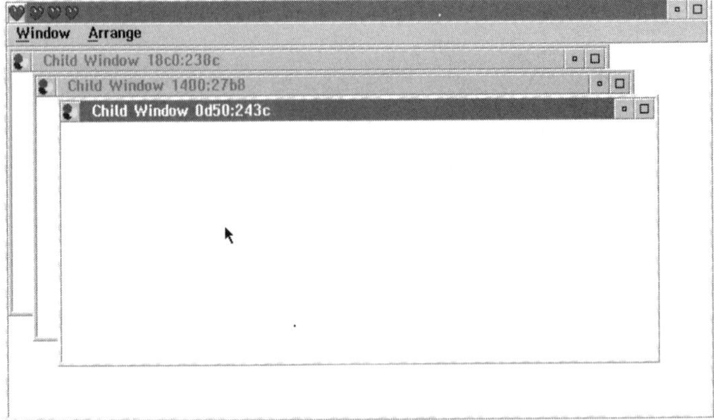

Figure 3.14.
Diagram of windows arranged in a cascaded fashion.

Here, you want to enumerate the child windows in reverse z-order (from bottom to top). You can't use the window enumeration functions because that returns windows in z-order from top to bottom. You can, however, do your own enumeration by querying the extreme bottom child window

```
hWndChild   = WinQueryWindow (hWnd, QW_BOTTOM);
```

and by repeatedly querying the previous child window

```
hWndChild = WinQueryWindow (hWndChild, QW_PREV);
```

until no more children exist. Here is where it gets a little tricky with iconic windows. When a frame window is minimized, a window of class `WC_ICONTEXT` is created to contain the text displayed below the icon. This `WC_ICONTEXT` window will enumerate as one of the child windows. PM helpfully assigns all `WC_ICONTEXT` windows an identifier of zero. As long as you don't use an identifier of zero for your child windows, you can query the identifier of the window and skip those that are zero:

```
while (hWndChild)
{
   /* Skip ICONTEXT windows and minimized windows */
   if ( WinQueryWindowUShort (hWndChild, QWS_ID) &&
        !IsWindowMinimized (hWndChild) )
   {
      GetNextWindowPos (ulChildCnt, &pSwp[ulChildCnt]);
      pSwp[ulChildCnt].fl = SWP_MOVE | SWP_SIZE | SWP_SHOW;

      /* If child is maximized then restore it */
      if (IsWindowMaximized (hWndChild))
         pSwp[ulChildCnt].fl |= SWP_RESTORE;

      pSwp[ulChildCnt++].hwnd = hWndChild;
```

```
    }

    /* Query the previous child frame window in the z-order */
    hWndChild = WinQueryWindow (hWndChild, QW_PREV);
}
```

For each noniconic, non-WC_ICONTEXT window, you call GetNextWindowPos to calculate the size and position for the next cascaded window. If the child window is currently maximized, you add the SWP_RESTORE flag so that the maximized child is restored in addition to being resized and positioned.

The CloseAllChildWindows function merely enumerates all the child windows and calls WinDestroyWindow to remove the window.

CreateChildWindow is called to create a new child window. Each child window is created with a titlebar, system menu, sizing border, minmax menu, and icon:

```
ULONG flChildFrameFlags  = FCF_TITLEBAR | FCF_SYSMENU | FCF_SIZEBORDER |
                           FCF_MINMAX   | FCF_ICON | FCF_NOBYTEALIGN;

if (hWndChildFrame = WinCreateStdWindow (hWnd, 0L, &flChildFrameFlags,
    "CHILD", "", 0L, 0L, ID_CHILDWINDOW, &hWndChild))
```

When we create a new child, we want it to be the active window. If the current active window is maximized, we must first restore it:

```
if (hWndActiveChild && IsWindowMaximized (hWndActiveChild))
     WinSetWindowPos (WinQueryWindow (hWndActiveChild, QW_PARENT),
          0L, 0L, 0L, 0L, 0L, SWP_RESTORE);
```

Because the client window made with WinCreateStdWindow creates the client window with no owner, you assign the owner of the client to be the frame:

```
WinSetOwner (hWndChild, hWndChildFrame);
```

The initial position of a newly created child window will be the next available cascaded window position:

```
GetNextWindowPos (ulNumChildren - 1L, &Swp);
WinSetWindowPos (hWndChildFrame, 0L, Swp.x, Swp.y, Swp.cx, Swp.cy,
      SWP_MOVE | SWP_SIZE | SWP_SHOW | SWP_ACTIVATE);
```

You are also keeping track of the number of child windows with a heart in the titlebar. Because a new child was just created, you force the titlebar to repaint. This can be done by invalidating the titlebar window:

```
WinInvalidateRect (WinWindowFromID(hWndFrame,FID_TITLEBAR),
    NULL, FALSE);
```

The IsWindowMaximized and IsWindowMinimized functions check the window style of the frame window for the WS_MAXIMIZED or WS_MINIMIZED flag. It is necessary to query the style of a frame window because client windows do not use those flags. Because you are always passing the handle of either the child's frame window or the child's client window, you can just check whether the identifier is `FID_CLIENT`. If so, query the parent window and use it:

```
if (WinQueryWindowUShort (hWnd, QWS_ID) == FID_CLIENT)
    hWnd = WinQueryWindow (hWnd, QW_PARENT);
```

`SwitchToNextChildWindow` will locate the next child below the currently active child window and move it to the top of the z-order while moving the currently active child window to the bottom of the z-order. To get the next child below the currently active child, you use `QW_NEXT` on the frame window of the active child.

```
while ( (hWndNext = WinQueryWindow (hWndNext, QW_NEXT)) &&
!WinQueryWindowUShort (hWndNext, QWS_ID))
{
}
```

As mentioned earlier, be sure you don't attempt to use a `WC_ICONTEXT` window. When the next window is found, two calls to `WinSetWindow` change the z-order of your windows. This ensures that if the active child window is maximized, it is restored as well:

```
WinSetWindowPos (hWndNext, HWND_TOP, 0, 0, 0, 0,
    SWP_ZORDER ¦ SWP_ACTIVATE);
WinSetWindowPos (hWndActiveFrame, HWND_BOTTOM, 0, 0, 0, 0,
   IsWindowMaximized (hWndActiveFrame) ? SWP_RESTORE ¦ SWP_ZORDER :
                                         SWP_ZORDER);
```

`TileChildWindows` is used to arrange the nonminimized child windows in a tiled fashion. (See Figure 3.15.)

Figure 3.15. Diagram of windows arranged in a tiled fashion.

The algorithm will arrange the child windows, moving from the upper-left corner to the right and attempting to have as many windows the same size as possible. Here, you enumerate the child windows in z-order from top to bottom, again skipping WC_ICONTEXT and minimized windows. If the child window is currently maximized, add in the SWP_RESTORE flag so that the maximized child is restored. For both cascading and tiling, be sure that the icon windows are not covered by the non-icon windows.

```
if (ulNumMinChildren)
   Rectl.yBottom += WinQuerySysValue (HWND_DESKTOP, SV_CYICON) * 2;
```

The bottom of the client rectangle used for calculations is shifted up to leave room for the icons if any minimized children exist.

Chapter 4

Common Dialogs

Introduction to Common Dialogs

The common dialogs greatly simplify the amount of work a programmer must do to perform a number of routine tasks. These dialogs provide the functionality for tasks most programs need to perform at one time or another, such as opening and saving files or selecting fonts.

In the past, every application development team was forced to write code to perform routine tasks, tasks that practically every application needed to perform. To make application development easier, PM provides dialogs that programmers may use in their code to perform these routine operations. Using these common dialogs in your application achieves more than relieving some of the coding burden. They provide a consistent interface for the user. Not only will your applications be consistent with each other, but also applications will be consistent even among programmers and unrelated applications if they use these common dialogs.

Practice with the CONTROL Sample Application

The concepts in this chapter will be far more intelligible if you have some hands-on experience with the common file dialogs. Open the control application that was installed from the distribution disk for Real-World Programming for OS/2. Use of the menu choices in this sample application should be fairly self-explanatory to anyone accustomed to a menu-windowing interface. You do not need to worry about backing up files, as you would normally, because the `SaveAs` choice in the application has been deliberately left unworking. Spend some time familiarizing yourself with the use of these controls.

The CONTROL sample application has two major parts. One demonstrates the common file API, and the other demonstrates the common font API. These are divided between the File and Font choices on the menu bar.

The File Menu

The File menu contains those menu choices that concern the common file dialogs. When you start the application and click the File menu choice, the application appears as illustrated in Figure 4.1.

Basic Open

The Basic Open menu choice, shown in Figure 4.2, displays the basic dialog box for enabling the user to choose a file to open. The file, however, is not read, and no data is written to the client area.

Open And Display

Open And Display enables the user to open any file for display in the client area. The client area processing is, however, only set up to display text files, so only these will appear in an intelligible form. Only the first few lines of text from the file are all that are displayed in the client area. No editing capabilities are provided.

Figure 4.1. Open and Save As menu.

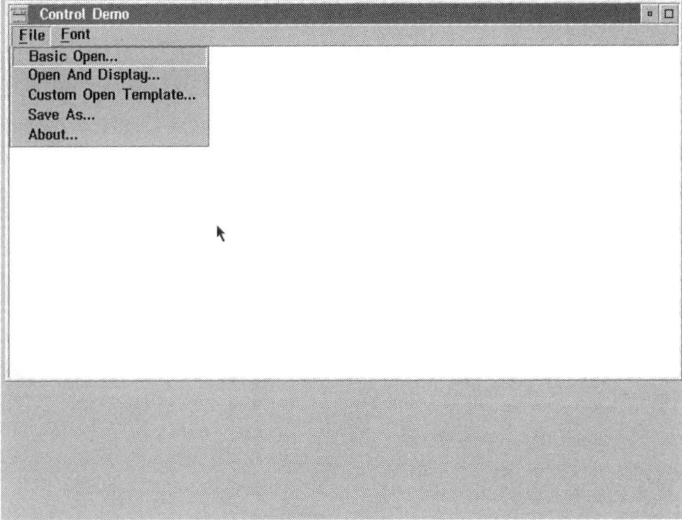

Figure 4.2. Basic File Open dialog.

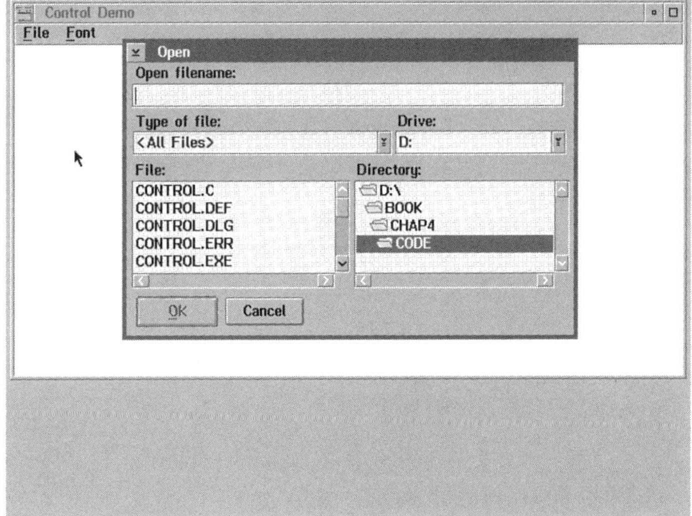

Custom Open Template

The Custom Open Template, shown in Figure 4.3, operates similarly to the Open And Display menu choice, with one important addition. Notice the checkbox for Save Directory. Try changing the file path to some directory other than that displayed when the application opens, open a file, then select Custom Open Template from the menu again. Notice that the dialog has returned to the directory that you chose earlier.

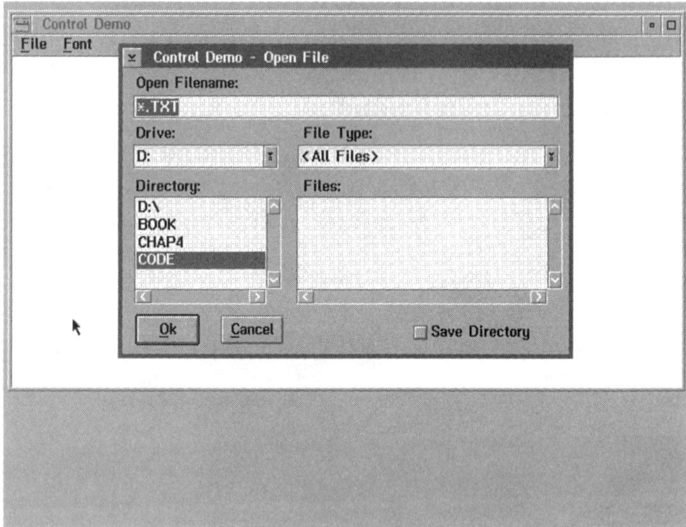

Figure 4.3. File Open dialog using a custom template.

Save As

The Save As option is included merely to show the workings of this common file dialog. No code for actually saving the files is included.

The Font Menu

The Font menu contains those choices that pertain to the common font dialogs. These are shown in Figure 4.4.

The Basic Font menu choice causes the Basic Font dialog to be displayed, as shown in Figure 4.5. The choices in the dialog should be fairly self-explanatory.

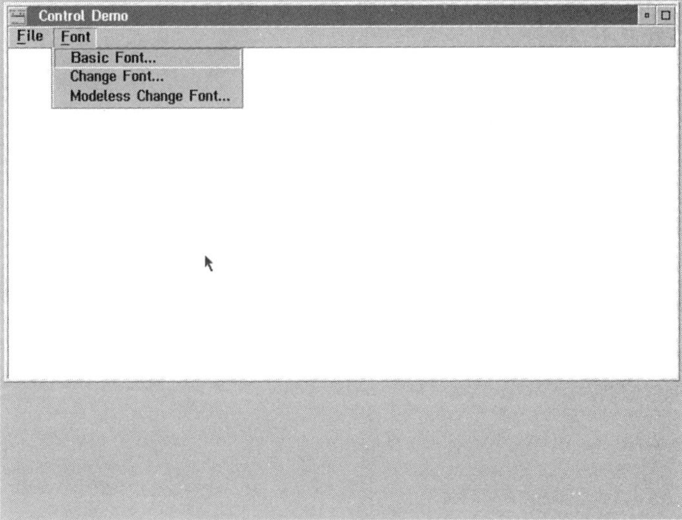

Figure 4.4. Font selection menu.

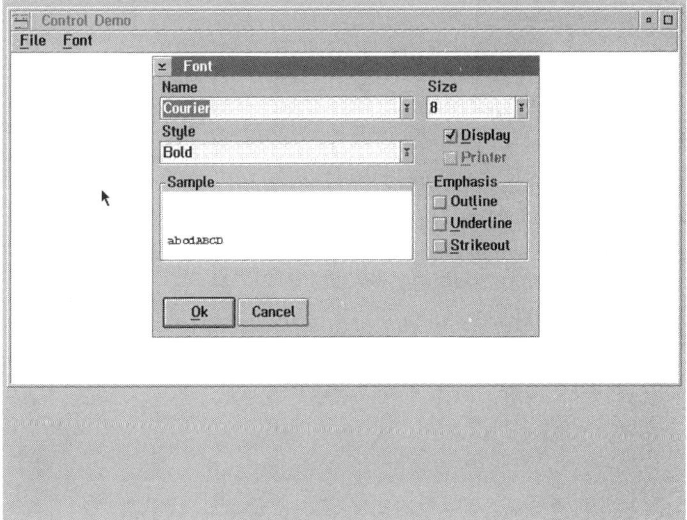

Figure 4.5. Basic Font selection dialog.

Change Font

The Change Font menu choice enables you to change the font for the displayed text. To use it, first choose Open And Display and select a valid text file to be displayed. Now, use Change Font to cause the text to be displayed in a different font.

The Reset button under Change Font sets the font selection back to what it was before you began changing it. Notice also that changes are not made to the displayed text until you select OK. Because Change Font, shown in Figure 4.6, is a modal dialog, this is the expected behavior. The user cannot continue the process until either OK or Cancel is selected in this dialog.

Figure 4.6. Change Font dialog.

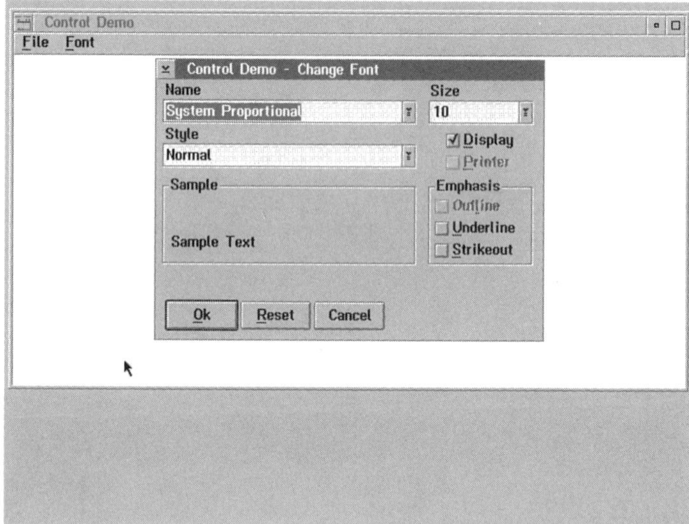

Modeless Change Font

The Modeless Change Font menu choice is similar to that of Change Font; however, it is a modeless. This means that the user may proceed with other processing in the application without selecting OK or Cancel. In fact, the Modeless Change Font dialog will remain open even if the user chooses to open another file.

Notice the Direct Update checkbox. (See Figure 4.7.) This will cause the font changes to be applied immediately to the displayed text. Otherwise, font changes may be applied to the displayed text by clicking the Apply button.

Development of the Sample

For both the common file and font dialogs, this sample application demonstrates more than a single scenario of their use. Several different ways of presenting the file and font data occur under each of the menu choices. Although each of the examples of using the common file dialogs has been combined in a single application, each is written somewhat independent of the previous samples. There will be, therefore, some redundant storage of data between calls to the dialog.

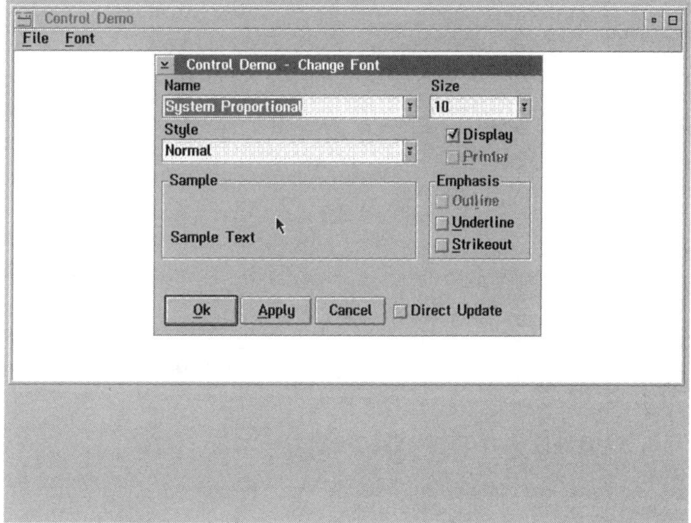

Figure 4.7. The Modeless Change Font dialog box.

File Dialog

The common file dialog is a set of functions and resources or dialog templates provided within PM. These provide list boxes and combination boxes that allow directories to be navigated and files to be selected. Only a single function call is needed to bring up a dialog box that would be far more complex to code individually. An edit window is also provided to enter a full path and filename or a wildcard file spec. This is certainly a welcome feature, because it prevents the necessity of coding an activity that is common to most applications. A file may be selected by double-clicking the filename in the files list box or pushing the OK button. The dialog may be closed by pushing the Cancel button or by using the escape key.

The common file dialog has three API entries. These are as follows:

`WinFileDlg`	Creates and displays the File Open or Save As dialog and returns the user's selection(s).
`WinDefFileDlgProc`	Default dialog procedure for the File Open or "Save As" dialogs.
`WinFreeFileDlgList`	Frees the memory allocated when the `FDS_MULTIPLESEL` flag is set in the fl field of the `FILEDLG` structure.

Let's take a closer look at the `WinFileDlg` function:

```
WinFileDlg(hwndParent,hwndOwner,pFileDlg);
```

`HWND hwndParent`	Window handle of the parent window of the created dialog box. The parent window may be `HWND_DESKTOP` or a valid window handle.
`HWND hwndOwner`	Window handle of the requested owner. PM will select the actual owner by searching up the parent chain beginning with `hwndOwner`. The first window that is a child of `hwndParent` will be set as the dialog box owner. If no children of `hwndParent` are found, the owner is set to NULL.
`PFILEDLGpFiledlg`	Pointer to a `FILEDLG` structure. The contents of the `pFiledlg` structure define the appearance, location, and behavior of the Open or Save As dialog.

Creating a Simple Application

We wrote the code in this book to make it easier to cannibalize. If you are adventurous, creating a basic file selection dialog in your application is not difficult. By adding a menu and four lines of code to the skeleton program from Chapter 2, "OS/2 Application Window Fundamentals," you can quickly create an application that displays a modal file selection dialog. Remember to declare the necessary file dialog structure, too.

First, initialize all fields of the `FILEDLG` structure to `NULL`. Then, set the required `cbSize` and `fl` fields in the structure. The flags indicate that an open dialog should be created and centered relative to its owner window:

```
memset(&FileDlg,0,sizeof(FILEDLG));
FileDlg.cbSize    = sizeof(FILEDLG);
FileDlg.fl        = FDS_CENTER ¦ FDS_OPEN_DIALOG;
WinFileDlg(HWND_DESKTOP,hWndFrame,(PFILEDLG)&FileDlg);
if (FileDlg.lReturn == DID_OK)
    WinSetWindowText(hWndFrame,(PSZ)FileDlg.szFullFile);
```

The `WinFileDlg` function returns `TRUE` if the dialog was successfully created and `FALSE` if an error occurs. Modal dialogs are created by default. Modal dialogs are those that will not return to the caller until the dialog has been dismissed. Dismissing a dialog is another way to describe terminating or closing a dialog. The term originates from the PM function `WinDismissDlg` that is used to destroy dialogs. The `FILEDLG` structure not only defines the type and location of the dialog, but also contains selections made in the dialog. The default file open dialog may be ended with either the OK or Cancel push buttons The `lReturn` field will indicate which control dismissed the dialog. If OK was selected, the `szFullFile` name will contain the full pathname of the selected file. If Cancel was chosen, the `szFullFile` parameter is undefined. In the previous sample, the filename will be set as the titlebar text if OK was selected.

The *FILEDLG* Structure

The FILEDLG structure contains many more fields than the two used in the previous example. To fully understand the ways the File Open dialog may be used, the FILEDLG structure must be examined. We will examine these before moving on to a more complex example. The FILEDLG structure is defined as follows:

ULONG	cbSize	Structure size in bytes.
ULONG	fl	Flags that define the dialog appearance, location, and behavior.

One of the following must be specified:

FDS_OPEN_DIALOG	Creates the Open dialog.
FDS_SAVEAS_DIALOG	Creates the Save As dialog.

Zero or more of the following may be added:

FDS_APPLYBUTTON	The Apply button is added to the dialog between the OK and Cancel buttons. This button should be used on modeless dialogs. You must supply your own dialog procedure to process this control's command messages.
FDS_CENTER	Centers dialog relative to owner window. This flag will override a dialog position specified by the X and Y parameters.
FDS_CUSTOM	Creates the dialog using the custom dialog template found in hMod with ID usDlgId. You must still supply the Open or Save As dialog type flag so that WinFileDlg knows how to process the control windows.
FDS_HELPBUTTON	The help button is added to the dialog. When the button is clicked, a WM_HELP message is sent to the owner window. If the owner is a frame window, it must be subclassed to receive the WM_HELP message.
FDS_MODELESS	The dialog is created modeless; the default is to create a modal dialog. When this flag is used, WinFileDlg returns the window handle of the created dialog.
FDS_PRELOAD_VOLINFO	This option queries the volume label for all drives before displaying the dialog. The values are placed in the drives combination box after the drive letter. If this flag is not specified, the volume label is displayed in the combo box when the directory is

		selected. Because all drives including removable are queried, using this option can increase significantly the time required to display the dialog.
FDS_INCLUDE_EAS		Always Loads EA information.
FDS_MULTIPLESEL		Allows multiple selections in the file list box. Selected strings are returned through the `papszFQFilename` parameter.
FDS_ENABLEFILELB		When the `FDS_SAVEAS_DIALOG` is specified, the file list box is disabled. Using this will enable the file list box.
FDS_FILTERUNION		The default behavior is to display those files that are the intersection of the file type and extended attribute filters. Use this flag to display the union of those filters.
ULONG	ulUser	Unused field reserved for application use.
LONG	lReturn	`WinDefFileDlgProc` will set this value to the ID of the control that resulted in the dismissal of the dialog. It is not the result value passed to the `WinDismissDlg` function. If your custom dialog callback calls `WinDismissDlg`, it must still set the `ulReturn` field to the desired control ID.
LONG	lSRC	If the `WinFileDlg` function fails, this field will contain one of the following errors codes: FDS_ERR_DEALLOCATE_MEMORY FDS_ERR_FILTER_TRUNC FDS_ERR_INVALID_DIALOG FDS_ERR_INVALID_DRIVE FDS_ERR_INVALID_FILTER FDS_ERR_INVALID_PATHFILE FDS_ERR_OUT_OF_MEMORY FDS_ERR_PATH_TOO_LONG FDS_ERR_TOO_MANY_FILE_TYPES FDS_ERR_INVALID_VERSION FDS_ERR_INVALID_CUSTOM_HANDLE FDS_ERR_DIALOG_LOAD_ERROR FDS_ERR_DRIVE_ERROR
PS	pszTitle	Pointer to a null-terminated string that is placed in the titlebar of the dialog. If this parameter is `NULL`, the default title for the open dialog is "Open" and "Save As" for the save dialog.
PSZ	pszOKButton	Pointer to a null-terminated string that contains the text to be placed in the OK push button. The default string is "OK."

PFNWP	pfnDlgProc	Application-supplied dialog procedure that will be called in place of WinDefFileDlgProc.
PSZ	pszIType	Extended-attribute type filter.
PAPSZ	papszITypeList	Pointer to an array of pointers that point to null-terminated file type strings. The end of the array is marked with a NULL pointer.
PSZ	pszIDrive	Pointer to a null-terminated string that contains the initial drive to display in the drives combo box. It must be a drive letter followed by a semicolon, for example, C:. If the drive provided is not valid, the first entry in the drives combo box is selected as the default drive. If this parameter is NULL, the current drive is used.
PAPSZ	papszIDriveList	Pointer to an array of pointers to null-terminated drive strings to be added to the drop-down list of logical drives. If this parameter is NULL, all available drives are displayed.
HMODULE	hMod	If the FDS_CUSTOM flag is set, WinFileDlg will attempt to load a dialog resource with the ID specified in the usDlgId field from this module. If hMod is NULL, the current executable is searched.
CHAR	szFullFile	Character array of CCHMAXPATH bytes. Before the call to WinFileDlg, this array may be initialized with the initial filename to display in the dialog. Wildcards may be used.
PAPSZ	papszFQFilename	Pointer to an array of pointers that point to null-terminated filename strings. There will be one entry for each file selected in the file list box. The number of entries in the array is indicated by the ulFQFCount parameter. The FDS_MULTIPLESEL flag must be used to allow multiple files to be selected. This memory should be freed by calling the WinFreeFileDlgList function.
ULONG	ulFQFCount	The number of pointers in the array pointed to by the papszFQFilename parameter.
USHORT	usDlgId	If the FDS_CUSTOM flag is set, WinFileDlg will attempt to load a dialog resource with this ID from the module specified in the hMod field.

SHORT	x	Screen X dialog coordinate, which is ignored if the FDS_CENTER flag is used.
SHORT	y	Screen Y dialog coordinate, which is ignored if the FDS_CENTER flag is used.
SHORT	sEAType	Selected extended-attribute type.

Using Nondefault Values

Let's take advantage of the features the dialog offers. First, let's provide a title string for the dialog. It will indicate which application is displaying the dialog. To do this, we call the `set_title` function, which will load the application name string from the resource file and concatenate a hyphen followed by the name of the dialog. The dialog name is dependent on the string ID passed as the second parameter to the `set_title` function. This string is then set as the title in the `pszTitle` parameter.

Rather than setting the file name in the titlebar, we read the selected file and display it in the client area. If `lReturn` is set to `DID_OK` when the dialog returns, the `load_file` function is called. It will open the file and read it into an allocated memory block pointed to by `pFileText`. If an error occurs during the loading process, a message box is posted. The file name is then copied to the `szFilePath` character array, and the client area is invalidated. Because we are primarily interested in displaying ASCII text files, we will set the initial file spec in the `FILEDLG` structure. The `szFullFile` that will return a selected file name can also be used to supply an initial file or wildcard search pattern. The `IDS_PATH` resource string ("*.TXT") is loaded into the `szFullFile` parameter. The function call to do this is as follows:

```
WinLoadString (hab,NULL,IDS_PATH,CCHMAXPATH,(PSZ)&FileDlg.szFullFile);
```

Rather than allowing all drives to be displayed, we will use the `papszIDriveList` parameter to display only the nonremovable drives available to the system.

This parameter points to an array of pointers to null-terminated strings that identify the drive letter to be added to the drives combo box. The string should include the drive letter followed by a colon. When the program starts, the `get_fixed_drives` function is called to initialize the `pDrivesList` variable. The drives type is queried by calling the `DosQueryFSAttach` function and requesting information level 1. The `iType` field of the returned buffer will indicate whether the drive is local or remote. After the drive is identified as local, the device is opened and queried by using the `DosDevIOCtl` function. If a drive is determined to be fixed, it is added to the `pDrivesList` pointer array. Before the file open dialog is posted, the `papszIDDrivelist` parameter is set to `pDrivesList`:

```
FileDlg.papszIDriveList = pDrivesList;
```

Now that the file is loaded, we need code that will display the text in the client window. For this, we will use the `WinDrawText` function. Data will be read from the file and output to the window formatted as a line of text within a supplied rectangle. Essentially, we are dividing the client

window into a group of rectangles, stacked one on top of the other. Each line of text will be drawn into a rectangle. To position the text correctly, we must know the client window size and the height of the font being used. The client window size is updated in the static `Rectl` variable when the `WM_SIZE` message is received. The new width and height of the window is passed in the high and low words of the `mp2` parameter:

```
case WM_SIZE:
    Rectl.xLeft   = Rectl.yBottom = 0;
    Rectl.xRight  = SHORT1FROMMP(mp2);
    Rectl.yTop    = SHORT2FROMMP(mp2);
    break;
```

The height of the current font is queried by calling `GpiQueryFontMetrics` with the Presentation Space handle returned from `WinBeginPaint`. In this example, we will calculate line spacing by adding `lMaxBaselineExt` and `lExternalLeading`. This is performed with the following function calls:

```
GpiQueryFontMetrics(hPS,sizeof(FONTMETRICS),
     (PFONTMETRICS)&FontMetrics);
cyHeight = FontMetrics.lMaxBaselineExt + FontMetrics.lExternalLeading;
```

Now that we have the client size and font height, the text can be output by calling `WinDrawText` and advancing the current position based on the number of characters drawn. After the end of the text is reached or the client area has been filled with text, the loop is exited:

```
lHeight = Rectl.yTop;
for ( iTotalDrawn = 0;
     (iTotalDrawn < ulTextSize) && (Rectl.yTop > 0);
     Rectl.yTop -= cyHeight)
{
   iDrawn = WinDrawText(hPS,
      min (0x1000,(ulTextSize - iTotalDrawn)),
      pFileText + iTotalDrawn,
      (PRECTL)&Rectl,CLR_BLACK,CLR_WHITE,
      DT_LEFT | DT_TOP | DT_WORDBREAK);
   if (iDrawn)
      iTotalDrawn += iDrawn;
   else
      iTotalDrawn++;
}
Rectl.yTop = lHeight;
```

To ensure visibility for the text displayed, the client window is registered with the `CS_SIZEREDRAW` style flag. This will cause the entire client window to be invalidated whenever the window is resized. The text will then be output based on the new client size. Now that our sample application is capable of opening and displaying files, let's add our custom dialog template.

Custom Template

It is possible to create your own File Open or Save dialog template and still have the `WinDefFileDlgProc` do all the processing for you. Some guidelines, though, must be followed.

The custom template must contain all the controls of the default dialog. Control windows must be the same style and ID of those in the default dialog template. Controls that are not needed should be hidden. The window ID range 0x000 to 0xFFF is reserved for the default control ID. To avoid any conflict, user defined additions should use ID values of 0x1000 (WM_USER) and greater.

Using the PM dialog editor, a custom open dialog is created. All the basic controls found in the standard dialog are present, but in a different order. In addition to the basic controls, a new checkbox button is added. This checkbox enables the user to specify whether the current directory should be retained. The current path and filename are saved as an atom in the variable `atSavePath`. (Atoms are PM features in which unique strings are assigned numeric identifiers. This saves space and allows the identifiers to be manipulated more easily than strings.)

Creating the custom file open dialog requires some additional parameters to be set. The `FDS_CUSTOM` flag is added to the `fl` field, and the `usDlgId` parameter is set to the ID assigned to the custom dialog. Notice that although we are providing a dialog template, `FDS_OPEN_DIALOG` or `FDS_SAVEAS_DIALOG` must still be specified. Without one of these flags, the dialog creation will fail. The `hMod` field must also be set to indicate where to search for the resources. Because the new dialog resource will be bound into the executable, the module handle may be set to NULL. A NULL module handle will cause `WinFileDlg` to search the current module for the requested resource.

`WinFileDlg` handles the processing for all the standard control windows. If your custom dialog template does not define additional controls, `WinDefFileDlgProc` can be used to process the dialog. Processing for any user-supplied controls, however, must be done in a user-supplied dialog procedure. To do that, the `pfnDlgProc` parameter of the `FILEDLG` structure is set to our private dialog procedure, `FileOpenDlgProc`. Providing a private callback subclasses the file open dialog. Anytime a window is subclassed, the previous callback, in this case `WinDefFileDlgProc`, should be called with all messages received. The callback must also be added to the `EXPORTS` section of the module definition file. With the exception of the function name, the callback function must be defined as follows:

```
MRESULT EXPENTRY FileOpenDlgProc(HWND,ULONG,MPARAM,MPARAM);
```

In our example here, the `FileOpenDlgProc` dialog callback only processes two messages, `WM_INITDLG` and `WM_COMMAND`. During the processing of the `WM_INITDLG` message, the initial state of the directory checkbox must be set. The common dialogs, unlike those created by calling `WinDlgBox`, do not pass a pointer to initialization data in the `mp2` parameter of the `WM_INITDLG` message. Data, however, may be shared between the caller and the dialog by using the `ulUser` field of the `FILEDLG` structure. How does the dialog get the pointer to the `FILEDLG` structure? The `OWL_USER` field of the dialog window contains a pointer to this structure that may be retrieved by calling `WinQueryWindowUlong`. When we have this pointer, the `ulUser` field is checked. If it contains a value, the Save Directory button is checked. This field will be initialized prior to the `WinFileDlg` function call to the atom handle of the saved path if one existed. After setting the button state, `WinDefFileDlgProc` is then called to allow any default initialization to occur.

This is performed with these lines:

```
case WM_INITDLG:
   pFileDlg = (PFILEDLG)WinQueryWindowULong(hWndDlg,QWL_USER);
   if (pFileDlg->ulUser)
      WinCheckButton(hWndDlg,DID_SAVE_DIR,1);
   break;
```

A WM_COMMAND message will be sent to the dialog when OK or Cancel is selected by the user. Part of the default processing by WinDefFileDlgProc for these controls is calling WinDismissDlg and setting the return code in the lReturn field of the FILEDLG structure. Notice that this field is not set by WinDismissDlg, but by WinDefFileDlgProc. If your custom dialog procedure dismisses the dialog, it should also set the return code in the FILEDLG structure. During the processing of the WM_COMMAND for the DID_OK control ID, WinDefFileDlgProc sets the szFullPath to the selected filename.

FileOpenDlgProc must return to the caller the state of the Save Directory checkbox. If the button is checked, the ulUser field of the FILEDLG structure will be set to the ID of the checkbox, DID_SAVE_DIR. The lReturn field may be used as an alternate method of returning a value to the caller. Notice that this will work only if WinDefFileDlgProc is called with the WM_COMMAND message first:

```
case WM_COMMAND:
   switch (SHORT1FROMMP(mp1))
   {
      case DID_OK:
      case DID_CANCEL:
      if(WinQueryButtonCheckstate(hWndDlg,DID_SAVE_DIR))
      {
         // Do the default processing
         WinDefFileDlgProc(hWndDlg,ulMessage,mp1,mp2);

         // Get the pointer to the FILEDLG structure
         pFileDlg = (PFILEDLG)WinQueryWindowULong(hWndDlg,
QWL_USER);
         pFileDlg->ulUser = DID_SAVE_DIR;
         return (0);
      }
      break;
   }
   break;
```

In the second example, the dialog was always created by using the file search spec "*.TXT" based on the files in the current directory. To make our custom File Open dialog smarter, we added the Save Directory checkbox. Now that the code exists in our dialog callback, to set and get the state of that checkbox, we must save and restore the directory. If, upon the return from the WinFileDlg function, lReturn is set to DID_OK and ulUser is set to DID_SAVE_DIR, the previous path atom is destroyed, and the file and directory contained in szFullFile are saved as the new path atom. If Cancel is selected, no changes to the current file or Save Directory state are made:

```
if (FileDlg.lReturn == DID_OK)
{
   if (atSavePath)
      atSavePath = WinDeleteAtom(hAtomTable,atSavePath);
   if (FileDlg.ulUser == DID_SAVE_DIR)
      atSavePath = WinAddAtom(hAtomTable,(PSZ)FileDlg.szFullFile);
   load_file((PSZ)&FileDlg.szFullFile);
}
```

Before we call the `WinFileDlg` function, the `set_path` function is called to initialize the `szFullFile` variable. You will recall that this parameter sets an initial file spec for the dialog. The `set_path` function takes two parameters. The first is a pointer to the `szFullFile` variable, and the second is the dialog type being created. If the `atSavePath` atom is non-NULL, the atom text containing the fully qualified pathname is retrieved. If the File Open dialog is to be created, the text of the saved path is returned. The default file save "*.TXT" is then concatenated at the end of the string. If the Save As dialog is to be created, the saved file and path are left unchanged. If `atSavePath` is NULL, the default "*.TXT" is used. The `ulUser` field is then initialized with the atom handle. This handle is checked during the processing of the `WM_INITDLG` message in the `FileOpenDlgProc` function.

Multiple File Selection

When the `FDS_MULTIPLESEL` flag is set in the `fl` field of the `FILEDLG` structure, the file selection list box is created to allow multiple selections. The selections are returned to the caller in the `papszFQFilename` parameter of the `FILEDLG` structure. The `papszFQFilename` points to an array of pointers that point to null-terminated file names. The number of entries will be contained in the `ulFQFCount`. The memory that these strings occupy is allocated by PM in the call to `WinFileDlg`. An application should make its own copy of the filenames and free this memory by calling the `WinFreeFileListDlg` function. The `WinFreeFileListDlg` takes the `papszFQFilename` as its only parameter:

```
WinFreeFileListDlg(FileDlg.papszFQFilename);
```

Save As Dialog

The Save As dialog uses the same template as the file open dialog. The default behavior is to disable the file selection list box. This enables the user to see the files in the current directory, but not select them. By disabling the list box, an existing file may not be accidentally selected by double-clicking it. An application should not rely on this alone to prevent an existing file from being overwritten, however. The list box may be enabled by setting the `FDS_ENABLEFILELB` flag in the `fl` field. If a file is currently being processed, a Save As dialog should preload the `szFullFile` with the path and file of that file. In this sample, the contents of `szFilePath` are copied to the `szFullFile` parameter. In a commercial application, the path and file should be saved and retrieved from an atom. This was demonstrated in the custom dialog template sample shown previously.

Font Dialog

The common font dialog provides an easy way to enumerate and display the fonts available for the screen or a print device. This dialog is created and manipulated in much the same manner as the file dialog. Before we discuss the common font dialog, however, a brief summary of font terminology is necessary. Chapter 7 "Creating and Manipulating PM Fonts and Text," provides a full discussion of all the font topics briefly touched on in this chapter.

Understanding the Basics of Fonts

A font is a collection of characters that share a common height and appearance. The collection can be any size, but most fonts you will work with have 256 characters. The height of a font is described in points, which is short for printer points. Each printer point is 1/72 inch. Although the height of a font can be described exactly, the appearance of a font is more difficult to pin down. Fonts are divided into families based on characteristics of the font. A major determinate of a font family is the presence of serifs. A serif is a fine line drawn at the end and perpendicular to the major strokes of a character. It often appears as a flaring of the stroke. Fonts without serifs are referred to as sans serif. Strokes are the lines used to draw the characters of the font. The width of those strokes are also used to classify the font in a family. OS/2 includes fonts from four families by default:

Serif fonts	***Sans serif fonts***
Times	Helvetica
Courier	
Symbol	

A font family may be further divided into a single font with a unique facename. The characters of that font will be representative of the family to which they belong. Certain font attributes can be applied to fonts of any family or face. These attributes do not change the basic appearance but do modify the manner in which the characters are displayed. For example, most fonts can be made italic or bold.

Font Representation

Now that we have some understanding about how fonts are classified, let's look at how they are represented. Font representation falls into two categories: outline and image. The characters of an outline font are described in terms of the graphics primitives that draw the font. Image font characters, on the other hand, are bitmaps. Both have advantages and disadvantages. Outline fonts are continuously scalable and may be displayed in any point size without a loss of quality. That quality comes at the expense of speed, however, because each character must be drawn when it is output. Image fonts display faster than outline fonts because a bitmap exists for each character in the font. Image fonts may not be scaled, however. An image font will require a bitmap for each point size it has available.

The Common Font API

With a little font terminology under our belt, let's look at the two functions available in the common font dialog API:

`WinFontDlg`	Creates and displays the font selection dialog and returns user selections.
`WinDefFontDlgProc`	Default font dialog procedure that handles all the processing of the control windows in the dialog.

The `WinFontDlg` function takes three parameters. The first two are the same as those for the `WinFileDlg` function, which are the window handles of the parent and owner, respectively. The third parameter is a pointer to a `FONTDLG` structure. It is this structure that defines the appearance and behavior of the dialog. Although creating the Basic Font selection dialog is easy, using it in an application requires some work on the application's behalf. Taking advantage of the features of the font dialog requires an understanding of the `FONTDLG` structure. This structure has some of the same fields as the `FILEDLG`, but many are specific to fonts:

`ULONG`	`cbSize`	Structure size in bytes.
`HPS`	`hpsScreen`	Handle to a screen presentation space from which fonts are to be enumerated. If `NULL`, a screen PS will be supplied.
`HPS`	`hpsPrinter`	Handle to a printer presentation space from which fonts are to be enumerated.
`PSZ`	`pszTitle`	Pointer to a null-terminated string that should be used as the title of the dialog. The default string is "Font."
`PSZ`	`pszPreview`	Pointer to a null-terminated string that should be used as the text displayed in the preview font window. The default string is "abcdABCD."
`PSZ`	`pszPtSizeList`	Pointer to a null-terminated string that is a list of point sizes to be displayed in the drop-down portion of the size combo box. The sizes are separated by spaces and defaults to "8 10 12 14 18 24."
`PFNWP`	`pfnDlgProc`	Application-supplied dialog procedure.
`PSZ`	`pszFamilyname`	Pointer to a null-terminated string that identifies an initial family name to display in the font name combo box. `pszFamilyname` is also used to return the selected font family name. It is, therefore, a required parameter. The memory pointed to by `pszFamilyname` should be at least `FACESIZE` in length.

`FIXED fxPointSize`	Initial point size to display preview font. This value is placed in the combo box edit field, but is not added to the drop-down list.
`ULONG fl`	Flags that define the dialog appearance, location, and behavior.
`FNTS_APPLYBUTTON`	The Apply button is added to the dialog between OK and Cancel. This button should be used on modeless dialogs to make a change take effect without closing the dialog. You must supply your own dialog procedure to process this control's command messages.
`FNTS_BITMAPONLY`	Only enumerate image fonts in the dialog box. When this option is selected, the Outline checkbox is disabled.
`FNTS_CENTER`	Centers dialog relative to owner window. This flag will override a dialog position specified by the X and Y parameters.
`FNTS_CUSTOM`	Creates the dialog using the custom dialog template found in `hMod` with the ID supplied in `usDlgId`.
`FNTS_FIXEDWIDTHONLY`	Only enumerate fixed pitch fonts in the dialog. A font is fixed pitch if the width of all characters is equal.
`FNTS_HELPBUTTON`	A help push button is added to the dialog. When the button is pushed, a `WM_HELP` message is sent to the owner window. If the owner is a frame window, it must be subclassed to receive the `WM_HELP` message.
`FNTS_INITFROMFATTRS`	The initial font displayed is created based on the contents of the `fAttrs` parameter. For a complete discussion of the `FATTRS` structure, see Chapter 7.
`FNTS_MODELESS`	The dialog is created modeless; the default is to create a modal dialog. When this flag is used, the `WinFontDlg` returns the window handle of the created dialog.
`FNTS_NOSYNTHESIZEDFONTS`	Fonts displayed in the dialog are not synthesized. Attributes such as bold or italic will not be added to base fonts.
`FNTS_OWNERDRAWPREVIEW`	A `WM_DRAWITEM` message is sent to the owner window allowing it to render the preview window. If this message is not processed, the

		default processing of the preview window occurs. The Outline, Underline, and Strikeout buttons are created as three state checkboxes.
FNTS_PROPORTIONALONLY		Only enumerate proportional fonts in the dialog. A Font is proportional if characters vary in width. For example, a capital "A" will be wider than a lower case "i."
FNTS_RESETBUTTON		The Reset push button is added to the dialog. When it is pushed, the dialog is reset to the values it was initialized with.
FNTS_VECTORONLY		Only enumerate outline fonts in the dialog.
ULONG	f lFlags	Additional flags that control the initial display of printer or screen fonts in the dialog. The default behavior is to display fonts enumerated from the screen and, if a PS for a print device is supplied, display printer fonts. These flags will disable the display of printer or screen fonts. One or both of these flags may be supplied as input.
FNTF_NOVIEWSCREENFONTS		Do not display fonts enumerated from the screen PS. The user may override by checking the Display checkbox in the dialog.
FNTF_NOVIEWPRINTERFONTS		If a PS for a print device is supplied, do not display fonts enumerated from that device. The user may override by checking the printer checkbox. If `hpsPrinter` is `NULL`, printer fonts are not displayed, the printer checkbox is disabled, and this flag has no effect. If the dialog was dismissed by selecting OK, one of these two flags will be set. They have no effect as an input parameter.
FNTF_SCREENFONTSELECTED		A screen font was selected in the dialog.
FNTF_PRINTERFONTSELECTED		A printer font was selected in the dialog.
ULONG	f lType	If a font was selected, this parameter will contain a facename attribute. This flag should be used as input to `GpiQueryFaceString` to create a compound facename that may be passed to `GpiCreateLogFont`: FTYPE_ITALIC 0x1 FTYPE_ITALIC_DONT_CARE 0x2

		FTYPE_OBLIQUE	0x4
		FTYPE_OBLIQUE_DONT_CARE	0x8
		FTYPE_ROUNDED	0x10
		FTYPE_ROUNDED_DONT_CARE	0x20
ULONG	f lTypeMask	When the FNTS_OWNERDRAWPREVIEW flag is set in the f l parameter, this field contains a mask of the type bits to use.	
ULONG	f lStyle	If a font was selected, this parameter will contain flags based on the selected emphasis checkboxes in the dialog. When creating the font, the fsSelection field of the FATTRS structure should be set to the contents of flStyle:	
		FATTR_SEL_UNDERSCORE	0x2
		FATTR_SEL_OUTLINE	0x8
		FATTR_SEL_STRIKEOUT	0x10
ULONG	f lStyleMask	When the FNTS_OWNERDRAWPREVIEW flag is set in the f l parameter, this field contains a mask of the style bits to use.	

The next two parameters control the color text display in the font preview window. When the FNTS_OWNERDRAWPREVIEW flag is set in the fl parameter, the CLR_NOINDEX value may be used to leave alone the foreground and background colors. The PM documentation states that the color value may be an indexed or RGB color value based on the color mode hpsScreen is set to. Only indexed colors seem to work:

LONG	clr Fore	Foreground (text) color of the font in the preview window.
LONG	clr Back	Background color of the text in the font preview window.
ULONG	ulUser	Unused field reserved for application use.
LONG	lReturn	WinDefFontDlgProc will set this value to the ID of the control that resulted in the dismissal of the dialog. It is not the result value passed to the WinDismissDlg function. If your custom dialog callback calls WinDismissDlg, it must still set the ulReturn field to the desired control ID.

LONG	lSRC	If the `WinFontDlg` function fails, this field will contain one of the following error codes: FNTS_ERR_INVALID_DIALOG FNTS_ERR_ALLOC_SHARED_MEM FNTS_ERR_INVALID_PARM FNTS_ERR_OUT_OF_MEMORY FNTS_ERR_INVALID_VERSION FNTS_ERR_DIALOG_LOAD_ERROR

If a font is selected, the following three parameters will contain font-sizing information taken from the `FONTMETRIC` structure of the selected font. They are not required to create a font of this type and are returned for informational purposes:

LONG	lEmHeight	When the dialog is dismissed, this parameter is updated with Em height of the current font.
LONG	lXHeight	When the dialog is dismissed, this parameter is updated with X height of the current font.
LONG	lExternalLeading	When the dialog is dismissed, this parameter is updated with external leading of the current font.
HMODULE	hMod	If the `FNTS_CUSTOM` flag is set, `WinFontDlg` will attempt to load a dialog resource with the ID specified in the `usDlgId` field from this module. If `hMod` is `NULL`, the current executable is searched.
FATTRS	fAttrs	If a font is selected, the `FATTRS` of the selected font will be returned in this parameter. If the `FNTS_INITFROMFATTRS` flag is set in the `fl` field, this is used as an input parameter to select the initial font to be displayed in the preview window.
SHORT	sNominalPointSize	When the dialog is dismissed, this parameter is updated with nominal point size of the font. For Image fonts, this will be the font height. For Outline fonts, this is the size the font was designed to be rendered. The size is returned in decipoints that are 1/720 inch. To convert to points, divide by 10.

If a font was selected, the following two parameters will contain weight and width flags that should be used as input to the `GpiQueryFaceString` function. It will create a compound facename that may be passed to `GpiCreateLogFont`:

USHORT	usWeight	Return parameter that indicates the thickness of the strokes used in the characters of the font. The most common font weights are normal and bold: FWEIGHT_ULTRA_LIGHT FWEIGHT_EXTRA_LIGHT FWEIGHT_LIGHT FWEIGHT_SEMI_LIGHT FWEIGHT_NORMAL FWEIGHT_SEMI_BOLD FWEIGHT_BOLD FWEIGHT_EXTRA_BOLD FWEIGHT_ULTRA_BOLD
USHORT	usWidth	Return parameter that describes the width of characters in this font: FWIDTH_ULTRA_CONDENSED FWIDTH_EXTRA_CONDENSED FWIDTH_CONDENSED FWIDTH_SEMI_CONDENSED FWIDTH_NORMAL FWIDTH_SEMI_EXPANDED FWIDTH_EXPANDED FWIDTH_EXTRA_EXPANDED FWIDTH_ULTRA_EXPANDED
SHORT	x	Screen X dialog coordinate; ignored if the FNTS_CENTER flag is used. Upon return, X is updated to the last screen X position regardless of the FNTS_CENTER flag.
SHORT	y	Screen Y dialog coordinate; ignored if the FNTS_CENTER flag is used. Upon return, Y is updated to the last screen Y position regardless of the FNTS_CENTER flag.
USHORT	usDlgId	If the FNTS_CUSTOM flag is set, WinFileDlg will attempt to load a dialog resource with this ID from the module specified in the hMod field.

USHORT	usFamilyBufLen	Size of the pszFamilyname in bytes. It is recommended that pszFamilyname be at least FACESIZE in length.
USHORT	usReserved	Reserved parameter must be NULL.

Basic Font Dialog

The common file dialog provides three combo boxes that allow selection of various font facenames, styles, and point sizes. A preview window allows the effect of current selections to be seen. Like the initial file open sample, the first font dialog sample uses the minimum set of parameters to display the dialog. As with the FILEDLG structure, the FONTDLG structure must be initialized to zeros and the size of the structure set in the cbSize field. An additional buffer that will hold the selected family name upon return must be allocated. The buffer pointed to by the pszFamilyname should be at least FACESIZE in length. This constant is defined in the toolkit header files as the maximum size of a font facename. Unlike the File Open dialog that doubled as the Save As dialog, no flags are required by default. We have used the FNTS_CENTER flag in place of specifying the default X and Y positions of the dialog. Finally, the foreground and background colors used in the font preview window must be provided. Here is an example of setting these:

```
szFamilyname[0] = 0;
memset((PCH)&FontDlg,0,sizeof(FONTDLG));
FontDlg.cbSize          = sizeof(FONTDLG);
FontDlg.pszFamilyname   = szFamilyname;
FontDlg.usFamilyBufLen  = FACESIZE;
FontDlg.fl              = FNTS_CENTER;
FontDlg.clrFore         = CLR_BLACK;
FontDlg.clrBack         = CLR_WHITE;
WinFontDlg(HWND_DESKTOP,hWndClient,(PFONTDLG)&FontDlg);
if (FontDlg.lReturn == DID_OK)
    WinSetWindowText(hWndFrame,(PSZ)FontDlg.pszFamilyname);
```

The WinFontDlg function returns TRUE if the dialog was successfully created and FALSE if an error occurs. If an error occurs, the lSRC parameter will contain an error code that identifies the reason for the failure. The dialog is by default modal and will return from the WinfontDlg function call when the user selects the OK or Cancel push buttons. The selected familyname will be contained in the pszFamilyname parameter if OK was selected; otherwise its contents are undefined. If OK was selected, the font familyname is set as the titlebar text.

Changing the Font

When a file is opened and displayed in the client area, it is output by using the default system proportional font. This font requires no creation or selection because it is present in the default presentation space unless changed by the application. The second font dialog sample presented here allows the font which is used to output the file text to be changed. Although the familyname returned in the first example is interesting, it alone is not sufficient to create a font selected in the dialog. Because we are more concerned with how the common font dialog is used than with all the interworking of the font creation process, we will cover only the basics. Chapter 7 provides a more in-depth coverage of the font creation process.

Font as Logical Resource

A font is considered to be a logical resource created by the `GpiCreateLogFont` function. A logical font is a description of a desired font from which PM will select a physical font. IN order for the letter to actually be written to an output device, the logical description of the font must finally be mapped to some physical representation. The logical font description is comprised of the facename, size, and attributes of a desired font. It is from this description that PM will map or choose the closest physical font available. A physical font is bitmap images or graphics primitives used to render the font. A new logical font is identified by a numeric value called a local identifier. This value is selected by the application and must be in the range of 1 to 254. After a logical font is created, the physical font to which it is mapped will not change.

The `GpiCreateLogFont` function takes these four parameters:

```
GpiCreateLogFont(hPS,pchName,lcid,pFattrs)
```

HPS	hPS	The handle to a presentation space in which this logical font is to be created.
PSTR8	pName	Pointer to an optional logical font name.
LONG	lLcid	The application-supplied local identifier to be associated with this logical font.
PFATTRS	pFattrs	Pointer to a FATTRS structure. This structure contains the definition of the logical font to be created.

It is the `pFattrs` parameter that we are most interested in here. It contains facename, sizes, and attributes that describe a logical font. You may recall that the `FONTDLG` structure also contains a `FATTRS` structure. When a font is selected by pressing OK in the dialog, the `fAttrs` parameter will contain the logical description of the selected font. The values returned in the `FATTRS` may then be passed to the `GpiCreateLogFont` function. When the `WinFontDlg` function returns and a font has been selected, the `FATTRS` portion of the `FONTDLG` is copied to the `Fattrs` variable in our sample application:

```
if (FontDlg.lReturn == DID_OK)
{
   set_font((PSZ)FontDlg.pszFamilyname);
   Fattrs = FontDlg.fAttrs;
}
```

The `Fattrs` variable will be passed to the `GpiCreateLogFont` function during the painting of the client window. After it is created, the local identifier must be set into the presentation space before the new logical font is used. This is done by using the `GpiSetCharSet` function. It takes two parameters: the first is the handle to the presentation space to set the created font into, and the second is the local identifier used when the font was created.

Now that we have a method of creating a font selected in font dialog, the second sample dialog will demonstrate changing the font used to output the text. Several new creation flags have been added to the `fl` field of the `FONTDLG` structure. To simplify the creation process, only image fonts will be displayed in the dialog. This is done by setting the `FNTS_BITMAPONLY` flag. The `FNTS_RESETBUTTON` flag has also been added. It creates a push button that, when pushed, returns the dialog to its initial creation state. The most important new flag added, however, is the `FNTS_INITFROMFATTRS` flag. This causes the font initially selected in the dialog to be created based on the contents of the `fAttrs` field of the `FONTDLG` structure. The `FATTRS` field will be initialized with the values saved from the last font selected in the dialog:

```
szFamilyname[0] = 0;
memset((PCH)&FontDlg,0,sizeof(FONTDLG));
FontDlg.cbSize          = sizeof(FONTDLG);
FontDlg.hpsScreen       = WinGetPS(hWnd);
FontDlg.pszFamilyname   = szFamilyname;
FontDlg.usFamilyBufLen  = FACESIZE;
FontDlg.pszPreview      = "Sample Text";
FontDlg.fl              = FNTS_RESETBUTTON ¦ FNTS_CENTER ¦
                          FNTS_INITFROMFATTRS ¦ FNTS_BITMAPONLY;
FontDlg.clrFore         = CLR_BLACK;
FontDlg.clrBack         = CLR_PALEGRAY;
FontDlg.fAttrs          = Fattrs;
FontDlg.pszTitle        = szBuff1;
set_title(szBuff1,IDS_FONT);
WinFontDlg(HWND_DESKTOP,hWndClient,(PFONTDLG)&FontDlg);
```

The only problem is that, until the dialog is created the first time, `Fattrs` is uninitialized. This variable can be initialized with the default font values during the `WM_CREATE` message. The function used to query the default font attributes does not take a pointer to a `FATTRS` structure, however. The `GpiQueryFontMetrics` function requires a presentation space handle and a pointer to a `FONTMETRICS` structure. Information about the font currently selected in the presentation space is returned in the `FONTMETRICS` structure. The `FATTRS` structure is a subset of `FONTMETRICS`, and after being initialized to zeros, the default font facename and height are copied to the `Fattrs` variable:

```
case WM_CREATE:
   // Query the height of the default font.
   hPS = WinGetPS(hWnd);
   memset(&Fattrs,0,sizeof(FATTRS));
   GpiQueryFontMetrics(hPS,sizeof(FONTMETRICS), (PFONTMETRICS)&FontMetrics);
   Fattrs.lMaxBaselineExt = FontMetrics.lMaxBaselineExt;
   Fattrs.usRecordLength = sizeof(FATTRS);
   strcpy((PSZ)Fattrs.szFacename, (PSZ)FontMetrics.szFacename);
   WinReleasePS(hWnd);
   szFilePath[0] = '\0';
   break;
```

The font can now be created in the requested size before outputting the file text during the `WM_PAINT` message:

```
GpiCreateLogFont(hPS,NULL,CLIENT_FONT,&Fattrs);
```

```
GpiSetCharSet(hPS,CLIENT_FONT);
GpiQueryFontMetrics(hPS,sizeof(FONTMETRICS),(PFONTMETRICS)&FontMetrics);
cyHeight = FontMetrics.lMaxBaselineExt + FontMetrics.lExternalLeading;
```

The `set_font` function has been added to update the titlebar with the current filename and font facename. The client window is then invalidated causing the file text to be redisplayed.

Making the Dialog Modeless

Although we have enabled the user to change the font which is used to display a file, the mechanism is cumbersome. There are two major drawbacks to the solution just presented. The first is that the user is required to select OK and close the dialog to see the changes to the font take effect. The font preview window helps, but it won't show how much of the text will fit in the client window. Each change of a font requires the dialog to be opened by selecting it from the menu. If the font is being changed frequently, this can become tiresome. The second problem results from creating the font dialog as modal. The `WinFontDlg` function will not return until the dialog is dismissed. This prevents any other interaction with the application while this dialog is displayed.

The solution to the first problem is to create the dialog with the Apply push button by adding the `FNTS_APPLYBUTTON` flag to the `fl` field of the `FONTDLG` structure. We will also need to add our private dialog callback, `FontDlgProc`, to handle the processing of the Apply button. As with the private file open dialog callback, the previous callback, `WinDefFontDlgProc`, should be called with unprocessed messages. With the exception of the function name, the callback function must be defined as follows:

```
MRESULT EXPENTRY FontDlgProc(HWND,ULONG,MPARAM,MPARAM);
```

When pushed, the Apply push button will send `FontDlgProc` a `WM_COMMAND` message with the first short value in `mp1` equal to `DID_APPLY_BUTTON`. When this message is received, the same code that was called in the previous example—when the `WinFontDlg` function returned with `lReturn` equal to `DID_OK`—is executed:

```
case DID_APPLY_BUTTON:
   set_font(pFontDlg->pszFamilyname);
   Fattrs = pFontDlg->fAttrs;
   return (0);
   break;
```

You may recall that this caused the application to add the new font facename to the titlebar and to redraw the client area using the new font. The `pFontDlg` pointer is a static variable that was initialized during the `WM_INTIDLG` message.

The solution to the second problem is to create the dialog as modeless rather than modal. `WinFontDlg` will immediately return the dialog handle of the created dialog when the `FNTS_MODELESS` flag is added to the `fl` field. The return value is the handle of the dialog if successful and 0 if an error occurs. The user will then be able to interact with the main application.

For example, the current file may be changed while the font dialog is displayed. When creating the dialog as modeless, remember that the `FONTDLG` structure passed to the `WinFontDlg` function must be valid for the life of the dialog. In the previous font dialogs, the structure was allocated as a local variable on the stack. When the `process_command` function returned, those variables were no longer valid. A new global structure, `FontDlg2`, is defined and used for the modeless font dialog initialization.

The dialog may be closed by selection of the OK or Cancel push button. Because the dialog is modeless, it will not return to the caller as was the case in the modal font dialog. Any code executed based on `lReturn` field of the `FONTDLG` structure must be done in the dialog. We must add code to process the `WM_COMMAND` message from the OK push button. We want to do exactly the same thing for the OK button processing as was done for the Apply button and then cause the dialog to be dismissed. Calling `WinDefFontDlgProc` with the OK command message will dismiss the dialog and have no effect for the Apply command. The code for OK and Apply button processing can, therefore, be identical:

```
case DID_APPLY_BUTTON:
case DID_OK_BUTTON:
   WinDefFontDlgProc(hWndDlg,ulMessage,mp1,mp2);
   set_font(pFontDlg->pszFamilyname);
   Fattrs = pFontDlg->fAttrs;
   return (0);
   break;
```

Although this change gives us the desired behavior for the OK and Apply buttons, it still requires the Apply or OK buttons to be pushed. What we would like is to have immediate feedback similar to that of the notebook controls. Notebooks typically do not have an OK button to put the changes into effect. When a selection is made, the change occurs. For example, the background page of the settings notebook allows a bitmap to be used as the background of the desktop or a folder. When a bitmap file is selected in the file combination box, the window is updated immediately. A new checkbox will be added to the dialog during the `WM_INITDLG` message. This checkbox will enable or disable the immediate updating of the client window. The `add_checkbox` function calculates the position of the control and creates the button. Because we know this dialog will have only three push buttons, the checkbox is created vertically centered on these rows of push buttons. The horizontal position is one character to the right of the Cancel button.

Font Notification Messages

In order to update the client window immediately, we must know when changes are made in the dialog. `FontDlgProc` will receive a number of notification messages when selections are made that alter the facename, point size, and style attributes.

The following are important font notification messages:

`FNTM_FACENAMECHANGED`	Sent when the font family name is changed by the user. The mp1 parameter will contain a pointer to the currently selected facename. The `mp2` parameter will contain zero.
`FNTM_FILTERLIST`	This message is sent to the dialog before strings are added to the family name, style name, and point size combo boxes. The `mp1` parameter will contain a pointer to the null-terminated string being added. The low word of the `mp2` parameter will identify the combo box the string is being added to. It may be one of the following:
`FNTI_FAMILYNAME`	The string is being added to the family name combo box (DID_NAME).
`FNTI_POINTSIZE`	The string is being added to the point size combo box (DID_SIZE).
`FNTI_STYLENAME`	The string is being added to the font style combo box (DID_STYLE). The high word of `mp2` contains information about the font being added. The high word of `mp2` contains information about the font being added. It will contain one or more of the following:
`FNTI_BITMAPFONT`	Font is a bitmap font.
`FNTI_DEFAULTLIST`	Font point size is from the default or application supplied point size string.
`FNTI_FIXEDWIDTHFONT`	Font is fixed width.
`FNTI_PROPORTIONALFONT`	Font is proportionally spaced.
`FNTI_SYNTHESIZED`	Font style is synthesized. This flag will only be set for `FNTI_STYLENAME`.
`FNTI_VECTORFONT`	Font is a vector font.The default processing in `WinFontDlgProc` will add the string if it meets the criteria of the `fl` flags set in the `FONTDLG` structure. If the font is added, `WinFontDlgProc` will return `TRUE`. Otherwise, `FALSE` is returned.
`FNTM_POINTSIZECHANGED`	Sent when the point size of the font is changed by the user. The `mp1` parameter will contain a pointer to the text in the point size entry field. The `mp2` parameter contains that point size in fixed notation.

FNTM_STYLECHANGED	Sent when any one of the style attributes such as underline or strikeout are changed. The mp1 parameter will contain a pointer to a STYLECHANGE structure. It contains information on the weight, width, and type of the font before and after the user made a change.
FNTM_UPDATEPREVIEW	Sent before the preview window is updated. The mp1 parameter will contain the window handle of the preview window. The mp2 parameter is zero.

The message that we are most interested in here is the FNTM_UPDATEPREVIEW message. It is sent after the FONTDLG structure has been updated and before the preview window is drawn. If the Direct Update checkbox is selected when this message is received, the client area is updated:

```
case FNTM_UPDATEPREVIEW:
   if(WinSendMsg(hWndUpdate,BM_QUERYCHECK,0,0))
   {
      // Update the display window.
      mReturn = WinDefFontDlgProc(hWndDlg,ulMessage,mp1, mp2);
      set_font(pFontDlg->pszFamilyname);
      Fattrs = pFontDlg->fAttrs;
      return (mReturn);
   }
   break;
```

Owner Draw Preview

If your application has some special requirements for the preview window, you can provide your own drawing routine. Setting the FNTS_OWNERDRAWPREVIEW flag in the fl field of the FONTDLG structure causes a WM_DRAWITEM message to be sent to the dialogs owner window whenever the preview window must be updated. Because this message is sent to the owner window and not the dialog, it is not necessary to supply your own dialog procedure. The mp1 parameter of the WM_DRAWITEM message will contain the ID of the window to be updated, in this case DID_SAMPLE. The mp2 parameter is a pointer to an OWNERITEM structure. It will contain the window handle of the preview window, a Presentation Space handle for the window, a rectangle defining the size preview window size, and various state flags. The pointer to the FONTDLG structure can be retrieved by querying the QWL_USER field of the parent of the preview window. If your application draws the preview window, return TRUE; otherwise, return FALSE if you want the dialog to draw the item.

The CONTROL Sample Application

The following sections contain the source code of the files in the CONTROL sample.

Files to Build the CONTROL Sample

COMMDLG.C
COMMDLG.DEF
COMMDLG.H
COMMDLG.ICO
COMMDLG.RC
CUSTOM.DLG

COMMDLG.C

```
/* -------------------------------
Common Dialogs Program
Real-World Programming for OS/2
Copyright (c)  1994 Blain, Delimon, and English
------------------------------- */


#define INCL_WIN
#define INCL_GPI
#define INCL_DOS
#define INCL_ERRORS
#include <os2.h>
#include <stdlib.h>
#include "commdlg.h"
#include "..\common\about.h"


#define DRIVE_REMOVABLE 2
#define DRIVE_FIXED     3
#define DRIVE_REMOTE    4

MRESULT EXPENTRY ClientWndProc (HWND,ULONG,MPARAM,MPARAM);
MRESULT EXPENTRY FileOpenDlgProc(HWND,ULONG,MPARAM,MPARAM);
MRESULT EXPENTRY FontDlgProc(HWND,ULONG,MPARAM,MPARAM);

HAB     hab;
HWND    hWndFrame,
        hWndClicnt,
        hFontDlg = 0;
PVOID   pMem;
PCHAR   pFileText    = 0;
PAPSZ   pDrivesList  = 0;
ULONG   ulTextSize   = 0;
ULONG   ulDrivesSize = 0;
int     cyHeight;
char    szBuff1[MAX_BUFF];
char    szFilePath[CCHMAXPATH];
char    szFamilyname[FACESIZE];
ATOM    atSavePath;
HATOMTBL     hAtomTable = 0;
FATTRS       Fattrs;
FONTDLG      FontDlg2;
```

```
int main()
{
   HMQ    hmq;
   QMSG   qmsg;
   ULONG flFrameFlags     = FCF_TITLEBAR ¦ FCF_SYSMENU ¦
                            FCF_SIZEBORDER ¦ FCF_MINMAX ¦
                            FCF_SHELLPOSITION ¦ FCF_TASKLIST ¦
                            FCF_ICON ¦ FCF_MENU;
   CHAR   szClientClass[] = "CLIENT";

   hab = WinInitialize (0);
   hmq = WinCreateMsgQueue (hab, 0);

   hAtomTable = WinQuerySystemAtomTable();

   DosAllocMem((PPVOID)&pMem,0x1000,PAG_READ ¦ PAG_WRITE);
   DosSubSet(pMem,DOSSUB_INIT ¦ DOSSUB_SPARSE_OBJ,8192);
   get_fixed_drives();

   WinRegisterClass (hab, szClientClass, ClientWndProc, CS_SIZEREDRAW,0);
   WinLoadString (hab, 0, IDS_APPNAME, sizeof(szBuff1), szBuff1);

   hWndFrame = WinCreateStdWindow (HWND_DESKTOP, WS_VISIBLE,
         &flFrameFlags,szClientClass, szBuff1,0,0, ID_APPNAME,
         &hWndClient);

   while (WinGetMsg (hab, &qmsg, 0, 0, 0))
   WinDispatchMsg (hab, &qmsg);

   WinDestroyMsgQueue (hmq);
   WinTerminate (hab);
   return (0);
}


HWND APIENTRY add_checkbox(HWND hWndDlg)
/*-------------------------------*/

This function will create a checkbox button in the lower right
hand corner of hWndDlg. The dialog is expected to be the standard
font selection dialog. The button is vertically aligned to the
center of the OK push button and horizontally aligned so that all
of the text is visible in the dialog.

/*-------------------------------*/
{
   HWND     hCheckBox;
   HPS      hPS;
   RECTL    DlgRectl;
   RECTL    ButtonRectl;
   int      iLength;
   PVOID    pData;
   FONTMETRICS FontMetrics;
   POINTL   Ptl[TXTBOX_COUNT + 1];
```

```
    // Get the sizes of the dialog and the cancel push button
    WinQueryWindowRect(hWndDlg,&DlgRectl);
    WinQueryWindowRect(WinWindowFromID(hWndDlg,DID_CANCEL),
          &ButtonRectl);
    WinMapWindowPoints(WinWindowFromID(hWndDlg,DID_CANCEL), hWndDlg,
          (PPOINTL)&ButtonRectl,2);

    // Load the checkbox text string
    DosSubAlloc(pMem,(PPVOID)&pData,MAX_BUFF);
    iLength = WinLoadString (hab,0,IDS_UPDATE,MAX_BUFF, (PSZ)pData);

    // Get the string extent and the average character width.
    hPS = WinGetPS(hWndDlg);
    GpiQueryTextBox(hPS,iLength,(PSZ)pData,TXTBOX_COUNT,Ptl);
    GpiQueryFontMetrics(hPS,sizeof(FONTMETRICS),
          (PFONTMETRICS)&FontMetrics);
    WinReleasePS(hPS);

    // Increase the height of the window by 50%
    Ptl[TXTBOX_TOPRIGHT].y += Ptl[TXTBOX_TOPRIGHT].y / 2;

    // Create the checkbox
    hCheckBox = WinCreateWindow (hWndDlg,WC_BUTTON, (PSZ)pData,
          WS_VISIBLE ¦ BS_AUTOCHECKBOX ¦ WS_TABSTOP,
    ButtonRectl.xRight + FontMetrics.lAveCharWidth,
    ButtonRectl.yBottom +
          ((ButtonRectl.yTop - ButtonRectl.yBottom) / 2) -
          (Ptl[TXTBOX_TOPRIGHT].y / 2),
    DlgRectl.xRight - ButtonRectl.xRight -
          (FontMetrics.lAveCharWidth + 1),
          Ptl[TXTBOX_TOPRIGHT].y,
          hWndDlg,HWND_TOP, DID_UPDATE_FONT,0,0);
    DosSubFree(pMem,pData,MAX_BUFF);
    return (hCheckBox);
}


void APIENTRY cleanup()
/*-------------------------------*/

This function is called to free the memory allocated and destroy
the application window.

/*-------------------------------*/
{
    if (pFileText)
       DosSubFree(pMem,pFileText,ulTextSize);
    if (pDrivesList)
       DosSubFree(pMem,pDrivesList,ulDrivesSize);
    DosFreeMem(pMem);
    WinDestroyWindow (hWndFrame);
}
```

```
void APIENTRY get_fixed_drives()
/*-------------------------------*/

This function will enumerate the drives available to this device
and create papszDriveList parameter of the FILEDLG structure. Only
nonremovable drives are placed in the list.

/*-------------------------------*/
{
   APIRET      RetCode;
   ULONG       ulBytes;
   PFSQBUFFER2 pfsq;
   HFILE       hDrive;
   ULONG       ulAction;
   int         nDrive;
   char        szDrive[3] = " :";
   PUSHORT     pDrives = 0;
   PULONG      pStringArray;
   PSZ         pDriveLetter;

   // Disable the exception handling when the drive door is open
   DosError (0);

   // Allocate the memory for the pDrives array
   DosSubAlloc(pMem,(PPVOID)&pDrives,sizeof(USHORT) * MAX_DRIVES);
   memset(pDrives,0,sizeof(USHORT) * MAX_DRIVES);
   DosSubAlloc(pMem,(PPVOID)&pfsq,1024);

   // Allocate memory for pDrivesList
   ulDrivesSize = ((MAX_DRIVES + 1) * sizeof(PLONG)) +
         (3 * MAX_DRIVES);
   DosSubAlloc(pMem,(PPVOID)&pDrivesList,ulDrivesSize);
   pStringArray = (PULONG)pDrivesList;
   memset((PSZ)pStringArray,0,ulDrivesSize);
   pDriveLetter = (PSZ)pStringArray + ((MAX_DRIVES + 1) *
         sizeof(PLONG));

   for (nDrive = 0; nDrive < MAX_DRIVES; nDrive++)
   {
      szDrive[0] = (CHAR)(nDrive + 'A');
      ulBytes    = 1024;

      // Query the file system to determine if it is a remote drive
      RetCode = DosQueryFSAttach ((PSZ)szDrive,0L, FSAIL_QUERYNAME,
               (PFSQBUFFER2)pfsq,&ulBytes);
      if (((RetCode == 0) || (RetCode == ERROR_BUFFER_OVERFLOW)) &&
          (pfsq->szName[0] == (UCHAR)szDrive[0]))
      {
         if (pfsq->iType == FSAT_REMOTEDRV)
            pDrives[nDrive] = DRIVE_REMOTE;
         else
            pDrives[nDrive] = DRIVE_FIXED;
      }
      else if (RetCode == ERROR_NOT_READY)
         // If drive not ready then assume removable
         pDrives[nDrive] = DRIVE_REMOVABLE;
```

```
      // If drive is not remote, determine if it is removeable
      if (pDrives[nDrive] == DRIVE_FIXED)
      {
         // Open the drive and issue a DSK_BLOCKREMOVABLE request
         if (!DosOpen ((PSZ)szDrive,(PHFILE)&hDrive, &ulAction,
               0L,0L,FILE_OPEN,OPEN_FLAGS_DASD ¦ OPEN_SHARE_DENYNONE,0L))
         {
            USHORT usType    = 0;
            BYTE   bCmd      = 0;
            ULONG  cbParmLen = 1L;
            ULONG  cbDataLen = 2L;

            if (!DosDevIOCtl (hDrive,8L,32L,(PVOID)&bCmd, 1L,&cbParmLen,
               (PVOID)&usType,2L,&cbDataLen))
               pDrives[nDrive] = (USHORT)((usType == 0) ? DRIVE_REMOVABLE:
               DRIVE_FIXED);
            else
               pDrives[nDrive] = 0;
         }
         DosClose (hDrive);
      }

      if (pDrives[nDrive] == DRIVE_FIXED)
      {
         // Only add fixed drives to the drives list
         *pStringArray = (ULONG)pDriveLetter;
         pStringArray++;
         *pDriveLetter++ = (nDrive + 'A');
         *pDriveLetter++ = ':';
         pDriveLetter++;
      }

}
      // Reenable exception handling
      DosError (1);

   // Free Temp memory
   DosSubFree(pMem,pDrives,sizeof(USHORT) * MAX_DRIVES);
   DosSubFree(pMem,(PVOID)pfsq,1024);
}


void APIENTRY load_file(PSZ pFileName)
/*--------------------------------*/

This function is called to open pFileName, allocate memory, read
the file into memory, and close the file. If an error occurs, a
message box is posted a string loaded from the resource.

/*--------------------------------*/
{
   ULONG      i;
   FILESTATUS FileStat;
   HFILE      hFile;
   ULONG      ulAction;
```

```
   if (!DosOpen(pFileName,(PHFILE)&hFile,(PULONG)&ulAction, 0,
       FILE_NORMAL,FILE_OPEN,
       OPEN_ACCESS_READONLY ¦ OPEN_SHARE_DENYNONE,0) )
   {
      if (pFileText)
      {
         DosFreeMem(pFileText);
         pFileText  = 0;
         ulTextSize = 0;
      }

      if (!DosQueryFileInfo(hFile,1,(PVOID)&FileStat,
          sizeof(FILESTATUS)))
      {
         ulTextSize = FileStat.cbFileAlloc;
         if (DosAllocMem((PPVOID)&pFileText,ulTextSize, fALLOC))
         {
            ulTextSize = 0;
            pFileText  = 0;
            post_error(hWndClient,IDS_MEMORY_ERROR);
            DosClose(hFile);
            return;
         }
      }

      if (DosRead(hFile,(PVOID)pFileText,ulTextSize, (PULONG)&ulAction))
      {
         post_error(hWndClient,IDS_READ_ERROR);
         WinInvalidateRect(hWndClient,0,FALSE);
      }
      else
      {
         for (i = 0; i < ulTextSize;i++)
         {
            // Remove NULL characters and carrige returns.
            if (*(pFileText + i) == 0)
               *(pFileText + i) = ' ';
            if (*(pFileText + i) == 0xD)
               *(pFileText + i) = ' ';
         }
         strcpy((PSZ)szFilePath,pFileName);
         set_font ((PSZ)Fattrs.szFacename);
      }
      DosClose(hFile);
   }
   else
      post_error(hWndClient,IDS_OPEN_ERROR);
}


USHORT APIENTRY post_error(HWND hWnd,USHORT usErrorID)
/*-------------------------------*/

This is a utility function which will post a message box with
a string loaded from the resource file.
```

```
/*-------------------------------*/
{
   WinLoadString (hab,0,usErrorID,MAX_BUFF,szBuff1);
   return ((USHORT)WinMessageBox(HWND_DESKTOP,hWnd, (PSZ)szBuff1,
      (PSZ)"Error",0,MB_OK ¦ MB_ICONHAND ¦ MB_APPLMODAL));
}


void APIENTRY process_command(HWND hWnd,MPARAM mp1,MPARAM mp2)
/*-------------------------------*/

All WM_COMMAND messages received by the client window will be
processed here.

/*-------------------------------*/
{
   FILEDLG FileDlg;
   FONTDLG FontDlg;

   switch(SHORT1FROMMP(mp1))
   {
      case IDM_OPEN1:
         // Create the default file open dialog.
         memset(&FileDlg,0,sizeof(FILEDLG));
         FileDlg.cbSize    = sizeof(FILEDLG);
         FileDlg.fl        = FDS_CENTER ¦ FDS_OPEN_DIALOG;
         WinFileDlg(HWND_DESKTOP,hWndClient, (PFILEDLG)&FileDlg);
         if (FileDlg.lReturn == DID_OK)
         WinSetWindowText(hWndFrame, (PSZ)FileDlg.szFullFile);
         break;

      case IDM_OPEN2:
         memset(&FileDlg,0,sizeof(FILEDLG));
         set_title(szBuff1, IDS_OPEN);
         FileDlg.pszTitle    = szBuff1;
         FileDlg.cbSize      = sizeof(FILEDLG);
         FileDlg.fl          = FDS_OPEN_DIALOG ¦ FDS_CENTER;
         FileDlg.papszIDriveList = pDrivesList;
         WinLoadString (hab,0,IDS_PATH,CCHMAXPATH,
            (PSZ)&FileDlg.szFullFile);
         WinFileDlg(HWND_DESKTOP,hWndClient, (PFILEDLG)&FileDlg);
         if (FileDlg.lReturn == DID_OK)
            load_file((PSZ)&FileDlg.szFullFile);
         break;

      case IDM_OPEN3:
         // Create a dialog with a custom dialog template and callback.
         memset(&FileDlg,0,sizeof(FILEDLG));
         FileDlg.cbSize      = sizeof(FILEDLG);
         FileDlg.pszTitle    = szBuff1;
         FileDlg.fl          = FDS_OPEN_DIALOG ¦ FDS_CUSTOM ¦ FDS_CENTER;
         FileDlg.hMod        = 0;
         FileDlg.usDlgId     = OPEN_DIALOG;
         FileDlg.ulUser      = atSavePath;
         FileDlg.pfnDlgProc = (PFNWP)FileOpenDlgProc;
```

```
   set_title(szBuff1,IDS_OPEN);
   set_path((PSZ)FileDlg.szFullFile,FDS_OPEN_DIALOG);
   WinFileDlg(HWND_DESKTOP,hWndClient, (PFILEDLG)&FileDlg);
   if (FileDlg.lReturn == DID_OK)
   {
      if (atSavePath)
         atSavePath = WinDeleteAtom(hAtomTable, atSavePath);
      if (FileDlg.ulUser == DID_SAVE_DIR)
         atSavePath = WinAddAtom(hAtomTable, (PSZ)FileDlg.szFullFile);
      load_file((PSZ)&FileDlg.szFullFile);
   }
   break;



case IDM_SAVEAS1:
   memset(&FileDlg,0,sizeof(FILEDLG));
   FileDlg.cbSize   = sizeof(FILEDLG);
   FileDlg.pszTitle = szBuff1;
   FileDlg.fl       = FDS_CENTER ¦ FDS_SAVEAS_DIALOG ¦
                      FDS_ENABLEFILELB;
   set_title(szBuff1,IDS_SAVE);
   strcat((PSZ)FileDlg.szFullFile,(PSZ)szFilePath);
   WinFileDlg(HWND_DESKTOP,hWndFrame, (PFILEDLG)&FileDlg);
   if (FileDlg.lReturn == DID_OK)
   {
      WinSetWindowText(hWndFrame, (PSZ)FileDlg.szFullFile);
      // Code to perform file save operation would go here.
   }
   break;

case IDM_FONT1:
   szFamilyname[0] = 0;
   memset((PCH)&FontDlg,0,sizeof(FONTDLG));
   FontDlg.cbSize          = sizeof(FONTDLG);
   FontDlg.pszFamilyname   = szFamilyname;
   FontDlg.usFamilyBufLen  = FACESIZE;
   FontDlg.fl              = FNTS_CENTER;
   FontDlg.clrFore         = CLR_BLACK;
   FontDlg.clrBack         = CLR_WHITE;
   WinFontDlg(HWND_DESKTOP,hWndClient, (PFONTDLG)&FontDlg);
   if (FontDlg.lReturn == DID_OK)
      WinSetWindowText(hWndFrame, (PSZ)FontDlg.pszFamilyname);
   break;

case IDM_FONT2:
   szFamilyname[0] = 0;
   memset((PCH)&FontDlg,0,sizeof(FONTDLG));
   FontDlg.cbSize          = sizeof(FONTDLG);
   FontDlg.hpsScreen       = WinGetPS(hWnd);
   FontDlg.pszFamilyname   = szFamilyname;
   FontDlg.usFamilyBufLen  = FACESIZE;
   FontDlg.pszPreview      = "Sample Text";
   FontDlg.fl              = FNTS_RESETBUTTON ¦ FNTS_CENTER ¦
         FNTS_INITFROMFATTRS ¦ FNTS_BITMAPONLY;
   FontDlg.flStyle         = FATTR_SEL_ITALIC;
```

```
         FontDlg.clrFore        = CLR_BLACK;
         FontDlg.clrBack        = CLR_PALEGRAY;
         FontDlg.fAttrs         = Fattrs;
         FontDlg.pszTitle       = szBuff1;
         set_title(szBuff1,IDS_FONT);
         WinFontDlg(HWND_DESKTOP,hWndClient, (PFONTDLG)&FontDlg);
         if (FontDlg.lReturn == DID_OK)
         {
            set_font((PSZ)FontDlg.pszFamilyname);
            Fattrs = FontDlg.fAttrs;
         }
         WinReleasePS(FontDlg.hpsScreen);
         break;

      case IDM_FONT3:
         szFamilyname[0] = 0;
         memset((PCH)&FontDlg2,0,sizeof(FONTDLG));
         FontDlg2.hpsScreen      = WinGetPS(hWnd);
         FontDlg2.cbSize         = sizeof(FONTDLG);
         FontDlg2.pszFamilyname  = szFamilyname;
         FontDlg2.usFamilyBufLen = FACESIZE;
         FontDlg2.pszPreview     = "Sample Text";
         FontDlg2.pfnDlgProc     = FontDlgProc;
         FontDlg2.clrFore        = CLR_BLACK;
         FontDlg2.clrBack        = CLR_PALEGRAY;
         FontDlg2.fl             = FNTS_CENTER ¦
                                   FNTS_INITFROMFATTRS ¦
                                   FNTS_BITMAPONLY ¦
                                   FNTS_APPLYBUTTON ¦
                                   FNTS_MODELESS;
         FontDlg2.fAttrs         = Fattrs;
         FontDlg2.pszTitle       = szBuff1;
         set_title(szBuff1,IDS_FONT);
         hFontDlg = WinFontDlg(HWND_DESKTOP,hWndClient,
               (PFONTDLG)&FontDlg2);
         if (!hFontDlg)
            post_error(hWnd,IDS_FONTDLG_ERROR);
         break;

      case IDM_ABOUT:
         WinLoadString (hab, 0, IDS_APPNAME, sizeof(szBuff1), szBuff1);
         DisplayAbout (hWnd, szBuff1);
         break;

      default:
         break;
   }
   return;
   mp2;
}


void APIENTRY set_font(PSZ pFacename)
/*-------------------------------*/

This function will set a new titlebar text string. The string is
```

```
comprised of the filename of the displayed file followed by the
facename of the font that the file is displayed in. The client
window is then invalidated. This function should be called after
the font is changed.

/*-------------------------------*/
{
   ULONG  ulSize;
   PVOID  pData;
   if (szFilePath[0])
   {
      ulSize  = strlen(szFilePath);
      ulSize += strlen(pFacename);
      DosSubAlloc(pMem,(PPVOID)&pData,ulSize);
      strcpy(pData,szFilePath);
      WinLoadString (hab,0,IDS_DASH,MAX_BUFF,szBuff1);
      strcat(pData,szBuff1);
      strcat(pData,pFacename);
      WinSetWindowText(hWndFrame,(PSZ)pData);
      DosSubFree(pMem,pData,ulSize);
   }
   else
      WinSetWindowText(hWndFrame,pFacename);
   WinInvalidateRect(hWndClient,0,FALSE);
}

void APIENTRY set_path(PSZ pFileSpec,USHORT usType)
/*-------------------------------*/

This function will initialze pFileSpec with a path and file spec
based on the contents of atSavePath atom. If it is NULL, the default
file spec is loaded; otherwise the atom text is retrieved.

/*-------------------------------*/
{
   char   szBuff[MAX_BUFF];
   ULONG  ulSize;
   PVOID  pData;
   PCHAR  pChar;

   WinLoadString (hab,0,IDS_PATH,MAX_BUFF, szBuff);
   if (atSavePath &&
      (ulSize = WinQueryAtomLength(hAtomTable,atSavePath) + 1))
   {
      DosSubAlloc(pMem,(PPVOID)&pData,ulSize);
      if(WinQueryAtomName (hAtomTable,atSavePath,pData, ulSize))
      {
         if (usType == FDS_OPEN_DIALOG)
         {
            // Find the beginning of the filename.
            pChar = (PCHAR)pData + ulSize - 1;
            while ((*pChar != '\\') && (pChar != pData))
               pChar--;
            if (*pChar == '\\')
            {
               pChar++;
```

```
                *pChar = '\0';
            }
            strcat(pData,szBuff);
        }
        strcpy (pFileSpec,(PSZ)pData);
      }
      DosSubFree(pMem,pData,ulSize);
   }
   else
      strcat(pFileSpec,szBuff);
}


void APIENTRY set_title(PSZ pTitle,USHORT usType)
/*--------------------------------*/

This function will build a dialog title string in the memory
pointed to by pTitle. The string is comprised of the application
name followed by a hyphen followed by the name of the dialog. The
usType parameter is the string id of the dialog name. All resources
are loaded from the string table in the resource file.

/*--------------------------------*/
{
   char   szBuff[MAX_BUFF];

   WinLoadString (hab,0,IDS_APPNAME,MAX_BUFF,pTitle);
   WinLoadString (hab,0,IDS_DASH,MAX_BUFF,szBuff);
   strcat(pTitle,szBuff);
   WinLoadString (hab,0,usType,MAX_BUFF,szBuff);
   strcat(pTitle,szBuff);
}


MRESULT EXPENTRY ClientWndProc (HWND hWnd, ULONG msg, MPARAM mp1,
                                  MPARAM mp2)
/*--------------------------------*/

This is the callback which handles the messages necessary to
maintain the client window.

/*--------------------------------*/
{
   static  RECTL Rectl;
   HPS     hPS;
   int     iDrawn;
   int     iTotalDrawn;
   LONG    lHeight;
   BOOL    bHandled = TRUE;
   FONTMETRICS FontMetrics;
   MRESULT     mReturn  = 0;

   switch (msg)
   {
      case WM_CREATE:
      // Query the height of the default font.
```

```
hPS = WinGetPS(hWnd);
memset(&Fattrs,0,sizeof(FATTRS));
GpiQueryFontMetrics(hPS,sizeof(FONTMETRICS),
      (PFONTMETRICS)&FontMetrics);
Fattrs.lMaxBaselineExt = FontMetrics.lMaxBaselineExt;
Fattrs.usRecordLength   = sizeof(FATTRS);
strcpy((PSZ)Fattrs.szFacename, (PSZ)FontMetrics.szFacename);
WinReleasePS(hWnd);
szFilePath[0] = '\0';
break;

case WM_PAINT:
   hPS = WinBeginPaint (hWnd,0,0);
   WinFillRect(hPS,&Rectl,CLR_WHITE);
   if (pFileText)
   {
      GpiCreateLogFont(hPS,0,CLIENT_FONT,&Fattrs);
      GpiSetCharSet(hPS,CLIENT_FONT);
      GpiQueryFontMetrics(hPS,sizeof(FONTMETRICS),
            (PFONTMETRICS)&FontMetrics);
      cyHeight = FontMetrics.lMaxBaselineExt +
      FontMetrics.lExternalLeading;
      lHeight = Rectl.yTop;
      for (iTotalDrawn = 0;
         (iTotalDrawn < ulTextSize) && (Rectl.yTop > 0);
         Rectl.yTop -= cyHeight)
      {
         iDrawn = WinDrawText(hPS,
            min (0x1000,(ulTextSize - iTotalDrawn)),
            pFileText + iTotalDrawn,
            (PRECTL)&Rectl,CLR_BLACK,CLR_WHITE,
            DT_LEFT | DT_TOP | DT_WORDBREAK);
         if (iDrawn)
            iTotalDrawn += iDrawn;
         else
            iTotalDrawn++;
      }
      Rectl.yTop = lHeight;
      GpiDeleteSetId(hPS,CLIENT_FONT);
   }
   WinEndPaint (hPS);
   break;

case WM_SIZE:
   Rectl.xLeft  = Rectl.yBottom = 0;
   Rectl.xRight = SHORT1FROMMP(mp2);
   Rectl.yTop   = SHORT2FROMMP(mp2);
   break;

case WM_ERASEBACKGROUND:
   WinFillRect((HPS)LONGFROMMP(mp1),PVOIDFROMMP(mp2), CLR_WHITE);
   mReturn = MRFROMLONG(0L);
   break;

case WM_COMMAND:
```

```
            process_command(hWnd,mp1,mp2);
            break;

         case WM_DESTROY:
            cleanup();
            break;

         default:
            bHandled = FALSE;
            break;
      }

      if (!bHandled)
         mReturn = WinDefWindowProc (hWnd,msg,mp1,mp2);

      return (mReturn);

}


MRESULT EXPENTRY FileOpenDlgProc(HWND hWndDlg,ULONG ulMessage,
                  MPARAM mp1,MPARAM mp2 )
/*--------------------------------*/

This dialog callback will handle the save directory option added
to a standard or custom file open dialog. All other processing is
handled by WinDefFildDlgProc.

/*--------------------------------*/
{
   PFILEDLG   pFileDlg;

   switch (ulMessage)
   {
      case WM_INITDLG:
         // Determine if the save directory button should be checked.
         pFileDlg = (PFILEDLG)WinQueryWindowULong(hWndDlg, QWL_USER);
         if (pFileDlg->ulUser)
            WinCheckButton(hWndDlg,DID_SAVE_DIR,1);
         break;


      case WM_COMMAND:
         switch (SHORT1FROMMP(mp1))
         {
            case DID_OK:
            case DID_CANCEL:
               if(WinQueryButtonCheckstate(hWndDlg, DID_SAVE_DIR))
               {
                  // Do the default processing
                  WinDefFileDlgProc(hWndDlg,ulMessage,mp1, mp2);

                  // Get the pointer to the FILEDLG structure
                  pFileDlg = (PFILEDLG)WinQueryWindowULong(hWndDlg,
QWL_USER);
```

```
                pFileDlg->ulUser = DID_SAVE_DIR;
                return (0);
             }
             break;
         }
         break;
   }
   return (WinDefFileDlgProc(hWndDlg,ulMessage,mp1,mp2));
}


MRESULT EXPENTRY FontDlgProc(HWND hWndDlg,ULONG ulMessage,
               MPARAM mp1,MPARAM mp2 )
/*---------------------------------*/

This dialog callback will handle the apply button and update
checkbox which is added during the WM_INITDLG message. All
other processing is handled by WinDefFontDlgProc.

/*---------------------------------*/
{
   static  PFONTDLG  pFontDlg;
   static  HWND      hWndUpdate;
   MRESULT mReturn;

   switch (ulMessage)
   {
      case WM_INITDLG:
         pFontDlg = (PFONTDLG)WinQueryWindowULong(hWndDlg, QWL_USER);
         hWndUpdate = add_checkbox(hWndDlg);
         break;

      case FNTM_UPDATEPREVIEW:
         if(WinSendMsg(hWndUpdate,BM_QUERYCHECK,0,0))
         {
            // Update the display window.
            mReturn = WinDefFontDlgProc(hWndDlg,ulMessage, mp1,mp2);
            set_font(pFontDlg->pszFamilyname);
            Fattrs = pFontDlg->fAttrs;
            return (mReturn);
         }
         break;

      case WM_COMMAND:
         switch (SHORT1FROMMP(mp1))
         {
            case DID_APPLY_BUTTON:
            case DID_OK_BUTTON:
               WinDefFontDlgProc(hWndDlg,ulMessage,mp1,mp2);
               set_font(pFontDlg->pszFamilyname);
               Fattrs = pFontDlg->fAttrs;
               return (0);
               break;
         }
         break;
   }
```

```
   return (WinDefFontDlgProc(hWndDlg,ulMessage,mp1,mp2));
}
```

COMMDLG.H

```
/* ------------------------------
Common Dialogs Header File
Real-World Programming for OS/2
Copyright (c)  1994 Blain, Delimon, and English
------------------------------ */

#define MAX_BUFF    128
#define MAX_DRIVES  26
#define ID_APPNAME    1

#define MAIN_MENU     1

#define IDM_OPEN1    10
#define IDM_OPEN2    11
#define IDM_OPEN3    12
#define IDM_SAVEAS1  13
#define IDM_ABOUT    14

#define IDM_FONT1    20
#define IDM_FONT2    21
#define IDM_FONT3    22

#define IDS_APPNAME          1
#define IDS_OPEN             2
#define IDS_SAVE             3
#define IDS_FONT             4
#define IDS_DASH             5
#define IDS_PATH             6
#define IDS_UPDATE           7
#define IDS_OPEN_ERROR       8
#define IDS_MEMORY_ERROR     9
#define IDS_READ_ERROR      10
#define IDS_FONTDLG_ERROR   11

#define    OPEN_DIALOG                 10
#define    DID_FILENAME_TXT           257
#define    DID_FILENAME_ED            258
#define    DID_DRIVE_TXT              259
#define    DID_DRIVE_CB               260
#define    DID_FILTER_TXT             261
#define    DID_FILTER_CB              262
#define    DID_DIRECTORY_TXT          263
#define    DID_DIRECTORY_LB           264
#define    DID_FILES_TXT              265
#define    DID_FILES_LB               266
#define    DID_HELP_PB                267
#define    DID_APPLY_PB               268
#define    DID_OK_PB                  DID_OK
#define    DID_CANCEL_PB              DID_CANCEL
```

```
#define CLIENT_FONT 2
#define DID_SAVE_DIR     WM_USER
#define DID_UPDATE_FONT  WM_USER

HWND     APIENTRY add_checkbox(HWND);
void     APIENTRY cleanup(void);
void     APIENTRY get_fixed_drives(void);
void     APIENTRY load_file(PSZ);
USHORT   APIENTRY post_error(HWND,USHORT);
void     APIENTRY process_command(HWND,MPARAM,MPARAM);
void     APIENTRY set_font(PSZ);
void     APIENTRY set_path(PSZ,USHORT);
void     APIENTRY set_title(PSZ,USHORT);
```

COMMDLG.RC

```
/* ------------------------------
Common Dialogs Resource File
Real-World Programming for OS/2
Copyright (c)  1994 Blain, Delimon, and English
------------------------------ */

#define INCL_WINSTDDLGS
#include <os2.h>
#include "commdlg.h"

RCINCLUDE custom.dlg
RCINCLUDE ..\common\about.dlg
```

CUSTOM .DLG

```
/* ------------------------------
Custom File Open Dialog
Real-World Programming for OS/2
Copyright (c)  1994 Blain, Delimon, and English
------------------------------ */

DLGTEMPLATE OPEN_DIALOG LOADONCALL MOVEABLE DISCARDABLE
   BEGIN
      DIALOG "Open File", OPEN_DIALOG, 27, 16, 277, 130, FS_SCREENALIGN ¦
            WS_VISIBLE, FCF_SYSMENU ¦ FCF_TITLEBAR
      BEGIN
         LTEXT         "Open Filename:", DID_FILENAME_TXT, 7, 119, 113, 8
         ENTRYFIELD    "", DID_FILENAME_ED, 8, 108, 260, 8, ES_MARGIN
         LTEXT         "Drive:", DID_DRIVE_TXT, 7, 96, 64, 8
         CONTROL       "", DID_DRIVE_CB, 6, 60, 90, 35, WC_COMBOBOX,
                       CBS_DROPDOWNLIST ¦ WS_GROUP ¦ WS_TABSTOP ¦
                       WS_VISIBLE
         LTEXT         "File Type:", DID_FILTER_TXT, 111, 96, 68, 8
         CONTROL       "", DID_FILTER_CB, 108, 60, 162, 35, WC_COMBOBOX,
                       CBS_DROPDOWNLIST ¦ WS_TABSTOP ¦ WS_VISIBLE
         LTEXT         "Directory:", DID_DIRECTORY_TXT, 7, 72, 78, 8
         LISTBOX       DID_DIRECTORY_LB, 7, 23, 89, 54, LS_HORZSCROLL
```

```
            LTEXT        "Files:", DID_FILES_TXT, 111, 72, 72, 8
            LISTBOX      DID_FILES_LB, 108, 23, 162, 48, LS_HORZSCROLL
            PUSHBUTTON   "~Ok", DID_OK, 7, 4, 40, 14, WS_GROUP ¦ BS_DEFAULT
            PUSHBUTTON   "~Cancel", DID_CANCEL, 60, 4, 40, 14
            AUTOCHECKBOX "Save Directory", DID_SAVE_DIR, 179, 5, 84, 10,
            WS_GROUP
        END
END
```

COMMDLG.DEF

```
NAME        CONTROL WINDOWAPI
DESCRIPTION 'OS/2 Common Dialogs  Blain, Delimon, & English, 1994'
STACKSIZE   32768
EXPORTS     ClientWndProc
            AboutDlgProc
            FileOpenDlgProc
            FontDlgProc

------------------------------
/*------------------------------*/
```

Chapter 5

Menus

Introduction

Menus are generally the command interface for windowing applications. A menu is simply a list of items from which the user can easily pick a command or operation. Menus are not just "special" areas within a frame window. Menus in OS/2 are, in fact, windows themselves. Their nature and operation are similar to other windows; they are frame control windows with a specifically defined behavior.

An application developer has tremendous control over the appearance of the menus. Most programmers and users who are familiar with windowing applications expect menus to be lists of text that represent choices. However, in OS/2, menu items can be much more than that. Menus are windows that contain lists of items. These items can be strings, bitmaps, or application-drawn pictures. Menu items can be added, changed, or deleted at any time as the application presents different information. They are not static structures that must remain constantly the same during the execution of the application.

Menus are windows that are owned by another window. This owner window is generally a frame window. Each of the items in the menu is given a unique identifier by the application developer. When the user chooses an item from the menu, this identifier is posted in a message to the owner window. Menus are defined most often within the resource file that accompanies the application. The examples within this book follow that practice. Look for the keyword `MENU` in the resource files for several of the examples in this book.

Types of Menus

Menus may be one of several different types. The most common types are discussed in this section.

The predefined window class `WC_MENU` defines a class of window. This type of window class presents a list of items to the user for selection. When a menu window is created, a block of memory is allocated to hold the list of menu items and the information associated with each menu item. (See Figure 5.1.)

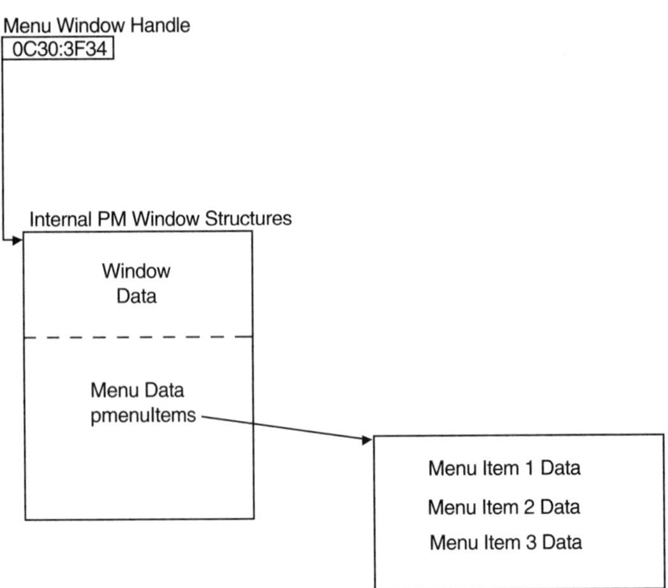

Figure 5.1.
PM internal menu data structure.

Associated with every menu item is information that describes its format and position in the menu list. The most basic type of menus are top-level menus, which are windows owned by a frame window. These menus are referred to as menu frame controls and are assigned an ID of either `FID_SYSMENU` (0x8002), `FID_MINMAX` (0x8004), or `FID_MENU` (0x8005). Each of these menus has a different format, but all are top-level menus.

A menu item can have a submenu associated with it, which is displayed when the menu item is selected. When a submenu is defined for a menu item, the window handle for that menu is stored in the menu item information. This window handle refers to another menu window, which again allocates a block of memory to store the list of menu items associated with it. (See Figure 5.2.)

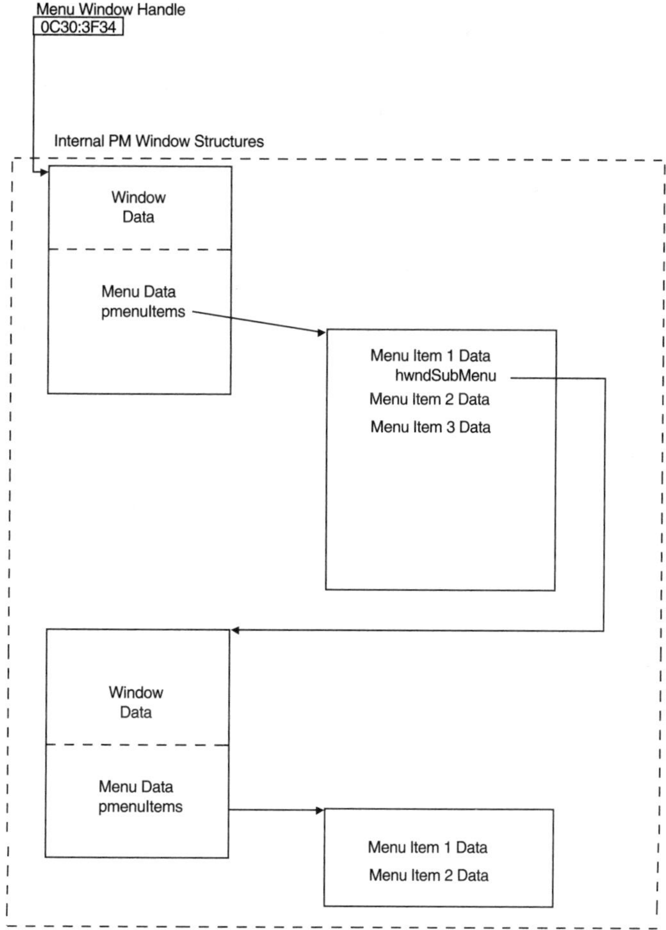

Figure 5.2.
PM internal submenu data structure.

Pull-Down and Cascaded Menus

A pull-down menu is a submenu that displays when a top-level menu item is selected. Pull-down menus have an ID that is defined by the application. If an item in a pull-down menu has a submenu defined for it, the submenu is referred to as a cascaded menu.

Pop-Up Menus

A menu can also appear by itself, without being associated with one of the menu frame controls. This type of menu is referred to as a pop-up menu and usually appears somewhere in the client area of a window or is associated with an icon.

Menu Components

The definition of a menu defines a hierarchy of menu items and submenus. Each menu item is defined by various styles and attributes. These components are discussed next.

Menu Hierarchy

Menu windows have a parent and an owner just like other windows. All top-level menus are owned by the application's frame window and all pull-down and cascaded menus are owned by their immediate predecessor in the menu hierarchy. Pop-up menus are owned by the window specified as its owner when it is displayed, usually the client window of an application. This ownership hierarchy is used to pass menu notification messages from one menu window to its owner.

Notification messages are passed from a menu window to its owner when a menu item is selected, a submenu is being displayed, a submenu is being closed, user input is received, or the owner is notified of many other window events. For example, when a menu is being created, the menu window sends the `WM_CONTROLHEAP` message to its owner. The owner window will either send this up to its owner or return the base address of the heap to use to allocate the block of memory required to store the list of menu items. When a menu item is selected, a `WM_MENUSELECT` message is sent to the menu's owner. If that window is another menu, that menu window will send the message up to its owner until it reaches a non-menu window.

Menu Window Styles

Menu windows have several flags that identify the type of menu to display. These style flags can be set by using:

```
WinSetWindowULong (hMenuWnd, QWL_STYLE, ulStyle)
```

or queried by using:

```
WinQueryWindowULong (hMenuWnd, QWL_STYLE)
```

These styles are set automatically by PM when the menu window is created or loaded, but there may be occasion to change these explicitly in the application. For example, if you want to take a top-level actionbar menu (`MS_ACTIONBAR`) and make it a submenu item, you would need to explicitly change the style bit so that it would display properly.

To change an actionbar menu to a pop-up menu, you would perform the following:

```
WinSetWindowULong (hWndMenu, QWL_STYLE,
   (WinQueryWindowULong (hWndMenu, QWL_STYLE) & ~MS_ACTIONBAR) | MS_POPUP);
```

The following is a list of menu styles with their associated value and appearance:

Style	*Value*	*Description*
MS_ACTIONBAR	0x00000001L	Menu items are displayed side-by-side horizontally.
MS_TITLEBUTTON	0x00000002L	The menu contains one or more of the system bitmaps (system menu, min button, max button, restore button, child system menu, close button).
MS_VERTICALFLIP	0x00000004L	Pull menu up rather than down from menu item. If used for an MS_ACTIONBAR window, all pull-down menus belonging to the actionbar are displayed above the menu item.
MS_ROOT	0x00000008L	Menu is the root of the menu hierarchy.
MS_POPUP	0x00000010L	Menu is a pop-up menu.

The MS_POPUP style provides a lot of opportunity to do some interesting things. An example of MS_POPUP is included in the sample application for this chapter.

Menu Items

As discussed earlier, a menu is defined by a list of menu items. Each menu item in a menu window is defined by an identifier and several styles and attributes. You must understand the MENUITEM structure to understand how each menu item is defined. The MENUITEM structure is defined in pmwin.h as follows:

```
typedef struct _MENUITEM { /* mi */
   SHORT   iPosition;
   USHORT  afStyle;
   USHORT  afAttribute;
   USHORT  id;
   HWND    hwndSubMenu;
   ULONG   hItem;
} MENUITEM;
typedef MENUITEM FAR *PMENUITEM;
```

The following is a description of each of the parameters:

iPosition The position of the item in the list of menu items, with 0 being the first item in the list.

afStyle The style of the menu item. This defines what kind of data is contained in the menu item and how the item is to be drawn.

Flag	*Value*	*Description*
MIS_TEXT	0x0001	Text item.
MIS_BITMAP	0x0002	Bitmap item.

continues

Flag	*Value*	*Description*
MIS_SEPARATOR	0x0004	Horizontal dividing line (only valid for pull-down and pop-up menus).
MIS_OWNERDRAW	0x0008	Item drawn by owner.
MIS_SUBMENU	0x0010	Item contains a pull-down or cascading menu window.
MIS_SYSCOMMAND	0x0040	Post a WM_SYSCOMMAND message rather than a WM_COMMAND message.
MIS_HELP	0x0080	Post a WM_HELP message rather than a WM_COMMAND message.
MIS_STATIC	0x0100	Information item that cannot be selected.
MIS_BUTTONSEPARATOR	0x0200	Menu button item. Items are displayed after a separator bar and can only be selected with the mouse or accelerator key.
MIS_BREAK	0x0400	Item is first item in a new row or column.
MIS_BREAKSEPARATOR	0x0800	Same as MIS_BREAK except it draws a separator between the row or column (only valid for pull-down and pop-up menus).

afAttribute — The attributes of the menu item. This defines how the menu item is displayed and whether the item can be selected.

Flag	*Value*	*Description*
MIA_NODISMISS	0x0020	When the item is selected, the menu containing this item should not be hidden before notifying the owner of the selection.
MIA_FRAMED	0x1000	Draw a frame around the item.
MIA_CHECKED	0x2000	Display checkmark next to the item.
MIA_DISABLED	0x4000	Item is disabled and cannot be selected.
MIA_HILITED	0x8000	Item is currently selected.

id — The identifier for the menu item. While this value does not have to be unique, it is recommended so as not to produce confusion to the application. Two menu items with the same identifier will post the same identifier with the WM_COMMAND, WM_SYSCOMMAND, or WM_HELP message and make it difficult for the application to determine the selection.

Flag	*Value*	*Description*
hwndSubMenu		If the menu item has the MIS_SUBMENU style, this field is the window handle of the pull-down or cascaded menu.
hItem		Handle to the object to be displayed for the item. If the MIS_BITMAP style is used, this is the handle to the bitmap; for MIS_OWNERDRAW, this can be any application defined value.

A mnemonic is a special way of selecting a menu item when the menu is displayed. When a menu is displayed, a menu item with a mnemonic can be selected simply by pressing the mnemonic key. The mnemonic character for a menu item is specified by preceding the character with a tilde. For example, to specify the character "F" as a mnemonic for the menu item "File," it would be defined as "~File."

Specifying Menus in the RC File

Perhaps the easiest way to define a menu is to do so in the resource file. A menu resource is defined in the resource file as follows:

```
MENU identifier
BEGIN
END
```

The identifier uniquely identifies the menu resource. You can substitute braces for the BEGIN and END statements.

```
MENU identifier
{
}
```

Each menu item is defined in the following format:

```
MENUITEM text, identifier, style, attribute
```

The text field describes the text used for the item or the name of the bitmap resource for MIS_BITMAP menu items. If the style or attribute fields are not specified, the item is assigned a style of MIS_TEXT, and no attributes are set for the item, indicating that the item is enabled. A submenu can be specified with the SUBMENU statement:

```
SUBMENU text, identifier, style, attribute
BEGIN
END
```

The field descriptions are the same as MENUITEM except that you are defining a pull-down or cascaded menu item. A submenu is defined just as the MENU is defined. The following example defines a menu with two pull-down menus and a MIS_HELP menu item. The first submenu contains three items with the first item checked and the third item specifying a cascaded menu.

The second submenu defines two columns of menu items with the first item in each column an `MIS_STATIC` item that cannot be selected:

```
MENU IDD_APPNAME
{
   SUBMENU "~Fill",               IDM_FILL
   {
      MENUITEM "~Black",          IDM_BLACK, 0, MIA_CHECKED
      MENUITEM "~White",          IDM_WHITE
      SUBMENU  "~Color",          IDM_COLOR
      {
         MENUITEM "~Red",         IDM_RED
         MENUITEM "~Green",       IDM_GREEN
         MENUITEM "~Blue",        IDM_BLUE
      }
   }
   SUBMENU "~Line Style",         IDM_LINE,        MIS_TEXT
   {
      MENUITEM "Horizontal", -1,
      MIS_STATIC, MIA_FRAMED
      MENUITEM "  Solid",        IDM_HORZSOLID,
      MENUITEM "  Dash",         IDM_HORZDASH,  0, MIA_CHECKED
      MENUITEM "  None",         IDM_HORZNONE,
      MENUITEM "Vertical",    -1,
            MIS_BREAKSEPARATOR ¦ MIS_STATIC, MIA_FRAMED
      MENUITEM "  Solid",        IDM_VERTSOLID,
      MENUITEM "  Dash",         IDM_VERTDASH,  0, MIA_CHECKED
      MENUITEM "  None",         IDM_VERTNONE
   }
   MENUITEM "Help", 0, MIS_TEXT ¦ MIS_BUTTONSEPARATOR ¦ MIS_HELP
}
```

Because the `"Horizontal"` and `"Vertical"` menu items are `MIS_STATIC` items and can never be selected, it is okay to assign them the same identifier, in this case `-1`.

A pop-up menu can be defined in the resource file in a similar manner. There is no special flag to set to define a pop-up menu. The following example defines a pop-up menu for selecting a color:

```
MENU COLOR_MENU
{
   MENUITEM "~Red",        IDM_RED
   MENUITEM "~Blue",       IDM_BLUE
   MENUITEM "~Green",      IDM_GREEN
   MENUITEM "~White",      IDM_WHITE
   MENUITEM "~Black",      IDM_BLACK
}
```

Menu Messages

Messages can be sent to a menu window to cause certain actions to be performed on that menu. These include messages to create new menus, add or delete menu items, change menu styles and

attributes, and query information about menu items. For a more thorough discussion of particular messages, consult the lists later in this chapter.

Menu Notification Messages

There are many messages sent by PM to the menu windows during the course of activating, drawing, and selecting menus and menu items. Many of these messages make their way up the owner chain to the frame or client window. These messages are mostly notification messages sent to indicate the occurrence of an event or activity. In some cases though, these messages are notification messages sent to a menu window to begin a particular activity. For example, the MM_SUMMON message is sent to a menu window when that menu is summoned and is to become active. It is possible for an application to use these notification messages to force menu activity for its own purpose. As an example, suppose an application wants the system menu to pop up when the user performs a certain action. The application can send the MM_STARTMENUMODE notification message to cause the system menu to appear.

For a more thorough discussion of particular messages, consult the lists near the end of this chapter.

Menu Item Selection

When a menu item is highlighted, the WM_MENUSELECT message is sent to the owner window. This message either contains the identifier of the currently highlighted menu item or the value 0xFFFF. This message can be used by an application to identify or display text related to the item. For example, many applications make use of a "hint" window, which is a window displaying a description of the currently selected menu item. When the WM_MENUSELECT message is received, the menu item identifier can be used to look up a text string and display it in the "hint" window. If the identifier is 0xFFFF, this indicates that the currently displayed pull-down or cascaded menu is being hidden.

When a menu item is selected with the mouse or the Enter key and the menu item does not have a submenu, the WM_MENUSELECT message is sent with the HIUSHORT of mp1 set to 1. If the application returns TRUE, PM will post either a WM_COMMAND, WM_SYSCOMMAND, or WM_HELP message. Returning FALSE will prevent the message from being posted. If the MIS_SYSCOMMAND style is set, a WM_SYSCOMMAND message is posted. If the MIS_HELP style is set, a WM_HELP message is posted. Otherwise, a WM_COMMAND message is posted. All these messages use the identifier of the selected menu item.

Menu Application

In our sample application, we will demonstrate all of the features of defining and creating menus, the various styles of menu items, the use of pop-up menus, and some of the undocumented menu messages. This begins with the basics of defining menu items and changing their attributes,

changing the menu item checkmark, defining bitmap menu items, and then how to use owner draw items in pop-up menus. Finally, we'll look at adding entries to the system menu.

Menu Application Files

The following are the files necessary to build the menu application:

MENU.C	Application file.
MENU.DEF	Module definition file.
MENU.H	Application include file.
MENU.ICO	Application icon.
MENU.RC	Application resource file.
MENUXTRA.H	This header file contains all the undocumented menu messages. We broke this out into a separate file so that you could use these in your other applications if you desire.

These are the various bitmap files used for bitmap menu items, checkmarks, and owner draw menus. You can use any bitmap editor that is compatible with OS/2 bitmaps to open these files and take a look at them. You could even make some modifications to them, if you wanted to see these changes in the version of the menu application that you create.

BMPITEM1.BMP
BMPITEM2.BMP
CHECK1.BMP
CHECK2.BMP
ODBLUE.BMP
ODGREEN.BMP
ODRED.BMP
UNCHECK1.BMP
UNCHECK2.BMP

MENU.C

```
/* --------------------------------
Menu Program
Real-World Programming for OS/2
Copyright (c) 1993, 1994 Blain, Delimon, and English
-------------------------------- */

#define INCL_WIN
#define INCL_GPI
#include <os2.h>
#include <stdio.h>
#include "menuxtra.h"
#include "menu.h"
#include "..\common\about.h"
```

```
MRESULT EXPENTRY ClientWndProc (HWND,ULONG,MPARAM,MPARAM);

HAB   hab;
CHAR  szTitle[64];
CHAR  szColor[24];
HWND  hWndFrame;              /* Application Frame window handle  */
HWND  hWndClient;             /* Application Client window handle */
HWND  hWndMenu;
HWND  hColorMenu;
HWND  hWndEditMenu;


/* Attributes set by menu */
LONG   lWindowColor    = 0x00FFFFFF;
LONG   lTextColor      = 0x00000000;
LONG   flCmd           = DT_CENTER ¦ DT_VCENTER;
CHAR   szText[40]      = "Menu Text String";
USHORT AlignFlags[6]   = { DT_LEFT, DT_CENTER, DT_RIGHT,
                         DT_TOP,  DT_VCENTER, DT_BOTTOM };
USHORT StyleFlags[3]   = { 0, DT_UNDERSCORE, DT_STRIKEOUT };
USHORT HAlign          = IDM_ALIGNCENTER,
       VAlign          = IDM_ALIGNMIDDLE,
       Style           = IDM_STYLENORMAL;
                         /*    RED       GREEN       BLUE */
LONG   lColorTable[3] = {0x00FF0000,0x0000FF00, 0x000000FF};
BOOL   bWindowColor    = TRUE;
BOOL   bUndoAvailable = FALSE;
BOOL   bSelected       = FALSE;

HBITMAP hbmCheck1,
        hbmUnCheck1,
        hbmCheck2,
        hbmUnCheck2;

int main()
{
   HMQ   hmq;
   QMSG  qmsg;
   ULONG flFrameFlags = FCF_TITLEBAR ¦ FCF_SYSMENU ¦ FCF_SIZEBORDER ¦
         FCF_MINMAX ¦ FCF_SHELLPOSITION ¦ FCF_TASKLIST ¦
         FCF_MENU ¦ FCF_ICON;
   CHAR  szClientClass[] = "CLIENT";

   hab = WinInitialize (0);
   hmq = WinCreateMsgQueue (hab, 0);

   WinRegisterClass (hab, szClientClass, ClientWndProc,
CS_SIZEREDRAW, 0);
   WinLoadString (hab, 0, ID_APPNAME, sizeof(szTitle), szTitle);


   hWndFrame = WinCreateStdWindow (HWND_DESKTOP, WS_VISIBLE,
         &flFrameFlags, szClientClass, szTitle, 0, 0, ID_APPNAME,
         &hWndClient);
```

```
   /* Set the source rectangle and draw the bitmap.  */
   Rectl.xLeft   = yOffset;
   Rectl.yBottom = 0L;
   Rectl.xRight  = yOffset + bmInfoOwnerDraw.cx / 4;
   Rectl.yTop    = bmInfoOwnerDraw.cy;
   WinDrawBitmap (poi->hps,(HBITMAP)poi->hItem,&Rectl,
         (PPOINTL)&poi->rclItem, 0L, 0L, ropCode);

   /* Turn off attributes by default */
   poi->fsAttribute =
      (poi->fsAttributeOld &= ~(MIA_CHECKED ¦ MIA_HILITED ¦
MIA_FRAMED));
   return;
}

VOID MeasureOwnerItem (POWNERITEM poi)
{
   BITMAPINFOHEADER bmInfoMenuAttached,
                    bmInfoMenuCheck,
                    bmInfoMenu;
   HBITMAP hbm = WinGetSysBitmap (HWND_DESKTOP, SBMP_MENUATTACHED);
   GpiQueryBitmapParameters (hbm,&bmInfoMenuAttached);
   GpiDeleteBitmap (hbm);
   hbm = WinGetSysBitmap (HWND_DESKTOP,SBMP_MENUCHECK);
   GpiQueryBitmapParameters (hbm,&bmInfoMenuCheck);
   GpiDeleteBitmap (hbm);
   GpiQueryBitmapParameters ((HBITMAP)poi->hItem, &bmInfoMenu);
   poi->rclItem.xRight = (bmInfoMenu.cx / 4) -
   bmInfoMenuAttached.cx - bmInfoMenuCheck.cx;
   poi->rclItem.yTop   = bmInfoMenu.cy;
   return;
}

VOID PlacePopup (HWND hWndOwner, HWND hWndMenu,
      ULONG x, ULONG y, BOOL bRight, ULONG ulFlags)
{
   /* We need to get the height of the menu because    WinPopupMenu will
   position the menu with the lower-left corner of the menu at the
   coordinates passed.  By sending a WM_ADJUSTWINDOWPOS message to
   the menu it will fill in the swp structure of the menu with its
   size.
   */
   SWP   Swp;
   ULONG ulStyle;

   ulStyle  = WinQueryWindowULong (hWndMenu,QWL_STYLE) & ~MS_ACTIONBAR;
   WinSetWindowULong (hWndMenu,QWL_STYLE,ulStyle);
   WinQueryWindowPos(hWndMenu, (PSWP)&Swp);
   Swp.fl                = SWP_MOVE ¦ SWP_SIZE;
   Swp.hwndInsertBehind = HWND_TOP;

   /* Set owner to frame here so that WM_MEASUREITEM messages are
   sent to the frame window for processing - in case menu is
ownerdraw */
   WinSetOwner  (hWndMenu,hWndOwner);
```

```
   WinSendMsg(hWndMenu, WM_ADJUSTWINDOWPOS, (MPARAM)(PSWP)&Swp, NULL);

   WinPopupMenu (hWndOwner,hWndOwner,hWndMenu,
         bRight ? x : x - Swp.cx, y - Swp.cy, 0,
         PU_HCONSTRAIN ¦ PU_VCONSTRAIN ¦ PU_KEYBOARD ¦
         PU_MOUSEBUTTON1 ¦ ulFlags);

   return;
}

VOID SetMenuCheckMarks (HPS hps, HWND hWndMenu)
{
   hbmCheck1   = GpiLoadBitmap (hps,0,IDBMP_CHECK1,0L,0L);
   hbmUnCheck1 = GpiLoadBitmap (hps,0,IDBMP_UNCHECK1,0L,0L);
   hbmCheck2   = GpiLoadBitmap (hps,0,IDBMP_CHECK2,0L,0L);
   hbmUnCheck2 = GpiLoadBitmap (hps,0,IDBMP_UNCHECK2,0L,0L);

   /* Set the checkmarks for the horizontal alignment */
   WinSetCheckMark (hWndMenu,IDM_ALIGNLEFT,hbmCheck1,TRUE);
   WinSetCheckMark (hWndMenu,IDM_ALIGNLEFT,hbmUnCheck1, FALSE);
   WinSetCheckMark (hWndMenu,IDM_ALIGNCENTER,hbmCheck1, TRUE);
   WinSetCheckMark (hWndMenu,IDM_ALIGNCENTER,hbmUnCheck1, FALSE);
   WinSetCheckMark (hWndMenu,IDM_ALIGNRIGHT,hbmCheck1,TRUE);
   WinSetCheckMark (hWndMenu,IDM_ALIGNRIGHT,hbmUnCheck1, FALSE);

   /* Set the checkmarks for the vertical alignment */
   WinSetCheckMark (hWndMenu,IDM_ALIGNTOP,hbmCheck2,TRUE);
   WinSetCheckMark (hWndMenu,IDM_ALIGNTOP,hbmUnCheck2, FALSE);
   WinSetCheckMark (hWndMenu,IDM_ALIGNMIDDLE,hbmCheck2, TRUE);
   WinSetCheckMark (hWndMenu,IDM_ALIGNMIDDLE,hbmUnCheck2, FALSE);
   WinSetCheckMark (hWndMenu,IDM_ALIGNBOTTOM,hbmCheck2, TRUE);
   WinSetCheckMark (hWndMenu,IDM_ALIGNBOTTOM,hbmUnCheck2, FALSE);
   return;
}

VOID SetOwnerDrawBitmapHandles (HPS hps, HWND hWndMenu)
{
  USHORT   usCnt;
  SHORT    sMenuID;
  HBITMAP  hBitmap;

  usCnt = LOUSHORT(WinSendMsg (hWndMenu, MM_QUERYITEMCOUNT, 0L,
                   0L));

  while (usCnt)
  {
    sMenuID = (SHORT)WinSendMsg (hWndMenu, MM_ITEMIDFROMPOSITION,
                 MPFROMSHORT(usCnt), MPVOID);

    /* The menu item id is the same as the bitmap id */
    hBitmap = GpiLoadBitmap (hps, 0, sMenuID, 0, 0);
    WinSendMsg (hWndMenu, MM_SETITEMHANDLE,
      MPFROMSHORT (sMenuID), (MPARAM)hBitmap);
    usCnt--;
  }
  return;
}
```

```
MRESULT EXPENTRY ClientWndProc (HWND hWnd, ULONG msg, MPARAM mp1,
                                MPARAM mp2)
{
   BOOL    bHandled = TRUE;
   MRESULT mReturn  = 0;
   HPS     hPS;

SHORT sMenuID;

   switch (msg)
   {
      case WM_CREATE:
         /* Retrieve the handle of the FID_MENU window */
         hWndMenu    = WinWindowFromID (WinQueryWindow(hWnd, QW_PARENT),
                            FID_MENU);

         /* Load the color pop-up menu */
         hColorMenu = WinLoadMenu (HWND_OBJECT,0, COLOR_MENU);

         hPS = WinGetPS (hWnd);

         /* Load and set the checkmark bitmaps */
         SetMenuCheckMarks (hPS, hWndMenu);

         /* Load and set the owner draw bitmap handles */
         SetOwnerDrawBitmapHandles (hPS,hColorMenu);

         WinReleasePS (hPS);

         /* Add the Edit menu item to the main menu */
         AddEditMenuItem (hWndMenu);

         /* Add the Bitmap menu item to the main menu */
         AddBitmapMenu (hWndMenu);

         /* Add the About menu item to the system menu */
         AddAboutToSystemMenu (WinQueryWindow (hWnd, QW_PARENT));
         break;

      case WM_DESTROY:
         /* Delete the bitmaps for the menu items */
         GpiDeleteBitmap (hbmCheck1);
         GpiDeleteBitmap (hbmUnCheck1);
         GpiDeleteBitmap (hbmCheck2);
         GpiDeleteBitmap (hbmUnCheck2);
         WinDestroyWindow (hColorMenu);
         break;

      case WM_BUTTON1DOWN:
         bWindowColor = TRUE;
         WinLoadString (hab, 0, IDS_WINDOWCOLOR, sizeof(szColor), szColor);
         sMenuID = (SHORT)WinSendMsg (hColorMenu, MM_ITEMIDFROMPOSITION,
                     MPFROMSHORT(0), MPVOID);
         WinSendMsg (hColorMenu, MM_SETITEMTEXT, MPFROMSHORT(sMenuID),
                   MPFROMP(szColor));
         /* Call WinDefWindowProc so that window is activated */
```

```
   mReturn = WinDefWindowProc (hWnd,msg,mp1,mp2);
   PlacePopup (hWnd, hColorMenu,
       SHORT1FROMMP(mp1),SHORT2FROMMP(mp1),FALSE,
       PU_NONE);  /* Allow button to be released */
   break;

case WM_BUTTON2DOWN:
   bWindowColor = FALSE;
   WinLoadString (hab, 0, IDS_TEXTCOLOR, sizeof(szColor), szColor);
   sMenuID = (SHORT)WinSendMsg (hColorMenu, MM_ITEMIDFROMPOSITION,
             MPFROMSHORT(0), MPVOID);
   WinSendMsg (hColorMenu, MM_SETITEMTEXT, MPFROMSHORT(sMenuID),
         MPFROMP(szColor));
   /* Call WinDefWindowProc so that window is activated */
   mReturn = WinDefWindowProc (hWnd,msg,mp1,mp2);
   PlacePopup (hWnd, hColorMenu,
         SHORT1FROMMP(mp1),SHORT2FROMMP(mp1),TRUE,
         PU_MOUSEBUTTON2DOWN);
   break;



case WM_COMMAND:
case WM_SYSCOMMAND:
   switch (LOUSHORT(mp1))
   {
      case IDM_ABOUT:
      DisplayAbout (hWnd, szTitle);
      break;

      case IDM_STYLENORMAL:
      case IDM_STYLEUNDERSCORE:
      case IDM_STYLESTRIKEOUT:
         WinCheckMenuItem (hWndMenu, Style, FALSE);
         Style = LOUSHORT(mp1);
         WinCheckMenuItem (hWndMenu, LOUSHORT(mp1), TRUE);
         flCmd &= ~(DT_UNDERSCORE ¦ DT_STRIKEOUT);
         flCmd ¦= StyleFlags[LOUSHORT(mp1) - IDM_STYLENORMAL];
         WinInvalidateRect (hWnd,NULL,FALSE);
         break;

      case IDM_ALIGNLEFT:
      case IDM_ALIGNCENTER:
      case IDM_ALIGNRIGHT:
         WinCheckMenuItem (hWndMenu, HAlign, FALSE);
         HAlign = LOUSHORT(mp1);
         WinCheckMenuItem (hWndMenu, LOUSHORT(mp1), TRUE);
         flCmd &= ~(DT_LEFT ¦ DT_CENTER ¦ DT_RIGHT);
         flCmd ¦= AlignFlags[LOUSHORT(mp1) - IDM_ALIGNLEFT];
         WinInvalidateRect (hWnd,NULL,FALSE);
         break;

      case IDM_ALIGNTOP:
      case IDM_ALIGNMIDDLE:
      case IDM_ALIGNBOTTOM:
```

```
            WinCheckMenuItem (hWndMenu, VAlign, FALSE);
            VAlign = LOUSHORT(mp1);
            WinCheckMenuItem (hWndMenu, LOUSHORT(mp1), TRUE);
            flCmd &= ~(DT_TOP ¦ DT_VCENTER ¦ DT_BOTTOM);
            flCmd ¦= AlignFlags[LOUSHORT(mp1) - IDM_ALIGNLEFT];
            WinInvalidateRect (hWnd,NULL,FALSE);
            break;

         case IDM_BMPITEM1:
         case IDM_BMPITEM2:
         {
            USHORT usChecked;

            /* Toggle the checkmark flag */
            usChecked =
                  LOUSHORT(WinIsMenuItemChecked (hWndMenu,
                  LOUSHORT(mp1)));
            usChecked ^= MIA_CHECKED;
            WinCheckMenuItem (hWndMenu, LOUSHORT(mp1), usChecked);
            break;
         }

         case IDBMP_ODITEM1:
         case IDBMP_ODITEM2:
         case IDBMP_ODITEM3:
         {
            USHORT usChecked;

            /* Toggle the checkmark flag */
            usChecked =
               LOUSHORT(WinIsMenuItemChecked (hColorMenu,
                  LOUSHORT(mp1)));
            usChecked ^= MIA_CHECKED;
            WinCheckMenuItem (hColorMenu, LOUSHORT(mp1), usChecked);

            /* Toggle the color field */
            if (bWindowColor)
               lWindowColor ^= lColorTable[LOUSHORT(mp1)-IDBMP_ODITEM1];
            else
               lTextColor   ^= lColorTable[LOUSHORT(mp1)-IDBMP_ODITEM1];
            WinInvalidateRect (hWnd,NULL,FALSE);
            break;
         }

         case SC_CLOSE:
           WinPostMsg (hWnd,WM_QUIT,0L,0L);
           break;

         default:
            bHandled = (msg == WM_COMMAND);
      }
      break;

   case WM_MEASUREITEM:
      MeasureOwnerItem ((POWNERITEM)mp2);
      break;
```

```
    case WM_DRAWITEM:
       DrawOwnerItem ((POWNERITEM)mp2);
       mReturn = (MRESULT)TRUE;
       break;

    case WM_INITMENU:
       if (SHORT1FROMMP(mp1) == IDM_EDIT)
       {
          ULONG ulFormat;
          WinEnableMenuItem ((HWND)mp2, IDM_UNDO, bUndoAvailable);
          WinEnableMenuItem ((HWND)mp2, IDM_COPY, bSelected);
          WinEnableMenuItem ((HWND)mp2, IDM_CUT,  bSelected);
          WinEnableMenuItem ((HWND)mp2, IDM_PASTE,
          WinQueryClipbrdFmtInfo (hab, CF_TEXT, &ulFormat));
       }
       else if ((HWND)mp2 == hColorMenu)
       {
          USHORT Pos;
          for (Pos = 0; Pos < 3; Pos++)
          {
             sMenuID = (SHORT)WinSendMsg (hColorMenu, MM_ITEMIDFROMPOSITION,
                       MPFROMSHORT(Pos+1), MPVOID);
             WinSendMsg (hColorMenu, MM_SETITEMATTR,
                       MPFROMSHORT(sMenuID),
                       MPFROM2SHORT(MIA_CHECKED,
                       bWindowColor ?
                       ((lWindowColor & lColorTable[Pos]) ? MIA_CHECKED : 0) :
                       ((lTextColor & lColorTable[Pos]) ? MIA_CHECKED : 0)));
          }
       }
       break;


    case WM_PAINT:
       hPS = WinBeginPaint (hWnd,0,0);
       {
          RECTL Rectl;
          GpiCreateLogColorTable (hPS,LCOL_RESET, LCOLF_RGB,0L,0L,NULL);
          WinQueryWindowRect (hWnd, &Rectl);
          WinFillRect (hPS, &Rectl, lWindowColor);
          WinDrawText (hPS,-1L, szText, &Rectl,
                lTextColor, lWindowColor, flCmd);
       }
       WinEndPaint (hPS);
       break;

    case WM_ERASEBACKGROUND:
       mReturn = (MRESULT)1;
       break;

    default:
       bHandled = FALSE;
       break;
}
```

```
   if (!bHandled)
      mReturn = WinDefWindowProc (hWnd,msg,mp1,mp2);

   return (mReturn);
}
```

MENU.H

```
/* ------------------------------
Menu Header File
Real-World Programming for OS/2
Copyright (c) 1993, 1994 Blain, Delimon, and English
------------------------------ */

#define ID_APPNAME              1
#define IDS_WINDOWCOLOR         2
#define IDS_TEXTCOLOR           3

#define IDBMP_CHECK1           50
#define IDBMP_UNCHECK1         51
#define IDBMP_CHECK2           52
#define IDBMP_UNCHECK2         53
#define IDBMP_BMPITEM1         54
#define IDBMP_BMPITEM2         55
#define IDBMP_ODITEM1          56
#define IDBMP_ODITEM2          57
#define IDBMP_ODITEM3          58

#define COLOR_MENU            100
#define IDC_COLOR             101

#define IDM_ALIGN             400
#define IDM_ALIGNLEFT         401
#define IDM_ALIGNCENTER       402
#define IDM_ALIGNRIGHT        403
#define IDM_ALIGNTOP          404
#define IDM_ALIGNMIDDLE       405
#define IDM_ALIGNBOTTOM       406

#define IDM_STYLE             500
#define IDM_STYLENORMAL       501
#define IDM_STYLEUNDERSCORE   502
#define IDM_STYLESTRIKEOUT    503

#define IDM_EDIT              600
#define IDM_UNDO              601
#define IDM_COPY              602
#define IDM_CUT               603
#define IDM_PASTE             604

#define IDM_ABOUT             700

#define BITMAP_MENU           800
#define IDM_BMPITEM1          801
#define IDM_BMPITEM2          802
```

MENUXTRA.H

The following is the code for the MENUXTRA.H header file. We could have simply included this code in the file MENU.H. However, we have broken it out here so that you may use it in your own applications if you desire. It contains undocumented menu messages and macros.

```
/* -------------------------------------------------------------------
              Undocumented PM Menu Messages Header File

                   Real World Programming for OS/2
         Copyright (c) 1993, 1994 Blain, Delimon, and English
------------------------------------------------------------------ */

#define WM_MENUCHAR                    0x003f
#define MM_MATCHMNEMONIC               0x01f0
#define MM_PORTHOLEINIT                0x01fb
#define MM_SETITEMCHECKMARK            0x0210

#define WinSetCheckMark(hWndMenu, id, hbm, bcheck) \
    ((BOOL)WinSendMsg(hWndMenu,MM_SETITEMCHECKMARK, \
    MPFROM2SHORT(id, (USHORT)bcheck), (MPARAM)hbm))
```

MENU.RC

```
/* ------------------------------
Menu Resource File
Real-World Programming for OS/2
Copyright (c) 1993, 1994 Blain, Delimon, and English
------------------------------ */

#include <os2.h>
#include "menu.h"

ICON ID_APPNAME MENU.ICO

/* Checkmark bitmaps */
BITMAP IDBMP_CHECK1      "CHECK1.BMP"
BITMAP IDBMP_UNCHECK1    "UNCHECK1.BMP"
BITMAP IDBMP_CHECK2      "CHECK2.BMP"
BITMAP IDBMP_UNCHECK2    "UNCHECK2.BMP"

/* Bitmap menu item bitmaps */
BITMAP IDBMP_BMPITEM1    "BMPITEM1.BMP"
BITMAP IDBMP_BMPITEM2    "BMPITEM2.BMP"

/* Ownerdraw bitmaps */
BITMAP IDBMP_ODITEM1     "ODRED.BMP"
BITMAP IDBMP_ODITEM2     "ODGREEN.BMP"
BITMAP IDBMP_ODITEM3     "ODBLUE.BMP"


STRINGTABLE LOADONCALL MOVEABLE
BEGIN
   ID_APPNAME       "Menu Application"
```

```
   IDS_WINDOWCOLOR   "Window Color"
   IDS_TEXTCOLOR     "Text Color"
END

MENU ID_APPNAME
{
   SUBMENU "~Style",            IDM_STYLE
   {
      MENUITEM "~Normal",       IDM_STYLENORMAL,0,MIA_CHECKED
      MENUITEM "~Underscore",   IDM_STYLEUNDERSCORE
      MENUITEM "~Strikeout",    IDM_STYLESTRIKEOUT
   }
   SUBMENU "~Alignment",        IDM_ALIGN,        MIS_TEXT
   {
      MENUITEM "Horizontal", -1,
               MIS_STATIC, MIA_FRAMED
      MENUITEM "  ~Left",       IDM_ALIGNLEFT,
      MENUITEM "  ~Center",     IDM_ALIGNCENTER,0,MIA_CHECKED
      MENUITEM "  ~Right",      IDM_ALIGNRIGHT,
      MENUITEM "Vertical",   -1,
               MIS_BREAKSEPARATOR ¦ MIS_STATIC, MIA_FRAMED
      MENUITEM "  ~Top",        IDM_ALIGNTOP,
      MENUITEM "  ~Middle",     IDM_ALIGNMIDDLE,0, MIA_CHECKED
      MENUITEM "  ~Bottom",     IDM_ALIGNBOTTOM,
   }
}

MENU COLOR_MENU
{
   MENUITEM "", IDC_COLOR, MIS_STATIC
   MENUITEM "", IDBMP_ODITEM1, MIS_OWNERDRAW ¦ MIS_BREAK
   MENUITEM "", IDBMP_ODITEM2, MIS_OWNERDRAW ¦ MIS_BREAK
   MENUITEM "", IDBMP_ODITEM3, MIS_OWNERDRAW ¦ MIS_BREAK
}

MENU BITMAP_MENU
{
   MENUITEM "#54", IDM_BMPITEM1, MIS_BITMAP
   MENUITEM "#55", IDM_BMPITEM2, MIS_BITMAP
}

rcinclude ..\common\about.dlg
```

MENU.DEF

```
NAME           MENU   WINDOWAPI
DESCRIPTION    'Menu Program (c) 1993, 1994 Blain, Delimon, & English'
PROTMODE
HEAPSIZE       4096
STACKSIZE      16384
EXPORTS        ClientWndProc
               AboutDlgProc
```

Using the Menu Application

Using the Menu application is fairly self-explanatory. After you have opened the program, you will see the Menu Application main window. Spend some time clicking the various menu choices and noting their effect on the displayed text. Take some time to note how the special checkmarks work. Figure 5.3 shows the Alignment pull-down menu, which uses the special checkmarks.

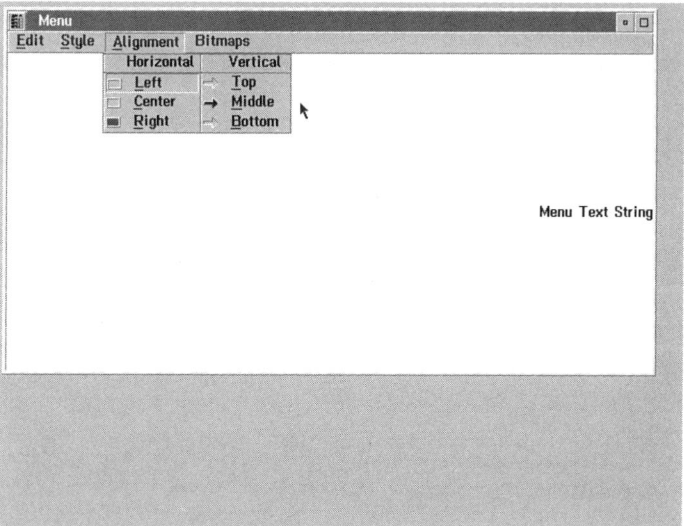

Figure 5.3.
Use of special checkmarks.

Clicking in the client area with the left mouse button will bring up a menu that enables you to change the color of the client area. The color for the client area is determined by a combination of the colors designated by buttons that are pressed. Notice that the pop-up menu remains open when you release the left mouse button.

Clicking with the right mouse button will open a pop-up menu that acts differently from the menu brought up with the left mouse button. The color for the text is set with the buttons in this pop-up menu in a way similar to setting text color for the client area. However, note that when you release the right mouse button, the pop-up menu disappears.

Basic Menu and Changing Menu Items

There are two ways to create a menu for use in your application: Load the menu from the resource file or dynamically build it in the code. We will do both here, but let's begin with a simple menu for our application that will be defined in the resource file. We begin with a main menu in our application with one menu item called "Style." This menu item will contain a submenu with three choices.

```
MENU ID_APPNAME
{
   SUBMENU "~Style",            IDM_STYLE
   {
      MENUITEM "~Normal",       IDM_STYLENORMAL,0,MIA_CHECKED
      MENUITEM "~Underscore",   IDM_STYLEUNDERSCORE
      MENUITEM "~Strikeout",    IDM_STYLESTRIKEOUT
   }
}
```

The first line gives our menu an identifier of `IDD_APPNAME`. We identify our first menu item as a submenu with the `SUBMENU` keyword, and it will be a text item (default) with an identifier of `IDM_STYLE`. Below the submenu, we list the three menu items that will appear in the pull-down menu. Notice that the first item will be checked initially as we have set the initial attribute to `MIA_CHECKED`.

Since this will be our actionbar menu, we want this menu to be set as the `FID_MENU` menu for our main window. This is done by using the `FCF_MENU` frame control flag when we create the main window. Using this flag tells PM to look for a menu resource with the identifier specified and load it as the main menu:

```
ULONG flFrameFlags = FCF_TITLEBAR ¦ FCF_SYSMENU ¦ FCF_SIZEBORDER ¦
            FCF_MINMAX ¦ FCF_SHELLPOSITION ¦ FCF_TASKLIST ¦
            FCF_MENU ¦ FCF_ICON;

hWndFrame = WinCreateStdWindow (HWND_DESKTOP, WS_VISIBLE,
    &flFrameFlags, szClientClass, szTitle, 0, 0, ID_APPNAME,
&hWndClient);
```

Alternately, we could leave the `FCF_MENU` flag off of the frame control flags and add the menu later with a call to `WinLoadMenu`.

Now that we have the basis for our menu, we can begin to add new menu items to our menu. Let's add an "Edit" menu item as the first item in the menu. We will want to include menu options for "Undo," "Copy," "Cut," and "Paste." The first step in dynamically creating a new menu is to create a menu handle:

```
hWndEditMenu = WinCreateMenu (HWND_OBJECT, NULL);
```

WinCreateMenu will create a window of class `WC_MENU`. Passing `NULL` for the menu template will create a menu window with no menu items. The ID for this menu window will be `FID_MENU`. So as not to cause confusion with the main menu window, we will rename it to `IDM_EDIT`:

```
WinSetWindowUShort (hWndEditMenu, QWS_ID, IDM_EDIT);
```

The style of this menu window is also `MS_ACTIONBAR ¦ WS_CLIPSIBLINGS ¦` MS_ROOT.

> **Note:** Although this is not the style for a submenu, PM will change the style to `MIS_SUBMENU ¦ WS_SAVEBITS ¦ WS_CLIPSIBLINGS` when the menu is inserted into the main menu.

We are now ready to begin adding the menu items to this menu. To add the items, we need to fill in the MENUITEM structure and send the MM_INSERTITEM message. We will initially want all of the menu items to be disabled:

```
MENUITEM mi;

   hWndEditMenu = WinCreateMenu (HWND_OBJECT, NULL);
   WinSetWindowUShort (hWndEditMenu, QWS_ID, IDM_EDIT);
   mi.iPosition   = MIT_END;
   mi.afStyle     = MIS_TEXT;
   mi.afAttribute = MIA_DISABLED;
   mi.id          = IDM_UNDO;
   mi.hwndSubMenu = 0;
   mi.hItem       = 0;
   WinSendMsg (hWndEditMenu, MM_INSERTITEM, &mi, "~Undo");
   mi.id          = IDM_COPY;
   WinSendMsg (hWndEditMenu, MM_INSERTITEM, &mi, "~Copy");
   mi.id          = IDM_CUT;
   WinSendMsg (hWndEditMenu, MM_INSERTITEM, &mi, "Cu~t");
   mi.id          = IDM_PASTE;
   WinSendMsg (hWndEditMenu, MM_INSERTITEM, &mi, "~Paste");
```

Let's insert a separator between the Undo and Copy menu items:

```
   mi.iPosition   = 1;
   mi.afStyle     = MIS_SEPARATOR;
   mi.afAttribute = 0;
   mi.id          = -1;
   WinSendMsg (hWndEditMenu, MM_INSERTITEM, &mi, "");
```

Now that the submenu is constructed, we can add it to the main menu as the first item in the menu:

```
   mi.iPosition   = 0;
   mi.afStyle     = MIS_TEXT | MIS_SUBMENU;
   mi.afAttribute = 0;
   mi.id          = IDM_EDIT;
   mi.hwndSubMenu = hWndEditMenu;
   WinSendMsg (hWndMenu, MM_INSERTITEM, &mi, "~Edit");
```

Figure 5.4 shows what this submenu looks like after inserting the edit menu item to the top-level menu.

Another way to add a submenu is to define it separately in the RC file, load it, and use that as the submenu handle in the menuitem structure. An example of this follows in the section on bitmap menu items.

With the edit menu in place, we will want to enable the menu items as appropriate. For example, we will want to enable the paste option if there is any data in the clipboard. Because we really only care about the clipboard when the submenu is about to be displayed, we can use the WM_INITMENU message to tell us the menu is about to be displayed and query the clipboard at that time.

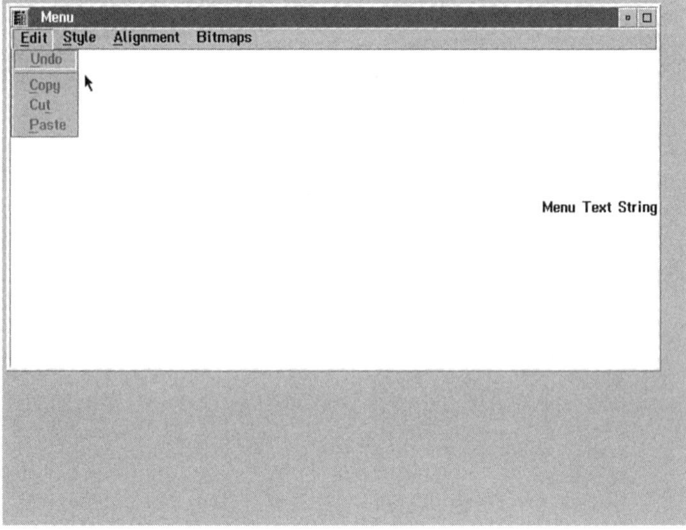

Figure 5.4. Dynamically added Edit submenu.

```
case WM_INITMENU:
   if (SHORT1FROMMP(mp1) == IDM_EDIT)
   {
      ULONG ulFormat;
      WinEnableMenuItem ((HWND)mp2, IDM_UNDO, bUndoAvailable);
      WinEnableMenuItem ((HWND)mp2, IDM_COPY, bSelected);
      WinEnableMenuItem ((HWND)mp2, IDM_CUT,  bSelected);
      WinEnableMenuItem ((HWND)mp2, IDM_PASTE,
      WinQueryClipbrdFmtInfo (hab, CF_TEXT, &ulFormat));
   }
```

To test this, start the menu application and select the "Edit" option. Notice that all the menu options are disabled. Now start the system editor and enter some text. Select the text and select the "Edit," and then the "Copy" options in the system editor. Now select the "Edit" option in the menu application. Notice that the "Paste" option is now enabled because there is data in the clipboard with the format `CF_TEXT`.

In our application, `bSelected` and `bUndoAvailable` are always set to `FALSE`, but would normally change during the course of the application.

Changing the Menu Item Checkmark

When a menu item has the `MIA_CHECKED` attribute, the system draws a default checkmark to the left of the menu item. This checkmark is shown in Figure 5.5.

In earlier versions of OS/2, if you did not want to use the system default checkmark, you had to define the menu item as a `MIS_OWNERDRAW` item and draw the entire menu item with a new checkmark. One of the newer undocumented features of OS/2 is the capability to change the checkmark that is used for each menu item. This is accomplished by sending a message to set both the bitmap used for the checked state and the bitmap used for the unchecked state. This undocumented message is provided here:

```
MM_SETITEMCHECKMARK         0x0210
     mp1 = MPFROM2SHORT (menuitemID,bchecked)
         menuitemID = ID of the menu item to set
         bchecked   = TRUE if bitmap is for the checked state
                      FALSE if bitmap is for the unchecked state
     mp2 = bitmap handle
```

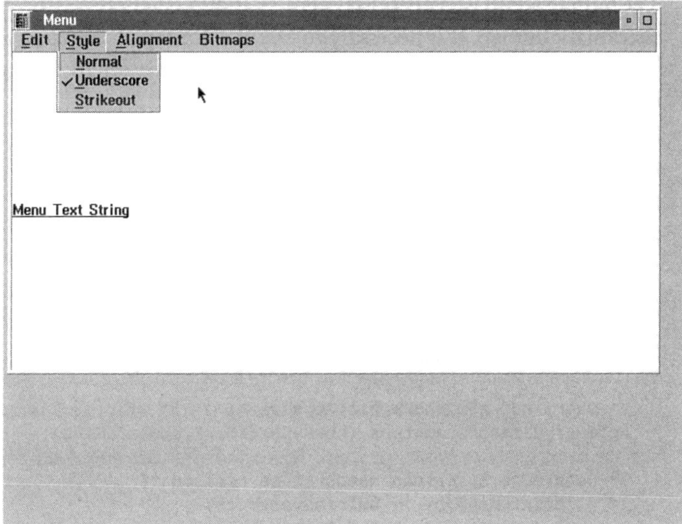

Figure 5.5.
A menu item marked with the default checkmark.

The checkmarks must be set for each menu item that we want to have using the new checkmarks. For example, if we have loaded two bitmaps and want to set them for menu items `IDM_ALIGNLEFT` and `IDM_ALIGNCENTER`, we would have to send four messages. If `hbmUnchecked` is our bitmap for the unchecked state and `hbmChecked` is our bitmap for the checked state, we would send the following messages:

```
WinSendMsg (hWndMenu, MM_SETITEMCHECKMARK,
   MPFROM2SHORT (IDM_ALIGNLEFT,FALSE), hbmUnchecked);
WinSendMsg (hWndMenu, MM_SETITEMCHECKMARK,
   MPFROM2SHORT (IDM_ALIGNLEFT,TRUE), hbmChecked);
WinSendMsg (hWndMenu, MM_SETITEMCHECKMARK,
   MPFROM2SHORT (IDM_ALIGNCENTER,FALSE), hbmUnchecked);
WinSendMsg (hWndMenu, MM_SETITEMCHECKMARK,
   MPFROM2SHORT (IDM_ALIGNCENTER,TRUE), hbmChecked);
```

It is not required to set both the checked and unchecked bitmaps. If you only set the bitmap for the unchecked state the system will use the default bitmap for the checked state.

for the third item in each column. To demonstrate the setting of a different checkmark bitmap, we will use two bitmaps for the first column and two different bitmaps for the second column. These are shown in figures 5.6 through 5.9.

Figure 5.6.
Image of `IDBMP_CHECK1` *checkmark image.*

Figure 5.7.
Image of `IDBMP_UNCHECK1` *checkmark image.*

Figure 5.8.
Image of `IDBMP_CHECK2` *checkmark image.*

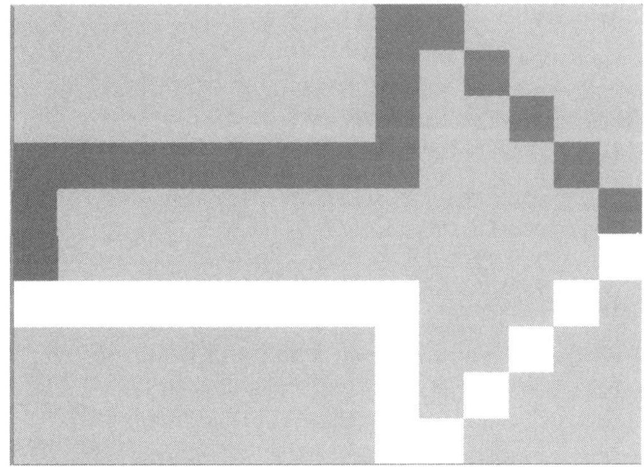

Figure 5.9.
Image of `IDBMP_UNCHECK2` *checkmark image.*

We use the `WinSetCheckMark` macro defined in the MENUXTRA.H file to set the checkmarks for each item in this submenu. (See figures 5.6 through 5.9). The bitmaps are set while processing the `WM_CREATE` message for the main window. Our bitmaps have been created with a width of 14 and a height of 10 so there is no need to call the `FitCheckMarkToSystem` function to resize them:

```
#define WinSetCheckMark(hWndMenu, id, hbm, bcheck) \
      ((BOOL)WinSendMsg(hWndMenu,MM_SETITEMCHECKMARK, \
      MPFROM2SHORT(id, (USHORT)bcheck), hbm))

VOID SetMenuCheckMarks (HPS hps, HWND hWndMenu)
{
   hbmCheck1   = GpiLoadBitmap (hps,0,IDBMP_CHECK1,0L,0L);
   hbmUnCheck1 = GpiLoadBitmap (hps,0,IDBMP_UNCHECK1,0L,0L);
   hbmCheck2   = GpiLoadBitmap (hps,0,IDBMP_CHECK2,0L,0L);
   hbmUnCheck2 = GpiLoadBitmap (hps,0,IDBMP_UNCHECK2,0L,0L);
```

```
    /* Set the checkmarks for the horizontal alignment */
    WinSetCheckMark (hWndMenu,IDM_ALIGNLEFT,hbmCheck1,TRUE);
    WinSetCheckMark (hWndMenu,IDM_ALIGNLEFT,hbmUnCheck1, FALSE);
    WinSetCheckMark (hWndMenu,IDM_ALIGNCENTER,hbmCheck1, TRUE);
    WinSetCheckMark (hWndMenu,IDM_ALIGNCENTER,hbmUnCheck1, FALSE);
    WinSetCheckMark (hWndMenu,IDM_ALIGNRIGHT,hbmCheck1,TRUE);
    WinSetCheckMark (hWndMenu,IDM_ALIGNRIGHT,hbmUnCheck1, FALSE);

    /* Set the checkmarks for the vertical alignment */
    WinSetCheckMark (hWndMenu,IDM_ALIGNTOP,hbmCheck2,TRUE);
    WinSetCheckMark (hWndMenu,IDM_ALIGNTOP,hbmUnCheck2, FALSE);
    WinSetCheckMark (hWndMenu,IDM_ALIGNMIDDLE,hbmCheck2, TRUE);
    WinSetCheckMark (hWndMenu,IDM_ALIGNMIDDLE,hbmUnCheck2, FALSE);
    WinSetCheckMark (hWndMenu,IDM_ALIGNBOTTOM,hbmCheck2, TRUE);
    WinSetCheckMark (hWndMenu,IDM_ALIGNBOTTOM,hbmUnCheck2, FALSE);
    return;
}
```

`SetMenuCheckMarks` is called during the `WM_CREATE` message processing for the application's main window:

```
case WM_CREATE:
    /* Retrieve the handle of the FID_MENU window */
    hWndMenu    = WinWindowFromID (WinQueryWindow(hWnd, QW_PARENT),
                  FID_MENU);

    ...
    hPS = WinGetPS (hWnd);

    /* Load and set the checkmark bitmaps */
    SetMenuCheckMarks (hPS, hWndMenu);

    ...
    break;
```

Bitmap Menu Items

So far we have dealt only with the `MIS_TEXT` menu style as the type of item to display. We can also have `MIS_BITMAP` and `MIS_OWNERDRAW` menu styles. Let's take a quick look at the `MIS_BITMAP` menu style. This style defines a bitmap handle to display in the menu item instead of text. The size of the menu item is adjusted by PM to contain the bitmap. The bitmap is displayed similarly to a text item; space is reserved to the left of the menu item for the checkmark, and space is reserved to the right for the submenu indicator.

We have defined a menu in the resource file called `BITMAP_MENU` that contains two menu items defined with the `MIS_BITMAP` style. We will add this menu as the last menu item in the main menu. (See Figure 5.10.)

```
#define IDBMP_BMPITEM1          54
#define IDBMP_BMPITEM2          55
```

```
BITMAP IDBMP_BMPITEM1    "BMPITEM1.BMP"
BITMAP IDBMP_BMPITEM2    "BMPITEM2.BMP"

MENU BITMAP_MENU
{
   MENUITEM "#54", IDM_BMPITEM1, MIS_BITMAP
   MENUITEM "#55", IDM_BMPITEM2, MIS_BITMAP
}
```

When a bitmap menu item is defined in the resource file, the text for the item is a string representation of the bitmap identifier. This string is the # character followed by the identifier:

```
VOID AddBitmapMenu (HWND hWndMenu)
{
   MENUITEM mi;

   mi.iPosition   = MIT_END;
   mi.afStyle     = MIS_TEXT | MIS_SUBMENU;
   mi.afAttribute = 0;
   mi.id          = BITMAP_MENU;
   mi.hwndSubMenu = WinLoadMenu (HWND_OBJECT,0,BITMAP_MENU);
   mi.hItem       = NULL;
   WinSendMsg (hWndMenu, MM_INSERTITEM, &mi, "Bitmaps");
   return;
}
```

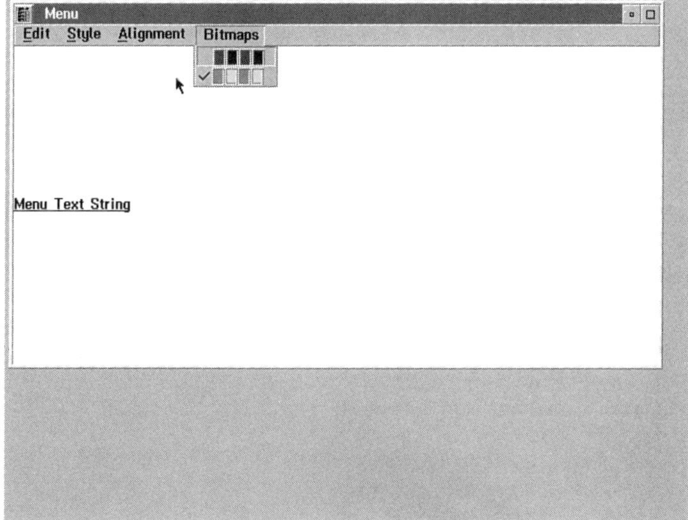

Figure 5.10.
A bitmap item selected with a checkmark.

To see what the bitmap item looks like with a checkmark (see Figure 5.10), we will toggle the checkmark attribute when the `WM_COMMAND` message is received for either of the two menu items.

```
case IDM_BMPITEM1:
case IDM_BMPITEM2:
{
   USHORT usChecked;

   /* Toggle to checkmark flag */
   usChecked =
      LOUSHORT(WinIsMenuItemChecked (hWndMenu, LOUSHORT(mp1)));
   usChecked ^= MIA_CHECKED;
   WinCheckMenuItem (hWndMenu, LOUSHORT(mp1), usChecked);
   break;
}
```

It is also possible to define a bitmap menu item for the actionbar. The definition of the menu item is the same as for any other item. When a menu window is destroyed, PM will delete bitmaps that we loaded implicitly by PM. These bitmaps are those specified for menu items in the resoure file. Bitmaps loaded by the application and set in menu items must be deleted by the application.

Ownerdraw Menu Items

Now we move on to an interesting aspect of menus, the `MIS_OWNERDRAW` menu item style. This style enables you to customize the appearance of your menu items because the application draws the menu item. We are going to create a pop-up menu with three `ownerdraw` menu items and draw each menu item in the appropriate state as requested.

When a `MIS_OWNERDRAW` item is to be displayed, the menu window sends a `WM_MEASUREITEM` to its owner window. This message gets passed up the menu chain until it reaches a frame window, which in turn sends it to the client window. The `WM_MEASUREITEM` is sent whenever the size of the menu needs to be determined and is used to retrieve the width and height of the item. This is used in calculating the entire size of the menu window. The width that is returned will be added to by PM to include the width of both the `SBMP_MENUCHECK` and the `SBMP_MENUATTACHED` bitmaps. The `SBMP_MENUATTACHED` bitmap is the arrow that is normally seen to the right of the menu item when the menu item includes a submenu.

If your menu items do not include submenus or you want to draw your own menu attached pointer, subtract the width of the `SBMP_MENUATTACHED` bitmap. In our case, our menu items will be bitmaps, including a separate bitmap for the checked state, and do not include submenus.

Whenever the menu item is to be drawn, a `WM_DRAWITEM` message is sent to its owner in the same way the `WM_MEASUREITEM` is sent. This message is sent when the item must be completely drawn, when the highlight state changes, or when the checkmark state changes. The application uses information passed in this structure to determine what state the menu item is in and draws the item appropriately.

Both these messages pass a pointer to an `OWNERITEM` structure:

```
typedef struct _OWNERITEM { /* oi */
   HWND    hwnd;            /* Window handle of menu containing menu
                                 item */
HPS     hps;             /* HPS to draw into */
   ULONG   fsState;         /* Style of the menu item */
   ULONG   fsAttribute;     /* New attribute of menu item */
   ULONG   fsStateOld;      /* Style of the menu item */
   ULONG   fsAttributeOld;  /* Old attribute of menu item */
   RECTL   rclItem;         /* Rectangle to draw into */
   LONG    idItem;          /* ID of menu item to draw */
   ULONG   hItem;           /* Handle of item for menu item */
} OWNERITEM;
```

The WM_MEASUREITEM passes the following information:

```
WM_MEASUREITEM     0x0037
   mp1 = SHORT1FROMMP(mp1) Identifier of the menu window
   mp2 = (POWNERITEM) Pointer to an owneritem structure to be filled in
```

The return value is ignored by the menu system in PM.

The client window procedure processes this message by filling in the rclItem.xRight and rclItem.yTop fields with the width and height of the item. Because we will be using bitmaps in our ownerdraw menu items, the width and height are set to the size of the bitmap:

```
case WM_MEASUREITEM:
   MeasureOwnerItem ((POWNERITEM)mp2);
   break;

VOID MeasureOwnerItem (POWNERITEM poi)
{
   BITMAPINFOHEADER bmInfoMenuAttached,
                    bmInfoMenuCheck,
                    bmInfoMenu;
   HBITMAP hbm = WinGetSysBitmap (HWND_DESKTOP, SBMP_MENUATTACHED);
   GpiQueryBitmapParameters (hbm,&bmInfoMenuAttached);
   GpiDeleteBitmap (hbm);
   hbm = WinGetSysBitmap (HWND_DESKTOP,SBMP_MENUCHECK);
   GpiQueryBitmapParameters (hbm,&bmInfoMenuCheck);
   GpiDeleteBitmap (hbm);
   GpiQueryBitmapParameters ((HBITMAP)poi->hItem, &bmInfoMenu);
   poi->rclItem.xRight = (bmInfoMenu.cx / 4) -
        bmInfoMenuAttached.cx - bmInfoMenuCheck.cx;
   poi->rclItem.yTop    = bmInfoMenu.cy;
   return;
}
```

Note that for the width of our menu item, we have subtracted the width of the SBMP_MENUATTACHED and SBMP_MENUCHECK bitmaps because we will draw everything ourselves, and we want the rectangle used in the WM_OWNERDRAW message to match the width of the bitmap. Remember that PM adds these widths back to our returned value so that the net result is that the resulting width of the menu item is the width of our bitmap.

The WM_DRAWITEM message passes the following information:

```
WM_DRAWITEM    0x0036
   mp1 = SHORT1FROMMP(mp1) Identifier of the menu window
   mp2 = (POWNERITEM) Pointer to an owneritem structure to be filled in
```

The return value is ignored by the menu system in PM.

Determination of what state to draw the menu item is done by looking at the fsAttribute field of the OWNERITEM structure. You can ignore the fsState and fsStateOld fields as they simply contain the menu item style. After drawing the menu item, you must tell PM if it should perform the default processing for the current attributes.

If you draw your own menu checkmarks or you do not use any, clear the MIA_CHECKED attribute of both the fsAttribute and fsAttributeOld fields, likewise for the MIA_HILITED and MIA_FRAMED attributes. For example, if you draw a menu item and the MIA_CHECKED attribute is set and you want the default checkmark drawn, leave the MIA_CHECKED attribute alone. On the other hand, if you do not want the system to draw the default checkmark, clear the MIA_CHECKED attribute in the OWNERITEM structure. You can use the following code:

```
((POWNERITEM)mp2)->fsAttribute =
     ( ((POWNERITEM)mp2)->fsAttributeOld &= ~MIA_CHECKED );
```

The MENU sample application shows a pop-up menu with three menu items. The pop-up menu is shown with each item aligned horizontally. (See Figure 5.11.) In order to show the six different states of a menu item, use a single bitmap with four different states already drawn in the bitmap. The offset of the portion of the bitmap to display is calculated in the DrawOwnerItem function called during the WM_DRAWITEM message processing.

We will only draw that portion of the bitmap that shows the current state. The UNHILITED and HILITED bitmap portions will also be used to show the disabled state—they will be drawn with the DBM_HALFTONE ROP code.

In defining our menus, we will use the hItem field of the MENUITEM to contain the bitmap handle for the menu item. This is set for each menu item after the menu has been loaded.

```
VOID SetOwnerDrawBitmapHandles (HPS hps, HWND hWndMenu)
{
   MENUITEM mi;
   USHORT   usCnt;

   usCnt = LOUSHORT(WinSendMsg (hWndMenu, MM_QUERYITEMCOUNT, 0L, 0L));

   while (usCnt)
   {
      WinSendMsg (hWndMenu, MM_QUERYITEMBYPOS,
         MPFROM2SHORT (usCnt,0), MAKE_16BIT_POINTER (&mi));
      /* The menu item id is the same as the bitmap id */
      mi.hItem = (ULONG)GpiLoadBitmap (hps,0,mi.id,0L,0L);
      WinSendMsg (hWndMenu, MM_SETITEMHANDLEBYPOS,
            MPFROM2SHORT (usCnt,0), (MPARAM)mi.hItem);
      usCnt-;
```

```
    }
    return;
}
```

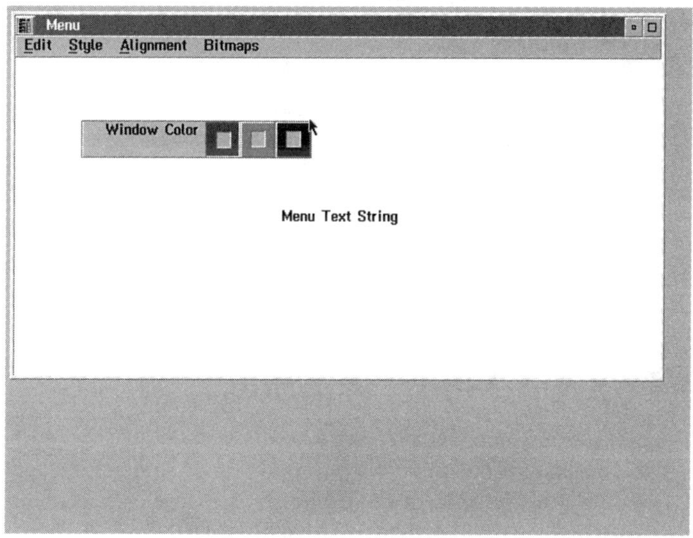

Figure 5.11.
Pop-up menu with owner-draw menu items.

We will draw the appropriate bitmap into the `hps` when we receive the `WM_DRAWITEM` message:

```
case WM_DRAWITEM:
   DrawOwnerItem ((POWNERITEM)mp2);
   mReturn = (MRESULT)TRUE;
   break;

VOID DrawOwnerItem (POWNERITEM poi)
{
   ULONG             yOffset;
   RECTL             Rectl;
   BITMAPINFOHEADER bmInfoOwnerDraw;
   ULONG             ropCode;

   /* Get the bitmap handle for the bitmap */
   GpiQueryBitmapParameters ((HBITMAP)poi->hItem, &bmInfoOwnerDraw);

   /* Determine the offset of the portion of the bitmap to draw */
   if (poi->fsAttribute & MIA_CHECKED)
      yOffset = bmInfoOwnerDraw.cx / 2;
   else
      yOffset = 0;
   if (poi->fsAttribute & MIA_HILITED)
      yOffset += bmInfoOwnerDraw.cx / 4;

   /* Determine ROP code to use */
   if (poi->fsAttribute & MIA_DISABLED)
```

```
      ropCode = DBM_HALFTONE;
   else
      ropCode = DBM_NORMAL;

   /* Set the source rectangle and draw the bitmap.  */
   Rectl.xLeft   = yOffset;
   Rectl.yBottom = 0L;
   Rectl.xRight  = yOffset + bmInfoOwnerDraw.cx / 4;
   Rectl.yTop    = bmInfoOwnerDraw.cy;
   WinDrawBitmap (poi->hps,(HBITMAP)poi->hItem,&Rectl,
         (PPOINTL)&poi->rclItem, 0L, 0L, ropCode);

   /* Turn off attributes by default */
   poi->fsAttribute =
       (poi->fsAttributeOld &= ~(MIA_CHECKED | MIA_HILITED |
       MIA_FRAMED));
   return;
}
```

Pop-Up Menu Window

Pop-up menu windows were also a new feature of OS/2 2.1. Although it was possible to simulate pop-up windows prior to this version, the addition of the `WinPopupMenu` API makes things a lot easier on the application developer. Essentially, a pop-up menu is much like a pull-down menu except that it can appear anywhere on the screen. The application has control over where the pop-up appears, the initial state of the pop-up, how menu selection occurs, and whether keyboard and mouse input are allowed. Normally, a pop-up menu is shown in response to some user input. For example, when the user presses the right mouse button in the client area, a pop-up may appear allowing the user to select a particular attribute.

The `WinPopupMenu` API is used to display a pop-up menu. The menu can be a menu loaded from a resource file with a call to `WinLoadMenu`, a menu created dynamically by the application with a call to `WinCreateMenu`, or a particular submenu extracted from an existing menu. One of the first things done in `WinPopupMenu` is to set the menu window style to `MS_ROOT | MS_POPUP | WS_SAVEBITS` and remove the `MS_ACTIONBAR` style. This allows you to use any existing menu because PM will set the menu style to fit the style of a pop-up window. The `WinPopupMenu` API is defined as follows:

```
BOOL WinPopupMenu (HWND hwndParent, HWND hwndOwner, HWND hWndMenu,
          LONG x, LONG y, ULONG idItem, USHORT fsOptions)

hwndParent - Parent window handle
hwndOwner  - Owner window handle
hWndMenu   - Popup window handle
x          - x-position of popup menu.  This position is relative to the
             parent window and specifies the lower-left corner of the
             menu.
y          - y-position of popup menu.  This position is relative to the
             parent window and specifies the lower-left corner of the
             menu.
```

```
idItem       - Identifier of menu item to select if PU_POSITIONONITEM or
               PUSELECTITEM are specified in fsOptions.
fsOptions    - Pop-up menu positioning and state options:
PU_POSITIONONITEM     - Position the popup so that the item specified by idItem is
                        directly below the pointer. The item specified by idItem is
                        selected.
PU_HCONSTRAIN         - Ensure that the menu does not extend beyond  the left or right
                        edge of the screen. Adjust the position of the menu as required.
PU_VCONSTRAIN         - Ensure that the menu does not extend beyond the top or bottom edge
                        of the screen. Adjust the position of the menu as required.
PU_NONE               - Menu is displayed and left up with no initial selection state. The
                        menu item idItem is selected if PU_SELECTITEM or PU_POSITIONONITEM
                        are specified.
PU_MOUSEBUTTON1DOWN   - Menu is displayed with mouse button 1 and
                        depressed and dismissed when mouse button 1 is released.
                        No menu item is initially selected.
PU_MOUSEBUTTON2DOWN   - Menu is displayed with mouse button 2 and
                        depressed and dismissed when mouse button 2 is released.
                        No menu item is initially selected.
PU_MOUSEBUTTON3DOWN   - Menu is displayed with mouse button 3 and depressed and dismissed
                        when mouse button 3 is released. No menu item is initially
                        selected.
PU_SELECTITEM         - Select the idItem if PU_NONE is specified.
                        If this item is in a submenu, then all owner
                        submenus in the menu hierarchy are displayed.
PU_MOUSEBUTTON1       - Mouse button 1 can be used for menu selection.
PU_MOUSEBUTTON2       - Mouse button 2 can be used for menu selection.
PU_MOUSEBUTTON3       - Mouse button 3 can be used for menu selection.
PU_KEYBOARD           - Keyboard can be used for menu selection.
```

If `PU_POSITIONONITEM` is specified, the x and y coordinates are screen coordinates and are not relative to the parent window. If `PU_MOUSEBUTTON1DOWN`, `PU_MOUSEBUTTON2DOWN`, or `PU_MOUSEBUTTON3DOWN` are specified, `PU_SELECTITEM` is ignored. If `PU_NONE` is specified but neither `PU_SELECTITEM` or `PU_POSITIONONITEM` are, the first item in the menu is selected.

As an example, if we have a pop-up menu that we want to display so that the menu remains up when the mouse is released, is constrained to the boundaries of the screen, has an item selected, and has all input devices available for selection, we would use the following flags:

```
PU_NONE ¦ PU_HCONSTRAIN ¦ PU_VCONSTRAIN ¦ PU_SELECTITEM ¦
PU_MOUSEBUTTON1 ¦ PU_MOUSEBUTTON2 ¦ PU_MOUSEBUTTON3 ¦ PU_KEYBOARD
```

If we want the menu to be dismissed when button 1 is released, assuming that button 1 was used to summon the pop-up, we would use the following flags:

```
PU_MOUSEBUTTON1DOWN ¦ PU_HCONSTRAIN ¦ PU_VCONSTRAIN ¦ PU_MOUSEBUTTON1
```

The call to `WinPopupMenu` returns immediately, and the menu is processed like any other menu window. The following code clip loads a pop-up menu and displays it as a pop-up menu when

the WM_BUTTON2DOWN message is received. The menu is constrained to the screen, and the keyboard and mouse button 2 are allowed for menu input. This menu will remain up after the mouse button is released, and the first menu item will be selected by default:

```
switch (msg)
{
   case WM_BUTTON2DOWN:
      if (!hWndPopupMenu)
         hWndPopupMenu = WinLoadMenu (HWND_OBJECT, 0, COLOR_MENU);
      WinPopupMenu (hWnd, hWnd, hWndPopupMenu,
         SHORT1FROMMP(mp1), SHORT2FROMMP(mp1), 0,
         PU_HCONSTRAIN ¦ PU_VCONSTRAIN ¦ PU_KEYBOARD ¦
         PU_MOUSEBUTTON2);
      break;
}
```

Note that the menu is only loaded once and not each time that the WinPopupMenu is called. The menu window handle is not destroyed when the menu is dismissed, so it is not necessary to load it every time. Doing so would result in a new menu window being created each time and would eventually utilize all the window resources in the system. However, you can use the WM_MENUEND notification message to know when the menu has been hidden and it is okay to destroy the pop-up window.

In our application, we will use a single pop-up menu to set both the window background color and the text color. The window background color will be set by activating the pop-up menu with mouse button 1, and the text color will be set by activating the pop-up menu with mouse button 2. Each version of the pop-up will behave differently. The pop-up menu is defined in the resource file:

```
/* menu.h */
#define COLOR_MENU           100
#define IDC_COLOR            101
#define IDBMP_ODITEM1         56
#define IDBMP_ODITEM2         57
#define IDBMP_ODITEM3         58

/* menu.rc */
MENU COLOR_MENU
{
   MENUITEM "", IDC_COLOR, MIS_STATIC
   MENUITEM "", IDBMP_ODITEM1, MIS_OWNERDRAW ¦ MIS_BREAK
   MENUITEM "", IDBMP_ODITEM2, MIS_OWNERDRAW ¦ MIS_BREAK
   MENUITEM "", IDBMP_ODITEM3, MIS_OWNERDRAW ¦ MIS_BREAK
}
```

The first menu item is a MIS_STATIC item with no text. The text for this item will be set to either "Window Color" or "Text Color" depending on the color that is being set. This field will act as a menu description field. The other three items are all MIS_OWNERDRAW menu items that will use the code discussed in the previous section. All items in this pop-up are aligned horizontally.

The specific color will be set when the menu items are selected. Two variables will contain the current settings for these colors. These color values are RGB (Red, Green, Blue) color values. If the `Red` button is selected, the color red will either be added or removed from the current color, likewise for `Green` and `Blue`:

```
LONG   lWindowColor    = 0x00FFFFFF;
LONG   lTextColor      = 0x00000000;
                       /*    RED         GREEN       BLUE    */
LONG   lColorTable[3] = {0x00FF0000,0x0000FF00,0x000000FF };

switch (msg)
{
   case WM_COMMAND:
   ...
   case IDBMP_ODITEM1:
   case IDBMP_ODITEM2:
   case IDBMP_ODITEM3:
   {
      USHORT usChecked;

      /* Toggle the checkmark flag */
      usChecked =
         LOUSHORT(WinIsMenuItemChecked (hColorMenu, LOUSHORT(mp1)));
      usChecked ^= MIA_CHECKED;
      WinCheckMenuItem (hColorMenu, LOUSHORT(mp1), usChecked);

      /* Toggle the color field */
      if (bWindowColor)
         lWindowColor ^= lColorTable[LOUSHORT(mp1)-IDBMP_ODITEM1];
      else
         lTextColor   ^= lColorTable[LOUSHORT(mp1)-IDBMP_ODITEM1];
      WinInvalidateRect (hWnd,NULL,FALSE);
      break;
   }
   ...
   break;
...
}
```

The pop-up menu is initialized during the `WM_INITMENU` message. This processing checks the menu items when the color is included in the current color setting:

```
case WM_INITMENU:
  ...
  else if ((HWND)mp2 == hColorMenu)
  {
    USHORT Pos;
    for (Pos = 0; Pos < 3; Pos++)
    {
      sMenuID = (SHORT)WinSendMsg (hColorMenu, MM_ITEMIDFROMPOSITION,
                     MPFROMSHORT(Pos+1), MPVOID);
      WinSendMsg (hColorMenu, MM_SETITEMATTR,
          MPFROMSHORT(sMenuID),
          MPFROM2SHORT(MIA_CHECKED,
```

```
          bWindowColor ?
          ((lWindowColor & lColorTable[Pos]) ? MIA_CHECKED : 0) :
          ((lTextColor & lColorTable[Pos]) ? MIA_CHECKED : 0)));
    }
  }
  break;
```

Our pop-up menu is loaded once during the `WM_CREATE` message processing, and the menu item bitmaps used in the `DrawOwnerItem` are set for each item:

```
/* Load the color pop-up menu */
hColorMenu = WinLoadMenu (HWND_OBJECT,0,COLOR_MENU);

/* Load and set the owner draw bitmap handles */
SetOwnerDrawBitmapHandles (hPS,hColorMenu);
```

With the pop-up menu loaded, we are ready to display it when the mouse button messages are received. We are going to do something quite a bit different in displaying our menus. Normally, the pop-up menu is displayed with the lower-left corner positioned at the pointer position. We want our pop-ups to display with either the upper-left or upper-right corner positioned at the pointer position. To do this, we will need to determine the size of the pop-up menu. When a menu is about to be displayed, PM sends a `WM_ADJUSTWINDOWPOS` message to the menu, and the menu window calculates its size and returns it in the `SWP` structure passed with the `WM_ADJUSTWINDOWPOS` message. This information can then be used to offset the current pointer position so that the pop-up menu displays with the upper corner aligned with the pointer. The function `PlacePopup` will handle this for us:

```
VOID PlacePopup (HWND hWndOwner, HWND hWndMenu,
         ULONG x, ULONG y, BOOL bRight, ULONG ulFlags)
{
   /* We need to get the height of the menu because WinPopupMenu will
   position the menu with the lower-left corner of the menu at the
   coordinates passed. By sending a WM_ADJUSTWINDOWPOS message to
   the menu it will fill in the swp structure of the menu with its
   size.
   */
   SWP   Swp;
   ULONG ulStyle;

   ulStyle  = WinQueryWindowULong (hWndMenu,QWL_STYLE) & ~MS_ACTIONBAR;
   WinSetWindowULong (hWndMenu,QWL_STYLE,ulStyle);
   WinQueryWindowPos(hWndMenu, (PSWP)&Swp);
   Swp.fl               = SWP_MOVE ¦ SWP_SIZE;
   Swp.hwndInsertBehind = HWND_TOP;

   /* Set owner to frame here so that WM_MEASUREITEM messages are
   sent to the frame window for processing - in case menu is ownerdraw */
   WinSetOwner  (hWndMenu,hWndOwner);
   WinSendMsg(hWndMenu, WM_ADJUSTWINDOWPOS, (MPARAM)(PSWP)&Swp, NULL);

   WinPopupMenu (hWndOwner,hWndOwner,hWndMenu,
         bRight ? x : x - Swp.cx, y - Swp.cy, 0,
         U_HCONSTRAIN ¦ PU_VCONSTRAIN ¦ PU_KEYBOARD ¦
```

```
         PU_MOUSEBUTTON1 | ulFlags);

   return;
}
```

The `hWndOwner` parameter is both the owner and parent of the pop-up. The `hWndOwner` window will receive all notification messages from the pop-up. `hWndMenu` is the handle of the pop-up menu; x and y are the coordinates of the current pointer position. The parameter `bRight` specifies if the menu should display to the right of the pointer or to the left of the pointer. `ulFlags` are additional flags for the `WinPopupMenu` call.

Before sending the `WM_ADJUSTWINDOWPOS` message, we must make sure the style of the menu window does not include the `MS_ACTIONBAR` style. This will cause the size calculation to be performed for a submenu rather than an actionbar menu style:

```
ulStyle  = WinQueryWindowULong (hWndMenu,QWL_STYLE) & ~MS_ACTIONBAR;
WinSetWindowULong (hWndMenu,QWL_STYLE,ulStyle);
```

Next, we query the current position of the menu and set the `fl` field to `SWP_MOVE | SWP_SIZE`. This tells PM that it needs to calculate a new size and position for the menu:

```
WinQueryWindowPos(hWndMenu, (PSWP)&Swp);
Swp.fl                 = SWP_MOVE | SWP_SIZE;
Swp.hwndInsertBehind = HWND_TOP;
```

The next step is very important, especially in our case, because we are using `ownerdraw` menu items. The owner of the menu window will be automatically set when the `WinPopupMenu` is called; however, at this point it will be whatever the previous owner was. In our case, it will initially be `HWND_OBJECT` because the menu was loaded with `HWND_OBJECT` as its owner. We set the owner of the menu window because, in calculating the size of the menu, PM will send a `WM_MEASUREITEM` message to the menu's owner for each `MIS_OWNERDRAW` menu item. We must make sure that our `ClientWndProc` receives those messages:

```
WinSetOwner  (hWndMenu,hWndOwner);
WinSendMsg(hWndMenu, WM_ADJUSTWINDOWPOS, (MPARAM)(PSWP)&Swp, NULL);
```

The `WM_ADJUSTWINDOWPOS` is sent to the window causing the calculation of the menu size. We then use the `Swp.cx` and `Swp.cy` fields to offset the position of the menu:

```
WinPopupMenu (hWndOwner,hWndOwner,hWndMenu,
      bRight ? x : x - Swp.cx, y - Swp.cy, IDBMP_ODITEM1,
      PU_HCONSTRAIN | PU_VCONSTRAIN | PU_KEYBOARD |
      PU_MOUSEBUTTON1 | ulFlags);
```

If `bRight` is `TRUE`, the menu will be positioned with the left corner of the menu at the pointer position. Otherwise, it will be positioned with the right corner of the menu at the pointer position.

In activating the pop-up menu, the pop-up used in setting the window color will be summoned by mouse button 1, and it will remain up after the mouse button is released. The text color pop-up menu will be summoned by mouse button 2, and it will be dismissed when mouse button 2 is released:

```
case WM_BUTTON1DOWN:
   bWindowColor = TRUE;
   WinLoadString (hab, 0, IDS_WINDOWCOLOR, sizeof(szColor), szColor);
   sMenuID = (SHORT)WinSendMsg (hColorMenu, MM_ITEMIDFROMPOSITION,
                     MPFROMSHORT(0), MPVOID);
   WinSendMsg (hColorMenu, MM_SETITEMTEXT, MPFROMSHORT(sMenuID),
       MPFROMP(szColor));
   /* Call WinDefWindowProc so that window is activated */
   mReturn = WinDefWindowProc (hWnd,msg,mp1,mp2);
   PlacePopup (hWnd, hColorMenu,
      SHORT1FROMMP(mp1),SHORT2FROMMP(mp1),FALSE,
      PU_NONE);  /* Allow button to be released */
   break;

case WM_BUTTON2DOWN:
   bWindowColor = FALSE;
   WinLoadString (hab, 0, IDS_TEXTCOLOR, sizeof(szColor), szColor);
   sMenuID = (SHORT)WinSendMsg (hColorMenu, MM_ITEMIDFROMPOSITION,
              MPFROMSHORT(0), MPVOID);
   WinSendMsg (hColorMenu, MM_SETITEMTEXT, MPFROMSHORT(sMenuID),
       MPFROMP(szColor));
   /* Call WinDefWindowProc so that window is activated */
   mReturn = WinDefWindowProc (hWnd,msg,mp1,mp2);
   PlacePopup (hWnd, hColorMenu,
       SHORT1FROMMP(mp1),SHORT2FROMMP(mp1),TRUE,
       PU_MOUSEBUTTON2DOWN);
   break;
```

There are three steps in handling each mouse message. The first step is to set the text of the first menu item to indicate the color that is being set. These strings are loaded from the resource file and the text set using the `MM_SETITEMTEXT` message. We set the global variable `bWindowColor` to indicate if we are setting the window color or text color. The next step is also important. PM uses the `WM_BUTTONxDOWN` messages to activate the window. When `WinDefWindowProc` receives the `WM_BUTTONxDOWN` message, it calls `WinSetActiveWindow` to activate the window that is beneath the pointer. If we do not pass the button down message to `WinDefWindowProc`, the window will not become active if it is not currently active. To see what would happen, remove the call to `WinDefWindowProc`, start the application, and then click another application so that the menu application is deactivated. Then click mouse button 1 in the client area of the menu application. The pop-up menu will appear, but the application will not become active.

Finally, we make the call to `PlacePopup` with the client window as the owner and passing the current pointer position as the x and y position. For `WM_BUTTON1DOWN`, we use the `PU_NONE` flag so that the menu remains up after the mouse button is released. For `WM_BUTTON2DOWN`, we use the `PU_MOUSEBUTTON2DOWN` flag so that the menu is dismissed when the mouse button is released. Notice the differences in the initial selection state of the pop-up when activated with the two mouse buttons.

Replacing the Actionbar Menu

In many Multiple Document Interface (MDI) applications, it is necessary to update the actionbar menu to reflect the selections for the currently selected child window. For example, one child window may require the following actionbar menu:

```
File     Edit     View     Style     Window
```

and a second child window may require the following actionbar menu:

```
Image    Options    Color    Window
```

There are two ways to handle the change in menu when a child window is activated. The first is to individually remove each menu item and insert the new items. This is time-consuming and rather undesirable. The second is to load two different menus and switch between the two. Remember that the actionbar window has an identifier of `FID_MENU` and that this menu is recognized by the frame window as a frame control window. All that is required is to replace the current `FID_MENU` window with the new `FID_MENU` and tell the frame window to redraw the menu frame control. To swap the menus, we could use the following `SwapActionBarMenu` function:

```
VOID SwapActionBarMenu (HWND hWndFrame, HWND hWndNewMenu)
{
   ULONG ulStyle;
   HWND hWndCurrentMenu = WinWindowFromID (hWndFrame, FID_MENU);

   /* If there is a current menu, change its parent and owner */
   if (hWndCurrentMenu)
   {
      WinSetParent (hWndCurrentMenu,
      WinQueryObjectWindow (HWND_DESKTOP),FALSE);
      WinSetOwner (hWndCurrentMenu,
      WinQueryObjectWindow (HWND_DESKTOP));
   }

   /* Make sure menu styles are properly set and identifer
is FID_MENU */
   ulStyle = WinQueryWindowULong (hWndNewMenu, QWL_STYLE);
   ulStyle ¦= MS_ROOT ¦ MS_ACTIONBAR ¦ WS_CLIPSIBLINGS;
   ulStyle &= ~WS SAVEBITS;
   WinSetWindowULong (hWndNewMenu, QWL_STYLE, ulStyle);
   WinSetWindowUShort (hWndNewMenu, QWS_ID, FID_MENU);

   /* Change parent and owner to frame window */
   WinSetParent (hWndNewMenu, hWndFrame, FALSE);
   WinSetOwner (hWndNewMenu, hWndFrame);

   /* Notify frame window of new frame control window */
   WinSendMsg (hWndFrame, WM_UPDATEFRAME, FCF_MENU, NULL);
   return;
}
```

We first check if there is an existing menu and effectively remove the menu from the frame by setting its parent and owner to the object window. The new menu must have the proper styles or else it will not format correctly; the identifier of the new menu window must be `FID_MENU`, or the frame window will not find it. The parent and owner of the new menu are set to the frame window. The `WM_UPDATEFRAME` is sent to the frame to notify it that a new menu control has been added, and it needs to reformat and redraw itself.

Assume that we have loaded two menus:

```
hWndMenu1 = WinLoadMenu (HWND_OBJECT, 0, MAIN_MENU1);
hWndMenu2 = WinLoadMenu (HWND_OBJECT, 0, MAIN_MENU2);
```

When child window 1 becomes active, we would call the following:

```
SwapActionBarMenu (hWndMDIFrame, hWndMenu1);
```

and when child window 2 becomes active, we would call this:

```
SwapActionBarMenu (hWndMDIFrame, hWndMenu2);
```

Using the Same Submenu in Multiple Menus

In an MDI application, there is usually one menu option that lists the current child window applications. This is usually the "Window" menu option, and as child windows are created and destroyed, menu items are added and removed from this pull-down menu. A "Window" menu item is defined for each actionbar menu, and each pull-down must be updated whenever a new item is added or removed. PM does not provide a way to specify the same submenu in multiple menus. In fact, if you call `MM_INSERTITEM` and use the same submenu window handle in more than one menu item, the submenu will display properly only for the last menu item that was added. Any other menu items attempting to display the submenu will have the submenu display, and the entire chain of menus above it will be dismissed. This is because the owner of the submenu is set when the item is inserted, and the owner of the menu is incorrect when it is displayed.

It would nice if we could somehow use the same submenu in multiple menu items and have the owner updated as required. This would be especially helpful for MDI application menus so that we could define the "Window" submenu once, update it as child windows are created and destroyed, and have it displayed properly for each actionbar menu. This can be accomplished by using the undocumented message `MM_PORTHOLEINIT` and the `MM_QUERYITEM` message. The `MM_PORTHOLEINIT` message is sent up the owner chain just prior to summoning the pop-up menu and gives us enough information to allow us to set the owner:

```
MM_PORTHOLEINIT     0x01fb
      SHORT1FROMMP (mp1)   =  position of submenu in the menu
      SHORT2FROMMP (mp1)   =  attribute of the menu item
      mp2                  =  menu handle containing the item
```

When the frame window receives this message, it can query the menu handle for the menu item at the specified position and set the owner of the submenu to the menu handle.

```
switch (msg)
{
   case MM_PORTHOLEINIT:
   {
      MENUITEM mi;
      SHORT    sMenuID;
      sMenuID = WinSendMsg ((HWND)mp2, MM_ITEMIDFROMPOSITION,
           SHORT1FROMMP(mp1), MPVOID);
      WinSendMsg ((HWND)mp2, MM_QUERYITEM, MPFROMSHORT(sMenuID),
           MPFROMP(&mi));
      if (WinQueryOwner (mi.hwndSubMenu,QW_OWNER) != (HWND)mp2)
      {
         WinSetOwner (mi.hwndSubMenu, (HWND)mp2);
         WinSetWindowUShort (mi.hwndSubMenu, QWS_ID, mi.id);
      }
      break;
   }
}
```

The `MM_ITEMIDFROMPOSITION` and `MM_QUERYITEM` messages retrieve the `MENUITEM` structure for the menu item at the specified position. If the owner of the submenu about to be displayed is not equal to the menu that is summoning it, we set the owner of the submenu to the summoning menu. We also set the identifier of the submenu to the identifier of the `MENUITEM` because this submenu may be referenced by many different identifiers.

You still need to set the submenu handle for each menu item that wants to share the particular submenu. This can be done when the item is added to the menu (`MM_INSERTITEM`) or changed later (`MM_SETITEM`).

Changing the System Menu

Finally, let's add an About option to the system menu. The system menu is just another menu window with an ID of `FID_SYSMENU`. (See Figure 5.12.) It contains one menu item, which is a bitmap menu item with a submenu. To add an item to the submenu, we must get the handle to the submenu. We do this by querying the first item in the system menu. Once we have that, we can append a separator and an `"About..."` menu item. Selecting this option in the application will display an informational dialog box. (See Figure 5.13.)

```
VOID AddAboutToSystemMenu(HWND hWndFrame)
{
  MENUITEM mi;
  HWND     hWndSysMenu;
  HWND     hWndSysSubMenu;
  SHORT    sMenuID;

  /* Query the menu item structure for the first menu item in the
     system menu */
```

```
    hWndSysMenu = WinWindowFromID (hWndFrame, FID_SYSMENU);
    sMenuID     = (SHORT)WinSendMsg (hWndSysMenu,
                  MM_ITEMIDFROMPOSITION,
                  MPFROMSHORT(0), MPVOID);
    WinSendMsg (hWndSysMenu, MM_QUERYITEM, MPFROMSHORT(sMenuID),
                MPFROMP(&mi));

    hWndSysSubMenu = mi.hwndSubMenu;
    mi.iPosition   = MIT_END;
    mi.afStyle     = MIS_SEPARATOR;
    mi.afAttribute = 0;
    mi.id          = -1;
    mi.hwndSubMenu = 0;
    mi.hItem       = 0;
    WinSendMsg (hWndSysSubMenu, MM_INSERTITEM, MPFROMP (&mi),
        NULL);
    mi.afStyle     = MIS_TEXT;
    mi.id          = IDM_ABOUT;
    WinSendMsg (hWndSysSubMenu, MM_INSERTITEM, MPFROMP (&mi),
      "About...");
    return;
  }
```

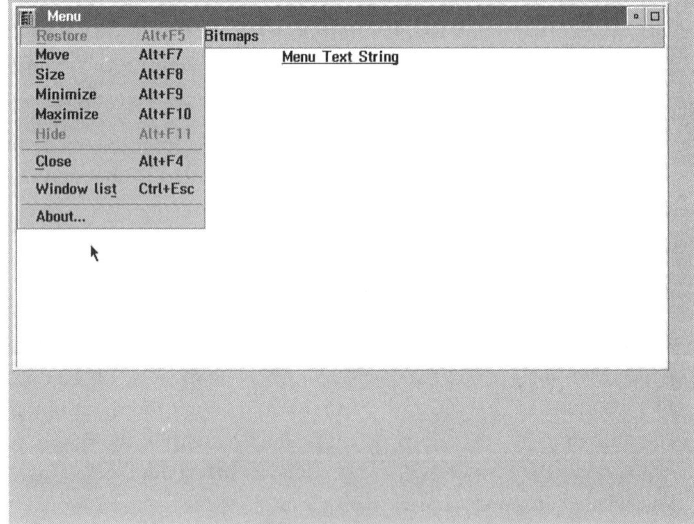

Figure 5.12.
System menu with added menu item.

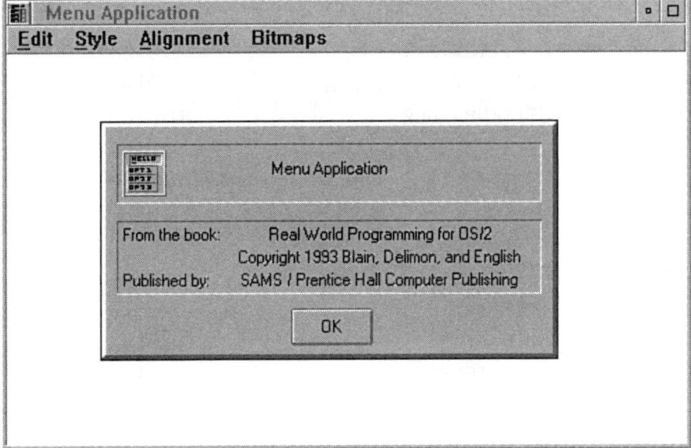

Figure 5.13.
About dialog box.

Menu Messages

Many of the common menu messages and some undocumented messages are discussed in the following section.

Menu Messages

The following is a list of the menu messages. This list is followed by a description of the more frequently used menu messages.

Message	*Value*	*Description*
`MM_INSERTITEM`	0x0180	Insert a menu item into a menu.
`MM_DELETEITEM`	0x0181	Delete a menu item from a menu.
`MM_QUERYITEM`	0x0182	Query `MENUITEM` structure of an item.
`MM_SETITEM`	0x0183	Set the `MENUITEM` structure of an item.
`MM_QUERYITEMCOUNT`	0x0184	Query number of items in menu.
`MM_STARTMENUMODE`	0x0185	Start menu selection of a menu
`MM_ENDMENUMODE`	0x0186	End all menu selections.
`MM_REMOVEITEM`	0x0188	Remove a menu item from a menu.
`MM_SELECTITEM`	0x0189	Set selection state of an item.
`MM_QUERYSELITEMID`	0x018a	Query the currently selected item `ID`.

continues

Message	*Value*	*Description*
MM_QUERYITEMTEXT	0x018b	Query the text of an item.
MM_QUERYITEMTEXTLENGTH	0x018c	Query the text length of an item.
MM_SETITEMHANDLE	0x018d	Set the bitmap or ownerdraw handle.
MM_SETITEMTEXT	0x018e	Set the text of an item.
MM_ITEMPOSITIONFROMID	0x018f	Query index of an item identifier.
MM_ITEMIDFROMPOSITION	0x0190	Query the identifier of an item.
MM_QUERYITEMATTR	0x0191	Query the attributes of an item.
MM_SETITEMATTR	0x0192	Set the attributes of an item.
MM_ISITEMVALID	0x0193	Query if item is selectable.
MM_QUERYITEMRECT	0x0194	Query bounding rectangle of an item.
MM_SUMMON	0x0196	Cause menu to be displayed.
MM_DISMISS	0x0197	Cause menu to be hidden.
MM_STARTTRACKING	0x0198	Capture mouse and begin tracking.
MM_SUMMONCHAIN	0x0199	Display menu and all owner menus.
MM_DISMISSCHAIN	0x019a	Hide menu and all owner menus.
MM_ISCHAINENABLED	0x019b	Are menu and all owners enabled.
MM_QUERYMENUSAVEDFOCUS	0x019c	Query window to receive focus at end.
MM_SETMENUSAVEDFOCUS	0x019d	Set window to receive focus at end.
MM_MATCHMNEMONIC	0x01f0	Find match of mnemonic char in menu.
MM_SETITEMCHECKMARK	0x0210	Set checkmark to display for item.

MM_INSERTITEM—0x0180

This message is sent to insert a menu item into a menu:

mp1 = pmenuitem (PMENUITEM)	Points to a MENUITEM structure for the item to insert.
mp2 = pItemText (PSTRL)	Text of menu item.

The return value specifies the index of the inserted item.

This example inserts the menu item Open File as the first item in the menu:

```
MENUITEM mi;
mi.iPosition    = 0;
mi.afStyle      = MIS_TEXT;
```

```
mi.afAttribute = 0;
mi.id          = 0x100;
mi.hwndSubMenu = NULL;
mi.hItem       = NULL;
WinSendMsg (hWndMenu, MM_INSERTITEM, &mi, "~Open File...");
```

The special identifier `MIT_END` can be used for the `iPosition` field to insert the item at the end of the list of items for the menu.

MM_DELETEITEM—0x0181

This message is sent to delete a menu item from a menu. It also destroys any submenu windows and deletes the bitmap associated with the menu item if the bitmap was not created by the application.

mp1 = SHORT1FROMMP(mp1)	Identifier of item to query.		
SHORT2FROMMP(mp1)	TRUE	Include submenus in the search.	
	FALSE	Do not include submenus in the search.	

mp2 is not used.

The return value specifies the number of items remaining in the menu.

This example deletes the menu item with identifier `0x101` from the menu and searches the submenus if it is not found in the menu:

```
WinSendMsg (hWndMenu, MM_DELETEITEM, MPFROM2SHORT(0x0101, TRUE), NULL);
```

MM_QUERYITEM—0x0182

This message is sent to retrieve the definition of a menu item. This message will not retrieve the text for `MIS_TEXT` items; use the `MM_QUERYITEMTEXT` message to retrieve the text.

mp1 = SHORT1FROMMP(mp1)		Identifier of item to delete.
SHORT2FROMMP(mp1)	TRUE	Include submenus in the search.
	FALSE	Do not include submenus in the search.
mp2 = pmenuitem (PMENUITEM)		Points to a `MENUITEM` structure to be filled in.

The return value is `TRUE` if the request is successful.

This example queries the definition for the menu item with identifier `0x101` from the menu and searches the submenus if it is not found:

```
MENUITEM mi;
WinSendMsg (hWndMenu, MM_QUERYITEM, MPFROM2SHORT(0x0101, TRUE), &mi);
```

MM_SETITEM—0x0183

This message is sent to set the definition of a menu item. The `iPosition` field of the `MENUITEM` structure is ignored because you cannot change the position of a menu item. If the submenu or bitmap handle is changing, the previous submenu window handle or bitmap handle is not deleted during the handling of this message.

Tmp1 =	SHORT1FROMMP(mp1)		Is reserved and set to zero.
	SHORT2FROMMP(mp1)	TRUE	Include submenus in the search.
		FALSE	Do not include submenus in the search.
mp2 =	pmenuitem (PMENUITEM)		Points to a MENUITEM structure for the item to set.

The return value is TRUE if the request is successful.

This example queries the current item definition for the menu with identifier 0x101 and changes the menu identifier to 0x202:

```
MENUITEM mi;
WinSendMsg (hWndMenu, MM_QUERYITEM, MPFROM2SHORT(0x0101, TRUE), &mi);
mi.id = 0x202;
WinSendMsg (hWndMenu, MM_SETITEM, MPFROM2SHORT(0,TRUE), &mi);
```

MM_QUERYITEMCOUNT—0x0184

This message is sent to query the number of items in the menu.

mp1 is not used.
mp2 is not used.

The return value is the number of items in the menu.

This example queries the number of items in the menu:

```
USHORT usCount = WinSendMsg (hWndMenu, MM_QUERYITEMCOUNT, 0, 0);
```

MM_STARTMENUMODE—0x0185

This message is sent to either the system menu (FID_SYSMENU) or actionbar menu (FID_MENU) when either the SC_SYSMENU or SC_APPMENU menu is summoned from the WM_SYSCOMMAND message. This message is ignored for pop-up menu windows. This message is generated when the system menu or application menu is activated by pressing and releasing the ALT key in an application window. It causes the submenu of the system menu or the actionbar menu to become active.

mp1 =	SHORT1FROMMP(mp1)	TRUE	Show the submenu of the first item.
		FALSE	Do not show the submenu of the first item.
	SHORT2FROMMP(mp1)	TRUE	Resume the user interaction of the currently active menu.
		FALSE	Resume the user interaction from the actionbar.

mp2 is not used.

The return value is TRUE if the request is successful.

When the window has a system menu and the ALT key is pressed and released, the following message is sent to the system menu window:

```
WinSendMSg (hWndSysMenu, MM_STARTMENUMODE, MPFROM2SHORT(TRUE, FALSE), 0);
```

If the ALT key is pressed and the window does not have a system menu but it does have an actionbar menu, the following message is sent to actionbar menu window:

```
WinSendMsg (hWndMenu, MM_STARTMENUMODE, MPFROM2SHORT(FALSE, FALSE), 0);
```

This example will cause the actionbar menu to become active and the first menu item to be selected (if the first item has a submenu, the submenu will be displayed):

```
WinSendMsg (hWndMenu, MM_STARTMENUMODE, MPFROM2SHORT(TRUE, FALSE), 0);
```

MM_ENDMENUMODE—0x0186

This message is sent to a menu window to terminate the menu selection. When the menu window receives this message, it sends the undocumented message MM_DISMISSCHAIN (0x019a) to the menu window, which causes the menu and all displayed submenus to be dismissed.

mp1 = SHORT1FROMMP(mp1)	TRUE	Dismiss the submenu window.
	FALSE	Do not dismiss the submenu window.

mp2 is not used.

The return value is zero.

This example uses the MM_ENDMENUMODE message to close the current menu processing:

```
WinSendMsg (hWndMenu, MM_ENDMENUMODE, MPFROMSHORT(TRUE), 0);
```

MM_REMOVEITEM—0x0188

This message is sent to remove a menu item from a menu. In contrast to the MM_DELETEITEM message, this message does not destroy any submenus or delete any bitmaps associated with the menu item.

mp1 = SHORT1FROMMP(mp1)		Identifier of item to remove.
SHORT2FROMMP(mp1)	TRUE	Include submenus in the search.
	FALSE	Do not include submenus in the search.

mp2 is not used.

The return value specifies the number of items remaining in the menu.

This example removes the menu item with identifier 0x101 from the menu and searches the submenus if it is not found in the menu:

```
WinSendMsg (hWndMenu, MM_REMOVEITEM, MPFROM2SHORT(0x0101, TRUE), NULL);
```

MM_SELECTITEM—0x0189

This message is sent to set the selection state of a menu item. If the item being selected is in a submenu that is not currently displayed, then the menu is summoned and displayed. If the item selected is in a submenu, the item is selected and the selection state of the menu owning the submenu is also set. This process continues up the menu hierarchy until the top-level menu is reached.

mp1 - SHORT1FROMMP(mp1)	MIT_NONE	Deselect all items in the menu.
	other	Identifier of item to select.
SHORT2FROMMP(mp1)	TRUE	Include submenus in the search.
	FALSE	Do not include submenus in the search.
mp2 - SHORT1FROMMP(mp2)		Reserved and set to zero.
SHORT2FROMMP(mp2)	TRUE	Dismiss the menu and post WM_COMMAND, WM_SYSCOMMAND, or WM_HELP message.
	FALSE	Do not dismiss the menu.

The return value is TRUE if the selection was made or MIT_NONE was specified. The return value is FALSE if the item is not selectable, the item was deselected, or MIT_NONE was not specified.

This example uses the MM_SELECTITEM message to select the menu item with identifier 0x302 and searches the submenus for the item, but does not dismiss the menu chain:

```
WinSendMsg (hWndMenu, MM_SELECTITEM, MPFROM2SHORT(0x302,TRUE),
    MPFROM2SHORT(0,FALSE));
```

MM_QUERYSELITEMID—0x018a

This message is sent to retrieve the identifier of the selected menu item.

mp1 = SHORT1FROMMP(mp1)		Reserved and set to zero.
SHORT2FROMMP(mp1)	TRUE	Find the selected item in the last submenu summoned.
	FALSE	Find the selected item in the menu specified.

mp2 is not used.

The return value is MIT_NONE if no menu item is specified or the identifier of the currently selected menu item.

This example retrieves the identifier of the selected item in the menu recursing the submenus to find the last submenu summoned:

```
SHORT sID = WinSendMsg (hWndMenu, MM_QUERYSELITEMID,
     MPFROM2SHORT(0,TRUE), 0);
```

MM_QUERYITEMTEXT—0x018b

This message is sent to retrieve the text for a specified menu item. This message only applies to menu items with the MIS_TEXT style. The length of the text to be copied can be queried with the MM_QUERYITEMTEXTLENGTH message. Only the specified menu is searched for the item and no submenus are searched.

mp1 = SHORT1FROMMP(mp1)	Identifier of item to query the text.
SHORT2FROMMP(mp2)	Maximum number of bytes to copy (includes the null termination character).
mp2 = pItemtext (PSTRL)	Pointer to buffer to copy text.

The return value is the length of the string copied to pItemText.

This example queries the text for the menu item with identifier 0x201:

```
CHAR szBuffer[80];
WinSendMsg (hWndMenu, MM_QUERYITEMTEXT,
    MPFROM2SHORT(0x201,sizeof(szBuffer)), szBuffer);
```

MM_QUERYITEMTEXTLENGTH—0x018c

This message is sent to retrieve the text length for a specified menu item. This message only applies to menu items with the MIS_TEXT style. Only the specified menu is searched for the item and no submenus are searched.

mp1 = Identifier of item to query.
mp2 is not used.

The return value is the length of the string.

This example queries the length of the text for the menu item with identifier 0x201:

```
SHORT sLen = WinSendMsg (hWndMenu, MM_QUERYITEMTEXTLENGTH,
   MPFROMSHORT(0x201), 0);
```

MM_SETITEMHANDLE—0x018d

This message is sent to change either the bitmap handle or owner draw handle for a specified menu item. This message only applies to menu items with the MIS_BITMAP or MIS_OWNERDRAW style.

mp1 = SHORT1FROMMP(mp1)	Identifier of item to query.
mp2 = Item handle.	

The return value is TRUE if the request is successful.

This example changes the bitmap handle of an MIS_BITMAP menu item with identifier 0x201;

```
HBITMAP hNewBitmap = GpiLoadBitmap (hPS, 0, IDB_NEWBITMAP, 0, 0);
WinSendMsg (hWnd, MM_SETITEMHANDLE, MPFROMSHORT(0x201), hNewBitmap);
```

MM_SETITEMTEXT—0x018e

This message is sent to change the text of a menu item for a specified menu item. This message only applies to menu items with the `MIS_TEXT` style.

`mp1 = SHORT1FROMMP(mp1)`	Identifier of item to query.
`mp2 = (PSTRL)`	Points to string.

The return value is `TRUE` if the request is successful.

This example changes the text of a `MIS_TEXT` menu item with identifier `0x201`:

```
WinSendMsg (hWnd, MM_SETITEMTEXT, MPFROMSHORT(0x201), "~Open File");
```

MM_ITEMPOSITIONFROMID—0x018f

This message is sent to retrieve the position of a menu item based on its identifier. The position returned is the menu item's position in the menu or submenu in which it was found.

`mp1 = SHORT1FROMMP(mp1)`		Identifier of item.
`SHORT2FROMMP(mp1)`	`TRUE`	Include submenus in the search to find the item.
	`FALSE`	Do not search submenus to find the item.

`mp2` is not used.

The return value is the zero-based index of the menu item if it is found or `MIT_NONE` if it is not found.

This example searches for the index of a menu item with identifier `0x201` and does not search submenus for the item:

```
SHORT sIndex = WinSendMsg (hWndMenu, MM_ITEMPOSITIONFROMID,
MPFROM2SHORT (0x201, FALSE), 0);
```

MM_ITEMIDFROMPOSITION—0x0190

This message is sent to retrieve the identifier of a menu item based on its position in the menu. This message will only search the menu that is specified.

`mp1 = SHORT1FROMMP(mp1)`	Position of item to find.
`SHORT2FROMMP(mp1)`	Reserved and set to zero.

`mp2` is not used.

The return value is the identifier of specified item or `MIT_NONE` if it was not found.

This example searches for the identifier of the menu item at position 2:

```
SHORT sID = WinSendMsg (hWndMenu, MM_ITEMIDFROMPOSITION,
MPFROM2SHORT (2, 0), 0);
```

MM_QUERYITEMATTR—0x0191

This message is sent to retrieve the current attributes of a menu item. The attributes returned are the current state values of the menu item ANDed with the attribute mask specified in mp2. It does not change any of the attributes of the menu item.

mp1 = SHORT1FROMMP(mp1)		Identifier of item to query.
SHORT2FROMMP(mp1)	TRUE	Include submenus in the search to find the item.
	FALSE	Do not search submenus to find the item.

mp2 = Requested attributes mask.

The return value is the current state of the attributes requested.

This example queries the attributes of the menu item with identifier 0x201 and does not search submenus. We are only interested in the MIA_CHECKED and MIA_DISABLED attributes:

```
USHORT usAttrs = WinSendMsg (hWndMenu, MM_QUERYITEMATTR,
   MPFROM2SHORT (0x201, FALSE), MIA_CHECKED ¦ MIA_DISABLED);
```

MM_SETITEMATTR—0x0192

This message is sent to set the current attributes of a menu item. Only those attributes specified by the attributes mask are modified by this message.

mp1 = SHORT1FROMMP(mp1)		Identifier of item to set.
SHORT2FROMMP(mp1)	TRUE	Include submenus in the search to find the item.
	FALSE	Do not search submenus to find the item.
mp2 = SHORT1FROMMP(mp2)		Attributes mask.
SHORT2FROMMP(mp2)		Attribute flags.

The return value is TRUE if the attributes were successfully modified.

This example sets the MIA_CHECKED flag of the menu item with identifier 0x201:

```
WinSendMsg (hWndMenu, MM_SETITEMATTR, MPFROM2SHORT(0x201, TRUE),
     MPFROM2SHORT(MIA_CHECKED,MIA_CHECKED));
```

MM_SETITEMCHECKMARK—0x0210 (UNDOCUMENTED MESSAGE)

This message is sent to set the checkmark bitmap that is displayed for a menu item when it is in the checked or unchecked state. If a bitmap is not specified for one of the states, the system default bitmap is used.

mp1 = MPFROM2SHORT (menuitemID,bchecked)

menuitemID		ID of the menu item to set.
bchecked	TRUE	Bitmap is for the checked state.
	FALSE	Bitmap is for the unchecked state.

mp2 = Bitmap handle.

The return value is TRUE if the request is successful.

This example sets the checkmark for both the unchecked and checked state of the menu item with identifier 0x201:

```
WinSendMsg (hWndMenu, MM_SETITEMCHECKMARK,
     MPFROM2SHORT (0x201,FALSE), hbmUnchecked);
WinSendMsg (hWndMenu, MM_SETITEMCHECKMARK,
     MPFROM2SHORT (0x201,TRUE), hbmChecked);
```

MM_MATCHMNEMONIC—0x01f0 (UNDOCUMENTED MESSAGE)

This message is sent within the menu code when the WM_CHAR message is being processed and the menu code is trying to find a mnemonic match for the character pressed. This message is not sent to the owner window, so you must subclass the menu window in order to receive this message.

mp1 = SHORT1FROMMP(mp1)	Character to match.
SHORT2FROMMP(mp1)	Number of submenu levels to search. 0 = none. 1 = top-level (this menu). 2 = top+first submenu. 3 = top+first 2 submenus (and so on). -1 = all.

mp2 = Pointer to hwnd of menu where match found.

The return value specifies both the index of the item in the menu that matched and the level of the match:

```
MRFROM2SHORT(hwndmenu,index)
```

In addition, *mp2 is updated to contain the window handle of the menu that contained the mnemonic.

Menu Notification Messages

The following is a list of the more important menu notification messages. This list is followed by a description on the use of the undocumented menu notification messages.

Message	*Value*	*Description*
WM_COMMAND	0x0020	Notification of menu selection.
WM_SYSCOMMAND	0x0021	Notification of system menu selection.
WM_HELP	0x0022	Notification of help item selection.
WM_INITMENU	0x0033	Menu is about to become active.

WM_MENUSELECT	0x0034	Menu item has been highlighted.
WM_MENUEND	0x0035	Menu is about to be hidden.
WM_DRAWITEM	0x0036	Draw the ownerdraw menu item.
WM_MEASUREITEM	0x0037	Determine the height of menu item.
WM_CONTROLHEAP	0x0039	Retrieve heaphandle for menu data.
WM_MENUCHAR	0x003f	Non-mnemonic menu char pressed.
WM_NEXTMENU	0x004e	Determine next menu to display.
MM_PORTHOLEINIT	0x01fb	Submenu about to be displayed.
WM_MENUHELP	0x0433	Help hook about to be called.

WM_MENUCHAR—0x003f (UNDOCUMENTED MESSAGE)

This message is sent from the menu code to its owner when the WM_CHAR message is being processed and the alphanumeric key pressed does not match any of the mnemonics in the displayed menu. It allows the application to specify which menu item should be selected in this case.

mp1 = Window handle of menu currently displayed
mp2 = SHORT1FROMMP(mp2) Character.
SHORT2FROMMP(mp2) Unused.

The return value specifies how PM should deal with this invalid character:

MRFROM2SHORT(0,0)	Character is invalid (beep).
MRFROM2SHORT(0,1)	Cancel the menu.
MRFROM2SHORT(position,2)	Select the menu item specified by position.

Any other return code means to ignore the character and do nothing. Normally, this message is passed to WinDefWindowProc, which returns 0L.

MM_PORTHOLEINIT—0x01fb (UNDOCUMENTED MESSAGE)

This message is sent from the menu code to its owner just prior to summoning a pop-up menu. Upon return from the processing of this message, PM will again retrieve the submenu handle for the selected item. This allows an application to replace the submenu just prior to the submenu being displayed.

mp1 = SHORT1FROMMP (mp1) Position of submenu in the menu.
SHORT2FROMMP (mp1) Attribute of the menu item.
mp2 = Menu handle containing the item.

The return code is ignored for this message.

Chapter 6

Presentation Spaces and Drawing

Introduction of GPI

When programming for the PC first began, most graphics libraries were homegrown. Later, compilers added libraries of drawing functions. As useful as these were, they were somewhat limited in scope and in availability for various devices. Still later, with the development of operating systems that supplied graphical user interfaces, drawing functions were made a part of the operating system.

OS/2 2.11 provides a rich set of functions, called drawing primitives, which may be used to render text and graphics on various devices. The drawing primitives are part of the device independent functions in GPI (Graphics Programming Interface). GPI defines a high-level graphics programming library that an application can code to. In other words, the programmer no longer must be concerned with setting specific pixels on specific devices, rounding off errors, and other such matters; they are built into the operating system.

The GPI programming model allows applications to use its 200-plus functions to output text, draw circles, lines, and arcs on any device. The functions of the library exist in the system DLL,

PMGPI. GPI is actually a thin layer on top of the OS/2 graphics engine. The graphics engine is the component that contains the algorithms to render filled areas, lines, and arcs and to perform clipping. Between the graphics engine and the hardware exists another component called a presentation driver. Presentation drivers are written to support an API called by the graphics engine. It is this driver's job to communicate the drawing requests to the hardware in a form that it can understand. When the presentation driver receives a call from the graphics engine, that driver may take one of three actions. It may call the hardware device directly, if it supports the primitive. It may further break the call into primitives that the device can understand, or it may pass the call back to the graphics engine to be broken down into yet simpler primitives.

The relationships among an application, the PMGPI DLL, the graphics engine, and presentation drivers are shown in Figure 6.1.

Figure 6.1.
Relationship of PMGPI, graphics engine, presentation drivers, and hardware.

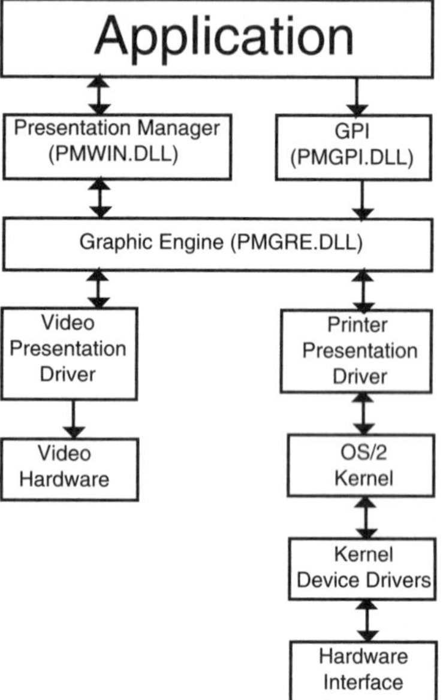

Presentation Spaces (PS)

An application interacts with GPI through a presentation space handle, or PS handle. This PS handle is device-independent; that is, no physical device, not even the screen, is associated with its operation. It is a logical or virtual drawing space. The handle is a 32-bit value that represents an internal data structure that defines the attributes applied to graphics primitives. Attributes are settings that control the colors and styles used when drawing GPI figures. For example, the fill color and line styles are set as attributes. All GPI functions require a PS handle. Associated with a device-independent PS is a device-specific 32-bit context handle. Device contexts (DCs) are the link between GPI and the physical device it represents. It is the device context that can be queried for device specific values such as resolution, size, and capabilities. The resolution, size, and so forth are determined by the specific physical characteristics of a device.

Types of Presentation Spaces

A PS may be retrieved or created in several ways. The easiest way is by calling the `WinBeginPaint` or `WinGetPS` functions. Although both return a PS handle, they are designed to be called at different times during program execution. When portions of your application's drawing area become invalid (require repainting), PM will place a `WM_PAINT` message in your application's queue. Calling `WinBeginPaint` in response to the paint message returns a PS handle that is clipped to the region that needs to be updated. This means that any drawing your application does will affect only the portion of the window that actually requires updating. For example, if a pop-up window from another application is moved over your window and then moved away, only a small portion of your window must be redrawn. On the other hand, when you call `WinGetPS`, the PS that you receive has no clipping region defined and enables you to draw on the entire client area.

Three types of PS handles exist, cached micro, micro, and normal. The cached micro PS offers the best performance and uses the least system resources of the three. It is drawn from a set of PS handles that are maintained by the window manager (PMWIN). These PS handles are available for short-term application use and may be used only on the display device. Retained graphics may not be used in a cached micro PS. Retained graphics is a type of graphic output. Primitives are stored in a segment that can be edited. In nonretained output, after a function is called, it is lost and must be called again to re-create the output.

A cached micro PS may be "checked out" by calling the `WinGetPS`, `WinGetScreenPS`, or `WinBeginPaint` functions. Before returning to the application, the attributes are reset to the system default values. After use, the PS is returned to the window manager by calling the `WinReleasePS` or `WinEndPaint` functions. Cached micro presentation spaces are best suited to windows that are updated frequently and don't require a large number of customized attributes. A good example would be a control window that updates a rectangle to indicate percentage of completion on an operation when a notification message is received. This is something like the thermometer control that we will show you how to build later in this chapter.

Unlike the cached micro PS handle, a micro PS handle is not automatically associated with the display device. You must associate it with a device context from a display window, memory, or printer. This enables you to print or create bitmaps in memory in addition to drawing directly to a window. When associated with a device, a micro PS may not be reassociated with any other device-context. Like the cached micro PS, it does not support retained graphics. A micro PS is created by calling the `GpiCreatePS` function. One of the parameters to the function is a device-context handle with which to associate the created PS. For display devices, the DC handle for the window may be retrieved by calling the `WinOpenWindowDC` function. The `WinOpenWindowDC`

hPS WinBeginPaint (hWnd, hPS, pRectl)

HWND	hWnd	Window handle for which to retrieve the cached micro PS handle.
HPS	hPS	Use NULLHANDLE.
PRECTL	pRect	Pointer to a RECTL structure that will contain the smallest bounding rectangle that contains the update region. Values are always in window coordinates.
HPS	hPS	If successful, the return value will be a PS that has been associated with the window device context. NULL is returned if a failure occurs. The returned PS is first reset to the default values, and then the update region is set as the clipping region in the PS.

Micro or Normal Presentation Spaces

hPS GpiCreatePS (hAB, hDC, pSizel, lOptions)

HAB	hAB	Handle to anchor block returned from the WinInitialize function.	
HDC	hDC	Device-context handle to associate with the PS to be created. If lOptions contains the GPIT_MICRO or GPI_ASSOC flags, the DC is required.	
PSIZEL	pSizel	Pointer to a SIZEL structure that defines the size of the created PS's page. If an hDC value is supplied, the page size is automatically set based on the dimensions of the device.	
LONG	lOptions	Bit flags used to define the units, format, type, and mode of the created PS.	
Units		Defines the meaning of each unit in a PS page:	
	PU_PELS		One unit equals 1 pel.
	PU_LOMETRIC		One unit equals .1 mm.
	PU_HIMETRIC		One unit equals .01 mm.
	PU_LOENGLISH		One unit equals .01 inches.
	PU_HIENGLISH		One unit equals .001 inches.
	PU_TWIPS		One unit equals 1/1440 inch.
	PU_ARBITRAY		Application defined.
Format		Format to be used for storing coordinates internally:	
	GPIF_LONG		Coordinates are stored as 4-byte integers.
	GPIF_SHORT		Coordinates are stored as 2-byte integers.
	GPIF_DEFAULT		Equivalent to GPIF_LONG.
Type		Presentation space type to create:	
	GPIT_MICRO		A micro PS is created. The GPIA_ASSOC flag must be set, and the hDC parameter must contain a device context with which to associate the created PS.

	GPIT_NORMAL	A normal PS is created.
Mode		Association action to be taken:
	GPIA_ASSOC	Associate the created PS with the supplied device context. hDC must contain a valid device context.
	GPIA_NOASSOC	Do not associate the created PS with a device context.

hPS WinBeginPaint (hWnd, hPS, pRectl)

HWND	hWnd	Window handle to retrieve the micro or normal PS handle for.
HPS	hPS	The PS handle returned from GpiCreatePS. NULLHANDLE may be used to retrieve a micro cached PS.
PRECTL	pRect	Pointer to a RECTL structure that will upon return contain the smallest bounding rectangle that contains the update region. Values are always in window coordinates.

If the function was successful and a presentation space was supplied as the second parameter, the return value will be the supplied PS. If NULLHANDLE was passed as the second parameter, the return value will be a micro cached PS. In either case, the current update region set as the clipping region is the returned PS.

GpiAssociate (hPS, hDC)

HPS	hPS	The PS handle to reassociate.
HDC	hDC	The device context to associate the hPS with. Note that in OS/2 2.0, you may not directly associate a PS from one DC to another. The GpiAssociate function must be called two times, first with NULLHANDLE as the second parameter, and second with the DC handle to associate the presentation space with. Attributes in the PS are reset to the defaults.

GpiDestroyPS (hPS)

HPS	hPS	The PS handle to be destroyed. It must first be disassociated from the current PS by calling the GpiAssociate function with a NULL hDC.

Device Contexts

As mentioned previously, the device context is the link between a PS and the physical device it represents. Like presentation spaces, a device context is identified by a handle. Using this handle, the resolution, device type, and capabilities of the physical hardware can be retrieved. An entire

API (called Device functions or DEV for short) is devoted to interacting with device contexts. We will look at these functions shortly, but first we examine window device-context handles.

Device contexts can be retrieved or created in several ways. For windows, a DC is created by calling the `WinOpenWindowDC` function and passing it the handle of the window for which a device-context handle is to be opened. If successful, the device-context handle returned is constant for the life of the window regardless of the type of PS used in that window. There is no equivalent `WinCloseWindowDC` function to free the DC handle when it is no longer required. It will be freed automatically when the window is destroyed. `WinOpenWindowDC` should be called only once for a given window; however, if you lose track of the window DC handle, you can use the `WinQueryWindowDC` function after a DC has been opened. In fact, you can create your own function called `WinGetDC`, which does all the work for you.

For example, observe the following:

```
HDC APIENTRY WinGetDC(HWND hWnd)
{
   hDC hDC
   if (!(hDC = WinQueryWindowDC(hWnd)))
      hDC = WinOpenWindowDC(hWnd);
   return (hDC);
}
```

If the DC for the window has already been opened, the `WinQueryWindowDC` will return the DC; otherwise, a DC is opened for this window. Using this function, you never need to worry about the state of the window device context.

For output devices other than a window, device contexts must be created by using one of the functions from the device API. The `DevOpenDC` function will create device contexts for use with metafiles, bitmap drawing, and device output. A device context should be opened when output is intended for a device other than a window. The `DevOpenDC` function takes the following parameters:

`DevOpenDC (hAB,lType,pszToken,lCount,pdod,hDC)`

HAB	hAB	Handle to anchor block returned from the `WinInitialize` function.
LONG	Type	This parameter identifies the type of device context to be created.
	OD_MEMORY	Creates a device context in which a bitmap may be set to draw "off screen" and then blt'd to a window or print device.
	OD_METAFILE	Creates a device context that can be used to create memory or disk metafiles.

	OD_METAFILE_NOQUERY	Creates a device context that can be used to create memory or disk metafiles, but that cannot be used for querying attributes.
	OD_QUEUED	Creates a device context for a printer or plotter that will use the print spooler to queue and send print jobs to physical print device.
	OD_DIRECT	Creates a device context that will output directly to a physical port. This option is a holdover from previous versions of OS/2 and should not be used by applications when performing normal print operations.
	OD_INFO	Creates a device context that may be queried for device-specific information and drawn into, but that will cause no output to occur. This DC type should be created when you need to know device information but are not currently printing.
PSZ	pszToken	Pointer to a null-terminated string that is an entry in an initialization file. Applications will generally use "*" to indicate that initialization data should be taken from the DEVOPENDATA passed to the function.
LONG	lCount	A long that identifies the number of parameters initialized in the DEVOPENDATA structure.
PDEVOPENDATA	pdod	Pointer to a DEVOPENDATA structure that provides the information required to create the DC.
HDC	hDC	A device-context handle with which to make the new device context compatible. If NULLHANDLE is used, compatibility with the display device is assumed.

If successful, the DevOpenDC function will return a device-context handle that may then be associated with a PS. A device context must be associated or linked with a PS before output can occur on that device. Chapter 13, "Printing," will look in depth at information and print device contexts.

Device Capabilities

After you have a device context, you can query the device to determine its capabilities by using the DevQueryCaps function. You may query one or all the values from the device including device resolution, color support, I/O support, and graphics capabilities. If you are using a feature of GPI not supported on all devices, utilize the DevQueryCaps function to determine whether the device supports it. You can also use this function to determine whether the device has built-in support for something PM is handling. For example, the following code determines whether the device can directly support wide lines outside a path:

```
DevQueryCaps (hDC,CAPS_ADDITIONAL_GRAPHICS,1,lAddGraphics);
if (lAddGraphic & CAPS_COSMETIC_WIDELINE_SUPPORT)
    bUsePaths = FALSE;
```

Coordinates

A coordinate system is a method of positioning items in an n-dimensional space. GPI coordinates are pairs of longs that define a position in a two-dimensional drawing space. An X value defines a position along the horizontal axis, and a Y value defines a position along the vertical axis. The point where the X- and Y-axes intersect defines the origin. The default origin (0,0) for a window PS is in the lower-left corner of the window, with X values increasing as you move to the right and Y values increasing as you move toward the top of the screen. In each PS, a current coordinate position is maintained. Many GPI primitives use the current position as the location to begin drawing from. The current position may be set or retrieved by using GpiMove and GpiQueryCurrentPosition, respectively. In some cases, GPI primitives update the current position. For example, GpiPartialArc, a function we use later in this chapter, updates the current position to the last point drawn in the arc.

Default Presentation Space Attributes

When a PS is created, associated with a new device context, or when a cached micro PS is retrieved, the attributes are set to the default system values. These defaults define such things as the current position, clipping paths, and the colors used when filling and outlining boxes and ellipses. The default attributes may also be reset in a PS by calling the GpiReset function. Table 6.1, found later in this chapter, contains the default PS attributes. The term default may be misleading here because PM enables you to change the default attributes for a PS by calling the GpiSetDefAttrs function. Because this function requires a handle to a PS, the default may be changed only for an existing PS, not for those created or retrieved in the future. Although you may change the default fill color from white to blue in the PS you created for your application, you cannot change the default fill color for all future PSs created by your process. Generally, changing the default attributes in a PS is not recommended even if your application modifies every attribute. All the potential benefits gained by changing these values is lost when they are reset with the GpiResetPS or GpiAssociate functions. A more efficient method is to maintain and set attributes as bundles.

BUNDLES

You are probably familiar with GPI "set" functions that modify attributes in a PS. For example, GpiSetBackColor will modify the background color used for fills, lines, and text. The most powerful function in the GPI attribute-setting arsenal, however, is also probably the one most overlooked. The GpiSetAttrs function enables you to set or reset single or multiple values in a bundle with a single function call. A bundle is a data structure that your application can use to set, query, and store drawing attributes. PM defines a set of five bundle structures. These define attributes that affect drawing across drawing primitives. They are as follows:

Type	*GPI Functions Affected*
AREA	The area bundle defines the current fill, color, and pattern used in functions such as GpiBox.
CHARACTER	The character bundle defines character attributes that affect the size, color, angle, and type of font used when text is output through functions such as GpiCharString.
IMAGE	The image bundle defines the color and mix mode used in monochrome bitmaps output by functions such as GpiBitBlt.
LINE	The line bundle defines the style and color of lines drawn as the outline of filled objects by functions such as GpiBox. Functions such as GpiPartialArc that draw lines but do not fill areas also use attributes in the line bundle.
MARKER	The marker bundle defines the color and style used when drawing markers with such functions as GpiPolyMarker.

The GpiSetAttrs function takes a pointer to a bundle structure that has been initialized by the caller. Based on the flags set, you can set one or all the values in a PS to a new value or to their defaults. The GpiSetAttrs function is defined as follows:

GpiSetAttrs (hPS, lPrimType, ulAttrMask, ulDefMask, pBundle)

HPS	hPS	Handle of the PS in which to change the attribute.
LONG	lPrimType	Identifies the bundle type to modify. It must be one of the following: PRIM_AREA PRIM_CHAR PRIM_IMAGE PRIM_LINE PRIM_MARKER

ULONG	ulAttrMask	Contains one or more flag values that indicate which attributes to set. The appropriate fields in the bundle structure must be initialized accordingly.
ULONG	ulDefMask	Contains one or more flags that indicate which attributes to reset to their default values. The corresponding flag must be set in the ulAttrMask.
PBUNDLE	pBundle	Pointer to a bundle of lPrimType.

The flags in the ulAttrMask indicate which fields have been initialized in the bundle and should be changed in the PS. To set the default value, you must set the flag of the desired attribute in both the ulAttrMask and ulDefMask parameters. The field in the bundle need not be initialized because it is ignored when the default is reset. The default may not be set by passing the default parameter in the field of the bundle. For example, assuming pAB is a pointer to an area bundle, the correct way to reset the area bundle background color is as follows:

```
GpiSetAttrs(hPS,PRIM_AREA,ABB_BACK_COLOR,ABB_BACK_COLOR,pAB);
```

Although the two following lines look good, they won't work as intended:

```
pAB->lBackColor = CLR_DEFAULT;
GpiSetAttrs(hPS,PRIM_AREA,ABB_BACK_COLOR,0,pAB);
```

All bundle types have four attributes in common: each has a foreground and background color, and each has a foreground and background mix mode. The foreground color defines the color used when drawing the primary or foreground of the primitive. What actually comprises the foreground varies from bundle to bundle, but it is best described as the main component of the primitive. For example, the foreground color in the character bundle defines the color of the characters that are output. For pattern sets, the foreground color is the color of the pattern lines. The background color defines how the remainder of the primitive is colored. In the character bundle, the background color is used to fill the space behind the characters. For pattern sets, the space between the actual pattern is defined by the background color. The mix mode for both foreground and background defines how their colors are combined with the color of the destination. The foreground mix mode may be set to one of 16 values, including overpaint and XOR. The background mix may be set to only one of four values.

Four functions exist for setting one of the previous four values in all bundles simultaneously, the GpiSetColor, GpiSetBkColor, GpiSetMix, and GpiSetBackMix. When an attribute must be set in all bundles, it is more efficient to set it by using one of the generic functions such as GpiSetColor. Rarely are all foreground colors set to the same value. In cases when they are, the GpiSetAttrs function should be used in place of a more global function. For example, assuming all variables are defined and initialized, the following will work:

```
GpiSetColor (hPS,CLR_RED);
GpiBox(hPS,DRO_FILL,ptl1,0,0);
GpiSetColor (hPS,CLR_BLUE);
GpiBox(hPS,DRO_FILL,ptl2,0,0);
```

The GpiBox function will use only the foreground color set in the area bundle (assuming a solid pattern fill). The foreground color set in the other four bundles are unused. Using the GpiSetAttrs function is much more efficient:

```
ab.lColor = CLR_RED;
GpiSetAttrs(hPS,PRIM_AREA,ABB_COLOR,0,pAB);
GpiBox(hPS,DRO_FILL,ptl1,0,0);
ab.lColor = CLR_BLUE;
GpiSetAttrs(hPS,PRIM_AREA,ABB_COLOR,0,pAB);
GpiBox(hPS,DRO_FILL,ptl2,0,0);
```

With the exception of the image bundle, the four remaining bundles have attributes other than color and mix mode that may be modified. We will examine the additional fields in those bundles.

AREA BUNDLE

The area bundle defines the color and pattern for filled areas. The area may be a simple rectangle or a complex polygon. When wide lines are drawn, they are filled with the current area bundle attributes. The area bundle has three additional fields that may be set to define the fill area.

usSet

The usSet parameter enables you to set a local identifier for a bitmap that will be used in the fill area. Monochrome bitmaps will use the foreground area bundle color for the foreground (black bits) of the bitmap. The background color will be used for the background (white bits) of the bitmap. Color bitmaps are not affected by the area bundle foreground and background colors.

usSymbol

The usSymbol parameter is used to specify a solid fill or one of the PM-defined hatch patterns for the fill area. Hatch patterns are intended to be a device-independent nonsolid fill type. Although the display and some printers may have the capacity to render bitmaps, plotters do not. Hatch patterns are implemented by all devices, including plotters. The patterns consist of horizontal, diagonal, and cross hatched lines of varying densities.

ptlRefPoint

The ptlRefPoint is an X and Y location that a bitmap or pattern fill is aligned to within the PS. It may be thought of as the point that bitmaps and patterns are "tiled" around. The entire area is filled regardless of the point supplied, even if that point is outside the fill area. The default pattern reference point is 0,0. If the reference point is modified, it should be modified for all subsequent painting. Failure to do this may result in a misalignment of the pattern or bitmap in a filled area after a partial repaint of that area.

CHARBUNDLE

As mentioned previously, the foreground color in the character bundle defines the color used when filling characters, whereas the background color will fill the space behind the characters. The default background mix mode, however, is BM_LEAVEALONE, which results in no background fill. The character bundle has nine additional fields that may be set to control the font, character size, and orientation when outputting text. Chapter 7, "Creating and Manipulating PM Fonts and Text," discusses these fields in more detail:

usSet	Local identifier that represents a logical font.
usPrecision	Character mode.
sizfxCell	Defines a character cell or box used in scaling outline fonts.
ptlAngle	Point that defines a new end point of the line that determines character baseline.
ptlShear	Point that defines a new end point of the line that determines how a character box is slanted relative to the baseline.
usDirection	Flag that defines the direction characters are drawn relative to the baseline.
usTextAlign	Flag values that define how a text string is aligned relative to the current position.
fxExtra	Specifies the amount of additional space added or subtracted between characters when a text string is output.
fxBreakExtra	Specifies the amount of additional space added or subtracted to the break character. The space character is most often the break character.

LINE BUNDLE

The line bundle affects primitives that output lines or that outline a filled area. For example, the GpiBox function uses the current line bundle attributes if the DRO_OUTLINE or DRO_OUTLINEFILL fill flags are used. The DRO_OUTLINE tells the function to leave the interior of the box unchanged and to outline it with the current line bundle attributes. DRO_OUTLINEFILL causes the box to be filled with the current area bundle attributes before being outlined. When the line style is other than solid, the background color will not be used to fill the gaps in the line as expected. To change the "background" of a dashed or dotted line, you must first draw a solid line with the foreground color set to the desired background color, and then draw the dashed or dotted line. The line bundle has five additional fields that define line attributes.

fxWidth

This parameter defines the width of cosmetic lines. Cosmetic lines are those not drawn as a result of a stroked path. Only two widths are supported, normal and thick. Normal widths are one device unit, and thick widths are two device units.

lGeomWidth

This field defines the geometric width of a line. The geometric width is used by GPI when drawing a "wide line" in a stroked path. When a primitive that renders lines is drawn in a path and the path is stroked, the normal line width is converted to a wide line. The new wide line is filled as an area; in fact, it is filled with the current area bundle fill attributes. This allows wide lines to be filled with patterns and bitmaps. The width is actually one pel wider than the `lGeomWidth` value.

ulType

`ulType` defines the line style used when drawing cosmetic lines. The default type is solid; however, several dotted and dashed styles along with invisible may be selected. The invisible line style can be used to update the current position in the PS without affecting the display. For example, the `GpiPartialArc` primitive begins drawing at the current location. Setting the line type to invisible and drawing the arc will cause the current position to be updated to the last point on the arc, but no screen or printer drawing will occur. This will be demonstrated later in this chapter. Geometric lines are not affected by this value.

ulEnd

This field defines the line end style for geometric lines. This style determines whether the end of the line should be rounded, flat, or square. Cosmetic lines are not affected by this setting. Line end styles are shown later in this chapter.

ulJoin

This field determines the appearance of connected lines drawn in a path. A connected line is one in which starting and ending points of separate primitives occur at the same point. Cosmetic lines are not affected by this setting. Line join styles are also shown later in this chapter.

MARKER BUNDLE

A marker is a symbol or character that is drawn centered over a given point. PM supplies a set of default markers that are often used to mark points on a chart or graph. Included in that set are a diamond, square, dot, and various stars.

usSet

The `usSet` field contains a local identifier that represents a logical font. This allows an application to use a character from any font as a custom marker. The `usSymbol` defines the character in the font to use as the marker.

usSymbol

If the default marker set is used, this field contains the ID (identification) of one of the system-supplied markers. If a custom marker set is set, this field will contain the code point (1-255) of the character to be used as the marker. For example, you could use a capital M as a custom marker.

sizefxCell

If the logical font defined by the `usSet` field is an outline font, this parameter defines a character cell or box used in scaling the character.

Color Models

In all the bundles discussed previously, you are able to set a foreground and background color. In PM, colors may be specified in one of two methods, as a color table index that identifies an RGB value or as an RGB value directly. An RGB value is a representation of a color based on the red, green, and blue content in that color. In the default PS, a logical color table is created by PM. To reference colors from this table, you use one of the predefined `CLR_` values. This is often referred to as indexed mode. You may create your own logical color table or modify an existing one with the `GpiCreateLogColorTable` function. An existing table may be modified by querying the current color table with the `GpiQueryLogColorTable`, changing the desired values, and re-creating a new logical color table with the `GpiCreateLogColorTable`. You may also use this function to switch into RGB mode. RGB mode enables you to supply RGB color values as the color value when one is required. Switching into RGB mode can be done as follows:

```
GpiCreateLogColorTable (hPS,LCOL_RESET,LCOLF_RGB,0,0,NULL);
```

Resetting the default color table is done as follows:

```
GpiCreateLogColorTable (hPS,LCOL_RESET,LCOLF_INDRGB,0,0,NULL);
```

GPI Drawing Primitives

In the following text is a summary of some of the more important GPI drawing functions. This certainly is not an exhaustive list because OS/2 has a great many drawing functions. This list, however, will give you a good place to start learning.

`GpiBox`	Draws a rectangle or rounded rectangle from the current position to a new point supplied to the function. The figure may be filled, outlined, or both.
`GpiFullArc`	Draws an ellipse (or circle) using the current arc parameters around the current position. Arc parameters define extent in the X and Y directions and shears.
`GpiLine`	Draws a straight line from the current position to a supplied end point.

GpiPartialArc	Draws a portion of an ellipse (or circle) using the current arc parameters based around a supplied center point from the current position. Arc parameters define extent in the X and Y directions and shears. A starting angle and sweep angle define the starting and ending points of the arc.
GpiPointArc	Draws an arc from the current position through a second point to an end point using the current arc parameters.
GpiPolyFillet	Draws a curved line (fillet) as a series of connecting arcs starting at the current position based on an array of points defining straight lines. Each arc is tangent to the midpoint of the supplied line segments. The end point is the same as the last point in the array.
GpiPolyFilletSharp	Draws one or more curved lines (fillets) using a sharpness value that will cause each curve to approximate an ellipse, hyperbola, or parabola.
GpiPolyLine	Draws one or more connected straight lines from the current position.
GpiPolySpline	Draws one or more connected Bézier splines from the current position.

Of the functions listed above only GpiBox and GpiFullArc are capable of filling their interiors as well as outlining their exterior. A fill control parameter determines if the shape is filled, outlined, or both. The fill control flags for both functions are as follows:

DRO_OUTLINE	Outline the ellipse or box.
DRO_FILL	Fill the interior of the ellipse or box.
DRO_OUTLINEFILL	Outline and fill the ellipse or box.

The current area bundle attributes determine the fill for rectangles and ellipses. The cosmetic line attributes are used to draw the boundary for all line and arc primitives and to outline boxes and ellipses when the fill control flag is set to DRO_OUTLINE or DRO_OUTLINEFILL.

Drawing a Thermometer

In Chapter 12, "Dynamic Link Libraries," we will create a custom thermometer control to show the amount of memory resources being used. This is a simple illustration of a thermometer filled with an area of color that depends on a ratio that makes sense in the application. Before a thermometer control can be created, a function to draw a thermometer must be written.

Before coding can begin, we must define the appearance of the thermometer and the GPI function used to draw it. A thermometer typically has a round bulb attached to a stem with a rounded top. Because real thermometers are made of glass, they are transparent with the exception of the mercury or other liquid that fills it. In our thermometer, the mercury will rise from the bulb to the top of the stem as the application-defined ratio increases.

To maintain a 3-D look, the outline of our thermometer will be drawn in white and shades of gray. This gives the appearance of a light source in the upper-left corner of the screen. The thermometer will therefore be consistent with the other default control windows such as push buttons. The thermometer will be drawn by using two functions, `DrawThermometer` and `DrawTemperature`. The first will draw the outline, bulb fill, and highlights. The second will draw the mercury in the stem. The temperature may then be drawn independent of the thermometer. The thermometer will be drawn within the supplied rectangle. If the rectangle is enlarged, the thermometer will be scaled with it. This leaves it up to the caller to define its size and position. Figure 6.2 shows the thermometer and the GPI primitives used to create it.

Figure 6.2.
Thermometer design.

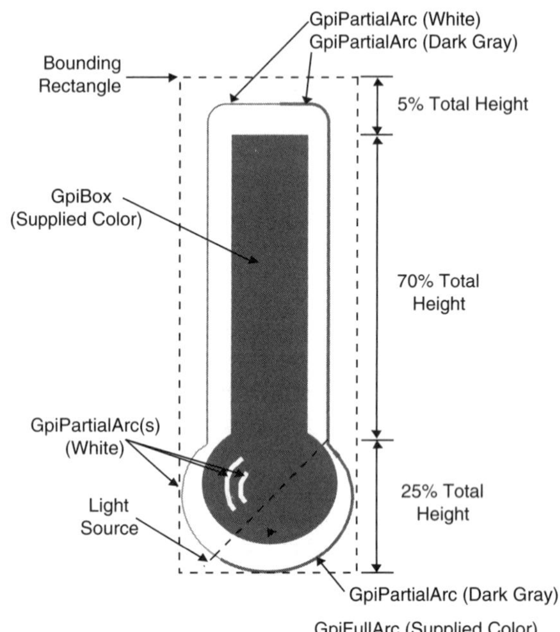

The outline could be drawn with `GpiPolyLine`. Calculating the points of the outline and the color transitions, however, would be too much trouble. The thermometer is best drawn as a series of lines and partial arcs. The bulb will be drawn first because the starting and ending point of its partial arc defines the starting location of the vertical lines that make up the stem. After some experimenting, we decided the bulb would occupy 25 percent of the bounding rectangle. The bulb rectangle is calculated, and the arc parameters are set. The arc parameters actually form a 2×2 matrix that scales and shears partial and full arcs. (See Figure 6.3.)

The `lP` parameter scales the ellipse in the X direction, whereas the `lQ` parameter scales it in the Y. The values are set to half the width and half the height of the rectangle bounding the bulb, respectively. The `lR` and `lS` parameters define shearing and are set to the default values:

```
arcparms.lP = (BulbRectl.xRight - BulbRectl.xLeft) / 2L;
arcparms.lQ = (BulbRectl.yTop - BulbRectl.yBottom) / 2L;
arcparms.lR = 0L;
arcparms.lS = 0L;
GpiSetArcParams(hPS, (PARCPARAMS)&arcparms);
```

Figure 6.3.
Arc parameters.

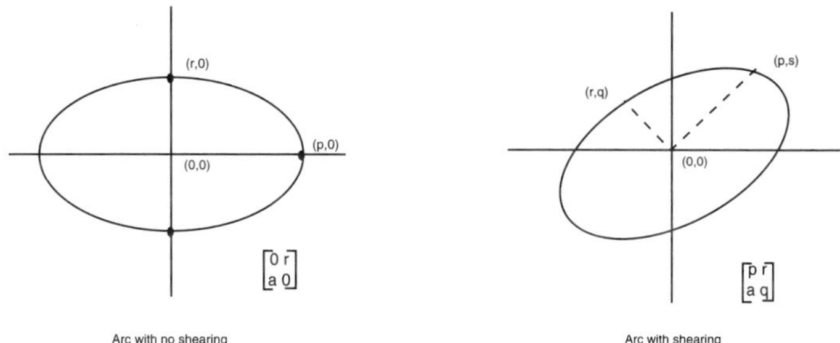

The center point of the arc is established based on the bulb rectangle and the X and Y scaling values:

```
lPtCenter.x = BulbRectl.xLeft + arcparms.lP;
lPtCenter.y = BulbRectl.yBottom + arcparms.lQ + 1;
```

The arc for the bulb must be drawn in two pieces; the highlighted side on the left will be drawn in white followed by the shaded side. The light source and the start angle for the first arc of the bulb will be at 120 degrees. The highlighted arc will continue for 90 degrees. Before the first arc can be drawn, we must establish the current position as the first point on the arc. This must be done because the `GpiPartialArc` function will draw a line from the current position to that point resulting in a stray line. To do this, set the line type to invisible and draw an arc with a start angle of 120 degrees and a sweep angle of zero:

```
fxStartAngle = MAKEFIXED(120,0);
lb.usType = LINETYPE_INVISIBLE;
GpiSetAttrs (hPS,PRIM_LINE,LBB_TYPE,0,(PBUNDLE)&lb);
GpiPartialArc(hPS,&lPtCenter,MAKEFIXED(1,0),fxStartAngle,MAKEFIXED(0,0));
GpiQueryCurrentPosition(hPS,(PPOINTL)&lStartPt);
```

After the arc is drawn, the current position is queried and retained for drawing the left side of the thermometer stem. When the current position is established, the line type is reset to solid, the color is changed to white, and the arc is drawn with a sweep angle of 90 degrees:

```
fxSweepAngle = MAKEFIXED(90,0);
lb.lColor = CLR_WHITE;
lb.usType = LINETYPE_SOLID;
GpiSetAttrs (hPS,PRIM_LINE,LBB_COLOR | LBB_TYPE,0,(PBUNDLE)&lb);
GpiPartialArc (hPS,&lPtCenter,MAKEFIXED(1,0),fxStartAngle,fxSweepAngle);
```

The current position is now the last point on the arc, so the shaded portion of the arc can be drawn without resetting the current position. After drawing the shaded portion of the bulb, the

current position is saved for drawing the right side of the stem. When the exterior of the bulb is drawn, the interior is filled. This is done now for two reasons. First, all the values needed to draw the full arc have been calculated. The center point is the same, and the X and Y arc scaling values can be reduced to leave a transparent gap between the outline and the mercury. Second, the bulb will always be drawn full regardless of the temperature:

```
arcparms.lP -= 4;
arcparms.lQ -= 4;
GpiSetArcParams(hPS, (PARCPARAMS)&arcparms);
ab.lColor = lColor;
GpiSetAttrs(hPS,PRIM_AREA,ABB_COLOR,0,(PBUNDLE)&ab);
GpiMove (hPS,&lPtCenter);
GpiFullArc(hPS,DRO_FILL,MAKEFIXED(1,0));
```

The bulb is filled by using the `GpiFullArc` function and the `DRO_FILL` flag. The ellipse will be filled with the caller-supplied color set into the area bundle. For a more 3-D effect, two reflections are drawn on the bulb. They are drawn by reducing the X and Y scaling factor and drawing a partial arc in white starting at 120 degrees and sweeping for 90 degrees.

The sides of the stem are then drawn by using the `GpiLine` function. The left side is drawn in white and the right in dark gray. After drawing the sides, the rounded top is drawn with two partial arcs as was done for the bulb. The code to draw the outline and the bulb for the thermometer will be put in the `DrawThermometer` function:

```
DrawThermometer (hPS,pRectl,lStyle,lColor,lBackColor,lPercent)
```

The `lColor` parameter will be used to fill the bulb and stem of the thermometer. The `lBackColor` parameter will be used to fill portions of the stem when `lPercent` is less than 100 percent. Finally, `lPercent` defines the amount of the stem that is filled with `lColor`. It may range from 0 to 100.

The actual drawing of the fill percentage is done in the `DrawTemperature` function. It takes a similar set of parameters as the `DrawThermometer` function:

```
DrawTemperature (hPS,pRectl,lColor,lBackColor,lPercent)
```

This function will be called from the `DrawThermometer` function after the outline and bulb are drawn. It will use the `GpiBox` function to paint first the unfilled percent at the top with `lBackColor`. The unfilled portion is drawn first because the 100 percent fill point within the rectangle will always be 5 percent from the top. The top of the bulb is dependent on its ending arc points. The filled percentage of the stem is then drawn by using `lColor`. In the sample program, the thermometer is drawn in the client area by default. (See Figure 6.4.) A timer may be started or stopped by selecting the Timer menu option under Thermometer. The timer causes the fill percentage of the thermometer to vary slowly from 0 to 100 percent.

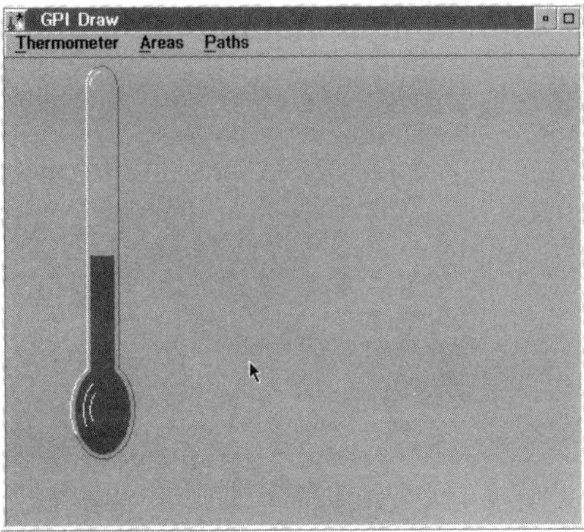

Figure 6.4.
GPI Draw thermometer.

Areas and Paths

PM provides two types of graphics objects comprised of a collection of drawing primitives: areas and paths. The primitives in an area define one or more closed figures that will be filled or filled and outlined by using the current area bundle and line bundle attributes, respectively. The primitives in a path, on the other hand, define a single area to be filled, outlined, or stroked. A stroked path results in a wide line. Both areas and paths have functions that mark their beginning and end. A completed area or path is referred to as a bracket. Before a figure in an area or path can be filled, it must be closed. If the primitives in an area bracket do not define a closed figure, an auto closure line is added by drawing a straight line from the last point to the first point of the figure. The closed figure is then filled based on the construction method for that bracket.

The fill method for an area or path may be alternate or winding. What these terms mean is made more clear by definitions that follow. Alternate fill is determined by the number of boundary lines that must be crossed by a line parallel to the X-axis from any given point in the figure to a point outside the figure. If an odd number of lines is crossed, the point at which the line originated is filled; otherwise, it is left unfilled. The direction the boundary lines are drawn does not affect the calculation. Figure 6.5 depicts alternate fill mode used when drawing several polygons.

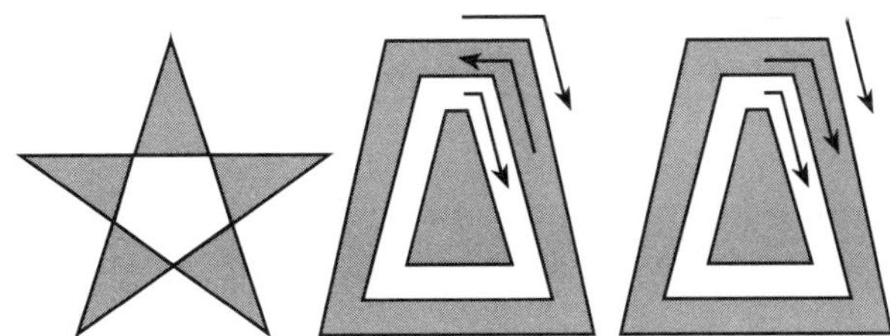

Figure 6.5.
Alternate fill mode.

The winding fill method uses the direction that boundary lines were drawn to determine if a point in the figure should be filled. Like alternate fill mode, an imaginary line is drawn from a point in the figure parallel to the X-axis to a point outside the figure. Rather than counting the number of boundary lines crossed, however, the direction of the crossed lines are tracked using a count. Starting with zero, for each line in a given direction, one is added to the count. When a boundary line drawn in the opposite direction is crossed, one is subtracted from the count. If the count is zero when the imaginary line exits, the closed figure at that point is not filled; otherwise, that point is filled. Figure 6.6 depicts winding fill mode used when drawing several polygons.

Figure 6.6.
Winding fill mode.

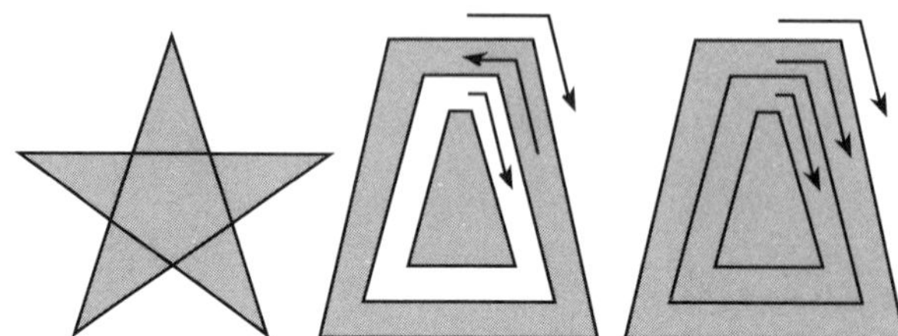

Areas

An area is started by calling the `GpiBeginArea` function. This function takes a PS and area fill options as its only parameters. The fill flags specify whether primitives drawn in the path should be outlined and whether alternate or winding fill mode should be used. The area flags are as follows:

`BA_BOUNDARY`	Draw boundary lines using the current linebundle attributes. This is the default.
or:	
`BA_NOBOUNDARY`	Do not draw boundary lines.
and:	
`BA_ALTERNATE`	Use alternate fill mode. This is the default.
or:	
`BA_WINDING`	Use winding fill mode.

The area bundle fill attributes set prior to the call to `GpiBeginArea` will be used to fill the one or more primitives that may be drawn in an area. These are sometimes referred to as the current attributes. You may set any valid combination of foreground and background colors and mix modes, pattern symbols, or fill patterns. The fill attributes may be changed within an area bracket; however, those changes will not affect the fill of objects in the current bracket. You can think of the current area fill attributes as a snapshot of the area bundle when `GpiBeginArea` was called. Area brackets are the only place where the term "current attributes" does not refer to the attributes last set. The line bundle attributes may also be changed within an area bracket; however, those changed will affect the next primitive drawn if the `BA_BOUNDRY` flag (or the default) has been used. As is true outside a path, only cosmetic boundary lines are drawn. You will recall that the geometric or wide lines are the result of a stroked path. After all figures are drawn, the area is completed by calling the `GpiEndArea` function. Before the `GpiEndArea` function returns, the figures are drawn in the target PS, and the area is destroyed. In the sample application, four stars are drawn in the client area when GpiBegin/EndArea menu item is selected. All four combinations of outline and fill methods are demonstrated.

Paths

A path may also be used to outline, fill, or stroke a figure with the current attributes. A completed path, however, may also be converted into a clipping boundary. The primitives within a path bracket define a single figure rather than the multiple figures drawn in an area. A path is started with the `GpiBeginPath` function and is initially empty. The `GpiBeginPath` function takes two parameters, a PS handle and a path identifier that must be 1.

A path bracket may not be started within an area bracket, nor may an area bracket begin within a path. As primitives are drawn in the path, points defining the figure are accumulated. If the starting and ending points in a path are not the same, the path is an open figure. Unlike an area, an auto closure line is not generated when a path is ended. You may still auto close the figure by using the `GpiCloseFigure` function. It will add points to the path that defines a line from the current position to the starting point. The `GpiCloseFigure` function must be called within a path bracket. Note that in OS/2 2.0, an outlined or filled path was limited to 1450 points; Version 2.1 and later have no restriction. The `GpiEndPath` function ends a path bracket. Unlike an area, the path is not rendered by the `GpiEndPath` function.

Although most GPI functions may be used in a path, there are some restrictions. The `GpiBox` and `GpiFullArc` functions can be used only with the `DRO_OUTLINE` option. Because each of these already defines a closed figure, if either is used, it may be the only function within a path bracket. Paths are the only method of creating nonrectangular clipping regions. The `GpiFullArc` function may be used to define an ellipse within a path that may then be converted to a clipping region. The `GpiBox` function, however, should generally be avoided within a path because filling a rectangle or defining a rectangular region can be accomplished more efficiently by other functions. For example, a rectangle defined by `GpiBox` may be filled by using the `DRO_FILL` option and a clipping region may be created with the `GpiCreateRegion` function. You also may not begin an area within a path or use image primitives such as `GpiBitBlt`. A complete list of functions valid in a path bracket is shown later in this chapter.

Unlike an area, closing a path does not render the image and destroy the path. You may recall that the interior of figures in an area are always filled. A path gives you much greater control of the rendering of the figure. When closed with the `GpiEndPath` function, a path may be outlined, filled, stroked, modified, set as a clipping region, or converted to a region.

Operation	*GPI function*
Fill path interior	`GpiFillPath`
Draw path boundary	`GpiOutlinePath`
Draw wide boundary lines	`GpiStrokePath`
Modify the path	`GpiModifyPath`
Set PS clip path	`GpiSetClipPath`
Convert path to a region	`GpiPathToRegon`

The sample application will define a path using two splines that define a football-shaped figure scaled to the client window size. When closed, the path will be filled, outlined, or stroked based on the selected menu option. The path is created as follows:

```
GpiBeginPath (hPS,1);
GpiMove (hPS,ptlSpline);
GpiPolySpline(hPS,3,&ptlSpline[1]);
GpiPolySpline(hPS,3,&ptlSpline[4]);
GpiEndPath (hPS);
```

Because path operations are varied, the fill method is not passed as a parameter to the `GpiBeginPath` function. If a path is to be filled, the desired method (alternate or winding) is passed to the `GpiFillPath` function. The `GpiFillPath` function will fill the interior of the figure by using the current area fill attributes. Current fill attributes for paths differ from the current attributes used for area fills: they are truly current. The attributes set when the `GpiFillPath` function is called will be used to fill the path. They may be changed before, during, and after a path bracket. If the figure is not closed, an auto closure line is added to the figure by the `GpiFillPath` function. Alternate or winding fill is determined by the same method as used in area brackets. After the figure is rendered, the path is destroyed before returning from `GpiFillPath`.

Boundary lines of a path may also be outlined by using the `GpiOutlinePath` function. The function takes a PS handle, a path identifier that must be 1, and a reserved option that must be 0. The outline of the path is drawn with the current cosmetic line bundle attributes. Unlike a filled path, an open figure is not auto closed. After the figure is outlined, the path is destroyed before returning from `GpiOutlinePath`.

A wide geometric line can be drawn on the boundries of a figure defined in a path by one of two methods. The path may be stroked or modified and filled. A path is stroked by using the `GpiStrokePath` function. This function will convert the current path points to points that follow the original boundary based on the geometric line parameters. These line parameters define the stroked line width, end, and joins styles. Geometric line width specifies the total line width, not the width on either side of the orignal boundary line. Line end styles define the appearance of the start and end points in a path. The first point drawn in the path is considered the starting point, and the last point drawn by the last primitive is the ending point. When multiple primitives are drawn in a path, join style determines the appearance of points that shared starting and ending points. The OS/2 2.0 path limit of 1,450 points applies to both a simple and stroked

path. A stroked path will have many more points than the simple path it is based on. Although there is no formula, limiting a path to be stroked to 500 points is a good guideline. This should only be a concern if your application may be run on versions of OS/2 prior to 2.1 since the point limit has been removed. Figure 6.7 depicts an outlined and stroked path.

Figure 6.7.
Outlined and stroked paths.

As mentioned in the discussion of line bundles three line end styles are defined: flat, square, and round. (See Figure 6.8.) Flat end style fills the geometric line inclusive of the end point, but not beyond. The end is drawn by a line that is perpendicular to the line direction. Flat end style is the default. Square line end style is also perpendicular to the current line direction; however, it fills one half the geometric line width beyond the end point of the orignal boundary line. The round end style also extends past the end point. It will draw as a circle whose center point is the original end point and whose radius is one half the geometric line width. In the sample application, the effect of changing line end styles can be seen when they are changed as a path is being stroked or converted and filled.

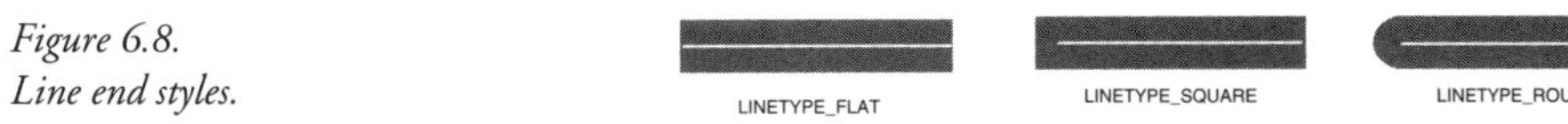

Figure 6.8.
Line end styles.

Three line join styles are also defined: beveled, mitered, and round. (See Figure 6.9.) They define the appearance of connected figures. Before the join style is applied, each line segment can be thought of as having an end style of flat. In the sample application, the effect of changing line join styles may be seen when they are changed as a path is being stroked or converted and filled.

A wide line can also be drawn by converting the path to a stroked path with the `GpiModifyPath` function. The `GpiModifyPath` function takes a PS handle, a path identifier that must be one, and a flag that defines the requested modification. Currently, one modification flag is defined. A path can be converted to a stroked path only by using the `MPATH_STROKE` flag. The current geometric line settings are used when converting the path. When converted, the path may be filled with the `GpiFillPath` function by using alternate or winding fill mode.

Regardless of its construction method, the wide line will be filled with the current area bundle fill attributes. The line bundle color and style have no effect on the figure. The sample program will actually fill the wide line with a vertical pattern.

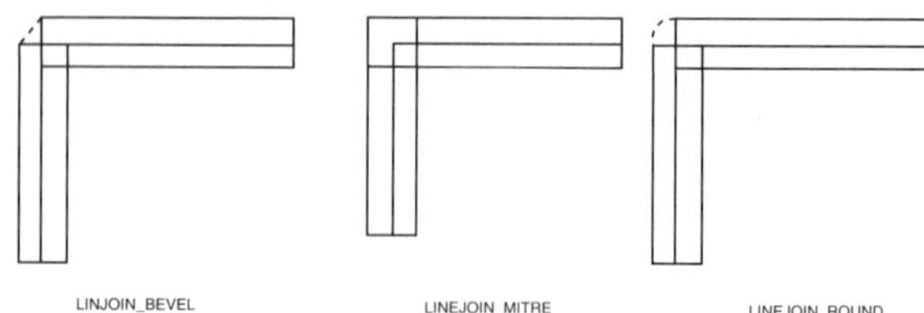

Figure 6.9.
Line join styles.

A path or modified path may also be set as a clipping area in the PS by using the `GpiSetClipPath` function. This function can reset the clipping path or define a new one that is the intersection of the current and new clip paths. After the `GpiSetClipPath` function is called, the path is no longer valid. As for a filled path, the clip path may be either alternate or winding. If the figure is not closed, an auto closure line is added to the figure before being set as the clip path. By using the `GpiModifyPath`, you can set a clip path that is the same as that defined by a stroked path. In the sample application, you may set the path or the stroked path of the football as the current clip path. When these options are selected, the screen is filled with a tiled bitmap image after the clip path has been set.

Resources

Resources are definitions of objects such as pointers, strings, and icons that are compiled by the resource compiler and bound to an executable or DLL. When a resource is loaded by a function such as `WinLoadPointer`, the process loading it becomes the owner. Threads created by this process will have access to those resources.

Resources that are created or loaded as part of one process may not be shared with another process. Initially, this may not seem like a large restriction; however, it should be considered when designing your application. For example, imagine that your application is comprised of a single executable and a DLL. If resources are loaded in the DLL and accessed by the executable, some conflicts could arise. Suppose your DLL loads and manages a group of cursors that the application can reference by index. If the DLL loads only one copy of the resources, the first instance of your application-process one-will have access to those pointer resources. If a second instance of your application is started—process 2—it will not have access to the loaded cursor resources because process 1 is the owner.

For this to work, the DLL would need to load the cursor resources and maintain the handles for each process.

Presentation Space Attribute Defaults

Whenever a PS is created, reset or associated with another DC the bundle attributes are reset to their default values. As a quick reference, the default values are listed by bundle type below in Table 6.1.

Table 6.1. Default Presentation Space Attributes.

Attribute	*Default Value*	*Functions to Query/Modify*
AREA BUNDLE		

Foreground Color	Display - `SYSCLR_WINDOWTEXT`
	Printer - Contrast to paper
		`GpiSet/QueryAttrs`
		`- ABB_COLOR`
		`- ab.lColor`
		`GpiSet/QueryColor`

Background Color	Display - `SYSCLR_WINDOW`
	Printer - Paper color
		`GpiSet/QueryAttrs`
		`- ABB_BACK_COLOR`
		`- ab.lBackColor`
		`GpiSet/QueryBackColor`

Foreground Mix Mode	`FM_OVERPAINT`	`GpiSet/QueryAttrs`
		`- ABB_MIX_MODE`
		`- ab.usMixMode`
		`GpiSet/QueryMix`

Background Mix Mode	`BM_LEAVEALONE`	`GpiSet/QueryAttrs`
		`-ABB_BACK_MIX_MODE`
		`- ab.usBackMixMode`
		`GpiSet/QueryBackMix`

Pattern Set	`LCID_DEFAULT`	`GpiSet/QueryAttrs`
		`- ABB_SET`
		`- ab.usSet`
		`GpiSet/QueryPatternSet`

Pattern Symbol	`PATSYM_SOLID`	`GpiSet/QueryAttrs`
		`- ABB_SYMBOL`
		`- ab.usSymbol`
		`GpiSet/QueryPattern`

Pattern Reference	(0,0)	`GpiSet/QueryAttrs`
		`- ABB_REF_POINT`
		`- ab.ptlRefPoint`
		`GpiSet/`
		`QueryPatternRefPoint`

continues

Table 6.1. continued

Attribute	*Default Value*	*Functions to Query/Modify*
CHARBUNDLE		
Foreground Color	Display - SYSCLR_WINDOWTEXT Printer - Contrast to paper	GpiSet/QueryAttrs - CBB_COLOR - cb.lColor GpiSet/QueryColor
Background Color	Display - SYSCLR_WINDOW Printer - Paper color	GpiSet/QueryAttrs - CBB_BACK_COLOR - cb.lBackColor GpiSet/QueryBackColor
Foreground Mix Mode	FM_OVERPAINT	GpiSet/QueryAttrs - CBB_MIX_MODE - cb.usMixMode GpiSet/QueryMix
Background Mix Mode	BM_LEAVEALONE	GpiSet/QueryAttrs - CBB_BACK_MIX_MODE - cb.usBackMixMode GpiSet/QueryBackMix
Character Angle	(1,0)	GpiSet/QueryAttrs - CBB_ANGLE - cb.ptlAngle GpiSet/QueryCharAngle
Character Shear	(0,1)	GpiSet/QueryAttrs - CBB_SHEAR - cb.ptlShear GpiSet/QueryCharShear
Character Direction	Left to Right	GpiSet/QueryAttrs - CBB_DIRECTION - cb.usDirection GpiSet/QueryCharDirection
Character Mode	CH_MODE1	GpiSet/QueryAttrs - CBB_MODE - cb.usPrecision GpiSet/QueryCharMode

Attribute	*Default Value*	*Functions to Query/Modify*
Extra Spacing All Characters	zero	GpiSet/QueryAttrs - CBB_ - cb.fxExtra GpiSet/QueryCharExtra
Extra Spacing Break Character Only	zero	GpiSet/QueryAttrs - CBB_ - cb.fxBreakExtra GpiSet/QueryCharBreakExtra
IMAGE BUNDLE		
Foreground Color	Display - SYSCLR_WINDOWTEXT Printer - Contrast to paper	GpiSet/QueryAttrs - IBB_COLOR - Ib.lColor GpiSet/QueryColor
Background Color	Display - SYSCLR_WINDOW Printer - Paper color	GpiSet/QueryAttrs - IBB_BACK_COLOR - ib.lBackColor GpiSet/QueryBackColor
Foreground Mix Mode	FM_OVERPAINT	GpiSet/QueryAttrs - IBB_MIX_MODE - ib.usMixMode GpiSet/QueryMix
Background Mix Mode	BM_LEAVEALONE	GpiSet/QueryAttrs - IBB_BACK_MIX_MODE - ib.usBackMixMode GpiSet/QueryBackMix
LINE BUNDLE		
Foreground Color	Display - SYSCLR_WINDOWTEXT Printer - Contrast to paper	GpiSet/QueryAttrs - LBB_COLOR - lb.lColor GpiSet/QueryColor
Background Color	Display - SYSCLR_WINDOW Printer - Paper color	GpiSet/QueryAttrs - LBB_BACK_COLOR - lb.lBackColor GpiSet/QueryBackColor

continues

Table 6.1. continued

Attribute	*Default Value*	*Functions to Query/Modify*

Foreground Mix Mode	`FM_OVERPAINT`	`GpiSet/QueryAttrs`
		- `LBB_MIX_MODE`
		- `lb.usMixMode`
		`GpiSet/QueryMix`

Background Mix Mode	`BM_LEAVEALONE`	`GpiSet/QueryAttrs`
		- `LBB_BACK_MIX_MODE`
		- `lb.usBackMixMode`
		`GpiSet/QueryBackMix`

Cosmetic Width	(1,0)	`GpiSet/QueryAttrs`
		- `LBB_WIDTH`
		- `lb.fxWidth`
		`GpiSet/QueryLineWidth`

Geometric Width	1	`GpiSet/QueryAttrs`
		- `LBB_GEOM_WIDTH`
		- `ib.lGeomWidth`
		`GpiSet/QueryLineWidthGeom`

Line Type	`LINETYPE_SOLID`	`GpiSet/QueryAttrs`
		- `LBB_TYPE`
		- `lb.ulType`
		`GpiSet/QueryLineType`

Geometric End Style	`LINEEND_FLAT`	`GpiSet/QueryAttrs`
		- `LBB_END`
		- `lb.ulEnd`
		`GpiSet/QueryLineEnd`

Geometric Join Style	`LINEJOIN_BEVEL`	`GpiSet/QueryAttrs`
		- `LBB_JOIN`
		- `lb.ulJoin`
		`GpiSet/QueryLineJoin`

MARKER BUNDLE		

Foreground Color	Display -
	`SYSCLR_WINDOWTEXT`
	Printer - Contrast to paper
		`GpiSet/QueryAttrs`
		- `MBB_COLOR`
		- `mb.lColor`
		`GpiSet/QueryColor`

Attribute	*Default Value*	*Functions to Query/Modify*
Background Color	Display - SYSCLR_WINDOW Printer - Paper color	GpiSet/QueryAttrs - MBB_BACK_COLOR - mb.lBackColor GpiSet/QueryBackColor
Foreground Mix Mode	FM_OVERPAINT	GpiSet/QueryAttrs - MBB_MIX_MODE - mb.usMixMode GpiSet/QueryMix
Background Mix Mode	BM_LEAVEALONE	GpiSet/QueryAttrs - MBB_BACK_MIX_MODE - mb.usBackMixMode GpiSet/QueryBackMix
Marker Set	LCID_DEFAULT	GpiSet/QueryAttrs - MBB_SET - mb.usSet GpiSet/QueryMarkerSet
Marker Symbol	MARKSYM_CROSS	GpiSet/QueryAttrs - MBB_SYMBOL - mb.usSymbol GpiSet/QueryMarker
Marker Box	(CAPS_MARKER_WIDTH, CAPS_MARKER_HEIGHT)	GpiSet/QueryAttrs - MBB_BOX - mb.sizfxCell GpiSet/QueryMarkerBox
Current position	(0,0)	GpiSet/QueryCurrentPosition GpiMove
Color table	Indexed	GpiCreate/ QueryLogColorTable GpiRealizeColorTable

Functions That Can Be Called in a Path Bracket

Function	*Restriction*
GpiBeginElement	
GpiBox	DRO_OUTLINE draw option only.
GpiCallSegmentMatrix	
GpiCharString	Current font must be outline.
GpiCharStringAt	Current font must be outline.
GpiCharStringPos	Current font must be outline.
GpiCharStringPosAt	Current font must be outline.
GpiCloseFigure	
GpiComment	
GpiCreateLogFont	Only outline fonts may be rendered.
GpiDeleteSetId	
GpiElement	
GpiEndElement	
GpiEndPath	
GpiFullArc	DRO_OUTLINE draw option only.
GpiLabel	
GpiLine	
GpiMarker	
GpiMove	
GpiOffsetElementPointer	
GpiPartialArc	
GpiPointArc	
GpiPolyFillet	
GpiPolyFilletSharp	
GpiPolyLine	
GpiPolyMarker	
GpiPolySpline	
GpiPop	
GpiPutData	
GpiQueryArcParams	
GpiQueryAttrMode	
GpiQueryCurrentPosition	
GpiSetArcParams	
GpiSetAttrMode	
GpiSetAttrs	
GpiSetCharAngle	
GpiSetCharBox	
GpiSetCharDirection	

Function	*Restriction*
GpiSetCharMode	
GpiSetCharSet	
GpiSetCharShear	
GpiSetColor	
GpiSetCp	
GpiSetCurrentPosition	
GpiSetEditMode	
GpiSetLineEnd	
GpiSetLineJoin	
GpiSetLineType	
GpiSetLineWidth	
GpiSetMarker	
GpiSetMarkerBox	
GpiSetMarkerSet	
GpiSetMix	
GpiSetModelTransformMatrix	

The Drawing Sample Application

The following files are needed to create the PMDRAW sample application:

ABOUT.DLG
DRAW.C
DRAW.DEF
DRAW.H
DRAW.ICO
DRAW.RC
STAR.BMP
STAR.DRW
THERMO.C
THERMO.H

DRAW.H

```
/* --------------------------------
GPI Drawing Header File
Real-World Programming for OS/2
Copyright (c) 1993-94 Blain, Delimon, and English
-------------------------------- */

#define ID_APPNAME     1
#define IDS_APPNAME    1
#define IDS_TIMERON    2
```

```
#define IDS_TIMEROFF   3
#define IDS_NOB_WIND   4
#define IDS_BOUND_WIND 5
#define IDS_NOB_ALT    6
#define IDS_BOUND_ALT  7


#define ID_STAR       50

#define IDM_DRAW               100
#define IDM_THERM              101
#define IDM_TIMER              102
#define IDM_ABOUT              103
#define IDM_AREAS              200
#define IDM_AREA_STARS         201
#define IDM_POLY_STARS         202
#define IDM_PATHS              300
#define IDM_FILL_PATH          301
#define IDM_OUTLINE_PATH       302
#define IDM_CONVERT_ALT_PATH   303
#define IDM_CONVERT_WIND_PATH  304
#define IDM_STROKE_PATH        305
#define IDM_CLIP_PATH          306
#define IDM_CLIP_STROKE_PATH   307
#define IDM_BEVEL              308
#define IDM_ROUND              309
#define IDM_MITRE              310
#define IDM_FLAT_END           311
#define IDM_ROUND_END          312
#define IDM_SQUARE_END         313


#define MAX_STRING 80

void  APIENTRY calculate_points(MPARAM);
void  APIENTRY process_command(HWND,MPARAM,MPARAM);
void  APIENTRY process_paint(HWND);
```

DRAW.C

```
/* ------------------------------
GPI Drawing Program
Real-World Programming for OS/2
Copyright (c) 1993-94 Blain, Delimon, and English
------------------------------ */

#define INCL_WIN
#define INCL_GPI
#define INCL_GPIPOLYGON
#include <os2.h>
#include "draw.h"
#include "thermo.h"
#include "..\common\about.h"
```

```
extern LONG APIENTRY GpiPolygons(HPS,ULONG,PPOLYGON,ULONG,ULONG);

#ifdef  POLYGON_EXCL
#undef  POLYGON_EXCL
#endif
#define POLYGON_EXCL 1

MRESULT EXPENTRY ClientWndProc (HWND,ULONG,MPARAM,MPARAM);



HAB     hab;
HWND    hWndFrame,
hWndClient;
HWND    hMenu;
CHAR    szTitle[64];
CHAR    szFontFace[]    = "8.Helv";

USHORT  usMode = IDM_THERM;
USHORT  usLineJoin = IDM_BEVEL;
USHORT  usLineEnd  = IDM_FLAT_END;
PVOID   pMem;
RECTL   ThermRectl;
int     iPercent = 0;
BOOL    bTimer = FALSE;
BOOL    bRising = TRUE;
POINTL  ptlStar [5][5];
POINTL  ptlSpline [7];
USHORT  usJoinStyles [] =
{LINEJOIN_BEVEL, LINEJOIN_ROUND, LINEJOIN_MITRE};
USHORT  usEndStyles [] =
{LINEEND_FLAT, LINEEND_ROUND, LINEEND_SQUARE};

int main()
{
   HMQ   hmq;
   QMSG  qmsg;
   ULONG flFrameFlags     = FCF_TITLEBAR | FCF_SYSMENU |
                            FCF_SIZEBORDER | FCF_MINMAX |
                            FCF_SHELLPOSITION | FCF_TASKLIST |
                            FCF_ICON | FCF_MENU;
   CHAR  szClientClass[] = "CLIENT";
   int   iClientHeight;

   hab = WinInitialize (0);
   hmq = WinCreateMsgQueue (hab, 0);

   WinRegisterClass (hab,szClientClass,ClientWndProc, CS_SIZEREDRAW,0);
   WinLoadString (hab,0,IDS_APPNAME,sizeof(szTitle), szTitle);

   DosAllocMem((PPVOID)&pMem,0x1000,PAG_READ | PAG_WRITE);
   DosSubSet(pMem,DOSSUB_INIT | DOSSUB_SPARSE_OBJ,8192);

   hWndFrame = WinCreateStdWindow (HWND_DESKTOP,0,
      &flFrameFlags,szClientClass, szTitle,0,0,ID_APPNAME, &hWndClient);
```

```
   iClientHeight = WinQuerySysValue(HWND_DESKTOP, SV_CYSCREEN) -
      WinQuerySysValue(HWND_DESKTOP,SV_CYICON);
   WinSetWindowPos (hWndFrame,HWND_TOP,0,
      WinQuerySysValue(HWND_DESKTOP,SV_CYSCREEN) -iClientHeight,
      WinQuerySysValue(HWND_DESKTOP,SV_CXSCREEN), iClientHeight,
         SWP_SHOW | SWP_ACTIVATE | SWP_ZORDER | SWP_SIZE | SWP_MOVE);

   hMenu  = WinWindowFromID (hWndFrame,FID_MENU);


   while (WinGetMsg (hab, &qmsg, 0, 0, 0))
      WinDispatchMsg (hab, &qmsg);

   WinDestroyWindow (hWndFrame);
   WinDestroyMsgQueue (hmq);
   WinTerminate (hab);
   DosFreeMem(pMem);
   return (0);
}


void APIENTRY calculate_points(MPARAM lNewSize)
/*-------------------------------*/

This function will update the point arrays for the stars and
splines when the window is resized.

/*-------------------------------*/
{
   int        i,j;
   int        X,Y;
   int        iWidth,iHeight;
   POINTL     ptl[5];

   /* Calculate the location of the 4 stars */
   iWidth  = SHORT1FROMMP(lNewSize);
   iHeight = SHORT2FROMMP(lNewSize);
   X = (iWidth / 3) - 1;
   Y = (iHeight / 2) - 1;
   ptl[0].x = -(X / 3);
   ptl[0].y = -(Y / 2);
   ptl[1].x = X / 2;
   ptl[1].y = Y / 6;
   ptl[2].x = -(X / 2);
   ptl[2].y = Y / 6;
   ptl[3].x = -ptl[0].x;
   ptl[3].y = ptl[0].y;
   ptl[4].x = 0;
   ptl[4].y = Y / 2;

   for (i = 0;i <= 4;i++)
   {
      if ((i == 0) || (i == 2))
         X = iWidth / 4;
      else
         X = iWidth - (iWidth / 4);
```

```
      if ((i == 2) || (i == 3))
         Y = iHeight / 4;
      else
         Y = iHeight - (iHeight / 4);

      for (j = 0;j <= 4;j++)
      {
         ptlStar[i][j].x = X + ptl[j].x;
         ptlStar[i][j].y = Y + ptl[j].y;
      }
   }

   /*  Calculate the points for the spline */
   ptlSpline[0].x = iWidth / 4;
   ptlSpline[0].y = iHeight / 2;
   ptlSpline[1].x = iWidth * 3 / 8;
   ptlSpline[1].y = iHeight * 3 / 4;
   ptlSpline[2].x = iWidth - ptlSpline[1].x;
   ptlSpline[2].y = ptlSpline[1].y;
   ptlSpline[3].x = iWidth - ptlSpline[0].x;
   ptlSpline[3].y = ptlSpline[0].y;
   ptlSpline[4].x = ptlSpline[2].x;
   ptlSpline[4].y = iHeight / 4;
   ptlSpline[5].x = ptlSpline[1].x;
   ptlSpline[5].y = ptlSpline[4].y;
   ptlSpline[6].x = ptlSpline[0].x;
   ptlSpline[6].y = ptlSpline[0].y;
}


void APIENTRY process_command(HWND hWnd,MPARAM mp1,MPARAM mp2)
/*--------------------------------*/

All WM_COMMAND messages received by the client window will be
processed here.

/*--------------------------------*/
{
   char szTemp [MAX_STRING];

   switch(SHORT1FROMMP(mp1))
   {
      case IDM_THERM:
         WinSendMsg (hMenu,MM_SETITEMATTR, MPFROM2SHORT(usMode,TRUE),
            MPFROM2SHORT(MIA_CHECKED,FALSE));
         WinSendMsg    (hMenu,MM_SETITEMATTR, MPFROM2SHORT(IDM_THERM,TRUE),
            MPFROM2SHORT(MIA_CHECKED,MIA_CHECKED));
         usMode = SHORT1FROMMP(mp1);
         WinInvalidateRect(hWndClient,0,FALSE);
         break;
      case IDM_TIMER:
         if (usMode != IDM_THERM)
         break;
         if (bTimer)
         {
```

```
      WinStopTimer(hab,hWnd,1);
      bTimer = FALSE;
      WinLoadString (hab,0,IDS_TIMERON,MAX_STRING, (PSZ)szTemp);
      WinSendMsg (hMenu,MM_SETITEMTEXT, MPFROMSHORT(IDM_TIMER),
            (MPARAM)szTemp);
   }
   else
   {
      WinStartTimer (hab,hWnd,1,0);
      bTimer = TRUE;
      WinLoadString (hab,0,IDS_TIMEROFF,MAX_STRING, (PSZ)szTemp);
      WinSendMsg (hMenu,MM_SETITEMTEXT, MPFROMSHORT(IDM_TIMER),
         (MPARAM)szTemp);
   }
   break;
case IDM_AREA_STARS:
case IDM_POLY_STARS:
case IDM_FILL_PATH:
case IDM_OUTLINE_PATH:
case IDM_CONVERT_ALT_PATH:
case IDM_CONVERT_WIND_PATH:
case IDM_STROKE_PATH:
case IDM_CLIP_PATH:
case IDM_CLIP_STROKE_PATH:
   if (bTimer)
      WinSendMsg(hWnd,WM_COMMAND, MPFROMSHORT(IDM_TIMER),0);
   WinSendMsg (hMenu,MM_SETITEMATTR, MPFROM2SHORT(usMode,TRUE),
      MPFROM2SHORT(MIA_CHECKED,FALSE));
   usMode = SHORT1FROMMP(mp1);
   WinSendMsg (hMenu,MM_SETITEMATTR, MPFROM2SHORT(usMode,TRUE),
      MPFROM2SHORT(MIA_CHECKED,MIA_CHECKED));
   WinInvalidateRect(hWndClient,0,FALSE);
   break;
case IDM_BEVEL:
case IDM_ROUND:
case IDM_MITRE:
   WinSendMsg (hMenu,MM_SETITEMATTR, MPFROM2SHORT(usLineJoin,TRUE),
      MPFROM2SHORT(MIA_CHECKED,FALSE));
   usLineJoin = SHORT1FROMMP(mp1);
   WinSendMsg (hMenu,MM_SETITEMATTR, MPFROM2SHORT(usLineJoin,TRUE),
      MPFROM2SHORT(MIA_CHECKED,MIA_CHECKED));
   WinInvalidateRect(hWndClient,0,FALSE);
   break;
case IDM_FLAT_END:
case IDM_ROUND_END:
case IDM_SQUARE_END:
   WinSendMsg (hMenu,MM_SETITEMATTR, MPFROM2SHORT(usLineEnd,TRUE),
   MPFROM2SHORT(MIA_CHECKED,FALSE));
   usLineEnd = SHORT1FROMMP(mp1);
   WinSendMsg (hMenu,MM_SETITEMATTR, MPFROM2SHORT(usLineEnd,TRUE),
      MPFROM2SHORT(MIA_CHECKED,MIA_CHECKED));
   WinInvalidateRect(hWndClient,0,FALSE);
   break;
case IDM_ABOUT:
   DisplayAbout (hWnd, szTitle);
   break;
```

```
   }
   mp2;
}


void APIENTRY process_paint(HWND hWnd)
/*-------------------------------*/

This function will paint the client area based on the current
display mode. The following modes are supported:

IDM_THERM              Draw a thermometer with the current fill
percentage.
IDM_AREA_STARS         Draw 4 stars with all combinations of fill

and outline using areas.
IDM_POLY_STARS         Draw 4 stars with all combinations of fill

and outline using the polygon primitive.
IDM_FILL_PATH          Fill a football shaped path created with 2
spines.
IDM_OUTLINE_PATH       Outline a football shaped path created with
2 spines.
IDM_CONVERT_ALT_PATH   Modifies a path and then fills it with
alternate fill mode.
IDM_CONVERT_WIND_PATH  Modifies a path and then fills it with
winding fill mode.
IDM_STROKE_PATH        Draw a football shaped wide line using 2
                          spines.
IDM_CLIP_STROKE_PATH   Converts a path and then select it as the
clipping region.
IDM_CLIP_PATH          Select the path created with 2 splines as a
clipping region and fill the client area with
bitmaps.

/*-------------------------------*/
{
   HPS        hPS;
   BOOL       bAreas = FALSE;
   RECTL      Rectl;
   POLYGON    poly;
   LINEBUNDLE lb;
   AREABUNDLE ab;
   HBITMAP    hBitmap;
   PSZ        pLabel;
   int        iRows, iColumns;
   int        i,j;
   BITMAPINFOHEADER bi;
   POINTL     ptl;


   WinSetPresParam(hWnd,PP_FONTNAMESIZE, strlen(szFontFace)+1,
         (PVOID)szFontFace);
   hPS = WinBeginPaint(hWnd,0,&Rectl);
   WinFillRect(hPS,(PRECTL)&Rectl,CLR_PALEGRAY);
   ab.lColor = CLR_BLUE;
```

```
switch (usMode)
{
   case IDM_THERM:
      DrawThermometer(hPS,(PRECTL)&ThermRectl,0,CLR_RED,
      CLR_PALEGRAY,iPercent);
      break;
   case IDM_AREA_STARS:
      bAreas    = TRUE;
      ab.lColor = CLR_RED;
   case IDM_POLY_STARS:
      DosSubAlloc(pMem,(PPVOID)&pLabel,MAX_STRING);

      GpiSetAttrs (hPS,PRIM_AREA,ABB_COLOR,0,&ab);
      poly.ulPoints = 5;

      GpiSetCurrentPosition (hPS,&ptlStar[0][0]);
      if (bAreas)
      {
         GpiBeginArea (hPS,BA_NOBOUNDARY ¦ BA_WINDING);
         GpiPolyLine (hPS,5L,&ptlStar[0][0]);
         GpiEndArea (hPS);
      }
      else
      {
         poly.aPointl = &ptlStar[0][0];
         GpiPolygons (hPS,1L,&poly,BA_NOBOUNDARY ¦ BA_WINDING,
                  POLYGON_EXCL);
      }
      i = WinLoadString (hab,0,IDS_NOB_WIND,MAX_STRING, pLabel);
      GpiCharStringAt (hPS,&ptlStar[0][2],i,pLabel);

      GpiSetCurrentPosition (hPS,&ptlStar[1][0]);
      if (bAreas)
      {
         GpiBeginArea (hPS,BA_BOUNDARY ¦ BA_WINDING);
         GpiPolyLine (hPS,5L,&ptlStar[1][0]);
         GpiEndArea (hPS);
      }
      else
      {
         poly.aPointl = &ptlStar[1][0];
         GpiPolygons (hPS,1L,&poly,BA_BOUNDARY ¦ BA_WINDING,
            POLYGON_EXCL);
      }
      i = WinLoadString (hab,0,IDS_BOUND_WIND,MAX_STRING, pLabel);
      GpiCharStringAt (hPS,&ptlStar[1][2],i,pLabel);

      GpiSetCurrentPosition (hPS,&ptlStar[2][0]);
      if (bAreas)
      {
         GpiBeginArea (hPS,BA_NOBOUNDARY ¦ BA_ALTERNATE);
         GpiPolyLine (hPS,5L,&ptlStar[2][0]);
         GpiEndArea (hPS);
      }
      else
```

```
      {
         poly.aPointl = &ptlStar[2][0];
         GpiPolygons (hPS,1L,&poly,BA_NOBOUNDARY ¦ BA_ALTERNATE,
               POLYGON_EXCL);
      }
      i = WinLoadString (hab,0,IDS_NOB_ALT,MAX_STRING, pLabel);
      GpiCharStringAt (hPS,&ptlStar[2][2],i,pLabel);

      GpiSetCurrentPosition (hPS,&ptlStar[3][0]);
      if (bAreas)
      {
         GpiBeginArea (hPS,BA_BOUNDARY ¦ BA_ALTERNATE);
         GpiPolyLine (hPS,5L,&ptlStar[3][0]);
         GpiEndArea (hPS);
      }
      else
      {
         poly.aPointl = &ptlStar[3][0];
         GpiPolygons (hPS,1L,&poly,BA_BOUNDARY ¦ BA_ALTERNATE,
               POLYGON_EXCL);
      }
      i = WinLoadString (hab,0,IDS_BOUND_ALT,MAX_STRING, pLabel);
      GpiCharStringAt (hPS,&ptlStar[3][2],i,pLabel);
      DosSubFree(pMem,pLabel,MAX_STRING);
      break;

   case IDM_FILL_PATH:
   case IDM_OUTLINE_PATH:
      ab.usSymbol      = PATSYM_HORIZ;
      ab.lColor        = CLR_WHITE;
      ab.lBackColor    = CLR_BLUE;
      ab.usBackMixMode = BM_OVERPAINT;
      GpiSetAttrs (hPS,PRIM_AREA,ABB_COLOR ¦ ABB_SYMBOL ¦
      ABB_BACK_COLOR ¦ ABB_BACK_MIX_MODE,0,&ab);
      GpiBeginPath (hPS,1);
      GpiMove (hPS,ptlSpline);

      GpiPolySpline(hPS,3,&ptlSpline[1]);
      GpiPolySpline(hPS,3,&ptlSpline[4]);
      GpiEndPath (hPS);

      if (usMode == IDM_FILL_PATH)
         GpiFillPath(hPS,1,FPATH_ALTERNATE);
      else
      {
         lb.lColor = CLR_RED;
         GpiSetAttrs(hPS,PRIM_LINE,ABB_COLOR,0,&lb);
         GpiOutlinePath(hPS,1,0);
      }
      break;

   case IDM_CONVERT_ALT_PATH:
   case IDM_CONVERT_WIND_PATH:
   case IDM_STROKE_PATH:
      ab.usSymbol    = PATSYM_VERT;
```

```
        ab.lColor     = CLR_BLUE;
        GpiSetAttrs (hPS,PRIM_AREA,ABB_COLOR ¦ ABB_SYMBOL,0,&ab);
        lb.lGeomWidth = 20;
        lb.usJoin = usJoinStyles[usLineJoin - IDM_BEVEL];
        lb.usEnd  = usEndStyles [usLineEnd - IDM_FLAT_END];
        GpiSetAttrs (hPS,PRIM_LINE,LBB_GEOM_WIDTH ¦ LBB_JOIN ¦ LBB_END,
              0,&lb);
        GpiBeginPath (hPS,1);
        GpiMove (hPS,ptlSpline);
        GpiPolySpline(hPS,3,&ptlSpline[1]);
        GpiPolySpline(hPS,3,&ptlSpline[4]);
        GpiEndPath (hPS);

        if (usMode == IDM_STROKE_PATH)
           GpiStrokePath(hPS,1,FPATH_ALTERNATE);
        else
        {
           GpiModifyPath (hPS,1,MPATH_STROKE);
           if (usMode == IDM_CONVERT_ALT_PATH)
              GpiFillPath(hPS,1,FPATH_ALTERNATE);
           else
              GpiFillPath(hPS,1,FPATH_WINDING);
        }
        break;

     case IDM_CLIP_STROKE_PATH:
     case IDM_CLIP_PATH:
        GpiBeginPath (hPS,1);
        GpiMove (hPS,ptlSpline);
        GpiPolySpline(hPS,3,&ptlSpline[1]);
        GpiPolySpline(hPS,3,&ptlSpline[4]);
        GpiEndPath (hPS);

        if (usMode == IDM_CLIP_STROKE_PATH)
        {
           lb.lGeomWidth = 20;
           lb.usJoin = usJoinStyles[usLineJoin - IDM_BEVEL];
           lb.usEnd  = usEndStyles [usLineEnd - IDM_FLAT_END];
           GpiSetAttrs (hPS,PRIM_LINE,LBB_GEOM_WIDTH ¦ LBB_JOIN ¦
                 LBB_END,0,&lb);
           GpiModifyPath (hPS,1,MPATH_STROKE);
        }
        GpiSetClipPath(hPS,1,FPATH_ALTERNATE ¦ SCP_AND);
        hBitmap = GpiLoadBitmap(hPS,0,ID_STAR,0,0);

        GpiQueryBitmapParameters(hBitmap, (PBITMAPINFOHEADER)&bi);
        iRows = Rectl.xRight / bi.cx;
        iColumns = Rectl.yTop / bi.cy;
        ptl.x = 0;
        ptl.y = 0;
        for (i = 0;i <= iRows;i++)
        {
           for (j = 0;j <= iColumns; j++)
           {
              WinDrawBitmap(hPS,hBitmap,0,&ptl,0,0, DBM_NORMAL);
              ptl.y += bi.cy;
```

```
            }
            ptl.y = 0;
            ptl.x += bi.cx;
         }
         break;
   }
   WinEndPaint (hPS);
}


void APIENTRY update_thermometer (HWND hWnd)
/*-------------------------------*/

This function will process the timer message for the thermometer
causing it to redraw cycling through the fill percentages 0 to 100.

/*-------------------------------*/
{
   HPS      hPS;

   hPS = WinGetPS(hWnd);
   DrawTemperature(hPS,(PRECTL)&ThermRectl,CLR_RED, CLR_PALEGRAY,
         iPercent);
   WinReleasePS (hPS);
   if (bRising)
   {
      iPercent++;
      if (iPercent > 100)
      {
         bRising = FALSE;
         iPercent--;
      }
   }
   else
   {
      iPercent--;
      if (iPercent < 0)
      {
         bRising = TRUE;
         iPercent++;
      }
   }
}



MRESULT EXPENTRY ClientWndProc (HWND hWnd, ULONG msg, MPARAM mp1,
                                MPARAM mp2)
/*-------------------------------*/

This is the application callback which handles the messages
necessary to maintain the client window.

/*-------------------------------*/
{
```

```
   BOOL    bHandled = TRUE;
   MRESULT mReturn  = 0;

   switch (msg)
   {
      case WM_CREATE:
         ThermRectl.xLeft   = 50;
         ThermRectl.yBottom = 50;
         ThermRectl.yTop    = 350;
         ThermRectl.xRight  = 100;
         break;

      case WM_COMMAND:
         process_command(hWnd,mp1,mp2);
         break;

      case WM_TIMER:
         update_thermometer(hWnd);
         break;

      case WM_PAINT:
         process_paint(hWnd);
         break;

      case WM_ERASEBACKGROUND:
         WinFillRect((HPS)LONGFROMMP(mp1),PVOIDFROMMP(mp2), CLR_PALEGRAY);
         mReturn = MRFROMLONG(0L);
         break;

      case WM_SIZE:
         calculate_points(mp2);
         break;

      default:
         bHandled = FALSE;
         break;
   }

   if (!bHandled)
      mReturn = WinDefWindowProc (hWnd,msg,mp1,mp2);

   return (mReturn);
}
```

DRAW.DEF

```
NAME           DRAW  WINDOWAPI
DESCRIPTION    'Draw Sample Program (c) Blain, Delimon, & English, 1993-94'
PROTMODE
HEAPSIZE       4096
STACKSIZE      32768
IMPORTS        GpiPolygons = PMGPI.650
EXPORTS        ClientWndProc
```

DRAW.RC

```
/* -----------------------------------
Draw Resource File
Real-World Programming for OS/2
Copyright (c) 1993-94 Blain, Delimon, and English
----------------------------------- */

#include <os2.h>
#include "draw.h"

ICON ID_APPNAME DRAW.ICO
BITMAP ID_STAR STAR.BMP

RCINCLUDE ..\common\about.dlg

MENU ID_APPNAME
BEGIN
   SUBMENU "~Thermometer",                  IDM_DRAW
      BEGIN
         MENUITEM "Display",                IDM_THERM, 0, MIA_CHECKED
         MENUITEM "Start Timer",            IDM_TIMER
         MENUITEM SEPARATOR
         MENUITEM "About...",               IDM_ABOUT
      END
   SUBMENU "~Areas",                        IDM_AREAS
      BEGIN
         MENUITEM "GpiBegin/EndArea",       IDM_AREA_STARS
         MENUITEM "GpiPolygons",            IDM_POLY_STARS
      END
   SUBMENU "~Paths",                        IDM_PATHS
      BEGIN
         MENUITEM "Fill Path",              IDM_FILL_PATH
         MENUITEM "Outline Path",           IDM_OUTLINE_PATH
         MENUITEM "Convert/Fill Path ALT", IDM_CONVERT_ALT_PATH
         MENUITEM "Convert/Fill Path WIND", IDM_CONVERT_WIND_PATH
         MENUITEM "Stroke Path",            IDM_STROKE_PATH
         MENUITEM "Clip To Path",           IDM_CLIP_PATH
         MENUITEM "Clip To Stroke Path",             IDM_CLIP_STROKE_PATH
         MENUITEM SEPARATOR
         MENUITEM "Line Join Bevel",        IDM_BEVEL, 0, MIA_CHECKED
         MENUITEM "Line Join Round",        IDM_ROUND
         MENUITEM "Line Join Mitre",        IDM_MITRE
         MENUITEM SEPARATOR
         MENUITEM "Line End Flat",          IDM_FLAT_END, 0, MIA_CHECKED
         MENUITEM "Line End Round",         IDM_ROUND_END
         MENUITEM "Line End Square",        IDM_SQUARE_END
      END
END

STRINGTABLE LOADONCALL MOVEABLE
BEGIN
   IDS_APPNAME      "GPI Draw"
   IDS_NOB_WIND     "BA_NOBOUNDARY ¦ BA_WINDING"
   IDS_BOUND_WIND   "BA_BOUNDARY ¦ BA_WINDING"
```

```
   IDS_NOB_ALT      "BA_NOBOUNDARY ¦ BA_ALTERNATE"
   IDS_BOUND_ALT    "BA_BOUNDARY ¦ BA_ALTERNATE"
   IDS_TIMERON      "Start Timer"
   IDS_TIMEROFF     "Stop Timer"
END
```

THERMO.H

```
/* --------------------------------
Thermometer Header File
Real-World Programming for OS/2
Copyright (c) 1993-94 Blain, Delimon, and English
-------------------------------- */

#define TS_SHOW_PERCENT  0x0001

BOOL  APIENTRY DrawThermometer (HPS,PRECTL,LONG,LONG,LONG, LONG);
BOOL  APIENTRY DrawTemperature (HPS,PRECTL,LONG,LONG,LONG);
```

THERMO.C

```
/* ------------------------------
Thermometer Drawing sample
Real-World Programming for OS/2
Copyright (c) 1993-94 Blain, Delimon, and English
------------------------------ */

#define INCL_WIN
#define INCL_GPI
#include <os2.h>
#include "thermo.h"



BOOL APIENTRY DrawTemperature (HPS hPS,PRECTL pRectl,LONG lColor,
                     LONG lBackColor,LONG lPercent)
/*------------------------------*/

This function will fill draw the vertical bar portion of the
thermometer. lColor is used to fill lPercent of the bar starting
at the top of the bulb. lBackColor is used to fill the remainder
of the bar. The rectangle identified by pRectl should be identical
to that supplied to DrawThermometer.

hPS         Presentation space to render in.
pRectl      Bounding box of the thermometer.
lColor      Color index used to fill bulb and stem of thermometer.
lBackColor  Color to fill the remainder of the stem (100 - lPercent).
lPercent    Amount to fill the thermometer. Valid range is 0 to 100.


/*------------------------------*/
{
```

```
   AREABUNDLE ab;
   RECTL      Rectl;
   int        iWidth  = (pRectl->xRight-pRectl->xLeft) / 3;
   int        iBoxHeight = pRectl->yTop - pRectl->yBottom;
   int        iBarHeight = (iBoxHeight * 70) / 100;

   /* Range check the percent */
   if (lPercent > 100)
      lPercent = 100;
   else if (lPercent < 0)
      lPercent = 0;

   Rectl.xLeft = pRectl->xLeft + iWidth;
   Rectl.yTop  = pRectl->yTop - (iBoxHeight * 5) / 100;
   if (lPercent)
      Rectl.yBottom = Rectl.yTop -
            ((iBarHeight * (100 - lPercent)) / 100);
   else
      Rectl.yBottom = Rectl.yTop - iBarHeight;
   Rectl.xRight  = pRectl->xRight - iWidth;

   ab.lColor = lBackColor;
   GpiSetAttrs(hPS,PRIM_AREA,ABB_COLOR,0,(PBUNDLE)&ab);
   GpiMove (hPS,(PPOINTL)&Rectl);
   GpiBox (hPS,DRO_FILL,(PPOINTL)&Rectl.xRight,0,0);

   Rectl.yTop = Rectl.yBottom - 1;
   Rectl.yBottom = pRectl->yBottom+(iBoxHeight * 20) / 100;
   ab.lColor = lColor;
   GpiSetAttrs(hPS,PRIM_AREA,ABB_COLOR,0,(PBUNDLE)&ab);
   GpiMove (hPS,(PPOINTL)&Rectl);
   GpiBox (hPS,DRO_FILL,(PPOINTL)&Rectl.xRight,0,0);
   return (TRUE);
}


BOOL APIENTRY DrawThermometer (HPS hPS,PRECTL pRectl,LONG lStyle,
               LONG lColor, LONG lBackColor, LONG lPercent)
/*-------------------------------*/

This function will draw the outine of a thermometer scaled to
the supplied rectangle in the give presentation space. The bulb
of the rectangle is filled with lColor and the remainder is drawn
by the DrawTemperature function.

hPS        Presentation space to render in.
pRectl     Bounding box of the thermometer.
lStyle     Currently undefined.
lColor     Color index used to fill bulb and stem of thermometer.
lBackColor Color to fill the remainder of the stem (100 - lPercent).
lPercent   Amount to fill the thermometer. Valid range is 0 to 100.

/*-------------------------------*/
{
   LINEBUNDLE lb;
```

```
    AREABUNDLE ab;
    ARCPARAMS  arcparms;
    POINTL     lPtCenter;
    POINTL     lStartPt;
    POINTL     lEndPt;
    POINTL     lPt;
    FIXED      fxStartAngle,fxSweepAngle;
    RECTL      BulbRectl;
    int        iBoxHeight = pRectl->yTop - pRectl->yBottom;

    /* Calculate the height of the bulb to be 25% of the total height */
    BulbRectl = *pRectl;
    BulbRectl.yTop = BulbRectl.yBottom+(iBoxHeight * 25)/100;

    /* define the bounding box for the arc */
    arcparms.lP = (BulbRectl.xRight - BulbRectl.xLeft) / 2L;
    arcparms.lQ = (BulbRectl.yTop - BulbRectl.yBottom) / 2L;
    arcparms.lR = 0L;
    arcparms.lS = 0L;
    GpiSetArcParams(hPS, (PARCPARAMS)&arcparms);

    /* Calculate the center point of bulb */
    lPtCenter.x = BulbRectl.xLeft + arcparms.lP;
    lPtCenter.y = BulbRectl.yBottom + arcparms.lQ + 1;

    /*------------------------------*/
    Draw the bulb
    /*------------------------------*/
    /* Draw an invisble arc from the current location to the
start angle */
    fxStartAngle = MAKEFIXED(120,0);
    fxSweepAngle = MAKEFIXED(90,0);
    lb.usType = LINETYPE_INVISIBLE;
    GpiSetAttrs (hPS,PRIM_LINE,LBB_TYPE,0,(PBUNDLE)&lb);
    GpiPartialArc (hPS,&lPtCenter,MAKEFIXED(1,0), fxStartAngle,
          MAKEFIXED(0,0));
    GpiQueryCurrentPosition(hPS,(PPOINTL)&lStartPt);

    /* Draw the left highlighted outline of the bulb */
    lb.lColor = CLR_WHITE;
    lb.usType = LINETYPE_SOLID;
    GpiSetAttrs (hPS,PRIM_LINE,LBB_COLOR ¦ LBB_TYPE,0, (PBUNDLE)&lb);
    GpiPartialArc (hPS,&lPtCenter,MAKEFIXED(1,0), fxStartAngle,
          fxSweepAngle);

    /* Draw the right shadowed outline of the bulb */
    fxStartAngle = MAKEFIXED(210,0);
    fxSweepAngle = MAKEFIXED(210,0);
    lb.lColor = CLR_DARKGRAY;
    GpiSetAttrs (hPS,PRIM_LINE,LBB_COLOR,0,(PBUNDLE)&lb);
    GpiPartialArc (hPS,&lPtCenter,MAKEFIXED(1,0), fxStartAngle,
          fxSweepAngle);
    GpiQueryCurrentPosition(hPS,(PPOINTL)&lEndPt);
```

```
/* Fill the bulb of the thermometer with the supplied color */
arcparms.lP -= 4;
arcparms.lQ -= 4;
GpiSetArcParams(hPS, (PARCPARAMS)&arcparms);
ab.lColor = lColor;
GpiSetAttrs(hPS,PRIM_AREA,ABB_COLOR,0,(PBUNDLE)&ab);
GpiMove (hPS,&lPtCenter);
GpiFullArc(hPS,DRO_FILL,MAKEFIXED(1,0));

/*-----------------------------*/
Draw the reflection on the bulb
/*-----------------------------*/
arcparms.lP = (arcparms.lP * 3) / 4;
arcparms.lQ = (arcparms.lQ * 3) / 4;
GpiSetArcParams(hPS, (PARCPARAMS)&arcparms);
fxStartAngle = MAKEFIXED(120,0);
fxSweepAngle = MAKEFIXED(90,0);
lb.usType = LINETYPE_INVISIBLE;
GpiSetAttrs (hPS,PRIM_LINE,LBB_TYPE,0,(PBUNDLE)&lb);
GpiPartialArc (hPS,&lPtCenter,MAKEFIXED(1,0), fxStartAngle,
      MAKEFIXED(0,0));

lb.lColor = CLR_WHITE;
lb.usType = LINETYPE_SOLID;
GpiSetAttrs (hPS,PRIM_LINE,LBB_COLOR ¦ LBB_TYPE,0, (PBUNDLE)&lb);
GpiPartialArc (hPS,&lPtCenter,MAKEFIXED(1,0), fxStartAngle,
      fxSweepAngle);

arcparms.lP = (arcparms.lP * 2) / 3;
arcparms.lQ = (arcparms.lQ * 2) / 3;
GpiSetArcParams(hPS, (PARCPARAMS)&arcparms);
fxStartAngle = MAKEFIXED(120,0);
fxSweepAngle = MAKEFIXED(90,0);
lb.usType = LINETYPE_INVISIBLE;
GpiSetAttrs (hPS,PRIM_LINE,LBB_TYPE,0,(PBUNDLE)&lb);
GpiPartialArc (hPS,&lPtCenter,MAKEFIXED(1,0), fxStartAngle,
      MAKEFIXED(0,0));

lb.lColor = CLR_WHITE;
lb.usType = LINETYPE_SOLID;
GpiSetAttrs (hPS,PRIM_LINE,LBB_COLOR ¦ LBB_TYPE,0, (PBUNDLE)&lb);
GpiPartialArc (hPS,&lPtCenter,MAKEFIXED(1,0), fxStartAngle,
      fxSweepAngle);

/*-----------------------------*/
Draw the sides
/*-----------------------------*/
/* Draw the right vertical side */
lb.lColor = CLR_DARKGRAY;
GpiSetAttrs (hPS,PRIM_LINE,LBB_COLOR,0,(PBUNDLE)&lb);
GpiMove(hPS,(PPOINTL)&lEndPt);
lPt.x = lEndPt.x;
lPt.y = pRectl->yBottom + ((iBoxHeight * 95) / 100);
GpiLine (hPS,&lPt);
```

```
/* Draw the left vertical side */
lb.lColor = CLR_WHITE;
GpiSetAttrs (hPS,PRIM_LINE,LBB_COLOR,0,(PBUNDLE)&lb);
lPt.x = lStartPt.x;
GpiMove(hPS,(PPOINTL)&lPt);
GpiLine (hPS,&lStartPt);

/*------------------------------*/
Draw the rounded top
/*------------------------------*/
/* Reset the rectangle for drawing the rounded top */
BulbRectl.xLeft   = lStartPt.x;
BulbRectl.yBottom = pRectl->yBottom+(iBoxHeight*90)/100;
BulbRectl.xRight  = lEndPt.x;
BulbRectl.yTop    = pRectl->yTop;

arcparms.lP = (BulbRectl.xRight - BulbRectl.xLeft) / 2L;
arcparms.lQ = (BulbRectl.yTop - BulbRectl.yBottom) / 2L;
GpiSetArcParams(hPS, (PARCPARAMS)&arcparms);

/* Calculate the center point for the rounded top arc */
lPtCenter.x = BulbRectl.xLeft + arcparms.lP;
lPtCenter.y = BulbRectl.yBottom + arcparms.lQ + 1;

/* Draw an invisble arc from the current location to the
   start angle */
fxStartAngle = MAKEFIXED(0,0);
fxSweepAngle = MAKEFIXED(120,0);
lb.usType = LINETYPE_INVISIBLE;
GpiSetAttrs (hPS,PRIM_LINE,LBB_TYPE,0,(PBUNDLE)&lb);
GpiPartialArc(hPS,&lPtCenter,MAKEFIXED(1,0), fxStartAngle,
      MAKEFIXED(0,0));

/* Draw the shaded side */
lb.lColor = CLR_DARKGRAY;
lb.usType = LINETYPE_SOLID;
GpiSetAttrs (hPS,PRIM_LINE,LBB_COLOR ¦ LBB_TYPE,0, (PBUNDLE)&lb);
GpiPartialArc (hPS,&lPtCenter,MAKEFIXED(1,0), fxStartAngle,
      fxSweepAngle);

/* Draw thehighlighed side */
fxStartAngle = MAKEFIXED(120,0);
fxSweepAngle = MAKEFIXED(60,0);
lb.lColor = CLR_WHITE;
GpiSetAttrs (hPS,PRIM_LINE,LBB_COLOR,0,(PBUNDLE)&lb);
GpiPartialArc (hPS,&lPtCenter,MAKEFIXED(1,0), fxStartAngle,
      fxSweepAngle);

/* Draw the reflection */
arcparms.lP = (arcparms.lP * 3) / 4;
arcparms.lQ = (arcparms.lQ * 3) / 4;
GpiSetArcParams(hPS, (PARCPARAMS)&arcparms);
fxStartAngle = MAKEFIXED(90,0);
fxSweepAngle = MAKEFIXED(90,0);
lb.usType = LINETYPE_INVISIBLE;
GpiSetAttrs (hPS,PRIM_LINE,LBB_TYPE,0,(PBUNDLE)&lb);
```

```
   GpiPartialArc (hPS,&lPtCenter,MAKEFIXED(1,0), fxStartAngle,
            MAKEFIXED(0,0));

   lb.lColor = CLR_WHITE;
   lb.usType = LINETYPE_SOLID;
   GpiSetAttrs (hPS,PRIM_LINE,LBB_COLOR | LBB_TYPE,0, (PBUNDLE)&lb);
   GpiPartialArc (hPS,&lPtCenter,MAKEFIXED(1,0), fxStartAngle,
         fxSweepAngle);

   DrawTemperature(hPS,pRectl,lColor,lBackColor,lPercent);
   return (TRUE);
}
```

Chapter 7

Creating and Manipulating PM Fonts and Text

Introduction

Throughout this book, we have been outputting text with various Graphics Programming Interface (GPI) functions. We even demonstrated changing the font in Chapter 4, "Common Dialogs," by selecting a new font in the common font selection dialog. The detail of enumerating, creating, scaling, and rendering of fonts has been largely ignored. This chapter will focus on all those topics and more.

Terminology

Before beginning, some definitions are in order. Knowing the words that describe the characteristics of fonts will make your work considerably easier.

Single-Byte and Double-Byte Characters

The term "font" appears in this book many times, but what exactly is a font? The term originates from printing, where a font describes a collection of characters that share a common height, style, and weight of typeface.

The collection of characters can be of any number in the real world of printing. Most computer fonts in the Western world are numbered with a single byte. This means there can be no more than 256 characters. The fonts we will be working with in this chapter have a single-byte character set (SBCS).

All the non-Asian languages supported by OS/2 use fonts from a single-byte character set. The Japanese, Chinese, and Korean languages use two bytes to represent the thousands of characters and ideographic symbols required by those languages.

Consequently, they use what is referred to as the double-byte character (DBCS). Using two bytes for each character increases the maximum character set from 255 to 65,536.

Point Size

The height of a font is described in points, which is short for printer points. Each printer point is 1/72 inch. Even with this exact measurement, a point size only approximates the height of the characters in the font. The height of the characters are up to the designer of the font.

Font Families

Fonts are divided into families based on the appearance characteristics of the font. A major determinate of a font family is the presence or absence of serifs. A serif is a fine line (relative to the stroke width) drawn at the end and perpendicular to the major strokes of a character. It often appears as a flaring of the stroke. Fonts without serifs are referred to as sans (from the French word without) serif. (See Figure 7.1.)

In Figure 7.1 the font on the left has serifs, whereas the font on the right does not. Strokes are the lines used to draw the characters of the font. The width of those strokes are also used to classify the font into a family.

A font family is comprised of one or more fonts with a unique typeface name. The word typeface is often used in place of a typeface name. The characters of those fonts will be representative of the family to which they belong. The facename for each font within a family will be unique, but often will be comprised of a base family name plus attribute modifiers. For example, Times New Roman Italic facename is comprised of the family name Times New Roman and the modifier Italic.

Figure 7.1.
Sample serif and sans serif characters.

Font Types

Font representation and rendering falls into two categories—outline and image. The characters of an outline font are described in terms of the graphics arcs and curves that draw the font. Image font characters, on the other hand, are bitmaps. Both have advantages and disadvantages. Outline fonts are continuously scalable, may be rotated, sheared, and displayed at larger point sizes without a loss of quality. Rotation changes the baseline angle against which text is output.

Shearing occurs when the characters in a font are slanted by modifying the character bounding box. An italic font can be thought of as a mildly sheared font. That quality and flexibility comes at the expense of speed, however, because each character must be drawn when output. The quality of outline fonts is not always superior to image fonts, however. At smaller sizes, image fonts are often easier to read than an outline font of an equivalent size because they were specifically designed for that size. Image fonts display faster than outline fonts because a bitmap exists for each character in the font. To support various device resolutions, an image font will require a bitmap for each character in each point size for each screen resolution it supports. In our sample program, we will enumerate and see all sizes available for each image font. Image fonts may not be scaled, rotated, or sheared.

Code Pages

Both outline and image fonts define characters based on code points. A code point is the actual numeric byte value of the character. It is from this value that mapping to the actual glyph displayed on output begins. For example, the code point 65 maps to the character glyph "A" in all single-byte character set code pages. A glyph is the picture or symbol associated with a given code point. When we said that single-byte character set fonts may define up to 256 characters, we were referring to the number of glyphs that can be represented; therefore, although all single-byte character set fonts will have 256 code points, it is not required that a glyph be defined for all of them. For example, a font that is decorative or ornamental may only define the first 128 characters. The mapping between code point and a character glyph is referred to as a code page. A code page may be based on either ASCII or EBCDIC. OS/2 defines many code pages for the application's use. The ASCII multilingual code page 850 is the PM default. Figure 7.2 demonstrates a single-code point (8E) being mapped to three different character glyphs.

Correct use of code pages is important to interacting with other applications and the system. You know that a code page is the mapping of a code point to character glyph. That might be all you would need to know if your application existed within a vacuum, but it does not. Code pages control how your application interacts with the system and other applications. For example, if your application uses keyboard input, the message queue code page will determine how characters are translated from the keyboard. This occurs because the keystroke's translation is based on the message queue code page and is performed before your application receives the message. You may change the default message queue code page by calling the `WinSetCp` function. A list of code pages available on the system may be retrieved by calling the `WinQueryCpList` function. It will return an array of code page IDs. If the code page used when text strings are created is not the same as the message queue code page, some characters might not display correctly. For example, say you are producing an international version of your application. You will need to ensure that the text editor used to create the translated string resources creates output in the code page of the target display font.

Figure 7.2.
Code point to glyph mapping.

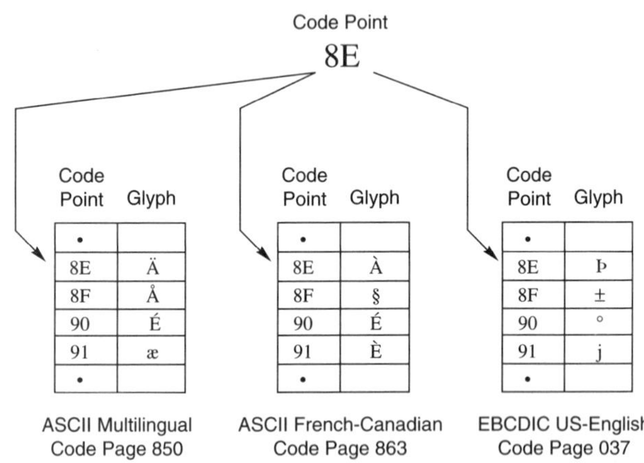

In addition to the message queue code page, each presentation space has a code page that may be set or queried. It defines what code page is used by the default font. It has no effect on fonts that are created and set into the presentation space. The PMFONT application enables you to change the code page that is used to create the font. Values may be selected from the code page menu.

While developing an application, various keyboard templates should be installed and tested on the system in conjunction with testing your application. The keyboard layout may be changed using the KEYB program. This is a utility that comes with OS/2. It will change the keyboard layout for all DOS and OS/2 sessions. Applications receive no notification of the change. KEYB takes a two-character abbreviation for the keyboard template to set as the current template. For example, GR will set the German keyboard template.

To aid in converting strings and characters from one code page to another, PM supplies two conversion functions, `WinCpTranslateChar` and `WinCpTranslateString`. Each requires an anchor block handle and a source and destination code page.

Font Styles

Style attributes may be applied to both outline and image fonts. Bold and italic are the most commonly used attributes. Again, outline and image fonts differ in the method by which these attributes are implemented for a font. What is normally thought of as a single outline font by the end user is often made up of a set of four fonts, one for each of the attribute combinations. For example, the Times New Roman font family is composed of the following four fonts:

Times New Roman	Base font.
Times New Roman Bold	Base font with embolding.
Times New Roman Bold Italic	Base font with embolding and italic.
Times New Roman Italic	Base font with italic.

Each font from this family is a separate physical resource, but applications often present them to the user as a single-font resource that can be made bold, italic, or both. The common font selection dialog discussed in Chapter 4 shows the font family name in the first combo box and a style that can be applied to that font in a separate combo box. Notice that the family name is not always the same as the base font facename. Unlike outline fonts, an image font does not include separate physical resources for each attribute combination desired. Image fonts can be made bold, italic, or bold italic by synthesizing the appearance desired. PM will create a character glyph based on the original bitmap. A bold font may be created by double-striking the base font at an offset in the X direction. Italics may be simulated by progressively offsetting the bits of the character starting at the bottom of the character.

Default Font

In many of the sample programs in this book, text was output by using one of the GPI output functions without setting or changing a font. Setting a font is not required because each presentation space has a default font resource set into it. When you call `WinGetPS`, `WinBeginPaint`, or `GpiCreatePS`, the default System Proportional font is set into that presentation space before returning. The System Proportional font is an image font supplied by the display driver to approximate a 12-point font based on the screen resolution of the device. Its character glyphs are defined based on code page 850.

Text Output Functions

PM supplies a group of functions that enables you to output character strings, using its currently selected font attributes. With the exception of the `WinDrawText` function, all GPI text output functions are limited to 512 characters. The GPI text function can be split into two groups, those with formatting and those without. In each group, one allows the current position to be specified and the other does not.

Nonformatting:

`GpiCharString`	Outputs a character string at the current location.
`GpiCharStringAt`	Outputs a character string starting at a supplied location.

Formatting:

`GpiCharStringPos`	Outputs a character string at the current location using a set of supplied formatting options.
`GpiCharStringPosAt`	Outputs a character string starting at a supplied location using a set of supplied formatting options.
`WinDrawText`	Outputs a character string in a bounding rectangle using a set of supplied formatting options.

Regardless of how the starting point is defined, all the GPI functions position the character string based on the character reference point. This point is defined as the intersection of the baseline and the vertical line that defines the left character cell boundary. As you can see in Figure 7.3, descenders are drawn below the reference point and ascenders are drawn above it.

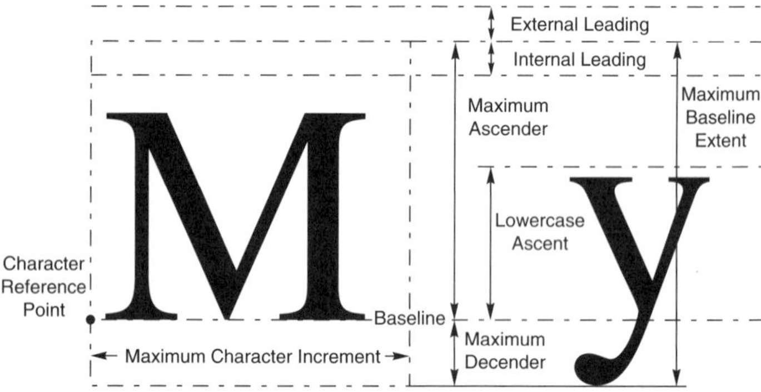

Figure 7.3.
Character reference point.

The `GpiCharString` function is the most basic of all character primitives. Text is output starting at the current location, and the current position is updated after each character is output. A starting position is not supplied. The `GpiCharStringAt` function is identical except it enables you to supply your own starting point. To best utilize these functions in your application, some thought is required. For example, if you are outputting multiple lines of text with no breaks or style changes in a line, it would be more efficient to use the `GpiCharStringAt` function to specify the starting position of each line. If a line of text includes a mixture of font styles, however, the first text style on a line could still be output by using the `GpiCharStringAt` function and the remainder of the line rendered with the `GpiCharString` function. Because the current position is updated when the characters are drawn, it would not be necessary to query the current location before outputting the second and subsequent text styles:

```
GpiCharStringAt (hPS,pPtl,lCount,pchString)
```

HPS	hPS	Handle of the presentation space to render the characters into.
PPOINTL	pPtl	Pointer to the point where text output will begin.
LONG	lCount	Length in bytes of the memory pointed to by pchString—the maximum is 512.
PCH	pchString	Pointer to a null-terminated string to output.

Expanding on basic text output function are the `GpiCharStringPos` and `GpiCharStringPosAt` functions. These two functions add formatting options to the previous functions giving the caller greater flexibility over the display of characters.

```
GpiCharStringPosAt (hPS,pPtl,pRectl,lOptions,lCount,pchString,paDX)
```

PRECTL	pRectl	Pointer to a bounding and/or clipping rectangle to be used if the `CHS_CLIP` or `CHS_OPAQUE` options are specified. Otherwise, the parameter is ignored.
LONG	lOptions	Flags that control the formatting of the output. It may be one or more of the following:
	CHS_CLIP	Clips the text drawn to the supplied rectangle defined by pRectl.
	CHS_LEAVEPOS	The current position is not updated. Without this flag, the current GPI position will be updated to the character reference point for where the next character would have been drawn.
	CHS_OPAQUE	The rectangle defined by pRectl is filled with the current background color in the `CHARBUNDLE`. This color may be set by Calling `GpiSetBackColor` or `GpiSetAttrs`.
	CHS_STRIKEOUT	The text string is drawn overstruck.
	CHS_UNDERSCORE	The text string is drawn underscored.
	CHS_VECTOR	This flag indicates that the paDX parameter contains pointer to an array of longs which supply incremental value to be used when spacing characters.
PLONG	paDX	Pointer to an array of longs used to position characters in the text string. This parameter is ignored if the `CHS_VECTOR` option flag is not used.

The `CHS_OPAQUE` option enables you to specify a rectangle to be filled with the current `CHARBUNDLE` background color. Notice that the rectangle can be independent of the location where the text is drawn. Two functions are available to set the background color. `GpiSetBackColor` will set the

background color in all bundles, and GpiSetAttrs can set the background color only of the CHARBUNDLE. For example, set a red background fill as follows:

```
GpiSetBackColor (hPS,CLR_RED);
```

or set the background color in the CHARBUNDLE as follows:

```
CHARBUNDLE cb;

cb.lBackColor = CLR_RED;
GpiSetAttrs(hPS,PRIM_CHAR,CBB_BACK_COLOR,0,(PBUNDLE)&cb);
```

The WinDrawText function is the most versatile of text output functions. It will output a stream of text formatted in a rectangle. You may recall that WinDrawText was used in Chapter 4 to display text in the client area of the sample application. The function is defined as follows:

```
WinDrawText (hPS,lCount,pchText,pRectl,lForeColor,lBackColor,ulCmd)
```

HPS	hPS	Handle of the presentation space to render the characters into.
LONG	lCount	The number of characters in the string pointed to by pchText. If the string is null terminated, -1 may be supplied and the length will be calculated.
PCH	pchText	Pointer to a null-terminated string to output.
PRECTL	pRectl	Pointer to an inclusive rectangle in which the text is to be formatted. The coordinates must be in world space.
LONG	lForeColor	Text foreground color, this parameter is not used if the DT_TEXTATRRS flag is set in the lCmd parameter.
LONG	lBackColor	Text background color, this parameter is not used if the DT_TEXTATRRS flag is set in the lCmd parameter. The character bundle background mix mode must set to BM_OVERPAINT or BM_XOR or the color is ignored.
ULONG	ulCmd	Flags which control the text formatting. One of the following horizontal alignment options may be supplied.
	DT_LEFT	Left justify the text in the rectangle. This is the default horizontal alignment.
	DT_CENTER	Center the text in the rectangle.
	DT_RIGHT	Right justify the text in the rectangle.
		One of the following vertical alignment options may be supplied.
	DT_TOP	Top justify the text in the rectangle. This is the default.
	DT_VCENTER	Center the text vertically in the rectangle.

DT_BOTTOM	Bottom justify the text in the rectangle.
	One or more of the following flags may be supplied.
DT_ERASERECT	Fill the background of the rectangle using lBackColor before rendering the text.
DT_EXTERNALLEADING	When the DT_TOP and DT_QUERYEXTENT flags are used the external leading for the current font is added to the bottom of the returned bounding rectangle.
DT_MNEMONIC	Convert mnemonic characters to an underline on the next character. For example: **~File** is output as File
DT_QUERYEXTENT	Do not output text only compute the bounding rectangle and return the result in pRectl.
DT_STRIKEOUT	Output all characters using the overstrike attribute.
DT_TEXTATTRS	Use the foreground and background colors in the character bundle set in the PS. lForeColor and lBackColor are ignored.
DT_WORDBREAK	Draw only words which will fit entirely within the rectangle defined by pRectl.

Note that the background color supplied will only fill the character cells if a background mix mode other than BM_LEAVEALONE is set in the character bundle. To fill the entire rectangle with the background use the DT_ERASERECT flag.

Text Spacing and Extents

Text output by the GPI functions are also affected by the direction, spacing, and alignment values set into a presentation space. Character direction controls the direction characters are output. The default is to output characters left to right along the baseline. The GpiSetCharDirection function enables you to change the horizontal direction to right to left or to output characters vertically. Vertical text is drawn either top to bottom or bottom to top along a line perpendicular to the baseline. The character reference point for vertical text is the center of the character cell as opposed to the left side of the cell used for horizontal text.

One method of altering the spacing of characters in a text string may be controlled by supplying an array of increment values to one of the GPI formatting text functions. This is useful if the increment value from character to character is modified in a nonlinear fashion. If the spacing of all characters output needs to be modified uniformly, however, the GpiSetCharExtra or GpiSetCharBreakExtra functions may be used. Each function takes a fixed value that modifies the default spacing. The GpiCharExtra function modifies the spacing of all characters, whereas

`GpiSetCharBreakExtra` changes only the spacing of the break character. The break character is defined by the font and may be retrieved from the `sBreakChar` field of the `FONTMETRIC` structure. This character is often, but not always, the space character. The break value may be negative or positive. Negative values result in less space between characters, and positive values result in more space between characters. The break character will be affected by both the character spacing and break character spacing. For example, if the character spacing was increased by one, but the break character spacing was decreased by one, there would be no effective change to the break character spacing.

In the sample application for this chapter, PMFONT, the character Extra and Break Character Extra for the selected font may be modified. Select the Rotation/Shear menu option on the display pop-up menu. Two slider controls enable you to dynamically modify the spacing of the currently displayed string.

When formatting text it is often necessary to determine the extent of the string prior to output. For example, in order center or right align a text string you will need to calculate the starting point. The `GpiQueryTextBox` may be used for just this purpose. It will take a supplied string and return an array of five points in world coordinates. The first four points will contain a parallelogram that encloses the output string. You may wonder why the bounds of the text string are defined by a parallelogram and not a rectangle. This is because GPI allows text to be slanted relative to the character baseline, this as know as shear. We will discuss character shear later in this chapter. The character baseline may be rotated so you may not assume that the top-left corner of the parallelogram is numerically less than bottom-right corner. The fifth point defines the concatenation point.

The `GpiQueryTextBox` function is defined as follows:

```
GpiQueryTextBox(hPS,lLength,pchString,lPtCount,pPtl)
```

`HPS`	`hPS`	Handle of the presentation space to use when calculating the text box. Note that all character bundle attributes set in the PS will affect the return values.
`LONG`	`lLength`	Number of characters to calculate extent of.
`PCH`	`pchString`	Pointer to the string to calculate the extent of.
`LONG`	`lPtCount`	Number of points which should be returned in the `pPtl` parameter. If all points are desired the `TXTBOX_COUNT` constant may be used.
`PPOINTL`	`pPtl`	Pointer to an array of `POINTL` structures. This must be at least `lPtCount` in length.

In the PMFONT sample, `GpiQueryTextBox` is used to calculate the position of centered text in the display window before rotation and shear are applied. It is then called again to query the points used to render a parallelogram around the text string.

Font Enumeration

Chapter 4 discussed using the common font selection dialog. It allows an application to add font selection quickly to an application. Choosing the font is only half the story, however. Creating and using a font requires you to know much that the common font dialog hides from you. In an effort to focus on the font dialog and not fonts, the sample program in Chapter 4 was limited in scope. It enabled you to select only from image fonts when changing the font used to display the text of the file. It also ignored how fonts were enumerated by PM and shown in the dialog. It gave you a taste of dealing with fonts, but left out the details. It's now time for the details.

You may be wondering where the common dialog got the font information to display in the combo boxes. All the items displayed were enumerated by PM to the dialog by calling the `GpiQueryFonts` function. The `GpiQueryFonts` function returns information about the font resources available to the application through the `FONTMETRICS` structure. The `GpiQueryFonts` function is defined as follows:

```
GpiQueryFonts (hPS,lOptions,pszFacename,plCount,lMetricLength,
pFontMetrics)
```

HPS	hPS	Presentation space handle for the device to enumerate `FONTMETRICS` from.
LONG	lOptions	Flags that control what type of font resources are included in the enumeration. It may be one or more of the following:
	QF_PUBLIC	Return fonts that are available to all processes. This includes fonts loaded using the `GpiLoadPublic-Fonts` function.
	QF_PRIVATE	Return fonts that have been loaded by calling `GpiLoadFonts` and are available only to the current process. If this flag is used alone and no private fonts have been loaded, no fonts will be returned by this function.
	QF_NO_DEVICE	Return fonts that are not device specific.
	QF_NO_GENERIC	Return fonts that are not device independent.
PSZ	pszFacename	Pointer to a null-terminated string that contains the font typeface name.
PLONG	plCount	Pointer to a long that contains the number of fonts to enumerate. The `pFontMetrics` parameter should be at least `lMetricLength * (plCount)` bytes long.

LONG	lMEtricLength	Length in bytes of the FONTMETRICS structure to be returned, sizeof(FONTMETRICS) is often used.
PFONTMETRICS	pFontMetrics	Pointer of the buffer to copy the requested array of FONTMETRICS to.

To determine the memory requirements for the desired set of fonts, the GpiQueryFonts function should be called with the lOptions and pszFacename set to the desired values and the contents of plCount and the pFontMetrics parameter set to zero. The return value will indicate the number of fonts meeting the search criteria. Memory can then be allocated for the size of the FONTMETRICS structure times the number of fonts. After the memory is allocated, calling GpiQueryFonts a second time with the contents of plCount set to the number of fonts returned on the first call and pFontMetrics pointing to the allocated memory, an array of FONTMETRICS structures will be returned. This structure contains all the detailed information necessary to create and manipulate the font. To give you a feel for the contents of the FONTMETRICS, the sample application in this chapter, PMFONT, will enumerate all the public and private fonts available and place the facename of the font in a list box. The names are added to the list box in the order they were received from PM. When the font is selected in the list box, the FONTMETRICS for that font are displayed along with a sample text string in the client window. The result is a font browser of sorts.

First, we must establish the number of fonts available:

```
ulCount = GpiQueryFonts (hPS,QF_PUBLIC | QF_PRIVATE,NULL,
&ulCount,(LONG)sizeof(FONTMETRICS),0);
```

If at least one font exists, memory is allocated and the fonts queried and then added to the list box.

```
if (ulCount)
{
   DosAllocMem ((PPVOID)&pFontMetrics,sizeof(FONTMETRICS) * (USHORT)ulCount,
      OBJ_TILE | PAG_READ | PAG_WRITE | PAG_COMMIT);
   GpiQueryFonts (hPS,QF_PUBLIC | QF_PRIVATE,NULL,
      &ulCount,(LONG)sizeof(FONTMETRICS),pFontMetrics);
   WinSendMsg (hLBox,LM_DELETEALL,NULL,NULL);

   for (i = 0; i < (int)ulCount; i++)
   {
      WinSendMsg (hLBox,LM_INSERTITEM,(MPARAM)LIT_END,
         (MPARAM)(pFontMetrics+i)->szFacename);
   }
}
return (pFontMetrics);
```

The client window of PMFONT is split vertically into two components. On the left side are the selection and information windows. The right side will be used to show a sample of the currently selected font. A list box is created to hold the font facenames of the enumerated fonts. It is created as a child of the client window and positioned in the upper-left corner of the screen.

The client window is also the owner window so that it will receive command and notification messages when a change in the list box selection is made.

The list box is displayed continually, and other "panel" windows are displayed below it. We define a panel window to be one that is part of a group of interchangeable windows that have the same size and are displayed at the same screen location. Although they are displayed at the same screen location, only one is visible at any point in time. Typically, a different panel will be used for each mode of operation. Each panel will have one or more children that display information and allow data entry. You might be thinking that a panel sounds a lot like a dialog; well it is, and it isn't.

Dialogs are an excellent way to group a feature or function of a program, but they can break the work flow of your application. A panel is created from a dialog template, but it is displayed as a part of the main application. Using the dialog template eliminates the cumbersome process of creating all the display windows individually. When the panel contains children that will accept focus, the default dialog procedure will process tabbing between windows for you. The panel is simply replaced with a new one when the operation mode of the program changes. Our first panel displays the `FONTMETRICS` for the selected font.

The *FONTMETRICS* Structure

The `FONTMETRICS` structure contains many fields that define the sizes, attributes, and descriptions of fonts. The characters of a font reside in a rectangle referred to as a cell. Each cell has a width and height, and the character must reside entirely within the cell. Along the bottom quarter of the cell is a horizontal line known as the baseline. The baseline is the logical line defining where the base of a character rests when drawn. The part of the character drawn above the baseline is the ascent, and that drawn below is the descent. Characters such as lowercase g, q, p, and j have descent and ascent, whereas most uppercase characters have only ascent. Figure 7.4 depicts ascent and descent for two characters.

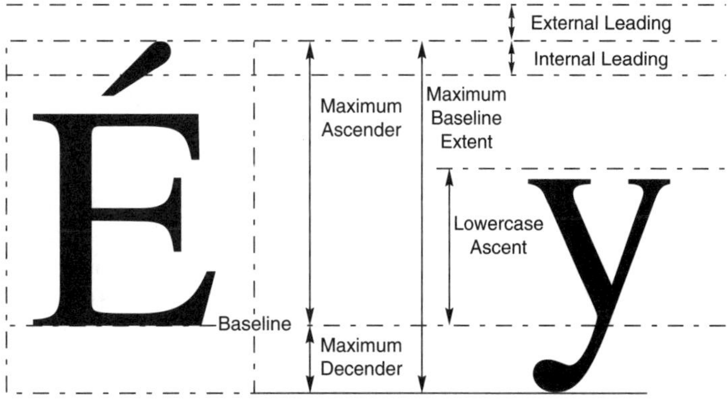

Figure 7.4. Character ascent and descent.

It might prove useful to run the PMFONT program and examine the contents of the metrics on your machine while we are describing the fields of the `FONTMETRICS` structure. The fields in boldface type are displayed in the FONTMETRICS panel of the PMFONT program. Sample output is depicted in Figure 7.5.

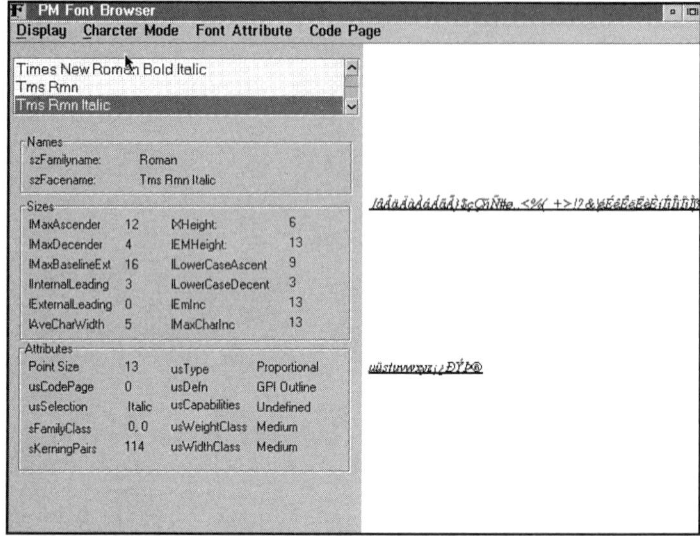

Figure 7.5.
PMFONT application.

CHAR szFamilyname — A null-terminated character array of `FACESIZE` length that will contain the font family name. `FACESIZE` is currently defined as 32. Do not, however, rely on this; use the `FACESIZE` constant when sizing arrays.

CHAR szFacename — A null-terminated character array of `FACESIZE` length that contains the facename of the font. The maximum length `(FACESIZE -1)` is adequate for the fonts shipped with OS/2, but too short for some of the Adobe type 1s that may be installed. For compatibility with older PM applications (1.x), `szFamilyname` and `szFacename` remain unchanged, but two new fields have been added to the `FONTMETRICS` structure. The `FamilyNameAtom` and `FaceNameAtom` fields will contain atoms if the font facename or family name exceeds `FACESIZE -1`. If this occurs, the `FM_TYPE_ATOMS` flag will be set in the `usType` field. Your application should check this flag

		and retrieve the atom text for the family and facename, rather than use the contents of the `szFamilyname` and `szFacename` fields.
USHORT	idRegistry	The IBM registered number. This field serves little or no value to an application.
USHORT	**usCodePage**	This field indicates which code page or code pages are supported by this font. You may recall that a code page defines the mapping between code points and character glyphs. It may be one of the following:
	0	All code pages are supported.
	65400	The font is special purpose or decorative and does not support any defined code page. The Symbol Set font shipped with OS/2 reports this code page.
	other	The code page supported by the font.
LONG	**lEmHeight**	This field contains the font point size in world coordinates.
LONG	**lXHeight**	This field contains the average ascent of the lowercase characters in the font.
LONG	**lMaxAscender**	This field contains the maximum height above the baseline for any character in the font. The character, however, is not identified.
LONG	**lMaxDescender**	This field contains the maximum depth below the baseline for any character in the font. As with the `lMaxAscender`, the character is not identified.
LONG	**lLowerCaseAscent**	This field contains the height of the tallest unaccented lowercase character in the font.
LONG	**lLowerCaseDescent**	This field contains the maximum depth below the baseline for any unaccented lowercase character in the font.
LONG	lInternalLeading	This field defines the space reserved at the top of the character cell for diacritics. Diacritics are accent marks that appear above a character. See Figure 7.4 as an example. This value is included in the `lMaxAscender` value.
LONG	**lExternalLeading**	This field contains a recommended amount of additional space to be used between lines of text rendered with this font. This value is not part of the character cell and all PM supplied fonts set this field to 0. Your application should consider using this value when spacing lines of text.
LONG	**lAveCharWidth**	This field contains the average width of the characters in the font based on their occurrence in the

		English language. For fixed pitch fonts, this value will be the actual width of each character cell and may be used for advancing caret and insertion points.
LONG	**lMaxCharInc**	This field is the cell width of the widest characters in the font.
LONG	**lEmInc**	This field contains the width of the EM square.
LONG	**lMaxBaselineExt**	This field contains the sum of the `lMaxAscender` and `lMaxDecender` fields.
SHORT	sCharSlope	This field contains the angle that a font slants from an imaginary line perpendicular to the baseline. (See Figure 7.6.) The angle is measured clockwise in degrees and minutes from this imaginary line. Degrees are stored in bits 0 through 9. Minutes are stored in bits 10 through 15. Bit 16 is unused.

Figure 7.6. Character slope.

SHORT	sInlineDir	This field contains an angle that determines the direction of output relative to the current position. (See Figure 7.7.) The angle is measured in degrees and minutes counterclockwise from the baseline. Fonts that are designed to be output left to right will have an angle of 0 degrees. Those intended to be output right to left will have an angle of 180 degrees.
SHORT	sCharRot	This field contains the angle that determines the rotation of the character glyphs to the default baseline. (See Figure 7.8.) The angle is measured in degrees and minutes counter-clockwise from that baseline. It is this angle that the characters use as a baseline.

Figure 7.7. Inline direction.

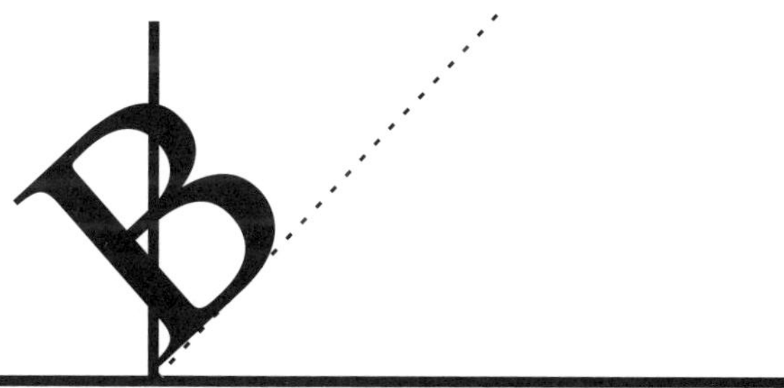

Figure 7.8. Character rotation.

USHORT usWeightClass

This field contains a value that classifies the stroke width of a font. There are currently nine weight classes defined:

```
FWEIGHT_DONT_CARE
FWEIGHT_ULTRA_LIGHT
FWEIGHT_EXTRA_LIGHT
FWEIGHT_LIGHT
FWEIGHT_SEMI_LIGHT
```

	FWEIGHT_NORMAL FWEIGHT_SEMI_BOLD FWEIGHT_BOLD FWEIGHT_EXTRA_BOLD FWEIGHT_ULTRA_BOLD Most fonts will fall into the light, normal, or bold weight classes.
USHORT usWidthClass	This field contains a value that classifies the character cell width of characters in this font based on other fonts of this type. The value identifies how the width of this font differs from the norm. Each flag represents a deviation percentage from the norm. The width class does not factor in the stroke width of the characters: FWIDTH_ULTRA_CONDENSED -50.0 percent FWIDTH_EXTRA_CONDENSED -37.5 percent FWIDTH_CONDENSED -25.0 percent FWIDTH_SEMI_CONDENSED -12.5 percent FWIDTH_NORMAL Reference FWIDTH_SEMI_EXPANDED +12.5 percent FWIDTH_EXPANDED +25.0 percent FWIDTH_EXTRA_EXPANDED +37.5 percent FWIDTH_ULTRA_EXPANDED +50.0 percent
SHORT sXDeviceRes	This field contains information on the horizontal resolution of the characters in the font. If the usDefn field has the FM_DEFN_OUTINE flag set, the value is the resolution at which the font was defined, or scanned. For outline fonts, this information is not useful. Otherwise, the font is an image font, and the value is the X resolution of the device the font was designed to be displayed on. The resolution is measured in pels per inch. The X resolution of the current device may be determined by calling the DevQueryCaps function with the CAPS_HORIZONTAL_FONT_RES flag. The horizontal device resolution is also measured in pels per inch.
SHORT sYDeviceRes	This field contains information on the vertical resolution of the characters in the font. If the usDefn field has the FM_DEFN_OUTINE flag set, the value is the resolution at which the font was defined or scanned. For outline fonts, this information is not useful. Otherwise, the font is an

		image font and the value is the Y resolution of the device the font was designed to be displayed on. The resolution is measured in pels per inch. The Y resolution of the current device may be determined by calling the `DevQueryCaps` function with the `CAPS_VERTICAL_FONT_RES` flag. The vertical device resolution is also measured in pels per inch.
SHORT	sFirstChar	This field contains the code point of the first character in the font.
SHORT	sLastChar	This field contains the code point of the last character in the font.
SHORT	sDefaultChar	This field defines the default code point for the font. When a code point outside the range of `sFirstChar` and `sLastChar` is specified, a replacement value must be supplied. This value identifies that point as an offset from `sFirstCharacter`, for example, `sDefaultCodePoint = sFirstChar + sDefaultChar`.
SHORT	sBreakChar	This field defines the offset from sFirstChar of the "break" codepoint. This value when added to `sFirstChar` typically identifies the code point of the space character.
SHORT	**sNominalPointSize**	This field contains information on the intended height values for the font. The value is the height in decipoints (1/720 inch) of the intended height. Divide by 10 to determine point size.
SHORT SHORT	sMinimumPointSize sMaximumPointSize	These two fields contain a recommended minimum and maximum point size value for this font. The value is set by the font creator and factors in the complexity of the font. As with the `sNominalPointSize` field, the value is measured in decipoints.
USHORT	**usType**	This field contains type information about the font:
	FM_TYPE_FIXED	The spacing between all characters in the font is constant.
	FM_TYPE_LICENSED	The font is licensed.
	FM_TYPE_KERNING	The font contains kerning information. The number of kerning pairs for the font will be set in the `sKerningPairs` field. The actual kerning pairs may be retrieved by calling the `GpiQueryKerningPairs` function when the font is set into a presentation space.

FM_TYPE_DBCS	The font is for double-byte code pages.
FM_TYPE_MBCS	The font is for a mixed single- and double-byte code page.
FM_TYPE_64K	Font exceeds 65,536 bytes.
FM_TYPE_FACETRUNC	The font facename exceeds FACESIZE -1, and the szFacename field does not contain the entire facename of the font.
FM_TYPE_FAMTRUNC	The font family name exceeds FACESIZE -1, and the szFamilyname field does not contain the entire family name of the font.
FM_TYPE_ATOMS	The contents of the FaceNameAtom and FaceNameAtom contain valid atoms.
USHORT usDefn	This field contains the flag that identifies the origin and representation of the font:
FM_DEFN_OUTLINE	The font is an outline font. If this bit is not set, it is an image font.
FM_DEFN_GENERIC	The font is understood by GPI and can be rendered on all devices. If this bit is not set, it is a device specific font.
USHORT fsSelection	This field contains flags that describe the attributes of this font. The flags will reflect only the attributes of the physical font, for example, outline fonts that typically provide four fonts with the following physical attributes normal, bold, italic, and bold italic. Image fonts, on the other hand, almost always have synthesized font attributes and, therefore, will infrequently have these flags set:
FM_SEL_ITALIC	The font is italic.
FM_SEL_UNDERSCORE	The font is underscored.
FM_SEL_NEGATIVE	The font has foreground and background colors reversed.
FM_SEL_OUTLINE	The font is designed with hollow characters.
FM_SEL_STRIKEOUT	The font has a strikeout as part of the character glyphs.
FM_SEL_BOLD	The font is bold.
USHORT usCapabilities	This field indicates that the characters of the font may not be mixed with graphics if the FM_CAP_NOMIX flag is set. The high byte of the field identifies the quality of the font. There are no system constants

		defined for these values, and the value is almost never set to a value other than undefined: 0 Undefined 1 Data processing quality 2 Data processing draft quality 3 Near letter quality 4 Letter quality
LONG	lSubscriptXSize	These fields contain the recommended width and height for subscripts and superscripts.
LONG	lSubscriptYSize	
LONG	lSuperscriptXSize	
LONG	lSuperscriptYSize	These fields contain the recommended X and Y offset for subscripts and superscripts relative to the baseline.
LONG	lSubscriptXOffset	
LONG	lSubscriptYOffset	
LONG	lSuperscriptXOffset	
LONG	lSuperscriptYOffset	
LONG	lUnderscoreSize	
LONG	lStrikeoutSize	This field contains the height of the underscore or strikeout stroke for the font.
LONG	lUnderscorePosition	This field contains the vertical position of the underscore relative to the baseline. Positive values are below the baseline and negative values are above the baseline.
LONG	lStrikeoutPosition	This field contains the vertical position of the strikeout relative to the baseline.
SHORT	**sKerningPairs**	This field contains the number of character pairs in the table of kerning pairs. To retrieve the character pairs, the font must be created and set into a presentation space. When this is done, the `GpiQueryKerningPairs` function is called to retrieve an array of kerning pairs.
SHORT	**sFamilyClass**	This field is intended to identify a font into a class and subclass. The specification was never widely published and is largely unimplemented by device fonts. The least significant byte identifies the family class, whereas the most significant byte contains the subclass.
ATOM	FamilyNameAtom	When the facename and/or `ATOM` `FaceNameAtom` family name exceed

	FACESIZE -1 bytes in length, the FM_TYPE_ATOMS flag will be set in the usType field, and these two fields will contain atom handles for the complete facename.
LONG lMatch	This field contains a unique ID for fonts enumerated from a given device at a given time. For example, all fonts enumerated from the display device will have a unique ID. If the value is greater than 0, the font is a generic GPI font; if negative, it is a device font. The lMatch field has no other significance and should not be saved (in a file, for example) along with other font selection information.
PANOSE panose	This structure identifies the PANOSE classification of the font. This classification system has superseded the sFamilyClass as a numeric means of selecting a font based on typographical characteristics. The PANOSE structure contains the following fields: bFamilyType bSerifStyle bWeight bProportion bContrast bStrokeVariation bArmStyle bLetterform bMidline bXHeight abReserved[2]

As you look through the fonts enumerated in the list box of the PMFONT sample, you will see many entries with the same name. This occurs primarily in image fonts that must have bitmaps for many point sizes and screen resolutions. Because we requested all public and private fonts, even imaged fonts that were not designed for this resolution are returned. Your application may eliminate these fonts by comparing the sXDeviceRes and xYDeviceRes fields of the FONTMETRICS structure to the horizontal and vertical pels per inch for your device. Those that do not match their respective values may be eliminated. For example, if your application is running on an 8514/A or XGA device at 1024×768, the horizontal and vertical resolution will be 120 pels per inch. Fonts that are designed for the standard VGA resolution (640×480) will have a horizontal and vertical resolution or 96 pels per inch.

When a font is selected in the list box, the contents of the FONTMETRICS panel are updated with the metrics for that font. Some of the items are converted from a numeric index to a string. For example, the weight and width values are displayed as the strings that describe those values. After updating the metrics, two text strings are output on the right side of the client area. The first, displayed in the upper third of the client, is comprised of the code points for the character glyphs from "a" to "z" in both uppercase and lowercase. The second string, displayed in the lower third of the client, contains the code points from 160 to 175. These values were selected to illustrate the variation of character glyphs based on the code page with which the font was created. We will elaborate on code pages a bit later; for now, all fonts will be created using the multilingual code page 850. Image fonts that are selected are displayed at their actual size, and outline fonts are displayed in their default size.

Creating Fonts

Before we can use any of the physical fonts available on this device, we must create a logical font resource and set that resource into a presentation space. A logical font is a description of a desired font from which PM will select a physical font. The font description is comprised of the facename, size, and attributes of a desired font. The creation of a logical font can be approached in two ways: you can do the mapping, or PM can do the mapping. Font mapping is a process of selecting a font from the available fonts that is the "best or closest match" to a requested font. Doing your own font mapping requires you to enumerate the available fonts, select the desired font, and create that font using values from the FONTMETRICS structure. When you let PM do the font mapping, you must simply supply the desired size and style information. The function to create a logical font is GpiCreateLogFont. You will notice that input parameter is not a pointer to a FONTMETRICS structure, but a pointer to a FATTRS structure. The FATTRS structure can be thought of as a subset of the FONTMETRICS structure:

```
GpiCreateLogFont (hPS,pName,lLcid,pFattrs)
```

HPS	hPS	Presentation space handle in which to create the logical font resource.
PSTR8	pName	Pointer to a null-terminated 8-character string that aids in description of a logical font.
LONG	lLcid	The local identifier used to refer to this font in this presentation space. Even though this parameter is a long, it must be in the range of 1 to 254. Because bitmap resources are also referred to by a local identifier, this value may not be the same as a currently defined bitmap LCID.
PFATTRS	Fattrs	Pointer to a FATTRS structure that describes the font to be created.

The GpiCreateLogFont function uses the contents of the supplied FATTRS structure as searching criteria to select a font. As mentioned, the FATTRS can be thought of as a subset of the FONTMETRICS structure. Let's look at the FATTRS structure and see how it's fields relate to those in the FONTMETRICS structure.

USHORT	usRecordLength	The length in bytes of the FATTRS structure.
USHORT	fsSelection	This parameter does not affect the font selection but the style to be applied to the selected font:
	FATTR_SEL_ITALIC	Makes the font italic.
	FATTR_SEL_UNDERSCORE	Underscores the characters.
	FATTR_SEL_STRIKEOUT	Overstrikes the characters.
	FATTR_SEL_BOLD	Emboldens the characters.
	FATTR_SEL_OUTLINE	Does not fill outline characters. This flag has no effect on image fonts.
LONG	lMatch	The font match identifier returned as the lMatch field of the FONTMETRIC structure. The match value is only valid for the device from which it was enumerated. Negative lMatch values indicate a device font. If lMatch is set to 0, PM attempts to select a font that meets the desired criteria.
CHAR	szFacename	A null-terminated character string of length FACESIZE that identifies the facename of the desired font. This is equivalent to the szFacename in the FONTMETRIC structure.
USHORT	idRegistry	The IBM registered number. If unknown this should be set to 0.
USHORT	usCodePage	The desired code page to use when creating the font. The default code page is used if 0 is specified. The current code page may be retrieved by calling the GpiQueryCp function. This value should generally be equal to the message queue code page.
LONG	lMaxBaselineExt	If the fsFontUse parameter does not have the FATTR_FONTUSE_OUTLINE flag set, this field contains the height of the requested image font. Otherwise, it should be set to 0.

LONG	lAveCharWidth	If the fsFontUse parameter does not have the FATTR_FONTUSE_OUTLINE flag set, this field contains the width of the requested image font. Otherwise, it should be set to 0.
USHORT	fsType	Defines the required font type:
	FATTR_TYPE_KERNING	A kerned font is required.
	FATTR_TYPE_MBCS	Mixed single- and double-byte code page required.
	FATTR_TYPE_DBCS	Double-byte code page required.
	FATTR_TYPE_ANTIALIASED	Antialiased font required.
USHORT	fsFontUse	Defines the intended use of the font:
	FATTR_FONTUSE_NOMIX	Text is not output with graphics.
	FATTR_FONTUSE_OUTLINE	An outline font is required.
	FATTR_FONTUSE_TRANSFORMABLE	Characters must be able to be scaled, sheared, and rotated.

If the function fails, it will return GPI_ERROR; otherwise, it will return the result of the creation. If FONT_MATCH is returned, the supplied LCID now refers to a font matching your selection criteria. If FONT_DEFAULT is returned, a match was not found, and the default font has been selected. For display devices, the default will be the System Proportional Font.

If the GpiCreateLogFont function was successful, the LCID for the font can now be set into a presentation space. The LCID can be thought of as an application-defined local handle that can be selected and unselected in a presentation space. The GpiSetCharSet function will "select" the supplied LCID into the supplied presentation space:

```
GpiSetCharSet (hPS,lLcid)
```

HPS	hPS	Presentation space handle to select lLcid into. This must be the same handle passed to the GpiCreateLogFont function when the local identifier was created.
LONG	lLcid	The local identifier used to refer to the font. To reset the default, use LCID_DEFAULT.

This font will now be used for all text output and query functions. When you are finished with a font resource, it should be freed. If the resource is currently set into a presentation space, the default value should be restored by calling the GpiSetCharSet function that is using LCID_DEFAULT as the lLcid value. The logical font resource may then be freed by calling the GpiDeleteSetId function. The default font for the device will be restored. For the display, the System Proportional font is reset:

```
GpiDeleteSetId (hPS,lLcid)
```

HPS	hPS	Presentation space handle to delete the lLcid from. This must be the same handle passed to the GpiCreateLogFont function when the local identifier was created.

LONG	lLcid	The local identifier used to refer to the font. To delete all logical font and bitmap identifiers, use LCID_ALL.

Both the GpiSetCharSet and the GpiDeleteSetId return TRUE if successful and FALSE if an error has occurred.

The presentation space in which the logical font resource is created is the only one in which that LCID is valid. A logical font resource may not be shared across multiple presentations spaces, even on the same device. That resource is also invalid after the presentation space it was created in is released. This has the potential to cause some performance problems in PM applications.

Mapping Fonts

The OS/2 documentation says that a font may be selected by setting only the lMatch and the usRecordLength fields in the FATTRS. While developing the sample application for this chapter, we were unable to create a font based on the lMatch and usRecordlength fields alone. The default font was selected even if the same presentation space handle was used for the enumeration and creation. When the szFacename from the FONTMETRICS szFacename was added, the desired font was successfully created. We, therefore, recommend that when creating a logical font, the FATTRS structure should be initialized with as much information as possible, even if you have a lMatch value.

If the lMatch field is set to 0, PM will attempt to select a font matching the supplied criteria. The chart in Figure 7.9 is a simplified description of the font selection process. Notice that if an image font of the desired width and height is not found, an outline font may be substituted for it.

When creating an application, a font of a given face name and point size is often needed to output text labels on controls such as rulers or status lines. This requires you to perform some simple mapping on your own. The PMFONT sample provides an example of selecting a font based on the criteria of face name and point size alone. The choose_font function will enumerate all fonts of the requested name. It then finds the closest point size match based on display resolution and a tolerance. If a suitable font is found then the list box entry item containing that fonts is selected. This causes that font along with it's metrics to be displayed. If you were creating a new font a FATTRS structure should be initialized with the lMatch and szFacename values from the selected FONTMETRICS structure. To access this feature from the Display menu select the Choose Font menu item. In the dialog box enter a face name and point size and select ok.

General Usage Tips

Many applications have several small windows that display program status and hint text to the user. In an effort to save screen space, the font used to display this information is often an image font smaller than the System Proportional font. Eight-point Helv font is frequently used because of its excellent readability. These windows might be updated by a notification message.

When that message is received, a presentation space handle is retrieved; the text is output; and the handle is released. If each of those three windows used a micro cached presentation space—as is most common—the eight-point Helv font must be created for each update and set into the presentation space before outputting the text. After the text has been drawn, the default font should be set back into the presentation space and the local identifier for the Helv font deleted. If the update of these windows is frequent, the overhead could slow down an application.

Figure 7.9.
Font mapping flowchart.

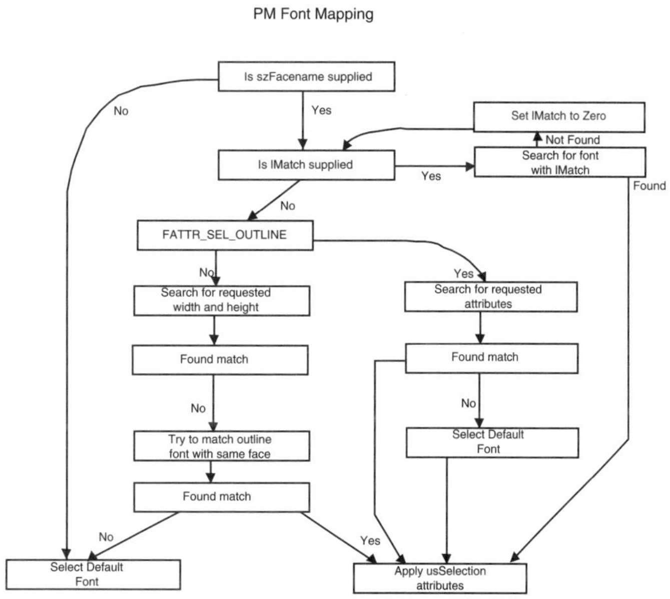

Dialogs that use a font other than the system font are excellent examples of this. When the default System Proportional font is used in a dialog, the creation and display speed is excellent. When the font is changed by using the `PRESPARAMS PP_FONTNAMESIZE` statement in the dialog template, the dialog display speed is noticeably slower. This occurs because even though all the control windows use the same font, each one must create, select, and delete that font. When the default System Proportional font is used, the creation is eliminated because it is the default presentation space font.

The whole point of this is to be aware of the font creation and selection model and use it to your advantage. For example, if you are a Windows developer moving to Presentation Manager, don't write your code like a Windows application using the PM API. When a font is created and selected into a presentation space, the display performance is excellent even for outline fonts. Your application, however, may not see this if it spends all its time creating fonts rather than using them. Our fictitious application with three status windows has several alternatives. The default system font could be used, or the three status windows could be combined into a single window.

The status windows could be eliminated and the text drawn on a reserved portion of the client area. The main drawing or display area often creates a presentation space for the duration of the application. Because a local identifier is valid for the life of a PS, the font must be created only once and set when needed.

Scaling, Shearing, and Rotating

When an image is created and set into a presentation space, its size is defined by the size of glyphs for the character. Outline fonts, on the other hand, must be scaled to the desired size before text can be output.

The characters of an outline are defined by a rectangle that has a width of `sXDeviceRes` and a height of `sYDeviceRes`. This rectangle, defined from fields in the `FONTMETRIC` structure, is referred to as the font definition space. From the font definition space, outline fonts are scaled to a second rectangle called the character box. The character box is an attribute that may be set into a presentation space. The height of the font definition space and the height of the character box correspond to the point size of the font. There is no limit to the size of the character box. When the character box is set, the width and height of the character box correspond to the resulting `lEMInc` and `lEMHeight` metrics. The character box is set by the function `GpiSetCharBox`:

```
GpiSetCharBox (hPS,pSizef)
```

`HPS`	`hPS`	Presentation space handle in which to set the character box.
`PSIZEF`	`pSizef`	Pointer to a `SIZEF` structure that contains the new width and height to set the character box to.

The character box is used primarily to size outline fonts. Although it won't size an image font, it may affect character spacing in certain character modes. We will explore this when character modes are discussed.

The default baseline is defined by a line originating at point 0,0 and extending to point 1,0 in a Cartesian coordinate system. This baseline is considered to have 0 degrees of rotation. The angle of rotation may be changed by calling the `GpiSetCharAngle`:

```
GpiSetCharAngle (hPS,pGradAngle)
```

`HPS`	`hPS`	Presentation space handle in which to set baseline angle.
`PGRADIENTL`	`pGradAngle`	Pointer to a `GRADIENTL` structure that defines a new end point of the angle vector which determines character baseline.

The `GRADIENTL` structure is comprised of two long values that define an X and Y point. Currently, `GRADIENTL` is identical to a `POINTL` structure. For future portability, however, the `GRADIENTL` type should be used. Because most of us think of rotation in terms of angle, not as

ordered pairs, we must convert the desired angle into a new X and Y point. The desired point may be calculated by the following formula:

```
X = radius * sin (angle) Y = radius * cos (angle)
```

The C library functions `sin` and `cos` expect angles defined as radians. A circle has 360 degrees, which is equivalent to 2 * PI radians. To determine the number of radians in a desired angle, we must multiply 2 * PI by the percent of the 360 degrees in which we are interested.

```
AngleInRadians = 2 * 3.1416 * DesiredAngle / 360
```

The radius is arbitrary, but should be large enough to provide an accurate point. The sample application has chosen 200, but your application may require a higher value.

In addition to modifying the baseline angle, PM enables you to modify the character shear angle. This angle defines how individual character cells are slanted relative to the baseline. `GpiSetCharAngle` will set the new point defining the shear angle:

```
GpiSetCharAngle (hPS,pPtl)
```

`HPS`	`hPS`	Presentation space handle in which to set shear angle.
`PPOINTL`	`pPtl`	Pointer to a `POINTL` structure that defines a new end point of the angle vector that determines character shear.

As with the baseline, the angle of character shear is specified as a point on the line that originates from point 0,0. The default point for character shear is 0,1, which translates to 90 degrees. This point is always relative to the baseline regardless of its angle. Any shear angle may be specified. Extreme shear angles may cause characters to display as a single line.

When text is output, characters are normally output left to right. The direction may be changed to one of three other values by the `GpiSetCharDirection` function:

```
GpiSetCharDirection (hPS,lDirection)
```

`HPS`	`hPS`	Presentation space handle in which to set character direction.

`LONG`	`lDirection`	A flag that defines the direction characters are drawn relative to the baseline. It may be one of the following:
		`CHDIRN_DEFAULT`
		`CHDIRN_LEFTRIGHT`
		`CHDIRN_TOPBOTTOM`
		`CHDIRN_RIGHTLEFT`
		`CHDIRN_BOTTOMTOP`

It appears there are four other directions that may be set; however, the `CHDIRN_DEFAULT` is initially equivalent to `CHDIRN_LEFTRIGHT`. The default may be changed to `CHDIRN_TOPBOTTOM`, `CHDIRN_RIGHTLEFT`, or `CHDIRN_BOTTOMTOP` using the `GpiSetDefAttrs` function. The `CHDIRN_RIGHTLEFT` flag will cause characters to be parallel to the baseline, but the current

position is advanced to the left after each character is drawn. Both CHDIRN_TOPBOTTOM and CHDIR_BOTTOMTOP flags will cause the characters to be drawn in columns 90 degrees to the baseline. CHDIRN_TOPBOTTOM rotates the character box 90 degrees clockwise and CHDIR_BOTTOMTOP 90 degrees counterclockwise.

Character Modes

A presentation space has three modes that control how characters use the current setting of the character attributes for angle, box, and shear. Outline fonts always use the current setting for angle, box, and shear and are never affected by character mode settings. Image fonts may be affected only by rotation and character box; the characters are never sheared. The current character mode may be set by calling the GpiSetCharMode function:

```
GpiSetCharMode (hPS,lMode)
```

HPS	hPS	Presentation space handle in which to set the character box.
LONG lMode		The new character mode to set. It may be one of the following: CM_DEFAULT CM_MODE1 CM_MODE2 CM_MODE3

The CM_DEFAULT mode is initially equivalent to CM_MODE1, but may be changed to CM_MODE2 or CM_MODE3 by the GpiSetDefAttrs function. CM_MODE1 allows the selection of a raster or outline font into the presentation space. Image fonts are positioned based on their metrics, and character box values are ignored. In CM_MODE2, the first character is positioned as in CM_MODE1, but the second and subsequent characters are positioned based on the width of the character box. The actual character glyphs are not stretched, but spacing between characters is increased. The vertical position of the characters is not affected. In CM_MODE2, characters also are rotated based on the current character angle. The glyphs, however, always maintain a perpendicular orientation to the default (1,0) baseline. The result is a stair-step effect when image fonts are rotated in CM_MODE2. The last mode, CM_MODE3, does not allow image fonts to be set into a presentation space.

Table 7.1 defines the default presentation space attributes that affect text output and the functions available to change them.

Table 7.1. Default values that affect text.

Character Attribute	*Default*	*Function(s) to Query/Modify*	
Angle	1,0	GpiSetCharAngle CharAngle GpiSetAttrs	GipQuer

Character Attribute	*Default*	*Function(s) to Query/Modify*	
Shear	0,1	GpiSetCharShear GpiQueryCharShear GpiSetAttrs	CBB_SHEAR
Direction	left to right	GpiSetCharDirection GpiQueryCharDirection GpiSetAttrs	CBB_DIRECTION
Mode	CH_MODE1	GpiSetCharMode GpiQueryCharMode GpiSetAttrs	CBB_MODE
Extra spacing all	zero	GpiSetCharExtra characters GpiQueryCharExtra GpiSetAttrs	CBB_EXTRA
Extra spacing break	zero	GpiSetCharBreakExtra character only GpiQueryCharBreakExtra GpiSetAttrs	CBB_BREAK_EXTRA
Foreground (text)	CLR_BLACK	GpiSetAttrs color	CBB_COLOR
Background color	DISPLAY_SYSCLR_WINDOW PRINTER_PAPER_COLOR	GpiSetAtts	CBB_BACK_COLOR
Foreground (text)	FM_OVERPAINT	GpiSetAttrs mix mode	CBB_MIX_MODE
Background	BM_LEAVEALONE	GpiSetAttrs	
Mix mode	CBB_BACK_MIX_MODE		

Rotation and Shear in PMFONT

To enable you to see how character modes, rotation, shear, and character box affect image and outline characters, a special panel has been added to PMFONT. This panel is displayed when the Rotation/Shear menu item is selected from the Display pop-up menu.

A sample text string in the currently selected font is displayed centered on the right side of the client window with a parallelogram drawn around it. The points of the parallelogram are

calculated by using the GpiQueryTextBox function. They define the bounds of the text string. On the shear panel are entry fields that control the width and height of the character box. The default size is 50×50 but you may change the size to any value. The character shear may be changed by entering a new X and Y point that defines a new end point for the baseline. A new baseline angle may also be specified by scrolling the spin control or by directly entering a value between 0 and 360. Notice that in character mode one (CM_MODE1), image fonts rotate around the logical 0,0 point, but the baseline remains unchanged. If you change the character mode to CM_MODE2, the characters are oriented along the modified baseline. The characters, however, remain perpendicular to the default baseline. You also will notice that the spacing between characters is wider. This occurs because the character box width affects the spacing of image fonts in CM_MODE2. The character shear may also be modified, but will affect only outline fonts. As with the baseline angle, you may supply a new X and Y point or dial in a new shear angle. The default shear is 90 degrees, which results in character boxes that are perpendicular to the baseline regardless of its angle. Angles less than 90 degrees cause the characters to slant to the right, and angles greater than 90 degrees will cause a slant to the left. Finally, a text entry field exists to enable you to enter your own text string to display.

Character Bundle Structure

This chapter has discussed many functions that modify character attributes. Almost all these functions are actually modifying the current character bundle in the presentation space. You may recall that when attribute bundles were discussed in Chapter 6, "Presentation Spaces and Drawing," the character bundle was excluded. Now that we understand more about fonts lets look at the character bundle. Like the other bundles the character bundle or CHARBUNDLE has a foreground and background color as well as a foreground and background mix mode. The foreground color defines the text color and the background color is the character cell fill color. Remember that setting the text background color requires changing the background mix mode from the default of BM_LEAVEALONE, otherwise the text is rendered with a transparent background. The remainder of the character bundle is comprised of fields that control character shear, rotation, size, direction, alignment, and the font selected. The type and format of the fields is the same as their GPI function equivalent. (See Table 7.2.) The CHARBUNDLE is modified by calling the GpiSetAttrs function. Fields specific to CHARBUNDLE are as follows:

usSet	Local identifier that represents a logical font. It must be between 1 and 254. The default may be reset by using the LCID_DEFAULT flag.
usPrecision	Character mode, it may be one of the following: CM_DEFAULT CM_MODE1 CM_MODE2 CM_MODE3
sizfxCell	Defines a character cell or box used in scaling outline fonts.
ptlAngle	Point that defines a new end point of the line which determines character baseline.

`ptlShear`	Point that defines a new end point of the line which determines how a character box is slanted relative to the baseline.
`usDirection`	Flag that defines the direction characters are drawn relative to the baseline.
`usTextAlign`	Flag values that define how a text string is aligned relative to the current position.
`fxExtra`	Specifies the amount of additional space added or subtracted between characters when a text string is output.
`fxBreakExtra`	Specifies the amount of additional space added or subtracted to the break character. The space character is most often the break character.

You will find in the `process_paint` function of PMFONT that character attributes for the metrics panel are set through the individual functions, and the shear panel sets them by using the `CHARBUNDLE`. Whenever possible, multiple attributes should be set by using the `GpiSetAttrs` function. For example, assuming the fields of the character bundle have been initialized, the following code clips accomplish the same task:

```
GpiSetCharSet   (hPS,CurrentCB.usSet);
GpiSetCharAngle (hPS,&CurrentCB.ptlAngle);
GpiSetCharShear (hPS,&CurrentCB.ptlShear);
GpiSetCharBox   (hPS,&CurrentCB.sizfxCell);
```

```
GpiSetAttrs(hPS,PRIM_CHAR,CBB_SET | CBB_ANGLE | CBB_SHEAR | CBB_BOX,0,&CurrentCB);
```

When resetting the default values by using the `GpiSetAttrs` function, you must set the `CBB_` flag for the field to reset in both the `ulAttrMask` and `ulDefault` values. The contents of that field are ignored and need not be initialized. Resist the temptation to attempt to reset a default value in the following way; it will not work:

```
CHARBUNDLE cb;

cb.usSet = LCID_DEFAULT;
GpiSetAttrs (hPS,PRIM_CHAR,CBB_SET,0,(PBUNDLE)&cb);
```

The current setting of the `CHARBUNDLE` may be retrieved by the `GpiQueryAttrs` function.

Table 7.2. Character functions and equivalent `CHARBUNDLE` fields and flags.

GPI Function	*CHARBUNDLE Field*	*CHARBUNDLE Flag*
`GpiSetCharSet()`	`usSet`	`CBB_SET`
`GpiSetCharBox()`	`sizfxCell`	`CBB_BOX`
`GpiSetCharShear()`	`pltShear`	`CBB_SHEAR`
`GpiSetCharMode()`	`usPrecision`	`CBB_MODE`

continues

Table 7.2. continued

GPI Function	*CHARBUNDLE Field*	*CHARBUNDLE Flag*
GpiSetCharDirection()	usDirection	CBB_DIRECTION
GpiSetCharExtra()	fxExtra	CBB_EXTRA
GpiSetCharBreakExtra()	fxBreakExtra	CBB_BREAK_EXTRA
GpiSetTextAlignment()	usTextAlign	CBB_TEXT_ALIGN

Logical Inches

To make fonts more legible on the display device, many applications display text according to a logical inch rather than a physical inch. A logical inch is typically 35 percent to 40 percent larger than an actual inch.

The PMFONT Application

The following files are necessary to build the PMFONT application:

PMFONT.C
PMFONT.DEF
PMFONT.DLG
PMFONT.H
PMFONT.ICO
PMFONT.RC
ABOUT.DLG
SLIDE.DLG

PMFONT.C

```
/* ---------------------------------------------------------------------
                         PM Font Program

                  Real World Programming for OS/2
            Copyright (c) 1993-94 Blain, Delimon, and English
------------------------------------------------------------------- */


#define INCL_DOS
#define INCL_WIN
#define INCL_GPI
#define INCL_GPILCIDS
#define INCL_DEV
#define INCL_WINERRORS
```

```
#include <stdio.h>
#include <string.h>
#include <math.h>
#include <stdlib.h>
#include <os2.h>
#include "pmfont.h"
#include "chap7.h"
#include "..\common\about.h"

BOOL APIENTRY GpiSetTextAlignment(HPS,LONG,LONG);

HAB  hab;
PVOID  pMem;
char   szBuff1[MAX_BUFF];
int    cxChar = 0;
int    cyChar = 0;
HWND   hWndMetrics = 0;
HWND   hWndShear = 0;
HWND   hMenu;
USHORT usDisplayMode  = IDM_METRICS;
USHORT usCharMode = IDM_CHMODE_ONE;
USHORT usSelection = 0;
USHORT usCurrentCP = 850;
USHORT usCurrentFontIndex = 0;
LONG   cxFontRes;
LONG   cyFontRes;
LONG   lHorzRes;
LONG   lVertRes;
double dRotSine;
double dRotCosine;
CHAR   szFontFace[] = "10.Helv";
CHAR   szDisplayStr[MAX_BUFF];
CHAR   szSpecialStr[MAX_STR];
CHAR   szUserStr[MAX_BUFF];
CHARBUNDLE CurrentCB;

GRADIENTL DefaultAngle = {0L,0L};
SIZEF     DefaultCharBox = {0,0};
FIXED     CharExtra = 0;
FIXED     BreakExtra = 0;

CHAR  *szWeights[] =
{
    "Ultra-light",
    "Extra-light",
    "Light",
    "Semi-light",
    "Medium",
    "Semi-bold",
    "Bold",
    "Extra-bold",
    "Ultra-bold"
};

CHAR  *szWidths[] =
```

```
{
    "Ultra-condensed",
    "Extra-condensed",
    "Condensed",
    "Semi-condensed",
    "Medium",
    "Semi-expanded",
    "Expanded",
    "Extra-expanded",
    "Ultra-expanded"
};

CHAR  *szQuality[]=
{
    "Undefined",
    "DP Quality",
    "DP Draft",
    "Near Letter Quality",
    "Leter Quality"
};

CHAR  *szFormat[]=
{
    "Device",
    "GPI"
};

CHAR  *szType[]=
{
    " Bitmap",
    " Outline"
};

CHAR  *szSelection[]=
{
    "",
    "Bold",
    " Italic",
    " Strikeout",
    " UnderScore",
    " Outline"
};

CHAR  *szSpacing[]=
{
    "Proportional",
    "Fixed"
};

int iCharModes[] =
{
    CM_MODE1,CM_MODE2,CM_MODE3
};

#define BUFF_SIZE 80
```

```
#define POINTSIZE_THRESHOLD 1

HDC          hDisplayInfoDC = 0;
HPS          hDisplayPS = 0;
HWND         hWndFrame,hWndClient;
HWND         hWndDC;
HWND         hFontLBox;
PFONTMETRICS pScreenFontMetrics = 0;


MRESULT APIENTRY ClientWndProc(HWND,ULONG,MPARAM,MPARAM);
MRESULT APIENTRY ChooseFontDlgProc(HWND,ULONG,MPARAM, MPARAM);
MRESULT APIENTRY MetricsWndProc(HWND,ULONG,MPARAM,MPARAM);
MRESULT APIENTRY ShearWndProc(HWND,ULONG,MPARAM,MPARAM);


int main ()
{
  HMQ    hmq;
  QMSG   qmsg;
  ULONG  flFrameFlags    = FCF_TITLEBAR ¦ FCF_SYSMENU ¦
                           FCF_SIZEBORDER ¦ FCF_MINMAX ¦
                           FCF_SHELLPOSITION ¦ FCF_TASKLIST ¦
                           FCF_ICON ¦ FCF_MENU;
  CHAR   szClientClass[] = "CLIENT";
  RECTL  Rectl;
  int    i = 0;
  int    iClientHeight;

  hab = WinInitialize (0);
  hmq = WinCreateMsgQueue (hab, 0);

  DosAllocMem((PPVOID)&pMem,0x1000,PAG_READ ¦ PAG_WRITE);
  DosSubSet(pMem,DOSSUB_INIT ¦ DOSSUB_SPARSE_OBJ,8192);

  WinRegisterClass (hab,szClientClass,ClientWndProc,CS_SIZEREDRAW ¦
    CS_CLIPCHILDREN, 0);
  WinLoadString (hab,0,IDS_APPNAME,sizeof(szBuff1),szBuff1);

  WinQueryWindowRect (HWND_DESKTOP,&Rectl);
  iClientHeight = WinQuerySysValue(HWND_DESKTOP,SV_CYSCREEN) -
                  WinQuerySysValue(HWND_DESKTOP,SV_CYICON);
  hWndFrame = WinCreateStdWindow (HWND_DESKTOP,0,&flFrameFlags,
    szClientClass,szBuff1,0,0,ID_APPNAME,&hWndClient);

  WinSetWindowPos (hWndFrame,HWND_TOP,0,
      WinQuerySysValue(HWND_DESKTOP,SV_CYSCREEN) - iClientHeight,
      WinQuerySysValue(HWND_DESKTOP,SV_CXSCREEN),iClientHeight,
      SWP_SHOW ¦ SWP_ACTIVATE ¦ SWP_ZORDER ¦ SWP_SIZE ¦ SWP_MOVE);

  hMenu  = WinWindowFromID (hWndFrame,FID_MENU);
  hWndDC = WinOpenWindowDC(hWndClient);

  WinEnableWindowUpdate(hWndClient,FALSE);
  if (create_controls(hWndClient))
  {
```

```
    WinEnableWindowUpdate(hWndClient,TRUE);
    WinShowWindow (hFontLBox,TRUE);
    WinSendMsg(hFontLBox,LM_SELECTITEM,MPFROMSHORT(0),
      MPFROMSHORT(TRUE));
    WinSetFocus(HWND_DESKTOP,hFontLBox);
    WinShowWindow (hWndMetrics,TRUE);
  }
  else
    return(0);

  while (WinGetMsg (hab,&qmsg,0,0,0))
    WinDispatchMsg (hab,&qmsg);

  WinDestroyMsgQueue (hmq);
  WinTerminate (hab);
  return 0;
}



VOID APIENTRY center_window (HWND hWnd)
{
    ULONG ulScrWidth, ulScrHeight;
    RECTL Rectl;

    ulScrWidth  = WinQuerySysValue (HWND_DESKTOP, SV_CXSCREEN);
    ulScrHeight = WinQuerySysValue (HWND_DESKTOP, SV_CYSCREEN);
    WinQueryWindowRect (hWnd, &Rectl);
    WinSetWindowPos (hWnd, HWND_TOP, (ulScrWidth-Rectl.xRight)/2,
        (ulScrHeight-Rectl.yTop)/2, 0, 0, SWP_MOVE | SWP_ACTIVATE);
    return;
}


VOID APIENTRY charbox_from_pointsize (FIXED fxPtSize,PSIZEF pSizef)
{
    pSizef->cx = MAKEFIXED( ((fxPtSize * cxFontRes) / 72),0);
    pSizef->cy = MAKEFIXED( ((fxPtSize * cyFontRes) / 72),0);
}


BOOL APIENTRY choose_font(PCH pFacename,int iPointSize)
/*-------------------------------------------------------------*/
/*-------------------------------------------------------------*/
{
  PFONTMETRICS pFM,pCurFM;
  ULONG        ulCount = 0L;
  BOOL         bFound = FALSE;
  HPS          hPS;
  int          i,iDelta;

  /* Do any fonts with the requested facename exist */
  hPS = WinGetScreenPS (HWND_DESKTOP);
  ulCount = GpiQueryFonts (hPS,QF_PUBLIC | QF_PRIVATE,pFacename,
```

```
(PLONG) &ulCount,(LONG)sizeof(FONTMETRICS),0);
  if (ulCount)
  {
    /* If so allocate memory and retrieve their metrics */
    DosAllocMem ((PPVOID)&pFM,sizeof(FONTMETRICS) * (USHORT)ulCount,
        OBJ_TILE ¦ PAG_READ ¦ PAG_WRITE ¦ PAG_COMMIT);
    GpiQueryFonts (hPS,QF_PUBLIC ¦ QF_PRIVATE,pFacename,
(PLONG) &ulCount,(LONG)sizeof(FONTMETRICS),pFM);

    /* Look through the list trying to find a match */
    pCurFM = pFM;
    while (!bFound && ulCount)
    {
      if (pCurFM->fsDefn & FM_DEFN_OUTLINE)
      {
        bFound = TRUE;
      }
      else if ( (pCurFM->sYDeviceRes == cyFontRes) &&
                (pCurFM->sXDeviceRes == cxFontRes) )
      {
        int iDelta = abs((pCurFM->sNominalPointSize / 10) - iPointSize);
        if (iDelta <= POINTSIZE_THRESHOLD)
          bFound = TRUE;
      }

      if (!bFound)
      {
        ulCount--;
        if (ulCount)
          pCurFM++;
      }
    }

    if (bFound)
    {
      /* Search the screen font list looking for the lMatch value
         and select that entry in the listbox. */
      bFound = FALSE;
      ulCount = (ULONG)WinSendMsg(hFontLBox,LM_QUERYITEMCOUNT,0,0);
      for (i = 0; !bFound && i <= (int)ulCount; i++)
      {
        if ((pScreenFontMetrics + i)->lMatch == pCurFM->lMatch)
        {
          /* Select that entry in the list box and stop the search */
          bFound = TRUE;
          WinSendMsg(hFontLBox,LM_SELECTITEM,MPFROMSHORT(i),
              MPFROMSHORT(TRUE));
        }
      }
    }
    DosFreeMem(pFM);
  }
  WinReleasePS(hPS);

  return (bFound);
```

```
}


void APIENTRY cleanup()
/*-----------------------------------------------------------------*/

   This function is called to free the memory allocated and destroy
   the application window.

/*-----------------------------------------------------------------*/
{
  if (pScreenFontMetrics)
      DosFreeMem(pScreenFontMetrics);
  DosFreeMem(pMem);
  if (hWndMetrics)
      WinDestroyWindow (hWndMetrics);
  if (hWndShear)
      WinDestroyWindow (hWndShear);
  WinDestroyWindow (hWndFrame);
}


void APIENTRY draw_grid(HPS hPS,PRECTL pRectl)
{
  POINTL   ptlGrid[4];

  ptlGrid[0].x = pRectl->xLeft;
  ptlGrid[0].y = pRectl->yTop / 2;
  ptlGrid[1].x = pRectl->xRight;
  ptlGrid[1].y = ptlGrid[0].y;
  ptlGrid[2].x = pRectl->xLeft +
                 ((pRectl->xRight - pRectl->xLeft) / 2);
  ptlGrid[2].y = pRectl->yBottom;
  ptlGrid[3].x = ptlGrid[2].x;
  ptlGrid[3].y = pRectl->yTop;
  GpiMove (hPS,&ptlGrid[0]);
  GpiLine (hPS,&ptlGrid[1]);
  GpiMove (hPS,&ptlGrid[2]);
  GpiLine (hPS,&ptlGrid[3]);
}


BOOL APIENTRY create_controls(HWND hWndClient)
/*-----------------------------------------------------------------*/

   This function will create the font selection listbox and load
   the metrics and rotation dialogs. The fonts will be added to the
   listbox and the default display strings are loaded. All windows
   are left hidden.

/*-----------------------------------------------------------------*/
{
  RECTL  ClientRectl;
  RECTL  MetricsRectl;
  HWND   hWndEdit;
```

```
  HPS     hPS;

  WinLoadString (hab, 0, IDS_DISPLAY_TEXT,MAX_BUFF,szDisplayStr);
  WinLoadString (hab, 0, IDS_SPECIAL_TEXT,MAX_STR,szSpecialStr);

  WinQueryWindowRect(hWndClient,(PRECTL)&ClientRectl);

  /* Load the Metrics Window */
  if (hWndMetrics = WinLoadDlg(hWndClient,hWndClient,MetricsWndProc,
      0,METRICS_DLG,0))
  {
    WinQueryWindowRect(hWndMetrics,(PRECTL)&MetricsRectl);
    WinSetWindowPos (hWndMetrics,HWND_TOP,
      cxChar,ClientRectl.yTop - MetricsRectl.yTop - (cyChar * 5),0,0,
      SWP_ZORDER | SWP_MOVE);
  }
  else
     return(FALSE);

  /* Create the font selection list box */
  if (hFontLBox = WinCreateWindow (hWndClient,WC_LISTBOX,0,
          0L,
          cxChar,ClientRectl.yTop - (cyChar * 4),
          MetricsRectl.xRight,cyChar * 3,
          hWndClient,HWND_TOP,FONT_LBOX,0,0))
  {
    WinSetPresParam(hFontLBox,PP_FONTNAMESIZE,strlen(szFontFace)+1,
      (PVOID)szFontFace);
    hPS = WinGetPS (hWndClient);
    pScreenFontMetrics = init_font_LBox(hFontLBox,hPS);
    WinReleasePS(hPS);
  }
  else
    return(FALSE);

  /* Load the Shear Window and leave it hidden */
  if (hWndShear = WinLoadDlg(hWndClient,hWndClient,ShearWndProc,
      0,SHEAR_DLG,0))
  {
    WinQueryWindowRect(hWndShear,(PRECTL)&MetricsRectl);
    WinSetWindowPos (hWndShear,HWND_TOP,
        cxChar,ClientRectl.yTop - MetricsRectl.yTop - (cyChar * 5),
        0,0,
        SWP_ZORDER | SWP_MOVE);
    WinLoadString (hab,0,IDS_USER_TEXT,MAX_STR,szUserStr);
    hWndEdit = WinWindowFromID(hWndShear,DID_USER_TEXT);
    WinSendMsg(hWndEdit,EM_SETTEXTLIMIT,MPFROMSHORT(MAX_STR),0);
    WinSetWindowText(hWndEdit,szUserStr);
  }
  else
    return(FALSE);
  return (TRUE);
}


USHORT APIENTRY post_error(HWND hWnd,USHORT usErrorID)
```

```
/*--------------------------------------------------------------*/

   This is a utility function which will post a message box with
   a string loaded from the resource file.

/*--------------------------------------------------------------*/
{
  WinLoadString (hab,0,usErrorID,MAX_BUFF,szBuff1);
  return ((USHORT)WinMessageBox(HWND_DESKTOP,hWnd,(PSZ)szBuff1,
      (PSZ)"Error",0,MB_OK ¦ MB_ICONHAND ¦ MB_APPLMODAL));
}


void APIENTRY process_command(HWND hWnd,MPARAM mp1,MPARAM mp2)
/*--------------------------------------------------------------*/

   All WM_COMMAND messages received by the client window will be
   processed here.

/*--------------------------------------------------------------*/
{
  USHORT usAction;
  USHORT usAttribute;

  switch(SHORT1FROMMP(mp1))
  {
    case IDM_METRICS:
      if (usDisplayMode != IDM_METRICS)
      {
        WinSendMsg (hMenu,MM_SETITEMATTR,
            MPFROM2SHORT(IDM_ROTATION,TRUE),
            MPFROM2SHORT(MIA_CHECKED,FALSE));
        WinSendMsg (hMenu,MM_SETITEMATTR,
            MPFROM2SHORT(IDM_METRICS,TRUE),
            MPFROM2SHORT(MIA_CHECKED,MIA_CHECKED));
        WinShowWindow(hWndMetrics,TRUE);
        WinShowWindow(hWndShear,FALSE);
        usDisplayMode = IDM_METRICS;
        /* Force a new font to be created */
        WinSendMsg(hWndClient,WM_CONTROL,
            MPFROM2SHORT(FONT_LBOX,LN_SELECT),0);
        WinInvalidateRect(hWndClient,0,FALSE);
      }
      break;

    case IDM_ROTATION:
      if (usDisplayMode != IDM_ROTATION)
      {
        WinSendMsg (hMenu,MM_SETITEMATTR,
            MPFROM2SHORT(IDM_METRICS,TRUE),
            MPFROM2SHORT(MIA_CHECKED,FALSE));
        WinSendMsg (hMenu,MM_SETITEMATTR,
            MPFROM2SHORT(IDM_ROTATION,TRUE),
            MPFROM2SHORT(MIA_CHECKED,MIA_CHECKED));
        WinShowWindow(hWndShear,TRUE);
        WinShowWindow(hWndMetrics,FALSE);
```

```
          usDisplayMode = IDM_ROTATION;
          WinInvalidateRect(hWndClient,0,FALSE);
        }
        break;

      case IDM_CHOOSE:
        /* Display the choose font dialog */
        WinDlgBox(HWND_DESKTOP,hWndFrame,
(PFNWP)ChooseFontDlgProc,0,CHOOSEFONT_DLG,(PVOID)0);
        break;

      case IDM_CHMODE_ONE:
      case IDM_CHMODE_TWO:
      case IDM_CHMODE_THREE:
        WinSendMsg (hMenu,MM_SETITEMATTR,
            MPFROM2SHORT(usCharMode,TRUE),
            MPFROM2SHORT(MIA_CHECKED,FALSE));
        WinSendMsg (hMenu,MM_SETITEMATTR,
            MPFROM2SHORT(MPFROMSHORT(mp1),TRUE),
            MPFROM2SHORT(MIA_CHECKED,MIA_CHECKED));
        usCharMode = SHORT1FROMMP(mp1);
        /* Force a new font to be created */
        WinSendMsg(hWndClient,WM_CONTROL,
            MPFROM2SHORT(FONT_LBOX,LN_SELECT),0);
        break;

      case IDM_ATTR_ITALIC:
      case IDM_ATTR_BOLD:
      case IDM_ATTR_UNDERSCORE:
      case IDM_ATTR_STRIKEOUT:
      case IDM_ATTR_OUTLINE:
        switch (SHORT1FROMMP(mp1))
        {
          case IDM_ATTR_ITALIC:
            usAttribute = FATTR_SEL_ITALIC;
            break;
          case IDM_ATTR_BOLD:
            usAttribute = FATTR_SEL_BOLD;
            break;
          case IDM_ATTR_UNDERSCORE:
            usAttribute = FATTR_SEL_UNDERSCORE;
            break;
          case IDM_ATTR_STRIKEOUT:
            usAttribute = FATTR_SEL_STRIKEOUT;
            break;
          case IDM_ATTR_OUTLINE;
            usAttribute = FATTR_SEL_OUTLINE;
            break;
        }

        if (usSelection & usAttribute)
        {
          usSelection &= ~usAttribute;
          usAction = 0;
        }
        else
```

```
WinFillRect(hPS,(PRECTL)&ClientRectl,CLR_WHITE);

/* Set up a clipping rectangle before drawing the text */
hClipRgn = GpiCreateRegion(hPS,1,&ClientRectl);
GpiSetClipRegion(hPS,hClipRgn,&hPrevRgn);

/* Update the character mode */
GpiSetCharMode (hPS,iCharModes[(usCharMode - IDM_CHMODE) - 1]);

if (usDisplayMode == IDM_METRICS)
{
  GpiSetCharAngle (hPS,&DefaultAngle);
  GpiSetCharSet   (hPS,DISPLAY_FONT);

  Pointl.x = PanelRectl.xRight + cxChar;
  Pointl.y = (ClientRectl.yTop / 3) * 2;
  GpiCharStringAt (hPS,&Pointl,strlen(szDisplayStr),
    (PSZ)szDisplayStr);

  Pointl.y = ClientRectl.yTop / 3;
  GpiCharStringAt (hPS,&Pointl,strlen(szSpecialStr),
    (PSZ)szSpecialStr);
}
else if(usDisplayMode == IDM_ROTATION)
{
  draw_grid(hPS,(PRECTL)&ClientRectl);

  GpiSetCharExtra(hPS,CharExtra);
  GpiSetCharBreakExtra(hPS,BreakExtra);

  iLength = strlen(szUserStr);

  /* Set the character set and box but reset the angle of rotation*/
  GpiSetAttrs(hPS,PRIM_CHAR,CBB_SET | CBB_BOX | CBB_ANGLE,
      CBB_ANGLE,&CurrentCB);

  /* Query the extent of the string before rotation or shearing */
  GpiQueryTextBox(hPS,iLength,(PCH)szUserStr,TXTBOX_COUNT,Ptl);
  Pointl.x = PanelRectl.xRight +
    ((ClientRectl.xRight - ClientRectl.xLeft) / 2);
  Pointl.y = ClientRectl.yTop / 2;

  if (Ptl[TXTBOX_BOTTOMLEFT].x < Ptl[TXTBOX_TOPRIGHT].x)
    xExtent=(Ptl[TXTBOX_BOTTOMLEFT].x - Ptl[TXTBOX_TOPRIGHT].x / 2);
  else
    xExtent=(Ptl[TXTBOX_TOPRIGHT].x - Ptl[TXTBOX_BOTTOMLEFT].x / 2);

  /* Calculate the starting point for the rotated string */
  dSine   = xExtent * dRotSine;
  dCosine = xExtent * dRotCosine;
  Pointl.x += ((LONG)dCosine * lHorzRes)/(LONG)lVertRes;
  Pointl.y += (LONG) dSine;

  /* Set the character angle and shear */
  GpiSetAttrs(hPS,PRIM_CHAR,CBB_ANGLE | CBB_SHEAR,0,&CurrentCB);
```

```
    /* Get the extents of the string with rotation and shearing */
    GpiQueryTextBox(hPS,iLength,(PCH)szUserStr,TXTBOX_COUNT,Ptl);

    for (i = 0; i < 5; i++)
    {
        Ptl[i].x += Pointl.x;
        Ptl[i].y += Pointl.y;
    }
    TempPoint = Ptl[2];
    Ptl[2] = Ptl[3];
    Ptl[3] = TempPoint;
    Ptl[4].x = Ptl[0].x;
    Ptl[4].y = Ptl[0].y;

    /* Draw a polygon which displays the text bounding box */
    GpiMove(hPS,(PPOINTL)&Ptl[TXTBOX_TOPLEFT]);
    GpiPolyLine(hPS,5L,Ptl);
    GpiCharStringPosAt (hPS,&Pointl,0L,CHS_LEAVEPOS,
        iLength,(PSZ)szUserStr,0);
  }
  GpiSetClipRegion(hPS,0,&hPrevRgn);
  WinEndPaint (hPS);
}



PFONTMETRICS APIENTRY init_font_LBox (HWND hLBox,HPS hPS)
/*-----------------------------------------------------------------*/

   This function will query metrics for supplied presentation space
   and then enumerate its public and private fonts.

/*-----------------------------------------------------------------*/
{
  HDC          hDC;
  PSZ          pFace;
  ULONG        ulSize = 0;
  ULONG        ulCount = 0;
  int          i;
  PVOID        pData;
  PFONTMETRICS pFontMetrics;
  HATOMTBL     hAtomTable = WinQuerySystemAtomTable();

  hDC = GpiQueryDevice(hPS);
  DevQueryCaps (hDC,CAPS_HORIZONTAL_RESOLUTION,1L,(PLONG)&lHorzRes);
  DevQueryCaps (hDC,CAPS_VERTICAL_RESOLUTION,1L,(PLONG)&lVertRes);
  DevQueryCaps (hDC,CAPS_HORIZONTAL_FONT_RES,1,&cxFontRes);
  DevQueryCaps (hDC,CAPS_VERTICAL_FONT_RES,1,&cyFontRes);

  ulCount = GpiQueryFonts (hPS,QF_PUBLIC ¦ QF_PRIVATE,0,

(PLONG) &ulCount,(LONG)sizeof(FONTMETRICS),0);
  if (ulCount)
  {
    DosAllocMem ((PPVOID)&pFontMetrics,
        sizeof(FONTMETRICS) * (USHORT)ulCount,
```

```
        OBJ_TILE ¦ PAG_READ ¦ PAG_WRITE ¦ PAG_COMMIT);
    GpiQueryFonts (hPS,QF_PUBLIC ¦ QF_PRIVATE,0,

(PLONG) &ulCount,(LONG)sizeof(FONTMETRICS),pFontMetrics);
    WinSendMsg (hLBox,LM_DELETEALL,0,0);

    for (i = 0; i < (int)ulCount; i++)
    {
#ifdef TOOLKT21
      /* If the facename has been truncated query the atom text */
      if ( ((pFontMetrics+i)->fsType & FM_TYPE_FACETRUNC) &&
            (ulSize = WinQueryAtomLength(hAtomTable,
            (pFontMetrics+i)->FaceNameAtom)) )
      {
        ulSize++;
        DosSubAlloc(pMem,(PPVOID)&pData,ulSize);
        if (WinQueryAtomName (hAtomTable,
           (pFontMetrics+i)->FaceNameAtom,pData,ulSize))
          pFace = pData;
        else
          pFace = (pFontMetrics+i)->szFacename;
      }
      else
#endif
            pFace = (pFontMetrics+i)->szFacename;

      WinSendMsg (hLBox,LM_INSERTITEM,(MPARAM)LIT_END,(MPARAM)pFace);

      if (ulSize)
          DosSubFree(pMem,pData,ulSize);
    }
  }
  return (pFontMetrics);
}


BOOL APIENTRY create_font(HPS hPS,int i,PFONTMETRICS pFontArray)
/*--------------------------------------------------------------*/

   This function will create a new font based on the current selection
   in the font listbox and style and codepage attributes set via the
   menu. The PS is first reset to the default character set attribute
   and character.

/*--------------------------------------------------------------*/
{
  FATTRS fattr;
  SIZEF  sizef;

  /* Reset the character box to the default size */
  sizef.cx = MAKEFIXED((pFontArray+i)->lEmInc,0);
  sizef.cy = MAKEFIXED((pFontArray+i)->lEmHeight,0);
  GpiSetCharBox (hPS,&sizef);
  GpiSetCharSet (hPS,LCID_DEFAULT);
  GpiDeleteSetId (hPS,DISPLAY_FONT);
```

```
  strcpy(fattr.szFacename,(PSZ)((pFontArray+i)->szFacename));
  fattr.usRecordLength  = sizeof(FATTRS);
  fattr.fsSelection     = usSelection;
  fattr.lMatch          = (pFontArray+i)->lMatch;
  fattr.idRegistry      = (pFontArray+i)->idRegistry;
  fattr.usCodePage      = usCurrentCP;
  fattr.lMaxBaselineExt = (pFontArray+i)->lMaxBaselineExt;
  fattr.lAveCharWidth   = (pFontArray+i)->lAveCharWidth;
  fattr.fsType          = 0;
  fattr.fsFontUse       = 0;
  return (GpiCreateLogFont (hPS,0,DISPLAY_FONT,&fattr));
}


void APIENTRY size_controls(MPARAM lNewSize)
/*-----------------------------------------------------------------*/

   This function will reposition the font selection listbox and the
   metrics and shear panel windows based on the new client window
   size.

/*-----------------------------------------------------------------/
{
  SHORT  sNewWidth  = SHORT1FROMMP(lNewSize);
  SHORT  sNewHeight = SHORT2FROMMP(lNewSize);
  RECTL  MetricsRectl;

  WinQueryWindowRect(hWndMetrics,(PRECTL)&MetricsRectl);
  WinSetWindowPos (hWndMetrics,HWND_TOP,
      cxChar,sNewHeight - MetricsRectl.yTop - (cyChar * 5),0,0,
      SWP_MOVE);

  WinQueryWindowRect(hWndShear,(PRECTL)&MetricsRectl);
  WinSetWindowPos (hWndShear,HWND_TOP,
      cxChar,sNewHeight - MetricsRectl.yTop - (cyChar * 5),0,0,
      SWP_MOVE);

  WinSetWindowPos (hFontLBox,HWND_TOP,
      cxChar,sNewHeight - (cyChar * 4),0,0,SWP_ZORDER | SWP_MOVE);
}


MRESULT EXPENTRY ClientWndProc (HWND hWnd, ULONG msg, MPARAM mp1,
                                MPARAM mp2)
/*-----------------------------------------------------------------*/

   This is the application callback which handles the messages
   necessary to maintain the client window.

/*-----------------------------------------------------------------*/
{
  MRESULT     mReturn  = 0;
  BOOL        bHandled = TRUE;
```

```
  FONTMETRICS FontMetrics;
  static HPS  hPS;
  SIZEL       sizel;

  switch(msg)
  {
    case WM_CREATE:
      /* Create a PS for the window */
      sizel.cx = sizel.cy = 0;
      hPS = GpiCreatePS(hab,WinOpenWindowDC(hWnd),(PSIZEL)&sizel,
        PU_PELS | GPIF_DEFAULT | GPIT_MICRO | GPIA_ASSOC);
      /* Query the height of the default font. */
      GpiQueryFontMetrics(hPS,sizeof(FONTMETRICS),
        (PFONTMETRICS)&FontMetrics);
      cyChar = FontMetrics.lMaxBaselineExt;
      cxChar = FontMetrics.lAveCharWidth;
      bHandled = FALSE;
      break;

    case WM_ERASEBACKGROUND:
      WinFillRect((HPS)LONGFROMMP(mp1),PVOIDFROMMP(mp2),CLR_WHITE);
      mReturn = MRFROMLONG(0L);
      break;

    case WM_SIZE:
      size_controls(mp2);
      break;

    case WM_COMMAND:
      process_command(hWnd,mp1,mp2);
      break;

    case WM_CONTROL:
      process_control (hWnd,hPS,mp1,mp2);
      break;

    case WM_PAINT:
      process_paint (hWnd,hPS);
      break;

    case WM_DESTROY:
      cleanup();
      break;

    default:
      bHandled = FALSE;
      break;
  }
  if (!bHandled)
    mReturn = WinDefWindowProc (hWnd,msg,mp1,mp2);

  return (mReturn);
}


MRESULT EXPENTRY ChooseFontDlgProc(HWND hWndDlg,ULONG ulMessage,
```

```
                                            MPARAM mp1,MPARAM mp2)
/*-----------------------------------------------------------*/
/*-----------------------------------------------------------*/
{
  static HWND hFacename;
  static HWND hPointSize;
  char   szFacename [FACESIZE];
  int    iPointSize;


  switch (ulMessage)
  {
      case WM_INITDLG:
        center_window(hWndDlg);
        hFacename  = WinWindowFromID(hWndDlg,DID_REQ_FACENAME);
        hPointSize = WinWindowFromID(hWndDlg,DID_REQ_POINTSIZE);
        WinSendMsg(hFacename,EM_SETTEXTLIMIT,MPFROMSHORT(FACESIZE),0);
        WinSendMsg(hPointSize,EM_SETTEXTLIMIT,MPFROMSHORT(2),0);
        WinEnableWindow(WinWindowFromID(hWndDlg,DID_OK),FALSE);
        break;

      case WM_CONTROL:
        if ( (SHORT2FROMMP(mp1) == EN_CHANGE) ||
             (SHORT2FROMMP(mp1) == MLN_CHANGE) )
        {
            if ( (WinQueryWindowTextLength(hFacename)) &&
                 (WinQueryWindowTextLength(hPointSize)) )
                WinEnableWindow(WinWindowFromID(hWndDlg,DID_OK),TRUE);
            else
                WinEnableWindow(WinWindowFromID(hWndDlg,DID_OK),FALSE);
        }
        break;

      case WM_COMMAND:
        switch (SHORT1FROMMP(mp1))
        {
            case DID_OK:
                /* Query the point size and convert it to an integer */
                WinQueryWindowText(hPointSize,FACESIZE,szFacename);
                iPointSize = atoi(szFacename);

                /* Query the facename */
                WinQueryWindowText(hFacename,FACESIZE,szFacename);

                if (choose_font(szFacename,iPointSize))
                    WinDismissDlg(hWndDlg,DID_OK);
                else
                {
                    WinAlarm(HWND_DESKTOP,WA_ERROR);
                    WinSetFocus(HWND_DESKTOP,hFacename);
                    WinSendMsg(hFacename,EM_SETSEL,
                      MPFROM2SHORT(0,FACESIZE + 1),0);
                    return ((MRESULT)1);
                }
                break;
        }
```

```
      default:
        break;
    }
    return (WinDefDlgProc(hWndDlg,ulMessage,mp1,mp2));
}


MRESULT EXPENTRY MetricsWndProc (HWND hWnd, ULONG msg, MPARAM mp1,
                                 MPARAM mp2)
/*-------------------------------------------------------------*/

   This dialog panel displays the metrics of the currently selected
   font. When the private WM_UPDATE_METRICS message is received the
   text of the child windows is updated with the contents of the
   fontmetrics pointed to by mp2.

/*-------------------------------------------------------------*/
{
  MRESULT      mReturn  = 0;
  BOOL         bHandled = TRUE;
  PFONTMETRICS pFM;
  CHAR         szTemp[80];

  switch(msg)
  {
    case WM_UPDATE_METRICS:
      pFM = (PFONTMETRICS)mp2;
      WinSetWindowText(WinWindowFromID(hWnd,DID_FAMILYNAME),
          pFM->szFamilyname);
      WinSetWindowText(WinWindowFromID(hWnd,DID_FACENAME),
          pFM->szFacename);
      ltoa(pFM->lLowerCaseAscent,(PSZ)szTemp,10);
      WinSetWindowText(WinWindowFromID(hWnd,DID_LOWERCASEASCENT),
        (PSZ)szTemp);

      ltoa(pFM->lXHeight,(PSZ)szTemp,10);
      WinSetWindowText(WinWindowFromID(hWnd,DID_XHEIGHT),
        (PSZ)szTemp);

      ltoa(pFM->lMaxAscender,(PSZ)szTemp,10);
      WinSetWindowText(WinWindowFromID(hWnd,DID_MAXASCENDER),
        (PSZ)szTemp);

      ltoa(pFM->lMaxDescender,(PSZ)szTemp,10);
      WinSetWindowText(WinWindowFromID(hWnd,DID_MAXDECENDER),
        (PSZ)szTemp);

      ltoa(pFM->lLowerCaseDescent,(PSZ)szTemp,10);
      WinSetWindowText(WinWindowFromID(hWnd,DID_LOWERCASEDECENT),
        (PSZ)szTemp);

      ltoa(pFM->lEmInc,(PSZ)szTemp,10);
      WinSetWindowText(WinWindowFromID(hWnd,DID_EMINC),(PSZ)szTemp);

      ltoa(pFM->lInternalLeading,(PSZ)szTemp,10);
      WinSetWindowText(WinWindowFromID(hWnd,DID_INTERNALLEADING),
```

```
  (PSZ)szTemp);

ltoa(pFM->lExternalLeading,(PSZ)szTemp,10);
WinSetWindowText(WinWindowFromID(hWnd,DID_EXTERNALLEADING),
  (PSZ)szTemp);

ltoa(pFM->lMaxBaselineExt,(PSZ)szTemp,10);
WinSetWindowText(WinWindowFromID(hWnd,DID_MAXBASELINEEXT),
  (PSZ)szTemp);

ltoa(pFM->lEmHeight,(PSZ)szTemp,10);
WinSetWindowText(WinWindowFromID(hWnd,DID_EMHEIGHT),
  (PSZ)szTemp);

ltoa(pFM->lAveCharWidth,(PSZ)szTemp,10);
WinSetWindowText(WinWindowFromID(hWnd,DID_AVECHARWIDTH),
  (PSZ)szTemp);

ltoa(pFM->lMaxCharInc,(PSZ)szTemp,10);
WinSetWindowText(WinWindowFromID(hWnd,DID_MAXCHARINC),
   (PSZ)szTemp);

ltoa (pFM->sNominalPointSize / 10,(PSZ)szTemp,10);
WinSetWindowText(WinWindowFromID(hWnd,DID_POINT_SIZE),
  (PSZ)szTemp);

ltoa(pFM->usCodePage,(PSZ)szTemp,10);
WinSetWindowText(WinWindowFromID(hWnd,DID_CODEPAGE),
  (PSZ)szTemp);

sprintf(szTemp,"%s%s%s%s%s",
  szSelection[(pFM->fsSelection & FM_SEL_BOLD)       ? 1 : 0],
  szSelection[(pFM->fsSelection & FM_SEL_ITALIC)     ? 2 : 0],
  szSelection[(pFM->fsSelection & FM_SEL_STRIKEOUT)  ? 3 : 0],
  szSelection[(pFM->fsSelection & FM_SEL_UNDERSCORE) ? 4 : 0],
  szSelection[(pFM->fsSelection & FM_SEL_OUTLINE)    ? 5 : 0]);
WinSetWindowText(WinWindowFromID(hWnd,DID_SELECTION),
  (PSZ)szTemp);

ltoa(pFM->sKerningPairs,(PSZ)szTemp,10);
WinSetWindowText(WinWindowFromID(hWnd,DID_KERNPAIRS),
  (PSZ)szTemp);

sprintf(szTemp,"%2i,%2i",LOBYTE(pFM->sFamilyClass),
  HIBYTE(pFM->sFamilyClass));
WinSetWindowText(WinWindowFromID(hWnd,DID_FAMILYCLASS),
  (PSZ)szTemp);

sprintf(szTemp,"%s",
    szSpacing[(pFM->fsType & FM_TYPE_FIXED) ? 1 : 0]);
WinSetWindowText(WinWindowFromID(hWnd,DID_TYPE),(PSZ)szTemp);

sprintf(szTemp,"%s%s",
    szFormat[(pFM->fsDefn & FM_DEFN_GENERIC) ? 1 : 0],
    szType[(pFM->fsDefn & FM_DEFN_OUTLINE) ? 1 : 0]);
WinSetWindowText(WinWindowFromID(hWnd,DID_DEFINITION),
```

```
        (PSZ)szTemp);

      WinSetWindowText(WinWindowFromID(hWnd,DID_CAPABILITIES),
          (PSZ)szQuality[(pFM->fsCapabilities >> 5)]);

      WinSetWindowText(WinWindowFromID(hWnd,DID_WEIGHTCLASS),
          (PSZ)szWeights[pFM->usWeightClass - 1]);

      WinSetWindowText(WinWindowFromID(hWnd,DID_WIDTHCLASS),
          (PSZ)szWidths[pFM->usWidthClass - 1]);
      break;

    case WM_ERASEBACKGROUND:
      WinFillRect((HPS)LONGFROMMP(mp1),PVOIDFROMMP(mp2),CLR_PALEGRAY);
      mReturn = MRFROMLONG(0L);
      break;

    case WM_COMMAND:
      break;

    default:
      bHandled = FALSE;
      break;
  }
  if (!bHandled)
    mReturn = WinDefDlgProc (hWnd,msg,mp1,mp2);

  return (mReturn);
}


MRESULT EXPENTRY ShearWndProc (HWND hWnd, ULONG msg, MPARAM mp1,
                               MPARAM mp2)
/*--------------------------------------------------------------*/

   This dialog panel displays the currently selected font and its
   bounding box. Controls on the panel all the user to change the
   point size, character shear, character orientation and spacing.

/*--------------------------------------------------------------*/
{
  MRESULT  mReturn  = 0;
  BOOL     bHandled = TRUE;
  CHAR     szTemp[20];
  int      iAngle;
  double   dSine;
  double   dCosine;
  SHORT    sPos;

  switch(msg)
  {
    case WM_INITDLG:
      CurrentCB.usSet = DISPLAY_FONT;
      charbox_from_pointsize (MAKEFIXED(0,DEFAULT_SIZE),
        &CurrentCB.sizfxCell);
```

```
  DefaultCharBox = CurrentCB.sizfxCell;
  ltoa (HIUSHORT(CurrentCB.sizfxCell.cy),szTemp,10);
  WinSetDlgItemText(hWnd,DID_CHAR_HEIGHT,szTemp);
  ltoa (HIUSHORT(CurrentCB.sizfxCell.cx),szTemp,10);
  WinSetDlgItemText(hWnd,DID_CHAR_WIDTH,szTemp);
  init_sliders_n_spinners(hWnd);
  break;

case WM_ERASEBACKGROUND:
  WinFillRect((HPS)LONGFROMMP(mp1),PVOIDFROMMP(mp2), CLR_PALEGRAY);
  mReturn = MRFROMLONG(0L);
  break;

case WM_COMMAND:
  switch (SHORT1FROMMP(mp1))
  {
    case DID_RESET_SIZE:
      ltoa (HIUSHORT(DefaultCharBox.cy),szTemp,10);
      WinSetDlgItemText(hWnd,DID_CHAR_HEIGHT,szTemp);
      ltoa (HIUSHORT(DefaultCharBox.cx),szTemp,10);
      WinSetDlgItemText(hWnd,DID_CHAR_WIDTH,szTemp);
      WinSendMsg(hWnd,WM_COMMAND,MPFROM2SHORT(DID_APPLY,0),0);
      break;
    case DID_RESET_ANGLE:
      WinSendDlgItemMsg(hWnd,DID_ROT_ANGLE,SPBM_SETCURRENTVALUE,
        MPFROMLONG(0),0);
      WinSendMsg(hWnd,WM_COMMAND,MPFROM2SHORT(DID_APPLY,0),0);
      break;
    case DID_RESET_SHEAR:
      WinSendDlgItemMsg(hWnd,DID_SHEAR_ANGLE,SPBM_SETCURRENTVALUE,
        MPFROMLONG(90),0);
      WinSendMsg(hWnd,WM_COMMAND,MPFROM2SHORT(DID_APPLY,0),0);
      break;
    case DID_APPLY:
      WinQueryDlgItemText(hWnd,DID_CHAR_WIDTH,20,szTemp);
      CurrentCB.sizfxCell.cx = MAKEFIXED(atol(szTemp),0);
      WinQueryDlgItemText(hWnd,DID_CHAR_HEIGHT,20,szTemp);
      CurrentCB.sizfxCell.cy = MAKEFIXED(atol(szTemp),0);
      WinQueryDlgItemText(hWnd,DID_ANGLEX,20,szTemp);
      CurrentCB.ptlAngle.x = atol(szTemp);
      WinQueryDlgItemText(hWnd,DID_ANGLEY,20,szTemp);
      CurrentCB.ptlAngle.y = atol(szTemp);
      WinInvalidateRect (hWndClient,0,FALSE);
      break;
  }
  break;

case WM_CONTROL:
  switch (LOUSHORT(mp1))
  {
    case DID_USER_TEXT:
      if (SHORT2FROMMP(mp1) == EN_CHANGE)
      {
        WinQueryWindowText(HWNDFROMMP(mp2),MAX_STR,szUserStr);
        WinInvalidateRect (hWndClient,0,FALSE);
      }
```

```
  break;
case DID_CHAR_EXTRA:
  sPos = (SHORT)WinSendDlgItemMsg(hWnd,DID_CHAR_EXTRA,
     SLM_QUERYSLIDERINFO,
     MPFROM2SHORT(SMA_SLIDERARMPOSITION,SMA_INCREMENTVALUE),
     0);
  CharExtra = MAKEFIXED(sPos - 10,0);
  WinInvalidateRect (hWndClient,0,FALSE);
  WinUpdateWindow(hWndClient);
  break;
case DID_BREAK_EXTRA:
  sPos = (SHORT)WinSendDlgItemMsg(hWnd,DID_BREAK_EXTRA,
     SLM_QUERYSLIDERINFO,
     MPFROM2SHORT(SMA_SLIDERARMPOSITION,SMA_INCREMENTVALUE),
     0);
  BreakExtra = MAKEFIXED(sPos - 10,0);
  WinInvalidateRect (hWndClient,0,FALSE);
  WinUpdateWindow(hWndClient);
  break;
case DID_ROT_ANGLE:
  if (SHORT2FROMMP(mp1) == SPBN_CHANGE)
  {
    if (WinSendMsg((HWND)mp2,SPBM_QUERYVALUE,&iAngle,
        MPFROM2SHORT(0,SPBQ_UPDATEIFVALID)))
    {
      dRotSine = sin(TWO_PIE * iAngle / 360.0);
      dSine    = 200.0 * dRotSine;
      dRotCosine = cos(TWO_PIE * iAngle / 360.0);
      dCosine = 200.0 * dRotCosine;
      CurrentCB.ptlAngle.x = ((LONG)dCosine * lHorzRes) /
        (LONG)lVertRes;
      CurrentCB.ptlAngle.y = (LONG) dSine;
      ltoa (CurrentCB.ptlAngle.x,szTemp,10);
      WinSetDlgItemText(hWnd,DID_ANGLEX,szTemp);
      ltoa (CurrentCB.ptlAngle.y,szTemp,10);
      WinSetDlgItemText(hWnd,DID_ANGLEY,szTemp);
      WinInvalidateRect (hWndClient,0,FALSE);
      WinUpdateWindow(hWndClient);
    }
  }
  break;
case DID_SHEAR_ANGLE:
    if (SHORT2FROMMP(mp1) == SPBN_CHANGE)
    {
      if (WinSendMsg((HWND)mp2,SPBM_QUERYVALUE,&iAngle,
          MPFROM2SHORT(0,SPBQ_UPDATEIFVALID)))
      {
        dSine   = 200.0 * sin(TWO_PIE * iAngle / 360.0);
        dCosine = 200.0 * cos(TWO_PIE * iAngle / 360.0);
        CurrentCB.ptlShear.x  = ((LONG)dCosine * lHorzRes) /
          (LONG)lVertRes;
        CurrentCB.ptlShear.y  = (LONG) dSine;
        ltoa (CurrentCB.ptlShear.x,szTemp,10);
        WinSetDlgItemText(hWnd,DID_SHEARX,szTemp);
        ltoa (CurrentCB.ptlShear.y,szTemp,10);
        WinSetDlgItemText(hWnd,DID_SHEARY,szTemp);
```

```
                WinInvalidateRect (hWndClient,0,FALSE);
                WinUpdateWindow(hWndClient);
              }
            }
            break;
      }
      break;

    default:
      bHandled = FALSE;
      break;
  }
  if (!bHandled)
    mReturn = WinDefDlgProc (hWnd,msg,mp1,mp2);

  return (mReturn);
}



BOOL APIENTRY init_sliders_n_spinners(HWND hWnd)
/*-----------------------------------------------------------------*/

   This function will initalize the tick marks and text for the
   slider controls which control character and break character
   spacing. A label is placed ever two tick marks. The spinners for
   rotation and shear angle are intialized by setting the range from
   0 to 360 and the default angles are set

/*-----------------------------------------------------------------*/
{
  SHORT   sIndex;
  CHAR    szTemp[4];
  HWND    hCharSliderWnd   = WinWindowFromID(hWnd,DID_CHAR_EXTRA);
  HWND    hBreakSliderWnd  = WinWindowFromID(hWnd,DID_BREAK_EXTRA);
  HWND    hRotAngleWnd     = WinWindowFromID(hWnd,DID_ROT_ANGLE);
  HWND    hShearAngleWnd   = WinWindowFromID(hWnd,DID_SHEAR_ANGLE);

  for (sIndex = -10;sIndex <= 10 ;sIndex ++)
  {
   itoa(sIndex,szTemp,10);
   WinSendMsg(hCharSliderWnd, SLM_SETTICKSIZE,
           MPFROM2SHORT(sIndex + 10, 3), 0);
   if ((sIndex & 0x01) == 0)
       WinSendMsg(hCharSliderWnd, SLM_SETSCALETEXT,
               MPFROMSHORT(sIndex + 10), MPFROMP(szTemp));

   WinSendMsg(hBreakSliderWnd, SLM_SETTICKSIZE,
           MPFROM2SHORT(sIndex + 10, 3), 0);

   if ((sIndex & 0x01) == 0)
       WinSendMsg(hBreakSliderWnd, SLM_SETSCALETEXT,
                MPFROMSHORT(sIndex + 10), MPFROMP(szTemp));
  }
  WinSendMsg (hCharSliderWnd,SLM_SETSLIDERINFO,
      MPFROM2SHORT(SMA_SLIDERARMPOSITION,SMA_INCREMENTVALUE),
```

```
        MPFROMSHORT(10));
    WinSendMsg (hBreakSliderWnd,SLM_SETSLIDERINFO,
        MPFROM2SHORT(SMA_SLIDERARMPOSITION,SMA_INCREMENTVALUE),
        MPFROMSHORT(10));

    WinSendMsg(hRotAngleWnd,SPBM_SETLIMITS,(MPARAM)360,(MPARAM)0);
    WinSendMsg(hRotAngleWnd,SPBM_SETTEXTLIMIT,MPFROMSHORT(3),0);
    WinSendMsg(hRotAngleWnd,SPBM_SETCURRENTVALUE,MPFROMLONG(0),0);

    WinSendMsg(hShearAngleWnd,SPBM_SETLIMITS,(MPARAM)360,(MPARAM)0);
    WinSendMsg(hShearAngleWnd,SPBM_SETTEXTLIMIT,MPFROMSHORT(3),0);
    WinSendMsg(hShearAngleWnd,SPBM_SETCURRENTVALUE,MPFROMLONG(90),0);

    return (TRUE);
}
```

PMFONT.H

```
/* ------------------------------
PM Font Header File
Real-World Programming for OS/2
Copyright (c) 1993-4 Blain, Delimon, and English
------------------------------ */

#define ID_APPNAME          1


#define IDM_DISPLAY        300
#define IDM_METRICS        301
#define IDM_ROTATION       302
#define IDM_ABOUT          303

#define IDM_CHOOSE 304
#define IDM_CHMODE         400
#define IDM_CHMODE_ONE     401
#define IDM_CHMODE_TWO     402
#define IDM_CHMODE_THREE   403

#define IDM_ATTRIBUTE        550
#define IDM_ATTR_ITALIC      551
#define IDM_ATTR_BOLD        552
#define IDM_ATTR_UNDERSCORE  553
#define IDM_ATTR_STRIKEOUT   554
#define IDM_ATTR_OUTLINE     555

#define IDM_CODEPAGE       600
#define IDM_CP037          037
#define IDM_CP273          273
#define IDM_CP274          274
#define IDM_CP277          277
#define IDM_CP278          278
#define IDM_CP280          280
#define IDM_CP282          282
#define IDM_CP284          284
#define IDM_CP285          285
```

```
#define IDM_CP297         297
#define IDM_CP437         437
#define IDM_CP850         850
#define IDM_CP852         852
#define IDM_CP857         857
#define IDM_CP860         860
#define IDM_CP861         861
#define IDM_CP863         863
#define IDM_CP865         865
#define IDM_CP1004       1004


#define IDS_APPNAME         1
#define IDS_DISPLAY_TEXT    2
#define IDS_SPECIAL_TEXT    3
#define IDS_USER_TEXT       4

#define DEFAULT_SIZE 30
#define MAX_BUFF   128

#define DISPLAY_FONT 1
#define MAX_WIDTHS   9
#define MAX_STR      40
#define TWO_PIE (2.0 * 3.14159)

#define WM_UPDATE_METRICS  WM_USER + 1

VOID     APIENTRY center_window(HWND);
BOOL     APIENTRY choose_font(PCH,int);
void     APIENTRY cleanup(void);
BOOL     APIENTRY create_controls (HWND);
BOOL     APIENTRY create_font(HWND,int,PFONTMETRICS);
void     APIENTRY draw_grid(HPS,PRECTL);
BOOL     APIENTRY init_print_info (void);
BOOL     APIENTRY init_sliders_n_spinners(HWND);
PFONTMETRICS  APIENTRY init_font_LBox (HWND,HPS);
USHORT   APIENTRY post_error(HWND,USHORT);
void     APIENTRY print_selected_font (void);
void     APIENTRY process_paint(HWND,HPS);
void     APIENTRY process_command(HWND,MPARAM,MPARAM);
void     APIENTRY process_control(HWND,HPS,MPARAM,MPARAM);
void     APIENTRY size_controls(MPARAM);
```

PMFONT.RC

```
/* --------------------------------
PM Font Resource File
Real-World Programming for OS/2
Copyright (c) 1993-94 Blain, Delimon, & and English
-------------------------------- */

#include <os2.h>
#include "chap7.h"
#include "pmfont.h"
```

```
RCINCLUDE pmfont.dlg
RCINCLUDE ..\common\about.dlg

ICON ID_APPNAME PMFONT.ICO

MENU ID_APPNAME
BEGIN
   SUBMENU "~Display",               IDM_DISPLAY
      BEGIN
         MENUITEM "Font Metrics",    IDM_METRICS,0, MIA_CHECKED
         MENUITEM "Rotation / Shear",  IDM_ROTATION
         MENUITEM "Choose Font",       IDM_CHOOSE
         MENUITEM "About...",          IDM_ABOUT
      END
   SUBMENU "~Charcter Mode",      IDM_CHMODE
      BEGIN
         MENUITEM "Mode 1",     IDM_CHMODE_ONE, 0, MIA_CHECKED
         MENUITEM "Mode 2",     IDM_CHMODE_TWO
         MENUITEM "Mode 3",     IDM_CHMODE_THREE
      END
   SUBMENU "Font Attribute",       IDM_ATTRIBUTE
      BEGIN
         MENUITEM "Italic",     IDM_ATTR_ITALIC
         MENUITEM "Bold",       IDM_ATTR_BOLD
         MENUITEM "Underscore", IDM_ATTR_UNDERSCORE
         MENUITEM "Strikeout",  IDM_ATTR_STRIKEOUT
         MENUITEM "Outline",    IDM_ATTR_OUTLINE
      END
   SUBMENU "Code Page",       IDM_CODEPAGE
      BEGIN
         MENUITEM "ASCII 437 US English",      IDM_CP437
         MENUITEM "ASCII 850 Multilingual", IDM_CP850,0, MIA_CHECKED
         MENUITEM "ASCII 852 Multilingual",    IDM_CP852
         MENUITEM "ASCII 857 Turkey",          IDM_CP857
         MENUITEM "ASCII 860 Portugese",       IDM_CP860
         MENUITEM "ASCII 861 Iceland",         IDM_CP861
         MENUITEM "ASCII 863 French-Canadian", IDM_CP863
         MENUITEM "ASCII 865 Norwegian",       IDM_CP865
         MENUITEM "ASCII 1004 Desktop Publishing", IDM_CP1004
         MENUITEM "EBCDIC 037 US English",       IDM_CP037,
         MIS_BREAKSEPARATOR
         MENUITEM "EBCDIC 273 Austrian/German",  IDM_CP273
         MENUITEM "EBCDIC 274 Belgian",          IDM_CP274
         MENUITEM "EBCDIC 277 Danish/Norwegian", IDM_CP277
         MENUITEM "EBCDIC 278 Finnish/Swedish",  IDM_CP278
         MENUITEM "EBCDIC 280 Italian",          IDM_CP280
         MENUITEM "EBCDIC 282 Portugese",        IDM_CP282
         MENUITEM "EBCDIC 284 Spanish",          IDM_CP284
         MENUITEM "EBCDIC 285 UK-English",       IDM_CP285
      END
END


STRINGTABLE PRELOAD MOVEABLE
BEGIN
```

```
   IDS_APPNAME        "PM Font Browser"
   IDS_DISPLAY_TEXT "AaBbCcDdEeFfGgHhIiJjKkLlMmNnOoPpQqRr"
                     "SsTtUuVvWwXxYyZz"
   IDS_SPECIAL_TEXT "áíóúñÑªº¿`^__¡«»"
   IDS_USER_TEXT      "Sample Text String"
END
```

PMFONT.DLG

```
/* ------------------------------
Chapter Dialogs
Real-World Programming for OS/2
Copyright (c) 1993-94 Blain, Delimon, and English
------------------------------ */

DLGINCLUDE 1 "CHAP7.H"

DLGTEMPLATE METRICS_DLG LOADONCALL MOVEABLE DISCARDABLE
BEGIN
   DIALOG  "Fontmetrics", METRICS_DLG, 105, 77, 210, 155,
            NOT FS_DLGBORDER
            PRESPARAMS PP_FONTNAMESIZE, "8.Helv"
   BEGIN
      GROUPBOX        "Names", -1, 4, 127, 204, 27
      LTEXT           "szFamilyname:", -1, 9, 138, 53, 8
      LTEXT           "szFacename:", -1, 9, 129, 50, 8
      LTEXT           "", DID_FAMILYNAME, 78, 138, 127, 8
      LTEXT           "", DID_FACENAME, 78, 129, 128, 8
      GROUPBOX        "Sizes", -1, 4, 61, 203, 64
      LTEXT           "lMaxAscender", -1, 9, 109, 60, 8
      LTEXT           "10", DID_MAXASCENDER, 69, 109, 20, 8
      LTEXT           "lMaxDecender", -1, 9, 100, 60, 8
      LTEXT           "10", DID_MAXDECENDER, 69, 100, 20, 8
      LTEXT           "lMaxBaselineExt", -1, 9, 91, 60, 8
      LTEXT           "10", DID_MAXBASELINEEXT, 69, 91, 20, 8
      LTEXT           "lInternalLeading", -1, 9, 82, 60, 8
      LTEXT           "10", DID_INTERNALLEADING, 69, 82, 20, 8
      LTEXT           "lExternalLeading", -1, 9, 73, 60, 8
      LTEXT           "10", DID_EXTERNALLEADING, 69, 73, 20, 8
      LTEXT           "lAveCharWidth", -1, 9, 64, 60, 8
      LTEXT           "10", DID_AVECHARWIDTH, 69, 64, 20, 8
      LTEXT           "lXHeight:", -1, 97, 109, 64, 8
      LTEXT           "10", DID_XHEIGHT, 169, 110, 20, 8
      LTEXT           "lEMHeight:", -1, 97, 100, 64, 8
      LTEXT           "10", DID_EMHEIGHT, 169, 101, 20, 8
      LTEXT           "lLowerCaseAscent", -1, 97, 91, 64, 8
      LTEXT           "10", DID_LOWERCASEASCENT, 169, 92, 20, 8
      LTEXT           "lLowerCaseDecent", -1, 97, 82, 64, 8
      LTEXT           "10", DID_LOWERCASEDECENT, 169, 83, 20, 8
      LTEXT           "lEmInc", -1, 97, 73, 64, 8
      LTEXT           "10", DID_EMINC, 169, 74, 20, 8
      LTEXT           "lMaxCharInc", -1, 97, 64, 64, 8
      LTEXT           "10", DID_MAXCHARINC, 169, 65, 20, 8
      GROUPBOX        "Attributes", 4, 3, 2, 204, 59
      LTEXT           "Point Size", -1, 9, 45, 49, 8
```

```
      LTEXT           "10", DID_POINT_SIZE, 69, 45, 20, 8
      LTEXT           "usCodePage", -1, 9, 35, 49, 9
      LTEXT           "850", DID_CODEPAGE, 69, 36, 20, 8
      LTEXT           "usSelection", -1, 9, 27, 49, 8
      LTEXT           "10", DID_SELECTION, 69, 27, 20, 8
      LTEXT           "sFamilyClass", -1, 9, 17, 49, 8
      LTEXT           "10", DID_FAMILYCLASS, 69, 18, 20, 8
      LTEXT           "sKerningPairs", -1, 9, 8, 53, 8
      LTEXT           "10", DID_KERNPAIRS, 69, 9, 20, 8
      LTEXT           "usType", -1, 97, 44, 53, 8
      LTEXT           "10", DID_TYPE, 150, 45, 54, 8
      LTEXT           "usDefn", -1, 97, 36, 53, 8
      LTEXT           "10", DID_DEFINITION, 150, 36, 54, 8
      LTEXT           "usCapabilities", -1, 97, 28, 53, 8
      LTEXT           "10", DID_CAPABILITIES, 150, 27, 54, 8
      LTEXT           "usWeightClass", -1, 97, 18, 53, 8
      LTEXT           "10", DID_WEIGHTCLASS, 150, 18, 54, 8
      LTEXT           "usWidthClass", -1, 97, 9, 53, 8
      LTEXT           "10", DID_WIDTHCLASS, 150, 9, 54, 8
   END
END

DLGTEMPLATE SHEAR_DLG LOADONCALL MOVEABLE DISCARDABLE
BEGIN
   DIALOG  "", SHEAR_DLG, 115, 55, 210, 157, NOT FS_DLGBORDER
            PRESPARAMS PP_FONTNAMESIZE, "8.Helv"
   BEGIN
      GROUPBOX      "Character Size", -1, 3, 133, 204, 22
      LTEXT         "Height", -1, 7, 138, 28, 8
      ENTRYFIELD    "", DID_CHAR_HEIGHT, 37, 139, 16, 7, ES_MARGIN
      LTEXT         "Width", -1, 59, 138, 20, 8
      ENTRYFIELD    "", DID_CHAR_WIDTH, 90, 139, 16, 7, ES_MARGIN
      PUSHBUTTON    "Reset", DID_RESET_SIZE, 170, 136, 32, 12
      GROUPBOX      "Character Angle", -1, 3, 108, 204, 22
      LTEXT         "X Point", 6, 7, 112, 30, 8
      ENTRYFIELD    "1", DID_ANGLEX, 37, 113, 16, 7, ES_MARGIN
      LTEXT         "Y Point", 7, 59, 112, 27, 8
      ENTRYFIELD    "0", DID_ANGLEY, 90, 113, 16, 7, ES_MARGIN
      PUSHBUTTON    "Reset", DID_RESET_ANGLE, 170, 111, 32, 12
      GROUPBOX      "Character Shear", -1, 3, 83, 204, 22
      LTEXT         "X Point", 4, 7, 87, 26, 8
      ENTRYFIELD    "0", DID_SHEARX, 37, 89, 16, 7, ES_MARGIN
      LTEXT         "Y Point", -1, 59, 87, 26, 8
      ENTRYFIELD    "1", DID_SHEARY, 90, 88, 16, 7, ES_MARGIN
      PUSHBUTTON    "Reset", DID_RESET_SHEAR, 170, 86, 32, 12
      GROUPBOX      "Character Spacing", -1, 3, 40, 204, 41
      LTEXT         "Char Extra", -1, 7, 60, 38, 8
      CONTROL       "", DID_CHAR_EXTRA, 66, 60, 140, 16, WC_SLIDER,
              SLS_HORIZONTAL | SLS_CENTER | SLS_LEFT |
              SLS_SNAPTOINCREMENT | SLS_HOMELEFT |
              SLS_PRIMARYSCALE1 | WS_GROUP | WS_TABSTOP |
              WS_VISIBLE
              CTLDATA 12, 0, 21, 0, 0, 0
      LTEXT         "Break Char Extra", 9, 7, 44, 57, 8
      CONTROL       "", DID_BREAK_EXTRA, 67, 44, 138, 16, WC_SLIDER,
              SLS_HORIZONTAL | SLS_CENTER | SLS_LEFT |
```

```
                SLS_SNAPTOINCREMENT ¦ SLS_HOMELEFT ¦
                SLS_PRIMARYSCALE1 ¦ WS_GROUP ¦ WS_TABSTOP ¦
                WS_VISIBLE
                CTLDATA 12, 0, 21, 0, 0, 0
      GROUPBOX       "Display Text", DID_POINTSIZE, 3, 14, 204, 22
      ENTRYFIELD     "", DID_USER_TEXT, 12, 19, 134, 7, ES_MARGIN
      DEFPUSHBUTTON "Apply", DID_APPLY, 164, 17, 35, 12
      LTEXT          "Angle", -1, 112, 112, 20, 8
      CONTROL        "", DID_ROT_ANGLE, 133, 112, 30, 12, WC_SPINBUTTON,
               SPBS_ALLCHARACTERS ¦ SPBS_NUMERICONLY ¦
               SPBS_MASTER ¦ SPBS_SERVANT ¦ SPBS_JUSTDEFAULT ¦
               SPBS_FASTSPIN ¦ WS_GROUP ¦ WS_TABSTOP ¦ WS_VISIBLE
      LTEXT          "Angle", -1, 113, 88, 20, 8
      CONTROL        "", DID_SHEAR_ANGLE, 134, 87, 30, 12, WC_SPINBUTTON,
               SPBS_ALLCHARACTERS ¦ SPBS_NUMERICONLY ¦
               SPBS_MASTER ¦ SPBS_SERVANT ¦
               SPBS_JUSTDEFAULT ¦ SPBS_FASTSPIN ¦
               WS_GROUP ¦ WS_TABSTOP ¦ WS_VISIBLE
   END
END

DLGTEMPLATE CHOOSEFONT_DLG LOADONCALL MOVEABLE DISCARDABLE
BEGIN
    DIALOG  "Choose Font", CHOOSEFONT_DLG, 31, 71, 147, 57, WS_VISIBLE, FCF_SYSMENU ¦
            FCF_TITLEBAR
    BEGIN
        LTEXT           "Facename:", -1, 8, 43, 48, 8
        ENTRYFIELD      "", DID_REQ_FACENAME, 59, 43, 79, 8, ES_MARGIN
        LTEXT           "Point Size:", -1, 8, 28, 48, 8
        ENTRYFIELD      "", DID_REQ_POINTSIZE, 59, 28, 21, 8, ES_MARGIN
        DEFPUSHBUTTON   "Ok", DID_OK, 26, 3, 40, 14
        PUSHBUTTON      "Cancel", DID_CANCEL, 79, 3, 40, 14
    END
END
```

PMFONT.DEF

```
NAME           PMFONT WINDOWAPI
DESCRIPTION    'PM Font Sample (c) 1993-94 Blain, Delimon, & English'
STACKSIZE      32768
EXPORTS        ClientWndProc
               MetricsWndProc
               ShearWndProc
               AboutDlgProc
               ChooseFontDlgProc
```

Font Class *sFamilyClass*

The following list is based on the sFamilyClass field. It turns out that the high-word and low-word values determine the fonts. Though this is not documented any place, to our knowledge, these are the font mappings that we have been able to determine. For example, if the high-word value is 1 and the low-word value is 3, the font will be Venetian.

High Word	*Low Word*	*Resulting Font*
0	Unclassified (No designation for font class or subclass has been assigned to this font)	
1	Old Style Serifs:	
	1	IBM Rounded Legibility
	2	Garalde
	3	Venetian
	4	Modified Venetian
	5	Dutch Modern
	6	Dutch Traditional
	7	Contemporary
	8	Calligraphic
2	Transitional Serifs:	
	1	Direct Line
	2	Script
3	Modern Serifs:	
	1	Italian
	2	Script
4	Clarendon Serifs:	
	1	Clarendon
	2	Modern
	3	Traditional
	4	Newspaper
	5	Stub Serif
	6	Monotone
	7	Typewriter

High Word	*Low Word*	*Resulting Font*
5	Slab Serifs:	
	1	Monotone
	2	Humanist
	3	Geometric
	4	Swiss
	5	Typewriter
6	Reserved	
7	Freeform Serifs:	
	1	Modern
8	Sans Serifs:	
	1	IBM Neo-Grotesque Gothic
	2	Humanist
	3	Low-x Round Geometric
	4	High-x Round Geometric
	5	Neo-Grotesque Gothic
	6	Modified Neo-Grotesque Gothic
	7	Reserved
	8	Reserved
	9	Typewriter Gothic
	10	Matrix
9	Ornamentals:	
	1	Engraver
	2	Black Letter
	3	Decorative
	4	Three Dimensional

continues

High Word	*Low Word*	*Resulting Font*
10	Scripts:	
	1	Unincal
	2	Brush Joined
	3	Formal Joined
	4	Monotone Joined
	5	Caligraphic
	6	Brush Unjoined
	7	Formal Unjoined
	8	Monotone Unjoined
11	Reserved	
12	Symbolic:	
	1-2	Reserved
	3	Mixed Serif
	4-5	Reserved
	6	Oldstyle Serif
	7	Neo-Grotesque Sans Serif

Chapter 8

Bitmaps and Palettes

Introduction

This chapter explains how to read a bitmap file from disk and display it in the client area of an OS/2 window. For this to be meaningful to you at all, we need to show the connection between two rather vast subjects. One is that of bitmaps, which are structures that define rows and columns of colored pixels. The other is how the color capabilities of display devices and the OS/2 operating system work. We treat both these subjects together here because they are intertwined. Unfortunately, this means that there are reams and reams of material we could include with this chapter, but we felt that abbreviating it somewhat would actually do you a better service.

Bitmaps

Bitmaps are fairly simple structures used to represent images which have been digitized. At least, the theory is simple. In practice, however, bitmaps can be difficult to work with. Conflicting file schemes and hardware limitations cause most of the trouble. In this chapter, we show how to display OS/2 bitmaps that use the BITMAPINFO2 structure. Of course, there are many others, including the older OS/2 BITMAPINFO type bitmaps, TIFFs, GIFs, PCX, and yet more. In addition, Windows bitmaps use the extension .BMP and are similar enough to OS/2

BITMAPINFO2 bitmaps that they can frequently be displayed using code written for OS/2 bitmaps. (We include an example with the code on the disk for this chapter.)

Bitmaps, as files or collections of data, have several distinct parts. They must have some means to represent the individual bits of color, and they must provide some indication about how to decipher these bits. However, there is no universal system for representing the data in a bitmap. The data may be compressed, or the bitmap may allow for the inclusion of resolution. It may encode the color information in different ways, or it may include fields in which the software creating the bitmap includes tags and labels. All the various bitmap types and the associated reasons for their technologies far exceed the scope of this book. Here we will focus narrowly on OS/2 bitmaps, those that use the BITMAPINFO2 structure. These bitmaps structures exhibit many of the characteristics of other bitmaps types, so they are a good place to start.

In this chapter we address the matter of displaying bitmaps and making palette changes primarily on the display device. Metafiles, memory contexts, and printer devices—although similar—act differently and warrant whole chapters to themselves.

In using the term OS/2 BITMAPINFO2 bitmaps (referred to in the remainder of the chapters as OS/2 bitmaps), we can really be speaking of different things. The term bitmap can in fact be a little confusing itself. It may refer to the bitmap information contained in a file, which can include file headers and color table information in addition to data for the pixels, or it may refer to the actual dots on the screen. It may also be referring to the internal data structure created with a call to `GpiCreateBitmap`. When considering bitmaps, it is important to keep these distinctions in mind.

General Bitmap File Structure

The bitmap, as a file, must contain some obvious pieces of data. These include data to describe the pixels, the encoded image bit data, its dimensions, some information about color if necessary, the size of the file, and other things.

In an OS/2 bitmap file, these pieces of data are grouped together in different logical structures. These are listed here in the order that they generally appear in a valid bitmap file:

- Bitmap File Header
- Bitmap Information Header Structure
- Bitmap Information Structure
- Bitmap bits

Notice in the following structures that the Bitmap Information Header Structure and the Bitmap Information Structure overlap. In other words they both begin at the same place in the file. The difference is that the Bitmap Information Structure has an additional field, `argbColor[1]`. This is the color information, which may or may not be present with the bitmap. The reasons for this are discussed in more detail later.

Bitmap files may also have a `BITMAPARRAYFILEHEADER2` structure at the beginning of the file when multiple versions of the same bitmap are contained in a file. This is done primarily for the purpose of providing icons and so forth that match the display resolution on which an application is running. We will not address these issues here because our purpose concerns displaying image bitmaps.

The Bitmap File Header

The following is the actual information for the Bitmap File Header structure copied from the include file which is part of the OS/2 toolkit. This data appears at the beginning of valid OS/2 bitmap files.

```
typedef struct _BITMAPFILEHEADER2
{
   USHORT    usType;
   ULONG     cbSize;
   SHORT     xHotspot;
   SHORT     yHotspot;
   ULONG     offBits;
   BITMAPINFOHEADER2 bmp2;
} BITMAPFILEHEADER2;
```

You can see that its structure is fairly logical and simple. Do not be confused by the `xHotspot` and `yHotspot` fields. Remember that pointers for graphical interfaces, like arrows and hourglasses and so forth, have an active point called the hotspot. These graphical interface elements are simply bitmaps with a defined hotspot, and they have the same structure as larger bitmaps used to display images. OS/2 icons also use the same structure. The fields in the Bitmap File header Structure are defined as follows:

`USHORT`	`usType`	Designates the type of bitmap in the file. For OS/2 bitmaps this may have one of the following values:
	`BFT_BMAP`	
	`BFT_ICON`	
	`BFT_POINTER`	
	`BFT_COLORICON`	
	`BFT_COLORPOINTER`	
`ULONG`	`cbSize`	Size in bytes of the file header structure.
`SHORT`	`xHotspot`	X coordinate for hotspot. This field is ignored for bitmaps.
`SHORT`	`yHotspot`	Y coordinate for hotspot. This field is ignored for bitmaps.
`ULONG`	`offBits`	Offset in bytes to the bitmap's pixel data in this file. This offset is from the beginning of the file.

BITMAPINFOHEADER2	bmp2	Contained within the file header structure is the bitmaps information header structure. This is described later.

The Bitmap Information Header

This structure follows the Bitmap File header structure. It contains data about the dimensions of the bitmap, what compression schemes were used with the bitmap and so forth. Its structure is reproduced here.

```
typedef struct _BITMAPINFOHEADER2
{
   ULONG  cbFix;
   ULONG  cx;
   ULONG  cy;
   USHORT cPlanes;
   USHORT cBitCount;
   ULONG  ulCompression;
   ULONG  cbImage;
   ULONG  cxResolution;
   ULONG  cyResolution;
   ULONG  cclrUsed;
   ULONG  cclrImportant;
   USHORT usUnits;
   USHORT usReserved;
   USHORT usRecording;
   USHORT usRendering;
   ULONG  cSize1;
   ULONG  cSize2;
   ULONG  ulColorEncoding;
   ULONG  ulIdentifier;
} BITMAPINFOHEADER2;
```

The fields for the BITMAPINFOHEADER2 structure have the following meanings:

ULONG	cbFix	Not all of this structure may be contained in the file. It is legal to chop it off after the field cBitCount. This field shows the length of the actual structure in the file. In our sample application we ignore all the fields after cBitCount except for the color table information.
ULONG	cx	Bitmap width in pels.
ULONG	cy	Bitmap height in pels.
USHORT	cPlanes	Number of color bit planes. Generally this field will have the value of 1.
USHORT	cBitCount	The number of bits per pel. This field can be used to determine the size of the palette necessary to represent the bitmap accurately. This is

		demonstrated in the sample.
ULONG	ulCompression	The bitmap data may be compressed in the file according to the following schemes:
	BCA_UNCOMP	The bitmap is not compressed.
	BCA_HUFFMAN1D	Modified Huffman encoding.
	BCA_RLE4	4-bit per pel run length encoding.
	BCA_RLE8	8-bit per pel run length encoding.
	BCA_RLE24	24-bit per pel run length encoding.

We do not address compression in this sample.

ULONG	cbImage	Byte length of the bitmap storage. This number is the size of the bitmap data only. It does not include the information and header structures.
ULONG	cxResolution	Horizontal resolution in units specified by usUnits.
ULONG	cyResolution	Vertical resolution in units specified by usUnits.
ULONG	cclrUsed	This is the number of color indexes used from the color table included with the bitmap. Strangely if this value is zero then all of them are used. If it is not zero, then it uses the number stored here beginning with the first index. For 24-bit bitmaps (which generally do not have a color table) this is the number of colors used by the bitmap.
ULONG	cclrImportant	Minimum number of colors for a satisfactory appearance of the bitmap. How somebody figures this out, we have no idea. Satisfactory is a rather ambiguous term. A better use for this field is that it is the count of colors listed in the color table for a 24-bit bitmap.
USHORT	usUnits	Generally this will have the value BRU_METRIC which is pels per meter.
USHORT	usReserved	Must be zero.
USHORT	usRecording	Default value BRA_BOTTOMUP means scan lines were recorded from the bottom to the top.
USHORT	usRendering	This field concerns the half-toning algorithm used. Something with which you are not often concerned with displaying the bitmap on a CRT. However, it may be useful for more advanced rendering on hardcopy devices. It may have the values:
	BRH_NOTHALFTONED	
	BRH_ERRORDIFFUSION	
	BRH_PANDA	
	BRH_SUPERCIRCLE	
ULONG	cSize1	Parameter used in connection with half-toning. Past our scope here.

ULONG	cSize2	Parameter used in connection with half-toning. Past our scope here.
ULONG	ulColorEncoding	For OS/2 bitmaps this will have the value BCE_RGB, meaning that color is encoded in RGB values.
ULONG	ulIdentifier	Applications may use this field for their own purposes.

The Bitmap Information

This structure is reproduced here.

```
typedef struct _BITMAPINFO2
{
   ULONG  cbFix;
   ULONG  cx;
   ULONG  cy;
   USHORT cPlanes;
   USHORT cBitCount;
   ULONG  ulCompression;
   ULONG  cbImage;
   ULONG  cxResolution;
   ULONG  cyResolution;
   ULONG  cclrUsed;
   ULONG  cclrImportant;
   USHORT usUnits;
   USHORT usReserved;
   USHORT usRecording;
   USHORT usRendering;
   ULONG  cSize1;
   ULONG  cSize2;
   ULONG  ulColorEncoding;
   ULONG  ulIdentifier;
   RGB2   argbColor[1];
} BITMAPINFO2;
```

Notice that it is identical to that of the BITMAPINFOHEADER2 with the exception of an additional field:

```
argbColor[1].
```

The BITMAPINFOHEADER2 and BITMAPINFO2 structures overlap in the file. This additional field is used to obtain an array of red, green, and blue (RGB) values. These RGB values are essentially a table of colors to which the indexes of the bitmaps bits should be mapped. In other words, if a bit within the bitmap has a color index of 5, then its point of color in the displayed bitmap should be mapped to color number 5 in this array. Colors on a CRT display are created by mixing varying RGB values for each pixel. RGB concepts are discussed more thoroughly later.

Twenty-four-bit bitmaps do not need this array. Because each bit in the bitmap may be described by a 24-bit value, there is sufficient color information available in the bit data itself that it does not need to be mapped by way of an index and table.

Displaying a Bitmap

Remember the bitmap data contained in the file is only one form of the bitmap. In order for it to appear in the client area of a window, several things must happen. Displaying a bitmap involves reading the information from the file, separating it into its component structures, then making the proper `Gpi` calls to create the displayed form. `GpiCreateBitmap` is a fairly straightforward function. You simply pass it a pointer to the bitmap data and some handles for the presentation space. It will create a bitmap that can be copied to the screen and return a handle to that bitmap. However, before we can go forward with demonstrating this process we must understand the concept of palettes.

Palettes

The coordination between the colors in the bitmap file and the capability of the display device are accomplished by the use of a palette. A palette is a software structure which is essentially a table of colors. Each presentation space can have a palette of different colors selected into that presentation space, or it may have no palette. Further, a palette can be selected into more than one presentation space simultaneously. Palettes may also exist without being selected into a presentation space.

Understand, however, that the process is not nearly as simple as copying a table of colors into the display device. If only it were! In order to maintain the general nature of the display device, and in order to enable it to display many different sorts of bitmaps, some mapping must take place between the requirements of the bitmap and the actual capabilities of the display hardware. The system must also maintain the system colors. In a multitasking environment, each of the applications that are running may be making its own particular demands on the display device. Some means must be provided in order to coordinate these different demands. Otherwise, there would be a total confusion of colors on the screen as the available colors were mapped and remapped.

In order to make it unnecessary for the application to be aware of the particular capabilities of every device on which it is running, some generalization is necessary. This generality appears in that the bitmap information is displayed in a window using the information for a palette selected into that window, which may or may not be the actual color information which was contained in the bitmap file. The burden of mapping 256 colors to 256 monochrome shades, for example, is hidden from the application.

Each bitmap may have its own color information contained within it. Some bitmaps have only two colors, white and black. Other bitmaps have 16 colors. Still others are called true color, in that each pixel of the bitmap is described by three 8-bit color values. In whatever way this information is contained in the bitmap file, whether TIFF or BMP, this color data must first be transformed into an OS/2 palette, which can be selected into a presentation space in order for it to be available for the display of that bitmap.

This transformation is accomplished by calling `GpiCreatePalette`. It has the general form:

```
hpal = GpiCreatePalette(hab, flOptions,lFormat, lCount, alTable);
```

Essentially this function accepts as input an array of RGB values of any length. If successful in creating a palette from this information it returns a handle to the palette. The application no longer needs to maintain the color information or memory to contain the color data after the palette is created. For our bitmap application here, we simply copy the RGB values into an array of unsigned longs along with a flag value in the upper byte, then pass this array off to `GpiCreatePalette`. For TIFF, GIFS, and other graphic file formats the method is very similar.

Palettes and Color Values

The term applying to arrays of colors and palettes get used fairly interchangeably, although they are not in fact the same thing. A palette is really only designated by its handle and the manipulation of it is done with the following listed functions. In OS/2 though, arrays of color values used to create palettes have only one form. That form is an array of unsigned longs. An unsigned long is four bytes in size. The upper byte is used as a flag value. The three bytes that follow it are the three values designating the component red, green, and blue values for that color. Each of these RGB value, obviously, can have a maximum value of 255.

For example, RGB values that are all zero would represent black. Values that were all 255 would represent white. 0, 255, 0 would make a bright green.

To put individual values in the array, use a formula:

```
(FLAG * 16777216) + (RED * 65536) + (GREEN * 256) + BLUE
```

`FLAG` is an OS/2 defined value which has the values and meanings described forthwith. `RED`, `GREEN`, and `BLUE` represent the unsigned short color values for each color component. In addition to using arithmetic C operators, you could also shift the bits into the upper bytes of a long value using the shift operators.

The values in the array should be ordered so that the most important colors have the lowest indices. These are considered first when the colors are remapped with a call to `WinRealizePalette`.

Palette Flags

PC_RESERVED

This flag is used in case the palette will be animated. It means that the color value might change frequently. Because there are a limited number of colors that most devices can display at any one time, whenever a change is made to the palette, other applications currently displayed must adjust for the color change. `PC_RESERVED` means that an application should not use that particular value because it will change frequently, constantly remapping it would cause the application to appear to flash and change in a confusing way to the user.

PC_EXPLICIT

`PC_EXPLICIT` designates the color as one of the devices physical colors. This is not a flag most programmers will use often. Most applications are not concerned with this level of control over the device.

The 0 Value

Zero is the customary value, and it is the one you should probably use most of the time.

The BMPPAL Application

The BMPPAL sample application demonstrates how to read a bitmap file from disk and display it in the client area. It also shows how to obtain parameters for both the bitmap and the display device. In addition it enables the user to modify the palette in use. This application is only a sample, and it is primarily designed to work with 256-color bitmaps and displays, because the color limitations demonstrate working with the palette more thoroughly.

We should emphasize again that the purpose of this application is to illustrate loading a bitmap from a file and manipulating its palette. We also demonstrate how to obtain the device capabilities for the display device. The important concept here is illustration. The techniques for manipulating the palette as well as displaying the capabilities and the bitmap parameters could and should be made far more elegant. We show the strings associated with the device capabilities right next to the value to be displayed so it will be easier to read. Using `WinLoadString`, although more efficient, would make the application unnecessarily dense. In addition, we use a single array in which we shift the palette values around, creating a new palette and palette handle each time. It would be more efficient to create several palette handles and to simply select them into the presentation space as needed. We do it this way so some connection can be seen among the various palette possibilities.

The general flow of activity in the application is as follows. Once the application has started, the user may either load a bitmap and display it or display the parameters for the screen device. If a

Using it, we obtain all the screen capabilities between CAPS_WIDTH and CAPS_COLOR_INDEX. Sometimes the use of this function can be a little confusing. What you actually receive as a result of making this call is a range of values. As an input value, you can designate the starting and ending place of the desired range. Output is placed in an array.

In other words, DevQueryCaps does not always return the same number of values or size of array. In fact, you can use it to obtain a single value as we do in the call to DevQueryCaps for the WM_CREATE message.

In our call here we want the screen capabilities in the range beginning with CAPS_WIDTH and ending with CAPS_COLOR_INDEX. We don't actually display all the values in this range, but it is more convenient to obtain them with this single call rather than making several calls.

The values are returned in the array alCaps. Most of the parameters have separate entries. For example, the value for the screen height is the second value in the array in our sample here. However, capabilities such as whether or not the device is able to load RGB color tables can only be obtained by or'ing in the flag CAPS_COLTABL_RGB_8 with the color table support entry, which is number 13 in our example here. These values and flags are listed in the section on DevQueryCaps later in the chapter.

Once again we should note that we have associated the strings that describe the device capabilities directly with the associated value here in the code. This just makes it easier to see. For a production application, you definitely would not want to do it this way, but it does help to see the words right next to the values involved.

IDM_QUERY_BIT_PARAM

Processing for this message is similar to that of IDM_QUERY_SCREEN. In this case though we obtain the parameters for the bitmap from the BITMAPINFOHEADER2 structure associated with the bitmap. Note that we did not directly copy these values into the header structure. They were written there when the bitmap was created with the call to GpiCreateBitmap in LoadBitmapFile.

IDM_EXIT

Before exiting we need to make sure the system colors are not scrambled, because they will remain in that state until explicitly changed by some other application. Resetting the palette exactly to its original state is not necessary because the window is closing and any other applications which were using the palette should remap it to their benefit. Really the only important colors in this situation are the system colors, so we want to be sure that they are not still overridden before the application quits. Therefore, we set our Override_Sys_Colors flag to FALSE, and call Set_Pal with the gray palette flag.

LoadBitmapFile

This function is called in response to the IDM_OPEN message in the window procedure. It performs most of the functionality necessary to read bitmap data from disk and create a bitmaps that can be displayed in an OS/2 presentation space.

First the common file dialogs are used to obtain a valid file. (See Chapter 4, "Common Dialogs," for more on common file dialogs.) Then the file is queried to obtain information about the file. In this case we are primarily interested in the size of the file. We obtain this with

```
if (DosOpen(Bitmap_File_Name, &hfFile, &cbRead, 0L,
  FILE_READONLY, OPEN_ACTION_OPEN_IF_EXISTS,
  OPEN_SHARE_DENYNONE, 0L))
  return 0;

if (DosQueryFileInfo( hfFile, 1, (PVOID) &File_Info,
  sizeof(FILESTATUS3)) != 0)
{
  DosClose(hfFile);
  return 0;
}

ulcbSize = File_Info.cbFile;
ReturnCode = DosAllocMem( &Mem_Buffer, ulcbSize, fALLOC );
```

Then allocate enough memory to hold the file and read it into memory. Only after the bitmap file data is in memory can we begin any significant processing.

Initially, of course, the file data is simply a collection of bytes which fill the allocated block. So we must first cast it to a type which is useful to the bitmap and palette functions. We presume first that this is a file which will have a BITMAPFILEHEADER2 structure at its beginning, so we cast the pointer to the memory as PBITMAPFILEHEADER2. This is performed with the lines

```
pbfh = (PBITMAPFILEHEADER2) Mem_Buffer;
```

The file may not in fact be a bmp2 file, but this will soon become apparent.

We next use a field in this BITMAPFILEHEADER2 structure to obtain a pointer to a BITMAPINFOHEADER2 structure. This happens at the line

```
pBitmap_Infoheader2 = (PBITMAPINFOHEADER2) &(pbfh->bmp2);
pBitmap_Info2 = (PBITMAPINFO2) pBitmap Infoheader2;
```

Notice that in the very next line we cast this same pointer to be of type pointer to BITMAPINFO2. This is done primarily to demonstrate that although the structures have different names, they do not occupy different locations in the data. They in fact overlap. Next we get a pointer to the actual bits which make up the bitmap.

```
pImage_Bits = (PBYTE) ((PBYTE)pbfh + pbfh->offBits);
```

You can see that there was considerable other stuff in this file besides the image data itself. Even at this point we do not have a valid bitmap which can be displayed. We have simply obtained information which may potentially be used to create a valid bitmap. The bitmap does not really exist, as far as OS/2 is concerned, until the call to `GpiCreateBitmap` returns successfully later in the code.

After getting our pointers set up, we calculate the number of colors necessary for this bitmap. This is determined by checking the for `cBitCount`. If this is a valid value, then we use the value from the colors used field in the bitmap data. If this is not one of the customary values, then we use the formula 2^N where N is the number of bits per pel to calculate the number of colors used.

Next we allocate memory sized to match this number and cast a pointer to this memory as unsigned long. Color values in OS/2 are kept as longs with the upper byte used as a flag and the following three containing the red, green, and blue component values. The color values associated with the bitmap are found using the `argbColor` field kept in the `BITMAPINFO2` structure.

Using the number of colors calculated, we use this pointer in a for loop to fill out the array of color values. The RGB and flag values are shifted into their respective bytes by multiplying. After the color values have been copied into the array of longs, we attempt to create a valid OS/2 palette, using this information.

```
hBitmapPal = GpiCreatePalette( hab,
  0, (ULONG) LCOLF_CONSECRGB,
  Colors_Used, BM_Color_Buffer );
```

It may be the case that none of this data was valid. Especially because Windows bitmaps have a similar, but different structure, to OS/2 bitmaps. If the color data turns out to be invalid, no harm is done though. The call to `GpiCreatePalette` will more than likely fail on invalid data. If `GpiCreatePalette` does not return an error then we set the global palette handle we use to this new palette handle.

The remainder of `LoadBitmapFile` attempts to use the bitmap data and palette to create a valid bitmap for the presentation space using the new palette if possible. So first we must obtain a handle to a presentation space. Next, if the new palette handle is valid, we select this palette into the presentation space. This is necessary so that the bitmap that is created will be able to use the color information in the palette. If the palette was not selected into the presentation space, then the operation of creating the bitmap would simply be unaware that it existed.

Set_Pal

This function has many lines of code in it, but it is really the most simple part of the sample application. It is essentially a large case statement. Each of the cases creates a new palette based on the palette flag passed in to the function.

Each of these cases involves filling out an array of values, whether by creating new values or shifting

around the old values, then calling GpiCreatePalette to create a new palette handle.

Important Palette- and Bitmap-Related Functions

The following are the functions used in connection with bitmaps and palettes that are important to address here. However, there are other related functions.

```
GpiAnimatePalette
GpiCreateBitmap
GpiCreatePalette
GpiDeletePalette
GpiQueryPalette
GpiQueryPaletteInfo
GpiSetPaletteEntries
GpiWCBitBlt
WinRealizePalette
DevQueryCaps
```

Each of these is described in detail in the following sections.

Animating the Palette

Animating the palette means causing the system to cycle through the available colors in turn. What this causes is the appearance of motion or change in the displayed image—if the image is rendered to take advantage of this. For instance, letters can be made to seem to fade to black if a black background is used and the palette is cycled through a series of light grays, darker grays, and ends with black. This function is not one that is often used, however, it is definitely useful for those that need it.

```
lChanged = GpiAnimatePalette(hpal, ulFormat,ulStart, ulCount, aulTable);
```

HPAL	hpal	Palette handle to be animated.
ULONG	ulFormat	This is the format of the entries in the color table, but in fact there is only one acceptable value, LCOLF_CONSECRGB, which is an array of RGB values. Because it's an unsigned long, each entry is four bytes long.
ULONG	ulStart	Color index with which to start the animation.
ULONG	ulCount	Number of elements in the color table.
PULONG	aulTable	Color table.

This function returns the number of remapped colors or the flag PAL_ERROR

Color indexes that are to be animated need the PC_RESERVED flag set, both in the palette currently

selected and in the color table. Elements that do not have this flag set are ignored. All presentation spaces using the same palette will have their colors animated by this call.

Creating Bitmaps

Creating bitmaps is performed by the function `GpiCreateBitmap`. As is the case with creating palettes, once the function has returned a handle successfully, the application no longer needs to maintain the memory in which the bitmap information was stored. In its general form the function is as follows:

```
GpiCreateBitmap(hps, pbmpNew, flOptions, pbInitData, pbmInfoTable)
```

HPS	hps	Presentation space in which the bitmap will be created. Bitmaps are always associated with a device even if the bitmap is only going to created in memory. The device is specified through the device context associated with the input presentation space to the call.
PBITMAPINFOHEADER2	pbmpNew	Bitmap information header structure. In our sample for this chapter, this information is copied from the bitmap file. However, you could fill out the structure with your own data to create a bitmap that was not read from a file.
ULONG	flOptions	When creating bitmaps from file data, use the flag `CBM_INIT` which causes the bitmap to be initialized with the bitmap pointed to by the parameter `pbInitData`.
PBYTE	pbInitData	Pointer to the data for the bitmap data.
PBITMAPINFO2	pbmInfoTable	This parameter points to the bitmap information table. It defines the format of the bits in `pbInitData`. It is ignored if `CBM_INIT` is not set.

If successful, this function returns the new bitmap handle that is not equal to zero. If it returns `GPI_ERROR` then use `WinGetLastError` to determine the problem.

This function has a number of other related functions that are not covered here because they have more specialized uses. They are:

GpiBitBlt	Copies a rectangle of bitmap information.

`GpiDeleteBitmap`	Deletes a bitmap.
`GpiDrawBits`	Draws a rectangle of bits in a bitmap.
`GpiLoadBitmap`	Loads a bitmap from a resource and returns a handle.
`GpiQueryBitmapBits`	Copies information from a bitmap to memory.
`GpiQueryBitmapDimension`	Returns width and height of a bitmap.
`GpiQueryBitmapParameters`	Returns information header for a bitmap.
`GpiQueryDeviceBitmapFormats`	Returns formats supported by the device driver.
`GpiSetBitmap`	Sets a bitmap as the currently selected bitmap in a memory device context.
`GpiSetBitmapBits`	Transfers data from storage to a bitmap.
`GpiSetBitmapDimension`	Sets a bitmap width and height in tenths of a millimeter.

Creating Palettes from Color Values

Palettes are created from arrays of RGB values. First fill the array with the desired color values, then call `GpiCreatePalette` to create the new palette and receive a handle to it.

```
GpiCreatePalette(hab, flOptions,lFormat, lCount, alTable)
```

HAB	hab	This is the anchor-block handle.
ULONG	flOptions	This parameter must have one of the following values: `LCOL_PURECOLOR` means that the system should not create a color using dot patterns of other colors; only solid, pure colors should be used. `LCOL_OVERRIDE_DEFAULT_COLORS` causes the system colors to be overridden by colors in the selected palette. This is only in effect while the palette is selected into a presentation space in the foreground. These values can be or'ed together. Options may also be set to zero, which is most often used.
LONG	lFormat	This parameter must have the value `LCOLF_CONSECRGB` which means the input table is RGB values as described above.
LONG	lCount	Number of elements in the input color table. It must be greater than 0.
PLONG	alTable	Array of color values as described above.

This function will return either the handle of the palette recently created or the flag `GPI_ERROR`. Use `WinGetLastError` to determine the problem. The palette will contain only those color entries that were input in the color table.

Note: It is not a good practice to create and use a palette that is larger than necessary for your application. Selecting and realizing the palette may cause other colors on the display to be remapped. Using a palette larger than necessary may cause a lot of unnecessary remapping.

You can create and select palettes that are larger than the value maximum `CAPS_COLOR_INDEX` (the number of valid indexes a device may use, returned by `DevQueryCaps`). However, a number of display device drivers do have bugs, in that they do not account for these larger palettes. We have seen them hang or perform inexplicably as a result of using palettes that are larger than they expect—unfortunate but true. So its best to be safe and check the maximum number the device can use.

Obtaining the Current Palette

```
GpiQueryPalette(hps)
```

Use this function to obtain the handle to the palette currently selected into the presentation space designated by the input parameter. Remember that palettes may be selected into more than one presentation space simultaneously.

`HPS`	`hps`	Handle for the presentation space from which the palette handle is desired.

If successful, `GpiQueryPalette` returns the palette handle. If it returns `NULLHANDLE`, it means that no palette is currently selected into that presentation space. If `PAL_ERROR` is returned, use `WinGetLastError` to determine the problem.

Querying Palette Values

Use `GpiQueryPaletteInfo` to obtain specific values in the currently selected palette in a presentation space. Remember that the values in the palette after it is selected may not be the same as those when the palette was created. For example, if the palette is not created to override the system colors, those will be present in the presentation space.

You may inquire about the whole palette or a sub-range of values.

```
GpiQueryPaletteInfo(hpal, hps, flOptions, ulStart, ulCount,aulArray)
```

`HPAL`	`hpal`	Input handle for the palette to be queried. If a palette handle other than `NULL` is used, information is returned for that palette, and the hps parameter is ignored.
`HPS`	`hps`	Presentation-space handle in which the palette is selected if the palette handle in `hpal` is `NULL`.

ULONG	flOptions	This is an input flag that can have only one value. LCOLOPT_INDEX means the index is to be returned for each RGB value in the aulArray parameter. Other flags are reserved and must be 0. Generally you will use 0 to obtain the actual RGB values.
ULONG	ulStart	Beginning index for values to be returned.
ULONG	ulCount	Number of elements to be returned. If this is set to 0, the number of elements required to return the palette information is returned.
PULONG	aulArray	This is an array to contain the output of the palette information when the call is successful. If on input the flag LCOLOPT_INDEX is specified, then the output is an array of alternating color indices and RGB values. In the form: index1, RGB value1, index2, RGB value2, ...

This function returns the number of elements successfully queried or PAL_ERROR. Use WinGetLastError to determine the problem. Zero is returned if no palette is selected into the presentation space.

If the palette is not loaded with a contiguous set of indices, QLCT_NOTLOADED is returned as the RGB value for values that lie outside the range.

Setting Palette Entries

GpiSetPaletteEntries is used to change the entries in a palette that already exists. This may be a palette that is currently selected into one or more presentation spaces. Remember that this is a logical palette. The actual physical palette will be remapped as best it can to match the desired changes.

The changes made by this function do not become apparent until WinRealizePalette is called.

```
GpiSetPaletteEntries(hpal, ulFormat, ulStart, ulCount, aTable)
```

HPAL	hpal	This is the palette handle in which entries will be changed.
ULONG	ulFormat	As in the other functions, this parameter can only have the value LCOLF_CONSECRGB, meaning that the color data is an array of RGB values.
ULONG	ulStart	Beginning index of values to be set.
ULONG	ulCount	Number of entries to be set.
PULONG	aTable	This contains the new palette definition data.

This function returns either TRUE or FALSE.

Copying Bitmap Data to the Presentation Space

Bitmaps may be display by copying them into a presentation space. This is frequently referred to as bit blitting, or blitting, the bitmap. In our sample here, we use the function `GpiWCBitBlt`, but there is another general purpose function for this also. It is `GpiBitBlt`. Essentially both functions involve using a bitmap handle to copy bitmap data into a presentation space. The parameter `lRop`, often referred to as the ROP code, is used to determine how the copied bitmap will be mixed with the bits already present in the presentation space.

The general form for the function is as follows:

```
GpiWCBitBlt(hpsTarget, hbmSource, lCount, aptlPoints, lRop, flOptions)
```

HPS	hpsTarget	The target presentation space into which the bitmap will be copied.
HBITMAP	hbmSource	Bitmap handle to be copied into the presentation space handle.
LONG	lCount	Number of pairs of points. It will always be equal to 4.
PPOINTL	aptlPoints	Point array for the rectangle in which the copying will take place. These are pairs of x- and y-coordinates based on the target and source space in the following order: Bottom-left corner of the target rectangle; top-right corner of the target rectangle; bottom-left corner of the source rectangle; top-right corner of the source rectangle.
LONG	lRop	Code to designate what mixing should take place between the source and target bits. The important codes for our purpose here are:
	ROP_SRCCOPY	Copy the source over the target.
	ROP_SRCAND	and the bits together.
	ROP_SRCINVERT	The source is xor'ed with the destination.
	ROP_SRCERASE	The sources is and'ed with the inverted destination.
	ROP_NOTSRCCOPY	The source is inverted.
	ROP_NOTSRCERASE	The source and destination are inverted then the two are and'ed together.
	ROP_MERGEPAINT	The inverted source is or'ed together with the destination.
ULONG	flOptions	This parameter governs how eliminated lines or columns are treated if a compression is performed. It may have the following values:

BBO_OR	or together eliminated rows if necessary.
BBO_AND	and together eliminated rows if necessary.
BBO_IGNORE	Ignore eliminated rows or columns.
BBO_PAL_COLORS	The color table associated with the BitmapInfoTable is a set of indices into the currently realized palette, instead of RGB colors.

Both source and target device contexts must be of the same physical device. In our case this will always be the case because we are blitting to the screen. Sometimes when the bitmap is copied, rows and columns may be deleted in order to make the bitmap fit. The flOptions parameter governs what happens to these eliminated rows and columns.

This function returns one of two values. GPI_OK means the copy was successful. GPI_ERROR means there was an error. Use WinGetLastError to determine the problem.

Realizing the Palette

Palettes do not become effective, even after they are selected into presentation spaces until WinRealizePalette is called. Being effective means that the colors in the physical devices palette are changed to accommodate as nearly as possible the new palette in the presentation space. Generally, you should expect to select a palette into a presentation space for display devices, then immediately call WinRealizePalette.

When the window has the input focus, the palette will be realized as well as can possibly be done. Otherwise, the realization is only achieved as well as it can be done after physical colors are allocated to the window with the input focus. If the palette is larger than the display device can support, then as many entries as possible are remapped in the device beginning with the lowest index of the palette. Remember also that some devices cannot change their physical palette, so the performance of this function is device dependent.

If entries in that palette are changed as a result of calling this function, a WM_REALIZEPALETTE message is sent to other applications by the system. The other applications will then need to update themselves in order to accommodate the changes. A palette may be successfully realized without any entries in the physical palette being made. In this case the WM_REALIZEPALETTE message is not sent.

A very important thing to note is that if the input presentation space handle to this function is currently associated with a device context of type OD_MEMORY, then this function does nothing other than return without error.

Do not call this function in response to a WM_SETFOCUS message, because a window's activation state is not known until processing of that message is finished.

```
WinRealizePalette(hwnd, hps, pcclr)
```

HWND	hwnd	Window handle.
HPS	hps	Presentation space handle.
PULONG	pcclr	This value is returned by the function and contains the number of physical palette entries changed. Zero means that the function realized all the entries without changing any entries in the display hardware's physical table.

This function returns either the number of colors remapped or PAL_ERROR. Use WinGetLastError to determine the problem.

WinGetLastError Return Values for Palettes and Bitmaps

In the case where a palette function fails, the cause can generally be determined by calling the function WinGetLastError and checking the flag returned. The following list are the flags that WinGetLastError may return. Not all GPI palette functions will return all these errors, we just collected them together here for the sake of quick reference.

PMERR_BITMAP_NOT_FOUND	A attempt was made to perform a bitmap operation on a bitmap that did not exist.
PMERR_HBITMAP_BUSY	An internal bitmap busy error was detected. The bitmap was locked by one thread during an attempt to access it from another thread.
PMERR_HDC_BUSY	This means that a device context was locked by another thread when the thread with the GPI call attempted to access it.
PMERR_INCOMPATIBLE_BITMAP	An attempt was made to select a bitmap or perform a BitBlt operation on a device context that was incompatible with the format of the bitmap.
PMERR_INCORRECT_DC_TYPE	An attempt was made to perform a bitmap operation on a presentation space associated with a device context of a type that is unable to support bitmap operations.
PMERR_INSUFFICIENT_MEMORY	Not enough memory was available to complete the operation.
PMERR_INV_BITBLT_MIX	An invalid lRop parameter was specified with a GpiBitBlt or GpiWCBitBlt function.

PMERR_INV_BITBLT_STYLE	An invalid options parameter was specified with a GpiBitBlt or GpiWCBitBlt function.
PMERR_INV_COLOR_DATA	The color table definition data specified with GpiCreateLogColorTable is not valid.
PMERR_INV_COLOR_OPTIONS	An invalid option parameter was specified for a logical color table or color query function.
PMERR_INV_COLOR_START_INDEX	The starting index parameter specified for a logical color table or color query function was invalid.
PMERR_INV_COORDINATE	An invalid coordinate value was specified.
PMERR_INV_HBITMAP	An invalid bitmap handle was specified.
PMERR_INV_HDC	This error can mean that either an invalid device context handle or an presentation space handle was specified.
PMERR_INV_HPAL	The color palette handle was not valid.
PMERR_INV_HPS	The handle to the presentation space was not valid.
PMERR_INV_INFO_TABLE	An invalid bitmap information table was specified.
PMERR_INV_LENGTH_OR_COUNT	An invalid length value was used as an input parameter.
PMERR_INV_RECT	An invalid rectangle parameter was specified.
PMERR_INV_USAGE_PARM	An invalid options parameter was used for GpiCreateBitmap.
PMERR_INVALID_HWND	The window handle was not valid.
PMERR_NO_BITMAP_SELECTED	An attempt has been made to operate on a memory device context that has no bitmap selected.
PMERR_NO_PALETTE_SELECTED	The realization of a palette failed because no palette was selected into that presentation space.
PMERR_PALETTE_BUSY	The owner of a palette cannot be reset while it is busy.
PMERR_PS_BUSY	The function failed because it attempted to use a presentation space that was in use by another thread.

Querying a Device's Capabilities

DevQueryCaps is a general purpose function for determining the capabilities of various devices installed on the system in which the application is running. This includes information about printer devices and even the mouse. Because all of its possible values far exceed what we need, we are going to list only those values with which this chapter and sample application are concerned. Consult the OS/2 Technical Library or the help file for the toolkit if you need information about how to use this function with these other devices.

The use of DevQueryCaps is fairly simple. You simply input a handle to a device context, a parameter in the list of possible parameters with which to begin, the number of parameters desired in the sequence that follows the input, and an array to hold the output as follows:

```
DevQueryCaps(hdc, lStart, lCount, alArray)
```

HDC	hdc	Handle for the device context about which the query is being made.
LONG	lStart	The number of the first item of information to be returned in the array. In the output array, it will be the item with index zero. These numbers are actually input as one of the defined flags. CAPS_FAMILY, for example, is the first defined number.
LONG	lCount	The number of items of information to be returned. It must be greater than zero.
PLONG	alArray	This array is returned filled with the values beginning with the input number and ending with the number of values input. If there are more array elements than values queried, the last values in the array are set to zero.

Capabilities Elements

The following is a list of the capabilities about which this function may return information. They are listed in their proper sequence. For example, CAPS_WIDTH, CAPS_HEIGHT, and CAPS_WIDTH_IN_CHARS are contiguous. Many of these entries also have flags defined that may be or'ed together with the entry in order to detect other capabilities of the device.

```
CAPS_FAMILY
CAPS_IO_CAPS
CAPS_TECHNOLOGY
CAPS_DRIVER_VERSION
CAPS_WIDTH
CAPS_HEIGHT
CAPS_WIDTH_IN_CHARS
CAPS_HEIGHT_IN_CHARS
CAPS_HORIZONTAL_RESOLUTION
CAPS_VERTICAL_RESOLUTION
CAPS_CHAR_WIDTH
CAPS_CHAR_HEIGHT
```

```
CAPS_SMALL_CHAR_WIDTH
CAPS_SMALL_CHAR_HEIGHT
CAPS_COLORS
CAPS_COLOR_PLANES
CAPS_COLOR_BITCOUNT
CAPS_COLOR_TABLE_SUPPORT
CAPS_MOUSE_BUTTONS
CAPS_FOREGROUND_MIX_SUPPORT
CAPS_BACKGROUND_MIX_SUPPORT
CAPS_VIO_LOADABLE_FONTS
CAPS_WINDOW_BYTE_ALIGNMENT
CAPS_BITMAP_FORMATS
CAPS_RASTER_CAPS
CAPS_MARKER_HEIGHT
CAPS_MARKER_WIDTH
CAPS_DEVICE_FONTS
CAPS_GRAPHICS_SUBSET
CAPS_GRAPHICS_VERSION
CAPS_GRAPHICS_VECTOR_SUBSET
CAPS_DEVICE_WINDOWING
CAPS_ADDITIONAL_GRAPHICS
CAPS_PHYS_COLORS
CAPS_COLOR_INDEX
CAPS_GRAPHICS_CHAR_WIDTH
CAPS_GRAPHICS_CHAR_HEIGHT
CAPS_HORIZONTAL_FONT_RES
CAPS_VERTICAL_FONT_RES
CAPS_DEVICE_FONT_SIM
CAPS_LINEWIDTH_THICK
```

Again, in this chapter we cannot possibly do justice to all these entries, so we will focus on those that are important for understanding the bitmaps, palettes, and the sample application. Each of the entries listed is discussed only in terms of the display device. However, for printer devices they may have additional or slightly altered meanings.

`CAPS_WIDTH`	Width of the screen in pels.
`CAPS_HEIGHT`	Height of the screen in pels.
`CAPS_COLORS`	Number of distinct colors supported at the same time.
`CAPS_COLOR_PLANES`	Number of color planes. In addition to thinking of screens as having a given width and height, you may also think of it as having a color depth, as if different colors of pixels could be stacked on top of each other. (The reason for this involves how color device hardware was historically built.)
`CAPS_COLOR_BITCOUNT`	The number of adjacent color bits for each pel.
`CAPS_COLOR_TABLE_SUPPORT`	This shows the type of loadable color table support the device provides. To find the value or in one of the following values with the returned entry.

Use the following flags or'ed together with the returned entry to determine further capabilities.

`CAPS_COLTABL_RGB_8`	This is 1 if RGB color table can be loaded, with a minimum support of 8 bits each for red, green, and blue.
`CAPS_COLTABL_RGB_8_PLUS`	This is 1 if a color table with other than 8 bits for each primary color can be loaded.
`CAPS_COLTABL_TRUE_MIX`	This is 1 if true mixing occurs when the logical color table has been realized.
`CAPS_COLTABL_REALIZE`	This is 1 if a loaded color table can be realized.
`CAPS_BITMAP_FORMATS`	This is the number of bitmap formats supported by the device.
`CAPS_ADDITIONAL_GRAPHICS`	This entry has a number of flags which may be or'ed in with it. In our case here we are only interested in whether or not the display device can make use of the palette manager functions. This is determined by or'ing in the `CAPS_PALETTE_MANAGER` flag.
`CAPS_PHYS_COLORS`	This is the maximum number of distinct colors available on the device.
`CAPS_COLOR_INDEX`	This is the maximum logical color-table index supported for this device. For the EGA and VGA drivers this value will be 63.

BMPPAL.C

```
#define INCL_DOSMEMMGR
#define INCL_WINSTDFILE
#define INCL_WINWINDOWMGR
#define INCL_WINMESSAGEMGR
#define INCL_WINHELP
#define INCL_WINFRAMEMGR
#define INCL_WINERRORS
#define INCL_WINPALETTE
#define INCL_WINPOINTERS
#define INCL_GPICONTROL
#define INCL_WINMENUS
#define INCL_WINDIALOGS
#define INCL_GPILCIDS
#define INCL_GPIPRIMITIVES
#define INCL_GPIPATHS
#define INCL_GPILOGCOLORTABLE
#define INCL_DOSSEMAPHORES
#define INCL_DOSPROCESS
#define INCL_DEV
#define INCL_WINSYS
```

```
#include <os2.h>
#include <string.h>
#include <stdlib.h>
#include <stdio.h>
#include <stdarg.h>
#include <math.h>
#include <time.h>
#include "bmppal.h"
#include "..\common\about.h"

HAB     hab;
HBITMAP hbmNewBitmap,
        hbmOld;
HPAL    hPal = NULLHANDLE,
        hBitmapPal  = NULLHANDLE;
HDC     hdc =  NULLHANDLE;
CHAR    szClassName[]   = "BMP_PAL",
        szTitle[64],
        szMessage[]     = "Bitmaps and Palettes";
BOOL    Bitmap_Loaded = FALSE,
        Pal_Capable = FALSE,
        Override_Sys_Colors = FALSE;
POINTL  Points[4];
HMTX    hmtxPS     = NULLHANDLE;
ULONG   Current_Palette = 0;
PVOID   P_Color_Memory = NULL;
PULONG  BM_Color_Buffer;
LONG    Colors_Used, Shift_Count=0;

LONG Format_Msg_Box(HWND, PSZ, ...);
HBITMAP LoadBitmapFile(HWND, PSZ);
LONG Set_Pal( ULONG, HWND );

int main( )
{
  QMSG   qmsg;
  ULONG  ctldata;
  HWND   hwndBMPPAL;
  HWND   hwndBMPPALFrame;
  HMQ    hmqBMPPAL;
  time_t seed;

  Points[0].x = 0;
  Points[0].y = 0;
  Points[1].x = 100;
  Points[1].y = 100;
  Points[2].x = 0;
  Points[2].y = 0;
  Points[3].x = 100;
  Points[3].y = 100;

  seed = time( NULL );
  srand( (ULONG) seed );
```

```
  hab = WinInitialize(0LU);
  hmqBMPPAL = WinCreateMsgQueue(hab, 0L);
  WinRegisterClass( hab, (PSZ)szClassName, (PFNWP) BMPPALWndProc,
    CS_SIZEREDRAW, 0LU);
  WinLoadString (hab, 0, ID_APPNAME, sizeof(szTitle), szTitle);

  ctldata = FCF_STANDARD;
  hwndBMPPALFrame = WinCreateStdWindow( HWND_DESKTOP,
    WS_VISIBLE, &ctldata, szClassName, szMessage, 0LU, NULLHANDLE,
    ID_APPNAME, &hwndBMPPAL );

  if (hwndBMPPALFrame == NULLHANDLE)
  {
    Format_Msg_Box(HWND_DESKTOP, "WinCreateStdWindow error: 0x%04x",
      WinGetLastError(hab));
    return 0;
  }
  WinSetPresParam( hwndBMPPALFrame, PP_FONTNAMESIZE,
    ( (ULONG) 10 ), ( (PSZ) "8.Courier") );

  WinShowWindow( hwndBMPPALFrame, TRUE );
  while( WinGetMsg( hab, (PQMSG)&qmsg, (HWND)NULLHANDLE, 0LU, 0LU ))
    WinDispatchMsg( hab, (PQMSG)&qmsg );

  if ( P_Color_Memory != NULL ) DosFreeMem( P_Color_Memory );
  if(hwndBMPPALFrame) WinDestroyWindow( hwndBMPPALFrame );
  if(hmqBMPPAL) WinDestroyMsgQueue( hmqBMPPAL );
  WinTerminate( hab );
  return 0;
}



MRESULT EXPENTRY BMPPALWndProc( HWND   hwnd, ULONG  msg, MPARAM mp1,
                                MPARAM mp2 )
{
  RECTL              rctlClient, rctlSize, rectDesk;
  ULONG              cclr;
  BITMAPINFOHEADER2 Bitmap_Param;
  char               String_Buffer[512];
  HPS                hps;
  LONG               alCaps[CAPS_PHYS_COLORS],
                     cxDesk,
                     cyDesk;
  APIRET             ReturnCode = 0;
  FILEDLG            FileDlg;
  switch (msg)
  {

/* The processing for this create message includes the call to check
   whether or not the display device can use palette manager
   capabilities. */

    case WM_CREATE:
      DosCreateMutexSem( (PSZ)NULL, &hmtxPS, 0UL, FALSE );
      hdc = WinOpenWindowDC(hwnd);
```

```
  /* Get device capabilities */
  DevQueryCaps( hdc, CAPS_ADDITIONAL_GRAPHICS, 1, alCaps );

  /* AND in flag to check if palette mgr. capable. */
  Pal_Capable = alCaps[0] & CAPS_PALETTE_MANAGER;
  break;

case WM_SIZE:
  WinQueryWindowRect(hwnd,&rctlSize);
  break;

case WM_COMMAND:
  switch (LOUSHORT(mp1))
  {
    case IDM_OPENFILE:
      /* Use common file dialogs to present bmp files. */
      memset(&FileDlg, 0, sizeof(FILEDLG));
      FileDlg.cbSize = sizeof(FILEDLG);
      FileDlg.fl = FDS_CENTER ¦ FDS_OPEN_DIALOG;
      strcpy(FileDlg.szFullFile, "*.bmp");
      WinFileDlg(HWND_DESKTOP, hwnd, (PFILEDLG)&FileDlg);

      if (FileDlg.lReturn == DID_OK)
      {
        /* Common dialog returned OK. */
        WinSetWindowText( WinQueryWindow(hwnd, QW_PARENT),
          (PSZ) FileDlg.szFullFile);
        /* Call BMPPAL function to process file. */
        Bitmap_Loaded = LoadBitmapFile( hwnd,
          (PSZ) FileDlg.szFullFile );

        if (Bitmap_Loaded)
        {
          /* If a file as successfully loaded, get the size of
             the desktop.  Check to see whether the bitmap
             is larger than the desktop.  If it is, then only
             display a piece of it. */

         WinQueryWindowRect( HWND_DESKTOP, &rectDesk );
         cxDesk = rectDesk.xRight - rectDesk.xLeft;
         cyDesk = rectDesk.yTop   - rectDesk.yBottom;

         if ( (Points[3].x >= cxDesk) ¦¦
              (Points[3].y >= cyDesk))
           WinSetWindowPos(WinQueryWindow(hwnd, QW_PARENT),
             HWND_TOP, cxDesk/3, cyDesk/3, Points[3].x/2,
             Points[3].y/2, ( SWP_SIZE ¦ SWP_MOVE ) );

        else
          WinSetWindowPos(WinQueryWindow(hwnd, QW_PARENT),
            HWND_TOP, (cxDesk-Points[3].x)/2,
            (cyDesk-Points[3].y)/2, Points[3].x+8,
            Points[3].y+62, ( SWP_SIZE ¦ SWP_MOVE ) );
        }
      }
      break;
```

```
/* The following cases are the result of menu choices made
   by the user.  We keep a flag of the current palette
   chosen then call the function that changes it. */

case IDM_SETPAL_RANDOM:
  Current_Palette = RANDOM_PAL;
  Set_Pal( Current_Palette, hwnd );
  break;

case IDM_SETPAL_GREEN:
   Current_Palette = GREEN_PAL;
   Set_Pal( Current_Palette, hwnd );
   break;

case IDM_SETPAL_DOWN:
   Current_Palette = DOWN_PAL;
   Set_Pal( Current_Palette, hwnd );
   break;

case IDM_SETPAL_UP:
   Current_Palette = UP_PAL;
   Set_Pal( Current_Palette, hwnd );
   break;

case IDM_SETPAL_GREY:
   Current_Palette = GREY_PAL;
   Set_Pal( Current_Palette, hwnd );
   break;

case IDM_SETPAL_RESET:
   Current_Palette = RESET_PAL;
   Set_Pal( Current_Palette, hwnd );
   break;

case IDM_OVERRIDE_SYS:
   Override_Sys_Colors = TRUE;
   Set_Pal( Current_Palette, hwnd );
   break;

case IDM_NO_OVERRIDE_SYS:
   Override_Sys_Colors = FALSE;
   Set_Pal( Current_Palette, hwnd );
   break;

/* The following case obtains and displays important
   parameters from the bitmap header structure read
   in with the bitmap file. */

case IDM_QUERY_BIT_PARAM:
   if ( Bitmap_Loaded )
   {
     Bitmap_Param.cbFix = sizeof(BITMAPINFOHEADER2);
     ReturnCode = GpiQueryBitmapInfoHeader( hbmNewBitmap,
                        &Bitmap_Param );

     if ( ReturnCode == TRUE )
```

```
      {
          Format_Msg_Box(hwnd,
            "Width:             %5lu\n"
            "Height:            %5lu\n"
            "Planes:            %5u\n"
            "Bits per pel:      %5u\n"
            "Color indexes used:%5lu\n"
            "Important indexes: %5lu\n",

             Bitmap_Param.cx,
             Bitmap_Param.cy,
             Bitmap_Param.cPlanes,
             Bitmap_Param.cBitCount,
             Bitmap_Param.cclrUsed,
             Bitmap_Param.cclrImportant);
      }
      else Format_Msg_Box(hwnd, "Could not read parameters.");
    }
    else
    {
       Format_Msg_Box(hwnd, "No bitmap is currently loaded.");
    }
    break;

/* This case obtains the important display parameters
   for the device, then presents them in a dialog box.
   Really the strings that follow should be loaded as resources;
   however, in the interest of clarity for this sample, we
   have inserted them directly in the code.*/

case IDM_QUERY_SCREEN:
  DevQueryCaps( hdc, CAPS_WIDTH, CAPS_COLOR_INDEX, alCaps );

  strcpy( String_Buffer, "Color table support:\n\0");
  if ( alCaps[13] & CAPS_COLTABL_RGB_8 )
      strcat(String_Buffer,
         "Able to load 8 bit RGB color tables.\n\0");
  else strcat(String_Buffer,
         "Unable to load 8 bit RGB color tables.\n\0");
  if ( alCaps[13] & CAPS_COLTABL_RGB_8_PLUS )
      strcat(String_Buffer,
         "Able to load RGB color tables other than 8 bit.\n\0");
  else strcat(String_Buffer,
         "Unable to load RGB color tables other than 8 bit.\n\0");
  if ( alCaps[13] & CAPS_COLTABL_TRUE_MIX )
      strcat(String_Buffer,
         "True mixing occurs when color table realized.\n\0");
  else strcat(String_Buffer,
         "No true mixing when color table realized.\n\0");
  if ( alCaps[13] & CAPS_COLTABL_REALIZE )
      strcat(String_Buffer,
         "Loaded color table can be realized.\n\0");
  else strcat(String_Buffer,
         "Loaded color table cannot be realized.\n\0");
  if ( Pal_Capable )
      strcat(String_Buffer,
```

```
                "Device supports palette functions.\n\0");
        else strcat(String_Buffer,
                "Device does not support palette functions.\n\0");

        Format_Msg_Box(hwnd,
           "Screen width:                       %5d\n"
           "Screen height:                      %5d\n"
           "Simultaneous distinct colors:       %5d\n"
           "Color planes:                       %5d\n"
           "Bits for each pel:                  %5d\n"
           "Number bitmap formats supported:    %5d\n"
           "Maximum distinct colors available:%5d\n"
           "Maximum logical color table index:%5d\n\n"
           "%s" ,
           alCaps[0], alCaps[1],
           alCaps[10], alCaps[11],
           alCaps[12],
           alCaps[19],
           alCaps[29], alCaps[30],
           String_Buffer);
        break;

     case IDM_ABOUT:
        DisplayAbout (hwnd, szTitle);
        break;

      /* Be sure to set the palette back before exiting.
         Otherwise, the system colors may still be
         overridden. */
      case IDM_EXIT:
        Override_Sys_Colors = FALSE;
        Current_Palette = GREY_PAL;
        Set_Pal( Current_Palette, hwnd );
        DosCloseMutexSem( hmtxPS );
        WinPostMsg(hwnd, WM_CLOSE, MPVOID, MPVOID);
        break;

      default:
         break;
   }
   break;

  case WM_PAINT:
    WinQueryWindowRect( hwnd, &rctlClient );
    hps = WinBeginPaint( hwnd, NULLHANDLE, &rctlClient );
    /* If a bitmap is loaded, obtain the semaphore select in
       the current palette, realize the palette, then blit
       the bitmap. */

    if ( Bitmap_Loaded )
    {
      WinRequestMutexSem( hmtxPS, SEM_INDEFINITE_WAIT );
      if(GpiSelectPalette(hps, hPal ) == PAL_ERROR)
      {
        DosReleaseMutexSem( hmtxPS );
        Format_Msg_Box(HWND_DESKTOP, "GpiSelectPalette Error %d %x",
```

```
          ReturnCode = WinGetLastError(hab), ReturnCode);
        }

        else
          if( WinRealizePalette(hwnd, hps, &cclr) == PAL_ERROR)
          {
            DosReleaseMutexSem( hmtxPS );
            Format_Msg_Box(HWND_DESKTOP,
               "WinRealizePalette Error 0x%04x",
                ReturnCode = WinGetLastError(hab));
          }

      else
      {
        GpiWCBitBlt( hps, hbmNewBitmap, 4L, Points,
          ROP_SRCCOPY, BBO_IGNORE);
        DosReleaseMutexSem( hmtxPS );
      }

    }

    WinEndPaint( hps );
    break;

    case WM_ERASEBACKGROUND:
      return (MRESULT) TRUE;

  default:
    return WinDefWindowProc(hwnd, msg, mp1, mp2);

  }
  return MRFROMLONG(0L);
}

/*******************************************************************/
/* The purpose of this function is to create a new palette based on
   the user's choice.  We only create palettes of 256 evenly
   shaded colors.  We could of course create these ahead of time and
   save them, but the re-creation is better for illustration.
   The essential operation of this procedure is performed by the
   call to GpiCreatePalette below.*/

LONG Set_Pal( ULONG Palette_Choice, HWND hwnd_passed )
{
  LONG    i, PalSize, index, ReturnCode = 0L;
  RECTL   Client_Rect;
  PVOID   P_Memory, P_Temp_Memory;
  PULONG  Palette_Buffer, Temp_Buffer;
  int     indexr1,indexr2, indexr3, Random_Number;
  ULONG   temp;

  if( Bitmap_Loaded )
  {
  /* Invalidate the window so it will repaint with the new palette.*/
```

```
WinQueryWindowRect( hwnd_passed, &Client_Rect );
WinInvalidateRect(  hwnd_passed, &Client_Rect, TRUE );

/* Check device palette size and allocate memory
   for palette. */

DevQueryCaps( hdc, CAPS_PHYS_COLORS, 1, &PalSize );
ReturnCode = DosAllocMem( &P_Memory, PalSize, fALLOC );
if(ReturnCode != 0)
{
   Format_Msg_Box(HWND_DESKTOP,
     "Could not allocate memory to create palette.");
   return 0L;
}
Palette_Buffer = (PULONG) P_Memory;

if( Pal_Capable )
{
  switch (Palette_Choice)
  {
    case RANDOM_PAL:
      for (i=0L; (ULONG)i < PalSize; i++)
      {
        Random_Number = rand();
        indexr1 = (int) (((float) PalSize - 1) *
          (float) Random_Number / (float) RAND_MAX);
        Random_Number = rand();
        indexr2 = (int) (((float) PalSize - 1) *
          (float) Random_Number / (float) RAND_MAX);
        Random_Number = rand();
        indexr3 = (int) (((float) PalSize - 1) *
          (float) Random_Number / (float) RAND_MAX);
        Palette_Buffer[i] = 0 * 16777216 +
          LONGFromRGB(indexr1, indexr2, indexr3);
      }
      break;

    case DOWN_PAL:
      Shift_Count—;
      temp = BM_Color_Buffer[0];
      for( i=0L; (ULONG) i < ( Colors_Used - 1); i++ )
        BM_Color_Buffer[i] = BM_Color_Buffer[i+1];
      BM_Color_Buffer[Colors_Used - 1] = temp;
      if ( Colors_Used < PalSize )
        for ( i = 0; i < Colors_Used; i++ )
          Palette_Buffer[i] = BM_Color_Buffer[i];
      else
        for ( i = 0; i < PalSize; i++ )
          Palette_Buffer[i] = BM_Color_Buffer[i];
      break;

    case UP_PAL:
      Shift_Count++;
      temp = BM_Color_Buffer[Colors_Used-1];
      for( i=(Colors_Used-1); (ULONG) i > 0; i— )
        BM_Color_Buffer[i] = BM_Color_Buffer[i-1];
```

```
  BM_Color_Buffer[0] = temp;
  if ( Shift_Count == Colors_Used ) Shift_Count = 0;
  if ( Colors_Used < PalSize )
    for ( i = 0; i < Colors_Used; i++ )
      Palette_Buffer[i] = BM_Color_Buffer[i];
  else
    for ( i = 0; i < PalSize; i++ )
      Palette_Buffer[i] = BM_Color_Buffer[i];
  break;

case GREEN_PAL:
  if (Colors_Used < PalSize)
  {
    for (i=0L; (ULONG)i < Colors_Used; i++)
    {
      index = (int) (255.0 * (float) i /
        (float) Colors_Used);
      Palette_Buffer[i] = 0 * 16777216 +
        LONGFromRGB(0, index, 0);
    }
    for (i=Colors_Used; (ULONG)i < PalSize; i++)
      Palette_Buffer[i] = 0 * 16777216 +
        LONGFromRGB(0, 0, 0);
  }
  else
  {
  for (i=0L; (ULONG)i < PalSize; i++)
    {
      index = (int) (255.0 * (float) i / (float) PalSize);
      Palette_Buffer[i] = 0 * 16777216 +
        LONGFromRGB(0, index, 0);
    }
  }
  break;

case GREY_PAL:
  if (Colors_Used < PalSize)
  {
    for (i=0L; (ULONG)i < Colors_Used; i++)
    {
      index = (int) (255.0 * (float) i /
        (float) Colors_Used);
      Palette_Buffer[i] = 0 * 16777216 +
        LONGFromRGB(index, index, index);
    }
    for (i=Colors_Used; (ULONG)i < PalSize; i++)
      Palette_Buffer[i] = 0 * 16777216 +
        LONGFromRGB(0, 0, 0);
  }
  else
  {
  for (i=0L; (ULONG)i < PalSize; i++)
    {
      index = (int) (255.0 * (float) i / (float) PalSize);
      Palette_Buffer[i] = 0 * 16777216 +
        LONGFromRGB(index, index, index);
```

```
    }
  }
  break;

case RESET_PAL:
  if( Shift_Count > 0 )
  {
    ReturnCode = DosAllocMem( &P_Temp_Memory,
      Shift_Count, fALLOC );
    if(ReturnCode != 0)
    {
       Format_Msg_Box(HWND_DESKTOP,
         "Could not allocate temporary memory for palette.");
       return 0L;
    }
    Temp_Buffer = (PULONG) P_Temp_Memory;
    for( i = 0; i < Shift_Count; i++ )
      Temp_Buffer[i] = BM_Color_Buffer[i];
    for( i = 0; i < (Colors_Used - Shift_Count); i++ )
      BM_Color_Buffer[i] = BM_Color_Buffer[i + Shift_Count];
    for( i = 0; i < Shift_Count; i++ )
      BM_Color_Buffer[i + (Colors_Used - Shift_Count)] =
        Temp_Buffer[i];
    Shift_Count = 0;
    DosFreeMem( P_Temp_Memory );
    }

  if( Shift_Count < 0 )
  {
    Shift_Count = 0-Shift_Count;
    ReturnCode = DosAllocMem( &P_Temp_Memory,
      Shift_Count, fALLOC );
    if(ReturnCode != 0)
    {
       Format_Msg_Box(HWND_DESKTOP,
         "Could not allocate temporary memory for palette.");
       return 0L;
    }
    Temp_Buffer = (PULONG) P_Temp_Memory;

    for( i = 0; i < Shift_Count; i++ )
      Temp_Buffer[i] =
         BM_Color_Buffer[Colors_Used-Shift_Count+i];
    for( i = (Colors_Used-1); i >= Shift_Count; i— )
      BM_Color_Buffer[i] = BM_Color_Buffer[i-Shift_Count];
    for( i = 0; i < Shift_Count; i++ )
      BM_Color_Buffer[i] = Temp_Buffer[i];
    Shift_Count = 0;
    DosFreeMem( P_Temp_Memory );
    }


    if ( Colors_Used < PalSize )
      for ( i = 0; i < Colors_Used; i++ )
        Palette_Buffer[i] = BM_Color_Buffer[i];
    else
```

```
            for ( i = 0; i < PalSize; i++ )
              Palette_Buffer[i] = BM_Color_Buffer[i];


          break;

        default:
        break;
        }

      /* If the user has indicated that the system colors should
         be overridden, then call GpiCreatePalette with
         LCOL_OVERRIDE_DEFAULT_COLORS, otherwise, use 0. */

      if (Override_Sys_Colors)
        hPal = GpiCreatePalette( hab, LCOL_OVERRIDE_DEFAULT_COLORS,
                                 (ULONG) LCOLF_CONSECRGB,
                                 PalSize, Palette_Buffer );
      else
        hPal = GpiCreatePalette( hab, (ULONG) 0,
                                 (ULONG) LCOLF_CONSECRGB,
                                 PalSize, Palette_Buffer );

      DosFreeMem( P_Memory );

      if ( hPal == NULLHANDLE ¦¦ hPal == GPI_ERROR )
      {
        Format_Msg_Box(HWND_DESKTOP,"GpiCreatePalette Error 0x%04x",
          ReturnCode = WinGetLastError(hab));
      }

    }
    else
    {
      Format_Msg_Box(HWND_DESKTOP,"Device is not palette capable");
    }
    }
}

/****************************************************************/
/* This is a handy function for displaying messages, particularly
   while debugging.  In consumer apps, you should use resource
   strings, but for our purposes here, this is excellent. */
/****************************************************************/

LONG Format_Msg_Box(HWND hwnd_PO, PSZ Format_String, ...)
{
  va_list Arg_List;
  PVOID   Buffer_Pointer;
  PSZ     String_Buffer;
  LONG    Item_Count;
  LONG    Return_Code;

  Return_Code = DosAllocMem( &Buffer_Pointer, 1024, fALLOC );
```

```
  if(Return_Code != 0) return 0L;

  String_Buffer = (PSZ) Buffer_Pointer;
  va_start(Arg_List, Format_String);
  Item_Count = vsprintf(String_Buffer, Format_String, Arg_List);

  WinMessageBox( HWND_DESKTOP, hwnd_PO, String_Buffer,
    "                                                    ",
    MSG_BOX_ID, ( MB_OK | MB_NOICON | MB_MOVEABLE ));

  if (!Return_Code) DosFreeMem( Buffer_Pointer );
  return Item_Count;
}

/***************************************************************/
/* This function is responsible for reading the bitmap data
   from disk and creating the bitmap. It returns a value
   signifying whether or not it was successful.
/***************************************************************/

HBITMAP LoadBitmapFile( HWND hWnd, PSZ Bitmap_File_Name )
{
  PBITMAPINFOHEADER2 pBitmap_Infoheader2 = NULL;
  PBITMAPFILEHEADER2 pbfh = NULL;
  PBITMAPINFO2       pBitmap_Info2 = NULL;
  ULONG              ulcbSize = 0L, cbRead = 0L;
  PVOID              Mem_Buffer = NULL, pImage_Bits = NULL;
  FILESTATUS3        File_Info;
  HFILE              hfFile;
  HPS                hps;
  BOOL               Value_To_Return;
  ULONG              i;
  APIRET             ReturnCode = 0;
  RECTL              Client_Rect;

  /* Reset parameters. */
  hbmNewBitmap = NULLHANDLE;
  Value_To_Return = FALSE;
  hBitmapPal = NULLHANDLE;
  hPal = NULLHANDLE;
  Override_Sys_Colors = FALSE;
  Shift_Count = 0;
  Current_Palette = GREY_PAL;


  WinQueryWindowRect( hWnd, &Client_Rect );
  WinInvalidateRect(  hWnd, &Client_Rect, TRUE );

  if( P_Color_Memory != NULL )
  {
    DosFreeMem( P_Color_Memory );
    P_Color_Memory = NULL;
  }
  /* Attempt to open the file obtained from the common
     file dialog. */
```

```
if (DosOpen(Bitmap_File_Name, &hfFile, &cbRead, 0L,
  FILE_READONLY, OPEN_ACTION_OPEN_IF_EXISTS,
  OPEN_SHARE_DENYNONE, 0L))
  return 0;

if (DosQueryFileInfo( hfFile, 1, (PVOID) &File_Info,
  sizeof(FILESTATUS3)) != 0)
{
  DosClose(hfFile);
  return 0;
}

/* Get the file size and allocate the memory to hold it. */
ulcbSize = File_Info.cbFile;
ReturnCode = DosAllocMem( &Mem_Buffer, ulcbSize, fALLOC );

if ( ReturnCode == 0 )
{
   ReturnCode = DosRead(hfFile, Mem_Buffer, ulcbSize, &cbRead);
   /* Cast the data to the structure which should be at the
      head of an OS/2 BMP2 file. */

   if ( ReturnCode == 0 )
   {
     /* Assign pointers to the bitmap header information and
        the data for the image bits. */

     pbfh = (PBITMAPFILEHEADER2) Mem_Buffer;
     pBitmap_Infoheader2 = (PBITMAPINFOHEADER2) &(pbfh->bmp2);
     pBitmap_Info2 = (PBITMAPINFO2) pBitmap_Infoheader2;
     pImage_Bits = (PBYTE) ((PBYTE)pbfh + pbfh->offBits);

     /* Check to see that the bits per pel is a value we can use.*/
     if( (pBitmap_Info2->cBitCount == 1) ||
         (pBitmap_Info2->cBitCount == 4) ||
         (pBitmap_Info2->cBitCount == 8))
     {
       if (pBitmap_Info2->cclrUsed)
         Colors_Used = pBitmap_Info2->cclrUsed;
       else
         Colors_Used = 1 << pBitmap_Info2->cBitCount;

       ReturnCode = DosAllocMem( &P_Color_Memory,
         Colors_Used, fALLOC );
       if(ReturnCode != 0)
       {
          Format_Msg_Box(HWND_DESKTOP,
            "Could not allocate memory for bitmap colors.");
          return FALSE;
       }
       BM_Color_Buffer = (PULONG) P_Color_Memory;
       for( i = 0; i < Colors_Used; i++ )
          BM_Color_Buffer[i] = 0;

       /* Copy the RGB value to a buffer compatible with
          a call to GpiCreatePalette. */
```

```
        for( i = 0; i < Colors_Used; i++)
        {
          BM_Color_Buffer[i] =
           pBitmap_Info2->argbColor[i].fcOptions * 16777216 +
           pBitmap_Info2->argbColor[i].bRed      * 65536    +
           pBitmap_Info2->argbColor[i].bGreen    * 256      +
           pBitmap_Info2->argbColor[i].bBlue;
        }
        /* Attempt to create the palette using the color information
           from the bitmap. */

        hBitmapPal = GpiCreatePalette( hab,
          0, (ULONG) LCOLF_CONSECRGB,
          Colors_Used, BM_Color_Buffer );

        if (hBitmapPal != GPI_ERROR) hPal = hBitmapPal;

        else  Format_Msg_Box(HWND_DESKTOP,
                "Bitmap palette could not be created.");
      }


      hps = WinGetPS (hWnd);
      /* If palette creation was successful, select it into the
         presentation space. */
      if ( hBitmapPal != GPI_ERROR)
         GpiSelectPalette( hps, hBitmapPal );

      /* Attempt to create a bitmap from the image bits. */
      hbmNewBitmap = GpiCreateBitmap (hps, pBitmap_Infoheader2,
        CBM_INIT, pImage_Bits, pBitmap_Info2 );

      if ( (hbmNewBitmap != 0) &&
           (hbmNewBitmap != GPI_ERROR) )
      {
        Value_To_Return = TRUE;
        /* Set the point structure to the bitmap size. */
        Points[1].x = pBitmap_Infoheader2->cx;
        Points[1].y = pBitmap_Infoheader2->cy;
        Points[3].x = pBitmap_Infoheader2->cx;
        Points[3].y = pBitmap_Infoheader2->cy;
      }

      else
      {
        Format_Msg_Box(HWND_DESKTOP,
          "Bitmap could not be created.");
      }
      WinReleasePS (hps);
    }
    DosFreeMem( &Mem_Buffer );
  }

  DosClose(hfFile);
  return( Value_To_Return );
}
```

BMPPAL.H

```
#define ID_APPNAME            1
#define ID_WINDOW             2
#define IDM_OPTIONS         100
#define IDM_OPENFILE        101
#define IDM_SETPAL_RANDOM   105
#define IDM_SETPAL_GREEN    106
#define IDM_SETPAL_DOWN     107
#define IDM_SETPAL_UP       108
#define IDM_SETPAL_GREY     109
#define IDM_SETPAL_RESET    110
#define IDM_OVERRIDE_SYS    111
#define IDM_NO_OVERRIDE_SYS 112
#define IDM_QUERY_BIT_PARAM 115
#define IDM_QUERY_SCREEN    116
#define IDM_ABOUT           120
#define IDM_EXIT            999

#define MSG_BOX_ID          1001

#define RANDOM_PAL          5001
#define GREEN_PAL           5002
#define DOWN_PAL            5003
#define GREY_PAL            5004
#define UP_PAL              5006
#define RESET_PAL           5007

#define LONGFromRGB(R,G,B) (LONG)(((LONG)R<<16)+((LONG)G<<8)+(LONG)B)

MRESULT EXPENTRY BMPPALWndProc( HWND, ULONG , MPARAM , MPARAM );
```

BMPPAL.DEF

```
NAME          SKELETON   WINDOWAPI
DESCRIPTION   'BMPPAL Program (c) Blain, Delimon, & English, 1994'
PROTMODE
HEAPSIZE      4096
STACKSIZE     32768

EXPORTS BMPPALWndProc
        AboutDlgProc
```

BMPPAL.RC

```
/* ---------------------------------------------------------------------
                      BMPPAL Resource File
                  Real World Programming for OS/2
           Copyright (c) 1994 Blain, Delimon, and English
--------------------------------------------------------------------- */

#include <os2.h>
#include "bmppal.h"
```

Contents of a Metafile

A metafile contains the encoded graphics primitives that make up a drawing. Most graphics primitives in OS/2 have an assigned numeric identifier and parameter format which is stored in the metafile. As graphics functions are called to draw within a metafile, the function and its parameters are encoded and stored. That is, each function is numbered. This number—and its associated parameters—are stored in sequence in the metafile.

Note: While it is possible to call any of the query functions or use calculations as parameters to graphics calls, only the result of those calls is stored in the metafile. The query functions or calculations themselves will not be stored.

Once recorded, a metafile can be edited in memory, saved to disk, or played into a presentation space. Encoded along with all of the graphics primitives is a metafile header. This header contains, among other important information, the following data related to the state of the presentation space used when the metafile was created:

- Logical color table
- Logical fonts
- Viewing transformation
- Page units
- Page dimensions

As a series of drawing instructions, metafiles may be rendered to screens, printers, plotters, or any other device whose driver can interpret a metafile. We will concern ourselves here with screen output only.

When playing the metafile, it is possible to override the values in the header to modify the image that the metafile represents. This will be covered when we discuss the playing of metafiles.

Creating a Metafile

The creation of a metafile is a relatively simple process. There is actually very little difference between creating a metafile and drawing in a window. The only real difference is that instead of using a screen or memory device context, a metafile device context is used. The creation and association of the presentation to use for the metafile device context is exactly the same as for any other device context.

A metafile device context can be created with the following code:

```
DEVOPENSTRUCT DevOpenStruct;
HDC           hDCMetaFile;
```

```
DevOpenStruct.pszLogAddress = (PSZ)NULL;
DevOpenStruct.pszDriverName = "DISPLAY";
hDCMetaFile = DevOpen (hAB, OD_METAFILE, "*", 2,
    (PDEVOPENDATA)&DevOpenStruct, (HDC)0);
```

Notice that the only difference in creating a metafile device context from creating a memory device context is the use of `OD_METAFILE` instead of `OD_MEMORY`. Once we have a metafile device context, the presentation space can be created and associated with it as follows:

```
HPS            hPSMetaFile;
SIZEL          Sizl = { 0, 0 };
hPSMetaFile = GpiCreatePS (hAB, hDCMetaFile, &Sizl,
   PU_PELS ¦ GPIA_ASSOC);
```

Once it is created, the graphics primitives are used to draw into this metafile presentation space. Figure 9.1 shows an example of a metafile image created by drawing a circle and a rectangle into a metafile presentation space.

Figure 9.1.
Example of a metafile image.

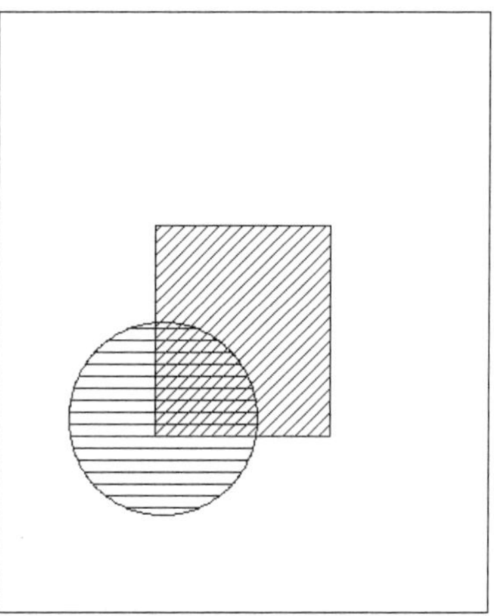

When we are done drawing into the metafile presentation space, it is disassociated from the device context. When the metafile device context is closed, a handle to the metafile is returned.

```
GpiAssociate (hPSMetaFile, (HDC)0);
GpiDestroyPS (hPSMetaFile);
hMetaFile = DevCloseDC (hDCMetaFile);
```

Saving a Metafile

A metafile handle is a reference to the block of memory containing the metafile information. The metafile can also be stored on disk using the `GpiSaveMetaFile` function.

```
BOOL APIENTRY GpiSaveMetaFile (HMF hmf, PSZ pszFilename);
```

HMF	hmf	Metafile handle
PSZ	pszFileName	Name of file to save the metafile data

The return value indicates if the file was successfully stored using the specified filename. If the filename specified by `pszFilename` already exists on the disk, `GpiSaveMetaFile` will not save the metafile to disk. OS/2 metafiles are normally stored using a file extension of ".MET."

To save our metafile to disk using the filename of "METAFILE.MET," we would use the following call:

```
GpiSaveMetaFile (hMetaFile, "METAFILE.MET");
```

Note: After a call to `GpiSaveMetaFile`, the metafile handle is no longer valid. If you wish to continue using the metafile after storing it on disk, you must explicitly reload the metafile file or make a copy of it prior to saving.

A metafile can be copied using the `GpiCopyMetaFile` function:

```
HMF APIENTRY GpiCopyMetaFile (HMF hmf);
```

HMF	hmf	Metafile handle

The return value is the handle to a copy of the original metafile. If we wanted to save our metafile to disk using the filename of "METAFILE.MET" and wanted to continue using the metafile, we would use the following calls:

```
hMetaFileCopy = GpiCopyMetaFile (hMetaFile);
GpiSaveMetaFile (hMetaFileCopy, "METAFILE.MET");
```

Loading a Disk Metafile

A metafile can be loaded from disk using the `GpiLoadMetaFile` function.

```
HMF APIENTRY GpiLoadMetaFile (HAB hab, PSZ pszFilename);
```

HMF	hmF	Metafile handle
PSZ	pszFileName	Name of file to save the metafile data

If the filename exists and it is a valid metafile, a metafile handle will be returned. To load the metafile we saved to disk using the filename of "METAFILE.MET," we would use the following call:

```
GpiLoadMetaFile (hAB, "METAFILE.MET");
```

Playing a Metafile

The graphics instructions contained in a metafile are executed when the metafile is "played." Your application has a tremendous amount of control over how the metafile is played. For example, you can choose to play the metafile using the viewing transformation specified in the metafile or using the current viewing transformation in the target presentation space. Overall there are seven elements that can be controlled by the `GpiPlayMetaFile` function.

Viewing Transformation	Specify whether to use the original viewing transformations in the metafile or the current viewing transformations in the target presentation space. This option allows the application to position and scale the metafile in the target presentation space different than the presentation space used for creating the metafile.
Local Identifiers	Specify whether to use the currently defined local identifiers (LCID) for pattern bitmaps and fonts or to load the pattern bitmaps and fonts from the metafile. This option allows the application to change the pattern bitmaps or fonts used by the metafile.
Presentation Space	Specify whether to use the size, page units, and default transformations of the presentation space used for creating the metafile or to use the parameters of the target presentation space.
Output of Image	Specify whether the actual drawing of the metafile occurs. This option allows the application to suppress output and query information about the presentation space or to change the presentation space parameters prior to actually drawing the metafile.
Logical Color Table	Specify whether to use the color table or palette from the metafile or the color table and palette defined in the target presentation space.
Realizable Color Table	Specify whether to realize the color table data from the metafile.
Default Attributes	Specify whether to use the default drawing attributes from the metafile or in the target presentation space.

All of these options are specified in a array of long values. This array is passed as a parameter to `GpiPlayMetaFile`:

```
LONG APIENTRY GpiPlayMetaFile (HPS hps, HMF hmf,
                LONG lCount1, PLONG alOptArray, PLONG plSegCount,
                LONG lCount2, PSZ pszDesc);
```

HPS	hps	Presentation space handle in which to play the metafile
HMF	hmf	Metafile handle
LONG	lCount1	Number of elements in the options array (alOptArray)
PLONG	alOptArray	Array of long values specifying the options for playing the metafile
PLONG	plSegCount	Must be zero (0)
LONG	lCount2	Size of pszDesc
PSZ	pszDesc	Buffer to contain metafile description specified in the DevOpenDC call that created the metafile

Note: The presentation space handle used to play a metafile must be a `GPIT_NORMAL` presentation space. The presentation space handle returned from `WinGetPS` and `WinBeginPaint` is a `GPIT_MICRO` presentation space.

The options array, `alOptArray`, is indexed using the following predefined option indexes:

Index	*Name*	*Value*
[0]	PMF_SEGBASE	Must be zero (0)
[1]	PMF_LOADTYPE	Viewing transformations
	LT_DEFAULT	(LT_NOMODIFY)
		LT_NOMODIFY
		LT_ORIGINALVIEW
[2]	PMF_RESOLVE	Must be zero (0)
[3]	PMF_LCIDS	LC_DEFAULT(LC_NOLOAD)
		LC_NOLOAD
		LC_LOADDISC
[4]	PMF_RESET	RES_DEFAULT (RES_NORESET)
		RES_NORESET
		RES_RESET
[5]	PMF_SUPPRESS	SUP_DEFAULT (SUP_NOSUPPRESS)
		SUP_NOSUPPRESS
		SUP_SUPPRESS
[6]	PMF_COLORTABLES	CTAB_DEFAULT (CTAB_NOMODIFY)
		CTAB_NOMODIFY
		CTAB_REPLACE
		CTAB_REPLACEPALETTE

Index	*Name*	*Value*
[7]	PMF_COLORREALIZABLE	CREA_DEFAULT (CREA_NOREALIZE) CREA_DOREALIZE CREA_NOREALIZE
[8]	PMF_DEFAULTS	DDEF_DEFAULT (DDEF_IGNORE) DDEF_IGNORE DDEF_LOADDISC

To play a metafile using the original viewing transformation, loading any required fonts and pattern bitmap resources from the metafile, using the color table from the metafile, and ignoring any default attributes in the metafile, we would use the following options and function calls:

```
LONG     alOptions [PMF_DEFAULTS+1];
alOptions [PMF_SEGBASE]         = 0L;
alOptions [PMF_LOADTYPE]        = LT_ORIGINALVIEW;
alOptions [PMF_RESOLVE]         = RS_DEFAULT;
alOptions [PMF_LCIDS]           = LC_LOADDISC;
alOptions [PMF_RESET]           = RES_DEFAULT;
alOptions [PMF_SUPPRESS]        = SUP_DEFAULT;
alOptions [PMF_COLORTABLES]     = CTAB_REPLACE;
alOptions [PMF_COLORREALIZABLE] = CREA_DEFAULT;
alOptions [PMF_DEFAULTS]        = DDEF_IGNORE;

GpiPlayMetaFile (hps, hmf, PMF_DEFAULTS, alOptions, 0, 0, NULL);
```

The metafile would be played using the options specified and at the coordinates originally used when the metafile was created. Later in this chapter, we will show how to modify the viewing transformation to display the metafile at a different location and size than it was originally drawn.

Deleting a MetaFile

Since a metafile is a resource and consumes memory, it is important to delete a metafile when it is no longer needed by the application. A metafile is deleted using the `GpiDeleteMetaFile` function:

```
BOOL  APIENTRY GpiDeleteMetaFile (HMF hmf);
```

HMF hmf   Metafile handle

The return value indicates if the metafile was successfully deleted. We must be careful when we talk about deleting a metafile. If we want to delete the metafile handle (in other words, the memory metafile) we use the `GpiDeleteMetaFile` function. To delete a disk metafile, we would use the `DosDelete` function to delete the file, just as we would delete any other disk file. The following calls are used to delete a metafile handle that has been used by our application and to delete the metafile that we saved to disk:

```
/* Delete metafile handle */
GpiDeleteMetaFile (hAB, hMetaFile);

/* Delete disk metafile */
DosDelete ("METAFILE.MET");
```

Additional Metafile Functions

There are three additional functions used to query and manipulate metafiles. These functions are used to query or modify a metafile in memory. The function `GpiQueryMetaFileLength` is used to query the size of the metafile:

```
LONG APIENTRY GpiQueryMetaFileLength (HMF hmf);
```

HMF	hmf	Metafile handle

The return value specifies the number of bytes occupied by the metafile. This value can be used to allocate a block of memory to contain the actual metafile bits. The metafile bits can be queried using the `GpiQueryMetaFileBits` function:

```
BOOL APIENTRY GpiQueryMetaFileBits (HMF hmf, LONG lOffset,
              LONG lLength, PBYTE pbData);
```

HMF	hmf	Metafile handle
LONG	lOffset	Offset from the start of the metafile
LONG	lLength	Number of bytes to query
PBYTE	pbData	Address of memory to receive the metafile bits

With the metafile bits in memory, they can be parsed and modified if necessary to change the contents of the metafile. The instructions or data can be updated in the metafile using the `GpiSaveMetaFileBits` function:

```
BOOL APIENTRY GpiSetMetaFileBits (HMF hmf, LONG lOffset,
              LONG lLength, PBYTE pbBuffer);
```

HMF	hmf	Metafile handle
LONG	lOffset	Offset from the start of the metafile
LONG	lLength	Number of bytes to write
PBYTE	pbData	Address of memory containing the metafile bits

Determining Metafile Boundaries

A metafile can be drawn using any coordinates that the metafile creator desires. It is not required that a metafile be created starting at coordinate (0,0) with the lower-left corner of the image residing at coordinate (0,0). Figure 9.2 illustrates a metafile and shows the boundary of all of the graphics primitives used in creating the metafile.

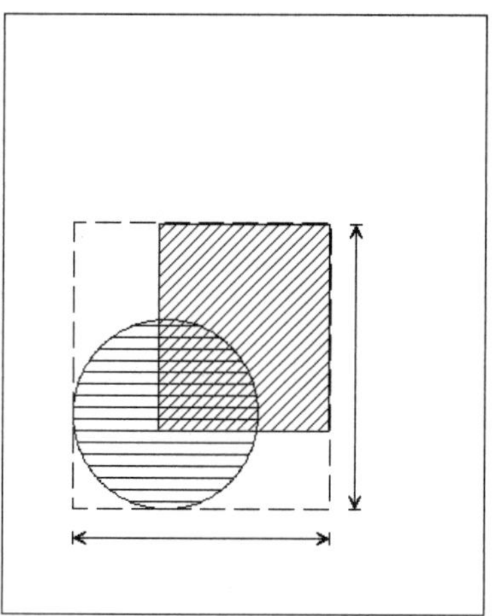

Figure 9.2.
Metafile boundary.

It is possible to determine the size and location of a metafile image by using several functions that control the drawing in a presentation space. To determine the metafile boundary before we actually display it, we must go through the process of playing the metafile without having any drawing performed. We cannot use the `SUP_SUPPRESS` option with the `GpiPlayMetaFile` function because this does not execute any of the drawing primitives within the metafile. The `GpiSetDrawControl` function can be used to allow us to play the metafile yet prevent any physical drawing to occur.

```
BOOL APIENTRY GpiSetDrawControl(HPS hps, LONG lControl, LONG lValue);
```

`HPS`	`hps`	Presentation space handle	
`LONG`	`lControl`	Drawing control to modify	
		`DCTL_DISPLAY`	Controls physical output to device
		`DCTL_BOUNDARY`	Accumulates boundary information
`LONG`	`lValue`	State of the specified drawing control	
		`DCTL_OFF`	Disables drawing control
		`DCTL_ON`	Enables drawing control

For the purpose of collecting boundary data for a metafile, the following three function calls are required:

```
GpiSetDrawControl (hPS, DCTL_DISPLAY, DCTL_OFF);
GpiSetDrawControl (hPS, DCTL_BOUNDARY, DCTL_ON);
GpiResetBoundaryData (hPSNew);
```

We turn off the physical output of the image and turn on the collection of boundary information. The `GpiResetBoundaryData` function is used to clear any previous boundary data that has been collected. At this point the metafile is played using the original metafile view. After the metafile is played, the boundary data is retrieved by using the `GpiQueryBoundaryData` function.

```
BOOL APIENTRY GpiQueryBoundaryData(HPS hps, PRECTL prclBoundary);
```

`HPS`	`hps`	Presentation space handle
`PRECTL`	`prclBoundary`	Address of RECTL structure to receive boundary information. The boundary data that is returned is in model space coordinates and must be converted to device space coordinates. This is done with the GpiConvert function.

To retrieve and convert the boundary data, the following two function calls are required:

```
GpiQueryBoundaryData (hPS, &MetafileRectl);
GpiConvert (hPSNew, CVTC_MODEL, CVTC_DEVICE, 2, (PPOINTL)&MetafileRectl);
```

Once we have the boundary of all of the graphics primitives in the metafile, we have enough information to change the location and size of the metafile when it is played.

Using Transformations

Up until this point, we have shown how to play a metafile using the original coordinates that were specified when the metafile was created. However, in most cases a metafile is created in a "generic" fashion using a given coordinate space. This can cause problems if our application needs to draw the metafile in a different location in the target presentation space or if we need to reduce or enlarge the metafile image.

One of the options specified in playing a metafile allows the application to use the viewing transformations of the target presentation space. This will allow us to translate and scale the coordinates in the metafile according to how we want the metafile played. We can think of the coordinates specified in a metafile as simply arbitrary units. These units are then translated according to the transformations defined in the target presentation space when the metafile is played.

There are four types of transformations provided by OS/2: translate, scale, rotate, and shear. For our purposes we are only interested in the translate and scale transformations. The translate transformation can be used to modify the position of the metafile. It simply specifies an offset to be added to each and every coordinate in the presentation space. A scale transformation can be used to modify the size of the metafile. It specifies a multiplier to be applied to each and every coordinate in the presentation space. We will not discuss the details of transformations and the various coordinate spaces in this book. The helper functions provided by OS/2 hide many of the details involved in using transformations. In the interest of keeping our discussion simple, we will not go into the mathematics.

To set up our transformation, the `GpiTranslate` and `GpiScale` helper functions can be used.

```
BOOL APIENTRY GpiTranslate (HPS hps, PMATRIXLF pmatlfArray,
               LONG lOptions, PPOINTL pptlTranslation);
```

`HPS`	`hps`	Presentation space handle
`PMATRIXLF`	`pmatlfArray`	Transform matrix

LONG	lOptions	Replacement option	
		TRANSFORM_REPLACE	Replace the previous matrix
		TRANSFORM_ADD	Combine this transformation with the transformation in the specified matrix PPOINTL pptlTranslation—Amount to translate each coordinate

```
BOOL APIENTRY GpiScale (HPS hps, PMATRIXLF pmatlfArray,
            LONG lOptions, PFIXED afxScale, PPOINTL pptlCenter);
```

HPS	hps	Presentation space handle	
PMATRIXLF	pmatlfArray	Transform matrix	
LONG	lOptions	Replacement option	
		TRANSFORM_REPLACE	Replace the previous matrix
		TRANSFORM_ADD	Combine this transformation with the transformation in the specified matrix afxScale scaling factor
PPOINTL	pptlCenter	Point at which the scaling occurs.	

Figure 9.3 shows the effect on the playing of our metafile if we were to translate the metafile so that it was positioned in the upper-left corner of our presentation space.

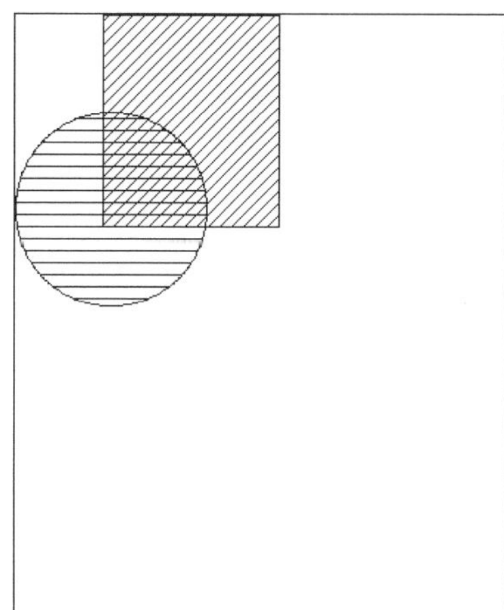

Figure 9.3. Translation of Metafile Coordinates.

Figure 9.4 shows the effect on the playing of our metafile if we were to scale the metafile so that is was reduced by 50 percent.

Figure 9.4.
Scaling of metafile coordinates.

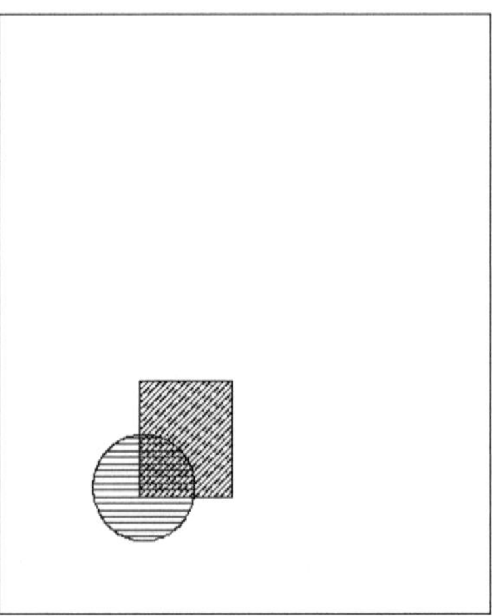

Once we have set up the desired translation and scaling effects, the transformation must be set into the target presentation space. This is done by using the `GpiSetDefaultViewMatrix` function:

```
BOOL APIENTRY GpiSetDefaultViewMatrix (HPS hps, LONG lCount,
              PMATRIXLF pmatlfArray, LONG lOptions);
```

`HPS`	`hps`	Presentation space handle	
`LONG`	`lCount`	Count of elements in pmatlfArray	
`PMATRIXLF`	`pmatlfArray`	Transformation matrix	
`LONG`	`lOptions`	Replacement option	
		`TRANSFORM_REPLACE`	Replace the previous matrix
		`TRANSFORM_ADD`	Combine this transformation with the transformation in the presentation space
		`TRANSFORM_PREEMPT`	Insert this transformation prior to the existing transformation in the presentation space

If we have our metafile boundary in the variable `MetafileRectl`, we can draw our metafile in the upper-left corner of our window with a reduction of 50 percent using the following calls:

```
/* Offset the x-coordinates by the negative of the metafile boundary.
   Offset the y-coordinates by the difference in the height of the
   window and top of the metafile boundary. */
Ptl.x = -MetafileRectl.xLeft;
Ptl.y = Rectl.yTop - MetafileRectl.yTop;
GpiTranslate (hps, &matlf, TRANSFORM_REPLACE, &Ptl);

/* Scale by 50% at the lower-left corner of where the metafile
   will be played. */
SizF.cx  = (FIXED)(65536 / 2);
SizF.cy  = (FIXED)(65536 / 2);
Ptl.y    = Rectl.yTop - (MetafileRect.yTop - MetafileRect.yBottom);
GpiScale (hps, &matlf, TRANSFORM_ADD, (PFIXED)&SizF, &Ptl);

/* Set the transformation into the presentation space */
GpiSetDefaultViewMatrix (hps, 9L, &matlf, TRANSFORM_REPLACE);

alOptions [PMF_SEGBASE]          = 0L;
alOptions [PMF_LOADTYPE]         = LT_NOMODIFY;
alOptions [PMF_RESOLVE]          = RS_DEFAULT;
alOptions [PMF_LCIDS]            = LC_LOADDISC;
alOptions [PMF_RESET]            = RES_DEFAULT;
alOptions [PMF_SUPPRESS]         = SUP_DEFAULT;
alOptions [PMF_COLORTABLES]      = CTAB_REPLACE;
alOptions [PMF_COLORREALIZABLE]  = CREA_DEFAULT;
alOptions [PMF_DEFAULTS]         = DDEF_IGNORE;

/* Play the metafile */
GpiPlayMetaFile (hps, hmf, PMF_DEFAULTS, alOptions, 0, 0, NULL);
```

Figure 9.5 shows the result of the previous code on our metafile. The metafile is located in the upper-left corner of the presentation space and it has been reduced by 50 percent.

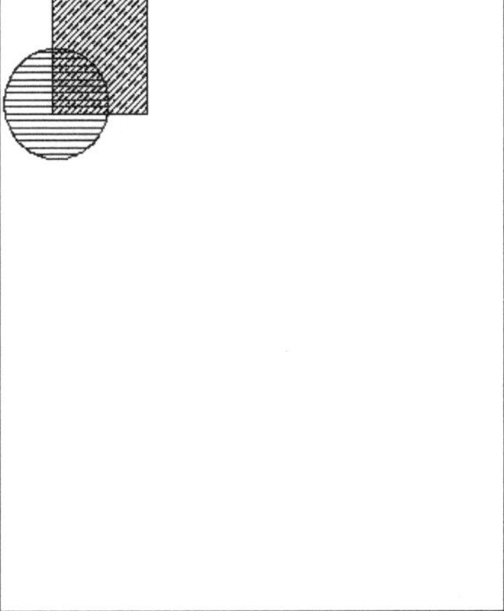

Figure 9.5. Translation and scaling of metafile coordinates.

Metafiles and the Clipboard

Metafiles are often used to exchange graphical data between applications through the system clipboard. Using a metafile format consumes much less memory than a bitmap of the image. Additionally, an application receiving a metafile through the clipboard may want to draw the image at a different size or location than where the original metafile was created. Using a metafile eliminates many potential problems when sharing graphical data.

A metafile is identified in the clipboard using the predefined clipboard format "`CF_METAFILE.`" The data that is maintained in the clipboard for a metafile is simply the metafile handle. A metafile can be placed into the clipboard using the `WinSetClipbrdData` function. Since the metafile handle is no longer valid after it has been placed into the clipboard, it is important to use a copy of the metafile if the metafile will continue to be used. The following code illustrates how to place a metafile into the clipboard:

```
if (WinOpenClipbrd (hab))
{
  hmfNew = GpiCopyMetaFile (hmf);
  WinEmptyClipbrd (hAB);
  WinSetClipbrdData (hAB, (ULONG)hmfNew, CF_METAFILE, CFI_HANDLE);
  WinCloseClipbrd (hAB);
}
```

To determine if a metafile handle is stored in the clipboard, again use the `CF_METAFILE` clipboard format identifier along with the `WinQueryClipbrdFmtInfo` function. The following code checks if a metafile is in the clipboard:

```
ULONG ulFormat;
WinQueryClipbrdFmtInfo (hAB, CF_METAFILE, &ulFormat);
```

Once it has been determined that a metafile is in the clipboard and you want to get a copy of it, use the `WinQueryClipbrdData` function to obtain the handle of the clipboard metafile.

Note: The handle to the metafile in the clipboard must not be used after the call to `WinCloseClipbrd`. Make a copy of the clipboard metafile before the call to `WinCloseClipbrd` if you need to use the metafile handle later.

The following code illustrates how to retrieve a copy of the metafile from the clipboard:

```
if (WinOpenClipbrd (hAB))
{
  hmfNew = (HMF)WinQueryClipbrdData (hAB, CF_METAFILE);
  hmfNew = GpiCopyMetaFile (hmfNew);
  WinCloseClipbrd (hAB);
}
```

The Metafile Application

The metafile sample application demonstrates most of the functionality and capabilities of creating and displaying metafiles. The application allows you to load and save a metafile file as well as create a new memory metafile. An interface to copy and paste metafiles to and from the clipboard also is provided. Finally, there are options for displaying the metafile in its normal state, scaled to fill the window, aligned with the upper-left corner of the window, and scaled and aligned within a user-specified tracking rectangle.

Using the Metafile Application

The main application window with a metafile displayed is shown in Figure 9.6. The application window contains the client window and an application-defined frame control. The frame control is actually a dialog box that displays the metafile boundary data and metafile presentation space size.

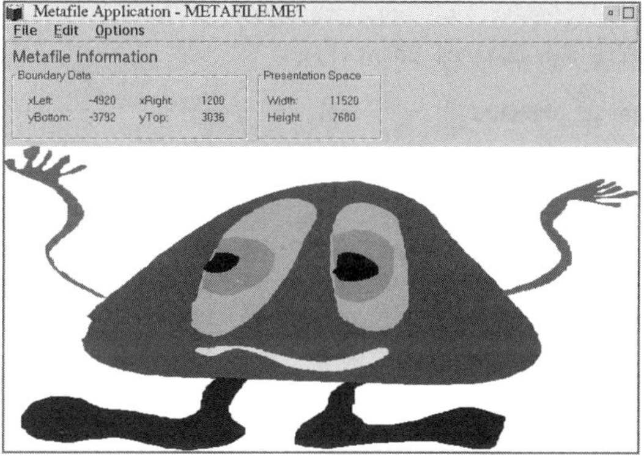

Figure 9.6.
Metafile application window.

Options from the "File" menu can be used to load, save, and create metafiles. The "Load Metafile" and "Save Metafile" options display the OS/2 common dialogs for opening and saving a file. The "Create Metafile" option will create a memory metafile and display it in the client area. Options from the "Edit" menu can be used to copy and paste metafiles to and from the clipboard. The "Options" menu item enables you to specify how the current metafile should be displayed. The "Normal" option will show the metafile as it was created. The "Scale to Fit Window" option will position and size the metafile so it fills the client window. The "Tracking Rectangle" option will position and size the metafile so it fills a rectangle outlined by tracking the mouse in the client area. The tracking rectangle can be changed by pressing and dragging the left mouse button. The "Upper-left Corner" option will position the metafile so the upper-left corner of the metafile boundary aligns with the upper-left corner of the client window.

```
#include "metafile.h"
#include "..\common\about.h"

/* Window and Dialog Functions  */
MRESULT EXPENTRY ClientWndProc (HWND,ULONG,MPARAM,MPARAM);
MRESULT EXPENTRY MetafileDlgProc (HWND,ULONG,MPARAM,MPARAM);
MRESULT EXPENTRY FrameSubclassProc (HWND hWnd, ULONG msg,
                                    MPARAM mp1, MPARAM mp2);

/* Local Functions              */
VOID CenterWindow (HWND hWnd);
HMF  CreateMetaFile (VOID);
PSZ  FindFileName (PSZ pszFileName);
VOID InitializeApplication (VOID);
BOOL OkayToReplace (PSZ pszFileName, PSZ pszTitle);
VOID PlayTheMetafile (HWND hWnd);
VOID QueryMetafileBounds (HMF hmf);
VOID QueryMetafilePSSize (HMF hmf);
VOID SetNewMetafile (HMF hmfNew);
VOID SetTitleText (PSZ pszFileName);
VOID TerminateApplication (VOID);

/* Global Variables             */
HAB       hab;                        /* Anchor block handle     */
CHAR      szTitle[128];               /* Application title string*/
HWND      hWndFrame,                  /* Frame window handle     */
          hWndClient,                 /* Client window handle    */
          hWndMenu,                   /* Main menu window handle */
          hDlgMetafile;               /* Frame control dlg handle*/
HDC       hdcWnd;                     /* HDC for client window   */
HMF       hmf        = 0;             /* Current metafile handle */
RECTL     MetafileRectl;              /* Current metafile bounds */
ULONG     ulDisplay  = IDM_SCALETOFIT; /* Display option          */
PFNWP     FrameWindowProc;            /* Frame window subclass   */
TRACKINFO TrackInfo;                  /* Mouse tracking data     */
FILEDLG   FileDlg;                    /* Common file dialog data */

/* --------------- Main Application Function ------------------ */

int main()
{
  HMQ   hmq;
  QMSG  qmsg;
  ULONG flFrameFlags    = FCF_STANDARD ¦ FCF_NOBYTEALIGN;
  CHAR  szClientClass[] = "CLIENT";

  hab = WinInitialize (0);
  hmq = WinCreateMsgQueue (hab, 0);

  WinLoadString (hab, 0, ID_APPNAME, sizeof(szTitle), szTitle);

  /* Register and create the client window class */
  WinRegisterClass (hab, szClientClass, ClientWndProc,
      CS_SIZEREDRAW ¦ CS_CLIPSIBLINGS, 0);

  /* Create the main application window */
```

```
  hWndFrame = WinCreateStdWindow (HWND_DESKTOP, 0, &flFrameFlags,
    szClientClass, szTitle, 0, 0, ID_APPNAME, &hWndClient);

  InitializeApplication ();

  /* Restore the window location and presentation parameters that
     were saved when the application was last run. */
  WinRestoreWindowPos ("RWPOS2", "METAFILE", hWndFrame);

  while (WinGetMsg (hab, &qmsg, 0, 0, 0))
      WinDispatchMsg (hab, &qmsg);

  /* Store the window location and presentation parameters so they
     can be restored on the next invocation of this program. */
  WinStoreWindowPos ("RWPOS2", "METAFILE", hWndFrame);

  TerminateApplication ();

  WinDestroyWindow (hWndFrame);
  WinDestroyMsgQueue (hmq);
  WinTerminate (hab);

  return (0);
}

/* --------------------- Local Functions --------------------- */

VOID CenterWindow (HWND hWnd)
{
  ULONG ulScrWidth, ulScrHeight;
  RECTL Rectl;

  ulScrWidth  = WinQuerySysValue (HWND_DESKTOP, SV_CXSCREEN);
  ulScrHeight = WinQuerySysValue (HWND_DESKTOP, SV_CYSCREEN);
  WinQueryWindowRect (hWnd,&Rectl);
  WinSetWindowPos (hWnd, HWND_TOP, (ulScrWidth-Rectl.xRight) / 2,
      (ulScrHeight - Rectl.yTop) / 2, 0, 0, SWP_MOVE | SWP_ACTIVATE);

  return;
}

HMF CreateMetaFile ()
{
  DEVOPENSTRUC     DevOpenData;
  SIZEL            Sizl;
  HDC              hDCMeta;
  HPS              hPSMeta;
  HMF              hmf;
  LINEBUNDLE       LineBundle;
  POINTL           Ptl;
  ULONG            ulInx;
  HBITMAP          hBitmap;
  BITMAPINFOHEADER bmi;
  POINTL           PtlBmp[4];

  /* Create a metafile DC */
```

```
memset (&DevOpenData, 0, sizeof(DEVOPENSTRUC));
DevOpenData.pszDriverName      = (PSZ)"DISPLAY";
hDCMeta = DevOpenDC (hab, OD_METAFILE, "*", 9L,
            (PVOID)&DevOpenData, 0);

/* Create a presentation space & associate it with the display DC */
Sizl.cx = Sizl.cy = 0;
hPSMeta = GpiCreatePS (hab, hDCMeta, &Sizl,
            PU_PELS | GPIF_DEFAULT | GPIT_NORMAL | GPIA_ASSOC);

/* Outline the area in which we will draw */
Ptl.x = Ptl.y = 0;
GpiSetCurrentPosition (hPSMeta, &Ptl);
Ptl.x = 400;
Ptl.y = 200;
GpiBox (hPSMeta, DRO_OUTLINE, &Ptl, 0, 0);

/* Output a random RGB color table */
GpiCreateLogColorTable (hPSMeta, LCOL_RESET, LCOLF_RGB, 0, 0, NULL);
LineBundle.lColor = 0;
Ptl.x = 0;
for (ulInx = 0; ulInx < 256; ulInx++)
{
  Ptl.y = 0;
  LineBundle.lColor = (rand () & 0xFF) |
                      ((rand () & 0xFF) << 8) |
                      ((rand () & 0xFF) << 16);
  GpiSetAttrs (hPSMeta, PRIM_LINE, LBB_COLOR, 0, &LineBundle);
  GpiSetCurrentPosition (hPSMeta, &Ptl);
  Ptl.y = 100;
  GpiLine (hPSMeta, &Ptl);
  Ptl.x++;
}

/* Load a bitmap and output to the metafile.  Make sure to use
   GpiWCBitBlt so the bitmap can be scaled with the rest
   of the metafile. */
hBitmap     = GpiLoadBitmap (hPSMeta, 0, ID_APPNAME, 0, 0);
bmi.cbFix   = sizeof(BITMAPINFOHEADER);
GpiQueryBitmapParameters (hBitmap, &bmi);
PtlBmp[0].x = 0;
PtlBmp[0].y = 200 - bmi.cy;
PtlBmp[1].x = bmi.cx;
PtlBmp[1].y = 200;
PtlBmp[2].x = 0;
PtlBmp[2].y = 0;
PtlBmp[3].x = bmi.cx;
PtlBmp[3].y = bmi.cy;
GpiWCBitBlt (hPSMeta, hBitmap, 4, PtlBmp, ROP_SRCCOPY, BBO_OR);
GpiDeleteBitmap (hBitmap);

/* Output a text string next to the bitmap */
Ptl.x = bmi.cx + 8;
Ptl.y = 200 - bmi.cy;
GpiCharStringAt (hPSMeta, &Ptl, 31,
  "Real-World Programming for OS/2");
```

```
   /* Disassociate the metafile presentation space from the metafile
      device context and destroy it. */
   GpiAssociate (hPSMeta, 0);
   GpiDestroyPS (hPSMeta);

   /* Retrieve the handle to the metafile by closing the metafile
      device context. */
   hmf = DevCloseDC (hDCMeta);

   return (hmf);
}

PSZ FindFileName (PSZ pszPath)
{
   /* Parse the path & locate the start of the filename in the path */

   PSZ pszCurrent = pszPath + strlen(pszPath);
   while (--pszCurrent >= pszPath)
     if (*pszCurrent == '\\')
       break;

   return (++pszCurrent);
}

VOID InitializeApplication ()
{
   /* Initialize the random number generator */
   srand (17);

   /* Initialize the Common File Dialog structure */
   memset (&FileDlg, 0, sizeof(FILEDLG));
   FileDlg.cbSize = sizeof(FILEDLG);

   /* Load the Metafile Information Dialog frame control window */
   hDlgMetafile = WinLoadDlg (hWndFrame, hWndFrame,
       MetafileDlgProc, 0L, IDD_METAFILE, NULL);

   /* Subclass the frame window so that we can add our new frame
      control window. */
   FrameWindowProc = WinSubclassWindow (hWndFrame, FrameSubclassProc);

   /* Get the handle to the main application menu window */
   hWndMenu        = WinWindowFromID (hWndFrame, FID_MENU);

   /* Initialize the mouse tracking information */
   TrackInfo.cxBorder          = 1;
   TrackInfo.cyBorder          = 1;
   TrackInfo.cxGrid            = 1;
   TrackInfo.cyGrid            = 1;
   TrackInfo.cxKeyboard        = 8;
   TrackInfo.cyKeyboard        = 8;
   TrackInfo.ptlMinTrackSize.x = 8;
   TrackInfo.ptlMinTrackSize.y = 8;
   WinSetRect (hab, &TrackInfo.rclTrack, 0, 0, 8, 8);
   TrackInfo.fs                = TF_SETPOINTERPOS;

   return;
```

```
}

BOOL OkayToReplace (PSZ pszFileName, PSZ pszTitle)
{
  FILEFINDBUF3 FileFindBuf3;
  ULONG        ulCount = 1;
  HDIR         hDir    = HDIR_SYSTEM;
  BOOL         bReturn = TRUE;

  /* Determine if the specified file already exists.  If so, then
     display a message box and ask if it is okay to replace the
     existing file. */

  if (!DosFindFirst (pszFileName, &hDir, FILE_NORMAL,
        (PVOID)&FileFindBuf3, sizeof(FileFindBuf3), &ulCount,
        FIL_STANDARD))
  {
    DosFindClose (hDir);
    if (WinMessageBox (HWND_DESKTOP, hWndClient,
          "File already exists! Replace file?", pszTitle, 0,
          MB_ICONEXCLAMATION | MB_MOVEABLE | MB_YESNO) == MBID_YES)
      DosDelete (pszFileName);
    else
      bReturn = FALSE;
  }

  return (bReturn);
}

VOID PlayTheMetafile (HWND hWnd)
{
  HPS      hps;
  LONG     alOptions [PMF_DEFAULTS+1];
  MATRIXLF matlf;
  RECTL    Rectl;
  POINTL   Ptl;
  POINTL   PtlMeta;
  SIZEL    Sizl;
  SIZEF    SizF;

  /* Handle the painting of the client window */
  hps = WinBeginPaint (hWnd, 0, 0);
  WinQueryWindowRect (hWnd, &Rectl);
  WinFillRect (hps, &Rectl, SYSCLR_PAGEBACKGROUND);
  WinEndPaint (hps);

  if (hmf)
  {
    Sizl.cx = Rectl.xRight;
    Sizl.cy = Rectl.yTop;

    /* Must create a presentation space here since the PS returned
       from WinGetPS/WinBeginPaint is a cache-presentation space and
       metafiles cannot be played into cache-presentation spaces. */
    hps = GpiCreatePS (hab, hdcWnd, &Sizl,
            PU_PELS | GPIF_DEFAULT | GPIT_NORMAL | GPIA_ASSOC);
```

```
/* Calculate the width and height of the metafile */
PtlMeta.x = MetafileRectl.xRight - MetafileRectl.xLeft;
PtlMeta.y = MetafileRectl.yTop - MetafileRectl.yBottom;

/* Set the default view matrix depending on the selected display
   option. */
switch (ulDisplay)
{
  case IDM_SCALETOFIT:
    /* First shift the metafile so that the lower-left corner
       aligns with (0,0) in the window. */
    Ptl.x = -MetafileRectl.xLeft;
    Ptl.y = -MetafileRectl.yBottom;
    GpiTranslate (hps, &matlf, TRANSFORM_REPLACE, &Ptl);

    /* Now scale the metafile so that it fits the window size.
       Make sure to scale around point (0,0) so the metafile
       remains at the location to which we just moved it. */
    SizF.cx  = (FIXED)((Rectl.xRight * 65536) / PtlMeta.x);
    SizF.cy  = (FIXED)((Rectl.yTop * 65536) / PtlMeta.y);
    Ptl.x    = 0;
    Ptl.y    = 0;
    GpiScale (hps, &matlf, TRANSFORM_ADD, (PFIXED)&SizF, &Ptl);

    GpiSetDefaultViewMatrix (hps, 9L, &matlf, TRANSFORM_REPLACE);
    break;

  case IDM_TRACKRECTANGLE:
    /* First shift the metafile so the lower-left corner
       aligns with the tracking rectangle */
    Ptl.x = TrackInfo.rclTrack.xLeft - MetafileRectl.xLeft;
    Ptl.y = TrackInfo.rclTrack.yBottom - MetafileRectl.yBottom;
    GpiTranslate (hps, &matlf, TRANSFORM_REPLACE, &Ptl);

    /* Now scale the metafile so it fits the tracking
       rectangle.  Make sure to scale around the lower-left corner
       of the tracking rectangle so the metafile remains at
       the location to which we just moved it. */
    SizF.cx  = (FIXED)(((TrackInfo.rclTrack.xRight -
                         TrackInfo.rclTrack.xLeft) * 65536) /
                         PtlMeta.x);
    SizF.cy  = (FIXED)(((TrackInfo.rclTrack.yTop -
                         TrackInfo.rclTrack.yBottom) * 65536) /
                         PtlMeta.y);
    Ptl.x    = TrackInfo.rclTrack.xLeft;
    Ptl.y    = TrackInfo.rclTrack.yBottom;
    GpiScale (hps, &matlf, TRANSFORM_ADD, (PFIXED)&SizF, &Ptl);

    GpiSetDefaultViewMatrix (hps, 9L, &matlf, TRANSFORM_REPLACE);
    break;

  case IDM_UPPERLEFT:
    /* Shift the metafile so that the upper-left corner
       aligns with the upper-left corner of the window */
    Ptl.x = -MetafileRectl.xLeft;
    Ptl.y = Rectl.yTop - MetafileRectl.yTop;
    GpiTranslate (hps, &matlf, TRANSFORM_REPLACE, &Ptl);
```

```
        GpiSetDefaultViewMatrix (hps, 9L, &matlf, TRANSFORM_REPLACE);
        break;
    }

    alOptions [PMF_SEGBASE]          = 0L;
    alOptions [PMF_LOADTYPE]         = LT_NOMODIFY;
    alOptions [PMF_RESOLVE]          = RS_DEFAULT;
    alOptions [PMF_LCIDS]            = LC_LOADDISC;
    alOptions [PMF_RESET]            = RES_DEFAULT;
    alOptions [PMF_SUPPRESS]         = SUP_DEFAULT;
    alOptions [PMF_COLORTABLES]      = CTAB_REPLACE;
    alOptions [PMF_COLORREALIZABLE] = CREA_DEFAULT;
    alOptions [PMF_DEFAULTS]         = DDEF_IGNORE;

    /* Play the metafile */
    GpiPlayMetaFile (hps, hmf, PMF_DEFAULTS, alOptions, 0, 0, NULL);

    /* Disassociate the presentation space and destroy it */
    GpiAssociate (hps, 0);
    GpiDestroyPS (hps);
  }

  return;
}

VOID QueryMetafileBounds (HMF hmf)
{
  DEVOPENSTRUC DevOpenData;
  HDC          hDCNew;
  HPS          hPSNew;
  LONG         alOptions [PMF_DEFAULTS + 1];
  SIZEL        Sizl;
  CHAR         szTmp[16];

  /* Create a display DC */
  memset (&DevOpenData, 0, sizeof(DEVOPENSTRUC));
  DevOpenData.pszDriverName = (PSZ)"DISPLAY";
  hDCNew = DevOpenDC (hab, OD_DIRECT, "*", 9, (PVOID)&DevOpenData, 0);

  /* Create a presentation space & associate it with the display DC */
  Sizl.cx = Sizl.cy = 0;
  hPSNew = GpiCreatePS (hab, hDCNew, &Sizl,
             PU_PELS | GPIF_DEFAULT | GPIT_NORMAL | GPIA_ASSOC);

  /* Turn drawing off and boundary collection on */
  GpiSetDrawControl (hPSNew, DCTL_DISPLAY, DCTL_OFF);
  GpiSetDrawControl (hPSNew, DCTL_BOUNDARY, DCTL_ON);
  GpiResetBoundaryData (hPSNew);

  /* Play the metafile into this presentation space.  Use the
     original metafile view and don't reset the presentation space. */
  alOptions [PMF_SEGBASE]          = 0L;
  alOptions [PMF_LOADTYPE]         = LT_ORIGINALVIEW;
  alOptions [PMF_RESOLVE]          = RS_DEFAULT;
  alOptions [PMF_LCIDS]            = LC_LOADDISC;
  alOptions [PMF_RESET]            = RES_NORESET;
  alOptions [PMF_SUPPRESS]         = SUP_NOSUPPRESS;
```

```
  alOptions [PMF_COLORTABLES]      = CTAB_REPLACE;
  alOptions [PMF_COLORREALIZABLE] = CREA_NOREALIZE;
  alOptions [PMF_DEFAULTS]         = DDEF_IGNORE;

  GpiPlayMetaFile (hPSNew, hmf, PMF_DEFAULTS+1, alOptions, 0L,
      0L, NULL);

  /* Collect the boundary data and convert to device units */
  GpiQueryBoundaryData (hPSNew, &MetafileRectl);
  GpiConvert (hPSNew, CVTC_MODEL, CVTC_DEVICE, 2L,
    (PPOINTL)&MetafileRectl);

  /* Destroy the presentation space and device context */
  GpiAssociate (hPSNew, 0);
  GpiDestroyPS (hPSNew);
  DevCloseDC (hDCNew);

  /* Update the metafile information dialog */
  sprintf (szTmp, "%8ld", MetafileRectl.xLeft);
  WinSetDlgItemText (hDlgMetafile, IDC_XLEFT, szTmp);
  sprintf (szTmp, "%8ld", MetafileRectl.yBottom);
  WinSetDlgItemText (hDlgMetafile, IDC_YBOTTOM, szTmp);
  sprintf (szTmp, "%8ld", MetafileRectl.xRight);
  WinSetDlgItemText (hDlgMetafile, IDC_XRIGHT, szTmp);
  sprintf (szTmp, "%8ld", MetafileRectl.yTop);
  WinSetDlgItemText (hDlgMetafile, IDC_YTOP, szTmp);

  return;
}

VOID QueryMetafilePSSize (HMF hmf)
{
  DEVOPENSTRUC DevOpenData;
  HDC          hDCNew;
  HPS          hPSNew;
  LONG         alOptions [PMF_DEFAULTS + 1];
  SIZEL        Sizl;
  CHAR         szTmp[16];

  /* Create a display DC */
  memset (&DevOpenData, 0, sizeof(DEVOPENSTRUC));
  DevOpenData.pszDriverName  = (PSZ)"DISPLAY";
  hDCNew = DevOpenDC (hab, OD_DIRECT, "*", 9, (PVOID)&DevOpenData, 0);

  /* Create a presentation space & associate it with the display DC */
  Sizl.cx = Sizl.cy = 0;
  hPSNew = GpiCreatePS (hab, hDCNew, &Sizl,
             PU_PELS | GPIF_DEFAULT | GPIT_NORMAL | GPIA_ASSOC);

  /* Save the current state of the presentation space */
  GpiSavePS (hPSNew);

  /* Play the metafile into this presentation space.  Reset the
     presentation space to the original in the metafile and suppress
     the actual playing of the metafile. */
  alOptions [PMF_SEGBASE]         = 0L;
  alOptions [PMF_LOADTYPE]        = LT_NOMODIFY;
```

```
   alOptions [PMF_RESOLVE]          = RS_DEFAULT;
   alOptions [PMF_LCIDS]            = LC_LOADDISC;
   alOptions [PMF_RESET]            = RES_RESET;
   alOptions [PMF_SUPPRESS]         = SUP_SUPPRESS;
   alOptions [PMF_COLORTABLES]      = CTAB_REPLACE;
   alOptions [PMF_COLORREALIZABLE] = CREA_NOREALIZE;
   alOptions [PMF_DEFAULTS]         = DDEF_IGNORE;

   if (GpiPlayMetaFile (hPSNew, hmf, PMF_DEFAULTS+1, alOptions,
          0, 0, NULL) == GPI_OK)
     /* Query the metafile PS Size */
     GpiQueryPS (hPSNew, &Sizl);
   else
     Sizl.cx = Sizl.cy = 0;

   /* Restore the state of the original presentation space */
   GpiRestorePS (hPSNew, -1);

   /* Destroy the presentation space and device context */
   GpiAssociate (hPSNew, 0);
   GpiDestroyPS (hPSNew);
   DevCloseDC (hDCNew);

   /* Update the metafile information dialog */
   sprintf (szTmp, "%8ld", Sizl.cx);
   WinSetDlgItemText (hDlgMetafile, IDC_WIDTH, szTmp);
   sprintf (szTmp, "%8ld", Sizl.cy);
   WinSetDlgItemText (hDlgMetafile, IDC_HEIGHT, szTmp);

   return;
}

VOID SetNewMetafile (HMF hmfNew)
{
   if (hmf)
     GpiDeleteMetaFile (hmf);
   hmf = hmfNew;

   QueryMetafileBounds (hmf);
   QueryMetafilePSSize (hmf);

   WinEnableMenuItem (hWndMenu, IDM_COPY, TRUE);
   WinEnableMenuItem (hWndMenu, IDM_SAVEMETAFILE, TRUE);
   WinInvalidateRect (hWndClient, NULL, FALSE);

   return;
}

VOID SetTitleText (PSZ pszFileName)
{
   CHAR   szTmp[CCHMAXPATH];

   strcpy (szTmp, szTitle);
   strcat (szTmp, " - ");
   strncat (szTmp, pszFileName, CCHMAXPATH - 3 - strlen(szTitle));
   WinSetWindowText (hWndFrame, szTmp);
```

```
  return;
}

VOID TerminateApplication ()
{
  return;
}

/* --------------- Window and Dialog Functions --------------- */

MRESULT EXPENTRY ClientWndProc (HWND hWnd, ULONG msg, MPARAM mp1,
                                MPARAM mp2)
{
  BOOL     bHandled = TRUE;
  MRESULT  mReturn  = 0;
  ULONG    ulFormat;
  HMF      hmfNew;

  switch (msg)
  {
    case WM_CREATE:
      /* Get the device context for the client window */
      hdcWnd = WinOpenWindowDC (hWnd);
      break;

    case WM_PAINT:
      PlayTheMetafile (hWnd);
      break;

    case WM_BUTTON1DOWN:
      WinDefWindowProc (hWnd, msg, mp1, mp2);
      if (ulDisplay == IDM_TRACKRECTANGLE)
      {
        /* Fill in the current position and size for the tracking
           rectangle and track the mouse */
        TrackInfo.rclTrack.xLeft    = SHORT1FROMMP(mp1);
        TrackInfo.rclTrack.yBottom  = SHORT2FROMMP(mp1);
        TrackInfo.rclTrack.xRight   = SHORT1FROMMP(mp1);
        TrackInfo.rclTrack.yTop     = SHORT2FROMMP(mp1);
        WinQueryWindowRect (hWnd, &TrackInfo.rclBoundary);
        TrackInfo.ptlMaxTrackSize.x = TrackInfo.rclBoundary.xRight;
        TrackInfo.ptlMaxTrackSize.y = TrackInfo.rclBoundary.yTop;

        if (WinTrackRect (hWnd, NULLHANDLE, &TrackInfo))
          WinInvalidateRect (hWnd, NULL, FALSE);
      }
      break;

    case WM_COMMAND:
      switch (SHORT1FROMMP(mp1))
      {
        case IDM_LOADMETAFILE:
          strcpy (FindFileName (FileDlg.szFullFile), "*.MET");
          FileDlg.fl = FDS_CENTER | FDS_OPEN_DIALOG;
          WinFileDlg (HWND_DESKTOP, hWnd, &FileDlg);
          if (FileDlg.lReturn == DID_OK)
          {
```

```
    hmfNew = GpiLoadMetaFile (hab, FileDlg.szFullFile);
    if (hmfNew != GPI_ERROR)
    {
      SetNewMetafile (hmfNew);
      SetTitleText (FindFileName (FileDlg.szFullFile));
    }
  }
  break;

case IDM_SAVEMETAFILE:
  FileDlg.fl = FDS_CENTER | FDS_SAVEAS_DIALOG |
               FDS_ENABLEFILELB;
  WinFileDlg (HWND_DESKTOP, hWnd, &FileDlg);
  if (FileDlg.lReturn == DID_OK)
  {
    /* GpiSaveMetaFile will not overwrite an
       existing file so we must check if a file
       with the specified name exists.  */

    if (OkayToReplace (FileDlg.szFullFile, "Save Metafile"))
    {
      /* Make a copy of the metafile since after the
         call to GpiSaveMetaFile, the metafile handle
         is no longer valid */
      hmfNew = GpiCopyMetaFile (hmf);
      GpiSaveMetaFile (hmfNew, FileDlg.szFullFile);

      /* Update the title to reflect new file name */
      SetTitleText (FindFileName (FileDlg.szFullFile));
    }
  }
  break;

case IDM_CREATE:
  hmfNew = CreateMetaFile ();
  if (hmfNew)
  {
      SetNewMetafile (hmfNew);
      SetTitleText ("Created");
  }
  break;

case IDM_COPY:
  if (WinOpenClipbrd (hab))
  {
    /* Make a copy of the metafile for the clipboard since
       after the call to WinSetClipbrdData, the metafile
       handle will no longer be valid. */
    hmfNew = GpiCopyMetaFile (hmf);
    WinEmptyClipbrd (hab);
    WinSetClipbrdData (hab, (ULONG)hmfNew,
        CF_METAFILE, CFI_HANDLE);
    WinCloseClipbrd (hab);
  }
  break;
```

```
        case IDM_PASTE:
          if (WinOpenClipbrd (hab))
          {
            /* Make a copy of the metafile from the clipboard */
            hmfNew = (HMF)WinQueryClipbrdData (hab, CF_METAFILE);
            hmfNew = GpiCopyMetaFile (hmfNew);
            WinCloseClipbrd (hab);
            if (hmfNew)
            {
              SetNewMetafile (hmfNew);
              SetTitleText ("clipboard");
            }
          }
          break;

        case IDM_NORMAL:
        case IDM_SCALETOFIT:
        case IDM_TRACKRECTANGLE:
        case IDM_UPPERLEFT:
          WinCheckMenuItem (hWndMenu, ulDisplay, FALSE);
          ulDisplay = (ULONG)SHORT1FROMMP(mp1);
          WinCheckMenuItem (hWndMenu, ulDisplay, TRUE);
          WinInvalidateRect (hWndClient, NULL, FALSE);
          break;

        case IDM_ABOUT:
          DisplayAbout (hWnd, szTitle);
          break;
      }
      break;

    case WM_INITMENU:
      if (SHORT1FROMMP(mp1) == IDM_EDIT)
      {
        /* Enable the paste option only if there is a metafile in
           the clipboard */
        WinEnableMenuItem ((HWND)mp2, IDM_PASTE,
            WinQueryClipbrdFmtInfo (hab, CF_METAFILE, &ulFormat));
      }
      break;

    default:
      bHandled = FALSE;
      break;
  }

  if (!bHandled)
    mReturn = WinDefWindowProc (hWnd,msg,mp1,mp2);

  return (mReturn);
}

MRESULT EXPENTRY FrameSubclassProc (HWND hWnd, ULONG msg, MPARAM mp1,
                                    MPARAM mp2)
{
  MRESULT mResult;
```

```
  ULONG   ulCnt;
  ULONG   ulInx;
  PSWP    pSwp;
  RECTL   Rectl;

  /* Call the original frame window procedure. */
  mResult = (*FrameWindowProc) (hWnd, msg, mp1, mp2);

  switch (msg)
  {
    case WM_QUERYFRAMECTLCOUNT:
      /* Tell OS/2 that there is one more frame control.  This tells
         OS/2 to allocate an additional SWP structure in the array
         that is passed in the WM_FORMATFRAME message. */
      ulCnt = (ULONG)mResult + 1;
      mResult  = (MRESULT)ulCnt;
      break;

    case WM_FORMATFRAME:
      /* Locate the window handle of the client window in the array
         of SWP structures.  When found, add our additional frame
         control window to the end of the list and resize the
         client window. */
      ulCnt = (ULONG)mResult;   /* Number of SWP entries used */
      pSwp  = (PSWP)mp1;
      for (ulInx = 0; ulInx < ulCnt; ulInx++)
        if (WinQueryWindowUShort (pSwp[ulInx].hwnd, QWS_ID) ==
             FID_CLIENT)
        {
          WinQueryWindowRect (hDlgMetafile, &Rectl);
          pSwp[ulCnt].fl    = pSwp[ulInx].fl;
          pSwp[ulCnt].hwnd = hDlgMetafile;
          pSwp[ulCnt].hwndInsertBehind =
                             pSwp[ulInx].hwndInsertBehind;
          pSwp[ulCnt].x     = pSwp[ulInx].x;
          pSwp[ulCnt].y     = pSwp[ulInx].y + pSwp[ulInx].cy -
                               Rectl.yTop;
          pSwp[ulCnt].cx    = pSwp[ulInx].cx;
          pSwp[ulCnt].cy    = Rectl.yTop;

          /* Adjust the height of the client window */
          pSwp[ulInx].cy   -= Rectl.yTop;

          /* Return one additional SWP structure */
          ulCnt++;
          mResult = (MRESULT)ulCnt;
          break;
        }
      break;
  }

 return (mResult);
}

MRESULT EXPENTRY MetafileDlgProc (HWND hWnd, ULONG msg, MPARAM mp1,
                                  MPARAM mp2)
```

```
{
  return (WinDefDlgProc (hWnd, msg, mp1, mp2));
}
```

METAFILE.DEF

```
NAME          METAFILE   WINDOWAPI
DESCRIPTION   'Metafile Program (c) Blain, Delimon, & English, 1994'
PROTMODE
STACKSIZE     16384
EXPORTS
    ClientWndProc      @1
    MetafileDlgProc    @2
    AboutDlgProc       @3
```

METAFILE.RC

```
/* ------------------------------------------------------------------
                         Metafile Resource File

                   Real-World Programming for OS/2
          Copyright (c) 1993, 1994 Blain, Delimon, and English
------------------------------------------------------------------ */

#include <os2.h>
#include "metafile.h"

ICON   ID_APPNAME METAFILE.ICO
BITMAP ID_APPNAME METAFILE.BMP

STRINGTABLE LOADONCALL MOVEABLE
BEGIN
    ID_APPNAME  "Metafile Application"
END

ACCELTABLE ID_APPNAME
BEGIN
    "L",      IDM_LOADMETAFILE,       CONTROL
    "l",      IDM_LOADMETAFILE,       CONTROL
    "S",      IDM_SAVEMETAFILE,       CONTROL
    "s",      IDM_SAVEMETAFILE,       CONTROL
    "R",      IDM_CREATE,             CONTROL
    "r",      IDM_CREATE,             CONTROL
    "C",      IDM_COPY,               CONTROL
    "c",      IDM_COPY,               CONTROL
    "P",      IDM_PASTE,              CONTROL
    "p",      IDM_PASTE,              CONTROL
    "F",      IDM_SCALETOFIT,         CONTROL
    "F",      IDM_SCALETOFIT,         CONTROL
    "N",      IDM_NORMAL,             CONTROL
    "n",      IDM_NORMAL,             CONTROL
    "T",      IDM_TRACKRECTANGLE,     CONTROL
    "t",      IDM_TRACKRECTANGLE,     CONTROL
```

unlike those of Microsoft Windows that are in ASCII text. This makes OS/2 INI files a little less approachable. Rather than using just any text editor, you need one specifically created to work with these files.

The OS/2 operating system provides a number of function calls to interact with INI files. For example, an application may want to save its current screen location and size. It should save this current screen location in an INI using functions from the profile management API. When the application is restarted, it should look for its INI file entry, again using functions from the profile management API. The application could then use the information it obtained from the INI file to resize itself accordingly.

INI files are files built using the profile management API within OS/2. This profile management API should also be used to add information to an INI file as well as delete information. This means that a consistent format is provided with which you and your applications may interact with these files. This interaction can involve not only data specific to the application, but also information contained within the operating system's INI files, and even other applications' data.

An application may create its own INI file or use the system INIs. OS/2 uses two INI files to store system data and configuration information. OS2.INI and OS2SYS.INI are the default names for the user and system profile files. These files can be found in the OS/2 directory on the drive where OS/2 was installed. These files have a considerable number of entries. Configuration information for system display colors is kept there along with information for print queues, settings for the serial ports, and much more.

Before we can start using INI files or programming for them, we have to learn their components. Even though INI files are binary files, all INI files that are created and modified using the Profile Management API have the same basic three-tiered layout.

These levels have the names:

Application name
Key name
Key data

At the highest level of organization is the application name. An INI file may have one or more application names. Each application name may, in turn, have one or more key names. Both the application name and the key name are null-terminated strings that may not exceed 1KB, including the terminating NULL character. Each key name has a data stream associated with it. This is the key data. This key data may be a null-terminated string or a block of binary data. Blocks of binary data should not exceed 64KB. For example, the default OS2INI file will contain the following:

```
PM_colors            <-   Application name
   DialogBackground  <-   Key name
       204 204 204   <-   Key data
```

In this example, the key data is also a null-terminated string. It should be noted that case is preserved in all stored strings.

One of the best ways to learn about the profile management API is to write an INI browser, as we have done here. Not only will this give you sample code for dealing with INI files, but also you will have a useful utility, especially because one is not provided with OS/2. The name of the INI browser we will be creating is INITOR. As always, if you intend to edit any system file, be sure to save a copy of that file in a safe place. One way of doing this is to let OS/2 automatically back up your current INI files each time you start your system. By adding the following line to your CONFIG.SYS file, you will always have a copy of your INI files as they existed at system start-up:

```
CALL=C:\OS2\XCOPY.EXE C:\OS2\OS2*INI C:\OS2\*.BAK
```

If your system boot drive is other than C, substitute the correct drive letter for your system.

The Profile Management API

Before we begin writing the INI file editor, let's look at the profile management API. This is a relatively small collection of system functions that assists your interaction with INI files. This API is made up of the following entries:

`PrfCloseProfile`	Closes a private profile file.
`PrfOpenProfile`	Opens a private profile file.
`PrfQueryProfile`	Retrieves full pathname for system initialization files (OS2.INI and OS2SYS.INI).
`PrfQueryProfileData`	Retrieves information from the profile file.
`PrfQueryProfileInt`	Retrieves an integer from the profile file.
`PrfQueryProfileSize`	Retrieves the size to hold the desired information from the INI file.
`PrfQueryProfileString`	Retrieves a string from the profile file.
`PrfReset`	Resets Presentation Manager initialization files with the new files.
`PrfWriteProfileData`	Writes or deletes binary data in the profile file.
`PrfWriteProfileString`	Writes or deletes a string in the profile file.

By the way, the term "profile file" is used almost interchangeably with the term "initialization file." Apparently, this follows a historical convention passed from Windows coding.

Reading from or writing to an INI file requires an initialization file handle HINI. An INI file must be opened to retrieve an INI file handle. The user and system profile files are opened by the system at start-up or as a result of a call to the `PrfReset` function. Private INI files, however, must be opened using the `PrfOpenProfile` function. To access the system INI files, three predefined handles are supplied by the operating system.

`HINI_USERPROFILE`	Read/Write user profile.
`HINI_SYSTEMPROFILE`	Read/Write system profile.
`HINI_PROFILE`	Read both user and system profile. Write user profile.

Enumerating the Entries in the INI File

Now that we have handles to access the system files, let's look at the `enum_app_names` function in INITOR. It takes two parameters, an INI file handle and the ID (identification) of a string to load and set in the title bar. This ID is, as usual, defined in the resource file. `enum_app_names` will enumerate all application names in the INI file by calling the `PrfQueryProfileString` function. The application names are then added to the application list box displayed by the INITOR application. The `PrfQueryProfileString` is defined as follows:

```
PrfQueryProfileString (hIni,pAppName,pKeyName,pDefault,pBuffer,ulBufferSize)
```

`HINI`	`hIni`	Initialization file handle.
`PSZ`	`pAppName`	Pointer to a null-terminated string that identifies the application name to be queried.
`PSZ`	`pKeyName`	Pointer to a null-terminated string that identifies the key name to be queried.
`PSZ`	`pDefault`	Pointer to a null-terminated string to be copied to `pBuffer` if the requested entry is not found.
`PSZ`	`pBuffer`	Pointer to the location that the return string is to be copied.
`ULONG`	`ulBuffSize`	Length in bytes of the memory pointed to by `pBuffer`.

`PrfQueryProfileString` performs a case-insensitive search for the string pointed to by `pKeyName` in the application section identified by `pAppName`. If a match is found, the key name data is copied to `pBuffer` and the number of bytes including the null terminator copied is returned. If a match is not found, the contents of `pDefault` are copied to `pBuffer`. If `pBuffer` is `NULL`, nothing is copied to `pBuffer` and 0 is returned. By specifying `NULL` for the `pAppName` parameter, `PrfQueryProfileString` returns all application names in the INI file as an array of null-terminated strings. The last string will be double null-terminated. If `NULL` is passed as the `pKeyName` parameter and `pAppName` is the pointer to a string that is found in the file, all key names in that application section are returned as an array of null-terminated strings. As with the enumerated application names, the last string will be double null-terminated.

Because the number and size of the entries in an INI file will vary, `enum_app_names` determines the space required to hold the application names by calling the `PrfQueryProfileSize` function. `PrfQueryProfileSize` takes a set of parameters similar to `PrfQueryProfileString`:

```
PrfQueryProfileSize (hIni,pAppName,pKeyName,pDataLength)
```

HINI	hIni	Initialization file handle.
PSZ	pAppName	Pointer to a null-terminated string that identifies the application name to be queried.
PSZ	pKeyName	Pointer to a null-terminated string that identifies the key name to be queried.
PULONG	pDataLength	Pointer to a ULONG that will contain the length of key name data if the function is successful.

enum_app_names will pass NULL for both the pAppName and pKeyName because we want to know the memory required to hold all the application names:

```
if (PrfQueryProfileSize(hini,NULL,NULL,(PULONG)&ulSize) && ulSize)
```

If the function is successful and the length returned in ulSize is non-NULL, memory is allocated and the strings are retrieved:

```
DosSubAlloc(pMem,(PPVOID)&pData,ulSize);
if(PrfQueryProfileString(hini,NULL,NULL,"No Entries",pData,ulSize))
```

The strings are copied to the memory pointed to by pData, and the actual number of bytes (including NULLs) copied to pData is returned. Because we already know the length of the returned data, the return length is ignored. The application list box is disabled, and its contents are deleted. Disabling the list box prevents redrawing after each string is added:

```
pCurrent = pData;
WinEnableWindowUpdate(hAppLBox,FALSE);
WinSendMsg (hAppLBox,LM_DELETEALL,NULL,NULL);
```

The array of application names is walked, and each string is added to the list box in ascending order:

```
while (*pCurrent)
{
   WinSendMsg (hAppLBox,LM_INSERTITEM, (MPARAM)LIT_SORTASCENDING, (MPARAM)pCurrent);
   while(*pCurrent)
      pCurrent++;
   pCurrent++;
}
```

When all items are added, the first item is selected and updates to the list box are reenabled. The memory used for the application names is freed. By selecting an entry in the list box, a WM_CONTROL message with a notification code of LN_SELECT is sent to the owner window. The owner window, INITOR's client, will call the enum_key_name function that will fill up the key name list box in a similar fashion:

```
WinSendMsg (hAppLBox,LM_SELECTITEM,MPFROMSHORT(0),
   MPFROMSHORT(TRUE));
WinEnableWindowUpdate(hAppLBox,TRUE);

DosSubFree(pMem,pData,ulSize);
```

After the key name list box is filled by the `enum_key_name` function, the first entry is selected causing another `WM_CONTROL` message to be sent to the owner window. This time the client window calls the `get_key_data` function. If a data item currently exists, the memory for it is freed, and the `PrfQueryProfileSize` function is called to determine the storage requirements of the new data. The data is retrieved by calling the `PrfQueryProfileData` function because the data may be a null-terminated string or a stream of binary data. The `PrfQueryProfileData` is defined as follows:

```
PrfQueryProfileData(hIni,pAppName,pKeyName,pKeyData,(PULONG)&ulKeySize))
```

`HINI`	`hIni`	Initialization file handle.
`PSZ`	`pAppName`	Pointer to a null-terminated string that identifies the application name to be queried.
`PSZ`	`pKeyName`	Pointer to a null-terminated string that identifies the key name to be queried.
`PSZ`	`pBuffer`	Pointer to the location that the data is to be copied. The return data is not nullterminated unless the last byte of the data stored was a `NULL`.
`PULONG`	`pDataLength`	Pointer to a `ULONG` that contains the length of buffer pointed to by `pBuffer`. If the function is successful, the value will be replaced with the number of bytes actually copied to `pBuffer`.

As with the `PrfQueryProfileString` function, the search is case-insensitive, and passing a `NULL` for either `pAppName` or `PKeyName` will have the same effect as described previously. If the data is successfully returned, the data window is invalidated causing the new data to be displayed.

Adding Entries

New application names, key names, and associated data may be added to an INI file with the `PrfWriteProfileData` or `PrfWriteProfileString` function. INITOR adds new entries to system or private INI files using both functions. Null-terminated strings may be added by selecting one of the menu options from the Add pop-up menu. Doing this will display a dialog that enables you to enter the application name, key name, and key data strings to add to the currently displayed INI file. The Add New Application option will leave all three edit windows uninitialized, and the Add New Key menu item will initialize the first edit window with the currently selected application name (see Figure 10.1).

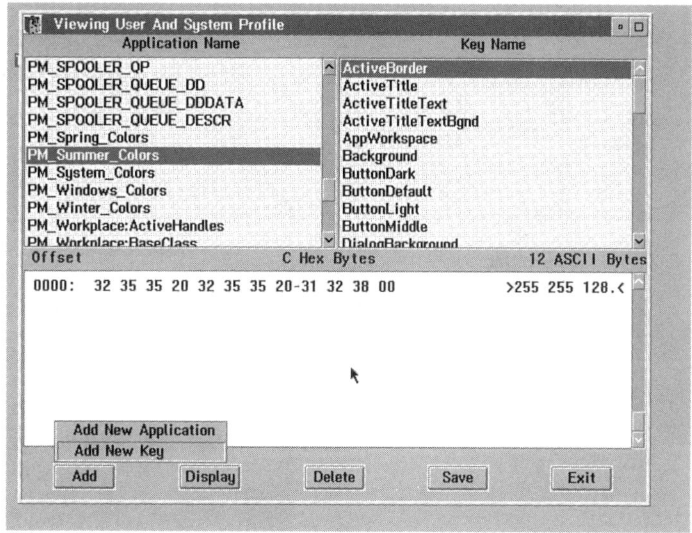

Figure 10.1.
Add New Key dialog ready to accept entry of Application Name, Key Name, and Key Data.

Because the application name and the key name may not exceed 1KB, the text limit for these edit controls is set to 1KB during the processing of the `WM_INITDLG` message:

```
WinSendMsg(hAppWnd,EM_SETTEXTLIMIT,MPFROMSHORT(MAX_TITLE),0;
WinSendMsg(hKeyWnd,EM_SETTEXTLIMIT,MPFROMSHORT(MAX_TITLE),0;
```

Because we are adding null-terminated strings to the current INI file, the `UPrfWriteProfileString` function may be used. It is defined as follows:

```
PrfWriteProfileString (hIni,pAppName,pKeyName,pBuffer)
```

`HINI`	`hIni`	Initialization file handle.
`PSZ`	`pAppName`	Pointer to a null-terminated string that identifies the application section to which data is to be added. If a section with this name does not currently exist, a new section with `pAppName` is added. Strings beginning with `PM_` are reserved for system use and should not be used.
`PSZ`	`pKeyName`	Pointer to a null-terminated string that identifies the key name section to which data is to be added. If a key with this name does not exist in the `pAppName` section, a new key with `pKeyName` is added.
`PSZ`	`pBuffer`	Pointer to a null-terminated string that is associated with the `pAppName pKeyName` pair. If the pair existed prior to the call, the current string is replaced with the contents of `pBuffer`. Otherwise, the new string identified by `pBuffer` is added to the file.

When all three edit fields in the Add dialog contain values and the OK button is selected, the text will be queried from the three edit windows. The Add dialog will attempt to add the new entry to the current INI file with the `PrfWriteProfileString` function. Because the application name and key name used a fixed length buffer, only the size of the key data must be queried:

```
WinQueryWindowText(hAppWnd,MAX_TITLE,szTitle);
WinQueryWindowText(hKeyWnd,MAX_TITLE,szKey);
ulLength = WinQueryWindowTextLength(hDataWnd);
DosSubAlloc(pMem,(PPVOID)&pData,ulLength);

if (pData && WinQueryWindowText(hDataWnd,ulLength,pData))
{
   if (!(PrfWriteProfileString(hCurrentIni,szTitle,szKey, pData)))
   {
      post_error(hWndDlg,ID_WRITE_ERROR);
   }
   DosSubFree(pMem,pData,ulLength);
   refresh_display();
}
else
   post_error(hWndDlg,ID_QTEXT_ERROR);
WinDismissDlg(hWndDlg,DID_OK);
return 0;
```

If the strings are successfully added, the `PrfWriteProfileString` function will return `TRUE`; otherwise, an error is posted.

INITOR allows the initial size and location of the main window to be set by the user. When the screen location option is selected from the Save pop-up menu, the current window coordinates are queried and written to the user profile file using the `PrfWriteProfileData` function. This function takes the same parameters as `PrfWriteProfileString` with the addition of a buffer size, as shown here:

```
PrfWriteProfileData (hIni,pAppName,pKeyName,pBuffer,ulBuffSize)
```

`ULONG`	`ulBuffSize`	Length in bytes of the memory pointed to by `pBuffer`.

The size parameter is used to specify the number of bytes pointed to by `bBuffer` to write to the INI file. INITOR queries the window rectangle of the frame and then converts the points to screen coordinates. The application and key name strings are loaded, and the data is written to the INI file:

```
WinQueryWindowRect(hWndFrame,(PRECTL)&Rectl);
WinMapWindowPoints(hWndFrame,HWND_DESKTOP,(PPOINTL)&Rectl,1;
WinLoadString (hab,0,ID_INITOR,MAX_TITLE,szTitle);
WinLoadString (hab,0,ID_LOCATION,MAX_TITLE,szKey);
if (!(PrfWriteProfileData(HINI_USERPROFILE,szTitle,szKey,
   (PVOID)&Rectl,sizeof(RECTL))))
   post_error(hWnd,ID_SAVEPOS_ERROR);
```

When INITOR is started, the entry defining the window location is queried from the user INI file by using the `PrfQueryProfileData` function. If found, the initial window size is set based on the saved coordinates; otherwise, the default screen location is used:

```
WinLoadString (hab,0,ID_INITOR,MAX_TITLE,szTitle);
WinLoadString (hab,0,ID_LOCATION,MAX_TITLE,szKey);

if (PrfQueryProfileData(HINI_USERPROFILE,szTitle,szKey, (PVOID)&Rectl,(PULONG)&ulSize))
   WinSetWindowPos (hWndFrame,HWND_TOP,
      Rectl.xLeft,Rectl.yBottom,Rectl.xRight,Rectl.yTop,
      SWP_SHOW ¦ SWP_ACTIVATE ¦ SWP_ZORDER ¦ SWP_SIZE ¦ SWP_MOVE);
else
   WinSetWindowPos (hWndFrame,HWND_TOP,0,
      WinQuerySysValue(HWND_DESKTOP,SV_CYSCREEN) - iClientHeight,
      WinQuerySysValue(HWND_DESKTOP,SV_CXSCREEN), iClientHeight,
      SWP_SHOW ¦ SWP_ACTIVATE ¦ SWP_ZORDER ¦ SWP_SIZE ¦ SWP_MOVE);
```

Deleting Entries

You may have noticed that there does not seem to be a function to delete entries from the INI file. The functions that are used to add entries, `PrfWriteProfileString` and `PrfWriteProfileData`, are also used to delete unwanted entries. An entire application section may be deleted by specifying the null-terminated application name and `NULL` for the key name and `pBuffer` parameters:

```
PrfWriteProfileString(hCurrentIni,pAppName,NULL,NULL);
```

An application key pair may be deleted by specifying the null-terminated application and key name strings and `NULL` for the `pBuffer` parameters:

```
PrfWriteProfileString(hCurrentIni,pAppName,pKeyName,NULL);
```

Although the previous examples used the `PrfWriteProfileSting` function, you may also use the `PrfWriteProfileData` function with the same parameters along with a zero for the `ulBuffSize` parameter. INITOR's pop-up Delete menu enables you to delete an application section or remove a single key name. This option should be used with caution when removing entries from the system or user INI files. Removing or changing a system entry could render your system unbootable.

The INITOR Sample Application

Before we begin to discuss the profile management API on which INITOR is based, we first want to tell you how the INITOR application code is organized. Like most OS/2 applications, the executable is created from a familiar set of files, including a C module, a resource file, an icon file, and others. For the INITOR application, these files are as follows:

INITOR.C	INITOR application's C code.
INITOR.DEF	Module definition file.
INITOR.H	An include file.
INITOR.ICO	The application's icon file.
INITOR.RC	INITOR's resource file.
INITOR.DLG	INITOR's dialog definition file.

INITOR.C

```
/* ----------------------------------
Initor Program
---------------------------------- */


#define INCL_WIN
#define INCL_GPI
#include <os2.h>
#include <stdlib.h>
#include "initor.h"

MRESULT EXPENTRY ClientWndProc (HWND,ULONG,MPARAM,MPARAM);
MRESULT EXPENTRY DataWndProc (HWND,ULONG,MPARAM,MPARAM);
MRESULT EXPENTRY AboutDlgProc(HWND,ULONG,MPARAM,MPARAM);
MRESULT EXPENTRY AddDlgProc(HWND,ULONG,MPARAM,MPARAM);

HAB     hab;
HWND    hWndFrame,
        hWndClient,
        hAppLBox,
        hKeyLBox,
        hAppTitle,
        hKeyTitle,
        hDataTitle,
        hDataFrame,
        hDataWnd,
        hVScroll;
PVOID   pMem;
PVOID   pKeyData  = NULL;
ULONG   ulKeySize = 0;
HWND    hButton[NUM_BUTTONS];
USHORT usSelectItem[NUM_BUTTONS] =
{
   IDM_ADD_KEY,
   IDM_DISPLAY_USERSYS,
   IDM_DELETE_KEY,
   IDM_SAVE_CHANGES,
   0
};
HWND hPopupMenu [NUM_BUTTONS] =
{
   NULLHANDLE,
NULLHANDLE,
NULLHANDLE,
NULLHANDLE,
NULLHANDLE, };
```

```
HINI hCurrentIni = NULLHANDLE ;

CHAR    szTitle[MAX_TITLE];
CHAR    szKey[MAX_TITLE];
CHAR    szBuff1[MAX_BUFF];
CHAR    szBuff2[MAX_BUFF];
CHAR    szFontFace[]    = "10.System Monospaced";
CHAR    szDataClass[]   = "DATA";
CHAR    szClientClass[] = "CLIENT";
int     nFixedFontWidth  = 0;
int     nFixedFontHeight = 0;
int     nSysFontHeight;
int     iButtonWidth;
int     iButtonHeight;
int     iButtonY;


int main()
{
   HMQ   hmq;
   QMSG  qmsg;
   RECTL Rectl;
   ULONG ulSize = sizeof(RECTL);
   ULONG flFrameFlags   = FCF_TITLEBAR | FCF_SYSMENU |
                          FCF_SIZEBORDER | FCF_MINMAX   |
                          FCF_SHELLPOSITION | FCF_TASKLIST |
                          FCF_NOBYTEALIGN;  //NOTE2
   int        iClientHeight;
   FRAMECDATA FrameData;

   hab = WinInitialize (0);
   hmq = WinCreateMsgQueue (hab, 0);

   DosAllocMem(&pMem,8192,PAG_READ | PAG_WRITE);
   DosSubSet(pMem,DOSSUB_INIT | DOSSUB_SPARSE_OBJ,8192);

   // NOTE 3
   WinRegisterClass (hab, szClientClass, ClientWndProc,CS_SIZEREDRAW, 0);
   FrameData.cb = sizeof(FRAMECDATA);
   FrameData.flCreateFlags = flFrameFlags;
   FrameData.hmodResources = 0;
   FrameData.idResources   = 0;
   WinLoadString (hab,0,ID_APPNAME,MAX_TITLE,szTitle);

   hWndFrame = WinCreateWindow (HWND_DESKTOP,WC_FRAME,
szTitle,0L,0,0,0,0,HWND_DESKTOP,HWND_TOP,10, &FrameData,NULL);

   WinSendMsg (hWndFrame,WM_SETICON,
   (MPARAM) WinLoadPointer(HWND_DESKTOP,0,ID_APPNAME),0);
   hWndClient = WinCreateWindow (hWndFrame,szClientClass,
      szClientClass,WS_VISIBLE | WS_CLIPCHILDREN,0,0,0,0,
      hWndFrame,HWND_TOP,FID_CLIENT,NULL,NULL);

   iClientHeight =
      WinQuerySysValue(HWND_DESKTOP,SV_CYSCREEN)
      WinQuerySysValue(HWND_DESKTOP,SV_CYICON);
```

```
   WinLoadString (hab,0,ID_INITOR,MAX_TITLE,szTitle);
   WinLoadString (hab,0,ID_LOCATION,MAX_TITLE,szKey);

   if (PrfQueryProfileData(HINI_USERPROFILE,szTitle,szKey,
(PVOID)&Rectl,(PULONG)&ulSize))
      WinSetWindowPos (hWndFrame,HWND_TOP,
         Rectl.xLeft,Rectl.yBottom,Rectl.xRight,Rectl.yTop,
         SWP_SHOW ¦ SWP_ACTIVATE ¦ SWP_ZORDER ¦ SWP_SIZE ¦ SWP_MOVE);
   else
      WinSetWindowPos (hWndFrame,HWND_TOP,0,
         WinQuerySysValue(HWND_DESKTOP,SV_CYSCREEN) - iClientHeight,
         WinQuerySysValue(HWND_DESKTOP,SV_CXSCREEN), iClientHeight,
            SWP_SHOW ¦ SWP_ACTIVATE ¦ SWP_ZORDER ¦ SWP_SIZE ¦ SWP_MOVE);

   create_controls(hWndClient);
   WinShowWindow (hAppLBox,TRUE);
   WinShowWindow (hKeyLBox,TRUE);
   enum_app_names(HINI_PROFILE,ID_HINIBOTH);

   while (WinGetMsg (hab, &qmsg, NULLHANDLE, 0, 0))
      WinDispatchMsg (hab, &qmsg);

   WinDestroyMsgQueue (hmq);
   WinTerminate (hab);
   return (0);
}

void APIENTRY change_ini_file(USHORT usCommand)
/*-------------------------------*/

This function changes the currently viewed INI file based on the
usCommand value. If a system INI file is to be displayed, the
current INI file handle is set to one of the three system handles.
If a private INI file is to be displayed, the file open dialog is
posted allowing the user to select a file. If OK is selected and
the file can be opened as an INI file, it will become the current
INI file viewed. The enum_app_names function is called to update
the display.

/*-------------------------------*/
{
   FILEDLG FileDlg;
   USHORT  usStringID = 0;
   HINI    hTempIni;
   HINI    hPrevIni = hCurrentIni;
   USHORT  usButtonNum =(USHORT)(usCommand-ID_FIRST_BUTTON);

   usSelectItem[1] = usCommand;
   switch(usCommand)
   {
      case IDM_DISPLAY_USER:
         hCurrentIni = HINI_USERPROFILE;
         usStringID  = ID_HINIUSER;
         break;
      case IDM_DISPLAY_SYS:
         hCurrentIni = HINI_SYSTEMPROFILE;
         usStringID  = ID_HINISYS;
         break;
```

```
        case IDM_DISPLAY_USERSYS:
           hCurrentIni = HINI_PROFILE;
           usStringID  = ID_HINIBOTH;
           break;
        case IDM_DISPLAY_PRIVATE:
           memset(&FileDlg,0,sizeof(FILEDLG));
           FileDlg.cbSize    = sizeof(FILEDLG);
           FileDlg.fl        = FDS_CENTER ¦ FDS_OPEN_DIALOG;
           FileDlg.pszTitle = "Select Private INI File";
           strcpy (FileDlg.szFullFile,"*INI");
           WinFileDlg(HWND_DESKTOP,hWndFrame, (PFILEDLG)&FileDlg);
           if ( (FileDlg.lReturn == DID_OK) &&
              (hTempIni=PrfOpenProfile(hab, FileDlg.szFullFile)))
           {
              if ( (hCurrentIni != HINI_SYSTEMPROFILE) &&
                   (hCurrentIni != HINI_USERPROFILE)   &&
                   (hCurrentIni != HINI_PROFILE) )
                 PrfCloseProfile(hCurrentIni);
              hCurrentIni = hTempIni;
              WinSetWindowText(hWndFrame, (PSZ)FileDlg.szFullFile);
           }
           break;
     }
     if (hPrevIni != hCurrentIni)
        enum_app_names(hCurrentIni,usStringID);
}


void APIENTRY cleanup()
/*------------------------------*/

This function is called to free the memory allocated, pop-up menus,
and windows created for the application

/*------------------------------*/
{
   int i;

   for (i = 0; i < NUM_MENUS; i++)
      WinDestroyWindow (hPopupMenu[i]);
   if (pKeyData)
   {
      DosSubFree(pMem,pKeyData,ulKeySize);
      pKeyData  = NULL;
      ulKeySize = 0;
   }
   DosFreeMem(pMem);
   WinDestroyWindow (hWndClient);
   WinDestroyWindow (hWndFrame);
}


void APIENTRY create_controls(HWND hWndClient)
/*------------------------------*/

This function will create the control windows that will display
the application names, key names, and key data for INI files. The
```

```
initial size is based on the size of their parent hWndClient. The
pop-up menus used by INITOR are also loaded.

/*------------------------------*/
{
   RECTL       Rectl;
   int         iButtonX;
   int         iColumn;
   int         i;
   FRAMECDATA  FrameData;
   FONTMETRICS fontMetrics;
   POINTL      Ptl[TXTBOX_COUNT + 1];
   LONG        lColor = CLR_PALEGRAY;
   HPS         hPS    = WinGetPS(hWndClient);
   ULONG       flFrameFlags = FCF_BORDER ¦ FCF_NOBYTEALIGN ¦

FCF_VERTSCROLL;

   WinQueryWindowRect(hWndClient,(PRECTL)&Rectl);
   GpiQueryFontMetrics(hPS,sizeof(FONTMETRICS),

(PFONTMETRICS)&fontMetrics);
   nSysFontHeight = fontMetrics.lMaxBaselineExt + 2;

   WinLoadString (hab,0,ID_APPLICATION,MAX_TITLE,szTitle);
   hAppTitle = WinCreateWindow (hWndClient,WC_STATIC,szTitle,
               WS_VISIBLE ¦ SS_TEXT ¦ DT_CENTER,
               0,Rectl.yTop - nSysFontHeight,
               Rectl.xRight / 2 - 1,nSysFontHeight,
hWndClient,HWND_TOP,1,NULL,NULL);
   WinSetPresParam(hAppTitle,PP_BACKGROUNDCOLORINDEX,

sizeof(PLONG),&lColor);

   WinLoadString (hab,0,ID_KEY,MAX_TITLE,szTitle);
   hKeyTitle = WinCreateWindow (hWndClient,WC_STATIC,szTitle,
               WS_VISIBLE ¦ SS_TEXT ¦ DT_CENTER,
               Rectl.xRight / 2,Rectl.yTop - nSysFontHeight,
               Rectl.xRight / 2 - 1,nSysFontHeight,
               hWndClient,HWND_TOP,1,NULL,NULL);
   WinSetPresParam(hKeyTitle,PP_BACKGROUNDCOLORINDEX,

sizeof(PLONG),&lColor);

   WinLoadString (hab,0,ID_DATA,MAX_TITLE,szTitle);
   hDataTitle = WinCreateWindow (hWndClient,WC_STATIC,szTitle,
                SS_TEXT ¦ DT_LEFT,
                0,Rectl.yTop / 2,
                Rectl.xRight,nSysFontHeight,
                hWndClient,HWND_TOP,1,NULL,NULL);

   WinSetPresParam(hDataTitle,PP_BACKGROUNDCOLORINDEX,

sizeof(PLONG),&lColor);
   WinSetPresParam(hDataTitle,PP_FONTNAMESIZE,strlen(szFontFace)+1,

(PVOID)szFontFace);
```

```
   hAppLBox = WinCreateWindow (hWndClient,WC_LISTBOX,NULL,
              LS_NOADJUSTPOS,
              1,Rectl.yTop / 2 + nSysFontHeight,
              Rectl.xRight / 2 - 2,Rectl.yTop / 2 -

(nSysFontHeight * 2 + 1),
              hWndClient,HWND_TOP,APP_LBOX,NULL,NULL);

   hKeyLBox = WinCreateWindow (hWndClient,WC_LISTBOX,NULL,
              LS_NOADJUSTPOS,
              (Rectl.xRight / 2) + 1,Rectl.yTop / 2 + nSysFontHeight,
              Rectl.xRight / 2 - 2,Rectl.yTop / 2 - (nSysFontHeight  * 2 + 1),
              hWndClient,HWND_TOP,KEY_LBOX,NULL,NULL);

   // Load the longest string to calculate button width
   WinLoadString (hab,0,ID_DISPLAY,MAX_TITLE,szTitle);
   GpiQueryTextBox(hPS,strlen(szTitle),szTitle,TXTBOX_COUNT, Ptl);
   iButtonWidth  = Ptl[TXTBOX_CONCAT].x +

(fontMetrics.lAveCharWidth * 2);
   iButtonHeight = nSysFontHeight + (nSysFontHeight / 3);
   iColumn       = Rectl.xRight / NUM_BUTTONS;
   iButtonX      = (iColumn - iButtonWidth) / 2;
   iButtonY      = nSysFontHeight / 2;

   WinRegisterClass (hab,szDataClass,DataWndProc,0,0);
   FrameData.cb = sizeof(FRAMECDATA);
   FrameData.flCreateFlags = flFrameFlags;
   FrameData.hmodResources = 0;
   FrameData.idResources   = 0;
   hDataFrame = WinCreateWindow (hWndClient,WC_FRAME,"",0L,
           0,0,0,0,hWndClient,HWND_TOP,11,&FrameData,NULL);

   hDataWnd = WinCreateWindow (hDataFrame,szDataClass,"",
              WS_VISIBLE,0,0,0,0,
              hDataFrame,HWND_TOP,FID_CLIENT,NULL,NULL);

   WinSetWindowPos (hDataFrame,HWND_TOP,
         1,iButtonHeight * 2,Rectl.xRight - 2,
         Rectl.yTop / 2 - 2 - (iButtonHeight * 2),
         SWP_SHOW ¦ SWP_ZORDER ¦ SWP_SIZE ¦ SWP_MOVE);

   for (i = 0; i < NUM_BUTTONS; i++)
   {
      WinLoadString (hab,0,ID_FIRST_BUTTON + i, MAX_TITLE, szTitle);
      hButton[i] = WinCreateWindow (hWndClient,WC_BUTTON, szTitle,
                   WS_VISIBLE ¦ BS_PUSHBUTTON,
                   (iColumn * i) + iButtonX,iButtonY,
                   iButtonWidth,iButtonHeight,
                   hWndClient,HWND_TOP,ID_FIRST_BUTTON + i,NULL,NULL);
   }
   WinReleasePS(hPS);

   // Update the title
   WinSendMsg(hDataWnd,WM_UPDATE_TITLE,0L,0L);
   WinShowWindow(hDataTitle,TRUE);
```

```
   for (i = 0; i < NUM_MENUS; i++)
      hPopupMenu[i]=WinLoadMenu(HWND_OBJECT,0,FIRST_MENU+i);

}


void APIENTRY enum_app_names(HINI hini,USHORT usStringID)
/*-------------------------------*/

This function will query the size required to hold all of the
application names for the current INI file. If the file contains
entries, a temporary block of memory is allocated and the application
names are queried from PM. The strings are then added to the
application name list box and the memory if freed. The first entry
in the list box is selected causing its owner, the client, to be
notifed. The client window will then fill the key name list box
by calling enum_key_name function.

/*-------------------------------*/
{
   PVOID pData;
   PBYTE pCurrent;
   ULONG ulSize = 0L;

   if (PrfQueryProfileSize(hini,NULL,NULL,(PULONG)&ulSize) && ulSize)
   {
      DosSubAlloc(pMem,(PPVOID)&pData,ulSize);
      if(PrfQueryProfileString(hini,NULL,NULL,

"No Entries",pData,ulSize))
      {
         pCurrent = pData;
         WinEnableWindowUpdate(hAppLBox,FALSE);
         WinSendMsg (hAppLBox,LM_DELETEALL,NULL,NULL);
         while (*pCurrent)
         {
            WinSendMsg (hAppLBox,LM_INSERTITEM,
(MPARAM)LIT_SORTASCENDING,(MPARAM)pCurrent);
            while(*pCurrent)
               pCurrent++;
            pCurrent++;
         }
         WinSendMsg (hAppLBox,LM_SELECTITEM,MPFROMSHORT(0),
            MPFROMSHORT(TRUE));
         WinEnableWindowUpdate(hAppLBox,TRUE);
         if (usStringID)
         {
            WinLoadString (hab,0,usStringID,MAX_TITLE, szTitle);
            WinSetWindowText(hWndFrame,(PSZ)szTitle);
         }
      }
      DosSubFree(pMem,pData,ulSize);
   }
   else
   {
      WinAlarm(HWND_DESKTOP,WA_WARNING);
      WinEnableWindowUpdate(hAppLBox,FALSE);
```

```
      WinSendMsg (hAppLBox,LM_DELETEALL,NULL,NULL);
      WinSendMsg (hAppLBox,LM_INSERTITEM,

(MPARAM)LIT_SORTASCENDING,"No Entries");
      WinSendMsg (hAppLBox,LM_SELECTITEM,

MPFROMSHORT(0),MPFROMSHORT(TRUE));
      WinEnableWindowUpdate(hAppLBox,TRUE);
      // No entries exist force the data window to free up its
      // data buffer and repaint.
      get_key_data("","");
      WinInvalidateRect(hDataWnd,NULL,FALSE);
   }
}


void APIENTRY get_key_data(PSZ pAppName,PSZ pKeyName)
/*-------------------------------*/

This function will attempt to query the key data for the current
application / key pair. If key data currently exists, it is freed
before the new entry is queried.  If successful, a message is sent
to the client to update the key data windows title with the size
of the new data, and the data window is invalidated.

/*-------------------------------*/
{
   if (pKeyData)
   {
      DosSubFree(pMem,pKeyData,ulKeySize);
      pKeyData  = NULL;
      ulKeySize = 0;
   }
   if (PrfQueryProfileSize(hCurrentIni,pAppName,pKeyName,

(PULONG)&ulKeySize) && ulKeySize)
   {
      DosSubAlloc(pMem,(PPVOID)&pKeyData,ulKeySize);
      if(PrfQueryProfileData(hCurrentIni,pAppName,pKeyName,

pKeyData,(PULONG)&ulKeySize))
      {
         // Update the title
         WinSendMsg(hDataWnd,WM_UPDATE_TITLE,0L,0L);
         // Force the data window to repaint
         WinInvalidateRect(hDataWnd,NULL,FALSE);
      }
   }
}


void APIENTRY enum_key_name(PSZ pAppName)
/*-------------------------------*/

This function will query the size required to hold all of the
key names for the current application name in the current INI file.
```

```
If the application name contains key strings, a temporary block of
memory is allocated, and the key names are queried from PM. The
strings are then added to the application name list box and the
memory if freed. The first entry in the list box is selected causing
its owner, the client, to be notifed. The client window will then
fill the data window by calling get_key_data.

/*-------------------------------*/
{
   PVOID pData;
   PBYTE pCurrent;
   ULONG ulSize = 0L;

   if (PrfQueryProfileSize(hCurrentIni,pAppName,NULL, (PULONG)&ulSize) && ulSize)
   {
      DosSubAlloc(pMem,(PPVOID)&pData,ulSize);
      if(PrfQueryProfileString(hCurrentIni,pAppName,NULL, "No Entries",pData,ulSize))
      {
         pCurrent = pData;
         WinEnableWindowUpdate(hKeyLBox,FALSE);
         WinSendMsg (hKeyLBox,LM_DELETEALL,NULL,NULL);
         while (*pCurrent)
         {
            WinSendMsg (hKeyLBox,LM_INSERTITEM,
(MPARAM)LIT_SORTASCENDING,(MPARAM)pCurrent);
            while(*pCurrent)
               pCurrent++;
            pCurrent++;
         }
         WinSendMsg (hKeyLBox,LM_SELECTITEM,MPFROMSHORT(0),
MPFROMSHORT(TRUE));
         WinEnableWindowUpdate(hKeyLBox,TRUE);
      }
      DosSubFree(pMem,pData,ulSize);
   }
   else
   {
      WinEnableWindowUpdate(hKeyLBox,FALSE);
      WinSendMsg (hKeyLBox,LM_DELETEALL,NULL,NULL);
      WinEnableWindowUpdate(hKeyLBox,TRUE);
      // No entries exist force the data window to free up its
      // data buffer and repaint.
      get_key_data("","");
      WinInvalidateRect(hDataWnd,NULL,FALSE);
   }
}


void APIENTRY size_controls(MPARAM lNewSize)
/*-------------------------------*/

Since the children are scaled to the client window size, this function
is called when the client window receives a WM_SIZE message. All
child windows are resized to fit the new client size. The buttons
will be repositioned but will not overlap.

/*-------------------------------*/
```

```
{
   SHORT sNewWidth  = SHORT1FROMMP(lNewSize);
   SHORT sNewHeight = SHORT2FROMMP(lNewSize);
   int   iButtonX;
   int   iColumn;
   int   i;

   WinSetWindowPos (hAppTitle,HWND_TOP,
         0,sNewHeight - nSysFontHeight,
         sNewWidth / 2 - 1,nSysFontHeight,
         SWP_SIZE ¦ SWP_MOVE);
   WinSetWindowPos (hKeyTitle,HWND_TOP,
         sNewWidth / 2,sNewHeight - nSysFontHeight,
         sNewWidth / 2 - 1,nSysFontHeight,
         SWP_SIZE ¦ SWP_MOVE);
   WinSetWindowPos (hDataTitle,HWND_TOP,
         0,sNewHeight / 2,sNewWidth,nSysFontHeight,
         SWP_SIZE ¦ SWP_MOVE);
   WinSetWindowPos (hAppLBox,HWND_TOP,
         1,sNewHeight / 2 + nSysFontHeight,
         sNewWidth / 2 - 2,
         sNewHeight / 2 - (nSysFontHeight * 2 + 1),
         SWP_SIZE ¦ SWP_MOVE);
   WinSetWindowPos (hKeyLBox,HWND_TOP,
         sNewWidth / 2 + 1,sNewHeight / 2 + nSysFontHeight,
         sNewWidth / 2 - 2,
         sNewHeight / 2 - (nSysFontHeight * 2 + 1),
         SWP_SIZE ¦ SWP_MOVE);

   iColumn  = (max (sNewWidth,iButtonWidth * NUM_BUTTONS)) /
                   NUM_BUTTONS;
iButtonX = (iColumn - iButtonWidth) / 2;

   for (i = 0; i < NUM_BUTTONS; i++)
      WinSetWindowPos (hButton[i],HWND_TOP,
         (iColumn * i) + iButtonX,iButtonY,0,0,SWP_MOVE);

   WinSetWindowPos (hDataFrame,HWND_TOP,
         1,iButtonHeight * 2,sNewWidth - 2,
         sNewHeight / 2 - 2 - (iButtonHeight * 2),
         SWP_SHOW ¦ SWP_ZORDER ¦ SWP_SIZE ¦ SWP_MOVE);
}


USHORT APIENTRY post_error(HWND hWnd,USHORT usErrorID)
/*-------------------------------*/

This is a utility function that will post a message box with
a string loaded from the resource file.

/*-------------------------------*/
{
   WinLoadString (hab,0,usErrorID,MAX_BUFF,szBuff1);
   return (WinMessageBox(HWND_DESKTOP,hWnd,szBuff1,
        (PSZ)"Error",0,MB_OK ¦ MB_ICONHAND ¦ MB_APPLMODAL));
}
```

```
void APIENTRY process_command(HWND hWnd,MPARAM mp1,MPARAM mp2)
/*-------------------------------*/

All WM_COMMAND messages received by the client window will be
processed here.  For each button command a popup menu is displayed.

/*-------------------------------*/
{
   PVOID   pKey;
   RECTL   Rectl;
   USHORT  usSelection;
   USHORT  usAddCmd     = IDM_ADD_KEY;
   USHORT  usCommand    = SHORT1FROMMP(mp1);
   USHORT  usButtonNum =(USHORT)(usCommand-ID_FIRST_BUTTON);

   switch(usCommand)
   {
      case ID_DELETE:
      case ID_DISPLAY:
      case ID_ADD:
      case ID_SAVE:
         WinQueryWindowRect (hButton[usButtonNum],
               (PRECTL)&Rectl);
         WinMapWindowPoints(hButton[usButtonNum],hWndFrame,
               (PPOINTL)&Rectl,2);
         WinPopupMenu(hWndFrame,hWndClient,
               hPopupMenu[usCommand - ID_FIRST_BUTTON],
               Rectl.xLeft + 1,Rectl.yTop + 1,
               usSelectItem[usButtonNum],
               PU_HCONSTRAIN ¦ PU_VCONSTRAIN ¦ PU_KEYBOARD ¦
               PU_MOUSEBUTTON1 ¦ PU_SELECTITEM);
         break;

      case ID_EXIT:
         WinPostMsg(hWndFrame,WM_QUIT,0,0);
         break;

      case IDM_ADD_APP:
         usAddCmd = IDM_ADD_APP;
      break;

case IDM_ADD_KEY:
         usSelectItem[0] = usCommand;
         WinDlgBox(HWND_DESKTOP,hWndFrame,(PFNWP)AddDlgProc,
               0,ADD_DLG,(PVOID)&usAddCmd);
         break;

      case IDM_ABOUT:
         WinDlgBox(HWND_DESKTOP,hWndFrame,
               (PFNWP)AboutDlgProc,0,ABOUT_DLG,

(PVOID)&usAddCmd);
         break;
```

```
        case IDM_REFRESH:
           refresh_display();
           break;
        case IDM_DISPLAY_USER:
        case IDM_DISPLAY_SYS:
        case IDM_DISPLAY_USERSYS:
        case IDM_DISPLAY_PRIVATE:
           if ( (usSelectItem[1] != usCommand) ||
              (usCommand == IDM_DISPLAY_PRIVATE) )
           {
              change_ini_file(usCommand);
           }
           break;

        case IDM_DELETE_APP:
        case IDM_DELETE_KEY:
           usSelectItem[2] = usCommand;
           usSelection = (USHORT)WinSendMsg (hAppLBox,
                         LM_QUERYSELECTION,
                         MPFROMSHORT(LIT_FIRST),NULL);
           if (usSelection != LIT_NONE)
           {
              WinSendMsg(hAppLBox,LM_QUERYITEMTEXT,
                 MPFROM2SHORT(usSelection,MAX_TITLE),
                 MPFROMP(szTitle));
              if (usCommand == IDM_DELETE_KEY)
              {
                 usSelection = (USHORT)WinSendMsg (hKeyLBox,
                               LM_QUERYSELECTION,
                               MPFROMSHORT(LIT_FIRST),NULL);
                 WinSendMsg(hKeyLBox,LM_QUERYITEMTEXT,
                       MPFROM2SHORT(usSelection,MAX_TITLE),
                       MPFROMP(szKey));
                 pKey = szKey;
              }
              else
                 pKey = NULL;
              if (!(PrfWriteProfileString(hCurrentIni,

szTitle,pKey,NULL)))
              {
                 post_error(hWnd,ID_DELETE_ERROR);
              }
              refresh_display();
           }
           else
              WinAlarm(HWND_DESKTOP,WA_NOTE);
           break;

        case IDM_SAVE_CHANGES:
           usSelectItem[3] = usCommand;
           break;
        case IDM_SAVE_LOCATION:
           usSelectItem[3] = usCommand;
           WinQueryWindowRect(hWndFrame,(PRECTL)&Rectl);
           WinMapWindowPoints(hWndFrame,HWND_DESKTOP,
```

```
                (PPOINTL)&Rectl,1);
         WinLoadString (hab,0,ID_INITOR,MAX_TITLE,szTitle);
         WinLoadString (hab,0,ID_LOCATION,MAX_TITLE,szKey);
         if (!(PrfWriteProfileData(HINI_USERPROFILE,szTitle,
                szKey,(PVOID)&Rectl,sizeof(RECTL))))
            post_error(hWnd,ID_SAVEPOS_ERROR);
         refresh_display();
         break;
   }
}

void APIENTRY process_control(HWND hWnd,MPARAM mp1,MPARAM mp2)
/*-------------------------------*/

This function will handle the control notifications passed to
the client window in the WM_CONTROL message. When an item is
selected in the application or key name list boxes, the remaining
list boxes and controls are updated.

/*-------------------------------*/
{
   USHORT usSelection;

   if (SHORT2FROMMP(mp1) == LN_SELECT)
   {
      usSelection = (USHORT)WinSendMsg (hAppLBox,
                     LM_QUERYSELECTION,
                     MPFROMSHORT(LIT_FIRST),NULL);
      WinSendMsg(hAppLBox,LM_QUERYITEMTEXT,
            MPFROM2SHORT(usSelection,MAX_TITLE),
            MPFROMP(szTitle));
      switch (LOUSHORT(mp1))
      {
         case APP_LBOX:
            enum_key_name(szTitle);
            break;
         case KEY_LBOX:
            usSelection = (USHORT)WinSendMsg (hKeyLBox,

LM_QUERYSELECTION,
                           MPFROMSHORT(LIT_FIRST),NULL);
            WinSendMsg(hKeyLBox,LM_QUERYITEMTEXT,
                  MPFROM2SHORT(usSelection,MAX_TITLE),
                  MPFROMP(szKey));
            get_key_data(szTitle,szKey);
            break;
      }
   }
}

void APIENTRY refresh_display()
/*-------------------------------*/

This is a utility that causes the current INI file to be reread
and updated on the display. The current selection is saved and
restored after the update. This prevents the list box from scrolling
```

```
to the top after updating an entry.

/*-------------------------------*/
{
   USHORT usCurrApp = (USHORT)WinSendMsg(hAppLBox,

LM_QUERYSELECTION,0,0);
   USHORT usCurrKey = (USHORT)WinSendMsg(hKeyLBox,

LM_QUERYSELECTION,0,0);

   enum_app_names(hCurrentIni,0);

   WinSendMsg(hAppLBox,LM_SELECTITEM,MPFROMSHORT(usCurrApp),
         MPFROMSHORT(TRUE));
   WinSendMsg(hKeyLBox,LM_SELECTITEM,MPFROMSHORT(usCurrKey),
         MPFROMSHORT(TRUE));
}


MRESULT EXPENTRY ClientWndProc (HWND hWnd, ULONG msg, MPARAM mp1,MPARAM mp2)
/*-------------------------------*/

This is the application callback which handles the messages
necessary to INITOR.

/*-------------------------------*/
{
   HPS     hps;
   BOOL    bHandled = TRUE;
   MRESULT mReturn  = 0;

   switch (msg)
   {
      case WM_PAINT:
         hps = WinBeginPaint (hWnd, NULLHANDLE,NULL);
         WinEndPaint (hps);
         break;

      case WM_ERASEBACKGROUND:
         WinFillRect((HPS)LONGFROMMP(mp1),PVOIDFROMMP(mp2),
               CLR_PALEGRAY);
         mReturn = MRFROMLONG(0L);
         break;

      case WM_COMMAND:
         process_command(hWnd,mp1,mp2);
         break;

      case WM_CONTROL:
         process_control(hWnd,mp1,mp2);
         break;

      case WM_SIZE:
         size_controls(mp2);
         break;

      case WM_DESTROY:
```

```
            cleanup();
            break;

         default:
            bHandled = FALSE;
            break;
   }

   if (!bHandled)
      mReturn = WinDefWindowProc (hWnd,msg,mp1,mp2);

   return (mReturn);
}


MRESULT EXPENTRY AboutDlgProc(HWND hWndDlg,ULONG ulMessage,
                              MPARAM mp1,MPARAM mp2)
/*-------------------------------*/

This is the callback for the application information dialog.

/*-------------------------------*/
{
   switch (ulMessage)
   {
      case WM_COMMAND:
      switch (SHORT1FROMMP(mp1))
      {
         case DID_OK:
            WinDismissDlg(hWndDlg,DID_OK);
            return 0;
      }
      break;
   }
   return (WinDefDlgProc(hWndDlg,ulMessage,mp1,mp2));
}


MRESULT EXPENTRY AddDlgProc(HWND hWndDlg,ULONG ulMessage,

MPARAM mp1,MPARAM mp2)
/*-------------------------------*/

This is the callback for the dialog which allows you to add items
to the current INI file. It will disable the OK button until all
three edit fields contain text.

/*-------------------------------*/
{
   static HWND hAppWnd;
   static HWND hKeyWnd;
   static HWND hDataWnd;
   USHORT usSelection;
```

```
    USHORT usAddCmd;
    ULONG  ulLength;
    PVOID  pData = NULL;

    switch (ulMessage)
    {
       case WM_INITDLG:
          hAppWnd  = WinWindowFromID(hWndDlg,DID_APP_NAME);
          hKeyWnd  = WinWindowFromID(hWndDlg,DID_KEY_NAME);
          hDataWnd = WinWindowFromID(hWndDlg,DID_KEY_DATA);
          usAddCmd = *((PUSHORT)mp2);
          WinSendMsg(hAppWnd,EM_SETTEXTLIMIT,
                MPFROMSHORT(MAX_TITLE),0);
          WinSendMsg(hKeyWnd,EM_SETTEXTLIMIT,
                MPFROMSHORT(MAX_TITLE),0);
          usSelection = (USHORT)WinSendMsg (hAppLBox,
                         LM_QUERYSELECTION,
                         MPFROMSHORT(LIT_FIRST),NULL);
          if ((usSelection != LIT_NONE) &&
              (usAddCmd == IDM_ADD_KEY))
          {
             WinSendMsg(hAppLBox,LM_QUERYITEMTEXT,
                   MPFROM2SHORT(usSelection,MAX_TITLE),
                   MPFROMP(szTitle));
             WinSetWindowText(WinWindowFromID(hWndDlg,
                   DID_APP_NAME), szTitle);
             WinSendMsg(hAppWnd,EM_SETREADONLY,
                   MPFROMSHORT(TRUE),0);
             WinSetFocus(HWND_DESKTOP,hKeyWnd);
             return ((MPARAM)1);
          }
          break;

       case WM_CONTROL:
          if ( (SHORT2FROMMP(mp1) == EN_CHANGE) ||
             (SHORT2FROMMP(mp1) == MLN_CHANGE) )
          {
             if ( (WinQueryWindowTextLength(hAppWnd)) &&
                   (WinQueryWindowTextLength(hKeyWnd)) &&
                   (WinQueryWindowTextLength(hDataWnd)) )
                WinEnableWindow(WinWindowFromID(hWndDlg,
                   DID_OK),TRUE);
             else
                WinEnableWindow(WinWindowFromID(hWndDlg,
                   DID_OK),FALSE);
          }
          break;

       case WM_COMMAND:
          switch (SHORT1FROMMP(mp1))
          {
             case DID_OK:

WinEnableWindow(WinWindowFromID(hWndDlg,DID_OK),
                   FALSE);

WinQueryWindowText(hAppWnd,MAX_TITLE,
```

```
                  szTitle);

WinQueryWindowText(hKeyWnd,MAX_TITLE,
                  szKey);

ulLength =WinQueryWindowTextLength(hDataWnd);

DosSubAlloc(pMem,(PPVOID)&pData,ulLength);
               if (pData && WinQueryWindowText (hDataWnd,ulLength,pData))
               {
                  if (!(PrfWriteProfileString(hCurrentIni,
                     szTitle,szKey,pData)))
                  {
                     post_error(hWndDlg,ID_WRITE_ERROR);
                  }
                  DosSubFree(pMem,pData,ulLength);
                  refresh_display();
               }
               else
                  post_error(hWndDlg,ID_QTEXT_ERROR);
               WinDismissDlg(hWndDlg,DID_OK);
               return 0;
         }
         break;
   }
   return (WinDefDlgProc(hWndDlg,ulMessage,mp1,mp2));
}


MRESULT EXPENTRY DataWndProc (HWND hWnd, ULONG msg,
                              MPARAM mp1, MPARAM mp2)
/*--------------------------------*/

This is the callback for INITOR's private data display window.
It will display data in both HEX and ASCII and allows scrolling.

/*--------------------------------*/
{
   static HPS  hPS;
   static int  iWndHeight;
   static int  iNumLines;
   static int  iTopLine = 1;
   BOOL        bHandled = TRUE;
   MRESULT     mReturn  = 0;

   switch (msg)
   {
      case WM_CREATE:
         hPS = init_data_window(hWnd);
         hVScroll = WinWindowFromID(hDataFrame,
                     FID_VERTSCROLL);
         break;

      case WM_PAINT:
```

```
        iNumLines = paint_data_window(hWnd,hPS,iTopLine);
        WinSendMsg(hVScroll,SBM_SETSCROLLBAR,
              MPFROMSHORT(iTopLine),
              MPFROM2SHORT(1,iNumLines));
        break;

     case WM_VSCROLL:
        switch (SHORT2FROMMP(mp2))
        {
           case SB_LINEDOWN:
              if (iTopLine < iNumLines)
              {
                 iTopLine++;
                 WinInvalidateRect(hDataWnd,NULL,FALSE);
              }
              break;
           case SB_LINEUP:
              if (iTopLine > 1)
              {
                 iTopLine--;
                 WinInvalidateRect(hDataWnd,NULL,FALSE);
              }
              break;
           case SB_SLIDERTRACK:
              if ((SHORT1FROMMP(mp2) >= 1) ||
                 (SHORT1FROMMP(mp2)) <= iNumLines)
              {
                 iTopLine = SHORT1FROMMP(mp2);
                 WinInvalidateRect(hDataWnd,NULL,FALSE);
              }
              else
                 WinAlarm(HWND_DESKTOP,WA_NOTE);
              break;
        }
        break;

     case WM_ERASEBACKGROUND:
        WinFillRect((HPS)LONGFROMMP(mp1),

PVOIDFROMMP(mp2),CLR_WHITE);
        mReturn = MRFROMLONG(0L);
        break;

     case WM_SIZE:
        iWndHeight = SHORT2FROMMP(mp2);
        break;

     case WM_UPDATE_TITLE:
        WinLoadString (hab,0,ID_DATA,MAX_BUFF,
           (PSZ)szBuff1);
        sprintf(szBuff2,szBuff1,ulKeySize,ulKeySize);
        WinSetWindowText(hDataTitle,(PSZ)szBuff2);
        break;

     case WM_DESTROY:
        GpiDeleteSetId(hPS,FIXED_FONT_LCID);
```

```
   iLength = strlen(pRetBuff);
   return (iLength);
}


int APIENTRY paint_data_window(HWND hWnd,HPS hPS,int iStartLine)
/*-------------------------------*/

This function will handle the painting of the data window. The
data is output after being formated by format_line. A maximum
of 16 bytes is displayed per line. The first line displayed
is determined by iStartLine.

/*-------------------------------*/
{
   RECTL   Rectl;
   PSZ     pData;
   POINTL  ptl;
   int     i,j;
   int     iSize;
   int     iPartialLine;
   int     iLineLength = MAX_LINE;
   int     iNumLines = ulKeySize / MAX_LINE;

   hPS = WinBeginPaint (hWnd,hPS,&Rectl);
   WinFillRect(hPS,&Rectl,CLR_WHITE);

   WinQueryWindowRect(hWnd,&Rectl);
   if ((ulKeySize) && (pKeyData))
   {
      if (iPartialLine = ulKeySize % MAX_LINE)
         iNumLines++;
      ptl.x = Rectl.xLeft + nFixedFontWidth;
      pData = (PSZ)pKeyData + ((iStartLine - 1) * 16);
      for (j = 1,i = iStartLine; i <= iNumLines; i++,j++)
      {
         ptl.y = (Rectl.yTop - nSysFontHeight * j);
         if ((i == iNumLines) && (iPartialLine))
            iLineLength = iPartialLine;
         iSize = format_line(szBuff1,pData,i,iLineLength);
         GpiCharStringAt (hPS,&ptl,iSize,szBuff1);
         pData += iLineLength;
      }
   }
   WinEndPaint (hPS);
   return (iNumLines);
}
```

INITOR.DEF

```
NAME            INITOR   WINDOWAPI
DESCRIPTION     'OS/2 INI Editor Program  Blain, Delimon, & English, 1994'
PROTMODE
STUB            'os2stub.exe'
```

```
HEAPSIZE       4096
STACKSIZE      32768
EXPORTS        ClientWndProc
               DataWndProc
               AboutDlgProc
```

INITOR.H

```
/* ---------------------------------
Initor Header File
--------------------------------- */

#define ID_ADD          10
#define ID_DISPLAY      11
#define ID_DELETE       12
#define ID_SAVE         13
#define ID_EXIT         14
#define ID_FIRST_BUTTON ID_ADD
#define ID_LAST_BUTTON  ID_EXIT
#define NUM_BUTTONS     5
#define NUM_MENUS       4

#define ID_APPNAME       51
#define ID_APPLICATION   52
#define ID_KEY           53
#define ID_DATA          54
#define ID_HINIUSER      55
#define ID_HINISYS       56
#define ID_HINIBOTH      57
#define ID_HINIPRIVATE   58
#define ID_DATA_HEADING  59
#define ID_TEST_DATA     60
#define ID_INITOR        61
#define ID_LOCATION      62
#define ID_WRITE_ERROR   63
#define ID_DELETE_ERROR  64
#define ID_SAVEPOS_ERROR 65
#define ID_QTEXT_ERROR   66

#define ADD_MENU        100
#define DISPLAY_MENU    101
#define DELETE_MENU     102
#define SAVE_MENU       103
#define EXIT_MENU       104
#define FIRST_MENU      ADD_MENU

#define IDM_DISPLAY_USER       200
#define IDM_DISPLAY_SYS        201
#define IDM_DISPLAY_USERSYS    202
#define IDM_DISPLAY_PRIVATE    203
#define IDM_REFRESH            204
#define IDM_ABOUT              205
#define DISPLAY_FIRST          IDM_DISPLAY_USER

#define IDM_DELETE_APP         300
```

```
#define IDM_DELETE_KEY        301

#define IDM_ADD_APP           400
#define IDM_ADD_KEY           401

#define IDM_SAVE_CHANGES      500
#define IDM_SAVE_LOCATION     501

#define MAX_TITLE     1024
#define MAX_BUFF      128
#define MAX_LINE      16

#define APP_LBOX      1
#define KEY_LBOX      2
#define DATA_WND      3

#define HEX_SIZE      47
#define HEX_START     7
#define ASCII_START   HEX_START + HEX_SIZE + 1


#define WM_UPDATE_DATA WM_USER + 1

#define FIXED_FONT_LCID 5

#define ADD_DLG                     1000
#define DID_APP_NAME                1001
#define DID_KEY_NAME                1002
#define DID_KEY_DATA                1003

#define ABOUT_DLG                   2000

#define WM_UPDATE_TITLE             WM_USER

void   APIENTRY change_ini_file(USHORT);
void   APIENTRY cleanup(void);
void   APIENTRY create_controls(HWND);
void   APIENTRY enum_app_names(HINI,USHORT);
void   APIENTRY enum_key_name(PSZ);
int    APIENTRY format_line(PSZ,PSZ,int,int);
void   APIENTRY get_key_data(PSZ,PSZ);
HPS    APIENTRY init_data_window(HWND);
int    APIENTRY paint_data_window(HWND,HPS,int);
USHORT APIENTRY post_error(HWND,USHORT);
void   APIENTRY process_command(HWND,MPARAM,MPARAM);
void   APIENTRY process_control(HWND,MPARAM,MPARAM);
void   APIENTRY refresh_display(void);
void   APIENTRY size_controls(MPARAM);
```

INITOR.RC

```
/* ----------------------------------
Initor Resource File
---------------------------------- */

#include <os2.h>
```

```
#include "initor.h"

RCINCLUDE initor.dlg

ICON ID_APPNAME INITOR.ICO

MENU ADD_MENU PRELOAD MOVEABLE DISCARDABLE
BEGIN
   MENUITEM "Add New Application",   IDM_ADD_APP
   MENUITEM "Add New Key",           IDM_ADD_KEY
END

MENU DISPLAY_MENU PRELOAD MOVEABLE DISCARDABLE
BEGIN
   MENUITEM "User Profile",          IDM_DISPLAY_USER
   MENUITEM "System Profile",        IDM_DISPLAY_SYS
   MENUITEM "User & System Profile", IDM_DISPLAY_USERSYS
   MENUITEM "Open Private...",       IDM_DISPLAY_PRIVATE
   MENUITEM "Refresh",               IDM_REFRESH
   MENUITEM "About Initor",          IDM_ABOUT
END

MENU DELETE_MENU PRELOAD MOVEABLE DISCARDABLE
BEGIN
   MENUITEM "Delete Application Section", IDM_DELETE_APP
   MENUITEM "Delete Selected Key",        IDM_DELETE_KEY
END

MENU SAVE_MENU PRELOAD MOVEABLE DISCARDABLE
BEGIN
   MENUITEM "Changes",               IDM_SAVE_CHANGES
   MENUITEM "Screen Location",       IDM_SAVE_LOCATION
END

STRINGTABLE LOADONCALL MOVEABLE
BEGIN
   ID_ADD            "Add"
   ID_DISPLAY        "Display"
   ID_DELETE         "Delete"
   ID_SAVE           "Save"
   ID_EXIT           "Exit"
   ID_APPNAME        "OS/2 INI File Editor"
   ID_APPLICATION    "Application Name"
   ID_KEY            "Key Name"
   ID_DATA           " Offset                   %1X Hex Bytes                  %4d ASCII
Bytes"
   ID_HINIUSER       "Viewing User Profile"
   ID_HINISYS        "Viewing System Profile"
   ID_HINIBOTH       "Viewing User And System Profile"
   ID_HINIPRIVATE    "Viewing %s"
   ID_INITOR         "INITOR"
   ID_LOCATION       "SCREEN POS"
   ID_WRITE_ERROR    "Update to initialization file failed"
   ID_DELETE_ERROR   "Error deleting initialization file entry"
   ID_SAVEPOS_ERROR "Unable to save current screen location"
```

```
   ID_QTEXT_ERROR    "Unable to retrieve key data text"
END
```

INITOR.DLG

```
/* -------------------------------------------------------------------
                              INITOR Dialog

                    Real World Programming for OS/2
            Copyright (c) 1994 Blain, Delimon, and English
------------------------------------------------------------------ */

DLGINCLUDE 1 "INITOR.H"

DLGTEMPLATE ADD_DLG LOADONCALL MOVEABLE DISCARDABLE
BEGIN
    DIALOG  "Add Section", ADD_DLG, 87, 61, 221, 116, FS_SCREENALIGN |
            WS_VISIBLE, FCF_SYSMENU | FCF_TITLEBAR
    BEGIN
        LTEXT           "Application Name:", -1, 6, 105, 81, 8
        LTEXT           "Key Name:", -1, 6, 79, 81, 8
        LTEXT           "Key Data:", -1, 6, 51, 81, 8
        ENTRYFIELD      "", DID_APP_NAME, 7, 93, 206, 8, ES_MARGIN |
                        WS_GROUP
        ENTRYFIELD      "", DID_KEY_NAME, 7, 66, 206, 8, ES_MARGIN
        MLE             "", DID_KEY_DATA, 5, 22, 210, 25, MLS_WORDWRAP |
                        MLS_VSCROLL | MLS_IGNORETAB
        DEFPUSHBUTTON   "~Ok", APP_LBOX, 49, 4, 40, 14, WS_DISABLED
        PUSHBUTTON      "~Cancel", KEY_LBOX, 130, 4, 40, 14
    END
END
```

Using INITOR

Looking at System Initialization Files

The INITOR INI editor is fairly self-explanatory. Remember that INIs in OS/2 follow a three-tiered structure. Because the data has a three-tiered layout, the editor we create, called INITOR, is designed to display the application name, key name, and key data at the same time. For this, two list boxes and an application-defined data window are used as shown in Figure 10.2, INITOR's application window. A row of buttons across the bottom of INITOR gives access to pop-up menus that display system or private INI files. These pop-up menus also enable you to add or delete entries in the open file.

Add the editor's icon to a window and open the application. Use the Display button at the bottom of the application's main window to open the desired INI. This button will give you a number of choices both for system INIs and private INIs. As always, before changing any file, especially a system file, ensure that you have a backup of that file in a safe place.

List boxes are provided in which the three tiers are displayed. The Application Name area represents the highest level of organization. Every entry in this is displayed. The next level down is the Key Name window. The entries displayed in this area change depending on which application name is highlighted. Every entry displayed in the Key Name area belongs to the highlighted application name. Spend some time clicking various application names to see the key names that may be associated with them.

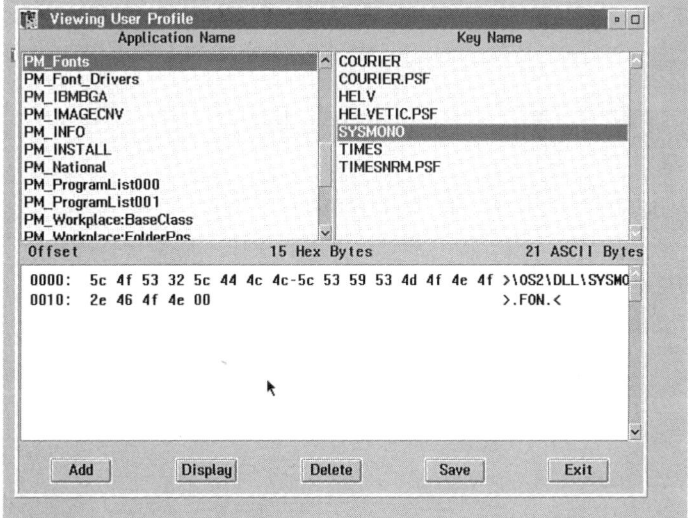

Figure 10.2.
INITOR's application window.

The most detailed area and the lowest in the hierarchy is in the Key Data window. This information may have a number of different formats depending on the application that placed the key data in the INI file. The INITOR application displays this data in both ASCII text and hexadecimal format. Once again, the data displayed in this area is the data associated with the entry highlighted in the previous level of the hierarchy. The data displayed will change depending on the Key Name that is highlighted.

Use INITOR to display entries from the user profile and the system profile. Spend some time exploring these system INIs so you can get a feel for the kind of entry they contain. Identify which entries are in the system INI file and which are in the user INI file. For example, the `PM_SPOOLER` application name contains entries in both the system and user INI files. An application will typically need to query entries from one of the system initialization files. If, for example, your application displays dates, you may want to query the date separator character configured by the user. A user may change this setting by settings in the country portion of the system settings. The `PM_National sDate` application/key combination found in the OS2.INI file will provide you with this information. You may even use the INITOR to change some of your system's settings, but wait until you are thoroughly familiar with the settings you are changing and their effect.

The remaining features follow the customary editing techniques that you would expect, with one important difference. The Save button also presents you with a choice to save the application's screen location. This is included simply to enable you to see an application saving data into an INI, which is used by a later instance of the application. Try moving the application far to one side of the screen, and then save its location. Click the Display button, and then click Refresh. Now, look for the INITOR entry in the User INI file. You may use the choices that appear with the Display button to choose the User INI file.

This application is a completely functional editor, so take some care with the changes you make to the INIs that are on your system, because no UNDO is provided.

Using Your Own INI File

Although INITOR saves its initial screen location in a system INI file, an application should store its configuration information in a private INI file. Using a private INI file prevents the loss of settings if OS/2 is reinstalled or the system INI files are rebuilt by the user. Pressing Alt+F1 for 20 seconds before the first OS/2 Logo panel appears will reset the default desktop configuration. You will recall that before data may be written to a private INI file, it must be opened by using the `PrfOpenProfile` function. If the file exists, it is opened; otherwise, a new file is created. An INI handle is returned if the function is successful, or NULL is returned if an error occurs. The `PrfOpenProfile` function requires an anchor block handle and a pointer to a null-terminated string that contains the filename:

```
HINI hIni = PrfOpenProfile(hab,pFullFileName);
```

When you select the Open Private menu item from the Display pop-up menu, INITOR invokes the common open file dialog. (See Figure 10.3.) You may then open or create any private INI file. Although most INIs use the INI file extension, it is not required. The `PrfOpenProfile` function will fail if the current system or user INI names are specified. Attempting to open an INI created by Windows applications in a WIN/OS2 session will also fail because these files are stored in different formats.

After a private profile file is opened or created, it may be queried or written to by using the same API as the system INIs. However, when your application is through updating the file, it should be closed by using the `PrfCloseProfile` function. This function takes the INI file handle returned from a `PrfOpenProfile` call as its only parameter. This function may not be used to close one of the system INIs. If successful, the function returns TRUE, or it returns FALSE if an error occurs.

When OS/2 is first installed, the system INI files are built by the MAKE.INI program from the INI.RC and INISYS.RC files found in the \OS2 directory. You may use this program to create new system INI files or a default INI file for your application. The input file is a standard PM resource script file where the entries are defined through string tables.

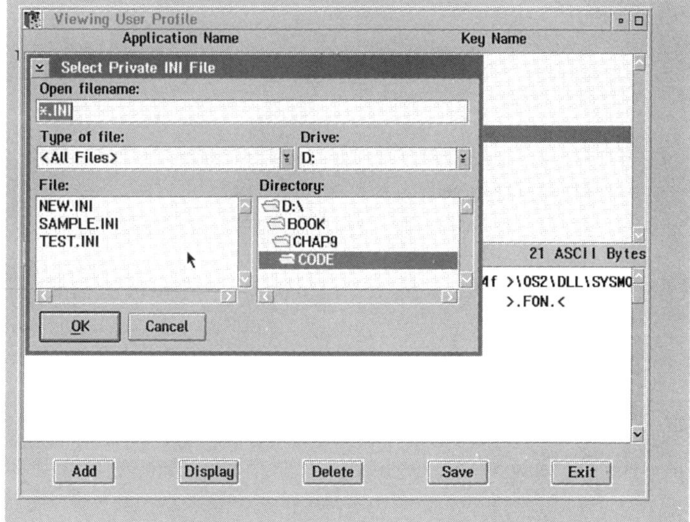

Figure 10.3.
Common open file dialog.

Spooler Functions-Additional Profile API

Applications written for OS/2 1.x were required to query the system INI files to retrieve information about the installed printers. This required intimate knowledge about how the data was stored in the INI files. When retrieved, the data had to be parsed before being used to open a device context with a printer driver. Although the information about printer and queue configurations is still stored in the system INI files in OS/2, a new group of functions have been added to insulate applications from knowing the details about how the data is stored. The Spooler API provides the following three functions for getting information on the configuration of the print subsystem:

`SplEnumQueue`	Enumerates queues on the local workstation.
`SplQueryQueue`	Returns information about a print queue and jobs in it.
`SplQueryDevice`	Returns information about a print device.

The `SplEnumQueue` will return a list of the print queues on a local or remote work station. The second parameter enables you to specify the level of detail required. By calling the function with `ulLevel` set to the desired information level and the `pBuffer` field set to `NULL`, the amount of storage space required may be determined:

```
SplEnumQueue (pszComputer,ulLevel,pBuffer,ulBuffSize,pcReturned,
pcTotal,pcbNeeded,pReserved)
```

`PSZ`	`pszComputer`	Pointer to a null-terminated string that identifies the name of the computer from which to enumerate queues. A

		NULL string indicates that the local workstation should be enumerated.
ULONG	ulLevel	Specifies the level of detail required. pBuffer will contain the following:

- An array of PRQINFO3 structures. Included in the PRQINFO3 structure are the queue name, description, priority, and type.
- An array of PRQINFO3 structures with each one followed by zero or more PRJINFO2 structures. The total number of PRQINFO3 structures will be returned in pcReturned. The cJobs field of the PRQINFO3 structure will indicate the number of PRJINFO2 structures that follow. The PRJINFO2 structure contains information on print jobs currently in the queue. Included in this information are the job's ID number, priority, position in the queue, and size.
- A null-terminated queue name string.
- An array of PRQINFO6 structures. The PRQINFO6 structure contains the same fields that the PRQINFO3 structure does, plus pointers to null-terminated strings that identify a remote computer name and a remote printer name.

PVOID	pBuffer	Pointer to the location return data is to be copied. Setting this field to NULL will cause the pcbNeeded to contain the memory required to hold the data for the requested information level.
ULONG	ulBuffSize	Length in bytes of the memory pointed to by pBuffer.
PULONG	pcReturned	Number of entries returned.
PULONG	pcTotal	Total number of entries available.
PULONG	pcbNeeded	Size in bytes of available information. A value of 0 specifies that the size is not known.
PVOID	pReserved	Reserved parameter, must be NULL.

The SplQueryQueue will return information about a specific print queue including any print jobs in it. The parameters to this function are similar to the SplEnumQueue function described previously. You can use this function in your application to track the status of a print job once submitted. By setting a timer and requesting level 4 information from the SplQueryQueue, the status of the print job, including position in the queue and job priority, may be displayed in a status line. The SplQueryQueue is defined as follows:

```
SplQueryQueue(pszComputer,pszQueueName,
    ulLevel,pBuffer,ulBuffSize,pcbNeeded)
```

PSZ	pszQueueName	Pointer to a null-terminated string that identifies the queue on which to return

information. The pszName field from the PRQINFO3 or PRQINFO6 should be used to provide this value.

As with the SplEnumQueue function, the memory required to hold the requested information may be determined by calling the function with the desired ulLevel and a NULL pBuffer. The bytes required will be returned in pcbNeeded.

If required, the SplQueryDevice function will return information about a device or port:

```
SplQueryDevice (pszComputer,pszPrintDevice,
     ulLevel,pBuffer,ulBuffSize,pcbNeeded)
```

PSZ	pszPrintDevice	Pointer to a null-terminated string that is either the name of the print device or port to query. ulLevel 0 requires a port name. Valid port names may be enumerated from the PM_SPOOLER_PORT application section of the system INI file. Level 1 is undefined and level 2 or 3 requires a print device name.
ULONG	ulLevel	Level of detail required.
0	pszPrintDevice	Pointer to a null-terminated string that indicates the port name to query.
2	pszPrintDevice	Pointer to a null-terminated string that indicates the print device to query.
3	pBuffer	Contains pointer PRDINFO3 structure. Included in PRDINFO3 structure are the time spent printing, the job ID, and the device timeout.
PVOID	pBuffer	Pointer to the location return data is to be copied.
ULONG	ulBuffSize	Length in bytes of the memory pointed to by pBuffer.
PULONG	pcbNeeded	Size in bytes of available information.

The following is a quick summary of important additional entries that may be in system INI files.

HINI_USERPROFILE	
PM_DEVICE_DRIVERS	This entry identifies the drivers installed on your system. The key data consists of the name of your device driver file without the extension, and the key data is the fully qualified pathname of the driver filename.

PM_Fonts	Your applications may include Type 1 fonts that can be installed on the PM desktop. Although these fonts may be installed by using a font palette, requiring a user to do this is undesirable. Those fonts may be installed by adding entries to this section where the key name is the filename of the AFM file and the data is the fully qualified pathname of the filename of the AFM file. Fonts in this section are public and are read by PM at system start-up. To make the fonts available without restarting, call `GpiLoadPublicFonts` for each facename contained in the font file added to the INI file.
PM_Font_Drivers	The key name entry is the name of a DLL that conforms to IFI (intelligent font interface) specification. The data is the fully qualified pathname to the DLL. The default entry describes the PMATM DLL supplied as part of OS/2.
PM_National	This application section contains various country specific settings for the display of dates, time, and monetary values.
PM_SPOOLER	
QUEUE	This entry contains the default queue name. If you have more than one printer installed on your machine, you may change this value by selecting the Set Default menu item of any print object. Applications are not informed of changes to this value, so you must select the Refresh option from the Display menu in INITOR to see the change.
PRINTER	In releases of OS/2, prior to 2.1, this contained the default printer. In 2.1, it remains for compatibility with 1.x applications and will contain the same value as the QUEUE keyname described previously.

SYS_DLLS	
LoadOneTime	This item contains the name of a DLL that is loaded at system start-up. The default is the single entry REXXINIT. Additional DLLs may be added by appending a comma followed by the DLL name. Each time the system is started, the initialization code for this DLL will be called. Changing this item is considered risky because a failure in the initialization of the DLL being added may prevent OS/2 from booting successfully.
LoadOncePerProcess	This item contains the name of a DLL that is loaded at the start-up of each process. The default is the single entry PMCTLS. Additional DLLs may be added by appending a comma followed by the DLL name.
HINI_SYSTEMPROFILE	
PM_SPOOLER_PRINTER	This application section contains entries for installed printer drivers.

The keyname is the physical device name, and the data string is defined as in the example that follows:

```
<addr>;<ddl>;<ql>;<netopt>;<timeout>;
ex. LPT1;PSCRIPT.HP LaserJet IIISi PS v52_3;HPLaserJ;;45;
```

<addr>	Address (ex. LPTn, COMn, IEEEn), which can be NULL (that is, not connected).
<ddl>	List of device drivers defined for the printer (comma between each name), which can be null. The first one is taken as the default.
<ql>	List of queues defined for the printer.
<netopt>	Network printer options, which may be omitted.
<timeout>	Timeout value in seconds.
PM_SPOOLER_PRINTER_DESCR	
PM_SPOOLER_QUEUE	
PM_SPOOLER_QUEUE_DD	
PM_SPOOLER_QUEUE_DESCR	
INI.RC and INISYS.RC files	

Chapter 13, "Printing," discusses the Spooler API in greater detail. Further, it outlines the conversion of profile queries to the appropriate spooler function.

Chapter 11

Memory Management

The Memory Architecture of OS/2

Many developers starting out programming for OS/2 have programmed for DOS. The clunky, segmented addressing architecture demanded by the chips on which DOS runs is notorious for its inefficiency and quirkiness. A 640KB limitation and competing and confusing schemes such as extended and expanded memory are the result of this segmented architecture. OS/2, running on the 80386 chip, is capable of leaving all this behind.

OS/2 has a linear address space. That is, the address of each byte that follows another is incremented by one. Some call this a "flat address space." Memory allocation in OS/2 takes advantage of the 32-bit protected mode of the Intel 80386 and 80486 processors. Because OS/2, as of this writing, runs on a chip that uses 32-bit pointers, 4GB of memory may be addressed. Not all this memory, however, is immediately available to an application, nor is the memory architecture as simple as the term "flat address space" implies.

Remember, OS/2 is a true multitasking operating system. This means that a number of different processes, which may have any number of threads, occupy the system memory simultaneously along with the operating system. If any process could access any place in memory at will, confusion and corruption would often be the result. Further, if the physical address space taken by one application was large, it might limit another from running. More often than not this would be the case because although memory is cheap, it's not yet free. Most systems do not have 4GB laying about for use. Most office and home systems have 8 physical megabytes available to the CPU, so some mechanism is necessary to allow applications to use a much larger virtual address space.

In OS/2, each process can access 512MB of linear address space. This area of memory is referred to as the process address space. The 512MB limit is incurred by the need to support both 16-bit and 32-bit applications. This 512MB of potential memory is, in fact, further limited to the amount of physical memory added to the amount of available hard disk memory.

To make this large address space available to multiple applications in the much smaller space of physical memory available on most machines, OS/2 uses a paged memory system. This 512MB of memory for each process is completely unrelated to the 512MB available to other processes that may be running on the machine. The total amount of committed memory for all processes, however, cannot exceed the amount of physical memory plus the available hard disk space.

The entire 4GB of address space is partitioned into private, shared, and system memory. Figure 11.1 illustrates how the address space is allocated to these three regions.

Of the 64MB reserved for private memory allocation, the first 64KB is reserved for operating system overhead. The address range from 448MB to 512MB is reserved for shared memory. Addresses above 512MB are in the OS/2 system space; these are where the operating system kernel is loaded. The remaining 384MB between addresses 64MB and 448MB is allocated as needed for either private or shared memory.

Private memory for each process grows upward (upward in value) from the bottom 64KB. This

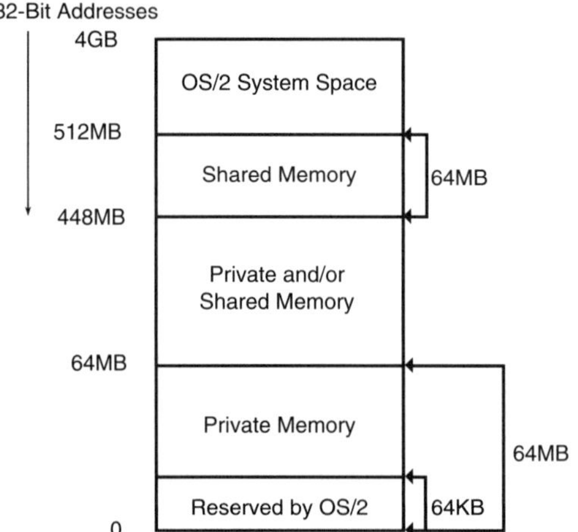

Figure 11.1.
OS/2 address space.

is true for every process running on the system. Shared memory starts at the top of the 512MB address space and grows downward. Shared memory is memory shared across processes. Keep in mind that a process is different from a thread. A process may have many threads, but processes are individuals to themselves. Shared memory is used to share memory across processes as well as for Dynamic Link Library (DLL) code and data. Private memory is composed of the application's code, data, heap, stack, and allocated nonshared memory objects.

Shared memory is allocated for all processes. For example, if several processes are running and one allocates 2MB of shared memory, this shared memory is allocated from the shared memory address space for all the processes. This is true even if some of the processes do not have access to the allocated memory.

16-Bit and 32-Bit Memory

To fully understand the allocation scheme, you will find it helpful to first understand the 16-bit segmented allocation scheme. Prior versions of OS/2 relied on the segmented memory model, and all memory was addressed by a 16-bit selector and 16-bit offset. Memory was allocated by blocks of up to 64KB, and a 16-bit segment selector was returned. Memory was then accessed by combining the 16-bit selector with a 16-bit offset, with all offsets starting at 0. Memory was allocated and accessible immediately after allocation. This architecture limits each segment to 64KB, so allocating blocks larger than 64KB required the segment register to be changed to match the desired portion of allocated memory.

OS/2 provides support for true 32-bit memory allocation and access, but it also still supports 16-bit segmented memory allocation for 16-bit applications. As it is possible for 32-bit applications and 16-bit applications to share data address spaces (shared memory) and also to pass memory addresses between each other, it is necessary to allow for differences in the addressing scheme. This support is provided by placing several restrictions on the 32-bit memory allocation process.

In the 32-bit world, all addresses are near addresses into what is called the FLAT address space. The FLAT address space, sometimes called linear address space, is the entire 4GB of addressable memory. Because the 16-bit world requires all segment offsets to start at 0, you can see that only those addresses in the 32-bit space that have 0 as the low word of their address should map to segment boundaries. This is done in OS/2 by what is called memory tiling, or TILED memory, which restricts the base linear addresses to multiples of 64KB. Figure 11.2 shows how the two addressing schemes can share the same memory space through tiling.

Notice that all selectors have the low 3-bits set and that the memory referenced starts on a 64KB multiple. Because the system reserves the first 64KB, it is never possible to have a selector value of 0. OS/2 enables you to force memory allocation to follow the TILED memory restriction when memory is allocated. Using this option does reduce the amount of available memory address space because the entire range of 64KB is reserved on such an allocation request. This is discussed later when we get into the memory management API.

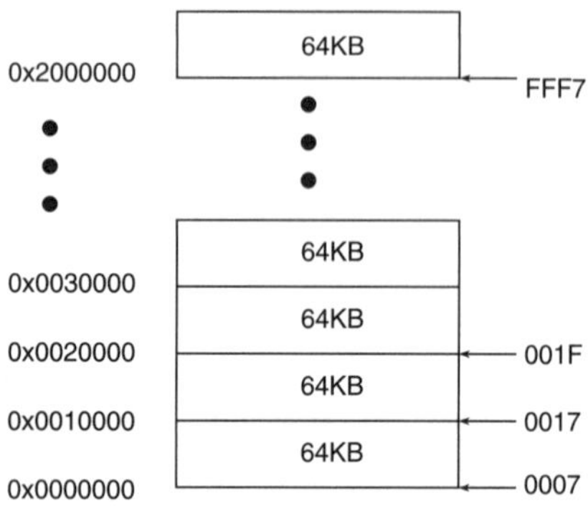

Figure 11.2.
Tiled memory architecture.

32-Bit Memory

The fundamental unit of memory for OS/2 memory management is the page. A page of memory is always 4,096 bytes, 4KB. If an application needs to allocate only 64 bytes of memory, this still causes a whole page, 4,096, to be allocated to contain that 64 bytes. If more than a page of memory is asked for, a page range is allocated. A page range is several contiguous pages.

The total virtual memory space available to a process is divided into pages. Each of these pages may be in one of only three states at any particular moment. These three states are as follows:

Free	The page has not been allocated.
Private	The process has allocated the page for use.
Shared	The page has been allocated as memory to be shared between processes.

Memory pages have an additional pair of characteristics. A memory page may be committed or uncommitted. Committed pages within memory objects have been allotted physical storage for the logical address range. Uncommitted pages are not yet backed by physical storage.

Memory allocation merely reserves a range of memory addresses in the process address space. It does not use any physical memory until the memory is committed and referenced. Memory commitment is the process of physically allocating memory from the system and assigning it to the address space that has been allocated. Requests to commit memory are done on a page basis. A page in memory cannot be accessed until the page has been committed. Attempts to access uncommitted memory will result in a protection violation.

Memory objects are allocated in units of 4KB pages. All memory requests are resolved to a page boundary. All pages allocated are fully addressable. A request to allocate 1 byte of memory will result in a 4KB page being allocated. The entire 4KB is available for use by the application. A request to allocate 4,097 bytes of memory will result in two 4KB pages being allocated. Again, the entire 8KB is available for allocation. For small memory requests, this can result in a lot of unused memory being allocated, thus reducing the amount of memory available for use. We will discuss ways to handle such requests more efficiently later in this chapter.

When an application no longer requires the use of a physical memory object, it can either be freed or decommitted. Decommitment allows the application to commit the memory again without the need for a memory allocation request.

Notice that applications do not actually allocate "pages" for their use. Applications or processes allocate memory, which is then set aside by the operating system in terms of pages. Applications allocate and use memory as memory objects. Memory objects are one or more pages. Processes or applications may allocate more than one memory object. These memory objects have the following characteristics:

- Each is allocated in increments of 4KB.
- Each has memory objects that are not relocatable.

The operating system reserves a linear address range when an application asks it to allocate memory. This address range, however, is not backed by physical memory until the memory is committed. Any attempt to use uncommitted memory will cause an access violation.

Memory may be committed when it is allocated, or it may be allocated as uncommitted and then committed at a later time. If the memory is committed when allocated, all of it is committed, and it is available for immediate use. If the memory is allocated as uncommitted, however, individual portions of the memory may be allocated at different times later. Allocated memory objects that are not committed are called by the peculiar term "sparse."

You can see that the best practice for memory management is to allocate a sparse memory object initially for as much space as the process might need. Later, parts of the memory object may be committed as needed. When a memory object is allocated as uncommitted, no physical memory is involved, so it is not wasteful to allocate several extra megabytes. Better yet, this practice actually optimizes the use of memory within the system. Pages are not given memory storage to back them up until they are both committed and referenced. No memory is wasted for unreferenced, committed pages.

Access to committed pages is further refined to have access rights: read, write, or execute. A fourth right, guard page, is also available but is not discussed here.

At any time, an application may change the access rights of a committed page of memory. It may also commit and decommit allocated pages on demand. Figure 11.3 shows an initial allocation request for 16KB of memory.

Notice that an entire range of 64KB of address space has been allocated. This is due to the current implementation of memory allocation in OS/2, which makes all memory allocation requests follow the TILED memory scheme.

Before accessing any of this memory, the application would have to make a request to commit the necessary pages. Figure 11.4 shows the result of a request by an application to commit the first 8KB of memory, starting at address 14F00000.

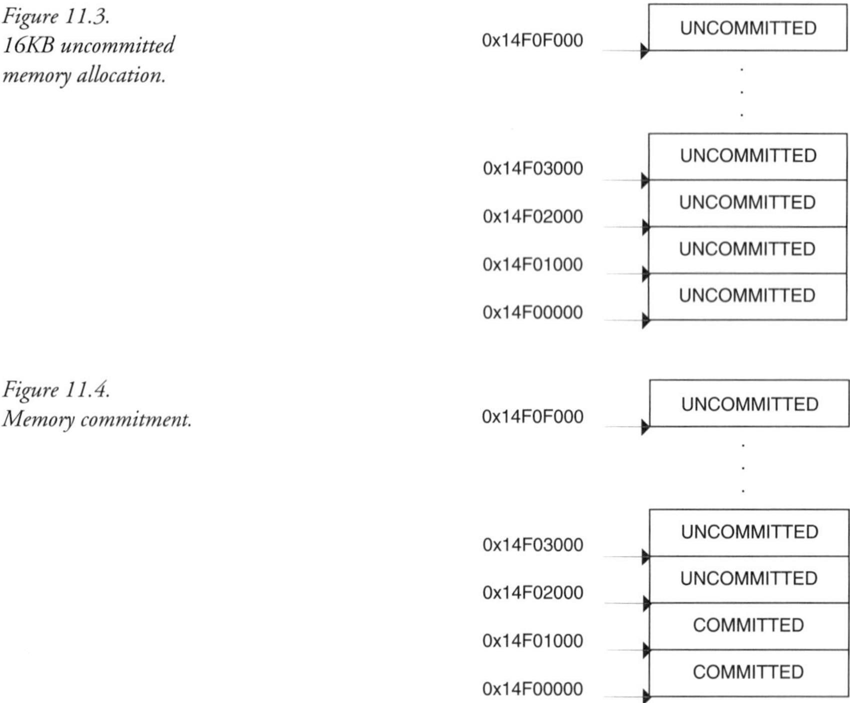

Figure 11.3. 16KB uncommitted memory allocation.

Figure 11.4. Memory commitment.

At this point, we are free to access memory in the range 14F00000 to 14F01FFF. Attempts to address 14F02000 would generate a protection violation.

Memory objects cannot be resized after allocation. An application, thus, must allocate the maximum amount of memory for a memory object and commit the memory as needed.

Committing and decommitting pages in a range of allocated memory as they are needed is a more efficient way of managing memory than requesting memory allocation and commitment every time. This, however, requires the application to keep track of how many pages have been committed so that memory requests to commit and decommit do not fail.

An easier way of handling such a situation is to allocate a memory object as a heap and use the memory suballocation functions to allocate and commit the memory as needed. The heap management functions in the operating system keep track of the committed and uncommitted pages and manage these pages as memory requests are made. Care must be taken when using a heap, as accessing memory above the requested amount of suballocated memory may write over memory allocated to another suballocated block of memory or destroy information maintained by the heap itself. Memory requests suballocated from a heap are rounded up to a multiple of 8 bytes.

The Memory Manager API

The memory management functions in OS/2 are divided into three categories: nonshared, suballocated, and shared. Some functions that are discussed as a part of the nonshared memory API are also available for use with shared memory.

NonShared Memory

Nonshared memory is allocated with the `DosAllocMem API`:

```
APIRET DosAllocMem (PPVOID ppBaseAddress, ULONG ulObjectSize,
ULONG ulAllocationFlags)
```

`PPVOID`	`ppBaseAddress`	Address of pointer to receive memory address.
`ULONG`	`ulObjectSize`	Maximum size of memory object to be allocated.
`ULONG`	`ulAllocationFlags`	Memory allocation flags: `PAG_READ` Allows read access. `PAG_EXECUTE` Allows execute access (executable code). `PAG_WRITE` Allows write access (includes read and execute access). `PAG_COMMIT` Commits all requested pages. `OBJ_TILE` Allocates memory on a 64KB boundary.

The following example allocates an 8KB memory object:

```
PBYTE pMem;
APIRET RetCode;
RetCode = DosAllocMem ((PPVOID) &pMem, 8192L, PAG_READ ¦ PAG_WRITE);
```

The memory object returned in `pMem` must be committed before it can be accessed. Memory can be committed at the same time it is allocated by using the `PAG_COMMIT` flag:

```
RetCode = DosAllocMem ((PPVOID) &pMem, 8192L,
           PAG_READ ¦ PAG_WRITE ¦ PAG_COMMIT);
```

The memory object returned in `pMem` can now be immediately accessed. Each page of a memory object is initialized to zeros the first time the page is read or written. The flag `fALLOC` can be used to request memory that is readable, writable, and committed:

```
#define fPERM  (PAG_EXECUTE + PAG_READ ¦ PAG_WRITE)
#define fALLOC (OBJ_TILE + PAG_COMMIT + fPERM)
```

Note: The current implementation of OS/2 always allocates memory as though the `OBJ_TILE` flag is set. If the `PAG_COMMIT` flag is set, however, only those pages required to satisfy the allocation request are committed. In the previous example, only the first four pages (8,192 bytes) would be committed, although 16 pages (64KB) are allocated. This may change in a future release of OS/2.

After the memory is allocated, it can be committed and decommitted as needed with the DosSetMem API:

```
APIRET DosSetMem (PVOID pBaseAddress, ULONG ulRegionSize,
                  ULONG ulAttributeFlags)
```

PVOID	pBaseAddress	Base address of memory object.		
ULONG	ulRegionSize	Size of memory to set.		
ULONG	ulAttributeFlags	Memory attribute flags:		
			PAG_COMMIT	Commits pages specified in ulRegionSize.
			PAG_DECOMMIT	Decommits pages specified in ulRegionSize starting at pBaseAddress.
			PAG_READ	Read access.
			PAG_EXECUTE	Execute access.
			PAG_WRITE	Write access.
			PAG_DEFAULT	Use default access.

If you are committing memory, you must also specify PAG_DEFAULT or at least one of these—PAG_READ, PAG_WRITE, or PAG_EXECUTE. PAG_DEFAULT sets the access rights of the page to the same rights as when the memory object was allocated.

The following example allocates an 8KB memory object and commits the first page of the object:

```
PBYTE pMem;
APIRET RetCode;
if ( !(RetCode = DosAllocMem ((PPVOID) &pMem, 8192L,
       PAG_READ | PAG_WRITE)) )
{
   RetCode = DosSetMem ((PVOID) pMem, 4096L,
             PAG_COMMIT | PAG_READ | PAG_WRITE);
}
```

Attempts to set the commitment state of a page of memory to a state to which it is already set will fail. The second call to DosSetMem in the following sequence will fail as the second page is already committed:

```
RetCode = DosSetMem ((PVOID) pMem, 8192L,
            PAG_COMMIT | PAG_READ | PAG_WRITE);
RetCode = DosSetMem ((PVOID) pMem+4096, 4096L,
            PAG_COMMIT | PAG_READ | PAG_WRITE);
```

DosSetMem can also be used to change the access rights of the committed pages of the memory object. The following example allocates and commits an 8KB memory object and then changes the access right of the first page from readable and writable to only readable:

```
PBYTE pMem;
APIRET RetCode;
if ( !(RetCode = DosAllocMem ((PPVOID)&pMem,8192L,fALLOC)) )
```

```
{
   RetCode = DosSetMem ((PVOID) pMem, 4096L, PAG_READ);
}
```

The first page is now readable, but the second page is still readable and writable. It is not possible to change the access rights for uncommitted memory.

It is important for you to remember that the access right of PAG_EXECUTE can be set for a page of memory only if the memory was originally allocated with PAG_EXECUTE.

When memory is no longer needed, you can release it with the DosFreeMem API:

```
APIRET DosFreeMem (PVOID pBaseAddress)
```

```
PVOID pBaseAddress     Base address of memory object
```

The following example allocates and commits an 8KB memory object and then releases it when done:

```
PBYTE pMem;
APIRET RetCode;
if ( !(RetCode = DosAllocMem((PPVOID)&pMem,8192L,fALLOC)) )
{
   .
   .
   .
   RetCode = DosFreeMem ((PVOID) pMem);
}
```

Any range of memory can be queried to determine its current state with the DosQueryMem API:

```
APIRET DosQueryMem (PVOID pBaseAddress,PULONG pulRegionSize,
                    PULONG pulAllocationFlags)
```

PPVOID	ppBaseAddress	Base address of memory object.
PULONG	pulRegionSize	Address of variable to receive region size.
PULONG	pulAllocationFlags	Address of variable to receive allocation flags.

DosQueryMem will scan the pages of memory starting at pBaseAddress and will return the allocation flags of the memory in the range specified. On input, pulRegionSize points to a variable containing the size, in bytes, of the amount of memory to scan. The range of memory pages scanned will stop when a page with attribute flags different from the first page is encountered, the number of pages requested is scanned, or the end of the allocated object is reached. On return, the variable pointed to by pulRegionSize will contain the actual number of bytes scanned.

The allocation flags include two new flags:

PAG_FREE	The memory pages are not allocated.
PAG_BASE	The first page specified is the first page of the allocated memory object.
PAG_SHARED	The memory pages are in a shared memory object. (This flag is returned only if the pages are committed.)

The following example queries the second page to see whether it is committed and writable:

```
ULONG ulMemSize = 4096L;
ULONG ulFlags;
if ( !(RetCode = DosQueryMem ((PVOID) (pMem+4096),
                 &ulMemSize, &ulFlags)) )
{
   if ( (ulFlags & (PAG_COMMIT | PAG_WRITE)) ==
         (PAG_COMMIT | PAG_WRITE)) )
   {
      .
      .
      .
   }
}
```

If every page of an allocated memory object has the same attributes, you can determine the amount of committed memory for the object with the following call:

```
ULONG ulMemSize = 0xFFFFFFFF;
ULONG ulFlags;
if ( (RetCode = DosQueryMem (pMem, &ulMemSize, &ulFlags)) ||
         !(ulFlags & PAG_COMMIT) )
   ulMemSize = 0L;
```

This example requests `DosQueryMem` to scan all memory pages starting at `pMem`. If `DosQueryMem` returns successful, we still need to check the flags because all memory may be uncommitted. The applications presented later demonstrate how to determine the amount of allocated and committed memory when all pages do not have the same attributes.

Suballocated Memory

There are several drawbacks to allocating, committing, and managing the pages of memory that your application may need.

- Your application must track which pages have been committed and must check this before each memory access.
- Small memory requests result in large amounts of address space being reserved.
- Small memory requests for committed pages result in at least 4KB of physical memory being used.
- Memory allocation requests for new blocks of memory will be slower than suballocating from already committed memory.

Consider the following memory requests:

```
DosAllocMem ((PPVOID) &pMem, 20L, fALLOC);
DosAllocMem ((PPVOID) &pMem, 32L, fALLOC);
```

This results in a total of 128KB of address space being reserved (64KB for each request) and 8KB of physical memory being used (4KB for each request). It would be more efficient if we could satisfy both requests in a single page of committed memory. This is made possible by using the heap management functions of OS/2. In using a heap, you allocate a block of memory and indicate to OS/2 that the block is to be managed as a heap. OS/2 will then satisfy memory requests from this heap by suballocating portions of this memory and returning the address to the application. OS/2 takes care of making sure the pages of memory are committed as necessary and of freeing them as they become available. Your application should never call `DosSetMem` to change any attribute of the memory used for suballocation, as this will cause unpredictable results. As an alternative, it is also possible for your application to commit the pages of the heap and avoid having the heap functions do any memory commitment.

The first step in using memory suballocation (heaps) is to allocate a block of memory for this purpose. This is done by using the `DosAllocMem` function. This allocated memory is then initialized for memory suballocation with the `DosSubSetMem` API, as follows:

```
APIRET DosSubSetMem (PVOID pOffset, ULONG ulFlags, ULONG ulSize)
```

`PVOID`	`pOffset`	Base address of memory object.	
`ULONG`	`ulFlags`	Memory suballocation flags:	
		`DOSSUB_INIT`	Initializes the memory for suballocation.
		`DOSSUB_SPARSE_OBJ`	Tells OS/2 to manage the commitment of the pages.
		`DOSSUB_GROW`	Increases the size of the memory used for suballocation.
		`DOSSUB_SERIALIZE`	More than one process will be suballocating memory from this block of memory.

The suballocation management for the heap uses 64 bytes of this memory to maintain control information. In addition, all suballocation requests are satisfied in multiples of 8 bytes. The minimum size that can be set, thus, is 72 bytes.

The `DOSSUB_INIT` flag is specified on the first call to `DosSubSetMem` so that the control information for the heap can be initialized.

Specify the `DOSSUB_SPARSE_OBJ` flag if you want OS/2 to manage the commitment of the pages. All pages in the range specified must be initially uncommitted. If the `DOSSUB_SPARSE_OBJ` flag is not set, all pages in the range specified must be committed before the call to DosSubSetMem. Because the heap must be updated as memory is suballocated, all pages must have minimum access rights of `PAG_READ` and `PAG_WRITE`.

The following example allocates 64KB for use as a heap and initializes it such that OS/2 will manage the commitment of pages:

```
if ( !(RetCode = DosAllocMem ((PPVOID) &pMem, 0x10000,
      PAG_READ ¦ PAG_WRITE)) )
{
   RetCode = DosSubSetMem (pMem,
         DOSSUB_INIT ¦ DOSSUB_SPARSE_OBJ, 0x10000);
}
```

The DOSSUB_GROW flag can be used to increase the amount of memory available for suballocation. When using this flag, the setting of the DOSSUB_SPARSE_OBJ flag must match the setting that was used on the initial call to DosSubSetMem. The DOSSUB_INIT flag is ignored if DOSSUB_GROW is specified. This example allocates 128KB for use as a heap, but only initializes the heap to use the first 64KB.

```
if ( !(RetCode = DosAllocMem ((PPVOID) &pMem, 0x20000,
         PAG_READ ¦ PAG_WRITE)) )
{
   RetCode = DosSubSetMem ((PVOID) pMem,
             DOSSUB_INIT ¦ DOSSUB_SPARSE_OBJ, 0x10000);
}
```

Later, the range of memory used for the heap can be increased by calling DosSubSetMem as follows:

```
RetCode = DosSubSetMem (pMem,
            DOSSUB_GROW ¦ DOSSUB_SPARSE_OBJ, 0x20000);
```

Notice that the base address used in the second call to DosSubSetMem must match that used in the first call.

If more than one process is going to perform memory suballocation from the same heap, it is necessary to specify the DOSSUB_SERIALIZE flag. Because OS/2 is a multitasking system, the system can interrupt one process, which could be in the middle of the code that is suballocating memory from the heap, to allow another process to continue which could also possibly call to have memory suballocated from the same heap. Because the first process may be in the middle of making updates to the control information for the heap and the second process may make updates as well, when the first process continues, the control information may be corrupted. Because the heap is then in a corrupted state, either the request to suballocate memory will never return or both processes will eventually cause a protection violation. By specifying the DOSSUB_SERIALIZE flag, OS/2 creates a semaphore for the heap and every request to suballocate or free memory from the heap starts with a request to gain access to the semaphore and releases it when it is done. This prevents more than one process from executing within the heap management code at the same time.

The first process to create the heap must allocate the memory as shared memory (discussed later) and must use the DOSSUB_INIT and DOSSUB_SERIALIZE flags. Other processes that want to share the heap must specify the DOSSUB_SERIALIZE flags without the DOSSUB_INIT flag. We will use this in an example later when we discuss shared memory.

When the heap has been initialized for suballocation, we can use the DosSubAllocMem API to request memory:

```
APIRET DosSubAllocMem (PVOID pOffset, PPVOID ppBlockOffset,
                       ULONG ulSize)
```

PVOID	pOffset	Base address of the heap.
PPVOID	ppBlockOffset	Address of pointer to receive memory address.
ULONG	ulSize	Amount of memory for use by the heap.

All memory requests are rounded up to the next multiple of 8 bytes. The following example requests 22 bytes from the heap allocated previously:

```
PBYTE  pSubMem;
APIRET RetCode;
RetCode = DosSubAllocMem (pMem, (PPVOID) &pSubMem, 22);
```

When the suballocate memory is no longer needed, you can release it with the `DosSubFreeMem` API:

```
APIRET DosSubFreeMem (PVOID pMem, PVOID pBlockOffset, ULONG ulSize)
```

PVOID	pMem	Base address of the heap.
PVOID	pBlockOffset	Address of pointer to receive memory address.
ULONG	ulSize	Size of memory to suballocate.

The amount of memory specified in `ulSize` will be rounded up to the next multiple of 8 bytes and, after rounding, must match the amount actually suballocated. The following example frees the memory requested in the previous example:

```
RetCode = DosSubFreeMem (pMem, pSubMem, 24);
```

When you are done with the heap, you must call the DosSubUnsetMem API to enable OS/2 to free the resources it has allocated to manage the heap:

```
APIRET DosSubUnsetMem (PVOID pMem)
```

PVOID	pMem	Base address of the heap.

All calls to DosSubSetMem must be matched with an equivalent call to `DosSubUnsetMem`. The memory used by the heap can then be freed with a call to `DosFreeMem` after `DosSubUnsetMem` has been called. The following example ends the use of the heap and frees the memory we allocated earlier:

```
if ( !(RetCode = DosSubUnsetMem ((PVOID) pMem)) )
{
   RetCode = DosFreeMem ((PVOID) pMem);
}
```

Shared Memory

Until now we have talked about memory allocated for the private use of a process. Shared memory is memory that can be addressed by multiple processes. Shared memory is used when two or more processes need to share data or when data is copied to or from the OS/2 clipboard. While

memory is allocated from the shared memory arena and the address space is reserved in the process address space of all processes, a process must explicitly gain access to the memory in order to access it.

Once access to shared memory is obtained, the processes must coordinate among themselves whenever the memory is updated. This is usually done using semaphores. No coordination is required when just reading the shared memory.

Shared memory is initially allocated by one process. So how do other applications know the address of the shared memory in order to access it? There are two methods for doing this. The first is to use *named* shared memory. In this case, shared memory is allocated, and a unique name is assigned to the memory. At that point, any application knowing the name of this memory can access it by referring to the same name. The second method is to use *unnamed* shared memory. In this case, shared memory is allocated, and the address of this memory is passed to the other applications. At that point, the other processes can access the memory. It is also possible for a process with access to a shared memory object to give access to another process.

When each process with access to shared memory is finished using the memory, each process must free the shared memory. This is because the shared memory object maintains a count of the number of processes that have gained access to it, and the physical memory assigned to the shared memory object is not freed until all processes using the memory have freed it. Failure of each process to free the shared memory will result in reducing the address space available for shared memory.

Shared memory is allocated by using the `DosAllocSharedMem` API:

```
APIRET APIENTRY DosAllocSharedMem (PPVOID ppb, PSZ pszName,
                ULONG cb, ULONG flag)
```

`PPVOID`	`ppb`	Address of pointer variable to receive the memory address.
`PSZ`	`pszName`	Name of the named shared memory object. This name has the form `\SHAREMEM\name`. `name` can be any name that meets the criteria for a valid OS/2 filename.
`ULONG`	`cb`	Maximum size of the memory object to be allocated.
`ULONG`	`flag`	Memory allocation flags:
	`PAG_READ`	Allows read access.
	`PAG_EXECUTE`	Allows execute access (executable code).
	`PAG_WRITE`	Allows write access (includes read and execute access).
	`PAG_COMMIT`	Commit pages when allocated.
	`OBJ_TILE`	Allocate on 64KB boundary.
	`OBJ_GETTABLE`	Memory is gettable by other processes.
	`OBJ_GIVEABLE`	Memory is giveable to other processes.

This function operates the same way as the `DosAllocMem` API, except that memory is allocated from the shared address space and there are some additional memory flags. To allocate named shared memory, the `pszName` field is set to the name of the object. The `OBJ_GETTABLE` and `OBJ_GIVEABLE` memory allocation flags are not allowed for named shared memory. To allocate unnamed shared memory, the `pszName` field is set to `NULL` and at least one of the `OBJ_GETTABLE` or `OBJ_GIVEABLE` flags must be specified. There are some macros defined in the BSEMEMF.H header file, which is included by the BSEDOS.H header file:

```
#define fSHARE      (OBJ_GETTABLE + OBJ_GIVEABLE)
#define fPERM       (PAG_EXECUTE + PAG_READ + PAG_WRITE)
#define fALLOCSHR   (OBJ_TILE + PAG_COMMIT + fSHARE + fPERM)
#define fGETNMSHR   (fPERM)
#define fGETSHR     (fPERM)
#define fGIVESHR    (fPERM)
```

After shared memory has been committed, the protection flags and commit state of the pages of memory can be changed with the `DosSetMem` API just as they were for nonshared memory. Shared memory can also be queried as before using the `DosQuerymem` API. If a page of shared memory has been committed, the additional flag of `PAG_SHARED` will be returned for the shared pages when `DosQueryMem` is used. Once a page of shared memory has been committed, it cannot be decommitted.

For named shared memory, the `DosGetNamedSharedMem` API is used by other processes to obtain access to the memory object:

```
APIRET APIENTRY DosGetNamedSharedMem (PPVOID ppBaseAddress,
              PSZ pszSharedMemName, ULONG ulAttributeFlags)
```

`PPVOID`	`ppBaseAddress`	Address of pointer to receive memory address.	
`PSZ`	`pszSharedMemName`	Name of the named shared memory object. This name has the form *\SHAREMEM\name*. *name* can be any name that meets the criteria for a valid OS/2 filename.	
`ULONG`	`ulAttributeFlags`	Desired access protection for the shared memory:	
		`PAG_READ`	Read access.
		`PAG_EXECUTE`	Execute access (executable code).
		`PAG_WRITE`	Write access (includes read and execute access).

If a named shared memory object with the specified name exists, the process is given access to the memory, and its address is returned in `ppBaseAddress`. The following example shows one process allocating 32KB of named shared memory and another process gaining access to it.

Process 1:

```
PVOID pMem;

if (!DosAllocSharedMem(&pMem,"\\SHAREMEM\\OBJECT1", 0x8000L,
      fPERM ¦ PAG_COMMIT ¦ OBJ_TILE))
{
   strcpy ((PSZ)pMem, "Hello, Process 2");
}
```

Process 2:

```
PVOID pMem;
if (!DosGetNamedSharedMem(&pMem,"\\SHAREMEM\\OBJECT1",
      fPERM))
{
   strcpy ((PSZ)pMem, "Hello to you, Process 1");
}
```

For unnamed shared memory, there are two ways that memory access can be obtained by a second process. The first is for the second process to use the `DosGetSharedMem` API:

```
APIRET APIENTRY DosGetSharedMem (PVOID pBaseAddress,
               ULONG ulAttributeFlags)
```

PVOID	pBaseAddress	The base address of the shared memory object.
ULONG	ulAttributeFlags	Desired access protection for the shared memory: PAG_READ — Read access. PAG_EXECUTE — Execute access (executable code). PAG_WRITE — Write access (includes read and execute access).

In order for the `DosGetSharedMem` request to succeed, the memory object must have been allocated with the `OBJ_GETTABLE` flag, and the requested `ulAttributeFlags` must be compatible with the current protection flags for the memory object. Note that the address passed in `pBaseAddress` must be the base address of the memory object. The following example shows one process allocating 32KB of unnamed shared memory, passing the address to the second process, and the second process gaining access to it.

Process 1:

```
#define WM_USER_SHARED_MEM    WM_USER+1

PVOID pMem;
HWND  hWndProcess2;

if (!DosAllocSharedMem (&pMem, NULL, 0x8000L,
      fPERM ¦ PAG_COMMIT ¦ OBJ_TILE ¦ OBJ_GETTABLE ¦
      OBJ_GIVEABLE))
{
   strcpy ((PSZ)pMem, "Hello, Process 2");
   WinSendMsg (hWndProcess2, WM_USER_SHARED_MEM,
         (MPARAM)pMem, 0L);
```

```
}
```

Process 2:

```
#define WM_USER_SHARED_MEM    WM_USER+1
PVOID pMem;
MRESULT EXPENTRY MainWndProcProc (HWND hWnd, ULONG msg,
         MPARAM mp1, MPARAM mp2)
{
   switch (msg)
   {
      ...
      case WM_USER_SHARED_MEM:
         pMem = (PVOID)mp1;
         if (!DosGetSharedMem (pMem, fPERM))
            strcpy ((PSZ)pMem, "Hello to you, Process 1");
         return (0L);
      ...
   }
   return (WinDefWindowProc (hWnd, msg, mp1, mp2));
}
```

In this example, we used a message (WM_USER_SHARED_MEM) to pass the address of the memory object to Process 2. It could also have been done other ways using interprocess communication or through global data in a DLL using a single data segment.

The second way for a process to gain access to unnamed shared memory is to have a process that currently has access to explicitly give access to another process. This is accomplished with the DosGiveSharedMem API:

```
APIRET APIENTRY DosGiveSharedMem (PVOID pBaseAddress,
            PID idProcessID, ULONG ulAttributeFlags)
```

PVOID	pBaseAddress	The base address of the shared memory object.	
PID	idProcessID	Process identifier of process to be given access.	
ULONG	ulAttributeFlags	Desired access protection for the shared memory:	
		PAG_READ	Read access.
		PAG_EXECUTE	Execute access (executable code).
		PAG_WRITE	Write access (includes read and execute access).

In order for the DosGiveSharedMem request to succeed, the memory object must have been allocated with the OBJ_GIVEABLE flag, and the requested ulAttributeFlags must be compatible with the current protection flags for the memory object. Note again that the address passed in pBaseAddress must be the base address of the memory object. The following example shows one process allocating 32KB of unnamed shared memory, giving access to it to another process, and then passing the address to the second process.

Process 1:

```
#define WM_USER_SHARED_MEM    WM_USER+1
```

Converting from Unshared to Shared Memory

There are many times when you have a memory object that is allocated as a private memory object, and you need to pass the information to another process or even copy it to the clipboard. In those circumstances, it is necessary to move the data to shared memory. The following function shows the steps to take a private memory object and convert it to a shared memory object. This process simply requires us to determine the size of the private memory object, allocate a shared memory object of the same size, and copy the data. The function `ConvertToSharedMemory` assumes that the committed pages of the private data object consist of contiguous pages starting at the base address.

```
PVOID ConvertToSharedMemory (PVOID pPrivateMem, BOOL bFree) {
/* Convert the private memory pointed to by pPrivateMem to shared
   memory. If bFree is specified, free the memory pointed
   to by pPrivateMem after creating the shared memory
   object. Return NULL if the convert fails.      */

   PVOID pSharedMem = NULL;
   ULONG ulSize;
   ULONG ulFlags;

   ulSize = 0xFFFFFFFFL;

   if ( !DosQueryMem (pPrivateMem, &ulSize, &ulFlag) &&
      (ulFlag & PAG_COMMIT) &&
      !DosAllocSharedMem (&pSharedMem, NULL, ulSize,
      (ulFlag & fALLOC) ¦ fSHARE) )
   {
      memcpy (pSharedMem, pPrivateMem, ulSize);
      if (bFree)
         DosFreeMem (pPrivateMem);
   }

   return (pSharedMem);
}
```

In order to successfully convert the pointer, there must be committed memory in the private memory object, and the shared memory object must be successfully allocated:

```
if ( !DosQueryMem (pPrivateMem, &ulSize, &ulFlag) &&
      (ulFlag & PAG_COMMIT) &&
      !DosAllocSharedMem (&pSharedMem, NULL, ulSize,
      (ulFlag & fALLOC) ¦ fSHARE) )
```

The flags used for the `DosAllocSharedMem` call are the existing flags for the private memory object (including the `PAG_COMMIT`) plus the `fSHARE` flags.

The MEMMAP Application

This sample application demonstrates most features and API calls needed to query memory within OS/2.

MEMMAP's Files

The files necessary to build the MEMMAP application are the following:

MEMMAP.DEF
MEMMAP.DLG
MEMMAP.C
MEMMAP.H
MEMMAP.RC
MEMMAP.ICO

MEMMAP.C

```
/* ----------------
MemMap Program
Real-World Programming for OS/2
Copyright (c) 1994 Blain, Delimon, and English
---------------- */

#define INCL_WIN
#define INCL_GPI
#define INCL_DOSERRORS
#include <os2.h>
#include <stdio.h>
#include "memmap.h"
#include "..\..\common\about.h"

/* Exported Functions */

MRESULT EXPENTRY MainDlgProc (HWND,ULONG,MPARAM,MPARAM);

/* Local Functions */

VOID  CenterWindow (HWND);
VOID  MemError (PSZ);
ULONG ParseItem (PSZ,ULONG);
VOID  QueryMemory (VOID);

HAB   hab;
CHAR  szTitle[64];
HWND  hWndFrame;
HWND  hWndMemList;
HWND  hWndStartAddress;
ULONG ulStartAddress    = 0L;
CHAR  szStartAddress[9] = "00000000";
PVOID pStartAddress     = (PVOID)szStartAddress;

/* Undocumented menu message */
#define MM_QUERYITEMBYPOS      0x01f3
#define MAKE_16BIT_POINTER(p)  \
((PVOID)MAKEULONG(LOUSHORT(p),(HIUSHORT(p) << 3) | 7))
```

```
int main()
{
   HMQ   hmq;
   QMSG  qmsg;

   hab = WinInitialize (0);
   hmq = WinCreateMsgQueue (hab, 0);

   WinLoadString (hab, 0, ID_APPNAME, sizeof(szTitle),
         szTitle);

   hWndFrame = WinLoadDlg (HWND_DESKTOP, HWND_DESKTOP,
         MainDlgProc, 0, ID_APPNAME, NULL);
   WinSendMsg (hWndFrame, WM_SETICON,
         (MPARAM)WinLoadPointer (HWND_DESKTOP, 0,
         ID_APPNAME), NULL);

   while (WinGetMsg (hab, &qmsg, 0, 0, 0))
      WinDispatchMsg (hab, &qmsg);

   WinDestroyWindow (hWndFrame);
   WinDestroyMsgQueue (hmq);
   WinTerminate (hab);
   return (0);
}

VOID AddAboutToSystemMenu(HWND hWndFrame)
{
   MENUITEM mi;
   HWND     hWndSysSubMenu;

   WinSendMsg (WinWindowFromID (hWndFrame, FID_SYSMENU),
         MM_QUERYITEMBYPOS, 0L, MAKE_16BIT_POINTER(&mi));
   hWndSysSubMenu = mi.hwndSubMenu;
   mi.iPosition   = MIT_END;
   mi.afStyle     = MIS_SEPARATOR;
   mi.afAttribute = 0;
   mi.id          = -1;
   mi.hwndSubMenu = 0;
   mi.hItem       = 0;
   WinSendMsg (hWndSysSubMenu, MM_INSERTITEM, MPFROMP (&mi),
         NULL);
   mi.afStyle     = MIS_TEXT;
   mi.id          = IDM_ABOUT;
   WinSendMsg (hWndSysSubMenu, MM_INSERTITEM, MPFROMP (&mi),
               "About...");
   return;
}

VOID CenterWindow (HWND hWnd)
{
   ULONG ulScrWidth, ulScrHeight;
   RECTL Rectl;

   ulScrWidth  = WinQuerySysValue (HWND_DESKTOP,
         SV_CXSCREEN);
```

```
   ulScrHeight = WinQuerySysValue (HWND_DESKTOP,
         SV_CYSCREEN);
   WinQueryWindowRect (hWnd,&Rectl);
   WinSetWindowPos (hWnd, HWND_TOP,
         (ulScrWidth-Rectl.xRight)/2,
         (ulScrHeight-Rectl.yTop)/2, 0, 0,
         SWP_MOVE ¦ SWP_ACTIVATE);
   return;
}

VOID MemError (PSZ pszMessage)
{
   WinMessageBox (HWND_DESKTOP, hWndFrame, pszMessage,
         "Memory Map", 0, MB_ERROR ¦ MB_OK);
   return;
}

ULONG ParseItem (PSZ szItem, ULONG CurPos)
{
   ULONG EndPos = CurPos + 8;
   ULONG ulMem  = 0;
   for (; CurPos < EndPos; CurPos++)
   {
      if (szItem[CurPos] != ' ')
         ulMem = ulMem*16 +
         ((szItem[CurPos] <= '9') ? (szItem[CurPos] - '0') :
         (szItem[CurPos] - 'A' + 10));
   }
   return (ulMem);
}

VOID QueryMemory ()
{
   char   szText[90];
   ULONG  ulAddress,
          ulEndAddress,
          ulPage,
          ulSize,
          ulFlags;
   APIRET RetCode;

   WinSetPointer (HWND_DESKTOP,
      WinQuerySysPointer (HWND_DESKTOP, SPTR_WAIT, FALSE));
   WinEnableWindowUpdate (hWndMemList, FALSE);
   ulAddress    = ulStartAddress;
   ulEndAddress = ulStartAddress + 0x02000000; /*32 MB max*/
   if (ulEndAddress > 0x20000000)
      ulEndAddress = 0x20000000;
   ulPage       = 0L;
   sprintf (szText,
      "%08lx  . . . . . . . . . . . . . . . . ",
      ulAddress);
   WinUpper (hab, 0, 0, szText);
   while (ulAddress < ulEndAddress)
   {
      ulSize = 0xFFFFFFFF;
```

```
    if (!(RetCode = DosQueryMem ((PVOID)ulAddress,
          &ulSize, &ulFlags)))
    {
       if (ulFlags == PAG_FREE)
          ulSize = 0x1000;
       else
          ulSize = (ulSize + 0xFFF) & 0xFFFFF000;
       if (ulFlags & PAG_BASE)
          szText[42] = '*';
       while (ulSize && (ulAddress < 0x20000000))
       {
          if (ulFlags & PAG_COMMIT)
             szText[10 + ulPage*2] = 'C';
          else if (!(ulFlags & PAG_FREE))
             szText[10 + ulPage*2] = 'A';
          ulAddress += 0x1000;
          ulSize    -= 0x1000;
          ulPage++;
          if (ulPage == 16)
          {
             if (ulFlags & PAG_SHARED)
                sprintf (&szText[43], "%s", "Shared ");
             else if (ulFlags & PAG_FREE)
                sprintf (&szText[43], "%s", "Free   ");
             else
                sprintf (&szText[43], "%s", "Private");
             if (WinInsertLboxItem (
                WinWindowFromID (hWndFrame, IDL_MEMLIST),
                      LIT_END, szText) < 0)
             break;
             ulPage = 0;
             sprintf (szText,
      "%08lx  . . . . . . . . . . . . . . . .          ",
                ulAddress);
             WinUpper (hab, 0, 0, szText);
          }
       }
    }
    else if (RetCode == ERROR_INVALID_ADDRESS)
    {
       ulAddress += 0x10000;
       sprintf (&szText[43], "%s", "Invalid");
       WinInsertLboxItem (WinWindowFromID (hWndFrame,
           IDL_MEMLIST), LIT_END, szText);
       sprintf (szText,
        "%08lx  . . . . . . . . . . . . . . . .          ",
          ulAddress);
       WinUpper (hab, 0, 0, szText);
    }
    else
    {
     sprintf(szText,"Error querying memory address %08lx",
          ulAddress);
       MemError (szText);
       break;
    }
}
```

```
   WinSetPointer (HWND_DESKTOP,
   WinQuerySysPointer (HWND_DESKTOP,SPTR_ARROW,FALSE));
   WinEnableWindowUpdate (hWndMemList, TRUE);
}


MRESULT EXPENTRY MainDlgProc (HWND hWnd, ULONG msg,
                  MPARAM mp1, MPARAM mp2)
{
   BOOL    bHandled = TRUE;
   MRESULT mReturn  = 0;

   switch (msg)
   {
      case WM_INITDLG:
         CenterWindow (hWnd);

         /* Add the About menu item to the system menu */
         AddAboutToSystemMenu (hWnd);

         hWndMemList = WinWindowFromID(hWnd, IDL_MEMLIST);
         hWndStartAddress=WinWindowFromID(hWnd,
            IDB_STARTADDRESS);

         WinSendMsg (hWndStartAddress, SPBM_SETTEXTLIMIT,
            (MPARAM)8, (MPARAM)0);
         WinSendMsg (hWndStartAddress, SPBM_SETARRAY,
            (MPARAM)&pStartAddress, (MPARAM)1L);
         WinSendMsg (hWndStartAddress, SPBM_SETCURRENTVALUE,
            (MPARAM)0L, (MPARAM)0L);
         WinSetFocus (HWND_DESKTOP, hWndStartAddress);
         WinPostMsg (hWnd, WM_COMMAND, (MPARAM)IDB_REFRESH,
            0L);
         break;

      case WM_CONTROL:
         switch (LOUSHORT(mp1))
         {
            case IDL_MEMLIST:
               if (HIUSHORT(mp1) == LN_SELECT)
               {
                  WinQueryLboxItemText (hWndMemList,
                  WinQueryLboxSelectedItem((HWND)mp2),
                  szStartAddress,9);
                  ulStartAddress = ParseItem(szStartAddress,
                                    0);
                  WinSendMsg (hWndStartAddress,
                              SPBM_SETARRAY,
                              (MPARAM)&pStartAddress,
                              (MPARAM)1L);
               }
               break;

            case IDB_STARTADDRESS:
               if (HIUSHORT(mp1) == SPBN_UPARROW)
                  ulStartAddress = (ulStartAddress+0x10000)
                                    & 0x1FFFFFFF;
```

```
            else if (HIUSHORT(mp1) == SPBN_DOWNARROW)
               ulStartAddress = (ulStartAddress-0x10000)
                                 & 0x1FFFFFFF;
            sprintf (szStartAddress,
                     "%08lx",ulStartAddress);
            WinUpper (hab, 0, 0, szStartAddress);
            WinSendMsg (hWndStartAddress, SPBM_SETARRAY,
                  (MPARAM)&pStartAddress, (MPARAM)1L);
            break;
         }
         break;

      case WM_COMMAND:
      case WM_SYSCOMMAND:
         switch (LOUSHORT(mp1))
         {
            case IDB_REFRESH:
               WinSendDlgItemMsg (hWndFrame, IDL_MEMLIST,
                       LM_DELETEALL, 0L, 0L);
               QueryMemory ();
               WinSendMsg (hWndMemList, LM_SELECTITEM,
                  (MPARAM)0, (MPARAM)TRUE);
               break;

            case IDM_ABOUT:
               DisplayAbout (hWnd, szTitle);
               break;

            case SC_CLOSE:
               WinPostMsg (hWnd, WM_QUIT, 0L, 0L);
               break;

            default:
               bHandled = (msg == WM_COMMAND);
         }
         break;

      default:
         bHandled = FALSE;
         break;
   }

   if (!bHandled)
      mReturn = WinDefDlgProc (hWnd, msg, mp1, mp2);

   return (mReturn);
}
```

MEMMAP.H

```
/* ----------------
MemMap Header File
Real-World Programming for OS/2
Copyright (c) 1994 Blain, Delimon, and English
---------------- */
```

```
#define ID_APPNAME         1

#define IDL_MEMLIST       10
#define IDB_REFRESH       11
#define IDT_PAGES         12
#define IDB_STARTADDRESS  13

#define IDM_ABOUT        100
```

MEMMAP.RC

```
/* ----------------
MemMap Resource File
Real-World Programming for OS/2
Copyright (c) 1994 Blain, Delimon, and English
---------------- */

#include <os2.h>
#include "memmap.h"

ICON ID_APPNAME MEMMAP.ICO

STRINGTABLE LOADONCALL MOVEABLE
BEGIN
   ID_APPNAME      "Memory Map Application"
END

rcinclude memmap.dlg
rcinclude ..\..\common\about.dlg
```

MEMMAP.DLG

```
/* ----------------
MemMap Dialog
Real-World Programming for OS/2
Copyright (c) 1994 Blain, Delimon, and English
---------------- */

DLGTEMPLATE ID_APPNAME LOADONCALL MOVEABLE DISCARDABLE
BEGIN
   DIALOG  "Memory Map", ID_APPNAME, 36, 17, 302, 165,
            WS_VISIBLE | FS_DLGBORDER,
            FCF_SYSMENU | FCF_TITLEBAR | FCF_DLGBORDER |
            FCF_TASKLIST | FCF_ICON;
   BEGIN
      LTEXT      "Address", -1, 15, 145, 37, 8
      LTEXT      "Page", -1, 139, 154, 24, 8
      LTEXT      "0 1 2 3 4 5 6 7 8 9 A B C D E F",
                  IDT_PAGES, 64, 145, 174, 8
                  PRESPARAMS PP_FONTNAMESIZE,
                  "10.System Monospaced"
      LTEXT      "Type", -1, 248, 145, 22, 8
      LTEXT      ". = Free  A = Allocated  C = Committed  * = Base",
                  -1, 77, 6, 207, 8
```

```
        LISTBOX     IDL_MEMLIST, 10, 36, 282, 107
                    PRESPARAMS PP_FONTNAMESIZE,
                    "10.System Monospaced"
        PUSHBUTTON "Refresh", 11, 8, 4, 45, 14
        LTEXT       "Start Address", DID_CANCEL, 9, 23, 60, 8
        CONTROL     "", IDB_STARTADDRESS, 73, 20, 64, 12,
                     WC_SPINBUTTON,
                     SPBS_ALLCHARACTERS ¦ SPBS_READONLY ¦
                     SPBS_MASTER ¦ SPBS_JUSTRIGHT ¦
                     SPBS_FASTSPIN ¦ WS_GROUP ¦ WS_TABSTOP ¦
                     WS_VISIBLE
                     PRESPARAMS PP_FONTNAMESIZE,
                     "10.System Monospaced"
    END
END
```

Using MEMMAP

Add the MEMMAP application icon to a window and open the program. You should see a display similar to Figure 11.5.

The MEMMAP application merely displays a map of the memory available to the MEMMAP process. The memory will be marked Free, Allocated, Committed, or Base.

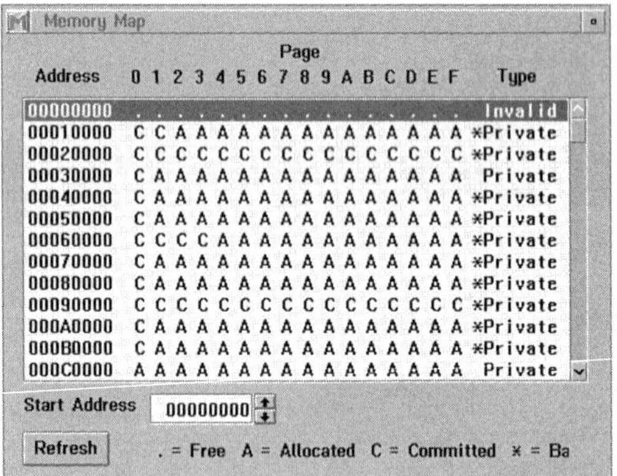

Figure 11.5.
MEMMAP application.

Remember base memory is the starting address of a block of memory. If a process allocated two pages of memory, the first page will be marked as base, the second will not. Take a look at the memory map that MEMMAP displays. Each asterisk signals the beginning of a new allocated block. Gaps indicate large blocks of memory.

Because the only memory available to the MEMMAP application is that which has been allocated for its own process, the map will not change much between differing instances of the application.

Understanding MEMMAP's Code

The code for MEMMAP is similar to that of the MEMORY sample application, which is detailed following the MEMMAP application. The major difference lies in the QueryMemory function, which is detailed in following text. Work through understanding this smaller portion of both applications before going on to tackle the MEMORY application.

The QueryMemory function will query 32MB of memory starting at ulStartAddress. We stop at 32MB because our list box can only hold so many entries. This function will check for all the features of paged memory allocation, as well as correct for a couple of OS/2 quirks.

We begin by calculating our ending address and ensuring that it is less than our 512MB limit. We now loop until we have reached the end of our range. The call to DosQueryMem queries the maximum memory size starting at our current address. Remember that if the address queried is the first page of a memory object, the PAG_BASE flag is set. If the page is not currently allocated, the PAG_FREE flag is set. Also, the DosQueryMem call will query pages until it finds a page with a memory flag different from the first page queried or until it finds the first page of the next allocated memory object.

Each call to DosQueryMem will start at the address in ulAddress and return the size of the memory pages that have the same flags as the first page at ulAddress. The ulFlags variable will contain those flags. Here, we discover a quirk in the DosQueryMem function. If the first page queried is free memory (PAG_FREE), the size of the memory object returned is not a believable value. In other words, we can be sure that only one page is marked as PAG_FREE. Do not use the size returned in ulSize as the size of contiguous PAG_FREE pages. For this reason, if the PAG_FREE bit is set, we reset ulSize to one 4KB page; otherwise, we round the size to a 4KB page boundary. At this point, we loop through the memory size returned, setting the appropriate page flags for allocated and committed pages.

We also output the type of memory object each 64KB block of memory represents (Shared, Free, or Private). At this point ulAddress contains the address of the first page past the memory object just processed. If the return code from DosQueryMem is ERROR_INVALID_ADDRESS, we are unable to query that address, so we skip that memory object and go to the next 64KB block.

Remember that a program can query memory only for the current process. It does not have access to another process's address space. This function, thus, only queries the memory allocated for the MemMap program. You, however, can use this function and add it to any program to query its allocated and committed memory.

The MEMORY Application

This sample application demonstrates allocating, committing, freeing, and changing the access rights to blocks of memory. It also utilizes the techniques from the MEMMAP program to display the status of each page of an allocated memory object.

MEMORY's Files

The files necessary to build the MEMORY application are the following:

MEMORY.C
MEMORY.H
MEMORY.DEF
MEMORY.RC
ALLOCATE.DLG
MEMORY.DLG
MEMORY.ICO

MEMORY.C

```
/* ----------------
Memory Program
Real-World Programming for OS/2
Copyright (c) 1994 Blain, Delimon, and English
---------------- */

#define INCL_WIN
#include <os2.h>
#include <stdio.h>
#include "memory.h"
#include "..\..\common\about.h"

#define WAIT_POINTER  WinSetPointer (HWND_DESKTOP, \
        WinQuerySysPointer (HWND_DESKTOP,SPTR_WAIT,FALSE));
#define ARROW_POINTER WinSetPointer (HWND_DESKTOP, \
        WinQuerySysPointer (HWND_DESKTOP,SPTR_ARROW,FALSE));

/* Exported Functions */

MRESULT EXPENTRY AllocateDlgProc (HWND,ULONG,MPARAM,MPARAM);
MRESULT EXPENTRY MainDlgProc (HWND,ULONG,MPARAM,MPARAM);

/* Local Functions */

VOID  CenterWindow (HWND);
VOID  ChangeAccessRights (USHORT);
VOID  ChangeCommitState (BOOL);
PSZ   FormatMemListItem (PVOID,LONG,ULONG,ULONG);
PSZ   FormatPageListItem (PVOID,ULONG);
VOID  MemError (PSZ);
ULONG ParseItem (PSZ,ULONG);
VOID  QueryMemory (SHORT);

HAB   hab;
CHAR  szTitle[64];
char  szListItem[40];
char  szPageItem[20];
HWND  hWndFrame,        /* Application Frame window handle */
```

```
HWND  hWndMemList,           /* Memory List box window handle    */
HWND  hWndPageList,          /* Page List box window handle      */
BOOL  bCommitted = FALSE;   /* Current settings in list box     */
BOOL  bShared    = FALSE;
BOOL  bRead      = TRUE;
BOOL  bWrite     = TRUE;
BOOL  bExecute   = TRUE;
BOOL  bTiled     = FALSE;

#define FONTNAMELEN 21   /* length + 1 */
CHAR  szListboxFont[] = "10.System Monospaced";

/* Undocumented menu message */
#define MM_QUERYITEMBYPOS      0x01f3
#define MAKE_16BIT_POINTER(p)  \
      ((PVOID)MAKEULONG(LOUSHORT(p),(HIUSHORT(p) << 3) | 7))

int main()
{
   HMQ   hmq;
   QMSG  qmsg;

   hab = WinInitialize (0);
   hmq = WinCreateMsgQueue (hab, 0);

   WinLoadString (hab, 0, ID_APPNAME, sizeof(szTitle),
                  szTitle);

   hWndFrame = WinLoadDlg (HWND_DESKTOP, HWND_DESKTOP,
   MainDlgProc, 0, ID_APPNAME, NULL);
   WinSendMsg (hWndFrame, WM_SETICON,
         (MPARAM)WinLoadPointer (HWND_DESKTOP, 0,
         ID_APPNAME), NULL);

   while (WinGetMsg (hab, &qmsg, 0, 0, 0))
      WinDispatchMsg (hab, &qmsg);

   WinDestroyWindow (hWndFrame);
   WinDestroyMsgQueue (hmq);
   WinTerminate (hab);
   return (0);
}

VOID AddAboutToSystemMenu(HWND hWndFrame)
{
   MENUITEM mi;
   HWND     hWndSysSubMenu;

   WinSendMsg (WinWindowFromID (hWndFrame, FID_SYSMENU),
         MM_QUERYITEMBYPOS, 0L, MAKE_16BIT_POINTER(&mi));
   hWndSysSubMenu = mi.hwndSubMenu;
   mi.iPosition   = MIT_END;
   mi.afStyle     = MIS_SEPARATOR;
   mi.afAttribute = 0;
   mi.id          = -1;
   mi.hwndSubMenu = 0;
```

```
   mi.hItem       = 0;
   WinSendMsg (hWndSysSubMenu, MM_INSERTITEM, MPFROMP (&mi),
               NULL);
   mi.afStyle     = MIS_TEXT;
   mi.id          = IDM_ABOUT;
   WinSendMsg (hWndSysSubMenu, MM_INSERTITEM, MPFROMP (&mi),
               "About...");
   return;
}

VOID CenterWindow (HWND hWnd)
{
   ULONG ulScrWidth, ulScrHeight;
   RECTL Rectl;

   ulScrWidth  = WinQuerySysValue (HWND_DESKTOP,
                 SV_CXSCREEN);
   ulScrHeight = WinQuerySysValue (HWND_DESKTOP,
                 SV_CYSCREEN);
   WinQueryWindowRect (hWnd,&Rectl);
   WinSetWindowPos (hWnd, HWND_TOP,
         (ulScrWidth-Rectl.xRight)/2,
         (ulScrHeight-Rectl.yTop)/2, 0, 0,
         SWP_MOVE | SWP_ACTIVATE);
   return;
}

PSZ FormatMemListItem (PVOID pMem, LONG lAllocRequest,
               ULONG ulAllocated, ULONG ulCommitted)
{
   sprintf (szListItem,"%08lx %8lx %8lx %8lx",
         (ULONG)pMem, (ULONG)lAllocRequest, ulAllocated,
         ulCommitted);
   WinUpper (hab, 0, 0, szListItem);
   return (szListItem);
}

PSZ FormatPageListItem (PVOID pMem, ULONG ulFlags)
{
   sprintf (szPageItem, "%08lx       ", pMem);
   szPageItem[9]  =
         (CHAR)(ulFlags & PAG_READ    ? 'R' : ' ');
   szPageItem[10] =
         (CHAR)(ulFlags & PAG_WRITE   ? 'W' : ' ');
   szPageItem[11] =
         (CHAR)(ulFlags & PAG_EXECUTE ? 'E' : ' ');
   szPageItem[12] =
         (CHAR)(ulFlags & PAG_COMMIT  ? 'C' : ' ');
   szPageItem[13] =
         (CHAR)(ulFlags & PAG_SHARED  ? 'S' : ' ');
   WinUpper (hab, 0, 0, szPageItem);
   return (szPageItem);
}

VOID MemError (PSZ pszMessage)
{
```

```
   WinMessageBox (HWND_DESKTOP, hWndFrame, pszMessage,
            "Memory Allocation", 0, MB_ERROR ¦ MB_OK);
   return;
}

ULONG ParseItem (PSZ szItem, ULONG CurPos)
{
   ULONG EndPos = CurPos + 8;
   ULONG ulMem  = 0;
   for (; CurPos < EndPos; CurPos++)
   {
      if (szItem[CurPos] != ' ')
         ulMem = ulMem*16 +
         ((szItem[CurPos] <= '9') ? (szItem[CurPos] - '0') :
         (szItem[CurPos] - 'A' + 10));
   }
   return (ulMem);
}

VOID ChangeAccessRights (USHORT usRights)
{
   ULONG ulAddress;
   SHORT sSel     = -1;
   ULONG ulFlags = 0L;
   BOOL  bError  = FALSE;

   WAIT_POINTER
   ulFlags = (ULONG)(usRights & 0x0007);
   while ((sSel = (SHORT)WinSendMsg (hWndPageList,
         LM_QUERYSELECTION, MPFROMSHORT(sSel),
         (MPARAM)NULL)) != LIT_NONE)
   {
      WinQueryLboxItemText (hWndPageList, sSel, szPageItem,
            20);
      ulAddress = ParseItem(szPageItem, 0);
      if (!DosSetMem ((PVOID)ulAddress, 0x1000, ulFlags))
      {
         ULONG ulNewFlags;
         ULONG ulSize = 0x1000;
         DosQueryMem ((PVOID)ulAddress, &ulSize,
               &ulNewFlags);
         WinSetLboxItemText (hWndPageList, sSel,
               FormatPageListItem ((PVOID)ulAddress,
               ulNowFlags));
      }
      else
      {
         char szError[40];
         if (szPageItem[12] != 'C')
         {
            if (!bError)
               MemError (
      "Cannot change access rights of decommitted pages");
            bError = TRUE;
         }
         else
```

```
            if (!bError)
               MemError (
                  "Unable to add any more list items");
            bError = TRUE;
         }
         ulAddress += 0x1000;
         ulSize    -= 0x1000;
      }
      ulSize      = 0xFFFFFFFF;
   }
   WinEnableWindowUpdate (hWndPageList, TRUE);
   WinSendMsg (hWndPageList, LM_SELECTITEM, (MPARAM)0L,
            (MPARAM)TRUE);
   sprintf (&szListItem[18], "%8lx %8lx", ulAllocated,
            ulCommitted);
   WinUpper (hab, 0, 0, szListItem);
   WinSetLboxItemText (hWndMemList, sSel, szListItem);
   ARROW_POINTER

   return;
}

MRESULT EXPENTRY AllocateDlgProc (HWND hWnd, ULONG msg,
MPARAM mp1, MPARAM mp2)
{
   LONG lMemAlloc;

   switch (msg)
   {
      case WM_INITDLG:
         CenterWindow (hWnd);
         WinCheckButton (hWnd,
            (bCommitted ? IDB_COMMITTED : IDB_UNCOMMITTED),
               TRUE);
         WinCheckButton (hWnd,
            (bShared ? IDB_SHARED : IDB_NONSHARED),TRUE);
         WinCheckButton (hWnd, IDB_READ,    bRead);
         WinCheckButton (hWnd, IDB_WRITE,   bWrite);
         WinCheckButton (hWnd, IDB_EXECUTE, bExecute);
         WinCheckButton (hWnd, IDB_TILED,   bTiled);
         WinSendDlgItemMsg (hWnd, IDB_NUMBYTES,
               SPBM_SETTEXTLIMIT,(MPARAM)7, (MPARAM)0);
         WinSendDlgItemMsg (hWnd, IDB_NUMBYTES,
               SPBM_SETLIMITS,
               (MPARAM)0x00100000,(MPARAM)1L);
         WinSendDlgItemMsg (hWnd, IDB_NUMBYTES,
               SPBM_SETCURRENTVALUE,(MPARAM)1,(MPARAM)0L);
         WinSendDlgItemMsg (hWnd, IDB_REPEAT,
               SPBM_SETTEXTLIMIT,(MPARAM)4, (MPARAM)0);
         WinSendDlgItemMsg (hWnd, IDB_REPEAT,
               SPBM_SETLIMITS,(MPARAM)9999L,(MPARAM)1L);
         WinSendDlgItemMsg (hWnd, IDB_REPEAT,
               SPBM_SETCURRENTVALUE, (MPARAM)1,(MPARAM)0L);
         WinSetFocus (HWND_DESKTOP,
         WinWindowFromID (hWnd, IDB_NUMBYTES));
         return ((MRESULT)TRUE);
```

```
case WM_COMMAND:
   switch (LOUSHORT(mp1))
   {
      case DID_OK:
         WinSendDlgItemMsg (hWnd, IDB_NUMBYTES,
            SPBM_QUERYVALUE,(MPARAM)&lMemAlloc,
            (MPARAM)0L);
         if (lMemAlloc)
         {
            ULONG flags = 0L;
            BOOL  bOkay;
            PVOID pMem;
            ULONG ulRepeat;

            if (lMemAlloc < 0)
               lMemAlloc = -lMemAlloc;
            bCommitted = WinQueryButtonCheckstate (hWnd, IDB_COMMITTED);
            bShared    = WinQueryButtonCheckstate (hWnd, IDB_SHARED);
            bRead      = WinQueryButtonCheckstate (hWnd, IDB_READ);
            bWrite     = WinQueryButtonCheckstate (hWnd, IDB_WRITE);
            bExecute   = WinQueryButtonCheckstate (hWnd, IDB_EXECUTE);
            bTiled     = WinQueryButtonCheckstate (hWnd, IDB_TILED);
            if (bCommitted)
               flags |= PAG_COMMIT;
            if (bShared)
               flags |= OBJ_GETTABLE | OBJ_GIVEABLE;
            if (bRead)
               flags |= PAG_READ;
            if (bWrite)
               flags |= PAG_WRITE;
            if (bExecute)
               flags |= PAG_EXECUTE;
            if (bTiled)
               flags |= OBJ_TILE;

            WinSendDlgItemMsg (hWnd, IDB_REPEAT,
               SPBM_QUERYVALUE,
               (MPARAM)&ulRepeat, (MPARAM)0L);

            while (ulRepeat--)
            {
               if (!bShared)
                  bOkay = !DosAllocMem ((PPVOID)&pMem,
                        lMemAlloc,flags);
               else
              bOkay =!DosAllocSharedMem((PPVOID)&pMem,
                      NULL,lMemAlloc, flags);
               if (bOkay)
               {
                  SHORT sSel;
            sSel=(SHORT)WinInsertLboxItem(hWndMemList,
                  LIT_SORTASCENDING,
                  FormatMemListItem (pMem, lMemAlloc,
                     0L, 0L));
                  QueryMemory (sSel);
                  WinSendMsg (hWndMemList,
```

```
                        LM_SELECTITEM,
                        (MPARAM)sSel, (MPARAM)TRUE);
                  }
                  else
                  {
                  MemError ("Unable to allocate memory");
                     break;
                  }
               }
            }

      /* FALL THROUGH */

         case DID_CANCEL:
            WinDismissDlg (hWnd, TRUE);
            return (0);
      }
      break;
   }
   return (WinDefDlgProc (hWnd, msg, mp1, mp2));
}


MRESULT EXPENTRY MainDlgProc (HWND hWnd, ULONG msg,
      MPARAM mp1, MPARAM mp2)
{
   SHORT   sSel;
   RECTL   Rectl;
   BOOL    bHandled       = TRUE;
   MRESULT mReturn        = 0;

   static  HWND hMenus[4] = { 0, 0, 0, 0 };

   switch (msg)
   {
      case WM_INITDLG:
         CenterWindow (hWnd);
         hWndMemList  = WinWindowFromID (hWnd, IDL_MEMLIST);
         hWndPageList = WinWindowFromID (hWnd,
               IDL_PAGELIST);

         /* Set the system monospaced font for the listboxes */
         WinSetPresParam (hWndMemList,
               PP_FONTNAMESIZE, FONTNAMELEN, szListboxFont);
         WinSetPresParam (hWndPageList,
               PP_FONTNAMESIZE, FONTNAMELEN, szListboxFont);

         /* Load the popup menus */
         hMenus[0] = WinLoadMenu (HWND_OBJECT, 0,
               FREE_MENU);
         hMenus[1] = WinLoadMenu (HWND_OBJECT, 0,
               SELECT_MENU);
         hMenus[2] = WinLoadMenu (HWND_OBJECT, 0,
               STATE_MENU);
         hMenus[3] = WinLoadMenu (HWND_OBJECT, 0,
               RIGHTS_MENU);
```

```
        /* Add the About menu item to the system menu */
        AddAboutToSystemMenu (hWnd);
        break;

    case WM_CONTROL:
        switch (LOUSHORT(mp1))
        {
            case IDL_MEMLIST:
                if (HIUSHORT(mp1) == LN_SELECT)
                    QueryMemory ((SHORT)WinQueryLboxSelectedItem((HWND)mp2));
                break;
        }
        break;

    case WM_COMMAND:
    case WM_SYSCOMMAND:
        switch (LOUSHORT(mp1))
        {
            case IDB_ALLOCATE:
                WinDlgBox (HWND_DESKTOP, hWnd,
                    AllocateDlgProc,
                    0, IDD_ALLOCATE, NULL);
                break;

            case IDB_SELECT:
            case IDB_FREE:
            case IDB_STATE:
            case IDB_RIGHTS:
                WinQueryWindowRect (WinWindowFromID(hWnd,
                    LOUSHORT(mp1)), &Rectl);
                WinMapWindowPoints (WinWindowFromID(hWnd,
                    LOUSHORT(mp1)), hWnd, (PPOINTL)&Rectl, 2);
                WinPopupMenu (hWnd, hWnd,
                    hMenus[LOUSHORT(mp1) / 100 - 1],
                    Rectl.xLeft, Rectl.yTop,
                    LOUSHORT(mp1) + 1,
                    PU_HCONSTRAIN | PU_VCONSTRAIN |
                    PU_KEYBOARD | PU_MOUSEBUTTON1 |
                    PU_SELECTITEM);
                break;

            case IDM_SELECT_NONE:
                WinSendMsg (hWndPageList, LM_SELECTITEM,
                    (MPARAM)LIT_NONE, 0L);
                break;

            case IDM_SELECT_ALL:
                {
                    SHORT sCount;
                    sCount = (SHORT)WinQueryLboxCount (hWndPageList);
                    while (sCount--)
                        WinSendMsg (hWndPageList,
                        LM_SELECTITEM,(MPARAM)sCount,
                        (MPARAM)TRUE);
                }
                break;
```

```
case IDM_COMMIT_SELECTED:
case IDM_DECOMMIT_SELECTED:
   ChangeCommitState (LOUSHORT(mp1) == IDM_COMMIT_SELECTED);
   break;

case IDM_READ:
case IDM_WRITE:
case IDM_EXECUTE:
case IDM_READWRITE:
case IDM_READEXECUTE:
case IDM_WRITEEXECUTE:
case IDM_READWRITEEXECUTE:
   ChangeAccessRights (LOUSHORT(mp1));
   break;

case IDM_FREE_SELECTED:
   if ( (sSel=(SHORT)WinQueryLboxSelectedItem (hWndMemList)) != LIT_NONE)
   {
      char szMem[9];
      ULONG ulMem;

      WinQueryLboxItemText (hWndMemList, sSel,
         szMem, 9);
      ulMem = ParseItem (szMem,0);
      if (!DosFreeMem ((PVOID)ulMem))
      {
         WinDeleteLboxItem (hWndMemList, sSel);
         WinSendMsg (hWndPageList, LM_DELETEALL,
            0L, 0L);
         if (sSel >= (SHORT)WinQueryLboxCount(hWndMemList))
            sSel--;
         WinSendMsg (hWndMemList, LM_SELECTITEM,
            (MPARAM)sSel, (MPARAM)TRUE);
      }
      else
         MemError ("Error freeing memory");
   }
   break;

case IDM_FREE_ALL:
   {
      char szMem[9];
      ULONG ulMem;
      while (WinQueryLboxItemText (hWndMemList,
            0, szMem, 9) >    0)
      {
         ulMem = ParseItem (szMem,0);
         if (!DosFreeMem ((PVOID)ulMem))
            WinDeleteLboxItem (hWndMemList, 0);
         else
         {
            MemError ("Error freeing memory");
            break;
         }
      }
```

```
                WinSendMsg (hWndPageList, LM_DELETEALL,
                     0L, 0L);
                break;
             }

          case IDM_ABOUT:
             DisplayAbout (hWnd, szTitle);
             break;

          case SC_CLOSE:
             WinDestroyWindow (hMenus[0]);
             WinDestroyWindow (hMenus[1]);
             WinDestroyWindow (hMenus[2]);
             WinDestroyWindow (hMenus[3]);
             WinPostMsg (hWnd, WM_COMMAND,
                (MPARAM)IDM_FREE_ALL, 0L);
             WinPostMsg (hWnd, WM_QUIT, 0L, 0L);
             break;

          default:
             bHandled = (msg == WM_COMMAND);
       }
       break;

    default:
       bHandled = FALSE;
       break;
 }

 if (!bHandled)
    mReturn = WinDefDlgProc (hWnd, msg, mp1, mp2);

 return (mReturn);
}
```

MEMORY.H

```
/* ----------------
Memory Header File
Real-World Programming for OS/2
Copyright (c) 1994 Blain, Delimon, and English
---------------- */

#define ID_APPNAME              1
#define IDD_ALLOCATE            2

#define IDL_MEMLIST            10
#define IDL_PAGELIST           11
#define IDB_ALLOCATE           12
#define IDB_FREE              100
#define IDB_SELECT            200
#define IDB_STATE             300
#define IDB_RIGHTS            400
```

```
#define IDB_NUMBYTES            20
#define IDB_COMMITTED           21
#define IDB_UNCOMMITTED         22
#define IDB_SHARED              23
#define IDB_NONSHARED           24
#define IDB_READ                25
#define IDB_WRITE               26
#define IDB_EXECUTE             27
#define IDB_TILED               28
#define IDB_REPEAT              29

#define FREE_MENU              100
#define SELECT_MENU            200
#define STATE_MENU             300
#define RIGHTS_MENU            400

#define IDM_FREE_SELECTED      101
#define IDM_FREE_ALL           102
#define IDM_SELECT_ALL         201
#define IDM_SELECT_NONE        202
#define IDM_COMMIT_SELECTED    301
#define IDM_DECOMMIT_SELECTED 302
#define IDM_READ               401
#define IDM_WRITE              402
#define IDM_READWRITE          403
#define IDM_EXECUTE            404

#define IDM_READEXECUTE 405
#define IDM_WRITEEXECUTE 406
#define IDM_READWRITEEXECUTE 407
#define IDM_ABOUT 500
```

MEMORY.RC

```
/* ---------------
Memory Resource File
Real-World Programming for OS/2
Copyright (c) 1994 Blain, Delimon, and English
--------------- */

#include <os2.h>
#include "memory.h"

ICON ID_APPNAME MEMORY.ICO

STRINGTABLE LOADONCALL MOVEABLE
BEGIN
   ID_APPNAME      "Memory Allocation Program"
END

rcinclude memory.dlg
rcinclude allocate.dlg
rcinclude ..\..\common\about.dlg
```

ALLOCATE.DLG

```
/* ----------------
Memory Allocation Dialog
Real-World Programming for OS/2
Copyright (c) 1994 Blain, Delimon, and English
---------------- */

DLGTEMPLATE IDD_ALLOCATE LOADONCALL MOVEABLE DISCARDABLE
BEGIN
   DIALOG  "Allocate Memory", IDD_ALLOCATE, -5, 53, 264, 72,
           WS_VISIBLE, FCF_SYSMENU ¦
           FCF_TITLEBAR
   BEGIN
      LTEXT            "Number of bytes", -1, 3, 58, 72, 8
      CONTROL          "", IDB_NUMBYTES, 76, 56, 64, 12,
                      WC_SPINBUTTON,
                      SPBS_NUMERICONLY ¦ SPBS_MASTER ¦
                      SPBS_JUSTRIGHT ¦ SPBS_FASTSPIN ¦
                      WS_TABSTOP ¦ WS_VISIBLE
      LTEXT            "Repeat", -1, 144, 58, 36, 8
      CONTROL          "", IDB_REPEAT,  181, 56, 30, 12,
                      WC_SPINBUTTON,
                      SPBS_NUMERICONLY ¦ SPBS_MASTER ¦
                      SPBS_JUSTRIGHT ¦ SPBS_FASTSPIN ¦
                      WS_TABSTOP ¦ WS_VISIBLE
      GROUPBOX         "Type",          -1, 3, 24, 87, 31
      AUTORADIOBUTTON "Committed",   IDB_COMMITTED, 9, 37,
                        58, 10, WS_TABSTOP
      AUTORADIOBUTTON "Uncommitted", IDB_UNCOMMITTED, 9, 27,
                        68, 10, WS_TABSTOP
      GROUPBOX         "Shareability",  -1, 97, 24, 77, 31
      AUTORADIOBUTTON "Shared",      IDB_SHARED, 101, 37,
                         44, 10, WS_TABSTOP
      AUTORADIOBUTTON "NonShared",   IDB_NONSHARED, 101, 27,
                         61, 10, WS_TABSTOP
      GROUPBOX         "Access Rights", -1, 181, 15, 77, 40
      AUTOCHECKBOX     "Read",         IDB_READ, 186, 37, 40,
                         10
      AUTOCHECKBOX     "Write",        IDB_WRITE, 186, 27, 40,
                         10
      AUTOCHECKBOX     "Execute",      IDB_EXECUTE, 186, 17,
                         40, 10
      AUTOCHECKBOX     "Tiled",        IDB_TILED, 102, 7, 31,
                         10, WS_GROUP
      DEFPUSHBUTTON    "OK",           DID_OK, 4, 4, 40, 14,
                         WS_GROUP
      PUSHBUTTON       "Cancel",       DID_CANCEL, 47, 4, 40,
                         14
   END
END
```

MEMORY.DLG

```
/* ---------------
Memory Dialog
Real-World Programming for OS/2
Copyright (c) 1994 Blain, Delimon, and English
--------------- */

MENU FREE_MENU PRELOAD
BEGIN
   MENUITEM "Free Selected Item", IDM_FREE_SELECTED
   MENUITEM "Free All Items",     IDM_FREE_ALL
END

MENU SELECT_MENU PRELOAD
BEGIN
   MENUITEM "Select All",   IDM_SELECT_ALL
   MENUITEM "Select None",  IDM_SELECT_NONE
END

MENU STATE_MENU PRELOAD
BEGIN
   MENUITEM "Commit Selected Pages",   IDM_COMMIT_SELECTED
   MENUITEM "Decommit Selected Pages", IDM_DECOMMIT_SELECTED
END

MENU RIGHTS_MENU PRELOAD
BEGIN
   MENUITEM "Read",                IDM_READ
   MENUITEM "Write",               IDM_WRITE
   MENUITEM "Execute",             IDM_EXECUTE
   MENUITEM "Read/Write",          IDM_READWRITE
   MENUITEM "Read/Execute",        IDM_READEXECUTE
   MENUITEM "Write/Execute",       IDM_WRITEEXECUTE
   MENUITEM "Read/Write/Execute",  IDM_READWRITEEXECUTE
END

DLGTEMPLATE ID_APPNAME LOADONCALL MOVEABLE DISCARDABLE
BEGIN
   DIALOG  "Memory Allocation", ID_APPNAME, 5, 11, 330, 153,
           WS_VISIBLE | FS_DLGBORDER,
           FCF_SYSMENU | FCF_TITLEBAR | FCF_DLGBORDER |
           FCF_TASKLIST | FCF_ICON;
   BEGIN
      LTEXT           "Address",    -1,   9, 137, 37, 8
      LTEXT           "Requested",  -1,  55, 137, 49, 8
      LTEXT           "Allocated",  -1, 109, 137, 41, 8
      LTEXT           "Committed",  -1, 156, 137, 48, 8
      LTEXT           "Address",    -1, 223, 137, 37, 8
      LTEXT           "Flags",      -1, 283, 137, 26, 8
      LISTBOX         IDL_MEMLIST, 5, 22, 208, 114,
                      WS_GROUP | WS_TABSTOP
      DEFPUSHBUTTON   "Allocate", IDB_ALLOCATE,   4, 4, 50,
                        14, WS_GROUP | WS_TABSTOP
      PUSHBUTTON      "Free",     IDB_FREE,      57, 4, 50,
                        14, WS_TABSTOP
```

```
        LISTBOX          IDL_PAGELIST, 222, 22, 102, 114,
                           WS_GROUP ¦ WS_TABSTOP ¦
                           LS_MULTIPLESEL ¦ LS_EXTENDEDSEL
        PUSHBUTTON       "Select",   IDB_SELECT,    171, 4, 50,
                           14, WS_GROUP ¦ WS_TABSTOP
        PUSHBUTTON       "State",    IDB_STATE,     224, 4, 50,
                           14, WS_TABSTOP
        PUSHBUTTON       "Rights",   IDB_RIGHTS,    277, 4, 50,
                           14, WS_TABSTOP
    END
END
```

MEMORY.DEF

```
NAME            MEMORY   WINDOWAPI
DESCRIPTION     'Memory Program (c) Blain, Delimon, & English, 1994'
PROTMODE
HEAPSIZE        4096
STACKSIZE       16384
EXPORTS         MainDlgProc
                AllocateDlgProc
```

Using the MEMORY Sample Application

The MEMORY application demonstrates committing, freeing, and changing the access rights to blocks of memory. Its use is also fairly explanatory. Remember though that you are making the changes only within a block of memory that is available to the MEMORY application. After starting the memory application, press the allocate button to allocate blocks of memory. The display for the allocated memory will appear similar to that shown in Figure 11.6.

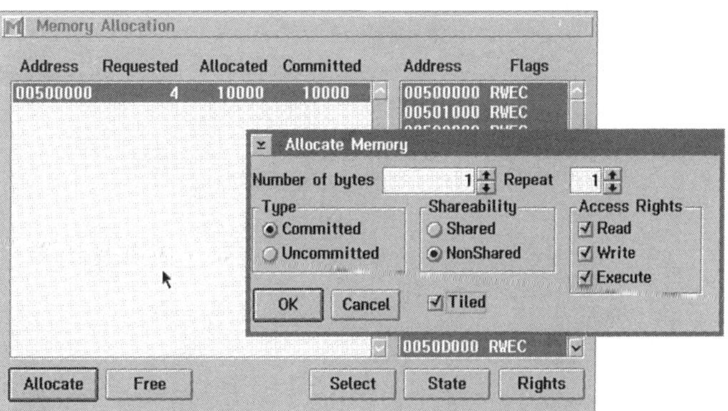

Figure 11.6.
MEMORY application.

Practice allocating both committed and uncommitted blocks of memory. Notice what state a particular block of memory must be in before its access rights can be changed. Notice also that the successive addresses for committed blocks of memory that are not shared grow upward.

Addresses for successive blocks of shared memory grow downward. This behavior is in keeping with how these blocks of memory are allocated by the system.

Understanding MEMORY's Code

Two macros will be used to set our current pointer. When we begin a time-consuming process, we will set the pointer to the SPTR_WAIT pointer and, when done, reset it to the SPTR_ARROW pointer:

```
#define WAIT_POINTER  WinSetPointer (HWND_DESKTOP, \
      WinQuerySysPointer (HWND_DESKTOP,SPTR_WAIT,FALSE));
#define ARROW_POINTER WinSetPointer (HWND_DESKTOP, \
      WinQuerySysPointer (HWND_DESKTOP,SPTR_ARROW,FALSE));
```

The CenterWindow function merely centers the dialog in the middle of the screen:

```
VOID CenterWindow (HWND hWnd)
{
   ULONG ulScrWidth, ulScrHeight;
   RECTL Rectl;

   ulScrWidth  = WinQuerySysValue (HWND_DESKTOP,
            SV_CXSCREEN);
   ulScrHeight = WinQuerySysValue (HWND_DESKTOP,
            SV_CYSCREEN);
   WinQueryWindowRect (hWnd,&Rectl);
   WinSetWindowPos (hWnd, HWND_TOP,
         (ulScrWidth-Rectl.xRight)/2,
         (ulScrHeight-Rectl.yTop)/2, 0, 0,
         SWP_MOVE | SWP_ACTIVATE);
   return;
}
```

To format our memory list items in the list box, the FormatMemListItem function takes the memory address, amount of memory originally requested, amount of memory actually allocated, and amount of memory currently committed and formats them using the sprintf function:

```
PSZ FormatMemListItem (PVOID pMem, LONG lAllocRequest,
      ULONG ulAllocated, ULONG ulCommitted)
{
   sprintf (szListItem,"%08lx %8lx %8lx %8lx",
         (ULONG)pMem, (ULONG)lAllocRequest, ulAllocated,
         ulCommitted);
   WinUpper (hab, 0, 0, szListItem);
   return (szListItem);
}
```

Likewise, the FormatPageListItem function takes the memory address and current page flags and formats them using the sprintf function. The memory page flags are checked individually and set in the string:

```
PSZ FormatPageListItem (PVOID pMem, ULONG ulFlags)
{
```

```
   sprintf (szPageItem, "%08lx       ", pMem);
   szPageItem[9]=(CHAR)(ulFlags & PAG_READ    ? 'R' : ' ');
   szPageItem[10]=(CHAR)(ulFlags & PAG_WRITE   ? 'W' : ' ');
   szPageItem[11]=(CHAR)(ulFlags & PAG_EXECUTE ? 'E' : ' ');
   szPageItem[12]=(CHAR)(ulFlags & PAG_COMMIT  ? 'C' : ' ');
   szPageItem[13]=(CHAR)(ulFlags & PAG_SHARED  ? 'S' : ' ');
   WinUpper (hab, 0, 0, szPageItem);
   return (szPageItem);
}
```

The MemError function is merely a consistent way for us to output our error messages using the WinMessageBox function:

```
VOID MemError (PSZ pszMessage)
{
   WinMessageBox (HWND_DESKTOP, hWndFrame, pszMessage,
      "Memory Allocation", 0, MB_ERROR ¦ MB_OK);
   return;
}
```

When a list box item is selected, we need to determine what memory address has been selected. Because each list box item is formatted as a string, the ParseItem function can be used to convert any portion of a string from its hexadecimal string value to an equivalent binary value. The first parameter szItem is the string to be parsed. The second parameter CurPos is the offset in szItem to start the conversion. The maximum size of our hexadecimal substrings is eight characters, so we look at the eight characters starting at position CurPos:

```
ULONG ParseItem (PSZ szItem, ULONG CurPos)
{
   ULONG EndPos = CurPos + 8;
   ULONG ulMem  = 0;
   for (; CurPos < EndPos; CurPos++)
   {
      if (szItem[CurPos] != ' ')
         ulMem = ulMem*16 +
         ((szItem[CurPos] <= '9') ? (szItem[CurPos] - '0') :
         (szItem[CurPos] - 'A' + 10));
   }
   return (ulMem);
}
```

The ChangeAccessRights function is used to set the access rights of the selected memory pages. The only parameter to this function is the new access rights to be set. Our menu items have conveniently been defined such that the low byte of their identifier is the new access rights, so we can just AND this identifier with 0x0007 to get the new access rights. We then loop, querying the next selected item in the memory page list until there are no more selected. Querying the text for each item, we call ParseItem to retrieve the memory address for the selected page. The call to DosSetMem will attempt to set the access rights of the page. Because we can change the access rights only for a committed page, the DosSetMem call will fail if the page is not committed. If the DosSetMem call is successful, we query the access rights of the page and reformat the item to be updated in the list box. It is necessary to query the memory again because decommitting a page will reset the access rights to those defined when the memory was allocated.

The ChangeCommitState function is used either to commit or decommit the selected memory pages. The only parameter is a flag indicating if the memory is to be committed or decommitted. Because the list box text for the memory list box has already been retrieved in QueryMemory, we can just call ParseItem on szListItem to get the current amount of committed memory for the selected item. This enables us to update the amount of committed memory as we make the updates.

We then loop, querying the next selected item in the memory page list until there are no more selected. Querying the text for each item, we call ParseItem to retrieve the memory address for the selected page. Because we want to leave the access rights unchanged for the page, if we are committing memory, we must set the access rights to their current settings. We can either call DosQueryMem to get them or look at the current flags in the list box string. The call to DosSetMem will attempt to commit or decommit the page. If the call to DosSetMem is successful, we query the memory to get its new flags. When a page is decommitted, its access rights are reset to those defined when the memory was allocated. We then update the amount of committed memory. When all selected pages have been processed, we must update the amount of committed memory in the memory list box.

The QueryMemory function is used to retrieve the current flags for each page of memory for each allocated memory object. The input to this function is the index in the list box of the selected memory object. We begin by querying the text for the selected item and deleting all the items in the page list box. The call to WinEnableWindowUpdate tells PM not to repaint the list box as we are making our updates. This prevents the window from repainting every time we add a new item. When we are done, we will reenable the painting of the list box.

The call to ParseItem converts the address portion of the string, so we have the base address for the memory object. We then repeatedly make calls to DosQueryMem to query the memory flags. Remember, if the address queried is the first page of a memory object, the PAG_BASE flag is set. If the page is not currently allocated, the PAG_FREE flag is set. Also, the DosQueryMem call will query pages until it finds a page with a different memory flag than the first page queried or it finds the first page of the next allocated memory object. Our loop will, thus, repeat until we either reach the end of the currently allocated object (PAG_FREE) or we reach the beginning of the next allocated memory object (PAG_BASE). We want to ignore the check for PAG_BASE on the first page because it will have the PAG_BASE flag set.

Each call to DosQueryMem will start at the address in ulAddress and return the size of the memory pages that have the same flags as the first page at ulAddress. The ulFlags variable will contain those flags. Our total allocated count can be incremented by ulSize, and ulCommitted is incremented if the PAG_COMMIT flag is set. We then add a page entry to the pages list box for each page in the queried memory. When the memory object has been completely queried, we reenable the list box updates and select the first item in the list box. We also update the allocated and committed totals in the memory list box.

AllocateDlgProc is the dialog function for the memory allocation dialog. When we receive the WM_INITDLG message, we can initialize all the controls in the dialog window. Because we save the last settings of each button from the last time the dialog was displayed, we use those values to either check or uncheck the buttons. Our spinners are initialized for their size, limits, and current value. Our dialog enables you to specify the amount of memory to allocate and its access rights, whether to commit the memory when it is allocated, whether it is private or shared memory, and whether it should be allocated out of the tiled arena. We also have the ability to repeat the memory request up to 9,999 times. When the WM_COMMAND message is received with the OK button pressed, we query the values input and current state of the buttons. Then, for each memory allocation request (the repeat count), we make the call to either DosAllocMem (private memory allocation) or DosAllocSharedMem (shared memory allocation). If the allocation is successful, we add an entry to the memory list box and call QueryMemory to fill the pages list box. When all memory requests have been made, we exit the dialog.

MainDlgProc is the dialog function for the main dialog of this program. When we receive the WM_INITDLG message, we query the handles and set the font for our two list boxes. We set the font to a monospaced font so that the columns in the list box align properly. The four different pop-up menus are also loaded at this time. If we receive a WM_CONTROL message from the memory list box and an item has been selected, we call QueryMemory to update the pages list box with the pages for the selected memory object. We receive a WM_COMMAND message for each button pressed in the dialog. If the command is IDB_ALLOCATE, we display the memory allocation dialog. If the command is IDB_SELECT, IDB_FREE, IDB_STATE, or IDB_RIGHTS, we display the pop-up menu directly above the button. The identifiers for the buttons and menus are the same. If IDM_SELECT_NONE is selected, we send the LM_SELECTITEM message to the pages list box with LIT_NONE specified so that no items are selected. If IDM_SELECT_ALL is selected, we send the LM_SELECTITEM message to the pages list box for each item in the list box. If one of the commit options is selected, we call ChangeCommitState. If one of the access rights options is selected, we call ChangeAccessRights. If IDM_FREE_SELECTED is selected, we call DosFreeMem on the selected memory object and remove it from the list box. After deleting the item, we select a new item. If IDM_FREE_ALL is selected, we call DosFreeMem on each item in the list box and remove it from the list box.

```
/* ----------------
Memory Header File
Real-World Programming for OS/2
Copyright (c) 1994 Blain, Delimon, and English
---------------- */

#define ID_APPNAME            1
#define IDD_ALLOCATE          2

#define IDL_MEMLIST          10
#define IDL_PAGELIST         11
#define IDB_ALLOCATE         12
#define IDB_FREE            100
#define IDB_SELECT          200
#define IDB_STATE           300
#define IDB_RIGHTS          400
```

```
#define IDB_NUMBYTES            20
#define IDB_COMMITTED           21
#define IDB_UNCOMMITTED         22
#define IDB_SHARED              23
#define IDB_NONSHARED           24
#define IDB_READ                25
#define IDB_WRITE               26
#define IDB_EXECUTE             27
#define IDB_TILED               28
#define IDB_REPEAT              29

#define FREE_MENU              100
#define SELECT_MENU            200
#define STATE_MENU             300
#define RIGHTS_MENU            400

#define IDM_FREE_SELECTED      101
#define IDM_FREE_ALL           102
#define IDM_SELECT_ALL         201
#define IDM_SELECT_NONE        202
#define IDM_COMMIT_SELECTED    301
#define IDM_DECOMMIT_SELECTED 302
#define IDM_READ               401
#define IDM_WRITE              402
#define IDM_READWRITE          403
#define IDM_EXECUTE            404
#define IDM_READEXECUTE        405
#define IDM_WRITEEXECUTE       406
#define IDM_READWRITEEXECUTE   407
#define IDM_ABOUT              408
```

Chapter 12

Dynamic Link Libraries

What is a DLL and How Does it Work?

Dynamic Link Libraries (DLLs) form the foundation of OS/2. They provide the key components in making OS/2 and the Presentation Manager (PM) work with your application. The DLL's importance to OS/2 is shown in that most of OS/2 and the Presentation Manager are implemented as DLLs. This chapter focuses on this important feature of OS/2 and demonstrates how to take advantage of the power it provides.

A DLL is a collection of code and/or resources maintained in a separate executable-like file that can be used by your application. A DLL, however, is not executable: It cannot be run by itself, but its functions and resources can be used by applications linked to it. You can think of a DLL as an extension of your application, but it also can be shared by multiple processes.

The concept of DLLs must not to be confused with processes or threads, which are entirely separate, unrelated mechanisms. Using a DLL does not make your application multithreaded. A DLL is an extension of your application; it is extra code. The code in a DLL executes on behalf of your process, but the activity in that DLL is still single threaded, unless it is explicitly defined otherwise by you, the programmer.

Most programmers are already familiar with static linking. Static linking occurs when you link your application with an external library of code. In static linking, the library actually contains the object code implementing the functions in the library. When you link your application with a static library, the required object code is pulled into your executable and becomes part of the executable file. Every application linked to a particular static library has its own copy of the same object code. The same object code, thus, is replicated for every application and takes up additional disk space. When the application is executed, the same object code is replicated in memory, taking up space each time. This is just one of the problems of static linking. Another problem is that if the library needs to be updated to correct a problem in the code or to add new logic to a function, every application linked to the library must be relinked and redistributed.

Herein lies the beauty of DLLs. A DLL provides services to your application much like a static library does, but can be replaced or updated without changing or updating your application. In addition, because multiple processes can share the code of a DLL, the amount of disk space and memory required for a program to run is reduced. The library created for a DLL is called an import library. This is a smaller file which has an extension of LIB. It contains no code, but does contain information about the names of the functions in the library and the necessary information to complete the linking process. The object code resides in a separate DLL file. When the application is loaded into memory, the OS/2 loader loads the DLL into memory (if it isn't already in memory) and resolves the addresses of the calls into the DLL with the actual addresses.

The obvious benefit here is that a DLL can be updated and replaced on the system. Then, all applications immediately have the latest code executing from the DLL. You can also add new functions to the DLL, allowing new applications to call these functions without disturbing the existing applications that are using the DLL.

It may help to take a look at the process of static linking and compare it with dynamic linking. First, take a look at static linking as pictured in Figure 12.1. In creating an application, assume we are making some external calls into a static library. Although the concept is the same for any static library, we will use the C functions `strcpy` and `strcmp` as examples. In compiling our application, whenever a call to an external function is identified, the compiler inserts a record in the file describing the name of the function to call. Because it does not know the address of the function, the record contains an unresolved reference.

Figure 12.1.
An application object module.

Application Object Module

Unresolved symbols
_strcpy
_strcmp

Application code
...
CALL ____ ;_strcpy
...
CALL ____ ;_strcmp
...
CALL ____ ;_strcmp
...

Taking a look at the static library, we can see that the object code for the functions in the library is contained within the library. (See Figure 12.2.)

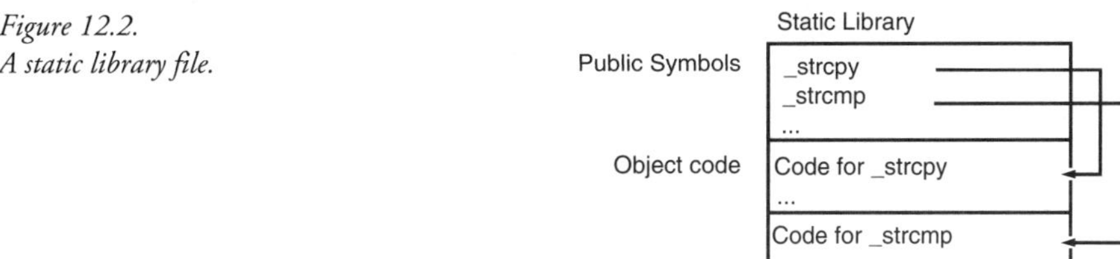

Figure 12.2.
A static library file.

During the linking process, the linker will look at the unresolved symbols in the application object module and search for those symbols in the libraries that it is linked to. When the linker locates a match, it resolves the symbol by copying the object code from the library into the executable file being constructed. The address of the function is then known, and all references to the external function are set to the new address of the function. (See Figure 12.3.)

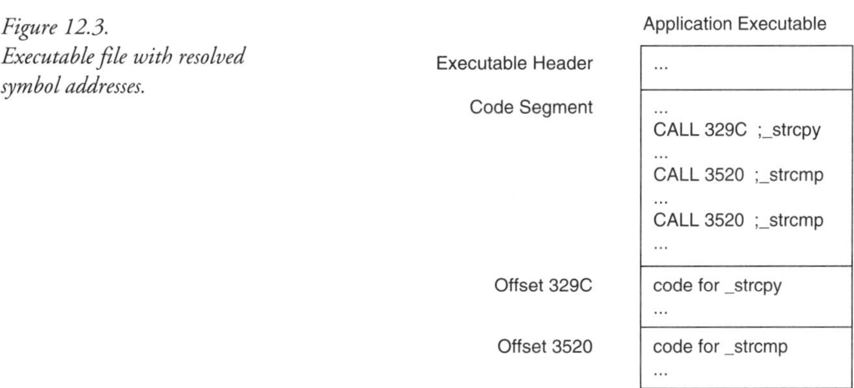

Figure 12.3.
Executable file with resolved symbol addresses.

The offsets shown are only arbitrary offsets and will depend on the actual size of the code. At this point, the executable is complete, and all the code is literally contained within it.

Compare this with dynamic linking. We will use our application object module shown previously. Let's assume we now have created a DLL that contains code for the `strcpy` and `strcmp` functions. This time, we use the import library created for the DLL. (See Figure 12.4.)

Notice that the import library contains no code. It does contain three items for each exported function: the name of the exported function, the name of the DLL containing the function, and the entry point for the function. The entry point can be either an ordinal or the internal name

of the function or both. We will look at how these entries are created in the next section. During the linking process, the linker will look at the un-resolved symbols in the application object module and search for those symbols in the libraries that it is linked to. When the linker locates a match this time, it resolves the symbol by inserting a relocation record into the executable. (See Figure 12.5.)

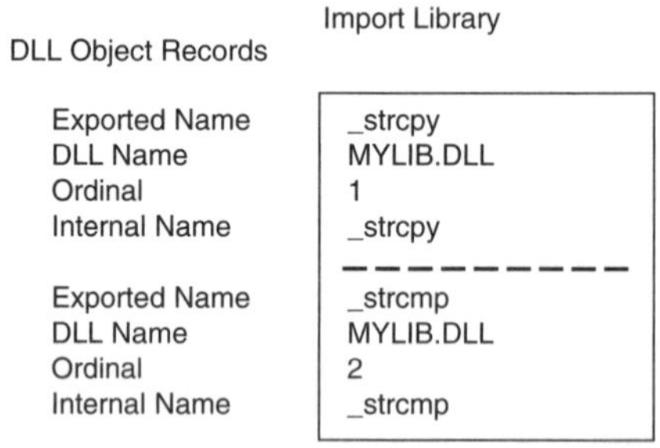

Figure 12.4.
An import library.

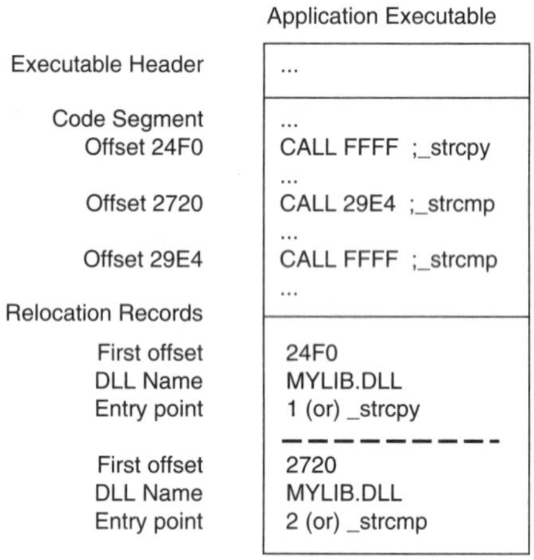

DLL Object Records	Import Library
Exported Name	_strcpy
DLL Name	MYLIB.DLL
Ordinal	1
Internal Name	_strcpy

Exported Name	_strcmp
DLL Name	MYLIB.DLL
Ordinal	2
Internal Name	_strcmp

Figure 12.5.
Executable file with DLL references.

	Application Executable
Executable Header	...
Code Segment	...
Offset 24F0	CALL FFFF ;_strcpy
	...
Offset 2720	CALL 29E4 ;_strcmp
	...
Offset 29E4	CALL FFFF ;_strcmp
	...
Relocation Records	
First offset	24F0
DLL Name	MYLIB.DLL
Entry point	1 (or) _strcpy

First offset	2720
DLL Name	MYLIB.DLL
Entry point	2 (or) _strcmp

The offsets shown are only arbitrary offsets and will depend on the actual size of the code. Each relocation record contains the offset of the first call to the function in the DLL. The instruction at that offset in the executable contains one of two values. If there is more than one call to the exported function, the instruction at that offset contains a CALL instruction with the address portion containing the offset of the next call to the same exported function. If the instruction at that offset is the last call in the application to that function, it contains a "CALL FFFF" instruction. Essentially, the linker has created a linked list of calls to each function that resides in a DLL.

At this point, the executable is complete, but where is the code for our external functions? The code is contained within the DLL. When the program is executed, the OS/2 loader attempts to resolve all the calls into the DLL. It does this by examining the relocation records in the application executable. After ensuring the DLL is loaded into memory, the OS/2 loader locates the appropriate entry in the DLL's entry table. With the actual address of the function in hand, it then walks the linked list of calls in the application and inserts this address. (See Figure 12.6.)

When a DLL is loaded, it is possible that the DLL itself is linked to other DLLs. The OS/2 loader performs the same process on the DLL as it does for the executable. It loads all necessary DLLs and resolves the addresses before attempting to resolve the addresses of the executable.

We just looked at one way a DLL is loaded into memory and how its exported function calls are resolved. There are actually several ways a DLL can be loaded into memory and its functions called. We will examine all the variations later in this chapter.

MYLIB.DLL

Executable Header	...
Code Segment Offset 7FCA	code for _strcpy ...
Offset 821E	code for _strcmp ...

Application Executable

Executable Header	...
Code Segment Offset 24F0	... CALL 7FCA ; _strcpy ...
Offset 2720	CALL 821E ; _strcmp ...
Offset 29E4	CALL 821E ; _strcmp ...

Figure 12.6.
An application executable file and DLL demonstrating address references.

How to Build a DLL

The purpose of a DLL is to provide code or resources that can be utilized by more than one process. For example, we could take the code from Chapter 3, "Window Management," that arranged child windows in various ways and put it into a DLL for all our applications to use. You may now be asking, "How do I create my own DLL?" In this section, we will show you how to do just that. We will begin by creating a basic DLL that contains two functions. We will use the `CenterWindow` function from the MINIMDI application, plus a function to fill a window with a specified color. In general, functions that could reside in an application can be placed into a DLL.

The components for building a DLL are the same as for an application. The main difference is in how the DLL is constructed. Those familiar with building 16-bit DLLs will notice it is no longer necessary to worry about DS != SS. Only one data and code segment exists for a 32-bit machine, and DS is always equal to SS.

The first step in building our DLL is to create the C file containing the code.

DLLSAMP.C

```
/* --------------------------------
              DLLSAMP Program
              Real-World Programming for OS/2
              Copyright (c)  1994 Blain, Delimon, and English
------------------------------- */

#define INCL_WIN
#define INCL_GPI

#include <os2.h>
#include "dllsamp.h"

VOID EXPENTRY CenterWindow (HWND hWnd)
{
   ULONG ulScrWidth, ulScrHeight;
   RECTL Rectl;

   ulScrWidth  = WinQuerySysValue (HWND_DESKTOP,
                       SV_CXSCREEN);
   ulScrHeight = WinQuerySysValue (HWND_DESKTOP,
                       SV_CYSCREEN);
   WinQueryWindowRect (hWnd, &Rectl);
   WinSetWindowPos (hWnd, HWND_TOP,
         (ulScrWidth-Rectl.xRight)/2,
         (ulScrHeight-Rectl.yTop)/2, 0, 0,
         SWP_MOVE ¦ SWP_ACTIVATE);
   return;
}

VOID EXPENTRY FillWindow (HWND hWnd, HPS hps, ULONG ulRGB)
{
   RECTL Rectl;
   BOOL  bRelease = FALSE;

   if (!hps)
   {
      hps = WinBeginPaint (hWnd, 0, 0);
      bRelease = TRUE;
   }
   WinQueryWindowRect (hWnd, &Rectl);
   /* Set color state in the hps to RGB mode */
   GpiCreateLogColorTable (hps, LCOL_RESET, LCOLF_RGB, 0L,
         0L, NULL);
   WinFillRect (hps, &Rectl, ulRGB);
   if (bRelease)
      WinEndPaint (hps);
   return;
}
```

Because a DLL is not an executable, there is no `main()` function. We did not define local functions here, but there is no restriction on doing so. For now, we have not defined global variables in this DLL. We will look at that part of DLLs later. All functions to be exported from a DLL should be defined with the EXPENTRY keyword. EXPENTRY defines the calling convention for the function to be a system call (_syscall or _System).

The file DLLSAMP.H contains the function prototypes for our exported functions so that applications or other DLLs wanting to use this DLL can include DLLSAMP.H to get these prototypes.

DLLSAMP.H

```
/* Exported Functions */
VOID EXPENTRY CenterWindow (HWND);
VOID EXPENTRY FillWindow (HWND, HPS, ULONG);
```

We can now compile this file just as we would for an executable producing our DLLSAMP.OBJ file. The key component in creating a DLL is the DEF file. The DEF file specifies that we are creating a DLL, and defines all the exported functions and how the data segments are assigned. Let's examine the format of the DEF file for our DLL.

DLLSAMP.DEF

```
LIBRARY       DLLSAMP
DESCRIPTION   'DLL Sample  1994 Blain, Delimon, & English'

DATA SINGLE

EXPORTS
   CenterWindow   @1
   FillWindow     @2
```

The first line contains the keyword "LIBRARY" rather than "NAME." The format of the LIBRARY statement is as follows:

```
LIBRARY [modulename] [module initialization]
```

modulename	Name of the DLL.
module initialization	
INITGLOBAL	Initialization code is called only when the DLL is first loaded (default).
INITINSTANCE	Initialization code is called for each process that loads the DLL.

The LIBRARY keyword tells the linker that it should create a DLL rather than an executable. After the keyword, LIBRARY is the name of the DLL. If the modulename is not specified, the name of the filename is used. Do not worry about the module initialization statement at this point as it will be discussed shortly.

The DATA statement defines the default characteristics of the data segments. Its format is as follows:

```
DATA  [loadtype] [access] [DGROUP type] [shareability] [privilege]
```

`loadtype`	
`PRELOAD`	Load data segment when DLL is loaded. For OS/2 2.0 and later, this keyword is ignored.
`LOADONCALL`	Load data segment on first access (default).
`READONLY`	Data segment can be read but not written.
`READWRITE`	Data segment can be read and written (default).
`DGROUP type`	
`NONE`	There is no DGROUP.
`SINGLE`	All instances of the DLL share the DGROUP (default).
`MULTIPLE`	Each instance of the DLL has its own DGROUP.
`shareability`	
`SHARED`	Data segment is shared among all instances of the DLL (default).
`NONSHARED`	Data segment is private to each instance.
`privilege`	
`IOPL`	Data segment can be accessed only from ring 2.
`NOIOPL`	Data segment can be accessed by ring 2 or ring 3 (default).

The `DGROUP` type and `shareability` are integrally related. If `SINGLE` is specified, `SHARED` is assumed. If `MULTIPLE` is specified, `NONSHARED` is assumed. Likewise, if `SHARED` is specified, `SINGLE` is assumed. If `MULTIPLE` is specified, `NONSHARED` is assumed. The `DATA` statement will become important when we discuss instance and global data segments. For now, we are safe to use `DATA SINGLE` because we do not really have any data in our DLL.

Next, we specify the functions that will be exported by our DLL. This is done with the `EXPORTS` statement:

```
EXPORTS
   export statement
   export statement
```

Each export statement can have one of several formats. In general, it uses the following format:

```
exported name [= internal name] [@ordinal]
```

`exported name`	The name of the function known outside of the DLL.
`internal name`	The name of the function known internally to the DLL.
`@ordinal`	Number assigned to the entry.

The simplest way to export a function is to list the function name:

```
EXPORTS    CenterWindow
```

Alternately, if we want the outside world to know the function by a different name, we can assign a different exported name and map it to the internal name:

```
EXPORTS    Center = CenterWindow
```

In this example, all applications and other DLLs would call the function by its exported name, `Center`. The linker would map those calls to the `CenterWindow` function. The `@ordinal` part is also an optional parameter. We can assign any ordinal number to our functions to speed the dynamic linking process. If we do not supply an ordinal, when the OS/2 loader is trying to match the function names in the application with those in the DLL, it must search for each function by name.

On the other hand, if there is an ordinal specified for the functions, the linker builds a table of functions indexed by their ordinal. The OS/2 loader, therefore, needs to look up the entry only by its index into this table. If you use ordinals, it is best to start at 1 and make them sequential. All ordinals must be unique within a DLL.

There is one caveat to using ordinals. Earlier, we talked about how you could replace a DLL on a system with a new one and have existing applications that utilize the DLL immediately use the new DLL. Remember also that the OS/2 loader matched the relocation records with the entries in the DLL's entry table. Without ordinals, the OS/2 loader does this matching by name, so as long as the exported function names remain the same in the new DLL, there is no problem. If, however, ordinals are specified, the relocation records reference the DLL entry by ordinal, not by name. Therefore, if you change the ordinal value for any function in the new DLL, the OS/2 loader will match that relocation record with whatever function now has that ordinal-potentially, a troublesome situation because the wrong function will be called. For this reason, it is best to delay using ordinals until the DLL is complete, and, once the ordinals are defined, do not reassign them.

To define an ordinal we would use the following:

```
EXPORTS CenterWindow    @1
```

We could also redefine the function name and assign an ordinal, as follows:

```
EXPORTS Center = CenterWindow @1
```

It is also possible to export variables. Variables can be exported using the same syntax as exported functions:

```
_DLLCount  @400
```

This exports the global DLL variable `_DLLCount`. An application can reference this variable by defining it as an external variable.

You may be wondering why there is no `STACK` keyword in the DEF file for a DLL. The `STACK` keyword is not relevant to DLL because DLLs do not have a stack. They use the same stack as the application. In other words, they share the application's stack.

We can now link our object file to create the DLL. Remember to link to the DLL version of your compiler's library. Our DLL is now created. The only thing left to do is to create the import library so that other modules can link to the DLL. To create the import library, we use the IMPLIB command:

```
IMPLIB DLLSAMP.LIB DLLSAMP.DEF
```

The `IMPLIB` command takes the DEF file and creates an import library based on those functions specified in the `EXPORTS` statement. The DLLSAMP.LIB library created from this is then used to link to other modules.

With the renaming capabilities of the `EXPORTS` statement, we can use a little trick to override any function defined by another library. For example, if we want to define some alternative to the PM function `WinCreateStdWindow`, we could define our own function `MyWinCreateStdWindow` that may do something in addition to calling `WinCreateStdWindow`. We would export our function as follows:

```
EXPORTS Win32CreateStdWindow = MyWinCreateStdWindow
```

The function name is actually `Win32CreateStdWindow` because the PMWIN.H header file defines `WinCreateStdWindow` to be `Win32CreateStdWindow`. After creating our import library, all we must do is ensure that our library is linked before the OS2386 library. The linker uses our `Win32CreateStdWindow` call rather than the OS2386 library. Our DLL is still free to call the original `Win32CreateStdWindow`, because it will link with OS2386 and its call will go directly to PM.

Although you may not want to rename PM functions often, this capability is useful for maintaining backward compatibility for DLLs that you may be distributing or using for your application. Let's say you have a function called `DoSomeWork` that currently defines two parameters and is exported with an ordinal:

```
VOID EXPENTRY DoSomeWork (BOOL bParm1, BOOL bParm2)
```

```
EXPORTS DoSomeWork  @10
```

Imagine that at some future point, you decide you need an additional parameter to this function. You have a problem because applications currently using this library will be passing only two parameters. Here are some steps to follow to make this work without breaking existing applications.

1. Make the changes to the function `DoSomeWork`:

   ```
   VOID EXPENTRY DoSomeWork (BOOL bParm1, BOOL bParm2, BOOL bParm3)
   ```

2. Define a stub function that takes the original two parameters and calls the new function with some default value for the third parameter:

```
VOID EXPENTRY DoSomeWork2 (BOOL bParm1, BOOL bParm2)
        {
            DoSomeWork (bParm1, bParm2, FALSE);
        }
```

3. Use the renaming capabilities of the EXPORTS statement to remap the ordinal to the stub function:

```
EXPORTS  DoSomeWork2  @10
               DoSomeWork   @11
```

All existing calls to the old DoSomeWork function still reference ordinal 10 that now will call the stub function. All new applications will call the modified DoSomeWork function at ordinal 11.

With our DLLSAMP.DLL built, we can call it from our application. The APPSAMP application simply makes calls into the DLLSAMP dynamic link library. The files for building APPSAMP are as follows:

APPSAMP.DEF
APPSAMP.RC
APPSAMP.H
APPSAMP.C
APPSAMP.ICO

APPSAMP.H

```
/* ------------------------------
          APPSAMP Header File
      Real-World Programming for OS/2
Copyright (c)  1994 Blain, Delimon, and English
 ------------------------------ */

#define ID_APPNAME 1

#define IDM_COLOR  100
#define IDM_RED    101
#define IDM_GREEN  102
#define IDM_BLUE   103

#define IDM_CENTER 200

#define IDM_ABOUT  300
```

APPSAMP.RC

```
/* ------------------------------
APPSAMP Resource File
Real-World Programming for OS/2
Copyright (c)  1994 Blain, Delimon, and English
 ------------------------------ */
```

```
#include <os2.h>
#include "appsamp.h"

/* Icons    */
ICON    ID_APPNAME        APPSAMP.ICO

STRINGTABLE LOADONCALL MOVEABLE
BEGIN
   ID_APPNAME      "DLL Sample Application (Implicit Load)"
END

MENU ID_APPNAME
{
   SUBMENU "~Color",           IDM_COLOR
   {
      MENUITEM "~Red",        IDM_RED
      MENUITEM "~Green",      IDM_GREEN
      MENUITEM "~Blue",       IDM_BLUE
   }
   MENUITEM "Cen~ter",         IDM_CENTER
   MENUITEM "",               -1,            MIS_SEPARATOR
   MENUITEM "~About",          IDM_ABOUT
}

rcinclude ..\..\common\about.dlg
```

APPSAMP.C

```
/* --------------------------------
            APPSAMP Program
        Real-World Programming for OS/2
Copyright (c)  1994 Blain, Delimon, and English
-------------------------------- */

#define INCL_WIN

#include <os2.h>
#include "appsamp.h"
#include "dllsamp.h"
#include "..\..\common\about.h"

MRESULT EXPENTRY ClientWndProc (HWND,ULONG,MPARAM,MPARAM);

HAB   hab;
HWND  hWndFrame = 0,
      hWndClient;
CHAR  szTitle[64];
ULONG ulColors[3] = { 0x00FF0000, 0x0000FF00, 0x000000FF };
ULONG ulCurrentColor = 0L;

int main()
{
   HMQ   hmq;
   QMSG  qmsg;
   ULONG flFrameFlags    = FCF_TITLEBAR | FCF_SYSMENU |
```

```
                  FCF_MENU ¦
                  FCF_SIZEBORDER ¦ FCF_MINMAX ¦ FCF_ICON ¦
                  FCF_SHELLPOSITION ¦ FCF_TASKLIST;
   CHAR  szClientClass[] = "CLIENT";

   hab = WinInitialize (0);
   hmq = WinCreateMsgQueue (hab, 0);

   WinRegisterClass (hab, szClientClass, ClientWndProc, 0,
         0);
   WinLoadString (hab, 0, ID_APPNAME, sizeof(szTitle),
         szTitle);

   hWndFrame = WinCreateStdWindow (HWND_DESKTOP, WS_VISIBLE,
         &flFrameFlags, szClientClass, szTitle, 0, 0,
         ID_APPNAME, &hWndClient);

   while (WinGetMsg (hab, &qmsg, 0, 0, 0))
      WinDispatchMsg (hab, &qmsg);

   WinDestroyWindow (hWndFrame);
   WinDestroyMsgQueue (hmq);
   WinTerminate (hab);
   return (0);
}

MRESULT EXPENTRY ClientWndProc (HWND hWnd, ULONG msg,
               MPARAM mp1, MPARAM mp2)
{
   HPS     hps;
   BOOL    bHandled = TRUE;
   MRESULT mReturn  = 0;

   switch (msg)
   {
      case WM_PAINT:
         hps = WinBeginPaint (hWnd,0,0);
         /* Call DLL function to fill the window */
         FillWindow (hWnd, hps, ulColors[ulCurrentColor]);
         WinEndPaint (hps);
         break;

      case WM_ERASEBACKGROUND:
         mReturn = MRFROMLONG(1L);
         break;

      case WM_COMMAND:
         switch (LOUSHORT(mp1))
         {
            case IDM_RED:
            case IDM_GREEN:
            case IDM_BLUE:
               ulCurrentColor = LOUSHORT(mp1) - IDM_RED;
               hps = WinGetPS (hWnd);
               /* Call DLL function to fill the window */
               FillWindow (hWnd, hps,
                     ulColors[ulCurrentColor]);
```

```
            WinReleasePS (hps);
            break;

         case IDM_CENTER:
            /* Call DLL function to center the window */
            CenterWindow (hWndFrame);
            break;

         case IDM_ABOUT:
            DisplayAbout (hWnd, szTitle);
            break;
      }
      break;

   default:
      bHandled = FALSE;
      break;
}

if (!bHandled)
   mReturn = WinDefWindowProc (hWnd,msg,mp1,mp2);

return (mReturn);
}
```

Our calls to `CenterWindow` and `FillWindow` are resolved by linking with the DLLSAMP.LIB import library. When APPSAMP is executed, the OS/2 loader will automatically load the DLLSAMP.DLL for us and handle the resolution of our function calls into the DLL. The APPSAMP application window is shown in Figure 12.7.

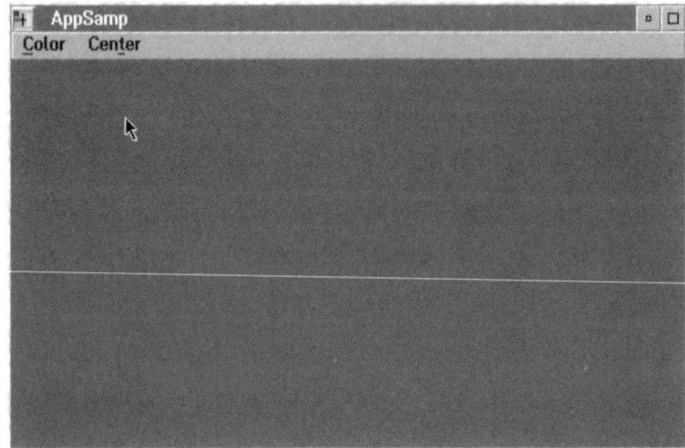

Figure 12.7. The APPSAMP primary window.

In our example, we used the library DLLSAMP.LIB to identify the functions that we used. In addition, we are resolved to using the names of the functions as they are defined in DLLSAMP.LIB. This process of using functions in a DLL is sometimes referred to as importing a function. The library does the importing for us automatically. It is possible to import functions from a DLL even without having a library file for the DLL. However, in either case, only functions exported from a DLL can be imported. This is done by using the `IMPORTS` statement in the DEF file for the application or DLL:

```
IMPORTS
      import statement
      import statement
      ...
```

The format of the `IMPORTS` statement is similar to the `EXPORTS` statement. In general, it uses the following format:

```
[imported name =] DLLname.exported name ¦ DLLname.ordinal
```

`imported name`	Name of the function used in the application.
`DLLname`	Name of the DLL.
`exportedname`	Name of the function exported from the DLL.
`ordinal`	Ordinal of the function exported from the DLL.

Use of the ordinal is only valid if the exported function has been exported with an ordinal. The simplest way to import a function is to list the function name:

```
IMPORTS   DLLSAMP.CenterWindow
```

Alternately, to assign a different name for the function to be used by our application, we could map the function using the following:

```
IMPORTS   Center = DLLSAMP.CenterWindow
```

To use the ordinal, we must assign a name to the function as it is used within the application. It may or may not be the same name as the function name in the DLL:

```
IMPORTS   CenterWindow = DLLSAMP.1
```

Just as we showed how a DLL can intercept the function call to `WinCreateStdWindow`, we can do the same to redirect our function call to a function within a DLL:

```
IMPORTS   Win32CreateStdWindow = DLLSAMP.MyCreateStdWindow
```

This remaps all calls to `Win32CreateStdWindow` to the `MyCreateStdWindow` function in the DLLSAMP.DLL.

Consider the situation in which you are linking two different import libraries; both using the same function name when you need to use both functions in your application. The linker will use the function it finds in the first import library specified during the linking process. You can use the `IMPORTS` statement to alias the two functions. If the function is `FillWindow`, we could define it as follows:

```
IMPORTS
      Lib1FillWindow = LIB1.FillWindow
      Lib2FillWindow = LIB2.FillWindow
```

When we want to call the `FillWindow` function of the LIB1 DLL, we would call it as `Lib1FillWindow()`. To call the `FillWindow` function of the LIB2.DLL, we would call it as `Lib2FillWindow`.

The LIBPATH Statement

Before we get too much farther, it is worth pausing for a minute to discuss how OS/2 finds the needed DLL to load. When dynamic linking is involved, OS/2 uses the `LIBPATH` statement in your CONFIG.SYS file to search for the DLL at load time. After a quick check of the DLLs already in memory, the OS/2 loader will search for the DLL using the `LIBPATH` statement. It is usually a good idea to include the current directory somewhere in the `LIBPATH` because most applications do not install their DLLs in a common DLL directory, but in the same directory as the executable.

For example:

```
LIBPATH=.;C:\OS2\DLL;C:\BIN\OS2;D:\TOOLKT20\BIN
```

The `LIBPATH` is not always used in the search. If the application attempts to load a DLL using runtime dynamic linking, it may not use the `LIBPATH` depending on how the name of the DLL is specified. We look at runtime dynamic linking next.

Runtime Dynamic Linking

The dynamic linking we have discussed so far is referred to as load-time dynamic linking. With load-time dynamic linking, the names of the DLLs linked against the application are specified at link time, and at load time, the system automatically searches for and loads these DLLs. This process is automatic; the application may even be unaware this is occurring. Load-time dynamic linking forces the DLL to be loaded into memory when the application is loaded. The DLL occupies memory in the system until the application terminates. If the functions in the DLL are used frequently, including during initialization, this is an appropriate method; however, what if we need to call into the DLL only under certain infrequent conditions? The DLL would be loaded the entire time and would be reserving and largely wasting a chunk of our shared memory addresses. What if we have multiple versions of a DLL, and we want to use a different one depending on the screen resolution? We wouldn't want all versions of the DLL to be linked with the application when we need only one of them.

The solution is runtime dynamic linking. With runtime dynamic linking, the DLL is explicitly loaded and unloaded by the application when it requires the DLL's code. The addresses of the functions to call are also retrieved as needed. The DLL, thus, is only in memory when it is required, and it is possible to selectively load a particular DLL.

Runtime dynamic linking is performed with the use of three functions: `DosLoadModule`, `DosQueryProcAddress`, and `DosFreeModule`. `DosLoadModule` is used to load the DLL into memory:

```
AIPIRET APIENTRY DosLoadModule(PSZ pszName, ULONG cbName,

          PSZ pszModname, PHMODULE phmod);
```

`pszName`	Buffer to return name of module that caused failure to load.
`cbName`	Size of `pszName`.
`pszModname`	The name of the DLL to load. If the LIBPATH is to be searched, this should be the name of the DLL without the DLL extension. Otherwise, this should be the full path of the DLL including the DLL extension.
`phmod`	Address of the module handle of the loaded DLL.

If the DLL is already loaded, `DosLoadModule` will return the handle to the DLL. If the DLL is not found or it is unable to load, a nonzero return code will be returned.

With the DLL loaded, we can use the module handle returned from `DosLoadModule` to query the addresses of the functions we want to call. `DosQueryProcAddr` is used to do this:

```
APIRET APIENTRY DosQueryProcAddr(HMODULE hmod,

     ULONG ordinal, PSZ pszName, PFN* ppfn);
```

`hmod`	Module handle of the DLL.
`ordinal`	Ordinal number of function to retrieve address. If this value is zero, the function is retrieved by name.
`pszName`	Name of function to retrieve address. This parameter is ignored if a nonzero ordinal is specified.
`ppfn`	Address to copy function address.

If the function is located in the DLL, the address of the function is returned in the variable referenced by `ppfn`. Otherwise, a nonzero return code is returned. Notice that it is possible to receive a nonzero return code when the function exists and the DLL is loaded in memory. OS/2 requires that `DosLoadModule` must be called at least once for a DLL to retrieve a function address with `DosQueryProcAddr`. This is true even if the DLL is loaded for the process by using load-time dynamic linking. If you receive the return code of `ERROR_INVALID_HANDLE`, you must call `DosLoadModule`, which will return the handle again and then reissue the call to `DosQueryProcAddr`.

When you are finished with the DLL and want to free it from memory, use the `DosFreeModule` function:

```
APIRET APIENTRY DosFreeModule(HMODULE hmod);
```

`hmod`	Module handle of the DLL to free.

If the DLL was initially loaded with a call to `DosLoadModule`, the DLL will be freed from this process. If no other processes are currently linked to the DLL, the DLL is released from memory. If the DLL was initially loaded as a result of load-time dynamic linking, the DLL remains linked to the process and is not released from memory.

Let's now rewrite APPSAMP to use runtime dynamic linking. We begin by removing the DLLSAMP library from the link command in our make file. This removes the load-time dynamic linking. In our example, we will load the DLL, query the function address, and free the DLL every time we want to call into the DLL. Although this will cause a lot of loading and unloading, it will demonstrate the procedure for runtime dynamic linking. In practice, you may want to load the DLL when it is first used and not release it until the application is terminating. We will call this application APPSAMP2. Because we will be retrieving the addresses of the functions using a generic PFN type definition, we will need to define a `typedef` for each of the functions. This will allow the compiler to perform the necessary type checking on the parameters. We add a `typedef` for each exported function to the DLLSAMP.H file. APPSAMP2.C contains the same code as APPSAMP.C except that the code for performing runtime dynamic linking has been added.

DLLSAMP.H

```
/* -------------------------------
           DLL Sample Header File
       Real-World Programming for OS/2
Copyright (c)  1994 Blain, Delimon, and English
------------------------------- */

/* Exported Functions */
VOID EXPENTRY CenterWindow (HWND);
VOID EXPENTRY FillWindow (HWND, HPS, ULONG);

/* Function typedefs for run-time dynamic linking */
#ifndef __IBMC__
typedef VOID (APIENTRY *PFNCENTERWINDOW) (HWND);
typedef VOID (APIENTRY *PFNFILLWINDOW) (HWND, HPS, ULONG);
#else
typedef VOID (APIENTRY _PFNCENTERWINDOW) (HWND);
typedef _PFNCENTERWINDOW *PFNCENTERWINDOW;
typedef VOID (APIENTRY _PFNFILLWINDOW) (HWND, HPS, ULONG);
typedef _PFNFILLWINDOW *PFNFILLWINDOW;
#endif
```

We also change the make file, resource file, and DEF to reference APPSAMP2 instead of APPSAMP. The only other changes are to the APPSAMP2 C file.

APPSAMP2.C

```
/* -------------------------------
             APPSAMP2 Program
       Real-World Programming for OS/2
Copyright (c)  1994 Blain, Delimon, and English
------------------------------- */

#define INCL_DOSMODULEMGR
#define INCL_WIN
```

```
#include <os2.h>
#include "appsamp.h"
#include "dllsamp.h"
#include "..\..\common\about.h"

MRESULT EXPENTRY ClientWndProc (HWND,ULONG,MPARAM,MPARAM);

VOID CallFillWindow (HWND, HPS);
VOID CallCenterWindow (HWND);

HAB   hab;
HWND  hWndFrame = 0,
      hWndClient;
CHAR  szTitle[64];
ULONG ulColors[3] = { 0x00FF0000, 0x0000FF00, 0x000000FF };
ULONG ulCurrentColor = 0L;

int main()
{
   HMQ   hmq;
   QMSG  qmsg;
   ULONG flFrameFlags = FCF_TITLEBAR ¦ FCF_SYSMENU ¦
                        FCF_MENU ¦ FCF_SIZEBORDER ¦
                        FCF_MINMAX ¦ FCF_ICON ¦
                        FCF_SHELLPOSITION ¦ FCF_TASKLIST;
   CHAR  szClientClass[] = "CLIENT";

   hab = WinInitialize (0);
   hmq = WinCreateMsgQueue (hab, 0);

   WinRegisterClass (hab, szClientClass, ClientWndProc, 0,
         0);
   WinLoadString (hab, 0, ID_APPNAME, sizeof(szTitle),
         szTitle);

   hWndFrame = WinCreateStdWindow (HWND_DESKTOP, WS_VISIBLE,
         &flFrameFlags, szClientClass, szTitle, 0, 0,
         ID_APPNAME, &hWndClient);

   while (WinGetMsg (hab, &qmsg, 0, 0, 0))
      WinDispatchMsg (hab, &qmsg);

   WinDestroyWindow (hWndFrame);
   WinDestroyMsgQueue (hmq);
   WinTerminate (hab);
   return (0);
}

VOID CallCenterWindow (HWND hWnd)
{
   CHAR             szTitle[40];
   CHAR             szFailBuff [CCHMAXPATH];
   HMODULE          hDLLModule;
   PFNCENTERWINDOW pfnCenterWindow;
```

```
   WinQueryWindowText (hWndFrame, sizeof(szTitle), szTitle);
   WinSetWindowText (hWndFrame, "Loading DLL");
   WinUpdateWindow (hWndFrame);
   if (!DosLoadModule (szFailBuff, sizeof(szFailBuff),
         "DLLSAMP", &hDLLModule))
   {
      if (!DosQueryProcAddr (hDLLModule, 0L, "CenterWindow",
            (PFN*)&pfnCenterWindow) ||
            !DosQueryProcAddr (hDLLModule, 0L,
               "CENTERWINDOW",
            (PFN*)&pfnCenterWindow))
         (*pfnCenterWindow) (hWnd);
      DosFreeModule (hDLLModule);
   }
   WinSetWindowText (hWndFrame, szTitle);
   return;
}

VOID CallFillWindow (HWND hWnd, HPS hps)
{
   CHAR           szTitle[40];
   CHAR           szFailBuff [CCHMAXPATH];
   HMODULE        hDLLModule;
   PFNFILLWINDOW pfnFillWindow;

   WinQueryWindowText (hWndFrame, sizeof(szTitle), szTitle);
   WinSetWindowText (hWndFrame, "Loading DLL");
   WinUpdateWindow (hWndFrame);
   if (!DosLoadModule (szFailBuff, sizeof(szFailBuff),
            "DLLSAMP", &hDLLModule))
   {
      /* FillWindow is ordinal #2 */
      if (!DosQueryProcAddr (hDLLModule,2L,NULL,
            (PFN*)&pfnFillWindow))
         (*pfnFillWindow) (hWnd, hps,
            ulColors[ulCurrentColor]);
      DosFreeModule (hDLLModule);
   }
   WinSetWindowText (hWndFrame, szTitle);
   return;
}

MRESULT EXPENTRY ClientWndProc (HWND hWnd, ULONG msg,
            MPARAM mp1, MPARAM mp2)
{
   HPS      hps;
   BOOL     bHandled = TRUE;
   MRESULT mReturn  = 0;

   switch (msg)
   {
      case WM_PAINT:
         hps = WinBeginPaint (hWnd,0,0);
         CallFillWindow (hWnd, hps);
         WinEndPaint (hps);
         break;
```

```
      case WM_ERASEBACKGROUND:
         mReturn = MRFROMLONG(1L);
         break;

      case WM_COMMAND:
         switch (LOUSHORT(mp1))
         {
            case IDM_RED:
            case IDM_GREEN:
            case IDM_BLUE:
               ulCurrentColor = LOUSHORT(mp1) - IDM_RED;
               hps = WinGetPS (hWnd);
               CallFillWindow (hWnd, hps);
               WinReleasePS (hps);
               break;

            case IDM_CENTER:
               CallCenterWindow (hWndFrame);
               break;

            case IDM_ABOUT:
               DisplayAbout (hWnd, szTitle);
               break;
         }
         break;

      default:
         bHandled = FALSE;
         break;
   }

   if (!bHandled)
      mReturn = WinDefWindowProc (hWnd,msg,mp1,mp2);

   return (mReturn);
}
```

The application window for APPSAMP2 is shown in Figure 12.8.

Figure 12.8.
The primary window for the application sample using a DLL.

When you compile your source files, data is normally placed in the automatic data segment. Initialized data is placed in the logical segment _DATA, and uninitialized data is placed in the logical segment _BSS or c_common. The name of the automatic data segment can be renamed using an option switch with most compilers. The code for the sample programs demonstrates this.

Global data is shared among all instances of the DLL. How is this accomplished? Let's start with a diagram of the DLL code and data segment for global data only. (See Figure 12.9.)

Figure 12.9. Global data segment for a DLL.

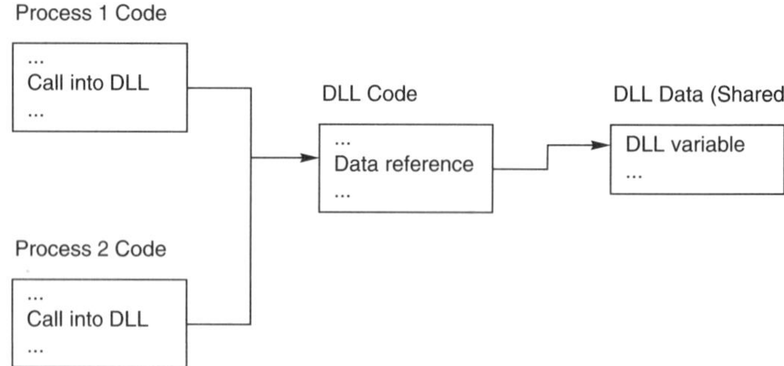

We see that the address for the data reference for both processes (instances) points to the same logical address in memory. This logical address maps to the same physical address for both processes. The type of data for the default data segment is defined in the DEF file with the DATA statement. To define a global, shared data segment, use the SINGLE keyword in the DEF file, for example:

```
DATA SINGLE SHARED
```

The shareability parameter of the DATA statement defines how all segments other than the default data segment are to be allocated. SHARED says all other segments are also global, and NONSHARED says all other segments are instance.

Keep in mind that data in global data segments is not protected from being updated by another process while one process is in the middle of using the current value. This is due to the preemptive nature of OS/2. One way to protect this type of activity is with semaphores. Another is to use instance data for those variables that do not need to be shared among processes.

Instance data is not shared among processes, and each process obtains its own copy of the data segment. Look at a diagram for instance data only. (See Figure 12.10.)

We see in this case that the address for the data reference for both processes points to the same logical address. This logical address, however, maps to two different physical memory addresses, depending on which process is currently active. How does this happen when the DLL code contains only one logical address? The key to this is in the use of the page table. When a process is executing, its page table is loaded and used for that process. When a task switch occurs and another process becomes active, the page table for that process is loaded into memory. Because all addresses in the code are logical addresses, it is possible for the same logical address to map to a different physical address. (See Figure 12.11.)

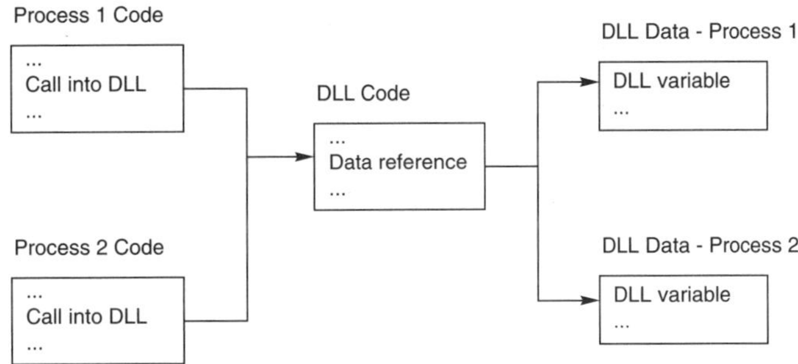

Figure 12.10. Instance data segment for a DLL.

The page table entries for two processes are shown. For process 1, logical address 0x09802000 has not been allocated, whereas for process 2, the same address has been allocated and assigned physical address 0x037E5000. Both process 1 and process 2 have logical address 0x09804000 allocated, but each points to a different physical address. Process 1 maps the logical address to physical address 0x0390F000, whereas process 2 maps to 0x037E6000. The logical address 0x1DC00000 is allocated to both processes, and it also maps to the same physical address. This is an example of shared data.

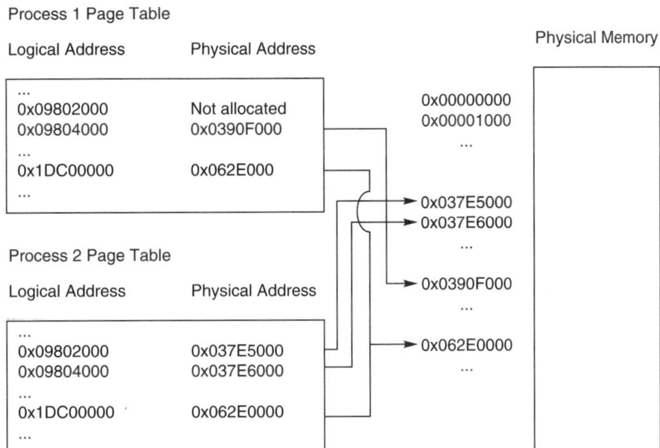

Figure 12.11. Demonstration of how the same logical address can map to a different physical address.

We can see that the DLL can refer to the same logical address and that OS/2 will take care of switching the page table and mapping the logical address to the correct physical address.

To define an instance, nonshared data segment, use the `MULTIPLE` keyword on the `DATA` statement in the DEF file.

```
DATA MULTIPLE NONSHARED
```

A quick look at an example shows the difference between these two methods. The same source code is used in both cases, but the DEF file will change to define the data as either global or instance. Assume we have a DLL coded with a global variable defined as `ulCount` which is incremented every time the function `IncrementCount` is called and the new count is returned to the caller:

```
/* DLL Code */

ULONG ulCount = 0L;

ULONG EXPENTRY IncrementCount ()
{
   return (++ulCount);
}
```

Assume we have an application that calls the `IncrementCount` only once and displays the count in the window. If we start the application twice, causing the DLL to be loaded for each process, we see different results for each case.

For the global data, the DEF file would contain the following `DATA` statement:

```
DATA SINGLE SHARED
```

The first process would call `IncrementCount`, and the return value would be 1. The second process would call `IncrementCount`, and the return value would be 2. This assumes the second process is started before the first one terminates. As long as there is a process linked to the DLL, the data segment remains loaded. Each successive call to `IncrementCount`, by either process, would continue to increment the same count.

For the instance data, the DEF file would contain the following `DATA` statement:

```
DATA MULTIPLE NONSHARED
```

The first process would call `IncrementCount`, and the return value would be 1. The second process would call `IncrementCount`, and the return value would again be 1. Each successive call to `IncrementCount` would increment the count maintained for the particular process making the call.

It is also possible to have both global and instance data segments for a DLL. This can be done in a single source file and with multiple source files. The key to defining both global and instance data is that first you must create multiple data segments defining the global data in the global data segment and the instance data in the instance data segment. Second, you must define the characteristics of these segments in the DEF file. The easiest approach is to use multiple source files with one file defining the instance data variables and to let all other variables be defined as global. Using this approach enables you to keep all the instance specific variables together, and you are free to define global variables in each source file as they are needed.

To begin, we must create a file to contain our instance-specific data. All variables that are to be private to an instance of a DLL are defined in that file. A technique I prefer is to define all instance-specific data items as part of a structure called `InstanceData`. Whenever an instance variable is being used, it is easily identified by the structure name `InstanceData`. We will use that in our example. We could create a file called DLLINST.H to contain the definition of the instance data structure, for example:

```
typedef struct tagINSTANCE_STRUCT
{
   ULONG ulFlags;
   HAB   hab;
   HMQ   hmq;
   HWND  hWndFrame;
} INSTANCEDATA_STRUCT;
```

The fields here are only arbitrary variables to illustrate our example. Next, we could define the file DLLINST.C to actually define the `InstanceData` structure, for example:

```
INSTANCEDATA_STRUCT InstanceData =
{
   0L,
   (HAB)0L,
   (HMQ)0L,
   (HWND)0L
};
```

Our `InstanceData` is initialized to zeroes, although you could initialize your variables to any value. The next step is to compile this file and redefine the default data segment. We give our instance data the name `_INSTANCEDATA`. All the compilers with which the sample code was tested for this book have different methods for defining a name for a data segment. Those compilers also differ in how variables are specified and placed into each data segment. Examine both the source code and the MAK file for the example program for this chapter for the compiler which you use.

The variable `InstanceData` is defined to reside in the data segment with name `_INSTANCEDATA`. Anytime an instance data variable is to be used, the `InstanceData` structure variable is used:

```
InstanceData.ulFlags
InstanceData.hab
InstanceData.hmq
InstanceData.hWndFrame
```

Because we have decided that all other data defined in our application is to be global data, we do not need to do anything special in defining those variables. They will be placed in a data segment other than `_INSTANCEDATA`. The final step is to define the `_INSTANCEDATA` segment as being nonshared and all others as being shared. The application's DEF file will contain the following statements:

```
DATA SINGLE SHARED

SEGMENTS
_INSTANCEDATA   CLASS 'FAR_DATA' NONSHARED PRELOAD
```

Examine your MAP file to find the exact name and class of the data segment containing your instance data.

As we saw earlier, the DATA SINGLE SHARED statement defines the automatic data segment to be SINGLE (global) and the default for all other segments to be SHARED (global). The SEGMENTS statement overrides the attributes for a segment defined. The format of the SEGMENTS statement is as follows:

```
SEGMENTS
   segment statement
   segment statement
   ...
```

Each segment statement defines the attributes for the segment. In general, the segment statement for DATA segments uses the following format:

```
segment-name [CLASS ['classname']] [segment-attribute]
```

segment-name	Name of the segment to be defined.
classname	Name of the class for the segment.
segment-attribute	PRELOAD | LOADONCALL
	READONLY | READWRITE
	IOPL | NOIOPL
	CONFORMING | NONCONFORMING
	SHARED | NONSHARED

Because we want the _INSTANCEDATA segment to be nonshared, we use the NONSHARED segment attribute.

Initialization and Termination

An important aspect of proper DLL maintenance is keeping track of the processes that are currently using the DLL. One way of doing this is to define a function in the DLL that is called by a process when the process starts and another function in the DLL that is called when it terminates. This relies on the application to behave properly and to make the calls at the proper time. An alternative, and a more practical method, is for the DLL to keep track of this activity. This is accomplished by using an Initialization/Termination function. It is called an Initialization/Termination function because OS/2 calls the function when the DLL is loaded for a process and when it is unloaded for a process.

The use of an initialization and termination function allows the DLL to perform any process-specific initialization and upon termination to clean up data or structures that were allocated. The initialization function for OS/2 DLLs has the following prototype:

```
ULONG _stdcall DLL_InitTerm (HMODULE hModule,
   ULONG ulTerminating);
```

`hModule`	Module handle of the DLL.
`ulTerminating`	Initialization/Termination flag.
`0x00`	DLL is initializing.
`0x01`	DLL is terminating.

Note: `_stdcall` in the preceding definition is changed to `_System` for the IBM C/Set compiler.

The return code indicates the success or failure of the DLL initialization code to OS/2. The function should return `FALSE` if the initialization is unsuccessful. OS/2 will then unload the DLL. If the DLL is being loaded as part of load-time dynamic linking, the application will fail to start. The function should return `TRUE` if the initialization is successful. The DLL will remain in memory until unloaded.

The same function is called when the DLL is being loaded and when it is being unloaded. The `ulTerminating` flag indicates that is occurring. If you are using the IBM C/Set compiler, this function will be called at initialization and termination. However, for the other compilers, defining this function alone does not guarantee the function will be called at initialization and termination. For these compilers, this entry point can be defined within an assembly language source file. The simplest assembly file to use is the following one.

DLLINIT.ASM

```
       .386p

INIT   SEGMENT        BYTE PUBLIC 'CODE'
       EXTRN          _DLL_InitTerm:near

assume CS:FLAT, DS:FLAT, ES:FLAT, SS:FLAT

INIT   ENDS
       END            _DLL_InitTerm
```

When this file is assembled and linked with the DLL, the function `DLL_InitTerm` is defined as the DLL entry point. The only remaining thing to specify for our `Initialization/Termination` function is when it should be called. This is defined in the DEF file in the `LIBRARY` statement. To have this function called only once when the first process loads the DLL, use the `INITGLOBAL` parameter, which is the default in the DEF file:

```
LIBRARY DLLSAMP INITGLOBAL
```

To have this function called for every process that loads the DLL, use the `INITINSTANCE` parameter, as in this sample statement:

```
LIBRARY DLLSAMP INITINSTANCE
```

If you need to perform both instance and global initialization, do this by defining a flag that is initialized to `TRUE` and set to `FALSE` after the first instance initializes. Thereafter, the global initialization is not performed because this flag is cleared:

```
BOOL bFirstInstance = TRUE;

ULONG _stdcall DLL_InitTerm (HMODULE hModule,
   ULONG ulTerminating)
{
   if (bFirstInstance)
   {
      perform global initialization
      bFirstInstance = FALSE;
   }
   perform instance initialization
}
```

Examples of global initialization may include allocating shared memory to be sub-allocated by the DLL, incrementing a count of processes linked to the DLL, or creating semaphores. Examples of instance initialization may include recording the process identifier, loading instance-specific resources, or gaining access to shared memory or semaphores.

C Runtime Functions in DLLs

Another point that we have not discussed so far is the use of the C runtime library functions. When C runtime library functions are used for an application, a call to the C runtime library initialization function is inserted into the start-up code. This is not done for DLLs when you define an alternate entry point as we just did. Because a DLL can have only one entry point, it may be necessary for you to explicitly call the C runtime library initialization function as part of your instance initialization. The name of the C runtime library initialization function will vary depending on the compiler you are using. Refer to your documentation to see if you are required to use certain C runtime library functions.

DosExitList

If you have created DLLs for OS/2 1.x, you are probably familiar with an "`exitlist`" handler. An `exitlist` handler is installed during initialization of a DLL and defines a function that is to be called when the current process terminates. With OS/2 now automatically calling the `Initialization/Termination` function, when the process terminates, it may no longer be necessary for you to install an `exitlist` handler. There are two circumstances when you may still want to have an `exitlist` handler even with an `Initialization/Termination` function.

The first circumstance is when the termination of your process requires you to clean up window or graphics objects. An example would be when your DLL creates a DC that is left open when the process terminates, which then requires the termination code to close and delete this DC. This requirement is due to the current sequence in which a process is cleaned up. When a process terminates the order of events is as follows:

1. Call all `exitlist` handlers by using the invocation order.
2. Call the `Initialization/Termination` functions of all 32-bit DLLs.

Because PMWIN and PMGPI install `exitlist` handlers for each process, their `exitlist` handler will be called before the 32-bit DLL termination function. Part of PMWIN and PMGPI cleanup involves destroying remaining windows and freeing bitmaps and other allocated graphics objects. An open DC, however, is not properly cleaned up by the system. By the time the 32-bit DLL termination code is called, both PMWIN and PMGPI have cleaned up, and calls into either DLL most likely will result in a failed function call. This particular sequence effectively eliminates the capability of the termination code to call into PMWIN or PMGPI to perform any cleanup. Installing an `exitlist` handler, thus, would be appropriate if you need to make calls into either DLL during termination.

The second circumstance is a more specialized reason, but nonetheless a useful tactic. If you don't want your DLL to be unloaded by OS/2 when `DosFreeModule` is called, you can install an `exitlist` handler. By installing an `exitlist` handler, you are effectively establishing a dependency with the OS/2 loader that the DLL cannot be unloaded until the process terminates. The reason is obvious. If you install an `exitlist` handler and have a call `DosFreeModule` actually free the DLL from memory, when the process terminates, the code will no longer be in memory, and the termination sequence will trap. After an `exitlist` handler is installed for a process, this dependency is established and is not removed, even if the `exitlist` handler is removed.

An `exitlist` handler is installed or removed by using the `DosExitList` function:

```
APIRET APIENTRY DosExitList(ULONG ordercode, PFNEXITLIST pfn);
```

`ordercode`		The low byte of the low word indicates the exitlist function:
	`EXLST_ADD`	(1) Add the function to the exitlist.
	`EXLST_REMOVE`	(2) Remove the function from the exitlist.
	`EXLST_EXIT`	(3) Transfer to the next function in the termination sequence. The high byte of the low word indicates the order in which the exitlist should be called. The exitlist functions are called in order based on their invocation order from lowest(0) to highest (255).
`pfn`		Function address to install.

To install the function DLL_ExitList as an exitlist handler:

```
DosExitList (EXLST_ADD ¦ 0x00007000, (PFNEXITLIST)DLL_ExitList);
```

The invocation order specified here is 112 (0x70). To remove an exitlist handler:

```
DosExitList (EXLST_REMOVE, (PFNEXITLIST)DLL_ExitList);
```

When the exitlist function has been called and it is through performing its function, it MUST tell OS/2 to continue with the next exitlist handler in the sequence. The last statement in the exitlist code must be as follows:

```
DosExitList (EXLST_EXIT, (PFNEXITLIST)DLL_ExitList);
```

Multiple exitlist handlers can be installed for the same process. The format of the exitlist function is as follows:

```
VOID EXPENTRY DLL_ExitList (ULONG ulCode);
```

ulCode		Code indicating reason for exitlist being called:
	TC_EXIT	(0) Terminating normally.
	TC_HARDERROR	(1) Hard-error encountered.
	TC_TRAP	(2) Trap operation (16-bit child process).
	TC_KILLPROCESS	(3) DosKillProcess.
	TC_EXCEPTION	(4) Exception operation (32-bit child process).

OS2.INI

Two entries are in the OS2.INI file which specify that certain DLLs be loaded at particular times. These entries should not be used indiscriminately to force your DLL to be preloaded, as that can affect system performance and memory usage. Both entries are under the application name "SYS_DLLS."

Application	*Key*	*Description*
SYS_DLLS	LoadOneTime	Load the DLLs listed when the system is booted.
SYS_DLLS	LoadPerProcess	Load the DLLs listed for every process that is started.

The format of the data for each of these entries is a list of DLLs separated by a space and finally terminated with a NULL byte. When these DLLs are loaded, OS/2 will automatically call the function with ordinal 1. If you decide you need to use this capability, ensure that you have a function with ordinal 1 defined which either performs some set-up on the first load or is just a stub function. No parameters are passed to this function.

There is an obvious possible conflict to this. If you install a DLL this way and the DLL causes a trap or hangs, it becomes difficult to reboot your system because this DLL will be automatically loaded each time. If you buy into using this capability, use it with caution—*caveat emptor!*

Resource-Only DLLs

You can also use DLLs to define resources to be loaded by multiple processes. Although you cannot directly share most resources among processes, you can use the resources of a DLL for your process. The resources for the DLL are bound into the DLL just as they are for an application-using the resource compiler. When you want to load a resource from a DLL, specify the module handle for the DLL rather than NULL (indicating the resources are in the executable).

Perhaps you have some bitmaps created for various screen resolutions. Because you probably don't want to bind every version of the bitmap into your executable, you can create resolution-specific DLLs, each containing the bitmaps and so on, required for that resolution. When your application is initializing, it can detect the screen resolution and perform runtime dynamic linking to load the appropriate resource DLL. The application can then load the resources using the module handle of the DLL and use the same resource identifier regardless of which DLL was loaded.

Thermometer Application

Our sample application will use extensively all the capabilities of DLLs as well as code from our earlier chapters on drawing and memory. We will create two general purpose DLLs, and our application will use them to assist in the display and operation of a basic dialog box. Both DLLs will use instance initialization, although only one will have both global and instance data.

The first DLL, CONTROLS.DLL, is a general purpose DLL demonstrating how you can define and create your custom window classes in a DLL. Having the classes defined in a DLL enables you to use those same window classes in many applications. The BEVEL control is a window that draws one of various forms of sculptured bevels. For example, we could have various bevel windows as shown in Figure 12.12.

The THERMOMETER control is a window that displays data shown as percentages on a thermometer. We will draw our thermometer using code we created earlier in the book. An example of our thermometer control showing a percentage of data is shown in Figure 12.13.

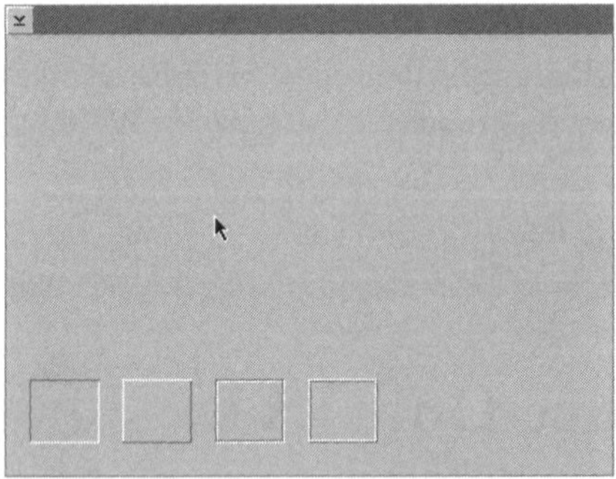

Figure 12.12.
Bevel window styles.

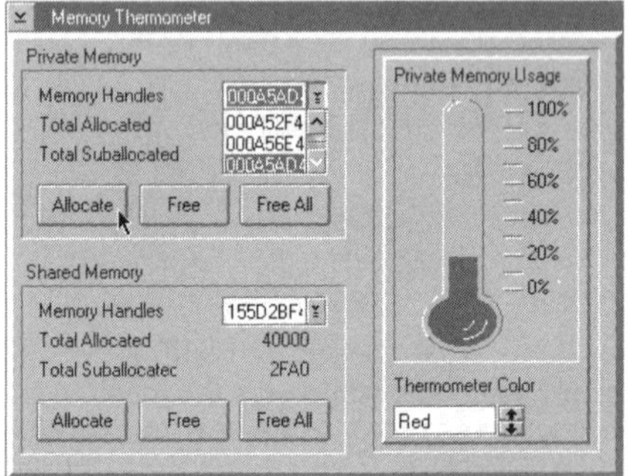

Figure 12.13.
Memory Thermometer application.

To allow any application using this DLL to use these window classes, we must register these two classes for each application. This will be handled through the use of instance initialization.

The second DLL, MEMDLL.DLL, is a general purpose DLL demonstrating how you can perform memory suballocation for both private and shared data. This DLL shows the usage of both instance and global data. In addition to providing memory suballocation for both private and shared data, it also performs memory cleanup when the application terminates.

Each application will have its own private memory suballocation object, and each will share a shared memory suballocation object. This DLL will also use instance initialization to create the private memory suballocation object and to gain access to the shared memory suballocation object. The shared memory suballocation object will be maintained in global data, and the private memory suballocation object will be maintained in instance data.

Let's take a detailed look at each DLL. We start with the CONTROLS.DLL. The first thing to define is the external interface for our two controls. This includes the names of the control class, the styles and messages for each control, and any additional functions to be exported. These are defined in CONTROLS.H.

CONTROLS.H

```
/* ------------------------------
Controls Header File
Real-World Programming for OS/2
Copyright (c)  1994 Blain, Delimon, and English
------------------------------ */

/**************************************************
GENERAL USE FUNCTIONS
**************************************************/

VOID EXPENTRY CenterWindow (HWND);


/**************************************************
BEVEL CONTROL
**************************************************/

#define BEVELCLASS        "BEVEL"

/* Use low word of style for private style flags */
#define BVS_BEVELIN      0x00000000
#define BVS_BEVELOUT     0x00000001
#define BVS_RECTANGLE    0x00000000
#define BVS_LINE         0x00000002
#define BVS_FILL         0x00000004
#define BVS_PREVID       0x00000008
#define BVS_PREVWINDOW   0x00000010

#define BVS_IDMASK       0x00008000

/* Bevel control messages */
#define BVM_SETCOLOR      WM_USER+1
#define BVM_SETTHICKNESS WM_USER+2
#define BVM_RESIZE        WM_USER+3


/**************************************************
THERMOMETER CONTROL
**************************************************/

#define THERMOMETERCLASS "THERMOMETER"

/* Use low word of style for private style flags */
#define THS_NOPERCENT     0x00000001

/* Thermometer control messages */
#define THM_SETRANGE      WM_USER+1
#define THM_SETVALUE      WM_USER+2
#define THM_SETCOLOR      WM_USER+3
```

This DLL also contains the `CenterWindow` function from our earlier example. The bevel control's class name is `BEVELCLASS`. Any application can use this identifier to create a window of this class.

mp1 = MAKELONG(fillcolorindex, backgroundcolorindex).
mp2 = Not used.

The default value is red with a pale gray background. To change the color to blue with a pale gray background, use the following:

```
WinSendMsg (hWndThermoCtl, THM_SETCOLOR,
      MAKELONG (CLR_BLUE, CLR_PALEGRAY), 0L);
```

With the definition of our controls, we move to defining the definition (DEF) file for the CONTROLS.DLL.

CONTROLS.DEF

```
LIBRARY         CONTROLS   INITINSTANCE
DESCRIPTION    'Controls DLL  1994 Blain, Delimon, & English'
PROTMODE

CODE           MOVEABLE
DATA           MOVEABLE SINGLE

EXPORTS
               CenterWindow          @1
               BevelWndProc          @2
               ThermometerWndProc    @3
```

The library is defined and named in our first line:

```
LIBRARY         CONTROLS   INITINSTANCE
```

The library name is CONTROLS, and we want our initialization code to be called for each instance of the DLL. Because we don't have a need for instance data, we define the data segment to be global data:

```
DATA           MOVEABLE SINGLE
```

CenterWindow is exported for use by other applications.

We have defined our DLL to be INITINSTANCE and, therefore, must define an initialization function. Our initialization function is defined in the CTLINIT.ASM file.

CTLINIT.ASM

```
; Controls DLL Initialization
; Define the initialization/termination entry point for the
; Controls DLL

      .386p
```

```
ifdef _ _TASM_ _
   model flat,pascal
endif

_TEXT     SEGMENT    DWORD USE32 PUBLIC 'CODE'
          EXTRN      _InitializeControlDll:near

ifdef _ _MASM386_ _
   ASSUME    CS: FLAT, DS: FLAT, ES: FLAT
endif

_DLLEntry:
          jmp _InitializeControlDll

_TEXT     ENDS
          END    _DLLEntry
```

This basic assembler file defines our initialization function as "`InitializeControlDLL`." This function will be called both when the DLL is loaded and when unloaded for each instance of the DLL.

Let's now take a look at our implementation of these controls.

CONTROLS.C

```
/* --------------------------------
              Controls DLL
        Real-World Programming for OS/2
Copyright (c)  1994 Blain, Delimon, and English
-------------------------------- */

/* Bevel Control
   Class Name  - BEVELCLASS
   Styles
      BVS_BEVELIN      - Draw bevel inwards
      BVS_BEVELOUT     - Draw bevel outwards
      BVS_RECTANGLE    - Draw a beveled rectangle
      BVS_LINE         - Draw a beveled trough or fence
      BVS_FILL         - Fill interior
      BVS_PREVID       - Size bevel to encompass all previous
                         sibling windows until window with
                         specified ID is reached. The windows
                         ID is specified as the ID of the
                         window to stop at; or'd with
                         BVS_IDMASK
                            x Position is horizontal
                               gap between bevel and windows
                            y Position is vertical gap
                               between bevel and windows
                            cx is border width (0 is nominal
                               width border)
      BVS_PREVWINDOW   - Size bevel to encompass previous
                         sibling window
```

```
                            x Position is horizontal gap
                               between bevel and windows
                            y Position is vertical gap
                               between bevel and windows
                            cx is border width (0 is nominal
                               width border)
   Messages
      BVM_SETCOLOR      - mp1 MAKELONG(bordercolorindex,
                        interiorcolorindex)
                         mp2 0L
      BVM_SETTHICKNESS - mp1 MPFROMSHORT (bevelthickness)
      BVM_RESIZE       - mp1 MAKELONG(horizontalgap,
                            verticalgap)

   Thermometer control
   Class Name  - THERMOMETER CLASS
   Messages
      THM_SETRANGE     - mp1 Low value of range
                         mp2 High value of range
      THM_SETVALUE     - mp1 Current value
      THM_SETCOLOR     - mp1 MAKELONG(fillcolorindex,
                            backgroundcolorindex)
*/

#define INCL_DOS
#define INCL_DOSERRORS
#define INCL_WIN
#define INCL_GPIPRIMITIVES

#include <os2.h>
#include "controls.h"

/* Window functions */

MRESULT EXPENTRY BevelWndProc (HWND,ULONG,MPARAM,MPARAM);
MRESULT EXPENTRY ThermometerWndProc(HWND,ULONG,MPARAM,
         MPARAM);

/* Undocumented WinDrawBorder flags */

#define DB_RAISED       0x0400
#define DB_DEPRESSED    0x0800
#define DB_TROUGH       0x1000
#define DB_FENCE        0x2000
#define DB_FIELD        0x4000
#define DB_CORNERBORDER 0x8000

/* Shared data placed into initialized variables data segment */

HMODULE hModDll = 0;

/* Bevel window extra bytes */

#define QWL_COLORS          0
#define QWS_THICKNESS       QWL_COLORS    + sizeof(ULONG)
#define BEVELEXTRA          QWS_THICKNESS + sizeof(USHORT)
```

```
/* Thermometer window extra bytes */

#define QWL_LOWERRANGE      0
#define QWL_UPPERRANGE      QWL_LOWERRANGE + sizeof(ULONG)
#define QWL_VALUE           QWL_UPPERRANGE + sizeof(ULONG)
#define QWL_COLOR           QWL_VALUE      + sizeof(ULONG)
#define THERMOMETEREXTRA    QWL_COLOR      + sizeof(ULONG)


#ifdef __IBMC__
ULONG _System _DLL_InitTerm (HMODULE hModule,
ULONG ulTerminating)
#else
ULONG _stdcall InitializeControlDll (HMODULE hModule,
ULONG ulTerminating)
#endif
{
   BOOL bResult;

   if (ulTerminating & 0x01)
      return (FALSE);
   else
   {
      /* Register the window control classes */
      bResult = WinRegisterClass ((HAB)0, BEVELCLASS,
                  BevelWndProc, CS_HITTEST | CS_SIZEREDRAW,
                  BEVELEXTRA) && WinRegisterClass ((HAB)0,
                  THERMOMETERCLASS, ThermometerWndProc,
                  CS_SIZEREDRAW, THERMOMETEREXTRA);
   }

   /* Save the module handle when we get loaded.  The module handle
   will be the same for all instances of the DLL */

   hModDll = hModule;

   return ((ULONG)bResult);
}


VOID EXPENTRY CenterWindow (HWND hWnd)
{
   ULONG ulScrWidth, ulScrHeight;
   RECTL Rectl;

   ulScrWidth  = WinQuerySysValue (HWND_DESKTOP,
                  SV_CXSCREEN);
   ulScrHeight = WinQuerySysValue (HWND_DESKTOP,
                  SV_CYSCREEN);
   WinQueryWindowRect (hWnd, &Rectl);
   WinSetWindowPos (hWnd, HWND_TOP,
         (ulScrWidth -Rectl.xRight)/2,
         (ulScrHeight-Rectl.yTop)/2, 0, 0,
         SWP_MOVE | SWP_ACTIVATE);
   return;
}
```

```
VOID QueryBorderRect (HWND hWnd, ULONG ulStyle,
      PRECTL pRectl)
{
   HWND   hWndPrev;
   SWP    Swp;
   USHORT usID;
   RECTL  RectlPrev;


   /* If style is BVS_PREVID, then size the bevel to encompass
   all previous sibling windows until a window with the
specifed ID is located.

   If style is BVS_PREVWINDOW, then size the bevel to encompass
   the previous sibling window. */

   WinSetRect ((HAB)0L, pRectl, 0L, 0L, 0L, 0L);

   if (ulStyle & BVS_PREVWINDOW)
   {
      if ((hWndPrev = WinQueryWindow (hWnd, QW_PREV)) != 0)
      {
         WinQueryWindowPos (hWndPrev, &Swp);
         WinSetRect ((HAB)0L, pRectl, Swp.x, Swp.y,
               Swp.x+Swp.cx, Swp.y+Swp.cy);
      }
   }
   else
   {
      hWndPrev = hWnd;
      usID     = WinQueryWindowUShort (hWnd, QWS_ID);
      usID    &= ~BVS_IDMASK;

      /* Union the bounding rectangle of all sibling windows
until window with ID usID is reached */

      while ((hWndPrev = WinQueryWindow (hWndPrev, QW_PREV)) != 0)
      {
         WinQueryWindowPos (hWndPrev, &Swp);
         WinSetRect ((HAB)0L, &RectlPrev, Swp.x, Swp.y,
                  Swp.x+Swp.cx, Swp.y+Swp.cy);
         WinUnionRect ((HAB)0L, pRectl, pRectl, &RectlPrev);
         if (WinQueryWindowUShort(hWndPrev,QWS_ID) == usID)
            break;
      }
   }
   return;
}

MRESULT EXPENTRY BevelWndProc (HWND hWnd, ULONG msg,
         MPARAM mp1, MPARAM mp2)
{
   BOOL    bHandled = TRUE;
   MRESULT mReturn  = 0;
   RECTL   Rectl;
   HPS     hps;
```

```
ULONG   ulStyle;
ULONG   ulDrawStyle;
ULONG   ulColors;
ULONG   ulThickness;

switch (msg)
{
   case WM_CREATE:
      /* Initialize border and interior colors */
      WinSetWindowULong (hWnd, QWL_COLORS,
         MAKELONG (SYSCLR_BUTTONDARK,
         SYSCLR_BUTTONMIDDLE));

      ulStyle = WinQueryWindowULong (hWnd, QWL_STYLE);
      if (ulStyle & (BVS_PREVID ¦ BVS_PREVWINDOW))
      {
         SWP    SwpBevel;

         /* Query bevel window parameters
            x Position specifies the horizontal gap
            between bevel and sibling windows
            y Position specifies the vertical gap between
            bevel and sibling windows
            cx specifies the width of the bevel */

         WinQueryWindowPos (hWnd, &SwpBevel);
         QueryBorderRect (hWnd, ulStyle, &Rectl);

         /* Position the bevel window */
         WinSetWindowPos (hWnd, 0,
            Rectl.xLeft   - SwpBevel.x,
            Rectl.yBottom - SwpBevel.y,
            Rectl.xRight  - Rectl.xLeft+(SwpBevel.x<< 1),
            Rectl.yTop - Rectl.yBottom+(SwpBevel.y << 1),
            SWP_MOVE ¦ SWP_SIZE);

         /* If width is zero use nominal width bevel */
         if (SwpBevel.cx == 0)
            SwpBevel.cx = 1;
         WinSetWindowUShort (hWnd, QWS_THICKNESS,
            (USHORT)SwpBevel.cx);
      }
      else
         WinSetWindowUShort (hWnd, QWS_THICKNESS, 1);
         break;

   case BVM_RESIZE:
      ulStyle = WinQueryWindowULong (hWnd, QWL_STYLE);
      if (ulStyle & (BVS_PREVID ¦ BVS_PREVWINDOW))
      {
         RECTL Rectl;

         QueryBorderRect (hWnd, ulStyle, &Rectl);

         /* Position the bevel window */
         WinSetWindowPos (hWnd, 0,
```

```
            Rectl.xLeft   - SHORT1FROMMP(mp1),
            Rectl.yBottom - SHORT2FROMMP(mp1),
        Rectl.xRight-Rectl.xLeft+(SHORT1FROMMP(mp1)<< 1),
      Rectl.yTop-Rectl.yBottom+(SHORT2FROMMP(mp1) << 1),
            SWP_MOVE | SWP_SIZE);
      }
      break;

   case BVM_SETCOLOR:
      /* LOUSHORT(mp1) == Border color
         HIUSHORT(mp1) == Interior color */
      WinSetWindowULong (hWnd, QWL_COLORS, (ULONG)mp1);

      /* Repaint bevel with new color */
      WinInvalidateRect (hWnd, NULL, FALSE);
      break;

   case BVM_SETTHICKNESS:
      WinSetWindowUShort (hWnd, QWS_THICKNESS,
         SHORT1FROMMP(mp1));
      break;

   case WM_PAINT:
      hps         = WinBeginPaint (hWnd,0,0);
      ulColors    = WinQueryWindowULong (hWnd,
                     QWL_COLORS);
      ulThickness = (ULONG)WinQueryWindowUShort (hWnd,
                     QWS_THICKNESS);
      ulStyle     = WinQueryWindowULong(hWnd,
                     QWL_STYLE) & 0x0000FFFF;

      ulDrawStyle = 0L;
      if (ulStyle & BVS_BEVELOUT)
         if (ulStyle & BVS_LINE)
            ulDrawStyle |= DB_FENCE;
         else
            ulDrawStyle |= DB_RAISED;
      else if (ulStyle & BVS_LINE)
               ulDrawStyle |= DB_TROUGH;
      else
          ulDrawStyle |= DB_DEPRESSED;
      if (ulStyle & BVS_FILL)
         ulDrawStyle |= DB_INTERIOR;

      WinQueryWindowRect (hWnd, &Rectl);
      WinDrawBorder (hps, &Rectl, ulThickness,
         ulThickness, LOUSHORT(ulColors),
         HIUSHORT(ulColors), ulDrawStyle);

      WinEndPaint (hps);
      mReturn = 0L;
      break;

   case WM_HITTEST:
      /* Allow mouse message to pass through this window */
      mReturn = (MRESULT)HT_TRANSPARENT;
      break;
```

```
      default:
         bHandled = FALSE;
         break;
   }

   if (!bHandled)
      mReturn = WinDefWindowProc (hWnd,msg,mp1,mp2);

   return (mReturn);
}

ULONG CalculatePercentage (HWND hWnd)
{
   LONG lLowerRange;
   LONG lUpperRange;
   LONG lValue;

   lLowerRange = WinQueryWindowULong (hWnd, QWL_LOWERRANGE);
   lUpperRange = WinQueryWindowULong (hWnd, QWL_UPPERRANGE);
   lValue      = WinQueryWindowULong (hWnd, QWL_VALUE);
   if (lUpperRange <= lLowerRange)
      return (1L);
   else
      return ( ((lValue - lLowerRange) * 100) /
         (lUpperRange - lLowerRange) );
}

VOID DrawPercentages (HPS hps, PRECTL pRectl)
{
   ULONG  ulTop;
   ULONG  ulBottom;
   POINTL Ptl;
   RECTL  Rectl;
   ULONG  ulHeight;

   Rectl.xLeft  = pRectl->xRight * 6 / 10;
   Rectl.xRight = pRectl->xRight * 3 / 4 - 2;
   Ptl.x        = pRectl->xRight * 3 / 4;

   ulTop        = pRectl->yTop * 95 / 100;
   ulBottom     = pRectl->yTop / 4;
   ulHeight     = ulTop - ulBottom;

   Rectl.yBottom = ulTop;
   Rectl.yTop    = Rectl.yBottom + 2;
   WinDrawBorder (hps, &Rectl, 1L, 1L, CLR_BLACK,
         CLR_WHITE,DB_FENCE);
   Ptl.y         = Rectl.yBottom - 2;
   GpiCharStringAt (hps, &Ptl, 4, "100%");

   Rectl.yBottom = ulBottom + (ulHeight * 9) / 10;
   Rectl.yTop    = Rectl.yBottom + 2;
   WinDrawBorder (hps, &Rectl, 1L, 1L, CLR_BLACK,
         CLR_WHITE,DB_TROUGH);

   Rectl.yBottom = ulBottom + (ulHeight * 8) / 10;
   Rectl.yTop    = Rectl.yBottom + 2;
```

```
    WinDrawBorder (hps, &Rectl, 1L, 1L, CLR_BLACK,
          CLR_WHITE,DB_FENCE);
    Ptl.y          = Rectl.yBottom - 2;
    GpiCharStringAt (hps, &Ptl, 3, "80%");

    Rectl.yBottom = ulBottom + (ulHeight * 7) / 10;
    Rectl.yTop    = Rectl.yBottom + 2;
    WinDrawBorder (hps, &Rectl, 1L, 1L, CLR_BLACK,
          CLR_WHITE,DB_TROUGH);

    Rectl.yBottom = ulBottom + (ulHeight * 6) / 10;
    Rectl.yTop    = Rectl.yBottom + 2;
    WinDrawBorder (hps, &Rectl, 1L, 1L, CLR_BLACK,
          CLR_WHITE,DB_FENCE);
    Ptl.y          = Rectl.yBottom - 2;
    GpiCharStringAt (hps, &Ptl, 3, "60%");

    Rectl.yBottom = ulBottom + (ulHeight * 5) / 10;
    Rectl.yTop    = Rectl.yBottom + 2;
    WinDrawBorder (hps, &Rectl, 1L, 1L, CLR_BLACK,
          CLR_WHITE,DB_TROUGH);

    Rectl.yBottom = ulBottom + (ulHeight * 4) / 10;
    Rectl.yTop    = Rectl.yBottom + 2;
    WinDrawBorder (hps, &Rectl, 1L, 1L, CLR_BLACK,
          CLR_WHITE,DB_FENCE);
    Ptl.y          = Rectl.yBottom - 2;
    GpiCharStringAt (hps, &Ptl, 3, "40%");

    Rectl.yBottom = ulBottom + (ulHeight * 3) / 10;
    Rectl.yTop    = Rectl.yBottom + 2;
    WinDrawBorder (hps, &Rectl, 1L, 1L, CLR_BLACK,
          CLR_WHITE,DB_TROUGH);

    Rectl.yBottom = ulBottom + (ulHeight * 2) / 10;
    Rectl.yTop    = Rectl.yBottom + 2;
    WinDrawBorder (hps, &Rectl, 1L, 1L, CLR_BLACK,
          CLR_WHITE,DB_FENCE);
    Ptl.y          = Rectl.yBottom - 2;
    GpiCharStringAt (hps, &Ptl, 3, "20%");

    Rectl.yBottom = ulBottom + (ulHeight * 1) / 10;
    Rectl.yTop    = Rectl.yBottom + 2;
    WinDrawBorder (hps, &Rectl, 1L, 1L, CLR_BLACK,
          CLR_WHITE,DB_TROUGH);

    Rectl.yBottom = ulBottom;
    Rectl.yTop    = Rectl.yBottom + 2;
    WinDrawBorder (hps, &Rectl, 1L, 1L, CLR_BLACK,
          CLR_WHITE,DB_FENCE);
    Ptl.y          = Rectl.yBottom - 2;
    GpiCharStringAt (hps, &Ptl, 2, "0%");

    return;
}
```

```
BOOL APIENTRY DrawTemperature (HPS hPS, PRECTL pRectl,
      LONG lColor, LONG lBackColor, LONG lPercent)
/*-------------------------------*/

This function will fill draw the vertical bar portion of the
thermometer. lColor is used to fill lPercent of the bar starting
at the top of the bulb. lBackColor is used to fill the remainder
of the bar. The rectangle identified by pRectl should be identical
to that supplied to DrawThermometer.

hPS        Presentation space to render in.
pRectl     Bounding box of the thermometer.
lColor     Color index used to fill bulb and stem of thermometer.
lBackColor Color to fill the remainder of the stem (100 - lPercent).
lPercent   Amount to fill the thermometer. Valid range is 0 to 100.


/*-------------------------------*/
{
   AREABUNDLE ab;
   RECTL       Rectl;
   int         iWidth =(pRectl->xRight - pRectl->xLeft) / 3;
   int         iBoxHeight = pRectl->yTop - pRectl->yBottom;
   int         iBarHeight = (iBoxHeight * 70) / 100;

   /* Range check the percent */
   if (lPercent > 100)
      lPercent = 100;
   else if (lPercent < 0)
      lPercent = 0;

   Rectl.xLeft = pRectl->xLeft + iWidth;
   Rectl.yTop  = pRectl->yTop - (iBoxHeight * 5) / 100;
   if (lPercent)
      Rectl.yBottom = Rectl.yTop -
         ((iBarHeight * (100 - lPercent)) / 100);
   else
      Rectl.yBottom = Rectl.yTop - iBarHeight;
   Rectl.xRight  = pRectl->xRight - iWidth;

   ab.lColor = lBackColor;
   GpiSetAttrs(hPS,PRIM_AREA,ABB_COLOR,0,(PBUNDLE)&ab);
   GpiMove (hPS,(PPOINTL)&Rectl);
   GpiBox (hPS,DRO_FILL,(PPOINTL)&Rectl.xRight,0,0);

   Rectl.yTop = Rectl.yBottom - 1;
   Rectl.yBottom=pRectl->yBottom+(iBoxHeight * 20) / 100;
   ab.lColor = lColor;
   GpiSetAttrs(hPS,PRIM_AREA,ABB_COLOR,0,(PBUNDLE)&ab);
   GpiMove (hPS,(PPOINTL)&Rectl);
   GpiBox (hPS,DRO_FILL,(PPOINTL)&Rectl.xRight,0,0);
   return (TRUE);
}
```

```
BOOL APIENTRY DrawThermometer (HPS hPS, PRECTL pRectl,
   LONG lStyle, LONG lColor, LONG lBackColor, LONG lPercent)
/*-------------------------------*/

This function will draw the outine of a thermometer scaled to
the supplied rectangle in the give presentation space. The bulb
of the rectangle is filled with lColor and the remainder is drawn
by the DrawTemperature function.

hPS        Presentation space to render in.
pRectl     Bounding box of the thermometer
lStyle     Currently undefined.
lColor     Color index used to fill bulb and stem of thermometer.
lBackColor Color to fill the remainder of the stem (100 - lPercent).
lPercent   Amount to fill the thermometer. Valid range is 0 to 100.

/*-------------------------------*/
{
   LINEBUNDLE lb;
   AREABUNDLE ab;
   ARCPARAMS  arcparms;
   POINTL     lPtCenter;
   POINTL     lStartPt;
   POINTL     lEndPt;
   POINTL     lPt;
   FIXED      fxStartAngle,fxSweepAngle;
   RECTL      BulbRectl;
   int        iBoxHeight = pRectl->yTop - pRectl->yBottom;

   /* Calculate the height of the bulb to be 25% of the total height */
   BulbRectl = *pRectl;
   BulbRectl.yTop=BulbRectl.yBottom+(iBoxHeight * 25) / 100;

   /* define the bounding box for the arc */
   arcparms.lP = (BulbRectl.xRight - BulbRectl.xLeft) / 2L;
   arcparms.lQ = (BulbRectl.yTop - BulbRectl.yBottom) / 2L;
   arcparms.lR = 0L;
   arcparms.lS = 0L;
   GpiSetArcParams(hPS, (PARCPARAMS)&arcparms);

   /* Calculate the center point of bulb */
   lPtCenter.x = BulbRectl.xLeft + arcparms.lP;
   lPtCenter.y = BulbRectl.yBottom + arcparms.lQ + 1;

/*-------------------------------*/
Draw the bulb
/*-------------------------------*/
/* Draw an invisble arc from current location to start angle */
   fxStartAngle = MAKEFIXED(120,0);
   fxSweepAngle = MAKEFIXED(90,0);
   lb.usType = LINETYPE_INVISIBLE;
   GpiSetAttrs (hPS,PRIM_LINE,LBB_TYPE,0,(PBUNDLE)&lb);
   GpiPartialArc (hPS,&lPtCenter,MAKEFIXED(1,0),
         fxStartAngle, MAKEFIXED(0,0));
   GpiQueryCurrentPosition(hPS,(PPOINTL)&lStartPt);
```

```
    /* Draw the left highlighted outline of the bulb */
    lb.lColor = CLR_WHITE;
    lb.usType = LINETYPE_SOLID;
    GpiSetAttrs (hPS,PRIM_LINE,LBB_COLOR ¦ LBB_TYPE,0,
          (PBUNDLE)&lb);
    GpiPartialArc (hPS,&lPtCenter,MAKEFIXED(1,0),
          fxStartAngle, fxSweepAngle);

    /* Draw the right shadowed outline of the bulb */
    fxStartAngle = MAKEFIXED(210,0);
    fxSweepAngle = MAKEFIXED(210,0);
    lb.lColor = CLR_DARKGRAY;
    GpiSetAttrs (hPS,PRIM_LINE,LBB_COLOR,0,(PBUNDLE)&lb);
    GpiPartialArc (hPS,&lPtCenter,MAKEFIXED(1,0),
          fxStartAngle, fxSweepAngle);
    GpiQueryCurrentPosition(hPS,(PPOINTL)&lEndPt);

    /* Fill the bulb of the thermometer with the supplied color */
    arcparms.lP -= 4;
    arcparms.lQ -= 4;
    GpiSetArcParams(hPS, (PARCPARAMS)&arcparms);
    ab.lColor = lColor;
    GpiSetAttrs(hPS,PRIM_AREA,ABB_COLOR,0,(PBUNDLE)&ab);
    GpiMove (hPS,&lPtCenter);
    GpiFullArc(hPS,DRO_FILL,MAKEFIXED(1,0));

/*--------------------------------*/
Draw the reflection on the bulb
/*--------------------------------*/
    arcparms.lP = (arcparms.lP * 3) / 4;
    arcparms.lQ = (arcparms.lQ * 3) / 4;
    GpiSetArcParams(hPS, (PARCPARAMS)&arcparms);
    fxStartAngle = MAKEFIXED(120,0);
    fxSweepAngle = MAKEFIXED(90,0);
    lb.usType = LINETYPE_INVISIBLE;
    GpiSetAttrs (hPS,PRIM_LINE,LBB_TYPE,0,(PBUNDLE)&lb);
    GpiPartialArc (hPS,&lPtCenter,MAKEFIXED(1,0),
          fxStartAngle, MAKEFIXED(0,0));

    lb.lColor = CLR_WHITE;
    lb.usType = LINETYPE_SOLID;
    GpiSetAttrs (hPS,PRIM_LINE,LBB_COLOR ¦
          LBB_TYPE,0,(PBUNDLE)&lb);
    GpiPartialArc (hPS,&lPtCenter,MAKEFIXED(1,0),
          fxStartAngle, fxSweepAngle);

    arcparms.lP = (arcparms.lP * 2) / 3;
    arcparms.lQ = (arcparms.lQ * 2) / 3;
    GpiSetArcParams(hPS, (PARCPARAMS)&arcparms);
    fxStartAngle = MAKEFIXED(120,0);
    fxSweepAngle = MAKEFIXED(90,0);
    lb.usType = LINETYPE_INVISIBLE;
    GpiSetAttrs (hPS,PRIM_LINE,LBB_TYPE,0,(PBUNDLE)&lb);
    GpiPartialArc (hPS,&lPtCenter,MAKEFIXED(1,0),
          fxStartAngle, MAKEFIXED(0,0));
```

```
   lb.lColor = CLR_WHITE;
   lb.usType = LINETYPE_SOLID;
   GpiSetAttrs (hPS,PRIM_LINE,LBB_COLOR |
         LBB_TYPE,0,(PBUNDLE)&lb);
   GpiPartialArc (hPS,&lPtCenter,MAKEFIXED(1,0),
         fxStartAngle, fxSweepAngle);

/*-------------------------------*/
Draw the sides
/*-------------------------------*/
   /* Draw the right vertical side */
   lb.lColor = CLR_DARKGRAY;
   GpiSetAttrs (hPS,PRIM_LINE,LBB_COLOR,0,(PBUNDLE)&lb);
   GpiMove(hPS,(PPOINTL)&lEndPt);
   lPt.x = lEndPt.x;
   lPt.y = pRectl->yBottom + ((iBoxHeight * 95) / 100);
   GpiLine (hPS,&lPt);

   /* Draw the left vertical side */
   lb.lColor = CLR_WHITE;
   GpiSetAttrs (hPS,PRIM_LINE,LBB_COLOR,0,(PBUNDLE)&lb);
   lPt.x = lStartPt.x;
   GpiMove(hPS,(PPOINTL)&lPt);
   GpiLine (hPS,&lStartPt);

/*-------------------------------*/
Draw the rounded top
/*-------------------------------*/
   /* Reset the rectangle for drawing the rounded top */
   BulbRectl.xLeft   = lStartPt.x;
   BulbRectl.yBottom=pRectl->yBottom+(iBoxHeight*90) / 100;
   BulbRectl.xRight  = lEndPt.x;
   BulbRectl.yTop    = pRectl->yTop;

   arcparms.lP = (BulbRectl.xRight - BulbRectl.xLeft) / 2L;
   arcparms.lQ = (BulbRectl.yTop - BulbRectl.yBottom) / 2L;
   GpiSetArcParams(hPS, (PARCPARAMS)&arcparms);

   /* Calculate the center point for the rounded top arc */
   lPtCenter.x = BulbRectl.xLeft + arcparms.lP;
   lPtCenter.y = BulbRectl.yBottom + arcparms.lQ + 1;

   /* Draw an invisble arc from current location to start angle */
   fxStartAngle = MAKEFIXED(0,0);
   fxSweepAngle = MAKEFIXED(120,0);
   lb.usType = LINETYPE_INVISIBLE;
   GpiSetAttrs (hPS,PRIM_LINE,LBB_TYPE,0,(PBUNDLE)&lb);
   GpiPartialArc (hPS,&lPtCenter,MAKEFIXED(1,0),
         fxStartAngle, MAKEFIXED(0,0));

   /* Draw the shaded side */
   lb.lColor = CLR_DARKGRAY;
   lb.usType = LINETYPE_SOLID;
   GpiSetAttrs (hPS,PRIM_LINE,LBB_COLOR |
         LBB_TYPE,0,(PBUNDLE)&lb);
```

```
   GpiPartialArc (hPS,&lPtCenter,MAKEFIXED(1,0),
         fxStartAngle, fxSweepAngle);

   /* Draw the highlighed side */
   fxStartAngle = MAKEFIXED(120,0);
   fxSweepAngle = MAKEFIXED(60,0);
   lb.lColor = CLR_WHITE;
   GpiSetAttrs (hPS,PRIM_LINE,LBB_COLOR,0,(PBUNDLE)&lb);
   GpiPartialArc (hPS,&lPtCenter,MAKEFIXED(1,0),
         fxStartAngle, fxSweepAngle);

   /* Draw the reflection */
   arcparms.lP = (arcparms.lP * 3) / 4;
   arcparms.lQ = (arcparms.lQ * 3) / 4;
   GpiSetArcParams(hPS, (PARCPARAMS)&arcparms);
   fxStartAngle = MAKEFIXED(90,0);
   fxSweepAngle = MAKEFIXED(90,0);
   lb.usType = LINETYPE_INVISIBLE;
   GpiSetAttrs (hPS,PRIM_LINE,LBB_TYPE,0,(PBUNDLE)&lb);
   GpiPartialArc (hPS,&lPtCenter,MAKEFIXED(1,0),
          fxStartAngle,MAKEFIXED(0,0));

   lb.lColor = CLR_WHITE;
   lb.usType = LINETYPE_SOLID;
   GpiSetAttrs (hPS,PRIM_LINE,LBB_COLOR ¦
         LBB_TYPE,0,(PBUNDLE)&lb);
   GpiPartialArc (hPS,&lPtCenter,MAKEFIXED(1,0),
         fxStartAngle, fxSweepAngle);

   DrawTemperature(hPS,pRectl,lColor,lBackColor,lPercent);
   return (TRUE);
}


MRESULT EXPENTRY ThermometerWndProc (HWND hWnd, ULONG msg,
      MPARAM mp1, MPARAM mp2)
{
   BOOL    bHandled = TRUE;
   MRESULT mReturn  = 0;
   RECTL   Rectl;
   HPS     hps;
   ULONG   ulColors;

   switch (msg)
   {
      case WM_CREATE:
         /* Initialize the window extra bytes */
         WinSetWindowULong (hWnd, QWL_LOWERRANGE, 0L);
         WinSetWindowULong (hWnd, QWL_UPPERRANGE, 0L);
         WinSetWindowULong (hWnd, QWL_VALUE, 0L);
         WinSetWindowULong (hWnd, QWL_COLOR,
               MAKELONG(CLR_RED,CLR_PALEGRAY));
         break;

      case THM_SETRANGE:
         WinSetWindowULong (hWnd, QWL_LOWERRANGE,
               (ULONG)mp1);
```

```
        WinRegisterClass ((HAB)0, BEVELCLASS, BevelWndProc,
              CS_HITTEST ¦ CS_SIZEREDRAW, BEVELEXTRA) &&
              WinRegisterClass ((HAB)0, THERMOMETERCLASS,
              ThermometerWndProc, CS_SIZEREDRAW,
              THERMOMETEREXTRA);
   }

   /* Save the module handle when we get loaded.  The module handle
   will be the same for all instances of the DLL */

   hModDll = hModule;

   return ((ULONG)bResult);
}
```

The `CenterWindow` function is the same one we used in our DLLSAMP and MINIMDI applications. Refer to the message processing code for the `WM_CREATE` message in CONTROLS.C. This code begins with the line:

```
case WM_CREATE:
```

`BevelWndProc` is the heart of the bevel control. When a bevel window is created, we must initialize the window extra bytes and possibly size the bevel window.

If either the `BVS_PREVID` or `BVS_PREVWINDOW` styles are specified, we use the `WinQueryWindow` function to traverse the previous sibling windows and accumulate their sizes and positions. When that is complete, `WinSetWindowPos` is used to set the bevel window's size and position. Remember that we must use the `x` and `y` fields of the bevel for its thickness and the `cx` field to increase the bevel's location and width to provide the gap between it and the sibling windows.

When we receive the `BVM_SETCOLOR` message, we need to save the new colors and cause it to repaint with the new colors. `WinInvalidateRect` is used to force the repaint:

```
   case BVM_SETCOLOR:
      /* LOUSHORT(mp1) == Border color
      HIUSHORT(mp1) == Interior color */
      WinSetWindowULong (hWnd, QWL_COLORS,(ULONG)mp1);

      /* Repaint bevel with new color */
      WinInvalidateRect (hWnd, NULL, FALSE);
      break;
```

When we receive the `BVM_SETTHICKNESS`, we simply save the new thickness. Typically, the thickness does not change, so we don't force it to repaint; however, adding a call to `WinInvalidateRect` would suffice:

```
case BVM_SETTHICKNESS:
   WinSetWindowUShort (hWnd, QWS_THICKNESS,
   SHORT1FROMMP(mp1));
   break;
```

All the drawing is performed during the `WM_PAINT` message. We first query the colors and thickness from the control's window extra bytes. Its style is queried from PM:

```
ulColors    = WinQueryWindowULong (hWnd, QWL_COLORS);
ulThickness = (ULONG)WinQueryWindowUShort (hWnd, QWS_THICKNESS);
ulStyle     = WinQueryWindowULong (hWnd, QWL_STYLE) & 0x0000FFFF;
```

Depending on the style, the various style flags are set for the call to `WinDrawBorder`. Our control makes use of several undocumented styles for the `WinDrawBorder` API. We query the rectangle of the control and paint it:

```
WinQueryWindowRect (hWnd, &Rectl);
WinDrawBorder (hps, &Rectl, ulThickness, ulThickness,
      LOUSHORT(ulColors), HIUSHORT(ulColors), ulDrawStyle);
```

Finally, we add code for the `WM_HITTEST` message. Notice that we registered the `BEVELCLASS` with `CS_HITTEST`. This allows our application to receive `WM_HITTEST` messages. Without this style, PM would automatically send all mouse messages to the control window. Because a bevel window is usually overlapping other sibling windows, the Z-order of these windows might prevent us from clicking on any one of those sibling windows because the mouse messages would be directed to the bevel window. With the `CS_HITTEST` class style, we can respond to the `WM_HITTEST` message with `HT_TRANSPARENT`, which tells PM we don't want mouse messages. They will then go to the next sibling window beneath the mouse pointer:

```
case WM_HITTEST:
/* Allow mouse message to pass through this window */
   mReturn = (MRESULT)HT_TRANSPARENT;
   break;
```

Thermometer WndProc has little to its code, but provides all the logic for the thermometer control window. During the `WM_CREATE` message, the window extra bytes are initialized:

```
case WM_CREATE:
   /* Initialize the window extra bytes */
   WinSetWindowULong (hWnd, QWL_LOWERRANGE, 0L);
   WinSetWindowULong (hWnd, QWL_UPPERRANGE, 0L);
   WinSetWindowULong (hWnd, QWL_VALUE, 0L);
   WinSetWindowULong (hWnd, QWL_COLOR,
      MAKELONG(CLR_RED,CLR_PALEGRAY));
   break;
```

The `THM_SETRANGE` processing merely stores the lower and upper ranges in the window extra bytes. Again, because this is typically done only once, we don't force a repaint, but `WinInvalidateRect` would suffice:

```
case THM_SETRANGE:
   WinSetWindowULong (hWnd, QWL_LOWERRANGE, (ULONG)mp1);
   WinSetWindowULong (hWnd, QWL_UPPERRANGE, (ULONG)mp2);
   break;
```

The `THM_SETVALUE` processing involves a little more. Upon receipt of this message, the value is stored in the window extra bytes and the fill color is retrieved. We must then update the thermometer with the new value. Our thermometer will be drawn in the thermometer window with its left edge at 20 percent of the window's width and its right edge at 60 percent of the window's width.

We then call the DrawTemperature function presented in the chapter on Presentation Spaces and Drawing:

```
case THM_SETVALUE:
   /* Set the new value */
   WinSetWindowULong (hWnd, QWL_VALUE, (ULONG)mp1);

   /* Query colors and thermometer size */
   ulColors = WinQueryWindowULong (hWnd, QWL_COLOR);
   WinQueryWindowRect (hWnd, &Rectl);
   if (!(WinQueryWindowULong (hWnd, QWL_STYLE) & THS_NOPERCENT))
   {
      Rectl.xRight  = (Rectl.xRight * 6) / 10;
      Rectl.xLeft  += (Rectl.xRight / 5);
   }
   Rectl.yTop-;

   /* Update the thermometer temperature */
   hps = WinGetPS (hWnd);
   DrawTemperature (hps, &Rectl, (LONG)((SHORT)ulColors),
         (LONG)(ulColors >> 16), CalculatePercentage(hWnd));
   WinReleasePS (hps);
   break;
```

The CalculatePercentage function takes the current value and computes the percentage value based on the lower and upper range. The WM_PAINT message processing is similar except that it must first paint the entire control and then call DrawPercentages to draw the tick marks with the percentage indicators. It then calls DrawThermometer, which draws the thermometer outline and then fills the thermometer by using the current percentage value:

```
case WM_PAINT:
   hps = WinBeginPaint (hWnd,0,0);
   WinQueryWindowRect (hWnd, &Rectl);

   /* Fill window with background color */
   ulColors = WinQueryWindowULong (hWnd, QWL_COLOR);
   WinFillRect (hps, &Rectl, (LONG)(ulColors >> 16));

   if (!(WinQueryWindowULong (hWnd, QWL_STYLE) & THS_NOPERCENT))
   {
      DrawPercentages (hps, &Rectl);

      Rectl.xRight  = (Rectl.xRight * 6) / 10;
      Rectl.xLeft  += (Rectl.xRight / 5);
   }
   Rectl.yTop-;

   DrawThermometer (hps, &Rectl, 0L,
      (LONG)((SHORT)ulColors),
      (LONG)(ulColors >> 16), CalculatePercentage(hWnd));

   WinEndPaint (hps);
   break;
```

Next, we move to MEMDLL. The external interface for this DLL is quite different. The MEMDLL DLL does not provide controls, but implements a memory suballocation module that tracks the size of each suballocated memory object and also tracks all the shared memory suballocated memory objects in order to clean up memory upon the termination of the process. The MEMDLL.H file defines the functions providing these services.

MEMDLL.H

```
/* -------------------------------
            MemDLL Header File
      Real-World Programming for OS/2
Copyright (c)  1994 Blain, Delimon, and English
------------------------------- */

PVOID   EXPENTRY PrivateAllocate (ULONG);
VOID    EXPENTRY PrivateFree (PVOID);
VOID    EXPENTRY PrivateQuery (PULONG,PULONG);
PVOID   EXPENTRY SharedAllocate (ULONG);
VOID    EXPENTRY SharedFree (PVOID);
VOID    EXPENTRY SharedQuery (PULONG,PULONG);
```

`PrivateAllocate` will suballocate a block of memory from a private memory object. The only parameter to this function is the size of the memory object to suballocate. `PrivateFree` will free a privately suballocated memory object. The only parameter to this function is the pointer to the memory object. Notice that the size of the memory object is not passed in as a parameter. This is because the MEMDLL.DLL will keep track of this information for each memory object. `PrivateQuery` will return the total amount of memory in the suballocation block and the total amount of memory that has currently been suballocated from that block. The first parameter is a pointer to a `ULONG` that will contain the allocation size of the suballocation block. The second parameter is a pointer to another `ULONG` that will contain the amount of memory that has been suballocated from the suballocation block.

The functions `SharedAllocate`, `SharedFree`, and `SharedQuery` are identical in functionality and parameters except they reference a shared memory block that is being used for suballocation among multiple processes.

Because we are defining both a private allocation block and a shared allocation block, we require both instance data and global data. In addition, we will need our initialization function to be called for each instance of the DLL. The definition (DEF) file for the MEMDLL. DLL looks like this.

MEMDLL.DEF

```
LIBRARY        MEMDLL   INITINSTANCE
DESCRIPTION   'Memory DLL  1994 Blain, Delimon, & English'
PROTMODE
```

```
CODE          MOVEABLE
DATA          MOVEABLE SINGLE SHARED

SEGMENTS
   _INSTANCEDATA         CLASS 'FAR_DATA' NONSHARED PRELOAD
   _INSTANCEDATA         CLASS 'DATA'     NONSHARED PRELOAD
   c_common              CLASS 'BSS'      NONSHARED PRELOAD

EXPORTS
   PrivateAllocate   @1
   PrivateFree       @2
   PrivateQuery      @3
   SharedAllocate    @4
   SharedFree        @5
   SharedQuery       @6
```

Like the CONTROLS.DLL, this one is defined as a library with instance initialization:

```
LIBRARY        MEMDLL   INITINSTANCE
```

Because we require both types of data segments, the default data segment type will be global, and we specifically identify all segments that will be private for each instance:

```
CODE          MOVEABLE
DATA          MOVEABLE SINGLE SHARED

SEGMENTS
   _INSTANCEDATA         CLASS 'FAR_DATA' NONSHARED PRELOAD
   _INSTANCEDATA         CLASS 'DATA'     NONSHARED PRELOAD
   c_common              CLASS 'BSS'      NONSHARED PRELOAD
```

Remember to check the output of your MAP file for the specific name for the segments and class name as they may change depending on which compiler you are using. Our size functions are exported here assigning each a unique ordinal value.

Because we have defined the DLL to be `INITINSTANCE`, our initialization entry point is defined as it was for the CONTROLS.DLL.

MEMINIT.ASM

```
; Memory DLL Initialization
; Define the initialization/termination entry point for the
; Memory DLL

    .386p

ifdef _ _TASM_ _
   model flat,pascal
endif

_TEXT   SEGMENT    DWORD USE32 PUBLIC 'CODE'
        EXTRN     _InitializeMemDll:near
```

```
ifdef _ _MASM386_ _
      ASSUME    CS: FLAT, DS: FLAT, ES: FLAT
endif

_DLLEntry:
      jmp _InitializeMemDll

_TEXT   ENDS
        END       _DLLEntry
```

The initialization function for this DLL is named "InitializeMemDLL" and will be called both when the DLL is loaded and when unloaded for each instance of the DLL.

The instance data we need to maintain for each instance of the DLL is defined in the MEMINST.H file.

MEMINST.H

```
/* --------------------------------
             MemInst Header File
       Real-World Programming for OS/2
Copyright (c)  1994 Blain, Delimon, and English
-------------------------------- */

/* MemDLL instance data structure */
typedef struct tagINSTANCE_STRUCT
{
   PVOID pMemPrivate;
   PVOID pMemSharedHead;
   ULONG ulTotalAlloc;
   ULONG ulTotalSubAlloc;
   ULONG ulTotalSharedSubAlloc;
} INSTANCEDATA_STRUCT;
```

We maintain the handle to the base of the private memory suballocation block in pMemPrivate. pMemSharedHead contains the handle of the last suballocated shared memory object for each instance. The shared memory handles are maintained by using a linked list that we will look at shortly. The size of the private memory suballocation block is stored in ulTotalAlloc, whereas the total amount of each type of suballocated memory for each instance is maintained in ulTotalSubAlloc and ulTotalSharedSubAlloc.

The instance data structure is instantiated and defined in the MEMINST.C file.

MEMINST.C

```
/* --------------------------------
Memory DLL Instance Data
Real-World Programming for OS/2
Copyright (c)  1994 Blain, Delimon, and English
-------------------------------- */
```

```
#include <os2.h>

#include "meminst.h"

#ifndef __ZORTECH__

/* IBMC compiler defines data segments with #pragma data_seg */
#ifdef __IBMC__
#pragma data_seg ( _INSTANCEDATA )
#endif

INSTANCEDATA_STRUCT InstanceData =
{
   NULL,              /* pMemPrivate            */
   NULL,              /* pMemSharedHead         */
   0L,                /* ulTotalAlloc           */
   0L,                /* ulTotalSubAlloc        */
   0L                 /* ulTotalSharedSubAlloc */
};
#else
/* Zortech Compiler does not have a command line switch to rename the
data segment.  Use the c_common data segment by not initializing
InstanceData. */
INSTANCEDATA_STRUCT InstanceData;
#endif
```

This file is compiled with the data segment name of `_INSTANCEDATA` so that the DEF file can define it as `NONSHARED`. All instance data can now be referenced in the `InstanceData` structure. Each instance of the DLL will receive its private copy of this instance data structure.

We now take a look at the code for the functions implementing the DLL.

MEMDLL.C

```
/* --------------------------------
                 Memory DLL
        Real-World Programming for OS/2
Copyright (c)  1994 Blain, Delimon, and English
-------------------------------- */

/*
Returned address is the allocated address plus the size of a
memory object header.

Private memory allocation stores the object size in the header.

Shared memory allocation stores the object size in the header.
It also maintains a linked list of the memory objects so that
memory can be cleaned up if a process terminates without freeing
all of its allocated shared memory.
*/

#define INCL_DOS
#define INCL_DOSERRORS
#define INCL_WIN
```

```
#include <os2.h>
#include <stdio.h>
#include "memdll.h"
#include "meminst.h"

#define PRIVATEALLOC     0x20000      /* 128 K */
#define SHAREDALLOC      0x40000      /* 256 K */

typedef struct tagPRIVATE_MEMORY_OBJECT
{
   ULONG ulSize;        /* Size of memory object  */
} PRIVATE_MEMORY_OBJECT;
typedef PRIVATE_MEMORY_OBJECT *PPRIVATE_MEMORY_OBJECT;

typedef struct tagSHARED_MEMORY_OBJECT
{
   PVOID pPrev;         /* Previous memory object */
   PVOID pNext;         /* Next memory object     */
   ULONG ulSize;        /* Size of memory object  */
} SHARED_MEMORY_OBJECT;
typedef SHARED_MEMORY_OBJECT *PSHARED_MEMORY_OBJECT;


/* Nonshared data in segment _INSTANCEDATA     */

extern INSTANCEDATA_STRUCT InstanceData;

/* Shared data placed into initialized variables data segment */

/* IBMC compiler defines data segments with #pragma data_seg */
#ifdef __IBMC__
#pragma data_seg (DATA32)
#endif

PVOID    pMemShared     = NULL;
BOOL     bFirstInstance = TRUE;
HMODULE hModDll         = 0;


#ifdef __IBMC__
ULONG _System _DLL_InitTerm (HMODULE hModule, ULONG ulTerminating)
#else
ULONG _stdcall InitializeMemDll (HMODULE hModule, ULONG ulTerminating)
#endif
{
   BOOL bResult;

   if (ulTerminating & 0x01)
   {
      PSHARED_MEMORY_OBJECT pMem =
         InstanceData.pMemSharedHead;

      /* Free all shared suballocated memory the app forgot to free */
      while (pMem)
      {
         PVOID pMemPrev = pMem->pPrev;
```

```
         if (!DosSubFreeMem (pMemShared, pMem,
               pMem->ulSize))
            pMem = (PSHARED_MEMORY_OBJECT)pMemPrev;
         else
            break;
      }

      /* Release access to semaphore used for shared memory
serialization */
      DosSubUnset (pMemShared);

      /* Free the private memory allocated for this instance */
      DosFreeMem (InstanceData.pMemPrivate);

      return (FALSE);
   }
   else
   {
      /* Allocate the private memory and initialize for suballocation */
      bResult = !DosAllocMem ((PPVOID)&InstanceData.pMemPrivate,
         PRIVATEALLOC, PAG_READ ¦ PAG_WRITE) &&
         !DosSubSet (InstanceData.pMemPrivate,
         DOSSUB_INIT ¦ DOSSUB_SPARSE_OBJ, PRIVATEALLOC);

      if (bResult)
      {
         if (bFirstInstance)
         {
            /* Allocate the shared memory and initialize for
suballocation.  Only allocate for first instance of DLL */
            bFirstInstance = FALSE;
            bResult =
               !DosAllocSharedMem ((PPVOID)&pMemShared,
                  NULL, SHAREDALLOC, PAG_READ ¦ PAG_WRITE ¦
                  fSHARE) && !DosSubSet (pMemShared,
                  DOSSUB_INIT ¦ DOSSUB_SPARSE_OBJ ¦
                  DOSSUB_SERIALIZE, SHAREDALLOC);

            /* Free shared memory if an error occurred */
            if (!bResult && pMemShared)
               DosFreeMem (pMemShared);
         }
         else
         {
            /* Get access to the shared memory and the semaphore used
            for memory suballocation of shared memory. */
            bResult =
               !DosGetSharedMem (pMemShared,
               PAG_READ ¦ PAG_WRITE) &&
               !DosSubSet (pMemShared,
               DOSSUB_SPARSE_OBJ ¦ DOSSUB_SERIALIZE,
               SHAREDALLOC);
         }
      }
      if (!bResult)
      {
```

```
            /* Free private memory if an error occurred */
            if (InstanceData.pMemPrivate)
               DosFreeMem (InstanceData.pMemPrivate);
         }
      }

   /* Save the module handle when we get loaded.  The module handle
   will be the same for all instances of the DLL */

   hModDll = hModule;

   return ((ULONG)bResult);
}

PVOID EXPENTRY PrivateAllocate (ULONG ulSize)
{
   PVOID pMem;

   /* Add room for the memory object header */
   ulSize += sizeof(PRIVATE_MEMORY_OBJECT);

   /* Align on 8 byte boundary */
   ulSize  = (ulSize + 7) & 0xFFFFFFF8;

   if (!DosSubAllocMem (InstanceData.pMemPrivate,
         &pMem, ulSize))
   {
      /* Save size in memory object header */
      ((PPRIVATE_MEMORY_OBJECT)pMem)->ulSize = ulSize;

      /* Data starts immediately after the memory object header */
      pMem = (PVOID)((ULONG)pMem +
              sizeof(PRIVATE_MEMORY_OBJECT));

      /* Increment total suballocation of private memory */
      InstanceData.ulTotalSubAlloc  += ulSize;
   }
   else
   {
      WinMessageBox (HWND_DESKTOP, HWND_DESKTOP,
         "Private Memory Suballocation Failure",
         "Memory Thermometer",
         0, MB_ERROR ¦ MB_OK);
      pMem = NULL;
   }

   return (pMem);
}

VOID EXPENTRY PrivateFree (PVOID pData)
{
   PPRIVATE_MEMORY_OBJECT pMem;
   ULONG                  ulSize;

   /* Set pointer to memory object header */
```

```
   pMem   = (PPRIVATE_MEMORY_OBJECT)((ULONG)pData -
            sizeof(PRIVATE_MEMORY_OBJECT));
   ulSize = pMem->ulSize;

   if (!DosSubFreeMem (InstanceData.pMemPrivate, pMem,
            ulSize))

      /* Decrement total suballocation of private memory */
      InstanceData.ulTotalSubAlloc  -= ulSize;

   else
      WinMessageBox (HWND_DESKTOP, HWND_DESKTOP,
            "Private Memory Free Failure",
            "Memory Thermometer",
            0, MB_ERROR | MB_OK);

   return;
}

VOID EXPENTRY PrivateQuery (PULONG pTotalAlloc,
      PULONG pTotalSubAlloc)
{
   *pTotalAlloc    = PRIVATEALLOC;
   *pTotalSubAlloc = InstanceData.ulTotalSubAlloc;
   return;
}

PVOID EXPENTRY SharedAllocate (ULONG ulSize)
{
   PVOID pMem;

   /* Add room for the memory object header */
   ulSize += sizeof(SHARED_MEMORY_OBJECT);

   /* Align on 8 byte boundary */
   ulSize  = (ulSize + 7) & 0xFFFFFFF8;

   if (!DosSubAllocMem (pMemShared, &pMem, ulSize))
   {
      /* Save size in memory object header */
      ((PSHARED_MEMORY_OBJECT)pMem)->ulSize = ulSize;
      ((PSHARED_MEMORY_OBJECT)pMem)->pNext  = NULL;
      ((PSHARED_MEMORY_OBJECT)pMem)->pPrev  =
      InstanceData.pMemSharedHead;
      if (InstanceData.pMemSharedHead)
         ((PSHARED_MEMORY_OBJECT)InstanceData.pMemSharedHead)->pNext = pMem;
      InstanceData.pMemSharedHead    = pMem;

      /* Data starts immediately after the memory object header */
      pMem = (PVOID)((ULONG)pMem +
            sizeof(SHARED_MEMORY_OBJECT));
      /* Increment total suballocation of shared memory */
      InstanceData.ulTotalSharedSubAlloc  += ulSize;
   }
   else
   {
```

```
      WinMessageBox (HWND_DESKTOP, HWND_DESKTOP,
         "Shared Memory Suballocation Failure",
         "Memory Thermometer",
         0, MB_ERROR | MB_OK);
      pMem = NULL;
   }

   return (pMem);
}

VOID EXPENTRY SharedFree (PVOID pData)
{
   PSHARED_MEMORY_OBJECT pMem;
   ULONG                 ulSize;

   /* Set pointer to memory object header */
   pMem    = (PSHARED_MEMORY_OBJECT)((ULONG)pData -
             sizeof(SHARED_MEMORY_OBJECT));
   ulSize = pMem->ulSize;
   if (pMem == InstanceData.pMemSharedHead)
   {
      if (pMem->pPrev)
         ((PSHARED_MEMORY_OBJECT)(pMem->pPrev))->pNext = NULL;
      InstanceData.pMemSharedHead = pMem->pPrev;
   }
   else
   {
      ((PSHARED_MEMORY_OBJECT)(pMem->pNext))->pPrev = pMem->pPrev;
      if (pMem->pPrev)
         ((PSHARED_MEMORY_OBJECT)(pMem->pPrev))->pNext = pMem->pNext;
   }

   if (!DosSubFreeMem (pMemShared, pMem, ulSize))
      /* Decrement total suballocation of private memory */
      InstanceData.ulTotalSharedSubAlloc  -= ulSize;
   else
      WinMessageBox (HWND_DESKTOP, HWND_DESKTOP,
         "Shared Memory Free Failure",
         "Memory Thermometer",
         0, MB_ERROR | MB_OK);

   return;
}

VOID EXPENTRY SharedQuery (PULONG pTotalAlloc,
      PULONG pTotalSharedSubAlloc)
{
   *pTotalAlloc          = SHAREDALLOC;
   *pTotalSharedSubAlloc = InstanceData.ulTotalSharedSubAlloc;
   return;
}
```

For our application, the private suballocation block will allocate 128KB, and the shared suballocation block will allocate 256KB:

```
#define PRIVATEALLOC      0x20000      /* 128 K */
#define SHAREDALLOC       0x40000      /* 256 K */
```

The DLL will track the size of each suballocation memory object. For private memory objects, this is done by suballocating an additional four bytes, storing the size at the beginning of the block, and returning a pointer starting immediately after the size. (See Figure 12.14.)

```
typedef struct tagPRIVATE_MEMORY_OBJECT
{
   ULONG ulSize;          /* Size of memory object  */
} PRIVATE_MEMORY_OBJECT;
typedef PRIVATE_MEMORY_OBJECT *PPRIVATE_MEMORY_OBJECT;
```

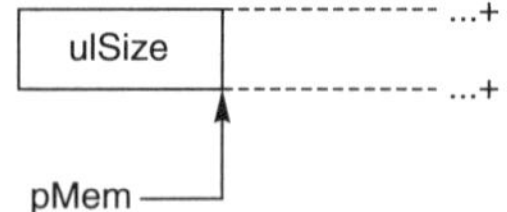

Figure 12.14. Tracking a private memory object.

When an instance terminates, we free all the memory in the private suballocation block. For shared memory objects, it is a little more complicated. We cannot merely free the shared memory suballocation block because other processes may be sharing this block of memory. In addition to tracking the size of each object, we must keep track of all currently suballocated memory objects for each process. This is done by using a linked list. Shared memory objects will have enough additional bytes allocated to store a `SHARED_MEMORY_OBJECT` header (see Figure 12.15):

```
typedef struct tagSHARED_MEMORY_OBJECT
{
   PVOID pPrev;           /* Previous memory object */
   PVOID pNext;           /* Next memory object     */
   ULONG ulSize;          /* Size of memory object  */
} SHARED_MEMORY_OBJECT;
typedef SHARED_MEMORY_OBJECT *PSHARED_MEMORY_OBJECT;
```

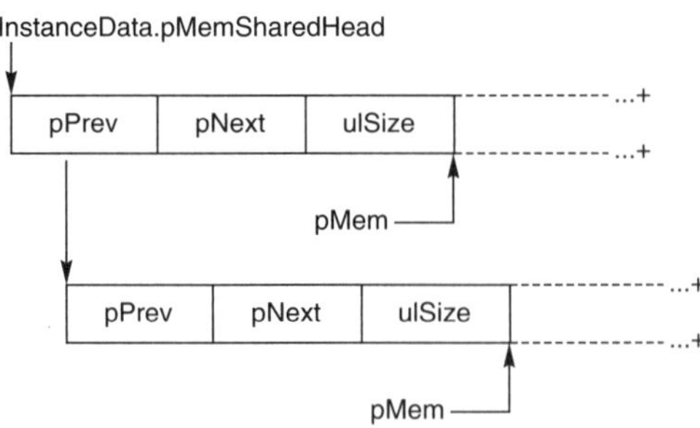

Figure 12.15. Tracking a shared memory object.

When a memory object is allocated, it is placed at the head of the list. `InstanceData.pMemSharedHead` will point to the last suballocated shared memory object. When a memory object is freed, it is removed from the linked list. Upon termination, the linked list for the process is walked, and all unfreed shared memory is freed.

The returned address starts immediately after this header information. Notice that because of the way we have defined the `PRIVATE_MEMORY_OBJECT` and `SHARED_MEMORY_OBJECT`, the size of a suballocated memory object can always be determined by subtracting `sizeof(ULONG)` from the pointer.

The global data segment for this DLL contains the handle for the shared memory block and a flag indicating whether this is the first DLL being initialized for the DLL. The instance data is referenced externally:

```
/* Nonshared data in segment _INSTANCEDATA      */
extern INSTANCEDATA_STRUCT InstanceData;

/* Shared data placed into initialized variables data segment */

/* IBMC compiler defines data segments with #pragma data_seg */
#ifdef __IBMC__
#pragma data_seg (DATA32)
#endif

PVOID   pMemShared     = NULL;
BOOL    bFirstInstance = TRUE;
HMODULE hModDll        = 0;
```

The initialization function, `InitializeMemDll`, is a little more involved than previous initialization functions. When the DLL is being initialized, we must allocate the private memory block and initialize it for suballocation:

```
   /* Allocate the private memory and initialize for suballocation */
bResult = !DosAllocMem ((PPVOID)&InstanceData.pMemPrivate,
      PRIVATEALLOC, PAG_READ ¦ PAG_WRITE) &&
      !DosSubSet (InstanceData.pMemPrivate,
      DOSSUB_INIT ¦ DOSSUB_SPARSE_OBJ, PRIVATEALLOC);
```

If this is the first instance, we allocate the shared memory block and initialize it for suballocation:

```
if (bResult)
{
   if (bFirstInstance)
   {
      /* Allocate the shared memory and initialize for
         suballocation.  Only allocate for first instance of
         DLL */
      bFirstInstance = FALSE;
      bResult =
         !DosAllocSharedMem ((PPVOID)&pMemShared, NULL,
         SHAREDALLOC, PAG_READ ¦ PAG_WRITE ¦ fSHARE) &&
         !DosSubSet (pMemShared,
         DOSSUB_INIT ¦ DOSSUB_SPARSE_OBJ ¦ DOSSUB_SERIALIZE,
         SHAREDALLOC);

      /* Free shared memory if an error occurred */
      if (!bResult && pMemShared)
         DosFreeMem (pMemShared);
   }
```

```
        CONTROL     "", IDC_THERMOMETER, 168, 38, 70, 78,
                    THERMOMETERCLASS, WS_VISIBLE
        CONTROL     "", IDC_THERMOMETER ¦ BVS_IDMASK, 3, 2, 1,
                    0, BEVELCLASS, BVS_BEVELIN ¦
                    BVS_RECTANGLE ¦ BVS_PREVID ¦ WS_VISIBLE
        LTEXT       "Thermometer Color",    -1,          164,
                    24, 77,  8
        CONTROL     "", IDC_THERMOCOLOR, 164, 13, 55, 12,
                    WC_SPINBUTTON, SPBS_READONLY ¦
                    SPBS_MASTER ¦ SPBS_JUSTLEFT ¦
                    SPBS_FASTSPIN ¦ WS_GROUP ¦ WS_TABSTOP ¦
                    WS_VISIBLE
        CONTROL     "", IDC_BEVEL4 ¦ BVS_IDMASK, 4, 2, 1, 0,
                    BEVELCLASS, BVS_BEVELOUT ¦ BVS_RECTANGLE ¦
                    BVS_PREVID ¦ WS_VISIBLE
        CONTROL     "", -1, 3, 2, 1, 0, BEVELCLASS,
                    BVS_BEVELIN ¦ BVS_RECTANGLE ¦
                    BVS_PREVWINDOW ¦ WS_VISIBLE
   END
END
```

The dialog makes extensive use of our BEVELCLASS control. A bevel is placed around the private memory, shared memory, and the thermometer. The dialog also defines a bevel around the bevel on the thermometer, and still another bevel around that bevel, each specifying a different gap. Remember that all units in this file are in dialog units and not pixels.

THERMO.H

```
/* -------------------------------
           Thermo Header File
      Real-World Programming for OS/2
Copyright (c)  1994 Blain, Delimon, and English
------------------------------- */

#define ID_APPNAME              1

#define IDC_BEVEL1             50
#define IDC_BEVEL2             51
#define IDC_BEVEL3             52
#define IDC_BEVEL4             53

#define IDC_PRIVATEALLOC      100
#define IDC_PRIVATESUBALLOC   101
#define IDC_PRIVATELIST       102
#define IDC_SHAREDALLOC       103
#define IDC_SHAREDSUBALLOC    104
#define IDC_SHAREDLIST        105
#define IDC_THERMOCOLOR       106
#define IDC_THERMOMETER       107

#define IDB_PRIVATEALLOC      200
#define IDB_PRIVATEFREE       201
#define IDB_PRIVATEFREEALL    202
#define IDB_SHAREDALLOC       203
```

```
#define IDB_SHAREDFREE        204
#define IDB_SHAREDFREEALL     205

#define IDM_ABOUT             300
```

THERMO.DEF

```
NAME            THERMO   WINDOWAPI
DESCRIPTION     'Thermometer  1994 Blain, Delimon, & English'
PROTMODE

HEAPSIZE        4096
STACKSIZE       16384

EXPORTS
      MainDlgProc    @1
      AboutDlgProc   @2
```

This should be nothing new to you at this point. We now look at the application itself.

THERMO.C

```
/* --------------------------------
                Thermo Program
        Real-World Programming for OS/2
Copyright (c)  1994 Blain, Delimon, and English
-------------------------------- */

#define INCL_DOS
#define INCL_WIN

#include <os2.h>
#include <stdio.h>
#include "thermo.h"
#include "memdll.h"
#include "controls.h"
#include "..\..\common\about.h"

/* Exported Functions */

MRESULT EXPENTRY MainDlgProc (HWND,ULONG,MPARAM,MPARAM);

/* Local Functions */

VOID  AddListItem (HWND,PVOID,ULONG);
VOID  FreeAllListItems (HWND,ULONG,BOOL);
VOID  FreeListItem (HWND,ULONG,BOOL);
ULONG ParseItem (PSZ);
VOID  SetNumberField (HWND,ULONG,USHORT);
VOID  UpdateNumbers (HWND);

/* Global Variables */

HAB      hab;                     /* Handle to anchor block       */
CHAR     szTitle[64];
```

```
/* Table of colors */
CHAR szColors[15][10] =
{
   "Black",
   "Blue",
   "Brown",
   "Cyan",
   "DarkBlue",
   "DarkCyan",
   "DarkGray",
   "DarkGreen",
   "DarkPink",
   "DarkRed",
   "Green",
   "Pink",
   "Red",
   "Yellow",
   "White"
};

/* Array of pointers to color strings (for spinner control) */
PVOID pszColors[15] =
{
   &szColors[0],
   &szColors[1],
   &szColors[2],
   &szColors[3],
   &szColors[4],
   &szColors[5],
   &szColors[6],
   &szColors[7],
   &szColors[8],
   &szColors[9],
   &szColors[10],
   &szColors[11],
   &szColors[12],
   &szColors[13],
   &szColors[14]
};

/* Table of color indexes matching the szColor entries */
SHORT sColorMap[15] =
{
   CLR_BLACK,
   CLR_BLUE,
   CLR_BROWN,
   CLR_CYAN,
   CLR_DARKBLUE,
   CLR_DARKCYAN,
   CLR_DARKGRAY,
   CLR_DARKGREEN,
   CLR_DARKPINK,
   CLR_DARKRED,
   CLR_GREEN,
   CLR_PINK,
   CLR_RED,
```

```
   CLR_YELLOW,
   CLR_WHITE
};

/* Undocument menu message */
#define MM_QUERYITEMBYPOS      0x01f3
#define MAKE_16BIT_POINTER(p)  \
      ((PVOID)MAKEULONG(LOUSHORT(p),(HIUSHORT(p) << 3) ¦ 7))

int main()
{
   HAB     hab;
   HMQ     hmq;

   hab = WinInitialize (0);
   hmq = WinCreateMsgQueue (hab, 0);

   WinLoadString (hab, 0, ID_APPNAME, sizeof(szTitle),
         szTitle);

   WinDlgBox (HWND_DESKTOP, HWND_DESKTOP, MainDlgProc, 0,
         ID_APPNAME, NULL);

   WinDestroyMsgQueue (hmq);
   WinTerminate (hab);
   return (0);
}

VOID AddAboutToSystemMenu(HWND hWndFrame)
{
   MENUITEM mi;
   HWND     hWndSysSubMenu;

   WinSendMsg (WinWindowFromID (hWndFrame, FID_SYSMENU),
         MM_QUERYITEMBYPOS, 0L, MAKE_16BIT_POINTER(&mi));
   hWndSysSubMenu = mi.hwndSubMenu;
   mi.iPosition   = MIT_END;
   mi.afStyle     = MIS_SEPARATOR;
   mi.afAttribute = 0;
   mi.id          = -1;
   mi.hwndSubMenu = 0;
   mi.hItem       = 0;
   WinSendMsg (hWndSysSubMenu, MM_INSERTITEM, MPFROMP (&mi),
         NULL);
   mi.afStyle     = MIS_TEXT;
   mi.id          = IDM_ABOUT;
   WinSendMsg (hWndSysSubMenu, MM_INSERTITEM, MPFROMP (&mi),
         "About...");
   return;
}

VOID AddListItem (HWND hWnd, PVOID pMem, ULONG ulCtlID)
{
   CHAR  szNumber[9];
   SHORT sIndex;
```

```
   /* Convert address to hexadecimal string */
   sprintf (szNumber, "%08lx", (ULONG)pMem);
   WinUpper (hab, 0, 0, szNumber);

   /* Insert formatted memory address into listbox */
   sIndex = (SHORT)WinSendDlgItemMsg (hWnd, ulCtlID,
         LM_INSERTITEM, (MPARAM)LIT_END, szNumber);

   /* Select the item just inserted */
   WinSendDlgItemMsg (hWnd, ulCtlID, LM_SELECTITEM,
         (MPARAM)sIndex, (MPARAM)TRUE);

   return;
}

VOID FreeAllListItems (HWND hWnd, ULONG ulCtlID,
    BOOL bPrivate)
{
   CHAR  szNumber[9];
   SHORT sIndex;

   /* Query number of items in the listbox */
   sIndex = (SHORT)WinSendDlgItemMsg (hWnd, ulCtlID,
         LM_QUERYITEMCOUNT, 0L, 0L);

   while (sIndex--)
   {
      /* Query the text of the last item in the listbox */
      WinSendDlgItemMsg (hWnd, ulCtlID,
         LM_QUERYITEMTEXT, MPFROM2SHORT(sIndex,9),
         szNumber);

      /* Convert text to address and free memory */
      if (bPrivate)
         PrivateFree ((PVOID)ParseItem (szNumber));
      else
         SharedFree ((PVOID)ParseItem (szNumber));
   }

   /* Delete all items in the listbox */
   WinSendDlgItemMsg (hWnd, ulCtlID, LM_DELETEALL, 0L, 0L);

   return;
}

VOID FreeListItem (HWND hWnd, ULONG ulCtlID, BOOL bPrivate)
{
   CHAR  szNumber[9];
   SHORT sIndex;

   /* Query the selected item in the listbox */
   sIndex = (SHORT)WinSendDlgItemMsg (hWnd, ulCtlID,
         LM_QUERYSELECTION, (MPARAM)LIT_FIRST, 0L);

   if (sIndex != LIT_NONE)
   {
```

```
      /* Query the text of the selected item in the listbox */
      WinSendDlgItemMsg (hWnd, ulCtlID,
         LM_QUERYITEMTEXT, MPFROM2SHORT(sIndex,9),
         szNumber);

      /* Convert text to address and free memory */
      if (bPrivate)
         PrivateFree ((PVOID)ParseItem (szNumber));
      else
         SharedFree ((PVOID)ParseItem (szNumber));

      /* Delete the selected item from the listbox */
      WinSendDlgItemMsg (hWnd, ulCtlID, LM_DELETEITEM,
           (MPARAM)sIndex, 0L);
   }

   /* Select the first item in the listbox */
   WinSendDlgItemMsg (hWnd, ulCtlID, LM_SELECTITEM,
         (MPARAM)0L, (MPARAM)TRUE);

   return;
}

ULONG ParseItem (PSZ szItem)
{
   ULONG CurPos = 0;
   ULONG ulMem  = 0;

   /* Convert hexadecimal string to number */
   for (; CurPos < 8; CurPos++)
      ulMem = ulMem*16 +
      ((szItem[CurPos] <= '9') ? (szItem[CurPos] - '0') :
      (szItem[CurPos] - 'A' + 10));

   return (ulMem);
}

VOID SetNumberField (HWND hWnd, ULONG ulNumber,
      USHORT usCtlID)
{
   CHAR    szNumber[9];

   /* Convert number to hexadecimal string */
   sprintf (szNumber, "%8lx", ulNumber);
   WinUpper (hab, 0, 0, szNumber);

   /* Set the text of the control */
   WinSetDlgItemText (hWnd, usCtlID, szNumber);

   return;
}

VOID UpdateNumbers (HWND hWnd)
{
   ULONG ulAlloc,
         ulSubAlloc,
```

```
        ulSharedAlloc,
        ulSharedSubAlloc;

   /* Query private memory allocation info */
   PrivateQuery (&ulAlloc, &ulSubAlloc);

   /* Query shared memory allocation info */
   SharedQuery (&ulSharedAlloc, &ulSharedSubAlloc);

   SetNumberField (hWnd, ulAlloc, IDC_PRIVATEALLOC);
   SetNumberField (hWnd, ulSubAlloc,
         IDC_PRIVATESUBALLOC);
   SetNumberField (hWnd, ulSharedAlloc,    IDC_SHAREDALLOC);
   SetNumberField (hWnd, ulSharedSubAlloc,
         IDC_SHAREDSUBALLOC);

   /* Free and Free All buttons are enabled only if memory allocated */
   WinEnableControl (hWnd, IDB_PRIVATEFREE, ulSubAlloc);
   WinEnableControl (hWnd, IDB_PRIVATEFREEALL, ulSubAlloc);
   WinEnableControl (hWnd, IDB_SHAREDFREE,
         ulSharedSubAlloc);
   WinEnableControl (hWnd, IDB_SHAREDFREEALL,
         ulSharedSubAlloc);

   /* Set private memory allocation amount as the thermometer value  */
   WinSendDlgItemMsg (hWnd, IDC_THERMOMETER, THM_SETVALUE,
         (MPARAM)ulSubAlloc, 0L);

   return;
}


MRESULT EXPENTRY MainDlgProc (HWND hWnd, ULONG msg,
         MPARAM mp1, MPARAM mp2)
{
   BOOL    bHandled = TRUE;
   MRESULT mReturn  = 0;
   PVOID   pMem;
   ULONG   ulAlloc,
           ulSubAlloc;

   switch (msg)
   {
      case WM_INITDLG:
         /* Center the dialog on the screen */
         CenterWindow (hWnd);

         /* Add the About menu item to the system menu */
         AddAboutToSystemMenu (hWnd);

         /* Set the thickness of the border around the dialog */
         WinSendDlgItemMsg (hWnd, IDC_BEVEL1,
               BVM_SETTHICKNESS, (MPARAM)4, 0L);

         /* Query the suballocation info to set thermometer range */
         PrivateQuery (&ulAlloc, &ulSubAlloc);
```

```
    WinSendDlgItemMsg (hWnd, IDC_THERMOMETER,
          THM_SETRANGE, 0L, (MPARAM)ulAlloc);
    WinSendDlgItemMsg (hWnd, IDC_THERMOMETER,
          THM_SETVALUE, 0L, 0L);
    WinSendDlgItemMsg (hWnd, IDC_THERMOMETER,
          THM_SETCOLOR,(MPARAM)MAKELONG(CLR_RED,
          CLR_PALEGRAY), 0L);

    /* Initialize the memory numbers */
    UpdateNumbers (hWnd);

    /* Initialize the thermometer color spinner control */
    WinSendDlgItemMsg (hWnd, IDC_THERMOCOLOR,
          SPBM_SETTEXTLIMIT, (MPARAM)9L, (MPARAM)0L);
    WinSendDlgItemMsg (hWnd, IDC_THERMOCOLOR,
          SPBM_SETARRAY, (MPARAM)pszColors,
          (MPARAM)15L);
    WinSendDlgItemMsg (hWnd, IDC_THERMOCOLOR,
          SPBM_SETCURRENTVALUE,
          (MPARAM)12L, (MPARAM)0L);

    /* Set the focus to the first pushbutton */
    WinSetFocus (HWND_DESKTOP,
    WinWindowFromID (hWnd, IDB_PRIVATEALLOC));
    break;

case WM_CONTROL:
    switch (LOUSHORT(mp1))
    {
       case IDC_THERMOCOLOR:
          if (HIUSHORT(mp1) == SPBN_ENDSPIN)
          {
             ULONG ulSelect;

             /* Query selection index from spinner */
             WinSendDlgItemMsg (hWnd, IDC_THERMOCOLOR,
              SPBM_QUERYVALUE, (MPARAM)&ulSelect, 0L);

/* Set the current color of the thermometer */
             WinSendDlgItemMsg (hWnd, IDC_THERMOMETER,
                THM_SETCOLOR,
                (MPARAM)MAKELONG(sColorMap[ulSelect],
                CLR_PALEGRAY),
                0L);
          }
          break;
    }
    break;

case WM_COMMAND:
case WM_SYSCOMMAND:
    switch (SHORT1FROMMP(mp1))
    {
       case IDB_PRIVATEALLOC:
          /* Allocate an arbitrary amount of 1000 bytes */
          if ((pMem = PrivateAllocate (1000L)) != 0)
```

```
                AddListItem (hWnd, pMem, IDC_PRIVATELIST);
             break;

          case IDB_PRIVATEFREE:
             FreeListItem (hWnd, IDC_PRIVATELIST, TRUE);
             break;

          case IDB_PRIVATEFREEALL:
             FreeAllListItems (hWnd, IDC_PRIVATELIST,
                TRUE);
             break;

          case IDB_SHAREDALLOC:
             /* Allocate an arbitrary amount of 1000 bytes */
             if ((pMem = SharedAllocate (1000L)) != 0)
                AddListItem (hWnd, pMem, IDC_SHAREDLIST);
             break;
          case IDB_SHAREDFREE:
             FreeListItem (hWnd, IDC_SHAREDLIST, FALSE);
             break;

          case IDB_SHAREDFREEALL:
             FreeAllListItems (hWnd, IDC_SHAREDLIST,
                FALSE);
             break;

          case IDM_ABOUT:
             DisplayAbout (hWnd, szTitle);
             break;

          case SC_CLOSE:
             WinDismissDlg (hWnd, FALSE);
             bHandled = TRUE;
             break;

          default:
             bHandled = (msg == WM_COMMAND);
       }

       /* If button was pressed then update the numbers */
       if (msg == WM_COMMAND)
          UpdateNumbers (hWnd);

       break;

    default:
       bHandled = FALSE;
       break;
 }

 if (!bHandled)
    mReturn = WinDefDlgProc (hWnd, msg, mp1, mp2);

 return (mReturn);
}
```

A bevel is defined around the entire edge of the dialog window. The thickness of this bevel is set during the WM_INITDLG message:

```
/* Set the thickness of the border around the dialog */
WinSendDlgItemMsg (hWnd, IDC_BEVEL1, BVM_SETTHICKNESS, (MPARAM)4, 0L);
```

The thermometer control is also initialized during the WM_INITDLG message. PrivateQuery is called to get the size of the private suballocation block, and this value is used to initialize the thermometer control:

```
   /* Query the suballocation info to set thermometer range */
   PrivateQuery (&ulAlloc, &ulSubAlloc);
   WinSendDlgItemMsg (hWnd, IDC_THERMOMETER, THM_SETRANGE,
         0L, (MPARAM)ulAlloc);
   WinSendDlgItemMsg (hWnd, IDC_THERMOMETER, THM_SETVALUE,
         0L, 0L);
   WinSendDlgItemMsg (hWnd, IDC_THERMOMETER, THM_SETCOLOR,
         (MPARAM)MAKELONG(CLR_RED, CLR_PALEGRAY), 0L);
```

The color of the thermometer can be changed by selecting a new color in the spinner control. The spinner control is initialized with the array of available colors:

```
   /* Initialize the memory numbers */
   UpdateNumbers (hWnd);

   /* Initialize the thermometer color spinner control */
   WinSendDlgItemMsg (hWnd, IDC_THERMOCOLOR,
         SPBM_SETTEXTLIMIT, (MPARAM)9L, (MPARAM)0L);
   WinSendDlgItemMsg (hWnd, IDC_THERMOCOLOR, SPBM_SETARRAY,
         (MPARAM)pszColors, (MPARAM)15L);
   WinSendDlgItemMsg (hWnd, IDC_THERMOCOLOR,
         SPBM_SETCURRENTVALUE, (MPARAM)12L, (MPARAM)0L);
```

When the SPBN_ENDSPIN notification is received, the current value is queried, and the thermometer color is changed with the THM_SETCOLOR message:

```
case WM_CONTROL:
   switch (LOUSHORT(mp1))
   {
      case IDC_THERMOCOLOR:
      if (HIUSHORT(mp1) == SPBN_ENDSPIN)
      {
         ULONG ulSelect;

         /* Query selection index from spinner */
         WinSendDlgItemMsg (hWnd, IDC_THERMOCOLOR,
               SPBM_QUERYVALUE, (MPARAM)&ulSelect, 0L);

         /* Set the current color of the thermometer */
         WinSendDlgItemMsg (hWnd, IDC_THERMOMETER,
            THM_SETCOLOR,
            (MPARAM)MAKELONG(sColorMap[ulSelect],
            CLR_PALEGRAY), 0L);
      }
      break;
   }
   break;
```

The Allocate button will cause the memory object to be suballocated by calling either `PrivateAllocate` or `SharedAllocate`. The returned address is inserted into the appropriate list box. The Free button will free the currently selected memory object by calling either `PrivateFree` or `SharedFree`. The Free All button will free all memory objects in the appropriate list box by calling either `PrivateFree` or `SharedFree` for each entry in the list box. After any one of these commands is processed, the numbers are updated by calls to `PrivateQuery` and `SharedQuery` in the `UpdateNumbers` function. At the end of the `UpdateNumbers` function, the current value of the thermometer is set.

```
/* Set private memory allocation amount as the thermometer value  */
WinSendDlgItemMsg (hWnd, IDC_THERMOMETER, THM_SETVALUE,
      (MPARAM)ulSubAlloc, 0L);
```

These two DLLs have been written to demonstrate the basics for creating general purpose DLLs. The CONTROLS.DLL demonstrated how to create private control classes and allow any application to use those controls. The MEMDLL DLL demonstrated how to use both instance and global data in managing memory and how to use the Initialization/Termination function to perform memory cleanup.

Chapter 13

Printing

Introduction

With only a few exceptions, most programs produce some type of printed output. One of the more time-consuming aspects of application development is ensuring that it prints correctly on a multitude of devices. In an effort to simplify the programmatic and user interaction with printers, OS/2 for version 2.0 introduced the concept of a print object to application printing. A print object is a logical print destination that is comprised of a spooler, a printer driver, and a queue driver. This object manages all aspects of a print job and adds new flexibility to OS/2.

This chapter is intended to provide you with a framework for interacting with the OS/2 print subsystem. To that end, this chapter shows you how to build a sample printing application called PRNT, which demonstrates printer selection, page display, form enumeration, and printing. Before examining how printing works in the later versions of OS/2, however, it's useful to briefly review printing in DOS, Windows 3.x, and OS/2 1.x .

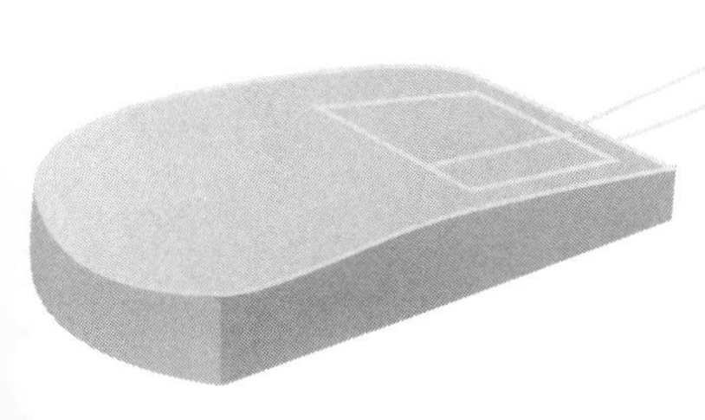

Some Printing Background: The DOS Days

Printing during the DOS days was very basic-text output was sent to a physical port (such as LPT1) as a series of characters. When the printer's buffer filled up, the application waited for the printer to catch up before sending more data, and the printer became a large bottleneck. With this came a tremendous burden. DOS applications that wanted to produce printed output other than basic text were required to write what amounted to a printer driver for each device it wished to support. Most applications relied on a set of drivers created and distributed by the software application's programmers. Raster printers often require special escape sequences for changing such items as font size, and graphics output on these printers was even more involved. Other devices such as PostScript or LaserJet printers required a completely different form of data. Also, the displayed text and graphics often had very little resemblance to the printed output.

The support burden for this was phenomenal. Printer manufacturers, of course, did not time the release of their new printers around software, so some incompatibility between revision levels was always likely, and the programming teams needed to support all these different printers was quite large. New printing technology, then as now, was being created all the time, so the shipping version of your software was always guaranteed to be out of date in comparison to the available printers.

Device Independence

One of the benefits that a device-independent programming interface provides is device support. This device independence really began to take hold in the IBM-compatible programming world with the release of Windows. Windows removed the direct interaction between display and print hardware from the application. OS/2 extends this device independence by providing such things as logical printers and logical queues.

Chapter 6, "Presentation Spaces and Drawing," discusses the device-independent model the GPI provides for output to the screen. Output was made more consistent by introducing the idea of presentation spaces. Using various presentation space handles, one for the screen and another for a physical printer, an application could call the same API function to produce output on the display and the printer. A printer driver provides the link from the graphics engine to a physical output device. The term *printer driver* is used to refer to a software component that controls various output devices such as plotters and printers. It is the printer driver's job to communicate the request to the hardware in a form it can understand. A printer driver is a stand-alone component that provides specific entry points that are called by the operating system. Although vendors may write their own printer drivers, drivers for many popular devices are supplied with the base system.

Printing Under OS/2 1.x and Windows 3.x

Before printing to a device can begin, a list of available devices must be determined. In both OS/2 1.x and Windows, the currently installed printer device drivers could be determined by querying entries from a system initialization file. Of the installed drivers, one is considered the default. The default driver is identified by a separate entry in the initialization file. In both environments, the entries are maintained through a print manager or control program.

The Windows system configuration files are simple text files with a well-documented format. This encourages users and programs to modify the system settings to suit their needs. The OS/2 system configuration files are written in a binary format and cannot be modified with a text editor, which makes modifications more difficult. In either case, the driver information is returned from system functions in a format that requires parsing before the information is useful. Included in the returned strings are the printer driver physical name and the hardware port to which the device is connected. Once installed, a printer driver can be configured from a printer properties dialog box. This dialog is part of the printer driver and allows setting of hardware personalities, along with default page orientation and size. A single PostScript printer driver, for example, can support 50 or more different brands and models of printer hardware.

In addition to printer properties, OS/2 introduced the concept of job properties. Job properties are properties that affect the appearance of a single print job without changing system-wide settings. The page orientation and number of copies are typical job properties. Each printer driver defines a second dialog that allows job properties to be set on an application-by-application basis.

OS/2 Print Objects

When a printer driver is installed in OS/2, it becomes a print object, which, from the end-user perspective, is in fact the printer. The name and hardware port connections can be modified on the settings page of the print objects notebook by the user. Although the print object is one logical unit, it is actually comprised of a queue driver and a printer driver.

In OS/2 1.x, a printer can be configured optionally with a queue if the user desires. From version 2.0 and later, all print objects include a queue. The default queue driver `PMPRINT`, or queue processor as it is sometimes called, is responsible for distributing print jobs to a single printer or among multiple printers. Print objects have the flexibility to allow multiple printers to be connected to a single queue. In businesses where many printers are available, this makes more efficient use of available printers possible. It allows the load to be balanced among multiple printers simultaneously. Multiple print queues may be connected to a single printer to allow printer sharing. A second queue processor, `PMPLOT`, is intended for use with plotters. It contains a reverse clipping engine that clips out overlapping objects before output is sent to the plotter.

PRQINFO3/PRQINFO6

PSZ	pszQueueName	Pointer to a null-terminated string that is the physical queue name. This name corresponds to a subdirectory under the spooler directory (typically, c:\spool). It also appears on the view page of the queue settings dialog. This value cannot be changed.
USHORT	uPriority	This parameter identifies the priority assigned to the queue. It may range from 1 to 9 (with 1 assigned as the highest priority).
USHORT USHORT	uStartTime uUntilTime	These parameters indicate the active hours of a queue, which ranges from `uStartTime` to `uUntilTime`. The format of both fields is the number of minutes past midnight.

USHORT	fsType	This value identifies the queue type that is set via the queue options on the queue settings notebook. It may be one of the following:
		`PRQ3_TYPE_RAW`
		Output is spooled in printer-specific format.
		`PRQ3_TYPE_QP_BYPASS`
		The spooler is configured to bypass the queue processor and send data directly to the printer driver.

PSZ	pszSepFile	Pointer to a null-terminated string that contains the path of a file that contains a separator file page. If set, the page(s) defined in the file are output between print jobs. If no pages are desired, `NULL` may be specified.
PSZ	pszQueueProc	Pointer to a null-terminated string that identifies queue processor for this queue. Current `PMPRINT` and `PMPLOT` are the only two processors defined.
PSZ	pszQueueParam	Pointer to a null-terminated string that contains queue parameters.
PSZ	pszComment	Pointer to a null-terminated string that contains the user-supplied queue description.

		This value is the descriptive name given by the user that appears in the icon text window and the title entry on the general page of printer settings.

`USHORT`	`fsStatus`	This field contains flags that identify the status of the queue. It may be one of the following:
		`PRQ3_PAUSED`
		The queue has been held.
		`PRQ3_PENDING`
		The queue is pending deletion.

`USHORT`	`cJobs`	The number of jobs in the queue.
`PSZ`	`pszPrinters`	Pointer to a null-terminated string that contains the print devices connected to this queue. This is often, but not always, equal to the queue name.
`PSZ`	`pszDriverName`	Pointer to null-terminated string that identifies the printers connected to the queue. It is in the form *<physical driver name>.<driver description>*. For example, if you install the HP LaserJet IIISi version of the PostScript driver, the entry is as follows: *PSCRIPT.HP LaserJet IIISi PS v52_3*
`PSZ`	`pDriverData`	Pointer to a device-specific block of data that identifies the default queue properties.

PRQINFO6 Only

`PSZ`	`pszRemoteComputerName`	Pointer to a null-terminated string that contains the name of a remote computer for which this queue has a local alias.
`PSZ`	`pszRemoteQueueName`	Pointer to a null-terminated string that contains the name of a remote queue for which this queue is a local alias.

The Queue and Printer details dialog box in the PRNT sample application provided with this book displays most of the fields of the `PRQINFO3` structure (along with other device information). When you select the printer information menu option on the Display menu, the installed print objects are enumerated using the `SplEnumQueue` function. The queue descriptions from

the pszComment field are added to the upper-left list box. Under that list box, several windows display the queue status, jobs, and a start and stop time. Three other entries display queue strings as follows:

Label in the dialog	*Field in PRQINFO3*
Queue Name:	pszName
Default Device:	pszDriverName
Print Devices:	pszPrinters

Identifying the Default Print Object

The new spooler API is still missing one function: SplQueryDefaultQueue. Determining the system default print object must be done using "the old way" by querying an entry in the system INI file. The physical name of the default queue may be found in the QUEUE entry of the PM_SPOOLER section of the user INI file. Using the physical name, a PRQINFO3 structure may be retrieved by calling the SplQueryQueue function. The physical name returned from the profile query ends in a semicolon. The semicolon should be removed before passing the name to the SplQueryQueue function. The following code fragment shows both functions being called:

```
/* Query the default printer */
ulSize = PrfQueryProfileString(HINI_PROFILE,"PM_SPOOLER",
         "QUEUE", 0,szTemp,MAX_BUFF);

if (ulSize)
{
   pStr = strchr(szTemp,';');
   *pStr = 0;
   SplQueryQueue(0,szTemp,3,0,0,&ulNeeded);
   if (ulNeeded && !(DosSubAlloc(pMem,
         (PPVOID)&pPrq3,ulNeeded)))
   {
      SplQueryQueue(0,szTemp,3,pPrq3,ulNeeded,&ulNeeded);
   }
}
```

Printer Versus Job Properties

When we reviewed the history of printing in DOS, Windows, and OS/2 1.x earlier in this chapter, we said that OS/2 introduced the concept of job properties. This, however, is not entirely true.

Windows 3.x added a function that printer drivers were required to implement in order to be considered 3.x-compliant. This function (ExtDeviceMode) allowed an application to retrieve and save printer configuration data, which could later be passed into a function that created a device context.

The ExtDeviceMode function allowed, but did not require, applications to implement printer job properties. What OS/2 brought to the table was a formalized job properties implementation. Printer drivers are required to implement a printer properties dialog and a job properties dialog. These are often two entirely separate dialog boxes for listing and choosing printer characteristics. The printer properties may be displayed by double-clicking on the printer driver icon on the printer driver page of any printer settings notebook. The job properties may be selected by selecting the job properties push button on the same page of the notebook.

Printer Properties

Printer properties define a base configuration for a print device. Hardware configuration of paper trays and installed font cartridges are typically found on this dialog. However, it may also include nonhardware items such as default paper orientation. Changes made in this dialog are written to the system INI file. Future jobs printed to this print object are affected by these settings. The saved settings are those which the pDriverData field of the PRQINF03/6 structure points to. An application does not post this dialog.

Job Properties

Job properties are properties that affect the appearance of a single print job without changing system-wide settings. Page orientation and number of copies and pages are typical items found on a job properties dialog. The job properties dialog may look identical to the printer properties dialog (as it does for the Epson driver) or it may be different. In either case, changes made in the job properties dialog are not saved to an INI file. Unless the application saves the modified driver data, the changes are lost.

Posting the Job Properties Dialog: *DevPostDeviceModes*

In Windows, the function that displays the configuration dialog is not a Windows API. It is actually a function exported from the printer driver. OS/2 has provided the DevPostDeviceModes system function, which handles the task of interacting with the configuration functions of all drivers. DevPostDeviceModes is used for retrieving the current driver settings with or without displaying the job properties dialog. Perhaps the most difficult part of using the function is supplying the correct device names. The DevPostDeviceModes function is defined as follows:

```
DevPostDeviceModes (hAB,pDriverData,pszDriverName,
                    pszDeviceName,pszName,ulOption)
```

HAB	hAB	Handle to anchor blocks returned from the WinInitialize function.
PDRIVDATA	pDriverData	Pointer to a memory block large enough to hold the printers DRIVDATA structure. The size in

		bytes of the DRIVDATA is returned if this parameter is NULL.
PSZ	pszDriverName	Pointer to a null-terminated string that contains the device driver name of the printer to query. This should be the portion that precedes the period in the string pointed to by the pszDriverName parameter in the PRQINFO3 structure. Using the example from above which is PSCRIPT.HP LaserJet IIISi PS v52_3, then the supplied string would be PSCRIPT.
PSZ	pszDevicename	Pointer to a null-terminated string that contains the device name of the printer to query. This should be the portion that follows the period in the string pointed to by the pszDriverName parameter in the PRQINFO3 structure. Using the example from above which is PSCRIPT.HP LaserJet IIISi PS v52_3, then the supplied string would be HP LaserJet IIISi PS v52_3.
PSZ	pszName	Pointer to a null-terminated string that contains the printer device name. This should be the same as the pszPrinters field of the PRQINFO3 structure.
ULONG	ulOption	A flag that tells the driver what action to take. It may be one of the following: DBDM_POSTJOBPROP. The job properties dialog is posted, and the updated driver data is returned when the user closes the dialog. DBDM_QUERYJOBPROP. The current driver data is returned without displaying the job properties dialog.

If successful, the function returns DEV_OK indicating that the returned driver data is valid. If the function fails, the driver data could be invalid and should not be used. By using the DPDM_QUERYJOBPROP flag, the current driver data is returned without displaying the dialog box. If the DBDM_POSTJOBPROP flag is used, the dialog is displayed. The DevPostDeviceModes function, however, does not provide a method for determining how the dialog was dismissed.

The PM documentation suggests that you always treat the returned data as if the OK button was selected. Another alternative is to save a copy of the driver data passed to the DevPostDeviceModes function and compare it with the returned data (replacing it if it is different). Because each device stores data in its own private format, it is invalid to pass the driver data to a different device. The get_job_properties function in the sample application provides a good example of calling the DevPostDeviceModes.

Once returned, the driver data may be supplied as input to a future call to DevPostDeviceModes. This causes the driver to display its configuration dialog with the same setting as when it was closed, assuming that the Cancel button was not selected. When an information or queued device context is created, the driver data should be passed in the DEVOPENSTRUC as input to DevOpenDC. This creates a DC with the desired job properties.

Creating an Information Device Context

Once the target print device is determined, an application needs to create an information device context, which can be used to determine device capabilities and physical dimensions. With this information, you can create a representation of the target print page in your client window. The queue and printer details dialog in the PRT program queries and displays various values returned from the DevQueryCaps function for the selected driver.

Although the chapter on presentation and drawing spaces discussed the DevOpenDC function, it deferred information and print device contexts to this chapter. You may recall that the device context is the link between a presentation space and the physical device it represents. Associated with the device context is a presentation space where all drawing occurs. A "print" device context and an associated presentation allow output to occur on a device other than the display. The "print" device context is a general term for those of type OD_QUEUED or OD_DIRECT. An information device context is basically the same as a "print" DC, except that no output occurs when the presentation space associated with it is drawn into. It allows your application to maintain a shadow of the current target print device and maintain a "what you see is what you get" (WYSIWYG) display. An info DC may be created by passing the OD_INFO flag as the type parameter to DevOpenDC function and initializing the DEVOPENSTRUCT correctly. The fields of the DEVOPENSTRUC as they apply to creating DCs of type OD_INFO are as follows:

PSZ	pszLogAddress	Pointer to a null-terminated string that is the port name the driver is connected to. The port may be queried using the SplQueryDevice function. If successful, the

		pszLogAddr of the returned PDRINFO3 structure contains the port name. This field should only be set to the port name when creating an info DC.
PSZ	pszDriverName	Pointer to a null-terminated string that contains the device driver name. This should be the portion that precedes the period in the string pointed to by the pszDriverName parameter in the PRQINFO3 structure. Using the example from above: PSCRIPT.HP LaserJet IIISi PS v52_3. The supplied string would be PSCRIPT.
PDRIVDATA	pdriv	Pointer to driver data returned from the DevPostDevice modes function.
PSZ	pszDataType	Pointer to a null-terminated string containing the format that data is to be queued in. PM_Q_STD allows the output to be metafiled; PM_Q_RAW leaves all data in device format.

For info device contexts, the remainder of the fields can be ignored by setting the lCount parameter passed to the DevOpenDC function to 4. If the DC is successfully created, a presentation space can be created and associated with it. The presentation space should be created with device-independent coordinates such as PU_LOMETRIC or PU_TWIPS. The presentation space for the client window should be created using the same coordinate system as the print info DC. This allows the same coordinates to be used when drawing to the PS for the client window or the PS for the printer. In the PRNT sample, we chose to use LOMETRIC. The following code clip creates an info device context and an associated presentation space using the LO_ENGLISH coordinate system.

```
DevOpenData.pszLogAddress = pPrd3->pszLogAddr;
DevOpenData.pszDriverName = szDriverName;
DevOpenData.pdriv         = pDD;
DevOpenData.pszDataType   = "PM_Q_STD";
if (pDI->hInfoDC = DevOpenDC (hab,OD_INFO,"*",4,
      (PVOID)&DevOpenData,0))
{
   sizel.cx = 0;
   sizel.cy = 0;
   if(!(pDI->hInfoPS = GpiCreatePS (hab,pDI->hInfoDC,&sizel,
         GPIA_ASSOC | GPIT_MICRO | PU_LOMETRIC)))
   {
      DevCloseDC(pDI->hInfoDC);
      pDI->hInfoDC = 0;
   }
   else
      get_page_metrics(pDI);
}
```

Notice that the `sizel` parameter has both `cx` and `cy` parameters set to `0`. This ensures that maximum page size is created. If the info DC is successfully created, the `GpiQueryPS` function can be called to determine the size of the created `PS`.

```
GpiQueryPS(pDI->hInfoPS,(PSIZEL)&pDI->PageSizel);
```

In the sample print application, when a print object is selected in the Queue and Printer details dialog box, an information device context is created. The info DC is then passed to the `DevQueryCaps` function to determine device capabilities and sizes. Some of the values that relate to printing are displayed within the device capabilities group box. Included here are the width and height of the print media in pels and device support for functions such as `GpiBitBlt` and `GpiSetPel`. The queue and printer details dialog is shown in Figure 13.1.

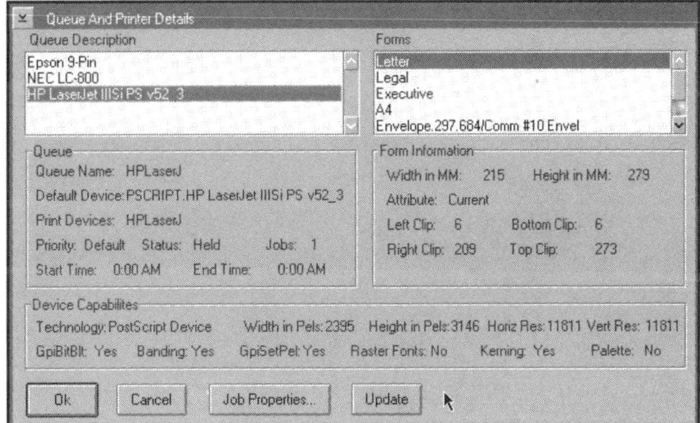

Figure 13.1.
Queue And Printer Details dialog.

Querying Device Forms

Many printers can be configured with multiple paper sources or bins. This allows print jobs to be printed on the desired paper sizes without waiting for the desired paper size to be added. Your application may determine the forms available on a print device by calling `DevQueryHardcopyCaps`. This function returns an array of `HCINFO` structures, one for each form type. In the `HCINFO` structure are the form name, sizes, and attributes. The attribute field indicates if the form is the current default form for the device (`HCAPS_CURRENT`) or if the form may be selected (`HCAPS_SELECTABLE`). If neither bit is set, the form is not installed on the device and should not be used. A form that is selectable may be specified by setting the form name in the spooler parameters of the `DEVOPENSTRUC` passed to `DevOpenDC`. The form name should follow the `FORM =` string. The form name should be taken from the `szFormname` field in the `HCINFO` structure (for example: `FORM=LETTER`).

The Queue and Printer details dialog demonstrates enumerating the forms using the DevQueryHardcopyCaps function. When a print object is selected, the forms are queried and added to the forms list box. Below the list box is the form width and height as returned from the device in millimeters. The attribute flags are displayed along with the offsets of the clipping limits of the page. Notice that many of the forms enumerated from a device have no attribute bits set and are not selectable. If a form is specified that is not currently installed in the printer, the job is held until that form is available.

Determining Page and Printable Area Size

Most print devices are unable to print on all portions of the physical page. The portion that can be drawn on by the printer is referred to as the printable area. This printable area size may be retrieved by calling the GpiQueryPS function after creating a device context. Be sure that the initial width and height used when creating the presentation space are set to 0. This ensures that the maximum presentation page is created.

The physical page size may be determined by using the width and height values from the HCINFO structure for the selected form. cx and cy need to be converted from millimeters to pels. This can be done by multiplying by the device resolution, which is in pels per meter, and dividing by 1,000 (the number of millimeters in a meter). Device resolution for the *X*- and *Y*-axis can be retrieved by calling the DevQueryCaps function and requesting CAPS_HORIZONTAL_RESOLUTION and CAPS_VERTICAL_RESOLUTION. Once the page size is calculated, the device points are converted into world coordinate space. For example, take a look at the following code clip:

```
DevQueryCaps (pDI->hInfoDC,CAPS_HORIZONTAL_RESOLUTION,1L,
      (PLONG) &PtlRes.x);
DevQueryCaps (pDI->hInfoDC,CAPS_VERTICAL_RESOLUTION,1L,
      (PLONG) &PtlRes.y);
pDI->PhyPageSizel.cx = (PtlRes.x * pHCInfo[i].cx) / 1000;
pDI->PhyPageSizel.cy = (PtlRes.y * pHCInfo[i].cy) / 1000;
GpiConvert(pDI->hInfoPS,CVTC_DEVICE,CVTC_WORLD,1,
     (PPOINTL)&pDI->PhyPageSizel);
```

There are two problems with the cx and cy fields of the HCINFO structure. While browsing the forms enumerated from the installed devices, you may have noticed the first one. The same form may have a different width and height based on the device driver that is selected. For example, the letter paper size may be reported to be 215 millimeters wide by one device and 216 by another. This occurs because different printer drivers are reporting different widths and heights for the same form size. The second problem is inherent in the use of millimeters as the unit of measurement. Millimeters do not provide a fine enough resolution to accurately define the page size of high resolution devices such as laser printers. Rounding may cause page size calculation to be in error.

Calculating Printer Offset

Printer offset is the difference between the origin of the physical page and the origin of the printable area. Using the physical page size, printable area, and printer offset, an accurate representation of the page may be drawn in the application. The printer offset may be calculated by converting `xLeftClip` and `yBottomClip` fields of the `HCINFO` structure to pels:

```
pDI->PrintOffsetSizel.cx = (PtlRes.x * pHCInfo[i].xLeftClip) / 1000;
pDI->PrintOffsetSizel.cy = (PtlRes.y * pHCInfo[i].yBottomClip) / 1000;
/* Convert from device to world coordinate space */
GpiConvert(pDI->hInfoPS,CVTC_DEVICE,CVTC_WORLD,1,
     (PPOINTL)&pDI->PrintOffsetSizel);
```

Some PM devices report a printer offset of 0; however, the presentation page size is not equal to the physical page size. It is also possible that the device will not return form information at all. If either of these situations occurs, an application can approximate the value by subtracting the printable area from the physical page size and dividing by two. Although not exact, this should be adequate for most needs. The physical page size may be retrieved by calling the `DevQueryCaps` function requesting the `CAPS_WIDTH` and `CAPS_HEIGHT` values:

```
DevQueryCaps (pDI->hInfoDC,CAPS_WIDTH,1L,(PLONG)&Ptl.x);
DevQueryCaps (pDI->hInfoDC,CAPS_HEIGHT,1L,(PLONG)&Ptl.y);
GpiConvert(pDI->hInfoPS,CVTC_DEVICE,CVTC_WORLD,1,&Ptl);
pDI->PrintOffsetSizel.cx = (pDI->PhyPageSizel.cx - Ptl.x) / 2L;
pDI->PrintOffsetSizel.cy = (pDI->PhyPageSizel.cy - Ptl.y) / 2L;
```

Basic Printing

Now that you can enumerate the installed print objects, create information device contexts, and query the device capabilities, you can look at the print process. Sending output to the printer is not much different from sending output to the screen. The same functions used to create figures and text on-screen are used when printing. The big difference is that the presentation space being drawn into is associated with a print device context (DC) in place of a window DC. Therefore, the first step in printing is to create an `OD_QUEUED` or `OD_DIRECT` device context.

Queued device contexts cause printed output to be queued on a spooler queue. Once added to the queue, the job can be held, deleted, or repeated, independent of the application. It is recommended that all PM applications create queued device contexts. Direct printing causes the spooler to be bypassed, causing the printing application to wait until the print job is complete (assuming that the printing was not done in a separate thread). Direct printing should be avoided unless security of the printed output must be maintained and access to spooler files and print objects cannot be limited. Spooled files are written to disk while waiting to be sent to the printer, and they may be copied if access to the spool directory is not limited. The spooler directory is specified on the spool path page of the spooler settings object. The default location for this object is in the system setup folder. If direct printing is required, a dedicated printer or output device should be used. Even with a dedicated device, it is possible for two jobs sent directly to the device to become intermixed.

Creating a print DC is very much like creating the information DC. In place of the `OD_INFO` type, the `OD_QUEUED` flags should be used. As with the info DC, the first four parameters of `DEVOPENSTRUCT` must be initialized at a minimum. Later in this chapter, we will use some of the other parameters, but let's discuss them now. The fields of the `DEVOPENSTRUC` as they apply to creating DCs of type `OD_QUEUED` are as follows:

`TPSZ`	`pszLogAddress`	Pointer to a null-terminated string that is the queue name from the `pszName` field of the `PRQINFO3` structure. Note that unlike the DCs of type `OD_INFO`, this is not the port name.
`PSZ`	`pszDriverName`	Pointer to a null-terminated string that contains the device driver name. This should be the portion that precedes the period in the string pointed to by the `pszDriverName` parameter in the `PRQINFO3` structure. Using the example from above: `PSCRIPT.HP LaserJet IIISi PS v52_3`. The supplied string would be `PSCRIPT`.
`PDRIVDATA`	`pdriv`	Pointer to driver data returned from the `DevPostDevice` modes function.
`PSZ`	`pszDataType`	Pointer to a null-terminated string containing the format that data is to be queued in. `PM_Q_STD` allows the output to be metafiled; `PM_Q_RAW` leaves all data in device format.
`PSZ`	`pszComment`	Pointer to a null-terminated string containing the document name that is used to describe this job once in the queue.
`PSZ`	`pszQueueProcName`	Pointer to a null-terminated string containing the name of the queue processor to be used for this job. If this parameter is `NULL`, the default queue processor PMPRINT is used. You may recall that PMPLOT may be optionally installed to clip output intended for a

		plotter. The default queue processor for the device is defined in the `pszPrProc` field of the `PRQINFO3` structure.
PSZ	pszQueueProcParams	Pointer to a null-terminated string containing queue processor parameters. This field may be `NULL`.

PSZ	pszSpoolerParams	Pointer to a null-terminated string containing spooler parameters. You may currently set the job priority and form used in the spooler parameters. If both are used, they should be separated by spaces:
		`FORM=<formname>.`
		Where formname is taken from the `szFormname` field of the `HCINFO` structure, if the form desired is not the current form or selectable, the job never prints.
		`PRTY=<priority>.`
		Where priority is a number ranging from 1 to 99, with 99 as the high. The default is 50 if no priority is specified. If the field is `NULL`, the job is printed on the current form using the default priority.

PSZ	pszNetworkParams	Pointer to a null-terminated string containing network parameters. This field is optional and may be `NULL`.

Once the print device context is created, the print job begins when the `DEVESC_STARTDOC` escape is sent to the printer. Escapes are commands your application sends to the printer to direct it to perform an action or return some information. The `STARTDOC` escape tells the printer that a new print job is starting and all subsequent output is part of the same job until the job is ended. A pointer to a string that specifies the document name may be passed in the input parameter of the `DevEscape` function. If a string is specified, it becomes the job name (even if a name is supplied in the `pszComment` field of the `DEVOPENSTRUC`). If no input is supplied, `pszComment` is used if not `NULL`; otherwise the job name is blank.

The presentation space must be associated with the DC prior to the `STARTDOC` escape. This may be done by creating the PS using the `GPI_ASSOC` flag or associating an existing PS with the print DC using the `GpiAssociate` function. After the PS is associated with the print DC, the `STARTDOC` escape should then be sent to the printer. Using the presentation space handle in any function prior to the `STARTDOC` is invalid. This includes attribute setting functions such as `GpiSetAttrs`, as well as the drawing primitives.

Once the print job is started, all GPI drawing is output to the printer. When a page is completed and another page exists, the DEVESC_NEWFRAME escape should be sent. This causes the printer to perform a page eject. If the job must be ended before it has completed, the DEVESC_ABORTDOC escape causes any output from the current job waiting to be sent to the printer to be cleared, and the job ends. This escape is typically used to implement a print cancel feature in an application. When the print job is complete, it is ended by sending the DEVESC_ENDDOC escape to the printer. The return parameter from the DevEscape function contains the job ID that can be used to track the progress of the print job in the queue if desired. If the DEVESC_ABORTDOC escape is used to cancel a print job, it is unnecessary to send the DEVESC_ENDDOC escape. The flow diagram in Figure 13.2 depicts the various steps of the printing process.

Printing in an Application

With all the basics in place, I can define the requirements for a simple print application called PRNT.EXE. PRNT allows the current application printer to be selected from a list of installed devices. Part of the selection process includes displaying the Job Properties dialog upon request. It must also display a representation of the print page and printable area in the client window. PRNT should have a print menu item that, when selected, posts a dialog to verify the requested print operation. If the print is confirmed, the print dialog is dismissed and a print status dialog is displayed during the duration of the print job. This dialog contains a cancel button that can abort the selected print job.

In order to manage all of the information about print devices, we will define the DEVICEINFO structure. Print DCs, physical and printable sizes, along with the pointers to driver data and form information are maintained in this structure. The application maintains one global variable of this type called CurrentDI. The information on the currently selected application printer is stored in this variable.

When the application starts, it calls the init_app function, which determines the default print device that becomes the current application default device. It then queries the current driver data from that device and creates an information DC used to draw a representation of the page in the client window. (See Figure 13.3.)

Up to this point, all drawing has been done in device units. This worked fine for drawing thermometers in control windows. However, because of the variation in resolution between the display and printer, a device-independent coordinate space must be used. A PS for the client area is created using the PU_LOMETRIC mapping mode. The mode was chosen arbitrarily from the defined coordinate spaces and could have been PU_TWIPS or PU_LOENGLISH. In order for the page to be entirely visible in the maximized client window, the viewing matrix is scaled to reduce page size by 50 percent. When the client window is drawn, the current print page is represented by a white rectangle with a black border. The printable area on the page is shown using a blue dashed line.

Figure 13.2.
The printing flowchart.

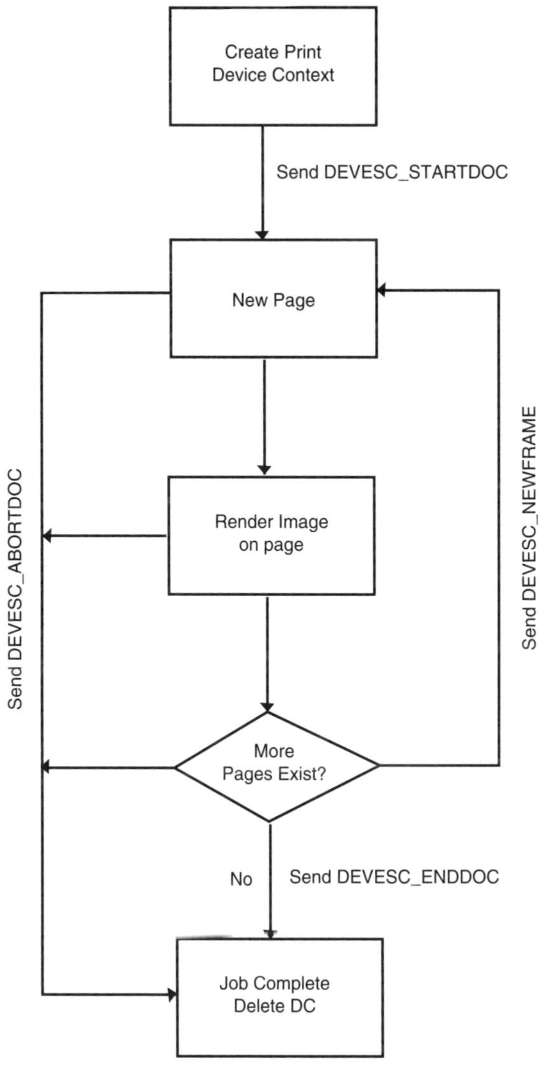

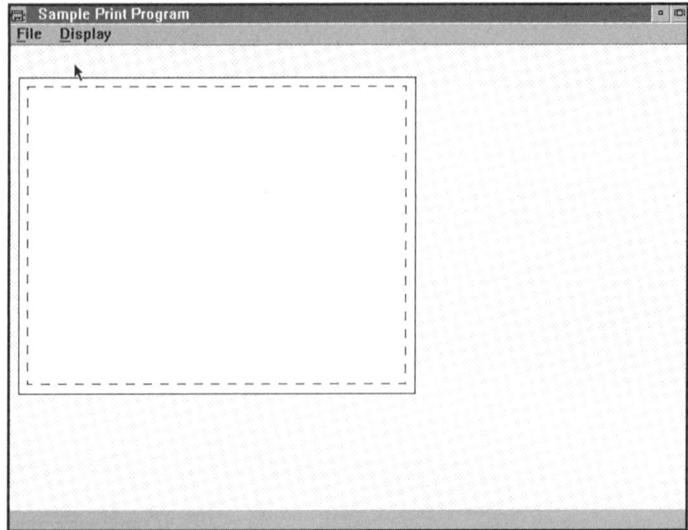

Figure 13.3.
PRNT application page representation.

The PRNT application contains a Print Selection dialog box. This dialog contains a list box that is filled with the installed print objects during the processing of the `WM_INITDLG` message. The Print Selection dialog box is shown in Figure 13.4.

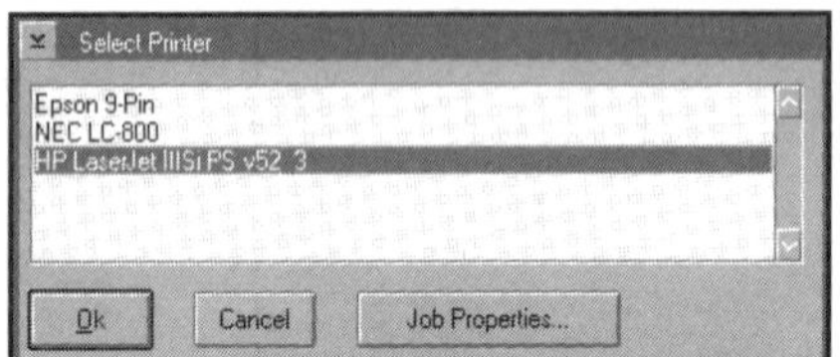

Figure 13.4.
Print object selection dialog.

After adding all objects, the application default printer is selected. The dialog also has a Job Properties push button, which, when pushed, posts the printers Job Properties dialog. The first time this dialog is displayed, the job properties for all devices will be their system default values. The Job Properties dialog for the postscript printer is shown in Figure 13.5.

Changes made to the job properties of the selected device should be maintained by the application. For example, if the user posts the Job Properties dialog and changes the page orientation from portrait to landscape, the next time that the Job Properties dialog is posted, landscape should still be selected. In order to maintain job properties of a printer, the driver data returned from the `DevPostDeviceModes` function must be saved. When the dialog box is dismissed by selecting the OK button, the selected device becomes the application default, and contents of the `CurrentDI` structure are updated accordingly. If Cancel is selected, the application default printer remains unchanged.

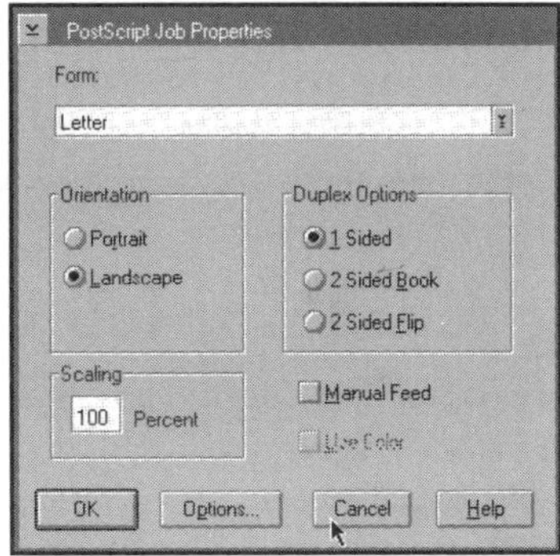

Figure 13.5.
The PostScript Job Properties dialog box.

When the Print menu item is selected, a print confirmation dialog is displayed. This dialog displays the name of the target printer and the document name. You may change the number of copies and priority of the print job through two spinner controls in the dialog. These selections are passed to the `DevOpenDC` function as queue processor and spooler parameters, respectively. If the OK button is selected, the values set in the copies and priority controls are retrieved, the dialog is closed, and the print status dialog is created. If Cancel is selected, the dialog is closed with no further action. Figure 13.6 shows the print confirmation dialog

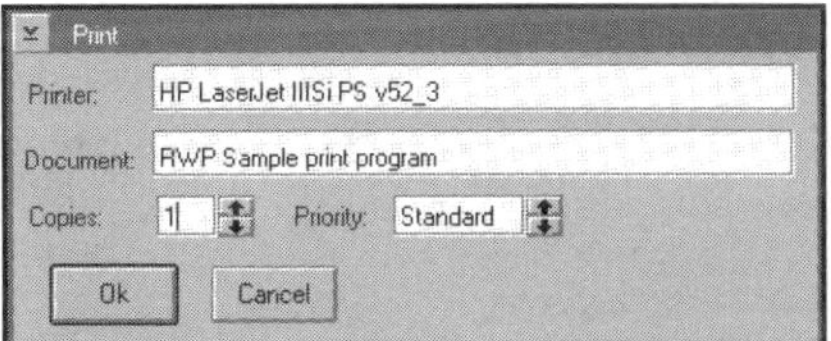

Figure 13.6.
Print confirmation dialog.

The print status dialog starts the print job, displays the status of that job, and allows the job to be canceled. When it receives the `WM_INITDLG` message, it initializes the printer and job name fields. It then sets the status field to "Initializing Printer" and posts a user defined `WM_START_PRINT` message to the client window. When the client window receives this message, it calls the `process_print` function. You may be wondering why `process_print` was not called directly from the dialog. Although this could have been done, you want that dialog to report only the status of the job, not to actually do the printing. The `process_print` function is responsible for creating the print device context and sending output to the printer. It first makes a copy of the data in the `CurrentDI`, which is passed into the `create_print_DC` function. This allows the function to be re-entrant when a printing thread is added in the chapter on threads and semaphores. If the DC is successfully created, a `WM_PRINT_STATUS` message is posted to the status dialog, which updates the status text accordingly.

When the job is completed, the DEVESC_ENDDOC escape is sent to the printer, and a status message indicating job completion is posted to the dialog. The print DC and PS are then destroyed, and the copy of the CurrentDI structure is freed. In nonthreaded print processing, the print status dialog is application modal; in the threaded version, it is not.

Tracking Your Print Job Using the Spooler API

Once your print job is in the queue, you can use the spooler API to track the status of submitted jobs in your application. You can also hold, delete, or copy the job. You could also write a single application that manages all queues and their jobs. Note that these functions will not work if the user disables the spooler. An application cannot change the status of the spooler; however, the spooler status may be retrieved by querying the QUEUE section of the PM_SPOOLER section in the system INI file. If the spooler is enabled, the data field is 1; otherwise, it is 0. Let's look at the spooler functions that manipulate print jobs.

SplControlDevice

This function enables you to control a print device. It may be paused or continued, and the current print job may also be restarted or deleted.

SplCopyJob

This function copies a job within a given print queue. Jobs may not be copied to another print queue. However, this restriction may be lifted in the future.

SplDeleteJob

This function deletes a specific job ID from a given print queue. The job ID is returned from the DEVESC_ENDDOC escape. Job IDs may also be retrieved from the SplEnumJob function.

SplEnumJob

This function can return an array of job IDs in the queue or an array of PRJINFO2 structures containing the status of each print job in the queue. The PRJINFO2 structure contains the job ID, priority, status, size, document name, title, and user name. The job status indicates whether the job is being held or whether an error occurs during processing.

An application that tracks the print job for the user can report out-of-paper errors or indicate whether the device is waiting for a form change.

SplHoldJob

This function holds a specific job in a given queue. A job may be held if it has not started printing. The job may be restarted with the `SplReleaseJob` function.

SplHoldQueue

This function changes the status of a print queue from released to held. All jobs in the queue awaiting the print device are held regardless of their individual status. The status of jobs currently printing is unaffected. The queue may be released using the `SplReleaseQueue` function.

SplPurgeQueue

This function removes all jobs in the queue awaiting the print device. Currently printing jobs are not affected.

SplQueryJob

This function queries information about a specific print job in a queue. A `PRJINFO2` or `PRJINFO3` structure is returned based on the requested information level. The `PRJINFO2` structure contains the job ID, priority, status, size, document name, title, and user name. The `PRJINFO3` structure contains that information along with more details, such as queue processor parameters and status string. The printer name, driver name, and data are also available.

SplReleaseJob

This function changes the status of a specific print job in the queue from held to released. The job is not sent to the printer if the queue is currently held.

SplReleaseQueue

This function changes the status of a print queue from held to released. Jobs in the queue that are not held are printed, provided that the requested form and other job-specific criteria are met by the print device or devices.

SplSetJob

This function modifies one or all parameters of a job, such as the number of copies or priority.

Installing Private Device Drivers

The spooler API provides the `SplCreateDevice` and `SplCreateQueue` functions to be used to add a new print object to the desktop. However, if your application requires a private device driver, you may add an entry to the `PM_DEVICE_DRIVERS` application section of the user system INI file. The section name should be the physical name of the installed driver. For example, if the name of the driver module was MYDRIVER.DRV, the section name would be `MYDRIVER`. The data for that section is the full path and filename of the device. Once installed, you may create a device context with that driver using the `DevOpenDC` function.

Converting Profile Queries to the Spooler Equivalents

This section is designed to assist you in converting code originally written for OS/2 version 1.x to 2.0 and later to 2.11. The INI file entries containing information on installed and default printers are listed. If you are developing new code, use the spooler API and ignore most of this section. You may find it helpful to use the INITOR program from the chapter, "Profile Management," and to browse through the entries as they are discussed. However, you should not depend on these entries for future versions of OS/2.

PM_SPOOLER

QUEUE

This entry contains the physical name of the default queue. The physical name may be found on the view page of a print object's settings notebook. If you have more than one printer installed on your machine, you may change this value by selecting the Set Default menu item of any print object.

Replacement Spooler API

Determining the default print object is unfortunately the one hole in the spooler API. As a result, the profile function `PrfQueryProfile` string must still be used to determine the system default printer. The `SplQueryQueue` may then be used to retrieve the queue description and other details in the `PRQINFO3` structure. The string returned ends in a semicolon, which should be removed before passing the name to the `SplQueryQueue` function. Selecting the default print object is not required. You can maintain an application default printer by writing the last selected device as private entries in an INI file. On program start-up, the entry can be read and the application default selected from the print objects returned from the `SplEnumQueue` function.

PRINTER

In releases of OS/2 prior to 2.1, this contained the default printer. In later versions, it remains for compatibility with 1.x applications and contains the same value as the QUEUE keyname described above.

Replacement Spooler API

No spooler API exists to retrieve this value.

PM_SPOOLER_PRINTER

This application section contains entries for installed printer drivers. The keyname is the physical device name, and the data string is defined as follows:

```
<addr>;<ddl>;<ql>;<netopt>;<timeout>;
```

For example, you might see the string:

```
ex. LPT1;PSCRIPT.HP LaserJet IIISi PS v52_3;HPLaserJ;;45;
```

The pieces of the string have the following meaning:

`<addr>`	The physical hardware address (for example, LPTn, COMn, IEEEn) to which the device is connected.
`<ddl>`	A list of device drivers defined for the printer (note the comma between each name), which can be NULL. The first one is taken as the default. The driver name is in the form *<printer driver name>.<hardware description>*.
`<ql>`	A list of queues defined for the printer; this contains the physical name of the queue the driver is associated with.
`<netopt>`	The network printer options, which may be omitted.
`<timeout>`	The timeout value in seconds.

Replacement Spooler API

This information may now be retrieved from the SplEnumQueue function.

PM_SPOOLER_PRINTER_DESCR

<printer name>

This entry contains the user-supplied printer description. Once again, this field remains for compatibility with 1.x applications. When a print object is installed, this entry contains the initial queue description, which may also be found in the PM_SPOOLER_QUEUE_DESC. This string

may be found in the title entry on the general page of the printer settings notebook, and it appears as the icon text of a print object. This entry will never be updated as the user changes the print object description.

Replacement Spooler API

The `pszComment` field of the `PRQINFO3/PRQINFO6` structure now contains the current queue description. This structure may be retrieved by calling `SplEnumQueue` or `SplQueryDevice`.

PM_SPOOLER_QUEUE_DESCR

<queue name>

This entry contained the user-supplied queue description. This value is the descriptive name given by the user that appears as the icon window text in the title entry on the general page of printer settings. Unlike `PM_SPOOLER_PRINTER_DESCR`, this field is updated when the queue name changes.

Replacement Spooler API

The `pszComment` field of the `PRQINFO3/PRQINFO6` structure now contains the current queue description. This structure may be retrieved by calling `SplEnumQueue` or `SplQueryDevice`. (See Figure 13.7.)

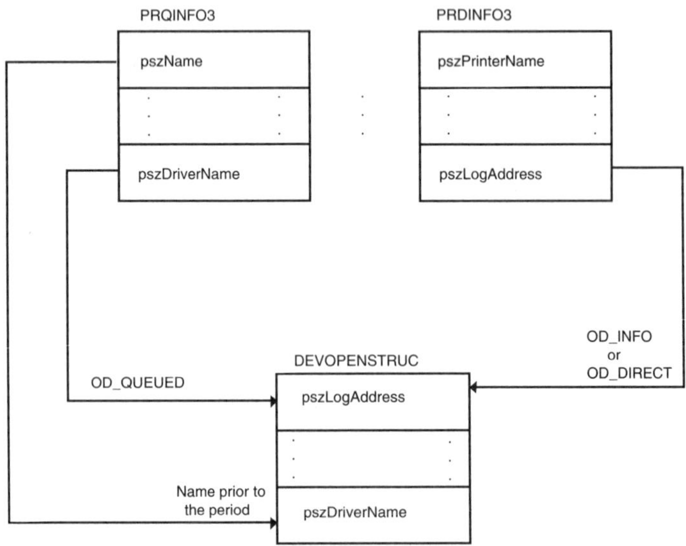

Figure 13.7. Relationship of the `PRQINFO3`, `DEVOPENSTRUC`, and `PRDINFO3` structures.

The PRNT Application

We have provided a fairly sophisticated little print application to illustrate these concepts. In order to use it, of course, you need an actual printer installed on your system. The following files are needed to build the PRNT application.

ABOUT.DLG
PRNT.DLG
DIALOG.H
PRNT.C
PRNTINFO.C
PRNT.DEF
PRNT.H
PRNT.ICO
PRNT.MAP
PRNT.RC

PRNT.DLG

```
/* ---------------------------------
Print Dialogs
Real-World Programming for OS/2
Copyright (c) 1994 Blain, Delimon, and English
--------------------------------- */

DLGINCLUDE 1 "DIALOG.H"

DLGTEMPLATE SELECT_PRINTER_DLG LOADONCALL MOVEABLE
DISCARDABLE
BEGIN
   DIALOG  "Select Printer", SELECT_PRINTER_DLG, 65, 89,
           253, 69, WS_VISIBLE, FCF_SYSMENU ¦ FCF_TITLEBAR
           PRESPARAMS PP_FONTNAMESIZE, "8.Helv"
   BEGIN
      LISTBOX         DID_QUEUE_NAMES, 5, 23, 241, 40
      DEFPUSHBUTTON   "~Ok", DID_OK, 4, 3, 40, 14
      PUSHBUTTON      "Cancel", DID_CANCEL, 56, 3, 40, 14
      PUSHBUTTON      "Job Properties...", DID_JOBPROPS,
                        107, 3, 84, 14
   END
END

DLGTEMPLATE PRINT_DLG LOADONCALL MOVEABLE DISCARDABLE
BEGIN
   DIALOG  "Print", PRINT_DLG, 72, 106, 250, 66, WS_VISIBLE,
           FCF_SYSMENU ¦ FCF_TITLEBAR
           PRESPARAMS PP_FONTNAMESIZE, "8.Helv"
   BEGIN
      LTEXT           "Printer:", -1, 7, 52, 37, 8
      ENTRYFIELD      "", DID_PRINTER, 48, 54, 196, 8,
                     ES_MARGIN
```

```
      LTEXT           "Document:", 106, 6, 37, 49, 8
      ENTRYFIELD      "", DID_DOCUMENT, 48, 39, 195, 8,
                     ES_MARGIN
      LTEXT           "Copies:", -1, 7, 24, 33, 8
      CONTROL         "", DID_COPIES, 47, 24, 30, 12,
                     WC_SPINBUTTON, SPBS_ALLCHARACTERS ¦
                     SPBS_MASTER ¦ SPBS_SERVANT ¦
                     SPBS_JUSTDEFAULT ¦ SPBS_FASTSPIN ¦
                     WS_GROUP ¦ WS_TABSTOP ¦ WS_VISIBLE
      LTEXT           "Priority:", -1, 89, 24, 27, 8
      CONTROL         "", DID_PRIORITY, 120, 24, 52, 12,
                     WC_SPINBUTTON, SPBS_ALLCHARACTERS ¦
                     SPBS_READONLY ¦ SPBS_MASTER ¦
                     SPBS_SERVANT ¦ SPBS_JUSTDEFAULT ¦
                     SPBS_JUSTLEFT ¦ SPBS_FASTSPIN ¦
                     WS_GROUP ¦ WS_TABSTOP ¦ WS_VISIBLE
      DEFPUSHBUTTON   "Ok", DID_OK, 14, 4, 40, 14
      PUSHBUTTON      "Cancel", DID_CANCEL, 63, 4, 40, 14
   END
END

DLGTEMPLATE PRINT_STATUS_DLG LOADONCALL MOVEABLE DISCARDABLE
BEGIN
   DIALOG  "Print Status", PRINT_STATUS_DLG, 94, 153, 240,
           61, WS_VISIBLE,
           FCF_SYSMENU ¦ FCF_TITLEBAR
           PRESPARAMS PP_FONTNAMESIZE, "8.Helv"
   BEGIN
      LTEXT           "Job:", -1, 5, 48, 31, 8
      LTEXT           "", DID_JOBNAME, 42, 48, 184, 8
      LTEXT           "Printer:", -1, 5, 36, 31, 8
      LTEXT           "", DID_PRINTER, 42, 37, 184, 8
      LTEXT           "Status:", -1, 5, 24, 31, 8
      LTEXT           "", DID_STATUS, 42, 25, 184, 8
      PUSHBUTTON      "Cancel", DID_CANCEL, 92, 4, 40, 14
      DEFPUSHBUTTON   "Ok", DID_OK, 91, 4, 40, 14
   END
END

DLGTEMPLATE QUEUE_INFO_DLG LOADONCALL MOVEABLE DISCARDABLE
BEGIN
   DIALOG  "Queue And Printer Details", QUEUE_INFO_DLG, 25,
           42, 378, 160, WS_VISIBLE, FCF_SYSMENU ¦
           FCF_TITLEBAR
           PRESPARAMS PP_FONTNAMESIZE, "8.Helv"
   BEGIN
      LISTBOX         DID_QUEUE_NAMES, 6, 117, 181, 36
      LTEXT           "Queue Description", -1, 8, 151, 90, 8
      GROUPBOX        "Queue", SELECT_PRINTER_DLG, 6, 55,
                     182, 59
      LTEXT           "Queue Name:", -1, 11, 98, 45, 8
      LTEXT           "", DID_QUEUE_NAME, 61, 98, 111, 8
      LTEXT           "Default Device:", -1, 11, 88, 50, 8
      LTEXT           "", DID_DEFAULT_DEVICE, 61, 88, 121, 8
      LTEXT           "Print Devices:", -1, 11, 78, 48, 8
```

```
LTEXT           "", DID_PRINTERS, 61, 78, 121, 8
LTEXT           "Priority:", -1, 11, 68, 26, 8
LTEXT           "", DID_PRIORITY, 38, 68, 24, 8
LTEXT           "Status:", -1, 70, 68, 25, 8
LTEXT           "", DID_STATUS, 98, 68, 30, 8
LTEXT           "Start Time:", -1, 11, 58, 39, 8
LTEXT           "", DID_START_TIME, 52, 58, 29, 8
LTEXT           "End Time:", -1, 98, 58, 38, 8
LTEXT           "", DID_END_TIME, 142, 58, 32, 8
LTEXT           "Jobs:", -1, 138, 68, 20, 8
LTEXT           "", DID_NUMBER_JOBS, 162, 68, 20, 8
LISTBOX         DID_FORMS, 197, 117, 173, 34
LTEXT           "Forms", -1, 198, 151, 27, 8
GROUPBOX        "Form Information", -1,196,55, 175, 59
LTEXT           "Width in MM:", -1, 204, 96, 44, 8
LTEXT           "", DID_FORM_CX, 257, 96, 18, 8
LTEXT           "Height in MM:", -1, 285, 96, 47, 8
LTEXT           "", DID_FORM_CY, 338, 96, 18, 8
LTEXT           "Left Clip:", -1, 204, 76, 29, 8
LTEXT           "", DID_LEFT_CLIP, 241, 76, 20, 8
LTEXT           "Bottom Clip:", -1, 273, 76, 38, 8
LTEXT           "", DID_BOTTOM_CLIP, 320, 76, 20, 8
LTEXT           "Attribute:", PRINT_STATUS_DLG, 204,
               86, 30, 8
LTEXT           "", DID_FORM_ATTR, 238, 86, 87, 8
LTEXT           "Right Clip:", -1, 204, 66, 32, 8
LTEXT           "", DID_RIGHT_CLIP, 241, 66, 20, 8
LTEXT           "Top Clip:", -1, 272, 66, 37, 8
LTEXT           "", DID_TOP_CLIP, 320, 66, 20, 8
GROUPBOX        "Device Capabilites", -1, 5,22,367, 30
LTEXT           "Technology:", -1, 11, 35, 40, 8
LTEXT           "", DID_TECHNOLOGY, 51, 35, 72, 8
LTEXT           "Width in Pels:", -1, 126, 35, 43, 8
LTEXT           "", DID_CAPS_WIDTH, 170, 35, 19, 8
LTEXT           "Height in Pels:", PRINT_DLG, 194, 35,
               47, 8
LTEXT           "", DID_CAPS_HEIGHT, 239, 35, 20, 8
LTEXT           "Horiz Res:", 106, 260, 35, 33, 8
LTEXT           "", DID_HORZ_RES, 293, 35, 20, 8
LTEXT           "Vert Res:", -1, 316, 35, 30, 8
LTEXT           "", DID_VERT_RES, 348, 35, 20, 8
LTEXT           "GpiBitBlt:", -1, 11, 25, 32, 8
LTEXT           "", DID_BITBLT, 44, 25, 20, 8
LTEXT           "Banding:", -1, 67, 25, 31, 8
LTEXT           "", DID_BANDING, 97, 25, 20, 8
LTEXT           "GpiSetPel:", -1, 123, 25, 35, 8
LTEXT           "", DID_SETPEL, 158, 25, 20, 8
LTEXT           "Raster Fonts:", -1, 184, 25, 44, 8
LTEXT           "", DID_RASTER_FONT, 228, 25, 20, 8
LTEXT           "Kerning:", -1, 256, 25, 29, 8
LTEXT           "", DID_KERNING, 286, 25, 20, 8
LTEXT           "Palette:", -1, 318, 25, 28, 8
LTEXT           "", DID_PALETTE, 347, 25, 20, 8
DEFPUSHBUTTON   "Ok", DID_OK, 6, 3, 40, 14
PUSHBUTTON      "Cancel", DID_CANCEL, 55, 3, 40, 14
```

```
      PUSHBUTTON       "Job Properties...", DID_JOBPROPS,
                         106, 3, 68, 14
      PUSHBUTTON       "Update", DID_UPDATE, 184, 3, 40, 14
   END
END
```

DIALOG.H

```
/* --------------------------------
Print Dialog Header File
Real-World Programming for OS/2
Copyright (c) 1994 Blain, Delimon, and English
-------------------------------- */

#define QUEUE_INFO_DLG              100
#define SELECT_PRINTER_DLG          102
#define PRINT_DLG                   103
#define PRINT_STATUS_DLG            104
#define STATUS_WND                  105
#define DID_QUEUE_NAMES             200
#define DID_PRIORITY                201
#define DID_STATUS                  202
#define DID_NUMBER_JOBS             203
#define DID_START_TIME              204
#define DID_END_TIME                205
#define DID_DEFAULT_DEVICE          206
#define DID_PRINTERS                207
#define DID_TECHNOLOGY              208
#define DID_FORMS                   209
#define DID_FORM_CX                 210
#define DID_FORM_CY                 211
#define DID_LEFT_CLIP               212
#define DID_BOTTOM_CLIP             214
#define DID_FORM_ATTR               215
#define DID_RIGHT_CLIP              216
#define DID_TOP_CLIP                217
#define DID_CAPS_WIDTH              218
#define DID_CAPS_HEIGHT             219
#define DID_HORZ_RES                220
#define DID_VERT_RES                221
#define DID_BITBLT                  222
#define DID_BANDING                 223
#define DID_SETPEL                  224
#define DID_RASTER_FONT             225
#define DID_KERNING                 226
#define DID_PALETTE                 227
#define DID_JOBPROPS                228
#define DID_UPDATE                  229
#define DID_PRINTER                 300
#define DID_DOCUMENT                301
#define DID_COPIES                  302
#define DID_JOB_LIST                400
#define DID_JOBNAME                 401
#define DID_QUEUE_NAME              240
```

PRNT.C

```
/* ------------------------------
Printing Sample Program
Real-World Programming for OS/2
Copyright (c) 1994 Blain, Delimon, and English
------------------------------ */

#define INCL_WIN
#define INCL_GPI
#define INCL_DEV
#define INCL_SPL
#define INCL_SPLDOSPRINT
#define INCL_WINERRORS
#define INCL_DOSPROCESS
#include <os2.h>
#include <string.h>
#include <stdio.h>
#include "prnt.h"
#include "dialog.h"
#include "..\common\about.h"

#define NERR_BuffTooSmall 2123

MRESULT EXPENTRY ClientWndProc (HWND,ULONG,MPARAM,MPARAM);
MRESULT EXPENTRY PrintInfoDlgProc (HWND,ULONG,MPARAM,MPARAM);
MRESULT EXPENTRY PrintStatusProc (HWND,ULONG,MPARAM,MPARAM);
MRESULT EXPENTRY PrintDlgProc (HWND,ULONG,MPARAM,MPARAM);
MRESULT EXPENTRY SelectPrinterDlgProc (HWND,ULONG,MPARAM,MPARAM);

HAB    hab;
HWND   hWndFrame,
       hWndClient;
HWND   hHintWnd;
HWND   hMenu;
CHAR   szTitle[64];
CHAR   szBuff1[MAX_BUFF];
CHAR   szFontFace[] = "8.Helv";
CHAR   szPM_Q_STD[] = "PM_Q_STD";
PVOID  pMem;
int    nSysFontHeight;
LONG   lColorWorkSpace;
USHORT usDraw = IDM_DISP_BLANK;
CHAR   szPriority[3][10] =
{
   "Low",
   "Standard",
   "High"
};

LONG lPriority[3] =
{
   1,50,99
};

/* Array of pointers to priority strings (for spinner control) */
```

```
PVOID pszPriorities[3] =
{
   &szPriority[0],
   &szPriority[1],
   &szPriority[2]
};


DEVICEINFO CurrentDI;

int main()
{
   HMQ   hmq;
   QMSG  qmsg;
   ULONG flFrameFlags    = FCF_TITLEBAR ¦ FCF_SYSMENU ¦
                        FCF_SIZEBORDER ¦ FCF_MINMAX ¦
                        FCF_SHELLPOSITION ¦ FCF_TASKLIST ¦
                        FCF_ICON ¦ FCF_MENU;
   CHAR  szClientClass[] = "CLIENT";

   hab = WinInitialize (0);
   hmq = WinCreateMsgQueue (hab, 0);

   WinRegisterClass (hab, szClientClass, ClientWndProc,
         CS_SIZEREDRAW, 0);
   WinLoadString (hab, 0, ID_APPNAME, sizeof(szTitle),
         szTitle);

   DosAllocMem((PPVOID)&pMem,0x1000,PAG_READ ¦ PAG_WRITE);
   DosSubSet(pMem,DOSSUB_INIT ¦ DOSSUB_SPARSE_OBJ,0x8000);

   hWndFrame = WinCreateStdWindow (HWND_DESKTOP, WS_VISIBLE,
      &flFrameFlags, szClientClass, szTitle, 0, 0,
      ID_APPNAME,           &hWndClient);

   hMenu  = WinWindowFromID (hWndFrame,FID_MENU);
   create_status_line(hWndClient);

   while (WinGetMsg (hab, &qmsg, 0, 0, 0))
      WinDispatchMsg (hab, &qmsg);

   WinDestroyWindow (hWndFrame);
   WinDestroyMsgQueue (hmq);
   WinTerminate (hab);
   DosFreeMem(pMem);
   return (0);
}


VOID APIENTRY center_window (HWND hWnd)
{
   ULONG ulScrWidth, ulScrHeight;
   RECTL Rectl;

   ulScrWidth  = WinQuerySysValue (HWND_DESKTOP,
         SV_CXSCREEN);
```

```
    ulScrHeight = WinQuerySysValue (HWND_DESKTOP,
          SV_CYSCREEN);
    WinQueryWindowRect (hWnd, &Rectl);
    WinSetWindowPos (hWnd, HWND_TOP,
          (ulScrWidth-Rectl.xRight)/2,
          (ulScrHeight-Rectl.yTop)/2, 0, 0,
          SWP_MOVE ¦ SWP_ACTIVATE);
    return;
}


BOOL APIENTRY create_info_DC(PPRQINFO3 pPrq3,
      PDEVICEINFO pDI)
\*-------------------------------*/

This function will intialize the pDI DEVICEINFO structure based
on the queue pointed to by pPrq3. If pDI contains an existing
entry, its info DC is destroyed and any form info is freed.
A new info DC is created and the get_page_metrics function is used
to initialize size information in the stucture.

/*-------------------------------*/
{
    PDRIVDATA     pDD;
    PPRDINFO3     pPrd3;
    DEVOPENSTRUC  DevOpenData;
    SIZEL         sizel;
    ULONG         ulNeeded = 0;
    int           i;
    CHAR          szDriverName[MAX_DEVICENAME];
    CHAR          szDeviceName[MAX_DEVICENAME];

    /* Free existing info DCs and PSs */
    if (pDI->hInfoPS)
    {
       GpiAssociate(pDI->hInfoPS,0);
       GpiDestroyPS(pDI->hInfoPS);
       pDI->hInfoPS = 0;
       DevCloseDC(pDI->hInfoDC);
       pDI->hInfoDC = 0;
    }
    if (pDI->pHCInfo)
    {
       DosSubFree(pMem,pDI->pHCInfo,(pDI->lSizeHC *
          sizeof(HCINFO)));
       pDI->pHCInfo = 0;
       pDI->lSizeHC = 0;
    }

    if ((i = strcspn(pPrq3->pszDriverName,".")) != 0)
    {
       strncpy((PSZ)szDriverName,
          (PSZ)pPrq3->pszDriverName,i);
       szDriverName[i] = '\0';
       strcpy((PSZ)szDeviceName,
          (PSZ)&pPrq3->pszDriverName[i + 1]);
```

```
   }

   if (SplQueryDevice(0,pPrq3->pszPrinters,3,0,0,
          &ulNeeded) != NERR_BuffTooSmall)
      return(FALSE);

   if (DosSubAlloc(pMem,(PPVOID)&pPrd3,ulNeeded))
      return (FALSE);
   if (SplQueryDevice(0,pPrq3->pszPrinters,3,(PVOID)pPrd3,
         ulNeeded, &ulNeeded) == 0)
   {
      if (pDI->pDrivData)
         pDD = pDI->pDrivData;
      else
         pDD = pPrq3->pDriverData;

      strcpy(pDI->szQueueDesc,pPrq3->pszComment);
      strcpy(pDI->szDriverName,pPrq3->pszDriverName);
      strcpy(pDI->szQueueName,pPrq3->pszName);

      DevOpenData.pszLogAddress = pPrd3->pszLogAddr;
      DevOpenData.pszDriverName = szDriverName;
      DevOpenData.pdriv         = pDD;
      DevOpenData.pszDataType   = (PSZ)szPM_Q_STD;


      if ((pDI->hInfoDC = DevOpenDC (hab,OD_INFO,"*",4,
            (PVOID)&DevOpenData,0)) != 0)
      {
         sizel.cx = 0;
         sizel.cy = 0;
         if (!(pDI->hInfoPS = GpiCreatePS (hab,pDI->hInfoDC,
               &sizel, GPIA_ASSOC ¦ GPIT_MICRO ¦
               PU_LOMETRIC)))
         {
            DevCloseDC(pDI->hInfoDC);
            pDI->hInfoDC = 0;
         }
         else
         {
            get_page_metrics(pDI);
         }
      }
   }
   else
      post_error(hWndClient,ID_ERR_FAIL_DEV_QUERY);

   DosSubFree(pMem,pPrd3,ulNeeded);
   return((BOOL)pDI->hInfoPS);
}


BOOL APIENTRY create_print_DC(PDEVICEINFO pDI)
/*-------------------------------*/

This function will create an OD_QUEUED device context based on the
```

contents of the pDI parameter. If successful, a presentation space is created and the DEVESC_STARTDOC escape is issued. The presentation space is then reset from indexed to RGB mode.

```
/*-------------------------------*/
{
   DEVOPENSTRUC  DevOpenStr;
   CHAR          szQueueProcParams[9];
   CHAR          szSpoolerParams[9];
   CHAR          szDriverName[MAX_DEVICENAME];
   int           i;

   memset((PVOID)&DevOpenStr, 0, sizeof(DevOpenStr));

   /* Set priority in spooler params */
   sprintf((PSZ)szSpoolerParams,(PSZ)"PRTY=%d",
         pDI->lPriority);
   /* Set number of copies in the queue processor params */
   sprintf((PSZ)szQueueProcParams,(PSZ)"COP=%d",
         pDI->lCopies);

   WinLoadString(hab,0,IDS_JOB_TITLE,sizeof(szBuff1),
         szBuff1);

   if ((i = strcspn(pDI->szDriverName,".")) != 0)
   {
      strncpy((PSZ)szDriverName,(PSZ)&pDI->szDriverName,i);
      szDriverName[i] = '\0';
   }

   DevOpenStr.pszLogAddress      = pDI->szQueueName;
   DevOpenStr.pszDriverName      = szDriverName;
   DevOpenStr.pdriv              = pDI->pDrivData;
   DevOpenStr.pszDataType        = (PSZ)szPM_Q_STD;
   DevOpenStr.pszComment         = (PSZ)szBuff1;
   DevOpenStr.pszQueueProcParams = (PSZ)szQueueProcParams;
   DevOpenStr.pszSpoolerParams   = (PSZ)szSpoolerParams;

   if ((pDI->hPrintDC = DevOpenDC(hab,OD_QUEUED,"*",9,
         (PVOID)&DevOpenStr,(HDC)0)) != 0)
   {
      if (!(pDI->hPrintPS = GpiCreatePS(hab,
            pDI->hPrintDC,(PSIZEL)
            &pDI->PageSizel,PU_LOMETRIC | GPIA_ASSOC )))
      {
         DevCloseDC(pDI->hPrintDC);
         pDI->hPrintDC = 0;
      }
      else
      {
         DevEscape(pDI->hPrintDC,DEVESC_STARTDOC,
            strlen(szBuff1), szBuff1,0,0);
         GpiCreateLogColorTable (CurrentDI.hPrintPS,
            LCOL_RESET, LCOLF_RGB,0,0,NULL);
      }
   }
```

```
         ptl.x = arcparms.lP;
         ptl.y = arcparms.lQ + 1;
         GpiMove (hPS,&ptl);
         GpiFullArc(hPS,DRO_OUTLINEFILL,MAKEFIXED(1,0));
         break;
      default:
         break;
   }
}


void APIENTRY draw_page_background(HPS hPS)
/*-------------------------------*/

This function draws the "print page" in the client area. The
physical page is drawn as a white rectangle with a black border
and the printable area is drawn as a blue dashed outline.

/*-------------------------------*/
{
   AREABUNDLE  ab;
   LINEBUNDLE  lb;
   POINTL      ptl;


   /* Draw the physical page white with a black border */
   ab.lColor = RGB_WHITE;
   GpiSetAttrs(hPS,PRIM_AREA,ABB_COLOR,0,(PBUNDLE)&ab);
   lb.lColor = RGB_BLACK;
   lb.usType = LINETYPE_SOLID;
   GpiSetAttrs(hPS,PRIM_LINE,LBB_COLOR |
         LBB_TYPE,0,(PBUNDLE)&lb);

   ptl.x = PAGE_OFFSET;
   ptl.y = (CurrentDI.cy - nSysFontHeight) - PAGE_OFFSET;
   GpiConvert(hPS,CVTC_DEVICE,CVTC_WORLD,1,(PPOINTL)&ptl);
   GpiMove(hPS,(PPOINTL)&ptl);
   ptl.x = CurrentDI.PhyPageSizel.cx + ptl.x;
   ptl.y = ptl.y - CurrentDI.PhyPageSizel.cy;
   GpiBox(hPS,DRO_OUTLINEFILL,(PPOINTL)&ptl,0,0);

   /* Outline the addressable portion of the page with a
      blue dashed line */
   lb.lColor = RGB_BLUE;
   lb.usType = LINETYPE_SHORTDASH;
   GpiSetAttrs(hPS,PRIM_LINE,LBB_COLOR |
         LBB_TYPE,0,(PBUNDLE)&lb);

   ptl.x = PAGE_OFFSET;
   ptl.y = (CurrentDI.cy - nSysFontHeight) - PAGE_OFFSET;
   GpiConvert(CurrentDI.hClientPS,CVTC_DEVICE,CVTC_WORLD,1,
         (PPOINTL)&ptl);
   ptl.x += CurrentDI.PrintOffsetSizel.cx;
   ptl.y -= CurrentDI.PrintOffsetSizel.cy;
   GpiMove(hPS,(PPOINTL)&ptl);
   ptl.x = CurrentDI.PageSizel.cx + ptl.x;
```

```
   ptl.y = ptl.y - CurrentDI.PageSizel.cy;
   GpiBox(hPS,DRO_OUTLINE,(PPOINTL)&ptl,0,0);
}


PPRQINFO3 APIENTRY enum_print_queues(HWND hWnd,
         HWND hWndLBox,PULONG pulSize,PULONG pulCount,
         PULONG pulCurrent)
/*-------------------------------*/

This function will enumerate the installed print queues and add
their description to hWndLBox.  The function returns a pointer
to an array of PPRQINFO3 structures if successful. The number of
entries in the array and the total size of the allocated memory
is returned in the pulCount and pulSize parameters respectfully.
The index of the current application default queue is returned in
the pulCurrent parameter.

/*-------------------------------*/
{
   ULONG     cReturned, cTotal, ulSize;
   int       i;
   PSZ       pName;
   PPRQINFO3 pQueueInfo = 0;

   ulSize = 0;
   SplEnumQueue(0,3,0,0L,(PULONG)&cReturned,(PULONG)&cTotal,
         (PULONG)&ulSize,0);

   if (pulCount)
      *pulCount = cTotal;

   if (!cTotal)
      post_error(hWnd,ID_NOQUEUE_ERROR);
   else if (!DosSubAlloc(pMem,(PPVOID)&pQueueInfo,ulSize))
   {
      /* Set the size in the return parameter */
      *pulSize = ulSize;

      SplEnumQueue(0,3,pQueueInfo,ulSize,(PULONG)&cReturned,
         (PULONG)&cTotal,(PULONG)&ulSize,0);

      WinEnableWindowUpdate(hWndLBox,FALSE);
      WinSendMsg (hWndLBox,LM_DELETEALL,0,0);
      for (i = 0;i < (int)cTotal; i++)
      {
         /* If the queue description is a NULL string then
            use the the queue name so the dialog won't have
            a blank entry */
         if (*pQueueInfo[i].pszComment)
            pName = pQueueInfo[i].pszComment;
         else
            pName = pQueueInfo[i].pszName;
         WinSendMsg (hWndLBox,LM_INSERTITEM,(MPARAM)LIT_END,
               (MPARAM)pName);
         if (strcmp(CurrentDI.szQueueDesc,pName) == 0)
```

```
            /* This is the current application default */
            *pulCurrent = i;
        }
        WinEnableWindowUpdate(hWndLBox,TRUE);
    }
    return(pQueueInfo);
}



VOID APIENTRY get_job_properties(PPRQINFO3 pQueueInfo,
         PDDINFO pDDInfo, ULONG ulOption)
/*------------------------------*/

This function will query or post job properties for the queue
identified by the pQueueInfo parameter. ulOptioh should be set
to DPDM_QUERYJOBPROP or DPDM_POSTJOBPROP.

/*------------------------------*/
{
    int    i;
    PSZ    pszTemp;
    CHAR   szDriverName[MAX_DEVICENAME];
    CHAR   szDeviceName[MAX_DEVICENAME];

    if ((i = strcspn(pQueueInfo->pszDriverName,".")) != 0)
    {
        strncpy((PSZ)szDriverName,
              (PSZ)pQueueInfo->pszDriverName,i);
        szDriverName[i] = '\0';
        strcpy((PSZ)szDeviceName,
              (PSZ)&pQueueInfo->pszDriverName[i + 1]);
    }
    else
    {
        strcpy((PSZ)szDriverName, pQueueInfo->pszDriverName);
        *szDeviceName = '\0';
    }

    pszTemp = (PSZ)strchr(pQueueInfo->pszPrinters, ',');
    if ( pszTemp )
    {
        *pszTemp = '\0' ;
    }

    if (pDDInfo->pDrivData == 0)
    {
        /* Allocate memory for the driver data */
        pDDInfo->lSizeDD = DevPostDeviceModes(hab,0,
              szDriverName,szDeviceName,
              pQueueInfo->pszPrinters,ulOption);
        DosSubAlloc(pMem,(PPVOID)&pDDInfo->pDrivData,
              pDDInfo->lSizeDD);
        pDDInfo->pDrivData->cb = sizeof(DRIVDATA);
        pDDInfo->pDrivData->lVersion = 0;
        strcpy(pDDInfo->pDrivData->szDeviceName,szDeviceName);
```

```
   }
   DevPostDeviceModes(hab,
         pDDInfo->pDrivData,szDriverName,szDeviceName,
         pQueueInfo->pszPrinters,ulOption);
}



VOID APIENTRY get_page_metrics(PDEVICEINFO pDI)
/*-------------------------------*/

This function will initialize the physical and printable page
sizes for the information DC in the pDI parameter.

/*-------------------------------*/
{
   POINTL   PtlRes;
   PHCINFO  pHCInfo;
   int      i;

   GpiQueryPS(pDI->hInfoPS,(PSIZEL)&pDI->PageSizel);
   pDI->lSizeHC = DevQueryHardcopyCaps(pDI->hInfoDC,0,0,0);
   if ( (pDI->lSizeHC > 0) &&
         (DosSubAlloc(pMem,(PPVOID)&pDI->pHCInfo,
         pDI->lSizeHC * sizeof(HCINFO)) == 0) )
   {
      DevQueryHardcopyCaps(pDI->hInfoDC,0,pDI->lSizeHC,
         pDI->pHCInfo);
      pHCInfo = pDI->pHCInfo;
      for (i = 0; i < pDI->lSizeHC; i++)
      {
         if (pHCInfo[i].flAttributes & HCAPS_CURRENT)
         {
            /* Calculate the physical page size */
            DevQueryCaps (pDI-   >hInfoDC,
               CAPS_HORIZONTAL_RESOLUTION,1L,
               (PLONG) &PtlRes.x);
            DevQueryCaps (pDI->hInfoDC,
               CAPS_VERTICAL_RESOLUTION,1L,
               (PLONG) &PtlRes.y);
            /* Convert from millimeters to pixels */
            pDI->PhyPageSizel.cx =
               (PtlRes.x * pHCInfo[i].cx) / 1000;
            pDI->PhyPageSizel.cy =
               (PtlRes.y * pHCInfo[i].cy) / 1000;
            /* Convert from device to world coordinate space */
            GpiConvert(pDI->hInfoPS,CVTC_DEVICE,
               CVTC_WORLD,1, (PPOINTL)&pDI->PhyPageSizel);

            pDI->PrintOffsetSizel.cx =
               (PtlRes.x * pHCInfo[i].xLeftClip) / 1000;
            pDI->PrintOffsetSizel.cy =
               (PtlRes.y * pHCInfo[i].yBottomClip) / 1000;
            /* Convert from device to world coordinate space    */
            GpiConvert(pDI->hInfoPS,CVTC_DEVICE,
               CVTC_WORLD,1,
```

```
                (PPOINTL)&pDI->PrintOffsetSizel);
             break;
          }
       }
    }
    else
    {
       pDI->pHCInfo = 0;
       pDI->lSizeHC = 0;
    }
}


HPS APIENTRY init_app(HWND hWnd)
/*-------------------------------*/

This function is called on program startup to intialize the
CurrentDI variable based on the system default queue. A PS is
created for the client window, the default viewing matrix is
modified, and the PS is changed from indexed to RGB mode.

/*-------------------------------*/
{
   PPRQINFO3 pPrq3;
   ULONG     ulSize;
   char      szTemp[MAX_BUFF];
   PSZ       pStr;
   ULONG     ulNeeded;
   MATRIXLF  matlfDefView;

   memset(&CurrentDI,0,sizeof(DEVICEINFO));
   CurrentDI.lCopies   = 1;
   CurrentDI.lPriority = 50;

   /* Query the default printer */
   ulSize = PrfQueryProfileString(HINI_PROFILE,"PM_SPOOLER",
         "QUEUE", 0,szTemp,MAX_BUFF);

   if (ulSize)
   {
      pStr = (PSZ)strchr(szTemp,';');
      *pStr = 0;
      SplQueryQueue(0,szTemp,3,0,0,&ulNeeded);
      if (ulNeeded && !(DosSubAlloc(pMem,(PPVOID)&pPrq3,
               ulNeeded)))
      {
         SplQueryQueue(0,szTemp,3,pPrq3,ulNeeded,&ulNeeded);
         get_job_properties(pPrq3,
            (PDDINFO)&CurrentDI.lSizeDD, DPDM_QUERYJOBPROP);
         create_info_DC(pPrq3,&CurrentDI);
         DosSubFree(pMem,pPrq3,ulNeeded);

         CurrentDI.hClientDC = WinOpenWindowDC(hWnd);
         CurrentDI.hClientPS = GpiCreatePS(hab,
               CurrentDI.hClientDC,
               (PSIZEL)&CurrentDI.ClientSizel,
```

```
                PU_LOMETRIC ¦ GPIF_LONG ¦ GPIT_NORMAL ¦
                GPIA_ASSOC);

          /* Scale the page to 50% */
          GpiQueryDefaultViewMatrix(CurrentDI.hClientPS,
                9,&matlfDefView);
          matlfDefView.fxM11 = MAKEFIXED(0,32768);
          matlfDefView.fxM22 = MAKEFIXED(0,32768);
          matlfDefView.lM31  = PAGE_OFFSET;
          matlfDefView.lM32  = 0;
          GpiSetDefaultViewMatrix(CurrentDI.hClientPS,9,
                &matlfDefView, TRANSFORM_REPLACE);

          /* Create an RGB color table */
          GpiCreateLogColorTable (CurrentDI.hClientPS,
                LCOL_RESET, LCOLF_RGB,0,0,NULL);
          lColorWorkSpace = WinQuerySysColor(HWND_DESKTOP,
                SYSCLR_APPWORKSPACE,0);
       }
    }

    if (!CurrentDI.hInfoDC)
    {
       /* Disable print menus */
       HWND hMenu = WinWindowFromID(WinQueryWindow(hWnd,
             QW_PARENT), FID_MENU);
       WinSendMsg (hMenu,MM_SETITEMATTR,
             MPFROM2SHORT(IDM_CHOOSE_PRINTER,TRUE),
             MPFROM2SHORT(MIA_DISABLED,FALSE));
       WinSendMsg (hMenu,MM_SETITEMATTR,
             MPFROM2SHORT(IDM_PRINTER_INFO,TRUE),
             MPFROM2SHORT(MIA_DISABLED,FALSE));
       WinSendMsg (hMenu,MM_SETITEMATTR,
             MPFROM2SHORT(IDM_PRINT,TRUE),
             MPFROM2SHORT(MIA_DISABLED,FALSE));
       /* Message box */
       post_error(hWnd,ID_ERR_NODEF_PRINTERS);
    }
    return (CurrentDI.hInfoDC);
}


USHORT APIENTRY post_error(HWND hWnd,USHORT usErrorID)
/*-------------------------------*/

This is a utility function which will post a message box with
a string loaded from the resource file.

/*-------------------------------*/
{
   WinLoadString (hab,0,usErrorID,MAX_BUFF,szBuff1);
   return (WinMessageBox(HWND_DESKTOP,hWnd,(PSZ)szBuff1,
         (PSZ)"Error",0,MB_OK ¦ MB_ICONHAND ¦
         MB_APPLMODAL));
}
```

```
void APIENTRY process_command(HWND hWnd,MPARAM mp1,
            MPARAM mp2)
/*-------------------------------*/

All WM_COMMAND messages received by the client window will be
processed here.

/*-------------------------------*/
{
   switch(SHORT1FROMMP(mp1))
   {
      case IDM_DISP_BLANK:
      case IDM_DISP_BOX:
      case IDM_DISP_ELLIPSE:
         WinSendMsg (hMenu,MM_SETITEMATTR,
               MPFROM2SHORT(usDraw,TRUE),
               MPFROM2SHORT(MIA_CHECKED,FALSE));
         usDraw = SHORT1FROMMP(mp1);
         WinSendMsg (hMenu,MM_SETITEMATTR,
               MPFROM2SHORT(usDraw,TRUE),
               MPFROM2SHORT(MIA_CHECKED,MIA_CHECKED));
         WinInvalidateRect(hWndClient,0,FALSE);
         break;
      case IDM_ABOUT:
         DisplayAbout (hWnd, szTitle);
         break;
      case IDM_CHOOSE_PRINTER:
         /* Display the queue selection dialog */
         WinDlgBox(HWND_DESKTOP,hWndFrame,
               (PFNWP)SelectPrinterDlgProc,0,
               SELECT_PRINTER_DLG,(PVOID)0);
         break;
      case IDM_PRINTER_INFO:
         /* Display the queue information dialog */
         WinDlgBox(HWND_DESKTOP,hWndFrame,
            (PFNWP)PrintInfoDlgProc,0,
            QUEUE_INFO_DLG,(PVOID)0);
         break;
      case IDM_PRINT:
         /* Confirm the print operation and print */
         if (WinDlgBox(HWND_DESKTOP,hWndClient,PrintDlgProc,
                0,PRINT_DLG, (PVOID)0) == DID_OK)
         {
            WinDlgBox(HWND_DESKTOP,hWndClient,
               PrintStatusProc,0,
               PRINT_STATUS_DLG,(PVOID)&mp1);
         }
         break;
      case IDM_PRINT_THREAD:
         /* Confirm the print operation and print in a thread */
         if (WinDlgBox(HWND_DESKTOP,hWndClient,
                  PrintDlgProc,0,PRINT_DLG,
                  (PVOID)0) == DID_OK)
         {
            WinLoadDlg(HWND_DESKTOP,hWndClient,
```

```
                  PrintStatusProc,0,
                  PRINT_STATUS_DLG,(PVOID)&mp1);
         }
         break;
      default:
         break;
   }
   return;
   mp2;
   hWnd;
}

#ifdef __IBMC__
#pragma linkage(process_print, system)
#endif

void APIENTRY process_print(HWND hPrintStatusDlg)
/*-------------------------------*/

This function perfoms the actual printing. A copy of the current
device settings are copied to an allocated memory block and a
print DC is created. If successful, the printing is done and the
job is completed. The print status dialog is updated via posted
WM_PRINT_STATUS messages.

/*-------------------------------*/
{
   PDEVICEINFO pDI;

   if (DosSubAlloc(pMem,(PPVOID)&pDI,
         sizeof(DEVICEINFO)) == 0)
   {
      *pDI = CurrentDI;

      if (create_print_DC(pDI))
      {
         WinPostMsg(hPrintStatusDlg,WM_PRINT_STATUS,
            (MPARAM)JOB_STARTED,0);
         draw_page(pDI->hPrintPS);
         DevEscape(pDI->hPrintPS,DEVESC_ENDDOC,0,0,0,0);
         WinPostMsg(hPrintStatusDlg,WM_PRINT_STATUS,
            (MPARAM)JOB_FINISHED,0);

         GpiAssociate(pDI->hPrintPS,0);
         GpiDestroyPS(pDI->hPrintPS);
         DevCloseDC(pDI->hPrintDC);
      }
      else
         WinPostMsg(hPrintStatusDlg,WM_PRINT_STATUS,
               (MPARAM)JOB_FAILED,0);
      DosSubFree(pMem,pDI,sizeof(DEVICEINFO));
   }
}


void APIENTRY process_size(MPARAM mp1,MPARAM mp2)
```

```
{
   POINTL   ptl;
   MATRIXLF matlfDefView;

   CurrentDI.cx = SHORT1FROMMP(mp2);
   CurrentDI.cy = SHORT2FROMMP(mp2);
   WinSetWindowPos (hHintWnd,HWND_TOP,0,0,SHORT1FROMMP(mp2),
         nSysFontHeight,SWP_SIZE ¦ SWP_MOVE);

   /* Reset the default view matrix before converting client size */
   ptl.x = PAGE_OFFSET;
   ptl.y = (CurrentDI.cy - nSysFontHeight)-PAGE_OFFSET + 1;
   GpiQueryDefaultViewMatrix(CurrentDI.hClientPS,9,
         &matlfDefView );
   matlfDefView.lM31  = 0;
   matlfDefView.lM32  = 0;
   GpiSetDefaultViewMatrix(CurrentDI.hClientPS,9,
      &matlfDefView, TRANSFORM_REPLACE);
   GpiConvert(CurrentDI.hClientPS,CVTC_DEVICE,
      CVTC_WORLD,1,(PPOINTL)&ptl);

   ptl.y = (ptl.y - CurrentDI.PhyPageSizel.cy) +
   CurrentDI.PrintOffsetSizel.cy;
   ptl.x = ptl.x + CurrentDI.PrintOffsetSizel.cx;
   matlfDefView.lM31 = (LONG)((float)ptl.x * 0.5);
   matlfDefView.lM32 = (LONG)((float)ptl.y * 0.5);
   GpiSetDefaultViewMatrix(CurrentDI.hClientPS,9,
         &matlfDefView, TRANSFORM_REPLACE);
   return;
   mp1;
}

MRESULT EXPENTRY ClientWndProc (HWND hWnd, ULONG msg,
         MPARAM mp1, MPARAM mp2)
/*--------------------------------*/

This is the application callback which handles the messages
necessary to maintain the client window.

/*--------------------------------*/
{
   HPS      hPS;
   RECTL    Rectl;
   TID      tid;
   BOOL     bHandled = TRUE;
   MRESULT  mReturn  = 0;

   switch (msg)
   {
      case WM_CREATE:
         hPS = init_app(hWnd);
         break;
      case WM_COMMAND:
         process_command(hWnd,mp1,mp2);
         break;
      case WM_PAINT:
```

```
            hPS = WinBeginPaint(hWnd,CurrentDI.hClientPS,
               (PRECTL)&Rectl);
            WinFillRect(hPS,(PRECTL)&Rectl,lColorWorkSpace);
            draw_page_background(hPS);
            draw_page(hPS);
            WinEndPaint (hPS);
            break;
         case WM_ERASEBACKGROUND:
            mReturn = MRFROMLONG(1L);
            break;
         case WM_MENUSELECT:
            display_hint(SHORT1FROMMP(mp1));
            bHandled = FALSE;
            break;
         case WM_SIZE:
            process_size(mp1,mp2);
            break;
         case WM_START_PRINT:
            if (SHORT1FROMMP(mp2) == IDM_PRINT)
               process_print((HWND)mp1);
            else
               DosCreateThread(&tid,(PFNTHREAD)process_print,
                  (ULONG)mp1, 0,0x2000);
            break;
         default:
            bHandled = FALSE;
         break;
   }

   if (!bHandled)
      mReturn = WinDefWindowProc (hWnd,msg,mp1,mp2);

   return (mReturn);
}



MRESULT EXPENTRY PrintDlgProc(HWND hWndDlg,
         ULONG ulMessage,MPARAM mp1, MPARAM mp2)
/*-------------------------------*/

This function will display the print confirmation dialog box. It
allows the user to verify the print destination and set the job
priority and print copies.

/*-------------------------------*/
{
   HWND  hWnd;
   ULONG ulSelect;

   switch (ulMessage)
   {
      case WM_INITDLG:
         center_window(hWndDlg);
         hWnd = WinWindowFromID(hWndDlg,DID_PRINTER);
         WinSetWindowText(hWnd,CurrentDI.szQueueDesc);
```

```
      WinSendMsg(hWnd,EM_SETREADONLY,(MPARAM)TRUE,0);

      hWnd = WinWindowFromID(hWndDlg,DID_DOCUMENT);
      WinLoadString(hab,0,IDS_JOB_TITLE,sizeof(szBuff1),
            szBuff1);
      WinSetWindowText(hWnd,szBuff1);
      WinSendMsg(hWnd,EM_SETREADONLY,(MPARAM)TRUE,0);

      /* Set the limits to the valid range for a queue
         processor */
      hWnd = WinWindowFromID(hWndDlg,DID_COPIES);
      WinSendMsg(hWnd,SPBM_SETLIMITS,(MPARAM)999,
            (MPARAM)1);
      WinSendMsg(hWnd,SPBM_SETCURRENTVALUE,
            MPFROMLONG(CurrentDI.lCopies),0);
      WinSetFocus(HWND_DESKTOP,hWnd);

      /* Initialize the priority spinner control */
      hWnd = WinWindowFromID(hWndDlg,DID_PRIORITY);
      WinSendMsg (hWnd,SPBM_SETTEXTLIMIT,(MPARAM)9L,
            (MPARAM)0L);
      WinSendMsg(hWnd,SPBM_SETARRAY,
            (MPARAM)pszPriorities, (MPARAM)3);
      WinSendMsg (hWnd,SPBM_SETCURRENTVALUE,(MPARAM)1,
            (MPARAM)0L);
      return ((MRESULT)TRUE);
   case WM_COMMAND:
      switch (SHORT1FROMMP(mp1))
      {
         case DID_OK:
            hWnd = WinWindowFromID(hWndDlg,DID_COPIES);
            WinSendDlgItemMsg(hWndDlg,DID_COPIES,
                  SPBM_QUERYVALUE,&CurrentDI.lCopies,
                  MPFROM2SHORT(0,SPBQ_UPDATEIFVALID));
            /* Query selection index from spinner */
            if(WinSendDlgItemMsg (hWndDlg, DID_PRIORITY,
                  SPBM_QUERYVALUE,(MPARAM)&ulSelect, 0L))
               CurrentDI.lPriority = lPriority[ulSelect];
            else
               CurrentDI.lPriority = 50;
            WinDismissDlg(hWndDlg,DID_OK);
            return 0;
      }
      break;
   case WM_CONTROL:
      switch (SHORT1FROMMP(mp1))
      {
         case DID_PRIORITY:
         if (HIUSHORT(mp1) == SPBN_ENDSPIN)
         {
            /* Query selection index from spinner */
            if(WinSendDlgItemMsg (hWndDlg, DID_PRIORITY,
                  SPBM_QUERYVALUE,(MPARAM)&ulSelect, 0L))
               CurrentDI.lPriority = lPriority[ulSelect];
            else
               CurrentDI.lPriority = 50;
```

```
            }
            break;
         }
         break;
   }
   return (WinDefDlgProc(hWndDlg,ulMessage,mp1,mp2));
}



MRESULT EXPENTRY PrintStatusProc(HWND hWndDlg,
         ULONG ulMessage, MPARAM mp1,MPARAM mp2)
/*--------------------------------*/

This function is the callback for the print job status dialog.
When the WM_INITDLG message is received a WM_START_PRINT message
is posted to the client window requesting the print job to be
started. When the WM_PRINT_STATUS message is received the text in
the status window is updated accordingly.

/*--------------------------------*/
{
   HWND  hWnd;
   LONG  lColor;

   switch (ulMessage)
   {
      case WM_INITDLG:
         center_window(hWndDlg);
         hWnd = WinWindowFromID(hWndDlg,DID_OK);
         WinShowWindow(hWnd,FALSE);

         hWnd = WinWindowFromID(hWndDlg,DID_JOBNAME);
         WinLoadString(hab,0,IDS_JOB_TITLE,
               sizeof(szBuff1),szBuff1);
         WinSetWindowText(hWnd,szBuff1);

         hWnd = WinWindowFromID(hWndDlg,DID_PRINTER);
         WinSetWindowText(hWnd,CurrentDI.szQueueDesc);

         hWnd = WinWindowFromID(hWndDlg,DID_STATUS);
         WinSetWindowText(hWnd,"Initializing Printer");

         WinPostMsg(hWndClient,WM_START_PRINT,
               (MPARAM)hWndDlg, (MPARAM)*(PULONG)mp2);
         break;
      case WM_PRINT_STATUS:
         hWnd = WinWindowFromID(hWndDlg,DID_STATUS);
         switch(SHORT1FROMMP(mp1))
         {
            case JOB_STARTED:
               WinSetWindowText(hWnd,"Starting Print Job");
               break;
            case JOB_CANCELED:
               WinSetWindowText(hWnd,"Print Job Cancelled");
               WinPostMsg(hWndDlg,WM_COMMAND,
```

```
                (MPARAM)DID_OK,0);
             break;
          case JOB_FAILED:
             lColor = CLR_RED;
             WinSetPresParam(hWnd,PP_FOREGROUNDCOLORINDEX,
                sizeof(PLONG), &lColor);
             WinSetWindowText(hWnd,"Print Job Failed");
             WinAlarm(HWND_DESKTOP,WA_ERROR);
             /* Switch the cancel button to an ok button */
             hWnd = WinWindowFromID(hWndDlg,DID_OK);
             WinShowWindow(hWnd,TRUE);
             hWnd = WinWindowFromID(hWndDlg,DID_CANCEL);
             WinShowWindow(hWnd,FALSE);
             break;
          case JOB_FINISHED:
             WinSetWindowText(hWnd,"Print Job Finished");
             WinPostMsg(hWndDlg,WM_COMMAND,
                   (MPARAM)DID_OK,0);
             break;
       }
       break;
    case WM_COMMAND:
       switch (SHORT1FROMMP(mp1))
       {
          case DID_CANCEL:
             hWnd = WinWindowFromID(hWndDlg,DID_STATUS);
             WinSetWindowText(hWnd,"Canceling Print Job");
             WinPostMsg(hWndClient,WM_ABORT_PRINT,0,0);
             return 0;
          case DID_OK:
             WinDismissDlg(hWndDlg,DID_OK);
             return 0;
       }
       break;
 }
 return (WinDefDlgProc(hWndDlg,ulMessage,mp1,mp2));
}


MRESULT EXPENTRY SelectPrinterDlgProc(HWND hWndDlg,
      ULONG ulMessage, MPARAM mp1,MPARAM mp2)
/*-------------------------------*/

This function is the callback for the printer selection dialog.
It will fill a list box with installed queue entries and post
job properties when requested. If OK is selected, the current
queue selection, along with it's last job properties, is set in
the CurrentDI variable.

/*-------------------------------*/
{
   static  PPRQINFO3 pQueueInfo;
   static  ULONG     ulSize = 0;
   static  HWND      hWndLBox;
   static  BOOL      bRedraw = FALSE;
   static  PDDINFO   pDDInfo;
```

```
static  ULONG     ulCount;
RECTL   Rectl;
int     i;
PDDINFO pDDI;
SHORT   sSelection;
ULONG   ulCurrent;

switch (ulMessage)
{
   case WM_INITDLG:
      center_window(hWndDlg);
      hWndLBox =    WinWindowFromID(hWndDlg,
            DID_QUEUE_NAMES);
      if (!(pQueueInfo = enum_print_queues(hWndDlg,
            hWndLBox, (PULONG)&ulSize,(PULONG)&ulCount,
            (PULONG)&ulCurrent)))
         WinDismissDlg(hWndDlg,DID_OK);
      else if (!DosSubAlloc(pMem,(PPVOID)&pDDInfo,
                  ulCount * sizeof(DDINFO)))
      {
         memset(pDDInfo,0,ulCount * sizeof(DDINFO));

         /* Preload the entry for the current printer with the
         saved values from CurrentDI */
         (pDDInfo + ulCurrent)->pDrivData = CurrentDI.pDrivData;
         (pDDInfo + ulCurrent)->lSizeDD = CurrentDI.lSizeDD;

         /* Select the current entry in the list box */
         WinSendMsg (hWndLBox,LM_SELECTITEM,
               MPFROMSHORT(ulCurrent),MPFROMSHORT(TRUE));
      }
      break;
   case WM_COMMAND:
      switch (SHORT1FROMMP(mp1))
      {
         case DID_OK:
            sSelection = (USHORT)WinSendMsg (hWndLBox,
                  LM_QUERYSELECTION,
                  MPFROMSHORT(LIT_FIRST), 0);
            if (!(pDDInfo + sSelection)->pDrivData)
            {
               get_job_properties(
                     &pQueueInfo[sSelection],
                     &pDDInfo[sSelection],
                     DPDM_QUERYJOBPROP);
               bRedraw - TRUE;
            }
            if ((pDDInfo + sSelection)->pDrivData)
            {
               /* If we are changing application default printers,
                  free up current driver data and replace it with
                  the driver data for the selected printer. */
               if ( CurrentDI.pDrivData &&
                     (CurrentDI.pDrivData !=
                     (pDDInfo + sSelection)->pDrivData) )
               {
```

```
            DosSubFree(pMem,CurrentDI.pDrivData,
                  CurrentDI.lSizeDD);
            CurrentDI.pDrivData =
               (pDDInfo + sSelection)->pDrivData;
            CurrentDI.lSizeDD =
               (pDDInfo + sSelection)->lSizeDD;
         }
         (pDDInfo + sSelection)->pDrivData = 0;
         (pDDInfo + sSelection)->lSizeDD = 0;
      }
      create_info_DC(&pQueueInfo[sSelection],
            (PDEVICEINFO)&CurrentDI);
      WinDismissDlg(hWndDlg,DID_OK);

      pDDI = pDDInfo;
      for (i = 0; i < (int)ulCount;i++)
      {
         if ((pDDI + i)->pDrivData)
            DosSubFree(pMem,(pDDI + i)->pDrivData,
            (pDDI + i)->lSizeDD);
      }
      DosSubFree(pMem,pDDInfo,
            ulCount * sizeof(DDINFO));
      DosSubFree(pMem,pQueueInfo,ulSize);
      if (bRedraw)
      {
         WinQueryWindowRect(hWndClient,
               (PRECTL)&Rectl);
         WinSendMsg(hWndClient,WM_SIZE,0,
            MPFROM2SHORT(Rectl.xRight,Rectl.yTop));
         WinInvalidateRect(hWndClient,0,TRUE);
      }
      break;
   case DID_CANCEL:
      WinDismissDlg(hWndDlg,DID_CANCEL);
      pDDI = pDDInfo;
      for (i = 0; i < (int)ulCount;i++)
      {
         /* Free up any allocated driver data except the
         current application default  */
         if ( (pDDI + i)->pDrivData &&
               (CurrentDI.pDrivData !=
               (pDDI + i)->pDrivData) )
            DosSubFree(pMem,(pDDI + i)->pDrivData,
            (pDDI + i)->lSizeDD);
      }
      DosSubFree(pMem,pDDInfo,
            ulCount * sizeof(DDINFO));
      DosSubFree(pMem,pQueueInfo,ulSize);
      break;
   case DID_JOBPROPS:
      sSelection = (USHORT)WinSendMsg (hWndLBox,
            LM_QUERYSELECTION,
            MPFROMSHORT(LIT_FIRST),0);
      if (sSelection != LIT_NONE)
      {
```

```
                get_job_properties(&pQueueInfo[sSelection],
                    &pDDInfo[sSelection],DPDM_POSTJOBPROP);
                 bRedraw = TRUE;
              }
              return 0;
        }
        break;
      default:
        break;
   }
   return (WinDefDlgProc(hWndDlg,ulMessage,mp1,mp2));
}
```

PRNTINFO.C

```
/* --------------------------------
Printing Sample Program
Real-World Programming for OS/2
Copyright (c) 1994 Blain, Delimon, and English
-------------------------------- */

#define INCL_WIN
#define INCL_GPI
#define INCL_DEV
#define INCL_SPL
#define INCL_SPLDOSPRINT
#include <os2.h>
#include <string.h>
#include <stdlib.h>
#include <stdio.h>
#include "prnt.h"
#include "dialog.h"


extern HAB   hab;
extern CHAR  szTemp[];
extern PVOID pMem;
CHAR   szYes[] = "Yes";
CHAR   szNo[]  = "No";


void APIENTRY free_info_DCs(PDEVICEINFO pDI,ULONG ulCount)
/*--------------------------------*/

This function will walk the array of DEVICEINFO structures destroy-
ing information device contexts and freeing memory allocated for
form arrays.

/*--------------------------------*/
{
   int i;
   for (i = 0; i < (int)ulCount;i++)
   {
      if ((pDI + i)->hInfoPS)
      {
```

```
         GpiAssociate((pDI + i)->hInfoPS,0);
         GpiDestroyPS((pDI + i)->hInfoPS);
         pDI->hInfoPS = 0;
         DevCloseDC((pDI + i)->hInfoDC);
         (pDI + i)->hInfoDC = 0;
      }
      if ((pDI + i)->pHCInfo)
      {
         DosSubFree(pMem,(pDI + i)->pHCInfo,
            ((pDI + i)->lSizeHC * sizeof(HCINFO)));
         (pDI + i)->pHCInfo = 0;
         (pDI + i)->lSizeHC = 0;
      }
   }
}


void APIENTRY query_device_info(HWND hWndDlg,
         PPRQINFO3 pPrq3, PDEVICEINFO pDI)
/*-------------------------------*/

This function will update fields of the queue info dialog based
on the supplied pPrq3 and pDI structures.

/*-------------------------------*/
{
   HWND     hWnd;
   int      index;
   PHCINFO pHCI;
   LONG     lDevCaps[CAPS_RASTER_CAPS + 1];
   CHAR     szTemp[MAX_BUFF];

   /* Update the device and default printer info */
   hWnd = WinWindowFromID(hWndDlg,DID_QUEUE_NAME);
   WinSetWindowText(hWnd,pPrq3->pszName);

   hWnd = WinWindowFromID(hWndDlg,DID_DEFAULT_DEVICE);
   WinSetWindowText(hWnd,pPrq3->pszDriverName);

   hWnd = WinWindowFromID(hWndDlg,DID_PRINTERS);
   WinSetWindowText(hWnd,pPrq3->pszPrinters);

   /* Update the queue priority */
   hWnd = WinWindowFromID(hWndDlg,DID_PRIORITY);
   index = ((pPrq3->uPriority > 7) ? ID_PRIORITY_HIGH :
         (pPrq3->uPriority > 3) ? ID_PRIORITY_DEF :
         ID_PRIORITY_MIN);
   WinLoadString (hab,0,index,MAX_BUFF,szTemp);
   WinSetWindowText(hWnd,szTemp);

   /* Update the queue status */
   hWnd = WinWindowFromID(hWndDlg,DID_STATUS);
   index = ((pPrq3->fsStatus == PRQ3_PAUSED) ?
         ID_STATUS_HELD : (pPrq3->fsStatus == PRQ_PENDING) ?
         ID_STATUS_PEND : ID_STATUS_NORM);
   WinLoadString (hab,0,index,MAX_BUFF,szTemp);
```

```
WinSetWindowText(hWnd,szTemp);

/* Update the number of jobs in the queue */
hWnd = WinWindowFromID(hWndDlg,DID_NUMBER_JOBS);
itoa(pPrq3->cJobs,szTemp,10);
WinSetWindowText(hWnd,szTemp);

/* Update the queue start and end time */
hWnd = WinWindowFromID(hWndDlg,DID_START_TIME);
index=(pPrq3->uStartTime > 779) ? pPrq3->uStartTime-720 :
         pPrq3->uStartTime;
sprintf(szTemp,"%2i:%02i %s",index / 60,
   pPrq3->uStartTime%60,(pPrq3->uStartTime>779)?"PM":
      "AM");
WinSetWindowText(hWnd,szTemp);

hWnd = WinWindowFromID(hWndDlg,DID_END_TIME);
index = (pPrq3->uUntilTime > 779) ? pPrq3->uUntilTime -
      720 : pPrq3->uUntilTime;
sprintf(szTemp,"%2i:%02i %s",index / 60,
   pPrq3->uUntilTime % 60,(pPrq3->uUntilTime > 779) ?
         "PM" : "AM" );
WinSetWindowText(hWnd,szTemp);

/* Query the forms available */
if ((!pDI->pHCInfo) &&
   (pDI->lSizeHC = DevQueryHardcopyCaps(pDI->hInfoDC,
         0,0,0)) > 0)
{
   /* Only query the forms the first time */
   if (DosSubAlloc(pMem,(PPVOID)&pDI->pHCInfo,
            (pDI->lSizeHC * sizeof(HCINFO))))
      pDI->pHCInfo = 0;
   else
      DevQueryHardcopyCaps(pDI->hInfoDC,0,pDI->lSizeHC,
         pDI->pHCInfo);
}
if (pDI->pHCInfo)
{
   hWnd = WinWindowFromID(hWndDlg,DID_FORMS);
   WinEnableWindowUpdate(hWnd,FALSE);
   pHCI = pDI->pHCInfo;
   WinSendMsg (hWnd,LM_DELETEALL,0,0);
   for (index = 0; index < pDI->lSizeHC; index++)
   {
      WinSendMsg (hWnd,LM_INSERTITEM,(MPARAM)LIT_END,
         (pHCI + index)->szFormname);
   }
   WinEnableWindowUpdate(hWnd,TRUE);
   WinSendMsg (hWnd,LM_SELECTITEM,(MPARAM)0,
         MPFROMSHORT(TRUE));
}
/* Query all of the desired metrics */
DevQueryCaps (pDI->hInfoDC,CAPS_FAMILY,CAPS_RASTER_CAPS,
      (PLONG)&lDevCaps);
```

```
    /* Update the device technology */
    hWnd = WinWindowFromID(hWndDlg,DID_TECHNOLOGY);
    WinLoadString (hab,0,lDevCaps[CAPS_TECHNOLOGY] +
          ID_TECH_BASE, MAX_BUFF,szTemp);
    WinSetWindowText(hWnd,szTemp);

    /* Update the device resolution */
    hWnd = WinWindowFromID(hWndDlg,DID_CAPS_WIDTH);
    itoa(lDevCaps[CAPS_WIDTH],szTemp,10);
    WinSetWindowText(hWnd,szTemp);

    hWnd = WinWindowFromID(hWndDlg,DID_CAPS_HEIGHT);
    itoa(lDevCaps[CAPS_HEIGHT],szTemp,10);
    WinSetWindowText(hWnd,szTemp);

    hWnd = WinWindowFromID(hWndDlg,DID_HORZ_RES);
    itoa(lDevCaps[CAPS_HORIZONTAL_RESOLUTION],szTemp,10);
    WinSetWindowText(hWnd,szTemp);

    hWnd = WinWindowFromID(hWndDlg,DID_VERT_RES);
    itoa(lDevCaps[CAPS_VERTICAL_RESOLUTION],szTemp,10);
    WinSetWindowText(hWnd,szTemp);

    hWnd = WinWindowFromID(hWndDlg,DID_BITBLT);
    WinSetWindowText(hWnd,
          (lDevCaps[CAPS_RASTER_CAPS] & CAPS_RASTER_BITBLT) ?
             szYes : szNo);

    hWnd = WinWindowFromID(hWndDlg,DID_BANDING);
    WinSetWindowText(hWnd,
         (lDevCaps[CAPS_RASTER_CAPS] & CAPS_RASTER_BANDING) ?
          szYes : szNo);

    hWnd = WinWindowFromID(hWndDlg,DID_SETPEL);
    WinSetWindowText(hWnd,
       (lDevCaps[CAPS_RASTER_CAPS] & CAPS_RASTER_SET_PEL) ?
       szYes : szNo);

    hWnd = WinWindowFromID(hWndDlg,DID_RASTER_FONT);
    WinSetWindowText(hWnd,
       (lDevCaps[CAPS_RASTER_CAPS] & CAPS_RASTER_FONTS) ?
       szYes : szNo);

    hWnd = WinWindowFromID(hWndDlg,DID_KERNING);
    WinSetWindowText(hWnd,
       (lDevCaps[CAPS_ADDITIONAL_GRAPHICS] &
       CAPS_GRAPHICS_KERNING_SUPPORT) ?
       szYes : szNo);

    hWnd = WinWindowFromID(hWndDlg,DID_PALETTE);
    WinSetWindowText(hWnd,
       (lDevCaps[CAPS_ADDITIONAL_GRAPHICS] &
          CAPS_PALETTE_MANAGER) ? szYes : szNo);
}
```

```
void APIENTRY query_form_info(HWND hWndDlg,PHCINFO pHCInfo)
/*-------------------------------*/

This function will update the form fields in the queue info dialog
based on the form pointed to by pHCInfo.

/*-------------------------------*/
{
   HWND    hWnd;
   int     i;
   CHAR    szTemp[MAX_BUFF];


   hWnd = WinWindowFromID(hWndDlg,DID_FORM_CX);
   itoa(pHCInfo->cx,szTemp,10);
   WinSetWindowText(hWnd,szTemp);

   hWnd = WinWindowFromID(hWndDlg,DID_FORM_CY);
   itoa(pHCInfo->cy,szTemp,10);
   WinSetWindowText(hWnd,szTemp);

   hWnd = WinWindowFromID(hWndDlg,DID_LEFT_CLIP);
   itoa(pHCInfo->xLeftClip,szTemp,10);
   WinSetWindowText(hWnd,szTemp);

   hWnd = WinWindowFromID(hWndDlg,DID_BOTTOM_CLIP);
   itoa(pHCInfo->yBottomClip,szTemp,10);
   WinSetWindowText(hWnd,szTemp);

   hWnd = WinWindowFromID(hWndDlg,DID_RIGHT_CLIP);
   itoa(pHCInfo->xRightClip,szTemp,10);
   WinSetWindowText(hWnd,szTemp);

   hWnd = WinWindowFromID(hWndDlg,DID_TOP_CLIP);
   itoa(pHCInfo->yTopClip,szTemp,10);
   WinSetWindowText(hWnd,szTemp);

   hWnd = WinWindowFromID(hWndDlg,DID_FORM_ATTR);
   if (pHCInfo->flAttributes & HCAPS_CURRENT)
   {
      WinLoadString (hab,0,ID_CAPS_CURRENT,MAX_BUFF,szTemp);
      if (pHCInfo->flAttributes & HCAPS_SELECTABLE)
      {
         strcat(szTemp,", ");
         i = strlen (szTemp);
         WinLoadString (hab,0,ID_CAPS_SELECTABLE,
            MAX_BUFF - i,&szTemp[i]);
      }
   }
   else if (pHCInfo->flAttributes & HCAPS_SELECTABLE)
      WinLoadString (hab,0,ID_CAPS_SELECTABLE,MAX_BUFF,
            szTemp);
```

```
   else
      WinLoadString (hab,0,ID_CAPS_NONE,MAX_BUFF,szTemp);
   WinSetWindowText(hWnd,szTemp);
}


MRESULT EXPENTRY PrintInfoDlgProc(HWND hWndDlg,
      ULONG ulMessage, MPARAM mp1,MPARAM mp2)
/*-------------------------------*/

This function is the callback for the queue and printer information
dialog. It will fill a list box with installed queue entries and
post job properties when requested. In addition the forms available
on the selected queue are queried and added to a second list box.
Details from the PRQINFO3, HCINFO, and various device capabilities
of the selected queue are displayed in the dialog.

/*-------------------------------*/
{
   static    PPRQINFO3   pQueueInfo;
   static    PDEVICEINFO pDI = 0;
   static    ULONG       ulSize   = 0;
   static    ULONG       ulDISize = 0;
   static    ULONG       ulCount  = 0;
   static    DDINFO      DDInfo;
   SHORT     sQueueSelect;
   SHORT     sFormSelect;
   HWND      hWndLBox;
   ULONG     ulCurrent;
   PHCINFO   pHCI;

   switch (ulMessage)
   {
      case WM_INITDLG:
         center_window(hWndDlg);
         hWndLBox = WinWindowFromID(hWndDlg,
               DID_QUEUE_NAMES);
         if (!(pQueueInfo = enum_print_queues(hWndDlg,
               hWndLBox, (PULONG)&ulSize,(PULONG)&ulCount,
               (PULONG)&ulCurrent)))
            WinDismissDlg(hWndDlg,DID_OK);
         else
         {
            DDInfo.lSizeDD = 0;
            DDInfo.pDrivData = 0;
            ulDISize = ulCount * sizeof(DEVICEINFO);
            DosSubAlloc(pMem,(PPVOID)&pDI,ulDISize);
            memset(pDI,0,ulDISize);
            WinSendMsg (hWndLBox,LM_SELECTITEM,
                 MPFROMSHORT(ulCurrent), MPFROMSHORT(TRUE));
         }
         break;
      case WM_COMMAND:
         switch (SHORT1FROMMP(mp1))
         {
            case DID_CANCEL:
```

```
case DID_OK:
   free_info_DCs(pDI,ulCount);
   DosSubFree(pMem,pQueueInfo,ulSize);
   DosSubFree(pMem,pDI,ulDISize);
   WinDismissDlg(hWndDlg,DID_OK);
   return 0;
case DID_JOBPROPS:
case DID_UPDATE:
   hWndLBox = WinWindowFromID(hWndDlg,
            DID_QUEUE_NAMES);
   sQueueSelect = (USHORT)WinSendMsg (hWndLBox,
         LM_QUERYSELECTION,
         MPFROMSHORT(LIT_FIRST),0);
   if (sQueueSelect != LIT_NONE)
   {
      if (SHORT1FROMMP(mp1) ==  DID_JOBPROPS)
      {
         get_job_properties(
             &pQueueInfo[sQueueSelect],
             (PDDINFO)&DDInfo,
              DPDM_POSTJOBPROP);
         if (DDInfo.pDrivData)
         {
            DosSubFree(pMem,
               DDInfo.pDrivData,
               DDInfo.lSizeDD);
            DDInfo.lSizeDD = 0;
            DDInfo.pDrivData = 0;
         }
      }
      free_info_DCs(pDI,ulCount);
      DosSubFree(pMem,pQueueInfo,ulSize);
      DosSubFree(pMem,pDI,ulDISize);
      pDI = 0;
      hWndLBox = WinWindowFromID(hWndDlg,
            DID_QUEUE_NAMES);
      if (!(pQueueInfo =
             enum_print_queues(hWndDlg,
             hWndLBox,(PULONG)&ulSize,
             (PULONG)&ulCount,
             (PULONG)&ulCurrent)))
         WinDismissDlg(hWndDlg,DID_OK);
      else
      {
         ulDISize = ulCount *
               sizeof(DEVICEINFO);
         DosSubAlloc(pMem,(PPVOID)&pDI,
               ulDISize);
         memset(pDI,0,ulDISize);
         WinSendMsg (hWndLBox,
               LM_SELECTITEM,
               MPFROMSHORT(sQueueSelect),
               MPFROMSHORT(TRUE));
      }
   }
   return 0;
```

```
            default:
               break;
         }
         break;

      case WM_CONTROL:
         if (SHORT2FROMMP(mp1) == LN_SELECT)
         {
            switch (LOUSHORT(mp1))
            {
               case DID_QUEUE_NAMES:
                  hWndLBox = WinWindowFromID(hWndDlg,
                        DID_QUEUE_NAMES);
                  sQueueSelect = (USHORT)WinSendMsg(
                        hWndLBox, LM_QUERYSELECTION,
                        MPFROMSHORT(LIT_FIRST),0);
                  if (sQueueSelect != LIT_NONE)
                  {
                    if (!(pDI + sQueueSelect)->hInfoDC)
                      create_info_DC(
                       (PPRQINFO3)&pQueueInfo[sQueueSelect],
                       (PDEVICEINFO)&pDI[sQueueSelect]);
                     query_device_info(hWndDlg,
                       (PPRQINFO3)&pQueueInfo[sQueueSelect],
                       (PDEVICEINFO)&pDI[sQueueSelect]);
                  }
                  break;
               case DID_FORMS:
                  hWndLBox = WinWindowFromID(hWndDlg,
                        DID_QUEUE_NAMES);
                  sQueueSelect = (USHORT)WinSendMsg
                        (hWndLBox, LM_QUERYSELECTION,
                        MPFROMSHORT(LIT_FIRST),0);

                  if ((pHCI=pDI[sQueueSelect].pHCInfo)!= 0)
                  {
                     hWndLBox = WinWindowFromID(hWndDlg,
                        DID_FORMS);
                     sFormSelect = (USHORT)WinSendMsg
                        (hWndLBox,
                        LM_QUERYSELECTION,
                        MPFROMSHORT(LIT_FIRST),0);
                     if (sFormSelect != LIT_NONE)
                        query_form_info(hWndDlg,
                        &(pHCI[sFormSelect]));
                  }
                  break;
            }
         }
         break;
   }
   return (WinDefDlgProc(hWndDlg,ulMessage,mp1,mp2));
}
```

PRNT.DEF

```
NAME            PRNT    WINDOWAPI
DESCRIPTION     'Print Sample Program  Blain, Delimon, & English, 1994'
PROTMODE
HEAPSIZE        4096
STACKSIZE       32768
EXPORTS         AboutDlgProc
                ClientWndProc
                PrintInfoDlgProc
                PrintStatusProc
                PrintDlgProc
                SelectPrinterDlgProc
```

PRNT.H

```
/* --------------------------------
Print Sample Header File
Real-World Programming for OS/2
Copyright (c) 1994 Blain, Delimon, and English
-------------------------------- */

/* Stringtable ID's */
#define ID_APPNAME              1
#define ID_NOQUEUE_ERROR        2
#define ID_PRIORITY_HIGH        3
#define ID_PRIORITY_DEF         4
#define ID_PRIORITY_MIN         5
#define ID_STATUS_HELD          6
#define ID_STATUS_PEND          7
#define ID_STATUS_NORM          8
#define ID_CAPS_CURRENT         9
#define ID_CAPS_SELECTABLE      10
#define ID_CAPS_NONE            11
#define ID_TECH_BASE            12
#define ID_TECH_UNKNOWN         ID_TECH_BASE
#define ID_TECH_PLOTTER         ID_TECH_BASE + 1
#define ID_TECH_RAST_DISP       ID_TECH_BASE + 2
#define ID_TECH_RAST_PRT        ID_TECH_BASE + 3
#define ID_TECH_RAST_CAM        ID_TECH_BASE + 4
#define ID_TECH_POSTSCRIPT      ID_TECH_BASE + 5
#define ID_ERR_NODEF_PRINTERS 18
#define ID_ERR_FAIL_DEV_QUERY 19

/* Menu ID's */
#define IDM_FILE                100
#define IDM_CHOOSE_PRINTER      101
#define IDM_PRINT               102
#define IDM_PRINT_THREAD        103
#define IDM_ABOUT               104

#define IDM_DISPLAY             200
#define IDM_DISP_BLANK          201
#define IDM_DISP_BOX            202
```

```
#define IDM_DISP_ELLIPSE      203
#define IDM_DISP_X            204
#define IDM_PRINTER_INFO      205

/* Help hint string ID's */
#define IDS_JOB_TITLE         105

#define MAX_BUFF              128
#define MAX_DEVICENAME         32
#define MAX_QUEUENAME          10
#define MAX_QUEUEDESC          64
#define MAX_DRIVERNAME        128

#define QUEUENAME_LENGTH    10
#define QUEUEDESC_LENGTH    64
#define DEVICENAME_LENGTH   32
#define DRIVERNAME_LENGTH   128

#define WM_START_PRINT      WM_USER
#define WM_ABORT_PRINT      WM_USER+1
#define WM_END_PRINT        WM_USER+2
#define WM_PRINT_STATUS     WM_USER+3

#define JOB_STARTED      100
#define JOB_CANCELED     101
#define JOB_FINISHED     102
#define JOB_FAILED       103

#define PAGE_OFFSET      10

typedef struct DEVICEINFO
{
   HDC       hInfoDC;
   HPS       hInfoPS;
   HDC       hPrintDC;
   HPS       hPrintPS;
   HDC       hClientDC;
   HPS       hClientPS;
   SIZEL     PageSizel;
   SIZEL     ClientSizel;
   SIZEL     PhyPageSizel;
   SIZEL     PrintOffsetSizel;
   LONG      lCopies;
   LONG      lPriority;
   CHAR      szQueueDesc[MAX_QUEUEDESC];
   CHAR      szQueueName[MAX_QUEUENAME];
   CHAR      szDriverName[MAX_DRIVERNAME];
   LONG      lSizeDD;
   PDRIVDATA pDrivData;
   PHCINFO   pHCInfo;
   LONG      lSizeHC;
   int       cx;
   int       cy;
} DEVICEINFO;
typedef DEVICEINFO *PDEVICEINFO;
```

```
typedef struct DDINFO
{
   LONG       lSizeDD;
   PDRIVDATA pDrivData;
} DDINFO;
typedef DDINFO *PDDINFO;

VOID       APIENTRY center_window(HWND);
BOOL       APIENTRY create_info_DC(PPRQINFO3,PDEVICEINFO);
BOOL       APIENTRY create_print_DC(PDEVICEINFO);
void       APIENTRY create_status_line(HWND);
void       APIENTRY display_hint(SHORT);
void       APIENTRY draw_page(HPS);
void       APIENTRY draw_page_background(HPS);
PPRQINFO3 APIENTRY enum_print_queues(HWND,HWND,PULONG,PULONG,PULONG);
void       APIENTRY free_info_DCs(PDEVICEINFO,ULONG);
VOID       APIENTRY get_job_properties(PPRQINFO3,PDDINFO,ULONG);
VOID       APIENTRY get_page_metrics(PDEVICEINFO);
HPS        APIENTRY init_app(HWND);
USHORT     APIENTRY post_error(HWND,USHORT);
void       APIENTRY process_print(HWND);
void       APIENTRY process_size(MPARAM,MPARAM);
void       APIENTRY process_command(HWND,MPARAM,MPARAM);
void       APIENTRY query_device_info(HWND,PPRQINFO3,PDEVICEINFO);
void       APIENTRY query_form_info(HWND,PHCINFO);
```

PRNT.RC

```
/* ----------------------------------
Print Sample Resource File
Real-World Programming for OS/2
Copyright (c) 1994 Blain, Delimon, and English
---------------------------------- */

#include <os2.h>
#include "prnt.h"
#include "dialog.h"

ICON ID_APPNAME PRNT.ICO

RCINCLUDE PRNT.DLG
RCINCLUDE ..\common\about.dlg

MENU ID APPNAME
BEGIN
   SUBMENU "~File",                      IDM_FILE
      BEGIN
         MENUITEM "Select Printer",    IDM_CHOOSE_PRINTER
         MENUITEM "Print",             IDM_PRINT
         MENUITEM "Print in a Thread", IDM_PRINT_THREAD
         MENUITEM SEPARATOR
         MENUITEM "About...",          IDM_ABOUT
      END
   SUBMENU "~Display",                 IDM_DISPLAY
```

```
      BEGIN
         MENUITEM "Blank page",        IDM_DISP_BLANK, 0,
                                       MIA_CHECKED
         MENUITEM "Box scaled to page",    IDM_DISP_BOX
         MENUITEM "Ellipse scaled to page",IDM_DISP_ELLIPSE
         MENUITEM SEPARATOR
         MENUITEM "Printer Information",   IDM_PRINTER_INFO
      END
END


STRINGTABLE LOADONCALL MOVEABLE
BEGIN
   ID_APPNAME             "Sample Print Program"
   ID_NOQUEUE_ERROR       "No Printers have been installed"
   ID_PRIORITY_HIGH       "High"
   ID_PRIORITY_DEF        "Default"
   ID_PRIORITY_MIN        "Low"
   ID_STATUS_HELD         "Held"
   ID_STATUS_PEND         "Pending Deletion"
   ID_STATUS_NORM         "Released"
   ID_CAPS_CURRENT        "Current"
   ID_CAPS_SELECTABLE     "Selectable"
   ID_CAPS_NONE           "No Attribute Set"
   ID_TECH_UNKNOWN        "Unknown"
   ID_TECH_PLOTTER        "Vector Plotter"
   ID_TECH_RAST_DISP      "Raster Display"
   ID_TECH_RAST_PRT       "Raster Printer"
   ID_TECH_RAST_CAM       "Raster Camera"
   ID_TECH_POSTSCRIPT     "PostScript Device"
   ID_ERR_NODEF_PRINTERS "A printer has not been installed, or all
                           printers have been deleted."
   ID_ERR_FAIL_DEV_QUERY "A call to SplQueryDevice has failed"
   IDS_JOB_TITLE          "RWP Sample print program"
   IDM_CHOOSE_PRINTER     "Change the current printer"
   IDM_PRINT              "Print to "
   IDM_PRINT_THREAD       "Print in a separate thread to "
   IDM_ABOUT              "Product information"
   IDM_DISP_BLANK         "Display an empty page"
   IDM_DISP_BOX           "Display a filled rectangle scaled to the
                           page"
   IDM_DISP_ELLIPSE       "Display a filled ellipse scaled to the page"
   IDM_DISP_X             "Display the ..."
   IDM_PRINTER_INFO       "Show information on all printers"
END
```

Chapter 14

Threads and Semaphores

Multitasking in OS/2

OS/2 is a multitasking operating system. This means lines of execution or processing do not simply start and then proceed continuously until termination. Individual lines of execution do not have sole use of the central processor and other system resources. Many different programs can be active on the system simultaneously.

Consider the common situation when an application, during its processing, is directed to output something to a printer. Printers are comparatively slow. If the application cannot continue its processing until the printer has completed outputting the data, the user must wait. Further, if the operating system has no means to spool the data for later delivery to the printer, every process, every application, must wait. To circumvent this, the central processor's time and attention can be divided among the various processes making demands on it. This is called multitasking.

Three Types of Multitasking

Multitasking within OS/2 is of three different sorts: sessions, processes, and threads. When taken together, these three divisions of multitasking within OS/2 improve the speed, responsiveness, and efficiency of the system. With a little thought, you can see the necessity for having these three different levels of multitasking.

Sessions

The highest level, one that will concern few programmers in OS/2, is the *session.* A session consists of one or more processes that have their own virtual console. The virtual console consists of a virtual screen and buffers for input from the keyboard and mouse. Sessions may be arranged in the familiar parent-child hierarchy. Sessions may start other sessions. Sessions may also end the processing of its child sessions, although it cannot end the processing of those sessions descendent from its children.

Processes

Within the session level is another level of multitasking. It is called the process. Each session contains at least one process, but it may contain many. It is convenient to think of an application as synonymous with the term *process.* A process is an application that has been loaded into memory and made ready for execution. Each process has a number of resources allocated for its use. These resources include memory, files, pipes, queues, semaphores, and others. Processes may create other processes. These too are arranged in a parent-child hierarchy. Child processes may inherit the resources owned by the parent process, except for memory. Child processes do not inherit the memory of their parent processes. Once again, the parent process may end the child process.

Threads

The lowest level of multitasking is called the *thread.* Different threads of execution within an application are what most programmers will be concerned with. Threads are lines of execution within a process. Each process has at least one thread, called the main thread. OS/2 creates this first thread for the application when it starts executing the process. To carry out tasks that are not related, other threads can be created by the process as it runs. For example, in the situation at the beginning of this chapter, the process could start another thread that sends data to the printer so that the main process may continue accepting input from the user. In this way, the application seems far more responsive to the user.

Threads are composed of CPU register values, a stack, and instructions. Threads do not own resources individually. A thread shares resources with the process that created it and all the other threads within the process. Threads are not organized in the previously described parent-child relationship for the other levels of multitasking. With one exception, all threads within a process are peers. For example, if one thread opens a file, that file is available to all the other threads. If one thread starts another thread which then opens a file, that file is still available to the thread that started it, as well as all the other threads. There is an exception to this peer relationship: Although the threads within a process are considered to be peers, if the first thread within a process ends, all other threads within that process also end. Threads can also suspend and resume the execution of other threads. This allows threads to coordinate access to time-critical resources.

Creating a thread is much faster than creating a new process. This is because the process resources do not have to be allocated for a new thread, but do for a new process. In addition, OS/2 can switch between threads much faster than it can switch between processes. There is no task switching involved, just the activity of setting the thread's CPU registers and current priority.

Threads and Time Slices

Because threads are the smallest unit of execution and time slices are the smallest unit of time parceled out for execution, these two are closely related. Time slices and threads are related by the concept of *dispatch priority*. Each thread is assigned a dispatching priority by the operating system. A thread's dispatch priority governs how often and for what length of time a thread will have the use of the central processor. Access is rotated among threads after the passage of a certain interval of time. This interval is based on the time slice.

Priority Classes and Priority Levels

When a thread is created, it is given a *priority class* and a *priority level*. Four priority classes are within OS/2. These are—in order of priority—time critical, fixed high, regular, and idle time. Within each of these classes, priority is further subdivided into priority levels. Each priority class has 32 priority levels within it. These are numbered from 0 to 31. Every thread marked time critical has a higher priority than those marked fixed high and so forth. Within each class, those with higher integer values for priority level are dispatched before those with lower values. For example, if two threads among several that are executing on a system are marked time critical, these two will always receive a time slice before any other thread on the system. However, if one of these two time-critical threads has a priority level set at 25 while the other has a priority level of 10, the thread with priority level 25 will always be executed first unless it is blocked or suspended.

Threads marked time critical are executed immediately and continuously. These threads are generally those that handle events which must receive immediate attention, such as communication ports and real-time events. Fixed high threads receive a time slice when no time-critical threads are waiting. Regular threads, as the name implies, is the classification most threads within the system will have. These are dispatched on the basis of I/O activity, whether they are running in the foreground or background, and use of the processor. Threads with idle time as their priority class receive time slices only when no other threads are waiting.

Applications can change the priority of threads. This is recommended in situations when other threads are waiting on a particular thread to finish a task before they can continue. However, it is best to change the priority level among the threads of your application, rather than give one thread the highest priority class and level in the system. Because the processor's time must be divided among all the applications and threads running on the system, gaming the system in this way would, in fact, degrade the overall performance.

OS/2 System Settings for Threads

OS/2 provides four settings related to threads that are configurable within the CONFIG.SYS file. These settings affect how the system allocates time slices and how it determines the priority of each thread. The maximum number of threads allowed in the system is controlled with the `THREADS` statement

```
THREADS=n
```

where n is the maximum number of threads (range 16...256). All threads begin with an initial priority setting. As time goes on and threads receive the CPU and more threads come into existence, some threads may receive more time slices than others. Some threads may also be involved in CPU intensive tasks that cause other threads to receive less and less CPU over time. OS/2 uses two schemes to monitor the priority of threads. `ABSOLUTE` priority means all threads within a priority class are assigned time slices based solely on their priority level. `DYNAMIC` priority means that the recent time-slice history of each thread is used to adjust the priority of threads dynamically. Threads that have not received much CPU relative to other threads in the same class will have their priorities temporarily adjusted upward to more evenly distribute the average CPU time per thread. The scheme that will be used is defined by using the `PRIORITY` statement:

```
PRIORITY=[ABSOLUTE ¦ DYNAMIC]
```

`ABSOLUTE`	Priorities are not adjusted according to system load.
`DYNAMIC`	OS/2 adjusts the priority so that the priority of threads within the same priority class do not hog the CPU (default).

When `DYNAMIC` priority is specified, the `MAXWAIT` directive establishes the maximum amount of time a thread will wait for the CPU before OS/2 adjusts its priority upward:

```
MAXWAIT=seconds
```

The interval of a time slice is specified with the `TIMESLICE` directive. Both a normal and maximum time slice interval can be specified. If a thread reaches the end of its time slice and is preempted by the system, its next time slice will be one tick longer as long as it has not reached the maximum time-slice interval. Both values are specified in milliseconds:

```
TIMESLICE=x[,y]
```

`x` =Normal length of a time slice before a thread gives up the CPU (minimum of 32).
`y` =Maximum length of a time slice (minimum of 32 and maximum of 65536).

Working with Threads

OS/2 provides a number of functions for working with threads. These enable you to perform tasks such as creating a thread, obtaining information on a thread, terminating a thread, and so forth.

`DosCreateThread` is used to create a new thread of execution. The new thread is created as an asynchronous thread and has access to all resources of the process in which it is executing. The initial priority of the new thread is the same as the thread making the `DosCreateThread` call. The format of `DosCreateThread` is as follows:

```
APIRET APIENTRY DosCreateThread(PTID ptid, PFNTHREAD pfn,
   ULONG param, ULONG flag, ULONG cbStack).
```

`PTID`	`ptid`	Address of a `TID` variable to receive a new thread identifier.
`PFNTHREAD`	`pfn`	Initial entry point of the thread.
`ULONG`	`param`	Single parameter passed to the initial thread function.
`ULONG`	`flag`	Flags setting the initial state of the thread: 0x00000001 Create thread in a suspended state. 0x00000002 Precommit all pages in the thread's stack. The default settings cause the thread to start immediately upon creation and to use the default method for committing the pages of the stack.
`ULONG`	`cbStack`	Size of the thread's stack. Minimum of 8KB is used by OS/2.

A new thread is created, and the function specified by the `pfn` parameter is the initial point of execution. A single parameter can be passed to the thread. If more than one parameter is required, this should be the address of a structure containing the data. Normally, a thread starts immediately upon creation. If you need to perform some additional setup or simply want the thread to wait until a particular event occurs, you can create the thread in a suspended state by setting the low bit of the flag parameter. The thread function is prototyped as follows:

```
typedef VOID (*PFNTHREAD)(VOID);
```

It, however, can have one parameter defined for it. For example, to create a new thread whose initial entry point is the function `ThermometerThread`, the following call can be used:

```
VOID ThermometerThread (HWND);

TID  ThreadID;
HWND hWndClient;

DosCreateThread (&ThreadID, (PFNTHREAD)ThermometerThread,
      (ULONG)hWndClient, 0, 0x5000);
```

ThermometerThread takes one parameter, which is the handle to a client window. The thread created in this example has a stack size of 20KB. Remember, while ThermometerThread is the initial entry point, the new thread can call any function within the process. It is also important to be sure that the parameter passed to the thread function is not passed in a register. For example, using the IBM C/Set compiler, this could be specified with the linkage program:

```
#pragma linkage (ThermometerThread,system)
```

A thread can terminate in several ways. The thread can terminate naturally by returning from the initial thread function or by calling DosExit. It will also terminate when DosKillThread is called with the thread's identifier or when thread 1 terminates. Normally, a thread will terminate itself by completing its processing and calling DosExit. The call to DosExit can also terminate the entire process, but this is not the normal case:

```
VOID APIENTRY DosExit(ULONG action, ULONG result);
```

ULONG	ulAction	Specifies entity to terminate: EXIT_THREAD — Current thread is terminated. EXIT_PROCESS — Current process is terminated, including all threads.
ULONG	result	Result code passed to any thread waiting for the process to terminate.

A thread may also decide to terminate itself when it receives a signal from another thread to terminate or when an error condition occurs. In any case, the call to DosExit for a thread normally appears as follows:

```
DosExit (EXIT_THREAD, 0L);
```

If thread 1 issues the call to DosExit, the entire process is terminated. A thread can also kill another thread with the DosKillThread function

```
APIRET APIENTRY DosKillThread(TID tid);
```

where TID tid is the thread identifier to kill.

It is not possible for a thread to kill itself with this function. If the thread identifier is 1, the entire process is terminated.

Now that you have looked at how to create and terminate a thread, look at how to control a thread while it is executing. Associated with every process is a Process Information Block. In addition, every thread has an associated Thread Information Block. As you might expect, these blocks contain information related to the current state of both the process and the individual thread. A thread can retrieve this information by calling DosGetInfoBlocks:

```
APIRET APIENTRY DosGetInfoBlocks(PTIB *pptib,PPIB *pppib);
```

`PTIB`	`*pptib`	Address of a `PTIB` pointer to receive the address of the Process Information Block (PIB).
`PPIB`	`*pppib`	Address of a `PPIB` pointer to receive the address of the Thread Information Block (TIB).

For example, a thread can retrieve this information with the following call:

```
PPIB   ppib;
PTIB   ptib;

DosGetInfoBlocks (&ptib, &ppib);
```

The `DosGetInfoBlocks` function is discussed in detail in Chapter 16, "Miscellaneous Topics."

We discussed earlier the mechanism by which OS/2 determines which thread to execute. Threads with a priority class of time critical are executed before those of fixed high. Fixed-high threads are executed before regular, and those are executed before idle-time threads. Within each class, a thread has a priority from 0 to 31. Higher priority threads within the same class obviously execute before those of a lower priority. This priority order is shown here:

Time Critical 31
30
:
0
Fixed High 31
30
:
0
Regular 31
30
:
0
Idle-Time 31
30
:
0

When a thread of higher priority is ready to execute, OS/2 will preempt any lower priority thread currently executing and allow the higher priority thread to execute. This occurs even if the lower priority thread has not completed its time slice. Threads of the same priority are allocated time slices in a round-robin scheme. Thread priorities can be changed with the `DosSetPriority` function. `DosSetPriority` allows any thread in a process to change the priority of any other thread in the process. It also allows a thread to change the priority of any thread in another process as long as the other thread's priority has not been changed from the default priority level:

```
APIRET APIENTRY DosSetPriority(ULONG scope, ULONG class,
   LONG delta, ULONG ultid);
```

ULONG	scope	Scope of the priority change:	
		PRTYS_PROCESS	All immediate threads of a process.
		PRTYS_PROCESSTREE	All threads and descendants of either the current process or a child process.
		PRTYS_THREAD	An individual thread.
ULONG	class	Priority class of the thread:	
		PRTYC_NOCHANGE	No change to priority class.
		PRTYC_IDLETIME	Idle-time priority class.
		PRTYC_REGULAR	Regular priority class.
		PRTYC_TIMECRITICAL	Time-critical priority class.
LONG	delta	Change to the priority: If PRTYC_NOCHANGE is specified for class, this is the relative change to the current priority. Valid values range from PRTYD_MINIMUM to PRTYD_MAXIMUM (-31 to 31). For all other class specifications, this is the absolute priority level within the class.	
ULONG	ultid	Process or thread identifier: If a scope of PRTYC_PROCESS or PRTYC_PROCESSTREE is specified, this is a process identifier. For a scope of PRTYS_THREAD, this is a thread identifier. Zero indicates the current process or thread.	

The following examples use the DosSetPriority function to set the priority of a thread to idle time:

```
DosSetPriority (PRTYS_THREAD, PRTYC_IDLETIME, 0, StatusThreadID);
```

to time critical with a priority level of 10:

```
DosSetPriority (PRTYS_THREAD, PRTYC_TIMECRITICAL, 10L, StatusThreadID);
```

and to increase the priority level of the current class by 1:

```
DosSetPriority (PRTYS_THREAD, PRTYC_NOCHANGE, 1L, 0L);
```

Typically, the priority of a thread is increased when the thread is performing some activity that needs to be completed before another thread can continue. For example, suppose one thread is recalculating the cells of a spreadsheet, and another thread is attempting to display a graph of

the new data but is waiting for the calculations to complete. The graph thread may increase the priority of the calculation thread so that the calculation thread receives most of the CPU time for the process, which allows the calculation thread to complete much faster.

Another mechanism used in controlling the execution of a thread is to temporarily suspend its execution. Suppose you have a thread that is searching the files on a disk for a text string. If another thread needs to save data to a file, it can temporarily suspend the search thread while writing the data to the disk. When the data has been saved to disk, it can resume the search thread. A thread can be suspended by calling `DosSuspendThread`, and it subsequently can be resumed by calling `DosResumeThread`. These two functions are described here:

```
APIRET APIENTRY DosSuspendThread(TID tid);
```

`TID`	`tid`	Thread identifier to suspend execution.

```
APIRET APIENTRY DosResumeThread(TID tid);
```

`TID`	`tid`	Thread identifier to resume execution.

Notice that it is possible to suspend and resume threads only within the scope of a process. It is not possible to suspend or resume threads belonging to another process.

To suspend a thread, you can issue the following call:

```
DosSuspendThread (ThreadID);
```

To resume it, issue the following call:

```
DosResumeThread (ThreadID);
```

A thread can also suspend itself for a specified amount of time by using the `DosSleep` function:

```
APIRET APIENTRY DosSleep(ULONG msec);
```

`ULONG`	`msec`	Number of milliseconds to suspend the current thread.

When `DosSleep` is called, the thread immediately relinquishes any remaining CPU time in its current time slice and suspends itself for approximately the amount of time specified. `DosSleep` can be used, for example, in a thread that is constantly displaying the status of the communications line. In this case, the thread will query and display the current line status and call `DosSleep` for a small amount of time, repeating this process until the thread is terminated. An example of this type of thread is shown in Chapter 15, "Communications Basics."

While a thread is suspended, it receives no CPU time regardless of that thread's priority class or priority level. This might create a problem if a thread containing a message queue is suspended. This problem is discussed in a later section about threading considerations.

Because all threads within a process share the data segment and resources of the process, you can foresee problems where two threads attempt to update the same data item or to use the same resource at once. The classic example is one of incrementing a counter. Look at the assembler code generated for the following statements:

```
ulCount++;
```

You might see an unoptimized sequence of instructions:

```
MOV EAX,[02BC]
INC EAX
MOV [02BC],EAX
```

Suppose you have two threads with each executing the instruction `ulCount++` at the same time. If the first thread executes the first two assembler instructions and then is preempted by the system, and thread 2 executes all three assembler instructions and is preempted so that thread 2 can continue, `ulCount` will contain an incorrect value:

```
Thread 1                  Thread 2                  ulCount
T                         MOV EAX,[02BC]            0
i                         INC EAX                   0
m                         MOV EAX,[02BC]            0
e                              INC EAX              0
                          MOV [02BC],EAX            1
|                         MOV [02BC],EAX            1
|
|
V
```

Notice that the final value of `ulCount` is 1, even though it was incremented twice and should contain the value 2. This is a basic example of the kind of problems that may arise with shared data. If a file handle is being shared and multiple threads are positioning the file pointer and reading or writing the file, there are more areas where contention might occur. One option is to suspend the other thread whenever a shared data item or resource is being updated and to resume it when completed. This, however, can be involved when multiple threads are being used.

A much more effective method is to protect shared data and resources with a critical section. While a thread is executing within a critical section, all other threads in the process are temporarily suspended. This way, the calling thread has exclusive access to the CPU for that process without being concerned about another thread in the current process interrupting it. Critical sections should be short and quick because you are suspending all other threads.

A critical section is entered with a call to `DosEnterCritSec` and exited with a call to `DosExitCritSec`. These functions appear as shown here:

```
APIRET APIENTRY DosEnterCritSec(VOID);

APIRET APIENTRY DosExitCritSec(VOID);
```

Using our example, you enclose the counter increment within a critical section as follows:

```
DosEnterCritSec();
ulCount++;
DosExitCritSec();
```

It is possible to nest critical sections. This can be done only by the thread that is executing within a critical section. A matching `DosExitCritSec` must be made for each `DosEnterCritSec` before other threads in the current process are allowed to continue executing.

An additional factor for declaring variables that will be shared among multiple threads is to ensure that the variable is not stored in a register. Because each thread has its own set of registers, this type of variable could not be shared. Use the volatile attribute if it is possible for the variable to be defined in a register.

The last thread API enables you to either wait for another thread to terminate or to check if another thread is still executing. `DosWaitThread` enables you to check the status of another thread:

```
APIRET APIENTRY DosWaitThread(PTID ptid, ULONG option);
```

`PTID`	`ptid`	Address of `TID` variable. On input, the thread ID (identification) specifies the thread to query. If the thread ID is zero, the next thread in the process to terminate is used. Upon return, the thread ID contains the ID of the thread that has terminated.
`ULONG`	`option`	Wait option: `DCWW_WAIT` — Do not return until the indicated thread has terminated. `DCWW_NOWAIT` — Return immediately with the status of the indicated thread.

The return code from this function indicates the status of the queried thread:

`NO_ERROR`	The thread has terminated (`DCWW_WAIT`).
`ERROR_THREAD_NOT_TERMINATED`	The thread has not terminated yet.
`ERROR_INVALID_THREADID`	An invalid thread ID was specified.

Suppose a thread is searching the disk for a file, and in another thread, the user presses a button to perform some action on that file. Because the second thread must wait for the search thread to complete, it could issue the following request:

```
if (!DosWaitThread (&SearchThread, DCWW_WAIT))
      /* continue */
```

If the search thread has terminated by the time this call is made, the call will return immediately; otherwise, it will not return until the `SearchThread` terminates.

The Thread Function

The function specified in the `DosCreateThread` call is the initial entry point of the thread. If a thread creates a message queue, that thread is considered a message queue thread; otherwise, it is a nonmessage queue thread. A message queue is required for any thread that must either create windows, send messages to other windows, or call functions that result in messages being sent to other windows. An application usually creates at least one message queue thread, the main thread.

A thread becomes a message queue thread by calling `WinCreateMsgQueue`. Windows created in one message queue thread cannot be deleted by another message queue thread.

Nonmessage queue threads do not have a message queue to worry about, so they do not have to call `WinPeekMsg` or `WinGetMsg` to retrieve messages from the queue. These threads can concentrate solely on performing the thread's task. Although nonmessage queue threads cannot create windows or cause messages to be sent to other windows, they can post messages to other windows.

Threading Considerations

When you design your threads and the operations to be performed in each, there are several areas of concern to keep in mind. These threading considerations are necessary to provide a well behaved thread that does not degrade overall system performance, or even cause your process to stop functioning.

Here are some general rules of thumb for creating threads:

- Do not assume any timing-related dependencies.

  A thread should not assume that another thread in the process will be executing a portion of code at any particular time. In other words, do not assume that another thread isn't modifying shared data that the current thread is manipulating. Threads should protect all shared data by either suspending competing threads, enclosing the code sequence in a critical section, or using semaphores.

- Do not suspend message queue threads.

  If a message queue thread must be suspended, it should be suspended only for a short time. This includes using critical sections in a message queue thread. While a message queue thread is suspended, it is unable to process messages sent to it. This includes messages sent while focus is changing (for example, `WM_QUERYFOCUSCHAIN`) or when the mouse is moved over a window created by the suspended thread (for example, `WM_HITTEST`). If the current focus window belongs to a thread that is suspended, when another thread attempts to obtain the focus, it will be unable to do so. This is because the thread attempting to gain the focus will be blocked while the `WM_QUERYFOCUSCHAIN` message is being sent by the system to the suspended thread.

- Be a good neighbor when it comes to changing thread priorities.

  Increases in thread priority should be done only on a temporary basis. If a nonmessage queue thread's priority is raised and it is a compute intensive thread, other threads with lower priority will not receive any CPU time. As long as the higher priority thread is in the ready state, it will starve out lower priority threads. This also goes for message queue threads that use `WinPeekMsg` loops and raise their priority above other threads. Even when there are no messages in the higher priority thread's message queue, the thread is continuously in a loop calling `WinPeekMsg` and is always in the ready state;

therefore, it will receive the CPU before a lower priority thread. Because there may be other threads of lower priority executing somewhere in the system, it is a good idea to insert a call to `DosSleep` somewhere in a `WinPeekMsg` loop. Using a small sleep interval of 5 to 10 milliseconds is usually enough to give, at least, some time to lower priority threads.

Semaphores

For processes or threads to coordinate their activities, some means of communication among them is necessary. This is accomplished with something termed "interprocess communication." OS/2 allows three different types of interprocess communication. They are *pipes, queues,* and *semaphores.* Pipes are buffers used to pass data between processes. Queues are ordered lists of elements to which more than one process may add an element. Semaphores are flags or signals maintained by the operating system. Semaphores allow processes to signal the start and finish of operations. They also permit the mutually exclusive ownership of resources by individual threads.

Semaphores are created and maintained in memory buffers by OS/2. Because a semaphore is always resident in memory, setting and clearing semaphores occurs rapidly. Threads use semaphores by setting or clearing a semaphore or by waiting for a semaphore to be set or released by another thread. While a thread is waiting for a semaphore, only the waiting thread is blocked. Other threads are allowed to continue executing. Using a semaphore is a more effective way of protecting access to a resource than is using a critical section. Remember, when `DosEnterCritSec` is used, all other threads in the process are suspended until the `DosExitCritSec` is called. In most cases, a resource is not shared among all threads of a process, so using a critical section needlessly stops nonconflicting threads from executing—which is not wise to do in so arbitrary a way. Further, a critical section cannot be used to protect a resource shared among processes, whereas a semaphore can.

OS/2 maintains three types of semaphores. These are event semaphores, mutual exclusion semaphores, and multiple wait semaphores. *Event semaphores* allow threads to signal other threads that a particular event has transpired. *Mutual exclusion semaphores* let threads cooperate in their access to resources. Essentially, a mutual exclusion semaphore allows threads to solely own a resource for a period so that threads can serialize their access to the resource. *Multiple wait semaphores* can be used in two ways. They allow threads to wait for a collection of resources to become available or for several events to occur. A flag may also be set for this type of semaphore, which allows the process to continue if any one of the events occurs or any one of the resources becomes available.

Semaphores may be private or shared. A private semaphore is available to all threads of a process. Shared semaphores are available for use by multiple processes. Semaphores are accessed by a handle assigned when the semaphore is created. Private semaphore handles are known by all threads of a particular process. Shared semaphore handles can be obtained by a process in two ways. The handle can be communicated to a process through a message, queue, or pipe, or even defined in the global data area of a DLL. A semaphore can also be given a name, and any process knowing its name can open it. Semaphores without names are called *anonymous semaphores.* Semaphores with names are called *named semaphores.* Semaphore names must conform to file system naming conventions and contain the prefix \SEM32\. For example, a legal semaphore name is \SEM32\RCVQUEUE. All named semaphores are considered shared. It is possible for two processes to attempt to create a named semaphore with the same name. In that case, the second attempt to create a semaphore with the same name will fail.

Each process sharing a semaphore must explicitly gain access to the shared semaphore by opening it. The process that initially creates the semaphore implicitly opens the semaphore. All other processes must issue a request to open it. When a process is done with a semaphore, it should close it. OS/2 maintains a count of the number of times a semaphore has been opened. This count is decremented each time the semaphore is closed. The semaphore is deleted when the count becomes zero. A thread may nest calls to open a semaphore, but must close it an equal number of times.

When a thread calls to wait for exclusive use of a semaphore or to wait for a semaphore event to be signalled, it specifies an amount of time to wait. If the specified time passes without gaining access to the semaphore or the event being posted, the semaphore request will timeout. Wait times are specified as milliseconds, `SEM_INDEFINITE_WAIT`, or `SEM_IMMEDIATE_RETURN`. The return code from the semaphore request will indicate whether the request was satisfied or timed out.

Event Semaphores

Event semaphores signal that an event has occurred. An event semaphore will be in one of two states. These two states are *reset* and *posted.* If an event semaphore is in the reset state, this conventionally means that the desired event has not occurred. The operating system, therefore, blocks threads and processes that are waiting on that semaphore. Blocked means execution for the thread is suspended. The threads waiting on the event cease activity until the semaphore changes to the posted state. When the semaphore is posted, all threads that were blocked on that thread, waiting for the event to occur, resume their execution.

Examples of when to use an event semaphore include giving another thread the following information:

- A file has been closed and is available for printing.
- A posted message has been processed.
- A file search has completed.
- A thread is about to terminate.

`DosCreateEventSem` is used to create a new event semaphore. An event semaphore's initial state (posted or reset) is specified in this call:

```
APIRET APIENTRY DosCreateEventSem (PSZ pszName, PHEV phev,
   ULONG flAttr, BOOL fState);
```

PSZ	pszName	Name of the semaphore or NULL (anonymous).
PHEV	phev	Address of event semaphore handle.
ULONG	flAttr	Semaphore attribute (ignored if pszName is NULL). DC_SEM_SHARED Shared semaphore.
BOOL	fState	Initial semaphore state: TRUE Semaphore is posted. FALSE Semaphore is reset.

The following call illustrates the creation of an anonymous shared event semaphore with an initial state of reset:

```
HEV hevEvent;

DosCreateEventSem (NULL, &hevEvent, DC_SEM_SHARED, FALSE);
```

The process of creating an event semaphore also has implicitly opened it. Other processes can open an event semaphore with the DosOpenEventSem function:

```
APIRET APIENTRY DosOpenEventSem (PSZ pszName, PHEV phev);
```

PSZ	pszName	Name of the semaphore or NULL (anonymous).
PHEV	phev	Address of event semaphore handle. If pszName is NULL: The event semaphore handle referenced by phev must be the handle of an existing anonymous semaphore. If pszName is not NULL: On input the event semaphore handle must be NULL; on output the event semaphore handle is updated with the semaphore handle.

The following call opens the semaphore created in the previous example:

```
DosOpenEventSem (NULL, &hevEvent);
```

When a process is done with a semaphore, it calls DosCloseEventSem:

```
APIRET APIENTRY DosCloseEventSem (HEV hev);
```

HEV	hev	Handle of the event semaphore.

The following call closes our semaphore:

```
DosCloseEventSem (hevEvent);
```

An event semaphore is reset to indicate the event has not occurred yet. While an event semaphore is in the reset state, all threads requesting the event semaphore will be blocked until it is posted. DosResetEventSem is used to reset the semaphore:

```
APIRET APIENTRY DosResetEventSem (HEV hev, PULONG pulPostCt);
```

HEV	hev	Handle of the event semaphore.
PULONG	pulPostCnt	Address of variable to receive the post count.

The post count is the number of times DosPostEventSem has been called since DosResetEventSem was last called. If the semaphore is already in the reset state when this function is called, the return code will be ERROR_ALREADY_RESET:

```
ULONG ulPostCount;
DosResetEventSem (hevEvent, &ulPostCount);
```

A thread signals an event by posting the event with DosPostEventSem:

```
APIRET APIENTRY DosPostEventSem (HEV hev);
```

HEV	hev	Handle of the event semaphore.

This call increments the post count of the semaphore. Threads waiting on the semaphore are unblocked and can continue executing:

```
DosPostEventSem (hevEvent);
```

When a thread needs to wait for an event to occur, it uses the DosWaitEventSem function. In specifying that it wants to wait for an event to occur, it can also indicate a time period to wait before continuing. If after the specified time period, the event has not occurred, the function returns ERROR_TIMEOUT.

```
APIRET APIENTRY DosWaitEventSem (HEV hev, ULONG ulTimeout);
```

HEV	hev	Handle of the event semaphore.
ULONG	ulTimeout	Maximum time period to wait for the semaphore (milliseconds). It can also be one of the following values: SEM_IMMEDIATE_RETURN — Zero timeout period. SEM_INDEFINITE_WAIT — No timeout period.

If you want to wait indefinitely for your semaphore to be posted, use the following call:

```
DosWaitEventSem (hevEvent, SEM_INDEFINITE_WAIT);
```

Finally, a thread can query the current post count for an event semaphore at any time. Remember that the post count is the number of times DosPostEventSem has been called since DosResetEventSem was last called:

```
APIRET APIENTRY DosQueryEventSem (HEV hev, PULONG pulPostCt);
```

HEV	hev	Handle of the event semaphore.
PULONG	pulPostCnt	Address of variable to receive the post count.

You can query the event semaphore with the following call:

```
ULONG ulPostCount;
DosQueryEventSem (hevEvent, &ulPostCount);
```

Mutual Exclusion Semaphores

Mutual exclusion semaphores prevent the simultaneous access of protected resources by different threads or processes. These semaphores are often referred to as "mutex" semaphores. A thread makes a request of the semaphore when getting ready to access a protected resource. If no other thread currently owns the semaphore, the request is granted, and the thread becomes the owner. On the other hand, if the semaphore is currently owned, the requesting thread is blocked. When done with the protected resource, the owning thread releases the semaphore. If there are outstanding requests for the semaphore, it is given to the blocked thread with the highest priority. If two blocked threads have the same priority, the request is satisfied in an `FIFO` order.

Examples of when to use a mutual exclusion semaphore include the following:

- Protecting write access to the same file handle.
- Protecting updates to a shared memory object.
- Protecting updates to a linked-list data structure.

`DosCreateMutexSem` is used to create a new mutex semaphore. A mutex semaphore's initial state (owned or unowned) is specified in this call:

```
APIRET APIENTRY DosCreateMutexSem (PSZ pszName, PHMTX phmtx,
   ULONG flAttr, BOOL fState);
```

`PSZ`	`pszName`	Name of the semaphore or `NULL` (anonymous).
`HMTX`	`phmtx`	Address of mutex semaphore handle.
`ULONG`	`flAttr`	Semaphore attribute (ignored if `pszName` is `NULL`). `DC_SEM_SHARED` Shared semaphore.
`BOOL`	`fState`	Initial semaphore state: `TRUE` Semaphore is owned. `FALSE` Semaphore is unowned.

The following call illustrates the creation of a named shared mutex semaphore with an initial state of unowned:

```
HMTX hmtxShared;
DosCreateMutexSem ("\\SEM32\\DEMO", &hmtxShared,
      DC_SEM_SHARED, FALSE);
```

The process creating a mutex semaphore also has implicitly opened it. Other processes can open a mutex semaphore with the `DosOpenMutexSem` function.

```
APIRET APIENTRY DosOpenMutexSem (PSZ pszName, PHMTX phmtx);
```

`PSZ`	`pszName`	Name of the semaphore or `NULL` (anonymous).
`PHMTX`	`phmtx`	Address of mutex semaphore handle. pszName is `NULL`: The mutex semaphore handle referenced must be the handle of an existing anonymous semaphore. pszName is not `NULL`: On input, the mutex semaphore handle must be `NULL`. On output, the mutex semaphore handle is updated with the semaphore handle.

The following call is used by another process to open the semaphore created in the previous example:

```
HMTX hmtxShared = (HMTX)NULL;
DosOpenMutexSem ("\\SEM32\\DEMO", &hmtxShared);
```

When a process is done with a semaphore, it calls `DosCloseMutexSem`.

```
APIRET APIENTRY DosCloseMutexSem (HMTX hmtx);
```

`HMTX`	`hmtx`	Handle of the mutex semaphore.

The following call closes our semaphore:

```
DosCloseMutexSem (hmtxShared);
```

A mutex semaphore is used to protect access to a shared resource. A thread should obtain ownership of a mutex semaphore before proceeding to use the shared resource. Ownership is requested with the `DosRequestMutexSem` function. If the semaphore is currently owned, the thread is blocked until either the semaphore is released by the current owner and the thread is granted ownership or the timeout period expires. In requesting ownership of the mutex semaphore, the thread also specifies a time period to wait before continuing. If after the specified time period the semaphore request is not granted, the function returns `ERROR_TIMEOUT`:

```
APIRET APIENTRY DosRequestMutexSem (HMTX hmtx, ULONG ulTimeout);
```

`HMTX`	`hmtx`	Handle of the mutex semaphore.
`ULONG`	`ulTimeout`	Maximum time period to wait for the semaphore (milliseconds).

It can also be one of the following values:

`SEM_IMMEDIATE_RETURN`	Zero timeout period.
`SEM_INDEFINITE_WAIT`	No timeout period.

The following call requests the mutex semaphore with a 10 second timeout:

```
APIRET RetCode;
RetCode = DosRequestMutexSem (hmtxShared, 10000L);
```

OS/2 keeps a count of the number of times DosRequestMutexSem is called for each mutex semaphore. This internal count is decremented each time the semaphore is released with a call to DosReleaseMutexSem. A thread may nest calls to DosRequestMutexSem, but must call DosReleaseMutexSem an equal number of times.

A thread releases a mutex semaphore by calling DosReleaseMutexSem:

```
APIRET APIENTRY DosReleaseMutexSem (HMTX hmtx);
```

HMTX hmtx Handle of the mutex semaphore.

If the request count for the semaphore becomes zero after this call, the thread with the highest priority that is waiting on a DosRequestMutexSem call for this semaphore is unblocked and allowed to execute.

To release ownership of our mutex semaphore, the following call is used:

```
DosReleaseMutexSem (hmtxShared);
```

At any point, a thread can query the mutex semaphore to determine who the current owner is and the number of DosRequestMutexSem calls without a matching DosReleaseMutexSem call:

```
APIRET APIENTRY DosQueryMutexSem (HMTX hmtx, PPID ppid,
   PTID ptid, PULONG pulCount);
```

HMTX	hmtx	Handle of the mutex semaphore.
PPID	ppid	Address of variable to receive process ID of semaphore owner.
PTID	ptid	Address of variable to receive thread ID of semaphore owner.
PULONG	pulCount	Address of variable to receive request count.

If the semaphore is currently unowned, the request count will be zero. You can query the mutex semaphore with the following code:

```
PID   pid;
TID   tid;
ULONG ulRequestCount;
DosQueryMutexSem (hmtxShared, &pid, &tid, &ulRequestCount);
```

Multiple Wait Semaphores

Multiple wait semaphores allow a process or thread to wait on several events to occur before proceeding. They can also be used to cause the thread or process to wait for several different resources to become available before proceeding. Multiple wait semaphores are often referred to as "muxwait" semaphores. Muxwait semaphores are lists of other event or mutex semaphores. These lists can be up to 64 entries in length consisting of either mutex or event semaphores. The two different types cannot be mixed in the same list. If a shared muxwait semaphore is created, all semaphores contained in the muxwait semaphore must be shared semaphores. Private mutex semaphores can mix both private and shared versions of the same semaphore type.

When muxwait semaphores are created, they can be flagged to operate in one of two ways. In the first case, if the muxwait semaphore consists of a list of events, threads will wait until all the semaphores have been posted. Similarly, if the muxwait semaphore consists of a list of mutex semaphores, threads will wait until all the mutex semaphores have been released before continuing. In the second way of operating, if the muxwait semaphore consists of a list of events, threads wait for any one of the event semaphores to be posted before continuing. If the muxwait semaphore consists of mutex semaphores, threads will wait until any one of the mutex semaphores has been released.

It is important to note at this point that just because a semaphore is contained within a muxwait semaphore, it does not change the use of that semaphore. In addition, a semaphore can be contained within multiple muxwait semaphores.

Here are examples of when to use a multiple wait semaphore:

- When requesting access to two or more shared memory objects where each shared memory object is protected by a mutex semaphore.
- When attempting to update multiple tables in a database where each table is protected by a mutex semaphore.
- When waiting for two calculation threads to complete, each signaling their completion by posting an event semaphore.

Before creating a muxwait semaphore, all semaphores to be contained in it must be created and opened. All the semaphores are then added to an array of `SEMRECORD` structures. The `SEMRECORD` structure contains two fields:

```
typedef struct
{
   HSEM  hsemCur;
         Handle of the semaphore (either event or mutex)
   ULONG ulUser;
         User-defined value
} SEMRECORD;
```

The `ulUser` field is defined solely for the application to identify the semaphore. This value is returned when a muxwait semaphore request is satisfied. A muxwait semaphore can contain at most 64 event or mutex semaphores. Assume you want to create a private muxwait semaphore made up of one shared mutex semaphore and one private mutex semaphore. You would create the semaphores and put the information in a `SEMRECORD` array:

```
SEMRECORD SemRecords[2];

DosCreateMutexSem ("\\SEM32\\DEMO", &SemRecords[0].hsemCur,
   DC_SEM_SHARED, FALSE);
SemRecords[0].ulUser = 0;
DosCreateMutexSem (NULL, &SemRecords[1].hsemCur, 0, FALSE);
SemRecords[0].ulUser = 1;
```

With the array SemRecords defined, the muxwait semaphore can be created with the DosCreateMuxWaitSem function:

```
APIRET APIENTRY DosCreateMuxWaitSem (PSZ pszName,
   PHMUX phmux, ULONG cSemRec, PSEMRECORD pSemRec,

   ULONG flAttr);
```

PSZ	pszName	Name of the semaphore or NULL (anonymous).
PHMUX	phmux	Address of muxwait semaphore handle.
ULONG	cSemRec	Number of semaphores contained in the array.
PSEMRECORD	pSemRec	Address of array of SEMRECORD structures defining the semaphores.
ULONG	flAttr	Semaphore attribute: DC_SEM_SHARED — Shared semaphore (ignored if pszName is NULL). DCMW_WAIT_ANY — Semaphore request is satisfied when any one of the semaphores is either posted or released. DCMW_WAIT_ALL — Semaphore request is satisfied only when all semaphores are either posted or released.

Using the array of two semaphores defined previously, you can now create a private muxwait semaphore that must have both semaphores to satisfy the request:

```
HMUX hmuxPrivateAll;
DosCreateMuxWaitSem (NULL, &hmuxPrivateAll, 2L, SemRecords,
   DCMW_WAIT_ANY);
```

The process creating a muxwait semaphore also has implicitly opened it. Other processes can open a muxwait semaphore with the DosOpenMuxWaitSem function. Remember that to successfully open a muxwait semaphore, a process must have individually opened each semaphore contained in the muxwait semaphore. Opening a muxwait semaphore does not automatically do this for a process:

```
APIRET APIENTRY DosOpenMuxWaitSem (PSZ pszName,

   PHMUX phmux);
```

PSZ	pszName	Name of the semaphore or NULL (anonymous).
PHMUX	phmux	Address of muxwait semaphore handle.

If a process creates a shared muxwait semaphore named \SEM32\MUXSHARE, another process can open it with the following call:

```
HMUX hmuxShare;

DosOpenMuxWaitSem ("\\SEM32\\MUXSHARE", &hmuxShare);
```

When a process is done with a muxwait semaphore, it calls `DosCloseMuxWaitSem`.

```
APIRET APIENTRY DosCloseMuxWaitSem (HMUX hmux);
```

HMUX	hmux	Handle of the muxwait semaphore.

The following call closes the shared semaphore previously opened:

```
DosCloseMuxWaitSem (hmuxShare);
```

Things get a little more complicated when a thread decides to wait or request a muxwait semaphore. First look at how a muxwait event semaphore operates. A thread waiting on a muxwait event semaphore will be triggered to continue execution in one of two ways depending on the wait attribute specified when the semaphore was created:

DCMW_WAIT_ANY	The muxwait semaphore request is triggered when any one of the event semaphores is posted.
DCMW_WAIT_ALL	The muxwait semaphore request is triggered when all the event semaphores are in the posted state at the same time. If any one of the event semaphores is in the reset state, the request is not triggered.

For a thread requesting a muxwait mutex semaphore, the thread will be blocked until the semaphore(s) is released. This will depend on the wait attribute specified when the semaphore was created:

DCMW_WAIT_ANY	The thread obtains ownership of the first semaphore in the list to be released. Semaphores are checked in the order they are defined in the `SEMRECORD` array. When the thread has obtained ownership of one of the semaphores, the thread is unblocked and all other semaphores defined in the muxwait semaphore remain unchanged.
DCMW_WAIT_ALL	The thread obtains ownership of all semaphores only when all semaphores are in the released state at the same time. All semaphores become owned at the same time.

It is an error for a thread to request a muxwait mutex semaphore if that thread currently owns one or more semaphores contained in the muxwait semaphore. For both types of muxwait semaphores, the thread is also unblocked if a timeout period is specified and the semaphore request is not satisfied within that timeout period. In this case, the return code will be ERROR_TIMEOUT. Requests of a muxwait semaphore are made with the DosWaitMuxWaitSem function:

```
APIRET APIENTRY DosWaitMuxWaitSem (HMUX hmux,
   ULONG ulTimeout, PULONG pulUser);
```

HMUX	hmux	Handle of the muxwait semaphore.
ULONG	ulTimeout	Maximum time period to wait for the semaphore (milliseconds). It can also be one of the following values: SEM_IMMEDIATE_RETURN — Zero timeout period. SEM_INDEFINITE_WAIT — No timeout period.
PULONG	pulUser	Address of variable to receive the user field from the SEMRECORD of the last semaphore that caused the semaphore request to be satisfied.

If the DosWaitMuxWaitSem request is successful, the ulUser field from the SEMRECORD of the last semaphore that caused the muxwait semaphore to be triggered or released is returned. The following call illustrates a request for the hmuxPrivateAll semaphore created earlier:

```
ULONG  ulUser;
APIRET RetCode;

RetCode = DosWaitMuxWaitSem (hmuxPrivateAll,
      SEM_INDEFINITE_WAIT, &ulUser);
```

It is possible to add new semaphores to an existing muxwait semaphore. To add a new semaphore, the process must have both the muxwait semaphore and the new semaphore open. A semaphore can be added even if other threads are currently waiting on the muxwait semaphore. The DosAddMuxWaitSem function is used to add a new semaphore. The semaphore must be the same type as the existing semaphores defined for the muxwait semaphore:

```
APIRET APIENTRY DosAddMuxWaitSem (HMUX hmux,

   PSEMRECORD pSemRec);
```

HMUX	hmux	Handle of the muxwait semaphore.
PSEMRECORD	pSemRec	Address of new SEMRECORD structure.

If you create a new private mutex semaphore, you can then add it to your private mutex semaphore as follows:

```
SEMRECORD SemRecord;
DosCreateMutexSem (NULL, &SemRecord.hsemCur, 0, FALSE);
SemRecord.ulUser = 2;

DosAddMuxWaitSem (hmuxPrivate, &SemRecord);
```

Notice that there is no significance to the fact you set the ulUser field to be equal to its index in the array. The ulUser field can contain any user-defined value.

Any threads currently waiting on the muxwait semaphore that do not have the newly added semaphore opened are immediately unblocked and receive a return code of ERROR_INVALID_HANDLE. Other threads that subsequently call DosWaitMuxWaitSem must also open the new semaphore. Any thread receiving an ERROR_INVALID_HANDLE return code can query all the semaphores contained by the muxwait semaphore by calling DosQueryMuxWaitSem. Then, the thread can open those semaphores it does not currently have open. It can determine which semaphores it does not have open by calling either DosQueryMutexSem or DosQueryEventSem and checking for a return code of ERROR_INVALID_HANDLE:

```
APIRET APIENTRY DosQueryMuxWaitSem (HMUX hmux,
   PULONG pcSemRec, PSEMRECORD pSemRec, PULONG pflAttr);
```

HMUX	hmux	Handle of the muxwait semaphore.
PULONG	pcSemRec	Address of count of SEMRECORD structures. On input, it is the maximum number of structures that will fit in the array addressed by pSemRec. On output, it is the number of structures copied into the array addressed by pSemRec.
PSEMRECORD	pSemRec	Address of array to receive the SEMRECORD structures.
PULONG	pflAttr	Address of variable to receive semaphore attributes specified when the semaphore was created. The flags may contain the following flags:

DC_SEM_SHARED	Shared semaphore (ignored if pszName is NULL).
DCMW_WAIT_ANY	Semaphore request is satisfied when anyone of the semaphores is either posted or released.
DCMW_WAIT_ALL	Semaphore request is satisfied only when all semaphores are either posted or released.

To query our private muxwait semaphore, you can issue the following call:

```
SEMRECORD SemRecords[10];
ULONG     ulCnt;
ULONG     ulAttr;

ulCnt = 10L;
DosQueryMuxWaitSem (hmuxPrivate, &ulCnt, SemRecords,

   &ulAttr);
```

The value returned in `ulCnt` should be three because there are three semaphores in the private muxwait semaphore (that is, the two original plus the one added afterward).

It is also possible to delete semaphores from a muxwait semaphore. This is done with the `DosDeleteMuxWaitSem` function:

```
APIRET APIENTRY DosDeleteMuxWaitSem (HMUX hmux, HSEM hSem);
```

`HMUX`	`hmux`	Handle of the muxwait semaphore.

When a semaphore is deleted from a muxwait semaphore, all threads currently waiting on the muxwait semaphore will be reevaluated. Deleting the semaphore may cause a thread to be triggered if the deleted semaphore was the only event preventing a `DCMW_WAIT_ALL` muxwait event semaphore from being triggered. It may also cause a thread to be unblocked if the deleted semaphore was the only semaphore preventing a `DCMW_WAIT_ALL` mutex semaphore from being released. Taking the result from the previous call to `DosQueryMuxWaitSem`, you can delete the first semaphore with the following call:

```
DosDeleteMuxWaitSem (hmuxPrivate, SemRecords[0].hsemCur);
```

Thread Demonstration Application

Many variables are involved in designing an effective multithreaded application. You must be concerned about protecting access to shared resources, setting the correct priorities of other threads when necessary, deciding whether a thread should contain a message queue, and, most important, deciding which functions should be executed in a thread. These design considerations and decisions can be made more competently with a good understanding of how the various parameters involved in multithreading affect the performance of the individual threads and the process as a whole. The application presented in this chapter is a multithreaded demonstration application that enables you to create both message queue and nonmessage queue threads. It is designed to enable you to modify dynamically various aspects of a thread so you can view the effect of the changes on the thread and the other threads in the process. Specifically, you can see the effects of the following:

- Creating additional message queue threads.
- Creating additional nonmessage queue threads.

```
#define IDC_THREADPRIORITY          201
#define IDC_STATE                   202
#define IDC_CRITSECTION             203
#define IDC_SEMAPHORE               204
#define IDC_THERMOMETER             205
#define IDC_KILL                    206
#define IDC_UPPRIORITY              207
#define IDC_DOWNPRIORITY            208

#define IDC_PERCENT                 300
#define IDC_PERCENTBAR              301
#define IDC_SUSPEND                 302
#define IDC_RESUME                  303
```

THREADS.RC

```
/* --------------------------------
Threads Resource File
Real-World Programming for OS/2
Copyright (c)  1994 Blain, Delimon, and English
-------------------------------- */

#include <os2.h>
#include "threads.h"
#include "..\common\controls.h"

ICON ID_APPNAME THREADS.ICO

MENU ID_APPNAME
{
   SUBMENU "~Threads",              IDM_THREADS
   {
      SUBMENU "~New Thread",       IDM_NEWTHREAD
      {
         MENUITEM "~Message Queue Thread", IDM_NEWQMSGTHREAD
         MENUITEM "~Sorting Thread", IDM_NEWSORTINGTHREAD
      }
      MENUITEM "~Kill All Message Queue Threads",
               IDM_KILLALLTHREADS
      MENUITEM "",                  -1,
               MIS_SEPARATOR
      MENUITEM "A~rrange",                     IDM_ARRANGE
      MENUITEM "",                  -1,
               MIS_SEPARATOR
      MENUITEM "~About...",         IDM_ABOUT
   }
}

STRINGTABLE LOADONCALL MOVEABLE
BEGIN
   ID_APPNAME       "Threads Demonstration Application"
END

rcinclude tid.dlg
```

```
rcinclude sort.dlg
rcinclude ..\common\about.dlg
```

TID.DLG

```
/* -------------------------------
Threads Dialog
Real-World Programming for OS/2
Copyright (c)  1994 Blain, Delimon, and English
------------------------------- */

DLGTEMPLATE IDD_TIDDLG LOADONCALL MOVEABLE DISCARDABLE
BEGIN
   DIALOG  "Dialog Title", IDD_TIDDLG, 34, 40, 80, 94,
            NOT FS_DLGBORDER ¦ NOT WS_SAVEBITS,
            FCF_NOBYTEALIGN
            PRESPARAMS PP_FONTNAMESIZE, "8.Helv"
   BEGIN
      CONTROL     "",            -1, 0,  0, 80, 94, BEVELCLASS,
                   BVS_BEVELIN ¦ BVS_RECTANGLE ¦ WS_VISIBLE
      LTEXT       "TID:",        -1, 4, 85, 33,  7
      LTEXT       "Priority:",   -1, 4, 79, 33,  7
      LTEXT       "State:",      -1, 4, 73, 33,  7
      RTEXT       "0000",        IDC_THREADID,          35, 85,
                    21,  7
      RTEXT       "0000",        IDC_THREADPRIORITY,   35, 79,
                   21,  7
      LTEXT       "Running",     IDC_STATE,             35, 73,
                   44,  7
      CONTROL     "", IDC_THERMOMETER, 27, 22, 27, 49,
               THERMOMETERCLASS, THS_NOPERCENT ¦ WS_VISIBLE
      PUSHBUTTON "Kill",       IDC_KILL,               1,  9,
               40, 10
      PUSHBUTTON "Up",         IDC_UPPRIORITY,        40,  9,
               20, 10
      PUSHBUTTON "Dwn",        IDC_DOWNPRIORITY,      60,  9,
               19, 10
      PUSHBUTTON "CritSec",    IDC_CRITSECTION,        1,  0,
               40, 10
      PUSHBUTTON "Semaphore", IDC_SEMAPHORE,          40,  0,
               39, 10
   END
END
```

SORT.DLG

```
/* -------------------------------
Sorting Thread Dialog
Real-World Programming for OS/2
Copyright (c) 1994 Blain, Delimon, and English
------------------------------- */

DLGTEMPLATE IDD_SORTINGDLG LOADONCALL MOVEABLE DISCARDABLE
```

```
BEGIN
  DIALOG  "Sorting Thread", IDD_SORTINGDLG, 56, 92, 128,
          47, 0,
          FCF_TITLEBAR ¦ FCF_NOBYTEALIGN ¦
          FCF_NOMOVEWITHOWNER
          PRESPARAMS PP_FONTNAMESIZE, "8.Helv"
  BEGIN
    LTEXT          "TID:",              -1,       4, 36,
              33,  7
    RTEXT          "0000",    IDC_THREADID,      35, 36,
              21,  7
    LTEXT          "Percent Complete:", -1,       5, 29,
              69,  7
    LTEXT          "%",                 -1,     103, 29,
              10,  7
    RTEXT          "0",     IDC_PERCENT,         82, 29,
              20,  7
    CONTROL        "", IDC_PERCENTBAR, 5, 18, 118, 10,
                   WC_STATIC, SS_TEXT ¦ WS_VISIBLE
    PUSHBUTTON     "Kill",    IDC_KILL,           4,  4,
              40, 10
    PUSHBUTTON     "Suspend", IDC_SUSPEND,       44,  4,
              40, 10
    PUSHBUTTON     "Up",      IDC_UPPRIORITY,    84,  4,
              20, 10
    PUSHBUTTON     "Dwn",     IDC_DOWNPRIORITY, 104,  4,
              20, 10
  END
END
```

THREADS.C

```
/* -------------------------------
Threads Program
Real-World Programming for OS/2
Copyright (c)  1994 Blain, Delimon, and English
------------------------------- */

#define INCL_DOSERRORS
#define INCL_DOS
#define INCL_WIN

#include <os2.h>
#include <stdio.h>
#include <stdlib.h>
#include "threads.h"
#include "..\common\controls.h"
#include "..\common\about.h"

/* Undocumented WinDrawBorder flag */
#define DB_RAISED       0x0400

/* Sorting thread structure        */
#define ARRAY_SIZE 4096
typedef struct
```

```
{
   HWND   hWndDlg;       /* Dialog window handle      */
   ULONG  ulCnt;         /* Number of entries to sort */
   ULONG  ulArray[1];    /* Array of data to sort     */
} SORTDATA;
typedef SORTDATA *PSORTDATA;

/* Window and Dialog Functions       */
MRESULT EXPENTRY ClientWndProc (HWND,ULONG,MPARAM,MPARAM);
MRESULT EXPENTRY TIDDlgProc (HWND,ULONG,MPARAM,MPARAM);
MRESULT EXPENTRY SortingDlgProc (HWND,ULONG,MPARAM,MPARAM);

/* Thread Functions                  */
#ifdef _ _WATCOM_ _VOID _ _stdcall ThermometerThread (HWND);
VOID _ _stdcall SortingThread (PSORTDATA);
#else
VOID ThermometerThread (HWND);
VOID SortingThread (PSORTDATA);
#endif

/* Local Functions                   */
VOID ArrangeThreadWindows (VOID);
VOID CreateSortingThread (HWND);
HWND CreateThreadWindow (HWND);
VOID DestroyThreadWindow (HWND);
VOID ThreadMessageLoop (HAB,HWND,HWND);

/* User-Defined messages             */
#define WM_USER_KILL              WM_USER+1
#define WM_USER_UPPRIORITY        WM_USER+2
#define WM_USER_DOWNPRIORITY      WM_USER+3
#define WM_USER_CRITSECTION       WM_USER+4
#define WM_USER_SEMAPHORE         WM_USER+5
#define WM_USER_PERCENTCOMPLETE WM_USER+6

/* Global Variables                  */
HAB       hab;                /* Handle to anchor block     */
HWND      hWndFrame,          /* Frame window handle        */
          hWndClient,         /* Client window handle       */
          hWndMainTID,        /* Main thread ID             */
          hWndMainThermo;     /* Main thermometer window    */
CHAR      szTitle[64];        /* Title string               */
RECTL     RectlTID;           /* Thread dialog size         */
HMTX      ThreadSem;          /* Thread semaphore           */
ULONG     ulThreadCnt   = 0;  /* Number of QMSG threads     */
SHORT     sScrollPos    = 0;  /* Current scroll position    */
SHORT     sScrollRange = 0;   /* Current scroll range       */


/* -------- Main Application Function ---------- */

int main()
{
   HMQ   hmq;
   ULONG flFrameFlags    = FCF_TITLEBAR ¦ FCF_SYSMENU ¦
                           FCF_ICON ¦
```

```
                        FCF_SIZEBORDER ¦ FCF_MINMAX    ¦
                        FCF_SHELLPOSITION ¦FCF_TASKLIST ¦
                        FCF_MENU ¦ FCF_NOBYTEALIGN ¦
                        FCF_VERTSCROLL;
CHAR  szClientClass[] = "CLIENT";
CHAR  szFailBuff [CCHMAXPATH];
HMODULE hDLLModule;

hab = WinInitialize (0L);
hmq = WinCreateMsgQueue (hab, 0L);

/* Load the controls dynamic link library */
if (DosLoadModule (szFailBuff, sizeof(szFailBuff),
      "CONTROLS", &hDLLModule))
{
   WinMessageBox (HWND_DESKTOP, HWND_DESKTOP,
         "Unable to load CONTROLS.DLL",
         "Real World Programming in OS/2",
         0, MB_OK ¦ MB_CRITICAL ¦ MB_MOVEABLE);
}
else
{
   WinRegisterClass (hab, szClientClass, ClientWndProc,
         CS_CLIPCHILDREN, 0);
   WinLoadString (hab, 0L, ID_APPNAME, sizeof(szTitle),
         szTitle);

   /* Create the main application window */
   hWndFrame = WinCreateStdWindow (HWND_DESKTOP, 0,
      &flFrameFlags, szClientClass, szTitle, 0, 0,
      ID_APPNAME, &hWndClient);

   WinShowWindow (hWndFrame, TRUE);

   /* Create main thread thermometer window */
   hWndMainTID    = CreateThreadWindow (hWndClient);
   hWndMainThermo = WinWindowFromID (hWndMainTID,
         IDC_THERMOMETER);
   WinEnableControl (hWndMainTID, IDC_KILL, FALSE);
   WinEnableControl (hWndMainTID, IDC_SEMAPHORE, FALSE);

   /* Create the thread semaphore */
   DosCreateMutexSem (NULL, &ThreadSem, 0L, FALSE);

   ThreadMessageLoop (hab, hWndMainTID, hWndMainThermo);

   /* Close the thread semaphore */
   DosCloseMutexSem (ThreadSem);

   DestroyThreadWindow (hWndMainTID);

   WinDestroyWindow (hWndFrame);

   /* Release the controls dynamic link library */
   DosFreeModule (hDLLModule);
}
```

```
   WinDestroyMsgQueue (hmq);
   WinTerminate (hab);

   return (0);
}


/* -------- Sorting Thread Function ---------- */

/*
The Sorting thread is responsible for sorting the array of unsigned long numbers.  The
input to this thread is the address of a SORTDATA structure.  This thread is for
demonstration only so it performs the very slow bubblesort.  A WM_USER_PERCENTCOMPLETE
message is posted to the dialog window as it completes each percent of the sorting
process.  When sorting is complete, the thread posts a 100% WM_USER_PERCENTCOMPLETE
message to the dialog and terminates itself.

This is a Nonmessage queue thread so it cannot send messages to
a Message queue thread.
*/

#ifdef _ _IBMC_ _#pragma linkage(SortingThread, system)
#endif

#ifdef _ _WATCOM_ _VOID _ _stdcall SortingThread (PSORTDATA pData)
#else
VOID SortingThread (PSORTDATA pData)
#endif
{
   ULONG ulInx,
         ulJnx,
         ulNewPercent,
         ulPercent,
         ulTotalComparisons,
         ulNumComparisons;

   /* Total number of comparisons = ulCnt! */
   ulTotalComparisons =
         (pData->ulCnt * (pData->ulCnt + 1)) / 2;
   ulNumComparisons    = 0;
   ulPercent           = 0L;

   /* Perform bubble sort */
   for (ulInx = 0; ulInx < (pData->ulCnt - 1); ulInx++)
   {
      for (ulJnx = ulInx+1; ulJnx < pData->ulCnt; ulJnx++)
         if (pData->ulArray[ulInx] > pData->ulArray[ulJnx])
         {
            /* Swap values using exclusive-or operation */
            pData->ulArray[ulInx] ^= pData->ulArray[ulJnx];
            pData->ulArray[ulJnx] ^= pData->ulArray[ulInx];
            pData->ulArray[ulInx] ^= pData->ulArray[ulJnx];
         }

         /* Increment number of comparisons done so far */
```

```
            ulNumComparisons += (pData->ulCnt - ulInx - 1);

            ulNewPercent =
               (ulNumComparisons * 100)/ ulTotalComparisons;
            if (ulNewPercent != ulPercent)
            {
               ulPercent = ulNewPercent;
               WinPostMsg (pData->hWndDlg,
                     WM_USER_PERCENTCOMPLETE,
                     (MPARAM)ulPercent, 0L);
            }
      }

      /* Post 100% completion message */
      WinPostMsg (pData->hWndDlg, WM_USER_PERCENTCOMPLETE,
            (MPARAM)100L, 0L);

      DosExit (EXIT_THREAD, 0L);
}


/* ------ Thermometer Thread Function ---------- */

/*
The Thermometer thread is responsible for simply incrementing
and decrementing the current thermometer value.  Most of the
thread processing is performed in the ThreadMessageLoop function.

Since this thread will be directly updating the dialog box control
windows, it must create a message queue.  Thus it will be a
Message queue thread.
*/

#ifdef _ _IBMC_ _#pragma linkage(ThermometerThread, system)
#endif

#ifdef _ _WATCOM_ _VOID _ _stdcall ThermometerThread (HWND hWnd)
#else
VOID ThermometerThread (HWND hWnd)
#endif
{
   HMQ    hmqThread;
   HAB    habThread;
   HWND   hWndTID,
          hWndThermo;

   /* Create message queue for this thread */
   habThread = WinInitialize (0L);
   hmqThread = WinCreateMsgQueue (hab, 0L);

   /* Create the thread window */
   hWndTID    = CreateThreadWindow (hWnd);
   hWndThermo = WinWindowFromID(hWndTID, IDC_THERMOMETER);

   ThreadMessageLoop (hab, hWndTID, hWndThermo);
```

```
   /* Destroy the thread's window */
   DestroyThreadWindow (hWndTID);

   /* Destroy the message queue for this thread */
   WinDestroyMsgQueue (hmqThread);
   WinTerminate (habThread);

   DosExit (EXIT_THREAD, 0L);
}


/* ---------- Local Functions ------------ */

VOID ArrangeThreadWindows ()
{
   HENUM hEnum;
   PSWP  pSwp;
   RECTL Rectl;
   ULONG ulNumPerRow,
         ulCnt = 0;
   HWND  hWndThread;

   /* Allocate memory to hold the SWP structures */
   if (!DosAllocMem ((PPVOID)&pSwp,
         sizeof(SWP)*ulThreadCnt, fALLOC))
   {
      /* Calculate number of thread windows that fit in each row */
      WinQueryWindowRect (hWndClient, &Rectl);
      ulNumPerRow = Rectl.xRight / RectlTID.xRight;
      if (ulNumPerRow == 0)
         ulNumPerRow++;

      /* Enter critical section so that the list of current
         windows remains unchanged while we enumerate */
      DosEnterCritSec ();

      /* Begin thread window enumeration */
      hEnum = WinBeginEnumWindows (hWndClient);

      /* Get handle to each thread window */
      while ((hWndThread = WinGetNextWindow (hEnum)) != 0)
      {
         pSwp[ulCnt].fl      = SWP_MOVE | SWP_NOADJUST |
               SWP_SHOW;
         pSwp[ulCnt].x =(ulCnt%ulNumPerRow) *
                RectlTID.xRight;
         pSwp[ulCnt].y       = Rectl.yTop -
            (((ulCnt / ulNumPerRow) + 1) * RectlTID.yTop);
         pSwp[ulCnt++].hwnd = hWndThread;
      }

      /* End Thread window enumeration */
      WinEndEnumWindows (hEnum);
```

```
        /* Exit the critical section since we have enumerated all the
        current windows */
        DosExitCritSec ();

        /* Arrange the tiled windwos */
        WinSetMultWindowPos (hab, pSwp, ulCnt);

        /* Set the scroll range and initial position */
        sScrollPos   = 0;
        sScrollRange = (SHORT)-pSwp[ulCnt-1].y;
        WinSendDlgItemMsg (hWndFrame, FID_VERTSCROLL,
              SBM_SETSCROLLBAR,
              MPFROMSHORT(0), MPFROM2SHORT(0,sScrollRange));

        /* Free the allocated memory    */
        DosFreeMem ((PVOID)pSwp);
     }

     return;
  }

  VOID CreateSortingThread (HWND hWnd)
  {
     TID             ThreadID;
     ULONG           ulInx;
     PSORTDATA       pData;
     RECTL           Rectl;
     POINTL          Ptl;

     /* Allocate a block of memory to contain the sorting data plus all
     of the array entries to sort */
     if (!DosAllocMem ((PPVOID)&pData,
           sizeof(SORTDATA) + ((ARRAY_SIZE - 1) *
           sizeof(ULONG)), fALLOC))
     {
        /* Initialize array as an array of descending numbers to be
        sorted in ascending order (worst case order) */
        for (ulInx = 0; ulInx < ARRAY_SIZE; ulInx++)
           pData->ulArray[ulInx] = ARRAY_SIZE - ulInx;

        pData->ulCnt = ARRAY_SIZE;

        /* Create dialog to display sorting status */
        pData->hWndDlg = WinLoadDlg (HWND_DESKTOP, hWnd,
        SortingDlgProc, 0L, IDD_SORTINGDLG, NULL);

        /* Create the sorting thread in a suspended state */
        DosCreateThread (&ThreadID, (PFNTHREAD)SortingThread,
              (ULONG)pData, 0x0001, 0x2000);

        WinSetWindowUShort (pData->hWndDlg, QWS_ID,
              (USHORT)ThreadID);
        WinSetDlgItemShort (pData->hWndDlg, IDC_THREADID,
              (USHORT)ThreadID, FALSE);
        WinSetWindowPtr (pData->hWndDlg, QWL_USER,
              (PVOID)pData);
```

```
      /* Position the sorting dialog */
      WinQueryWindowRect (pData->hWndDlg, &Rectl);
      Ptl.x = Ptl.y = 0L;
      WinMapWindowPoints (hWndFrame, HWND_DESKTOP, &Ptl,
            1L);
      WinSetWindowPos (pData->hWndDlg, 0L,
         Ptl.x + (ThreadID & 1) * Rectl.xRight,
         ((ThreadID & 7) >> 1) * Rectl.yTop,
         0L, 0L, SWP_MOVE | SWP_SHOW);

      /* Start the thread */
      DosResumeThread (ThreadID);
   }

   return;
}

HWND CreateThreadWindow (HWND hWnd)
{
   HWND   hWndTID;

   hWndTID = WinLoadDlg (hWnd, hWnd, TIDDlgProc, 0L,
         IDD_TIDDLG, NULL);

   /* Increment count of message queue threads within a critical
   section since multiple threads may be calling this function
   at the same time */
   DosEnterCritSec();
   ulThreadCnt++;
   DosExitCritSec();

   WinSetWindowPos (hWndTID, HWND_BOTTOM, 0L, 0L, 0L,
           0L,SWP_ZORDER);
   ArrangeThreadWindows ();

   return (hWndTID);
}

VOID DestroyThreadWindow (HWND hWnd)
{
   WinDestroyWindow (hWnd);

   /* Decrement count of message queue threads within a critical
   section since multiple threads may be calling this function
   at the same time */
   DosEnterCritSec();
   ulThreadCnt--;
   DosExitCritSec();

   return;
}

VOID ThreadMessageLoop (HAB hab, HWND hWndMain,
   HWND hWndThermo)
{
   APIRET RetCode;
```

```
   QMSG   qmsg;
   PPIB   ppib;
   PTIB   ptib;
   BOOL   bContinue          = TRUE;
   ULONG  ulValue            = 0L;
   LONG   lIncDec            = 1L;
   LONG   lPriority          = 0L;
   ULONG  ulCurPriority      = 0L;
   BOOL   bDoCriticalSection = FALSE;
   BOOL   bDoSemaphore       = FALSE;
   BOOL   bHaveSemaphore     = FALSE;

/* Message processing loop for a thread.  Peek messages from the
message queue and dispatch them as the default.  If the message
requires special processing then do it here.  This function
executes on behalf of each thread that calls it so the message
processing is per thread using each thread's stack space. */

   do
   {
      while (bContinue &&
         WinPeekMsg (hab, &qmsg, 0L, 0L, 0L, PM_REMOVE))
      {
         switch (qmsg.msg)
         {
            case WM_QUIT:
            case WM_USER_KILL:
               bContinue = FALSE;

               /* Force release of semaphore */
               ulValue      = 0L;
               bDoSemaphore = FALSE;
               break;

            case WM_USER_UPPRIORITY:
               /* Increase thread priority */
               lPriority++;
               DosSetPriority (PRTYS_THREAD, PRTYC_REGULAR,
                     lPriority, 0L);
               if (lPriority == PRTYD_MAXIMUM)
                  WinEnableControl (hWndMain,
                        IDC_UPPRIORITY, FALSE);
               WinEnableControl (hWndMain, IDC_DOWNPRIORITY,
                     TRUE);
               break;

            case WM_USER_DOWNPRIORITY:
               /* Decrease thread prioity */
               lPriority--;
               DosSetPriority (PRTYS_THREAD, PRTYC_REGULAR,
                  lPriority, 0L);
               if (lPriority == 0L)
                  WinEnableControl (hWndMain,
                     IDC_DOWNPRIORITY, FALSE);
               WinEnableControl (hWndMain, IDC_UPPRIORITY,
                     TRUE);
```

```
         break;

      case WM_USER_CRITSECTION:
         bDoCriticalSection = !bDoCriticalSection;
         break;

      case WM_USER_SEMAPHORE:
         bDoSemaphore = !bDoSemaphore;
         break;

      default:
         WinDispatchMsg (hab, &qmsg);
   }
}

/* No more messages in the queue */

/* Update thread priority in the dialog if it has changed */
DosGetInfoBlocks (&ptib, &ppib);
if (ulCurPriority != (ptib->tib_ptib2)->tib2_ulpri)
{
   ulCurPriority = (ptib->tib_ptib2)->tib2_ulpri;
   WinSetDlgItemShort (hWndMain, IDC_THREADPRIORITY,
      (USHORT)ulCurPriority, FALSE);
}

/* If the user has indicated that this thread should enter a
critical section, then enter a critical section and sleep
for 100 milliseconds */
if (bDoCriticalSection)
{
   WinSetDlgItemText (hWndMain, IDC_STATE,
      "Crit Sec");
   DosEnterCritSec ();
   DosSleep (100L);
   DosExitCritSec ();
   WinSetDlgItemText (hWndMain, IDC_STATE,
         bHaveSemaphore ? "Semaphore" : "Running");
}

/* Update thread thermometer value */
WinSendMsg (hWndThermo, THM_SETVALUE, (MPARAM)ulValue,
      0L);

/* If the thermometer value is zero, then reverse direction and
check if the semaphore should be requested or released */
if (ulValue == 0)
{
   lIncDec = 1L;

   /* If this thread has the semaphore, then release it */
   if (bHaveSemaphore)
   {
      bHaveSemaphore = FALSE;
      WinSetDlgItemText (hWndMain, IDC_STATE,
            "Running");
```

```
            DosReleaseMutexSem(ThreadSem);
         }

         /* If the user has indicated this thread should request
         the semaphore each time the thermometer value reaches
         zero, then request it.  If after 2 seconds the thread
         hasn't received the semaphore, then continue on anyway.*/
         if (bDoSemaphore)
         {
            WinSetDlgItemText (hWndMain, IDC_STATE,
                  "Req Sem");
            RetCode = DosRequestMutexSem (ThreadSem, 2000L);
            if (RetCode == 0L)
            {
               bHaveSemaphore = TRUE;
               WinSetDlgItemText (hWndMain, IDC_STATE,
                  "Semaphore");
            }
            else if (RetCode == ERROR_TIMEOUT)
               WinSetDlgItemText (hWndMain, IDC_STATE,
                  "Sem Timeout");
            else if (RetCode == ERROR_SEM_OWNER_DIED)
               WinSetDlgItemText (hWndMain, IDC_STATE,
                  "Sem Owner Died");
            else
               WinSetDlgItemText (hWndMain, IDC_STATE,
                  "Sem Req Error");
         }

         /* Give lower priority threads a chance to do something */
         DosSleep (5L);

      }
      else if (ulValue == 100)
         lIncDec = -1L;
      ulValue += lIncDec;

   } while (bContinue);

   return;
}

/* -------- Window and Dialog Functions -------- */

MRESULT EXPENTRY ClientWndProc (HWND hWnd, ULONG msg,
      MPARAM mp1, MPARAM mp2)
{
   BOOL     bHandled = TRUE;
   MRESULT  mReturn  = 0;
   RECTL    Rectl;
   HPS      hps;
   HENUM    hEnum;
   TID      ThreadID;
   HWND     hWndThread;
   SHORT    sNewScrollPos;
```

```
switch (msg)
{
   case WM_PAINT:
      hps = WinBeginPaint (hWnd,0L,NULL);
      WinQueryWindowRect (hWnd, &Rectl);
      WinFillRect (hps, &Rectl, CLR_PALEGRAY);
      WinEndPaint (hps);
      break;

   case WM_SIZE:
      ArrangeThreadWindows ();
      break;

   case WM_INITMENU:
      if (SHORT1FROMMP(mp1) == IDM_THREADS)
         WinEnableMenuItem ((HWND)mp2,
         IDM_KILLALLTHREADS, (ulThreadCnt > 1L));
      break;

   case WM_VSCROLL:
      sNewScrollPos = sScrollPos;
      switch (SHORT2FROMMP(mp2))
      {
         case SB_LINEUP:
            sNewScrollPos--;
            break;

         case SB_LINEDOWN:
            sNewScrollPos++;
            break;

         case SB_PAGEUP:
            sNewScrollPos -= (SHORT)RectlTID.yTop;
            break;

         case SB_PAGEDOWN:
            sNewScrollPos += (SHORT)RectlTID.yTop;
            break;

         case SB_SLIDERPOSITION:
            sNewScrollPos = SHORT1FROMMP(mp2);
            break;
      }

      sNewScrollPos = (SHORT)max (0, min (sNewScrollPos,
            sScrollRange));
      if (sNewScrollPos != sScrollPos)
      {
         WinScrollWindow (hWndClient, 0L,
            sNewScrollPos - sScrollPos, NULL, NULL, 0,
            NULL, SW_SCROLLCHILDREN | SW_INVALIDATERGN);
         sScrollPos = sNewScrollPos;
         WinSendDlgItemMsg (hWndFrame, FID_VERTSCROLL,
            SBM_SETPOS, MPFROMSHORT(sScrollPos), 0L);
         WinUpdateWindow (hWndClient);
      }
```

```
         break;

       case WM_COMMAND:
          switch (LOUSHORT(mp1))
          {
             case IDM_NEWQMSGTHREAD:
                DosCreateThread (&ThreadID,
                   (PFNTHREAD)ThermometerThread,
                   (ULONG)hWndClient, 0, 0x5000);
                break;

             case IDM_NEWSORTINGTHREAD:
                CreateSortingThread (hWnd);
                break;

             case IDM_KILLALLTHREADS:
                hEnum = WinBeginEnumWindows (hWnd);
                while (hWndThread = WinGetNextWindow (hEnum))
                {
                   /* Don't kill the main thread */
                   if (WinQueryWindowUShort
                         (hWndThread, QWS_ID) > 1L)
                      WinPostMsg (hWndThread, WM_USER_KILL,
                         0L, 0L);
                }
                WinEndEnumWindows (hEnum);
                break;

             case IDM_ARRANGE:
                ArrangeThreadWindows ();
                break;

             case IDM_ABOUT:
                DisplayAbout (hWnd, szTitle);
                break;
          }

       default:
          bHandled = FALSE;
          break;
    }

    if (!bHandled)
       mReturn = WinDefWindowProc (hWnd,msg,mp1,mp2);

    return (mReturn);
}

MRESULT EXPENTRY TIDDlgProc (HWND hWnd, ULONG msg,
      MPARAM mp1, MPARAM mp2)
{
   PPIB     ppib;
   PTIB     ptib;
   MRESULT mReturn  = 0L;
   BOOL     bHandled = TRUE;
```

```
switch (msg)
{
   case WM_INITDLG:
      /* Initialize thread dialog values */
      DosGetInfoBlocks (&ptib, &ppib);
      WinSetWindowUShort (hWnd, QWS_ID,
         (USHORT)((ptib->tib_ptib2)->tib2_ultid));
      WinSetDlgItemShort (hWnd, IDC_THREADID,
         (USHORT)((ptib->tib_ptib2)->tib2_ultid), FALSE);
      WinSetDlgItemShort (hWnd, IDC_THREADPRIORITY,
         (USHORT)((ptib->tib_ptib2)->tib2_ulpri), FALSE);
      WinEnableControl (hWnd, IDC_DOWNPRIORITY, FALSE);

      /* Set thermometer attributes */
      WinSendDlgItemMsg (hWnd, IDC_THERMOMETER,
         THM_SETRANGE, 0L, (MPARAM)100L);
      WinSendDlgItemMsg (hWnd, IDC_THERMOMETER,
         THM_SETVALUE, 0L, 0L);
      WinSendDlgItemMsg (hWnd, IDC_THERMOMETER,
         THM_SETCOLOR,
         MPFROM2SHORT((ptib->tib_ptib2)->tib2_ultid % 15,
         CLR_PALEGRAY), 0L);

      /* Store the size of the thread dialog window */
      WinQueryWindowRect (hWnd, &RectlTID);
      break;

   case WM_COMMAND:
      switch (LOUSHORT(mp1))
      {
         case IDC_KILL:
            WinPostMsg (hWnd, WM_USER_KILL, 0L, 0L);
            break;

         case IDC_UPPRIORITY:
            WinPostMsg (hWnd, WM_USER_UPPRIORITY, 0L,
                  0L);
            break;

         case IDC_DOWNPRIORITY:
            WinPostMsg (hWnd, WM_USER_DOWNPRIORITY, 0L,
                  0L);
            break;

         case IDC_CRITSECTION:
            WinPostMsg (hWnd, WM_USER_CRITSECTION, 0L,
                  0L);
            break;

         case IDC_SEMAPHORE:
            WinPostMsg (hWnd, WM_USER_SEMAPHORE, 0L, 0L);
            break;
      }
      break;

   default:
```

```
            bHandled = FALSE;
            break;
      }

      if (!bHandled)
         mReturn = WinDefDlgProc (hWnd, msg, mp1, mp2);

      return (mReturn);
}

MRESULT EXPENTRY SortingDlgProc (HWND hWnd, ULONG msg,
      MPARAM mp1, MPARAM mp2)
{
   TID      ThreadID;
   HPS      hps;
   HWND     hWndCtl;
   RECTL    Rectl;
   MRESULT mReturn  = 0L;
   BOOL     bHandled = TRUE;

   switch (msg)
   {
      case WM_USER_PERCENTCOMPLETE:
         /* Update the percent complete bar in the dialog */
         WinSetDlgItemShort (hWnd, IDC_PERCENT,
               (USHORT)mp1, FALSE);
         hWndCtl = WinWindowFromID (hWnd, IDC_PERCENTBAR);
         WinQueryWindowRect (hWndCtl, &Rectl);
         hps = WinGetPS (hWndCtl);
         WinDrawBorder (hps, &Rectl, 1L, 1L,
             SYSCLR_BUTTONDARK,
            SYSCLR_BUTTONMIDDLE, DB_RAISED);
         WinInflateRect (hab, &Rectl, -1L, -1L);
         Rectl.xRight = (Rectl.xRight * (ULONG)mp1) / 100;
         WinFillRect (hps, &Rectl, SYSCLR_ACTIVETITLE);
         WinReleasePS (hps);

         /* If sorting is 100% complete then beep and destroy the
         status window */
         if ((ULONG)mp1 == 100L)
         {
            DosBeep (1000L, 75L);
            DosBeep (800L, 75L);
            /* A process would now use the sorted array. Since
            this is a demonstration, just free the memory */
            DosFreeMem (WinQueryWindowPtr (hWnd, QWL_USER));
            WinDestroyWindow (hWnd);
         }
         break;

      case WM_COMMAND:
         ThreadID = (TID)WinQueryWindowUShort (hWnd,
               QWS_ID);
         switch (LOUSHORT(mp1))
         {
            case IDC_KILL:
```

```
                DosKillThread (ThreadID);
                DosFreeMem (WinQueryWindowPtr (hWnd,
                      QWL_USER));
                WinDestroyWindow (hWnd);
                break;

             case IDC_SUSPEND:
                WinSetDlgItemText (hWnd, IDC_SUSPEND,
                   "Resume");
                WinSetWindowUShort (
                      WinWindowFromID (hWnd, IDC_SUSPEND),
                      QWS_ID, IDC_RESUME);
                DosSuspendThread (ThreadID);
                break;

             case IDC_RESUME:
                WinSetDlgItemText (hWnd, IDC_RESUME,
                   "Suspend");
                WinSetWindowUShort (
                      WinWindowFromID (hWnd, IDC_RESUME),
                      QWS_ID, IDC_SUSPEND);
                DosResumeThread (ThreadID);
                break;

             case IDC_UPPRIORITY:
                /* Increase the priority */
                DosSetPriority (PRTYS_THREAD, PRTYC_NOCHANGE,
                      1L, ThreadID);
                break;

             case IDC_DOWNPRIORITY:
                /* Decrease the priority */
                DosSetPriority (PRTYS_THREAD, PRTYC_NOCHANGE,
                      -1L, ThreadID);
                break;
          }
          break;

       default:
          bHandled = FALSE;
          break;
    }

    if (!bHandled)
       mReturn = WinDefDlgProc (hWnd, msg, mp1, mp2);

    return (mReturn);
}
```

We are doing something a little differently for our main message processing loop. Normally, an application uses a `WinGetMsg` loop to retrieve and process messages; however, `WinGetMsg` does not return from the call until a message is placed in the message queue. Because this demonstration is showing the active CPU time of a thread, we want to continuously update the thermometer to show the thread's activity. For that reason, we are using a `WinPeekMsg` loop to pull messages from the queue. As long as messages are in the queue, they will be retrieved and processed. When there are no more messages, the thread will increment or decrement its counter and update the thermometer. When a new message queue thread is created, it calls CreateThreadWindow. CreateThreadWindow loads a dialog window for the thread and increments the count of the number of message queue threads. Because it is possible for two threads to be in the process of creating or even for a thread to be terminating while another is being created, we must protect the ulThreadCnt variable. This is done by enclosing the incrementing of the counter in a critical section:

```
DosEnterCritSec();
ulThreadCnt++;
DosExitCritSec();
```

Likewise, the counter is protected in DestroyThreadWindow when the counter is being decremented:

```
DosEnterCritSec();
ulThreadCnt-;
DosExitCritSec();
```

Before examining the message processing loop and the threads, let's look at the window and dialog functions and their processing of the commands. First, we look at ClientWndProc. When the Message Queue Thread menu option is selected, an IDM_NEWMSGTHREAD command is received. This is handled by creating a new thread starting at the function ThermometerThread:

```
case IDM_NEWQMSGTHREAD:
   DosCreateThread (&ThreadID,
      (PFNTHREAD)ThermometerThread,
      (ULONG)hWndClient, 0, 0x5000);
   break;
```

Remember that when a new thread is created, its initial priority is the same as the thread that creates it. In this case, that is thread one. Selecting Sorting Thread will generate an IDM_NEWSORTINGTHREAD command, which is handled by calling CreateSortingThread:

```
case IDM_NEWSORTINGTHREAD:
   CreateSortingThread (hWnd);
   break;
```

CreateSortingThread will create a nonmessage queue sorting thread by allocating a block of memory to contain the 4KB array of unsigned long integers. The sorting thread needs to receive a couple of items of information specific to the thread. This is passed to the thread in a SORTDATA structure:

```
typedef struct
{
   HWND    hWndDlg;          /* Dialog window handle      */
   ULONG   ulCnt;            /* Number of entries to sort */
   ULONG   ulArray[1];       /* Array of data to sort     */
} SORTDATA;
```

The SORTDATA structure contains the handle of the dialog window to post its messages to and the array of data to sort. With the dialog window loaded, it creates the thread starting at the function SortingThread:

```
DosCreateThread (&ThreadID, (PFNTHREAD)SortingThread,
      (ULONG)pData, 0x0001, 0x2000);
```

Note that this thread is created in a suspended state. This is needed so that the creating thread can initialize the dialog fields with the thread identifier. After all post thread creation setup is complete, the thread is started:

```
DosResumeThread (ThreadID);
```

All the message queue threads can be killed by selecting Kill All Message Queue Threads. The IDM_KILLALLTHREADS command is processed by enumerating all windows that are children of the client window. After the dialog window for a message queue thread is created, its identifier is set to the thread's identifier. When the windows are enumerated, we can check the identifier to ensure that we do not kill thread 1. Message queue threads are killed by posting a message to the dialog window that will be handled by the thread.

The dialog function for the message queue threads is contained in TIDDlgProc. This function responds to all messages generated by the buttons by posting a user message back to the dialog window indicating the action to perform. Because TIDDlgProc is executing on behalf of each thread, we could handle the WM_COMMAND message in the message loop without posting another message. We will soon look at how each of these messages are handled in the message loop.

The dialog function for the nonmessage queue threads is contained in SortingDlgProc. The dialog created for the sorting thread is owned by thread 1, and thus the dialog function executes as part of thread 1. As sorting is being performed, the thread posts a WM_USER_PERCENTCOMPLETE message with the current percentage contained in the mp1 parameter. The dialog function updates the status bar and percent fields. If sorting is 100 percent complete, the application normally does something with the sorted data. We aren't doing anything with it, so we free the allocated memory (pointer saved in the QWL_USER field of the dialog window). When a command message is received by the dialog function, the thread responds by killing, suspending, or resuming the sorting thread:

```
case IDC_KILL:
   DosKillThread (ThreadID);
   DosFreeMem (WinQueryWindowPtr (hWnd, QWL_USER));
   WinDestroyWindow (hWnd);
   break;

case IDC_SUSPEND:
   WinSetDlgItemText (hWnd, IDC_SUSPEND, "Resume");
   WinSetWindowUShort (
      WinWindowFromID (hWnd, IDC_SUSPEND),
      QWS_ID, IDC_RESUME);
   DosSuspendThread (ThreadID);
   break;

case IDC_RESUME:
   WinSetDlgItemText (hWnd, IDC_RESUME, "Suspend");
```

```
        WinSetWindowUShort (
           WinWindowFromID (hWnd, IDC_RESUME),
           QWS_ID, IDC_SUSPEND);
        DosResumeThread (ThreadID);
        break;
```

When a change in priority is requested, we either increment or decrement the priority without modifying the priority class:

```
     case IDC_UPPRIORITY:
        /* Increase the priority */
        DosSetPriority (PRTYS_THREAD, PRTYC_NOCHANGE, 1L,
        ThreadID);
        break;

     case IDC_DOWNPRIORITY:
        /* Decrease the priority */
        DosSetPriority (PRTYS_THREAD, PRTYC_NOCHANGE, -1L,
           ThreadID);
        break;
```

ThreadMessageLoop handles all the message processing for all the message queue threads. Again, remember that this function is called on behalf of each thread. Though it is the same code, it is using the message queue and stack for the thread that is currently active. This function simply enters into a loop. At the top of the loop, the function retrieves any messages from the queue and either handles them locally or dispatches them. There is only one way out of this function, and that is to set bContinue to TRUE. This is done if either the WM_QUIT or WM_USER_KILL message is received. If the WM_USER_UPPRIORITY or WM_USER_DOWNPRIORITY message is received, the thread adjusts its priority:

```
  DosSetPriority (PRTYS_THREAD, PRTYC_REGULAR,
        lPriority, 0L);
```

This time we use the other variation of DosSetPriority where we specify an explicit priority class and an absolute priority level. When the WM_USER_CRITSECTION or the WM_USER_SEMAPHORE message is received, the corresponding flag is toggled. When there are no more messages to process, the function exits the WinPeekMsg loop where the thread priority field is updated. If this thread is performing critical section simulation, the thread enters into a critical section for 1/10 second:

```
  DosEnterCritSec ();
  DosSleep (100L);
  DosExitCritSec ();
```

When the thermometer value reaches zero, we check whether the thread owns the semaphore. If so, the thread releases the semaphore:

```
if (bHaveSemaphore)
{
   bHaveSemaphore = FALSE;
   WinSetDlgItemText (hWndMain, IDC_STATE, "Running");
   DosReleaseMutexSem(ThreadSem);
}
```

If the thread is using the semaphore simulation, the thread requests the semaphore with a timeout of two seconds:

```
RetCode = DosRequestMutexSem (ThreadSem, 2000L);
```

Each time the thermometer value reaches zero, it also calls `DosSleep` for 5 milliseconds—this is to be somewhat of a good neighbor. If there are lower priority threads, they may be starved out by a higher priority thread. This is possible especially with this simulation, where the thread is constantly checking the message queue and processing with little chance for delay or interruption. Threads that use `WinGetMsg` do not have to worry about adding a `DosSleep` call, because the thread will only be doing something as long as messages are in the queue.

Finally, we look at the thread functions themselves. `ThermometerThread` is the message queue thread. It creates a message queue, calls `CallThreadWindow` to get its dialog window, and calls `ThreadMessageLoop` to process all the thread messages and update the thermometer. When the thread receives the `WM_QUIT` or `WM_USER_KILL` message, the thread returns from `ThreadMessageLoop`, destroys the message queue, and terminates the thread.

`SortingThread` has less to be concerned about because it does not have a message queue. This thread simply performs its function and terminates when done. In this case, it does the bubblesort while posting the `WM_USER_PERCENTCOMPLETE` message to the dialog. It also is possible for this thread to update directly the status bar in the dialog window by getting the handle to the presentation space and drawing directly into it. Because we also are updating fields in the dialog, the drawing code was kept with the field update code.

Thread Observations

Running the thread demonstration program will show you a lot about how threads work and how changing the various parameters affect all the other threads. Here are suggestions for what to try and watch for.

ACTION	Create an additional message queue thread.
RESULT	Notice that the rate at which the thermometers are updated slows. This is because the CPU time is being distributed among more threads now.
ACTION	Create multiple message queue threads. Increase the priority of one thread by clicking the Up button.
RESULT	Notice that the rate at which the higher priority thread updates its thermometer increases, while all other threads slow down considerably. This is because as long as the higher priority thread is ready to run, it will receive the next time slice before any lower priority threads. The other threads will slowly change because the higher priority thread is periodically calling DosSleep.

ACTION	Create multiple message queue threads. Click the CritSec button for one of the threads.
RESULT	Notice that all the thermometers' changes seem jumpy. This occurs because each time the thread that is clicked changes its thermometer value, it enters a critical section. Entering a critical section causes all other threads to be suspended until the critical section is exited.
ACTION	Create multiple message queue threads. Click the Semaphore button for two or more threads.
RESULT	Only one of the threads with semaphores enabled should be updating its thermometer at any time. This occurs because each time one thread's thermometer value reaches zero, it requests the semaphore. Because only one thread can own the semaphore at a time, the other threads will be blocked until the semaphore is released. The only exception to this is when the semaphore requests timeout, in which case the timed-out thread will become unblocked and continue. You will see this occur when you have several message queue threads with semaphores enabled in each.
ACTION	Create multiple message queue threads. Move the mouse over each thread window.
RESULT	The thermometer for the thread under the mouse will be updated at a higher rate while the mouse is being moved. Moving the mouse over a window causes a WM_HITTEST message to be sent to the window under the mouse. Sending this message causes the priority of the window receiving the message to be increased temporarily so it can respond quickly to the message.
ACTION	Create a sorting thread window.
RESULT	Again, notice that the thermometers for the message queue windows will be updated at a slower rate.
ACTION	Create multiple sorting thread windows. Move the mouse over the sorting thread windows.
RESULT	Notice that the sorting threads do not execute at a faster rate, in general. This is because the dialog windows are created by thread 1, and it is thread 1 that is receiving the WM_HITTEST messages, not the sorting threads. There is, therefore, no need to increase the priority of the sorting thread in order to respond to the message sent.
ACTION	Create multiple message queue threads. Create a sorting thread window. Suspend the sorting thread. Move the mouse over the sorting thread window.
RESULT	The thermometer for thread 1 will change at a faster rate than the other message queue thermometers. This is because the sorting dialog window is created by thread 1, and it is thread 1 that is receiving the WM_HITTEST messages, thus getting a temporary boost in priority.

It is worth noting that in most multithreaded applications, only one message queue thread is dedicated to processing messages, while all other threads are for performing specific functions such as drawing, calculating, or printing. As mentioned earlier, this application is used to demonstrate visually the effect of various changes to threads. Experiment with creating different threads and trying different options. You may be surprised how well OS/2 handles the various situations, and more important, you may see how to optimize your threads.

In addition to this application, several other applications in this book use multithreading. The Printing application shows how an application prints. With a few minor alterations, the application is changed to perform the printing in a thread. In the file PRNT.C, the `WM_START_PRINT` message is modified to call `DosCreateThread`:

```
case WM_START_PRINT:
   if (SHORT1FROMMP(mp2) == IDM_PRINT)
      process_print((HWND)mp1);
   else
      DosCreateThread(&tid,(PFNTHREAD)process_print,
         (ULONG)mp1, 0,0x2000);
   break;
```

Because the `process_print` function makes a copy of the `DEVICEINFO` data, each print thread will have its own copy and can print independently of other activity in the application. Note, however, that the print application is merely printing predefined graphics commands. If your application, for example, is printing the contents of a file currently being edited, additional work must be done either to make a copy of the file to be printed or to synchronize updates to the file with what is currently being printed by the print thread.

In the application for communications, a separate thread is used to monitor the status of the communications port and another thread to process input from the communications port. Among the miscellaneous applications at the end of the book, multithreading is used to perform a file search on any drive while enabling the user to continue interacting with the application.

and received by the ASYNC device driver as part of the normal operation of OS/2 and occurs while other activities and applications are executing. The driver coordinates requests to send and receive data from the applications. Because we are running in a multitasking environment and the system must deal with hardware interrupts, it is not always possible for the hardware to be ready when a request to send data occurs. Likewise, the hardware may receive data from the remote connection when the application is not ready to receive it.

To support these contingencies, the driver makes use of a transmit queue and a receive queue. The transmit queue is used to buffer the data sent from the application for which data has not yet been transmitted or sent to the physical hardware. To buffer data means that it is stored in a sequential manner until the facility is available to send it or act on it. The receive queue is used to buffer the data received from the physical hardware that has not yet been requested from the application. The driver is responsible for coordinating the flow of data through these buffers and talking with the physical hardware.

We can illustrate the flow of data in both directions. When an application wants to transmit data, it makes a call to the ASYNC device driver to send the data. As shown in Figure 15.1, the driver places the data into the transmit queue.

Figure 15.1.
Transmit queue data buffer.

Figure 15.2 illustrates the hardware's retrieval of data from the transmit queue. When the hardware signals the driver that it is ready to transmit, the driver then hands off the data to the hardware.

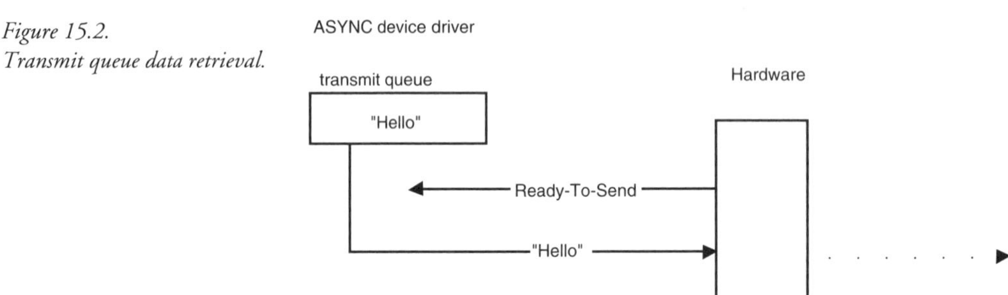

Figure 15.2.
Transmit queue data retrieval.

Just the opposite activity occurs when data is received by the device driver. Figure 15.3 illustrates the hardware copying the data into the receive queue. When the hardware receives data, it signals the ASYNC device driver that data has been received and is ready to be retrieved. The driver places the data into the receive queue.

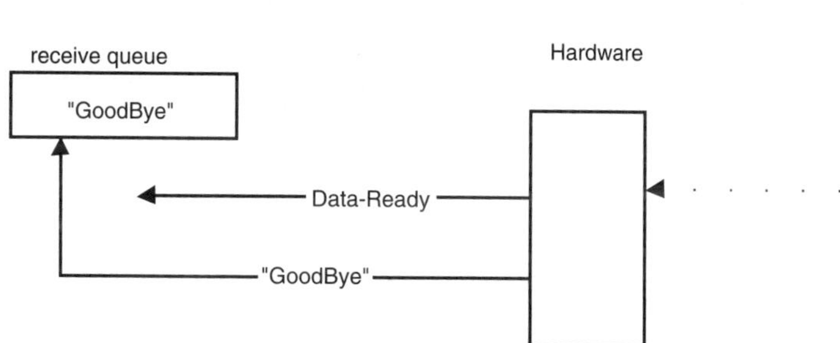

Figure 15.3.
Receive queue data buffering.

When the application requests data from the ASYNC device driver, the driver satisfies the request by moving the data from the receive queue to the application. Figure 15.4 illustrates this process.

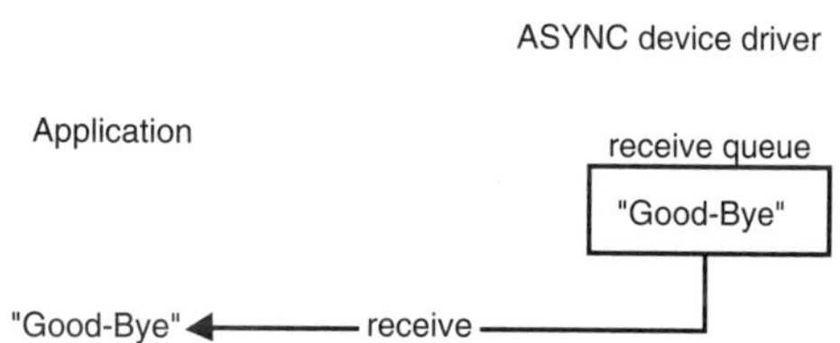

Figure 15.4.
Receive queue data retrieval.

The ASYNC device driver is capable of supporting multiple communications ports at the same time. Each port has its own set of transmit and receive buffers. The ASYNC device driver also supports a feature called *Extended Hardware Buffering.* This is a feature of the hardware that allows the hardware to buffer data itself and only send the buffer when a hardware interrupt occurs. Normally, the hardware operates in character mode whereby the hardware services one character at a time. Transmission and receipt of each character requires separate interrupts. This requires quite a bit of overhead for the hardware. With Extended Hardware Buffering, the hardware can send multiple characters with a single interrupt. This can significantly reduce the number of interrupts that must occur and improve the throughput of the data.

As coordinator of all communication activities between the application and hardware, it is the responsibility of the ASYNC driver to manage the flow of data and monitor various events. There are several hardware settings and states of flow control that can be set by an application.

Hardware Settings

There are a number of terms used for data communications. It is necessary to understand their meaning in order to work with communications effectively.

The baud rate refers to the rate at which data is transferred. This value is specified in bits per second (bps) and must match the current speed setting of the hardware device. Examples of the baud rate are 1200 bps and 2400 bps.

The data bits specify the number of bits that contain data in each character transferred. Valid values are 5 through 8.

The stop bits specify the number of bits that are used to separate each character. Valid values are 1, 1.5, and 2.

Parity refers to the type of parity checking performed on the data. Parity checking is used to check that the data is transferred successfully and that no data has been lost. Valid values are none, even, odd, mark, and space.

Read timeout enabling allows you to indicate how long to wait when requesting data from the driver. There are three options. If a request is made to read data and there is no data available, the request can fail immediately and return. This is called no-wait read timeout. Using this timeout, your application is not forced to wait around for data to appear. If the same request is made and no data is available within a specified amount of time, the request fails and returns. This is called normal read timeout. Finally, if the request is made but it should not return until some data is available, this is called wait-for-something timeout. Wait-for-something timeout can return without any data, but only after a specified period of time.

Write timeout is similar to read timeout except it refers to the amount of time to wait for the driver to transmit the data sent to it. If the driver sends data to the hardware and should wait until all data is transmitted, then it is called infinite timeout. If the driver should only wait on the hardware for a specified time and return even if all data has not been transmitted, it is referred to as normal timeout.

All timeout periods are specified in hundredths of a second.

Flow Control

Flow control determines how the ASYNC driver behaves when the receive and transmit queues contain a certain level of data. When Receive Flow Control is enabled, the driver will send an XOFF character when the receive queue is nearly full. This tells the remote driver to cease transmitting data until it receives the XON character.

When the receive queue drops back down to about half full, it transmits the XON character, which tells the remote driver that it is okay to transmit more data. When Transmit Flow Control is enabled, the driver responds to the XOFF and XON characters by suspending the transmission of data when it receives the XOFF character and resuming transmission when it receives the XON character. It is still possible for an application to transmit data when the driver has received the XOFF character and is not currently transmitting. The application can perform a "transmit immediate" operation, which forces the character to be sent.

It is possible for an error to occur during the transmission of data. Examples of errors are parity errors caused by a noisy transmission line. Another error is a full receive queue. If error replacement character processing is enabled, the driver will substitute all characters in error with an error replacement character.

When the driver detects a break condition on the line, it can likewise notify the application. If break replacement character processing is enabled, the driver will notify the application by inserting the specified break character into the receive queue.

The driver can also filter out null characters (0x00). This is called null stripping. When null stripping is enabled, all null characters that the driver receives are thrown away.

Communicating with the ASYNC Device Driver

Before using the ASYNC device driver, it must be installed when your system boots. The driver is installed by placing the appropriate `DEVICE` statement in the CONFIG.SYS file:

```
DEVICE=C:\OS2\COM.SYS
```

A communications port, COM2 for example, is opened just as any other file is opened. Use the `DosOpen` function to open a file named COMx, where x is the number of the communications port. To open the COM2 port, for example, issue the following call:

```
HFILE hFile;
ULONG ulAction;

DosOpen ("COM2", &hFile, &ulAction, 0L, FILE_NORMAL,
      FILE_OPEN,OPEN_ACCESS_READWRITE ¦ OPEN_SHARE_DENYNONE,

      0L);
```

Notice that the access mode of `OPEN_SHARE_DENYNONE` allows multiple processes to share the communications port. To prevent other processes from opening the same communications port, use `OPEN_SHARE_DENYREADWRITE`. To write data out of the communications port, use the `DosWrite` function; to read data, use the `DosRead` function. When communications is complete and you want to terminate use of the port, call the `DosClose` function. You can see how similar this operation is to working with files.

The *DosDevIOCtl* Function

When the port has been opened and a file handle returned, an application can communicate with the ASYNC device driver via the `DosDevIOCtl` function. The `DosDevIOCtl` function contains many subfunctions that specify the particular action for the device driver to perform.

This is one of the more confusing functions to use in OS/2. It can be used for interaction with the serial port, as well as the video driver, keyboard, mouse, and other things. As you might imagine, given that it can be used with so many different subsystems, the structure of the input and output parameters for the function is generic. Take a look at the function definition below. The first three parameters are easily understood. They are a handle to a device, the category of subfunction, and the specific function within that category. In our case here, the only functions with which we are concerned are those that involve the serial port. These are category 01. Within this category are 27 other subfunctions that govern serial communications. The confusing part is the generic means needed for input and output parameters for all the possible subfunctions:

The particulars of the `DosDevIOCtl` function are listed below:

```
APIRET APIENTRY DosDevIOCtl(HFILE hDevice, ULONG category,

      ULONG function, PVOID pParams, ULONG cbParmLenMax,

      PULONG pcbParmLen, PVOID pData, ULONG cbDataLenMax,

      PULONG pcbDataLen)
```

Parameter Descriptions:

Parameter	***Description***
`hDevice`	File handle returned from `DosOpen`.
`category`	Device category. `IOCTL_ASYNC`—Asynchronous Device Support function—Device function. There are others, but this is the only one with which we are concerned here.
`pParams`	Input parameter list for function.
`cbParmLenMax`	Maximum length of data in `pParams`.
`pcbParmLen`	Pointer to variable to receive length of return parameters in `pParams`.
`pData`	Pointer to output data area.
`cbDataLenMax`	Maximum length of data in `pData`.
`pcbDataLen`	Pointer to variable to receive length of return parameters in `pData`.

Let's make a quick rundown of each of the `IOCTL_ASYNC` functions and the parameters specified for each.

ASYNC_SETBAUDRATE—Set Baud Rate

Input data:
`USHORT`—Baud rate

Example:

```
USHORT usBaudRate = 1200;
DosDevIOCtl (hFile, IOCTL_ASYNC, ASYNC_SETBAUDRATE,
   (PVOID)&usBaudRate, sizeof(USHORT), NULL, NULL,

   0L,NULL);
```

ASYNC_SETLINECTRL—Set Line Characteristics

Input data:

`LINECONTROL`—Line control information. This is the structure:

```
typedef struct _LINECONTROL
```

Its fields and the allowable values are listed below:

`BYTE`	`bDataBits`	
	`0x05`	5 data bits
	`0x06`	6 data bits
	`0x07`	7 data bits
	`0x08`	8 data bits
`BYTE`	`bParity`	
	`0x00`	None
	`0x01`	Odd
	`0x02`	Even
	`0x03`	Mark
	`0x04`	Space
`BYTE`	`bStopBits`	
	`0x00`	1 stop bit
	`0x01`	1.5 stop bits
	`0x02`	2 stop bits
`BYTE`	`fTransBreak`	
	`0x00`	No break character transmitted.
	`0x01`	Transmit break character.

Example:

```
LINECONTROL LineControl;
LineControl.bDataBits   = 8;       /* 8 data bits    */
LineControl.bParity     = 0x00;    /* Parity None    */
LineControl.bStopBits   = 0x00;    /* 1 stop bit     */
LineControl.fTransBreak = 0x01;    /* Transmit break */
DosDevIOCtl (hFile, IOCTL_ASYNC, ASYNC_SETLINECTRL,
   &LineControl, sizeof(LINECONTROL), NULL, NULL, 0L,
   NULL);
```

ASYNC_TRANSMITIMM—Transmit Byte Immediate

Input Data:
CHAR—Character to transmit

Example:

```
CHAR ch = 'X';
DosDevIOCtl (hFile, IOCTL_ASYNC, ASYNC_TRANSMITIMM,
     &ch, sizeof(CHAR), NULL, NULL, 0L, NULL);
```

ASYNC_SETBREAKOFF—Turn Off Break Character

Output Data:
USHORT—Communications error flags

RX_QUE_OVERRUN	Receive queue is full.
RX_HARDWARE_OVERRUN	New character received before last character processed. New character is lost.
PARITY_ERROR	Parity error detected.
FRAMING_ERROR	Framing error detected.

Example:

```
USHORT usComError;
DosDevIOCtl (hFile, IOCTL_ASYNC, ASYNC_SETBREAKOFF,
   NULL, 0L, NULL, (PVOID)&usComError,

   sizeof(USHORT),NULL);
```

ASYNC_SETMODEMCTRL—Set the Modem Control Signals

Input Data:
MODEMSTATUS—Modem control masks

This is the structure:

```
typedef struct _MODEMSTATUS
```

Its fields and allowable values are listed below:

BYTE fbModemOn	Specifies Flags to Turn On
DTR_ON	Set DTR flag
RTS_ON	Set RTS flag
BYTE fbModemOff	Specifies Flags to Turn Off
DTR_OFF	Clear DTR flag
RTS_OFF	Clear RTS flag

Note: If both DTR_ON and DTR_OFF are specified, the flag is turned on. If both RTS_ON and RTS_OFF are specified, the flag is also turned on.

Output Data:
USHORT—Communications error flags

The following flags are valid:

RX_QUE_OVERRUN	Receive queue is full.
RX_HARDWARE_OVERRUN	New character received before last character processed. New character is lost.
PARITY_ERROR	Parity error detected.
FRAMING_ERROR	Framing error detected.

Example:

```
MODEMSTATUS ModemStatus;
USHORT      usComError;
ModemStatus.fbModemOn  = DTR_ON ¦ RTS_ON;
ModemStatus.fbModemOff = 0;
DosDevIOCtl (hFile, IOCTL_ASYNC, ASYNC_SETMODEMCTRL,
   (PVOID)&ModemStatus, sizeof(MODEMSTATUS), NULL,
   (PVOID)&usComError, sizeof(USHORT), NULL);
```

ASYNC_SETBREAKON—Turn On Break Character

Output Data:
USHORT—Communications error flags

The following flags are valid:

RX_QUE_OVERRUN	Receive queue is full.
RX_HARDWARE_OVERRUN	New character received before last character processed. New character is lost.
PARITY_ERROR	Parity error detected.
FRAMING_ERROR	Framing error detected.

Example:

```
USHORT usComError;
DosDevIOCtl (hFile, IOCTL_ASYNC, ASYNC_SETBREAKON,
   NULL, 0L, NULL, (PVOID)&usComError,

   sizeof(USHORT),NULL);
```

ASYNC_STOPTRANSMIT—Turn Off Transmission (XOFF Received)

Example:

```
DosDevIOCtl (hFile, IOCTL_ASYNC, ASYNC_STOPTRANSMIT,
   NULL, 0L, NULL, NULL, 0L, NULL);
```

ASYNC_STARTTRANSMIT—Turn On Transmission (XON Received)

Example:

```
DosDevIOCtl (hFile, IOCTL_ASYNC, ASYNC_STARTTRANSMIT,
   NULL, 0L, NULL, NULL, 0L, NULL);
```

ASYNC_SETDCBINFO—Set Device Control Block Information

Input Data:
DCBINFO—Device control block information

This is the structure:

```
typedef struct _DCBINFO
```

It has the following fields and defined values:

USHORT	usWriteTimeout	Write timeout time period (hundredths of a second).
USHORT	usReadTimeout	Read timeout time period (hundredths of a second).
BYTE	fbCtlHndShake	Specifies control and handshaking modes:
	MODE_DTR_CONTROL	Enable DTR Control Mode.
	MODE_DTR_HANDSHAKE	Enable DTR Control input handshaking.
	MODE_CTS_HANDSHAKE	Enable CTS output handshaking.
	MODE_DSR_HANDSHAKE	Enable DSR output handshaking.
	MODE_DCD_HANDSHAKE	Enable DCD output handshaking.
	MODE_DSR_SENSITIVITY	Enable DSR input sensitivity.

Note: MODE_DTR_CONTROL and MODE_DTR_HANDSHAKE cannot be specified together.

BYTE	fbFlowReplace	Specifies flow control and replacement character modes:
	MODE_AUTO_TRANSMIT	Enables auto transmit flow control (XON and XOFF).
	MODE_AUTO_RECEIVE	Enables auto receive flow control (XON and XOFF).
	MODE_ERROR_CHAR	Enables error replacement character.
BYTE	fbFlowReplace	Specifies flow control and replacement character modes:
	MODE_NULL_STRIPPING	Enables null stripping.
	MODE_BREAK_CHAR	Enables break replacement control (XON and XOFF).
	0x20	Enables full duplex flow control.
	MODE_RTS_CONTROL	Enables RTS control mode.
	MODE_RTS_HANDSHAKE	Enables RTS input handshaking.
	MODE_TRANSMIT_TOGGLE	Toggles RTS on transmit.
BYTE	fbTimeout	Specifies timeout process for device:
	MODE_NO_WRITE_TIMEOUT	Enables write infinite.
	MODE_READ_TIMEOUT	Enables normal read.
	MODE_WAIT_READ_TIMEOUT	Enables wait-for-something read.
	MODE_NOWAIT_READ_TIMEOUT	Enables no-wait read.
	0x08	Disables extended hardware buffering.
	0x10	Enables extended hardware buffering.
	0x18	Automatic protocol override.
	0x20	Extended buffer size of 4 characters.
	0x40	Extended buffer size of 8 characters.
	0x60	Extended buffer size of 16 characters.
	0x80	Transmit buffer size of 16 characters.

Note: Extended buffer size is 1 character unless otherwise specified. Transmit buffer size is 1 character unless otherwise specified.

BYTE	bErrorReplacementChar	Character inserted when character in error received.
BYTE	bBreakReplacementChar	Character inserted when break detected in line.
BYTE	bXONChar	Character used for XON signal.
BYTE	bXOFFChar	Character used for XOFF signal.

Example:

```
DCBINFO DCBInfo;
DCBInfo.usWriteTimeout = 0;
DCBInfo.usReadTimeout  = 0;
DCBInfo.fbCtlHandShake = MODE_DTS_CONTROL;
DCBInfo.fbFlowReplace  = 0;
DCBInfo.fbTimeout      = MODE_NO_WRITE_TIMEOUT ¦
                         MODE_READ_TIMEOUT;
DCBInfo.bErrorReplacementChar = '\0';
DCBInfo.bBreakReplacementChar = '\0';
DCBInfo.bXONChar              = 0x11;
DCBInfo.bXOFFChar             = 0x13;
DosDevIOCtl (hFile, IOCTL_ASYNC, ASYNC_SETDCBINFO,
   &DCBInfo, sizeof(DCBINFO), 0L, NULL, 0L, NULL);
```

ASYNC_GETBAUDRATE—Query the Baud Rate

Output Data:
USHORT—Baud rate

Example:

```
USHORT usBaudRate;
DosDevIOCtl (hFile, IOCTL_ASYNC, ASYNC_GETBAUDRATE,
   NULL, 0L, 0L, (PVOID)&usBaudRate, sizeof(USHORT),

   NULL);
```

ASYNC_GETLINECTRL—Query Line Characteristics

Output data:
LINECONTROL—Line control information

This is the structure:

```
typedef struct _LINECONTROL
```

It has the following fields and allowable values:

BYTE	bDataBits	
	0x05	5 data bits
	0x06	6 data bits
	0x07	7 data bits
	0x08	8 data bits
BYTE	bParity	
	0x00	None
	0x01	Odd.
	0x02	Even
	0x03	Mark
	0x04	Space
BYTE	bStopBits	
	0x00	1 stop bit
	0x01	1.5 stop bits
	0x02	2 stop bits
BYTE	fTransBreak	
	0x00	No break character transmitted.
	0x01	Transmit break character.

Example:

```
LINECONTROL LineControl;
DosDevIOCtl (hFile, IOCTL_ASYNC, ASYNC_GETLINECTRL,
   NULL,0L,0L,(PVOID)&LineControl,

   sizeof(LINECONTROL), L);
```

ASYNC_GETCOMMSTATUS—Get Communication Status Flags

Output Data:
BYTE—Communications status flags

The following flags are defined:

TX_WAITING_FOR_CTS	Transmit waiting for CTS signal.
TX_WAITING_FOR_DSR	Transmit waiting for DSR signal.
TX_WAITING_FOR_DCD	Transmit waiting for DCD signal.
TX_WAITING_FOR_XON	Transmit waiting because XOFF character was received.
TX_WAITING_TO_SEND_XON	Transmit waiting because XOFF character was transmitted.
TX_WAITING_WHILE_BREAK_ON	Transmit waiting because break character is being transmitted.

`TX_WAITING_TO_SEND_IMM`	Transmit waiting to send the character immediately.
`RX_WAITING_FOR_DSR`	Receive waiting for DSR signal.

Example:

```
BYTE CommStatus;
DosDevIOCtl (hFile, IOCTL_ASYNC, ASYNC_GETCOMMSTATUS,
   NULL, 0L, 0L, (PVOID)&CommStatus, sizeof(BYTE), NULL);
```

ASYNC_GETLINESTATUS—Query Data Transmission Status

Output Data:
BYTE—Transmission status flags

`WRITE_REQUEST_QUEUED`	Write request in progress or queued.
`DATA_IN_TX_QUE`	Data exists in transmit queue.
`HARDWARE_TRANSMITTING`	Hardware current transmitting data.
`CHAR_READY_TO_SEND_IMM`	Character ready to be transmitted immediately.
`WAITING_TO_SEND_XON`	Waiting to transmit XON (automatically).
`WAITING_TO_SEND_XOFF`	Waiting to transmit XOFF (automatically).

Example:

```
BYTE LineStatus;
DosDevIOCtl (hFile, IOCTL_ASYNC, ASYNC_GETLINESTATUS,
   NULL, 0L, 0L, (PVOID)&LineStatus, sizeof(BYTE), NULL);
```

ASYNC_GETMODEMOUTPUT—Query Modem Control Output Status

Output Data:
BYTE—Modem output status flags

The following flags are defined:

`DTR_ON`	DTR signal is on (Data-Terminal-Ready).
`RTS_ON`	RTS signal is on (Request-To-Send).

Example:

```
BYTE ModemOutputFlags;
DosDevIOCtl (hFile, IOCTL_ASYNC, ASYNC_GETMODEMOUTPUT,
   NULL, 0L, 0L, (PVOID)&ModemOutputFlags, sizeof(BYTE),

   NULL);
```

ASYNC_GETMODEMINPUT—Query Modem Control Input Status

Output Data:
BYTE—Modem input status flags

The following flags are defined:

CTS_ON	CTS signal is on.	(Clear-To-Send)
DSR_ON	DSR signal is on.	(Data-Set-Ready)
RI_ON	RI signal is on.	(Ring-Indicator)
DCD_ON	DCD signal is on.	(Data-Carrier-Detect)

Example:

```
BYTE ModemInputFlags;
DosDevIOCtl (hFile, IOCTL_ASYNC, ASYNC_GETMODEMINPUT,
   NULL, 0L, 0L, (PVOID)&ModemInputFlags, sizeof(BYTE),

   NULL);
```

ASYNC_GETINQUECOUNT—Query Number of Characters in Receive Queue

Output Data:
RXQUEUE—Receive queue information

This is the structure:

```
typedef struct _RXQUEUE
```

It has the following fields and allowable values:

USHORTcch	Number of characters in the receive queue.
USHORT cb	Size of the receive queue.

Example:

```
RXQUEUE ReceiveQueue;
DosDevIOCtl (hFile, IOCTL_ASYNC, ASYNC_GETINQUECOUNT,
   NULL, 0L, 0L, (PVOID)&ReceiveQueue, sizeof(RXQUEUE),

   NULL);
```

ASYNC_GETOUTQUECOUN—Query Number of Characters in Transmit Queue

Output Data:
RXQUEUE—Transmit queue information

	MODE_ERROR_CHAR	Error replacement character enabled.
	MODE_NULL_STRIPPING	Null stripping enabled.
	MODE_BREAK_CHAR	Break replacement control (XON and XOFF) enabled.
	0x20	Full duplex flow control enabled.
	MODE_RTS_CONTROL	RTS control mode enabled.
	MODE_RTS_HANDSHAKE	RTS input handshaking enabled.
	MODE_TRANSMIT_TOGGLE	Toggle RTS on transmit.
BYTE	fbTimeout	Specifies timeout process for device:
	MODE_NO_WRITE_TIMEOUT	Write infinite enabled.
	MODE_READ_TIMEOUT	Normal read enabled.
	MODE_WAIT_READ_TIMEOUT	Wait-for-something read enabled.
	MODE_NOWAIT_READ_TIMEOUT	No-wait read enabled.
	0x08	Extended hardware buffering disabled.
	0x10	Extended hardware buffering enabled.
	0x18	Automatic protocol override.
	0x20	Extended buffer size of 4 characters.
	0x40	Extended buffer size of 8 characters.
	0x60	Extended buffer size of 16 characters.
	0x80	Transmit buffer size of 16 characters.
BYTE	bErrorReplacementChar	Character inserted when character in error received.
BYTE	bBreakReplacementChar	Character inserted when break detected in line.
BYTE	bXONChar	Character used for XON signal.
BYTE	bXOFFChar	Character used for XOFF signal.

Example:

```
DCBINFO DCBInfo;
DosDevIOCtl (hFile, IOCTL_ASYNC, ASYNC_GETDCBINFO,
   NULL, 0L, 0L, (PVOID)&DCBInfo, sizeof(DCBINFO), NULL);
```

Phone Application

The application for this chapter demonstrates both the transmission and receipt of data through one of the communication ports. It also makes use of multiple threads and event semaphores. Because we are dealing with asynchronous events on the communications port, we never know exactly when we will be receiving data or possibly even when data is being transmitted. For that reason, we will establish a receive data thread. This way the application is not forced to wait around for data, keeping the user on hold. The application can continue processing and interacting with the user even though no data is immediately available. We will also establish a communications status thread that will constantly poll the various status and update the flags in the window.

The phone application will have two data viewing areas: a local connection area and remote connection area. These windows are shown in Figure 15.5. The local connection area will consist of an entry window and a history window. The entry window will be used to enter text to be transmitted. The history window will contain a list of the last 100 lines of transmitted text. The remote connection area will consist of a display window and a history window. The display window will show the current line of text being received. The history window will contain a list of the last 100 lines of received text. At the bottom of the window will be a set of communications status LEDs. These LEDs will be constantly updated as the communication status flags change.

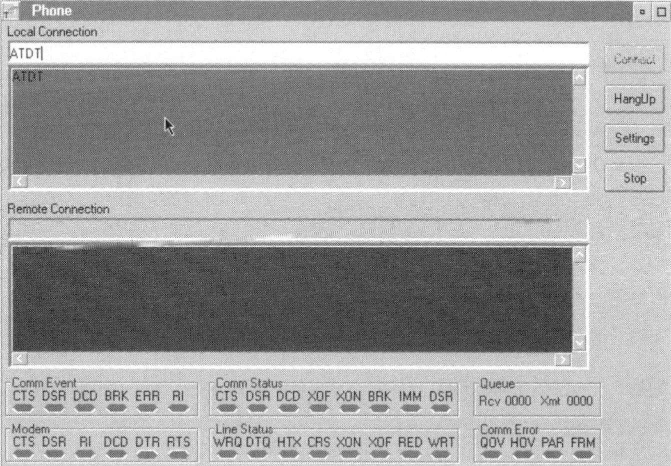

Figure 15.5.
Phone application window.

Although you can start this sample application without having the communications driver or a COM port installed, obviously it won't do much. If your system has a modem or even a debug terminal attached, you will be able to see and do much more with this sample. In some ways a debug terminal is even more illustrative because you can see the characters going out to the debug terminal as well as those returning from the debug terminal's keyboard.

On the right side of the window are five buttons. The Connect button will attempt to open the communications port using the current settings. The HangUp button will close the currently open session. The Settings button will display a settings dialog that enables you to change the settings for each port. The Stop button will cause transmission to be stopped (XOFF). When transmission is stopped, the text of this button will change to Start. Pressing Start will restart transmission (XON). The Abort button displays an information dialog box.

While a session is active, you enter the text to be sent in the local entry window. Press Enter to transmit the line of text. Double-clicking any entry in the local history list will cause the text on that line to be copied to the local entry window for editing. As data is received from the remote site, the data is displayed in the remote display window; and when the carriage return is received, the line of text is moved to the remote history window. Pressing the Settings button will display the settings dialog box, as shown in Figure 15.6.

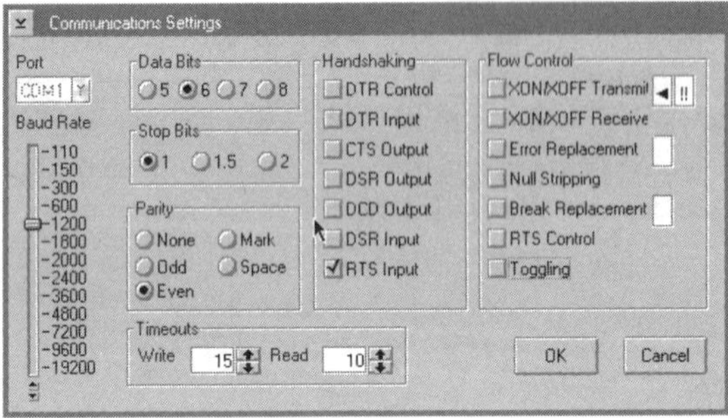

Figure 15.6.
The settings dialog.

The settings dialog does not include all possible settings, but it does provide a majority of the possible flags. The following list describes the acronyms used in this dialog.

RTS	Request to Send.
CTS	Clear to Send.
DSR	Data Set Ready.
DCD	Carrier Detect.
DTR	Data Terminal Ready.

When the application starts, it attempts to go out and retrieve the current settings for all of the communications ports. If it is unable to do so, it initializes the settings to some default settings. Selecting a port from the Port combo box will change the settings to reflect the port's settings.

You can set the desired port settings in this dialog. Notice that setting the Write and Read timeouts to any value other than zero will adversely impact performance as the `DosWrite` and `DosRead` will incur timeout processing. If you have a debug terminal attached to your computer, you can start a session with it using the communications port to which it is attached. For example, to start a TTY-like session, you might use the following settings:

Baud Rate:	9600
Data Bits:	8
Stop Bits:	1
Parity:	None
Read Timeout:	0
Write Timeout:	0

You should check the settings on your debug terminal for the exact values to use.

Let's take a quick look at how the application is structured with its three threads. Figure 15.7 shows the three major components of the application and their interaction with each other. The main application will create a message queue and be known as the message queue thread. It will be responsible for managing the application windows and dialogs and for establishing the connection and writing data to the communications port.

The receive data thread is solely responsible for reading data from the communications port and notifying the main thread when there is data in the application's receive buffer to be displayed. It will coordinate access to the application's receive buffer through an event semaphore.

The third thread is the communications status thread. It's sole responsibility is to constantly query the communication status and notify the main thread when any of the sets of flags has changed. Because the receive data and communications status threads are not message queue threads, they cannot send messages to any windows, so all notifications to the main thread are through posted messages.

Main Thread

We will use the CONTROLS.DLL from Chapter 12, "Dynamic Link Libraries," which defines a bevel control. In addition, we define a new control called an LED control. An LED control is an on/off indicator with a maximum three-character text field displayed above the indicator. It is modeled on the lights generally found on external modems.

The LED control is defined in LED.C, and the state is set or cleared by sending a `WM_ENABLE` message to the control.

Figure 15.7.
Phone application thread interaction.

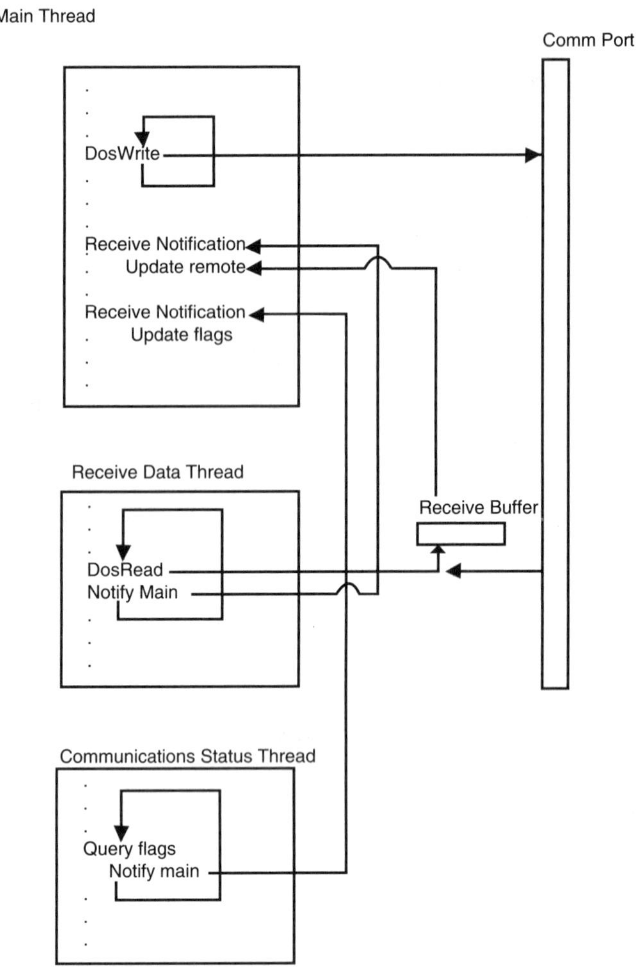

LED.C

```
/* ---------------------------------
               LED Control
      Real-World Programming for OS/2
Copyright (c) 1994 Blain, Delimon, and English
-------------------------------- */

/* LED Control
Class Name  - LEDCLASS
Messages
WM_ENABLE - MPFROMSHORT (enablestate)
*/
```

```
#define INCL_WIN
#define INCL_GPI

#include <os2.h>
#include "led.h"
#include "phone.h"

/* Window and Dialog Functions */
MRESULT EXPENTRY LEDWndProc      (HWND,ULONG,MPARAM,MPARAM);

/* Window extra bytes */
#define QWS_ENABLED          0
#define QWL_TEXT             QWS_ENABLED + sizeof(USHORT)
#define LEDEXTRA             QWL_TEXT    + sizeof(ULONG)

/* Local Functions */
VOID RedrawLED (HWND,HPS,USHORT);

/* Global Variables */
HBITMAP  hbmLED;                /* LED bitmap (contains 2 states) */
ULONG    ulLEDCount = 0;        /* Number of LED controls         */
ULONG    bmWidth;               /* Width of each bitmap state     */
ULONG    bmHeight;              /* Height of bitmap               */


/* ---------- Local Functions ---------- */

VOID RedrawLED (HWND hWnd, HPS hps, USHORT usEnabled)
{
   BOOL   bRelease = FALSE;
   ULONG   ulTxt;
   RECTL   Rectl;
   POINTL Ptl;

   if (!hps)
   {
      bRelease = TRUE;
      hps = WinGetPS (hWnd);
   }

   WinQueryWindowRect (hWnd, &Rectl);

   /* Draw text with bottom 1 pel above bitmap */
   Rectl.yBottom = bmHeight + 1;
   ulTxt = WinQueryWindowULong (hWnd, QWL_TEXT);
   WinDrawText (hps, -1, (PSZ)&ulTxt, &Rectl, 0L, 0L,
         DT_CENTER ¦ DT_BOTTOM ¦ DT_TEXTATTRS);

   /* Draw bitmap state */
   Ptl.x = (Rectl.xRight - bmWidth) >> 1;
   Ptl.y = 0;
   Rectl.xLeft   = usEnabled ? 0 : bmWidth;
   Rectl.xRight  = Rectl.xLeft + bmWidth;
   Rectl.yBottom = 0L;
   Rectl.yTop    = bmHeight;
```

```
   WinDrawBitmap (hps, hbmLED, &Rectl, &Ptl, 0L, 0L,
         DBM_NORMAL);

   if (bRelease)
      WinReleasePS (hps);

   return;
}

/* ---------- External Function ---------- */

VOID RegisterLEDClass (HAB hab)
{
   WinRegisterClass (hab, LEDCLASS, LEDWndProc, 0,
      LEDEXTRA);

   return;
}

/* ---------- Window Function ---------- */

MRESULT EXPENTRY LEDWndProc (HWND hWnd, ULONG msg,
      MPARAM mp1, MPARAM mp2)
{
   BOOL              bHandled = TRUE;
   MRESULT           mReturn  = 0;
   RECTL             Rectl;
   HPS               hps;
   ULONG             ulText;
   PSZ               pszText;
   BITMAPINFOHEADER bi;

   switch (msg)
   {
      case WM_CREATE:
         /* Initial state is disabled */
         WinSetWindowUShort (hWnd, QWS_ENABLED, 0);

      /* Save 3 character LED text in window extra bytes as a long */
         pszText = ((PCREATESTRUCT)mp2)->pszText;
         ulText  = (pszText[2] << 16) ¦ (pszText[1] << 8) ¦
                  pszText[0];
         WinSetWindowULong (hWnd, QWL_TEXT, ulText);

         /* Set font in the control */
         WinSetPresParam (hWnd, PP_FONTNAMESIZE,
               FONTNAMELEN, HELV8FONT);

         /* Load the LED bitmap when first LED control is created */
         if (!ulLEDCount)
         {
            hps = WinGetPS (hWnd);
            hbmLED = GpiLoadBitmap (hps, 0, IDB_LED, 0L,
                                    0L);
            GpiQueryBitmapParameters (hbmLED, &bi);
                     bmWidth  = bi.cx >> 1;
```

```
            bmHeight = bi.cy;
            WinReleasePS (hps);
         }
         ulLEDCount++;
         break;

      case WM_ENABLE:
         WinSetWindowUShort (hWnd, QWS_ENABLED,
            SHORT1FROMMP(mp1));
         RedrawLED (hWnd, 0, SHORT1FROMMP(mp1));
         break;

      case WM_PAINT:
         hps = WinBeginPaint (hWnd,0,0);
         WinQueryWindowRect (hWnd, &Rectl);
         WinFillRect (hps, &Rectl, CLR_PALEGRAY);
         RedrawLED (hWnd, hps, WinQueryWindowUShort (hWnd,
                  QWS_ENABLED));
         WinEndPaint (hps);
         break;

      case WM_DESTROY:
         if (!(-ulLEDCount))
         GpiDeleteBitmap (hbmLED);
         break;

      default:
         bHandled = FALSE;
         break;
   }

   if (!bHandled)
      mReturn = WinDefWindowProc (hWnd,msg,mp1,mp2);

   return (mReturn);
}
```

LED.H

```
/* -------------------------------
        LED Control Header File
      Real-World Programming for OS/2
Copyright (c) 1994 Blain, Delimon, and English
------------------------------- */

/**************************************************
LED CONTROL
**************************************************/

#define LEDCLASS   "LED"

/* Control registration function */
VOID RegisterLEDClass (HAB);
```

Files Required to Build the Phone Application

The following files are required to build the phone application:

LED.C
LED.H
LED.BMP
PHONE.C
PHONE.H
PHONE.RC
PHONE.DEF
PHONE.ICO
SETTINGS.DLG
STATUS.DLG
BUTTONS.DLG
CONTROLS.DLL

PHONE.C

```
/* --------------------------------
       Phone Communications Program
     Real-World Programming for OS/2
Copyright (c) 1994 Blain, Delimon, and English
-------------------------------- */

#define INCL_DOS
#define INCL_DOSDEVIOCTL
#define INCL_WIN
#define INCL_GPI
#define INCL_ERRORS

#include <os2.h>
#include <stdio.h>
#include "phone.h"
#include "..\common\controls.h"
#include "led.h"
#include "..\common\about.h"

/* Window and Dialog Functions      */
MRESULT EXPENTRY ClientWndProc   (HWND,ULONG,MPARAM,MPARAM);
MRESULT EXPENTRY SettingsDlgProc (HWND,ULONG,MPARAM,MPARAM);
MRESULT EXPENTRY StatusDlgProc   (HWND,ULONG,MPARAM,MPARAM);

/* Thread Functions                 */
VOID CommStatusThread (ULONG);
VOID ReceiveDataThread (ULONG);

/* Local Functions                  */
VOID ConnectToPort (HWND);
VOID DeInitializeControls (HWND);
VOID HangUpFromPort (HWND);
```

```
VOID InitializeAppWindow (HWND);
VOID InitializeControls (HWND,BOOL);
VOID PositionWindows (ULONG,ULONG);
VOID QueryBaudRate (ULONG);
VOID QueryDCBInfo (ULONG);
VOID QueryLineCtrl (ULONG);
VOID QueryValidCommPorts (VOID);
BOOL SetPortSettings (HWND);
VOID ToggleTransmit (HWND);
VOID TransmitLine (VOID);

/* User-Defined messages            */
#define WM_USER_RECEIVEQUEUE    WM_USER+1
#define WM_USER_TRANSMITQUEUE   WM_USER+2
#define WM_USER_COMSTATUS       WM_USER+3
#define WM_USER_TRANSMITSTATUS  WM_USER+4
#define WM_USER_COMEVENT        WM_USER+5
#define WM_USER_COMERROR        WM_USER+6
#define WM_USER_MODEMINPUT      WM_USER+7
#define WM_USER_MODEMOUTPUT     WM_USER+8
#define WM_USER_RCVLIST         WM_USER+9
#define WM_USER_RCVTEXT         WM_USER+10

/* Baud Rate Information */
typedef struct tagBAUDRATE
{
   CHAR  szTxt[6];        /* Text format of baud rate */
   ULONG ulValue;         /* Numeric format of baud rate */
} BAUDRATE;

/* Communications Port Information */
typedef struct tagPORTINFO
{
   ULONG       BaudIndex;
   ULONG       BaudRate;
   DCBINFO     DCBInfo;
   LINECONTROL LineControl;
} PORTINFO;

/* Global Variables                  */
HAB      hab;
HWND     hWndFrame,
         hWndClient,
         hWndButtons,
         hWndStatus,
         hWndSettings,
         hWndLocalTitle,
         hWndLocalEdit,
         hWndLocalList,
         hWndLocalBevel1,
         hWndLocalBevel2,
         hWndRemoteTitle,
         hWndRemoteText,
         hWndRemoteList,
         hWndRemoteBevel1,
         hWndRemoteBevel2;
```

```
CHAR     szTitle[64];
TID      StatusThreadID;   /* ID of CommStatus thread */
TID      ReadThreadID;     /* ID of ReceiveData thread */
HEV      hevRcvQueue;    /* Receive Queue Event Semaphore */
HFILE    hFile;          /* Open Comm Port file handle */
CHAR     szCom[5] = "COM ";
PORTINFO PortInfo[4];    /* Array of comm port settings   */
ULONG    ulPort = 0;     /* Currently selected port index */
ULONG    ulNumPorts = 0; /* Number of comm ports supported*/
BOOL     bConnected=FALSE; /*Communications currently open */
BOOL     bTransmitting=TRUE; /*Data transmission enabled     */
CHAR     szReceiveBuffer[255]; /* Receive Queue buffer */
USHORT   usNextPos = 0;  /* Next char pos in receive queue*/
ULONG    ulNumLocalLines  = 0L, /* # of lines in Local listbox   */
         ulNumRemoteLines = 0L;    /* # of lines in Remote listbox  */

/* Current line and status flags */
RXQUEUE     ReceiveQueue    = { 0, 0 };
RXQUEUE     TransmitQueue   = { 0, 0 };
BYTE        ComStatus       = 0;
BYTE        TransmitStatus  = 0;
USHORT      ComEvent        = 0;
USHORT      ComError        = 0;
BYTE        ModemInput      = 0;
MODEMSTATUS ModemOutput     = { 0, 0 };

/* Baud Rate Table */
BAUDRATE BaudRates[13] =
   {{ "110",     110L },
   { "150",     150L },
   { "300",     300L },
   { "600",     600L },
   { "1200",   1200L },
   { "1800",   1800L },
   { "2000",   2000L },
   { "2400",   2400L },
   { "3600",   3600L },
   { "4800",   4800L },
   { "7200",   7200L },
   { "9600",   9600L },
   { "19200", 19200L }
};


/* -------- Main Application Function ---------- */

int main()
{
   HMQ   hmq;
   QMSG  qmsg;
   ULONG flFrameFlags     = FCF_TITLEBAR ¦ FCF_SYSMENU ¦
                            FCF_ICON ¦
                            FCF_SIZEBORDER ¦ FCF_MINMAX ¦
                            FCF_TASKLIST ¦FCF_SHELLPOSITION ¦
                            FCF_NOBYTEALIGN;
```

```
    CHAR  szClientClass[] = "CLIENT";

    hab = WinInitialize (0);
    hmq = WinCreateMsgQueue (hab, 0);

    WinRegisterClass (hab, szClientClass, ClientWndProc, 0,
                      0);
    WinLoadString (hab, 0, ID_APPNAME, sizeof(szTitle),
                   szTitle);

    /* Create the main application window */
    hWndFrame = WinCreateStdWindow (HWND_DESKTOP, 0,
          &flFrameFlags, szClientClass, szTitle, 0, 0,
          ID_APPNAME, &hWndClient);

    /* Create child windows */
    InitializeAppWindow (hWndClient);

    /* Show the main window in a maximized state */
    WinSetWindowPos (hWndFrame, 0, 0L, 0L, 0L, 0L,
          SWP_MAXIMIZE ¦ SWP_SHOW);

    while (WinGetMsg (hab, &qmsg, 0, 0, 0))
       WinDispatchMsg (hab, &qmsg);

    WinDestroyWindow (hWndFrame);
    WinDestroyMsgQueue (hmq);
    WinTerminate (hab);
    return (0);
}

/* ---- CommStatus Thread Function ------ */

/*
The CommStatus thread is responsible for querying the current
communications line and status flags and determining if any
of the flags have changed.  For each set of flags or values that
has changed, a message is posted to the main message queue thread
so that it can update the LED controls.

Access to the communication port file handle (hFile) is protected
within a critical section.

This is a Non-Message queue thread so it cannot send messages to
a message queue thread.
*/

VOID CommStatusThread (ULONG ulThreadParam)
{
   RXQUEUE      NewReceiveQueue,
                NewTransmitQueue;
   BYTE         NewComStatus,
                NewTransmitStatus,
                NewModemInput;
   USHORT       NewComEvent,
                NewComError;
```

```
MODEMSTATUS NewModemOutput;

do
{
   /* Query all of the line and status flags */

   DosEnterCritSec ();

   DosDevIOCtl (hFile, IOCTL_ASYNC, ASYNC_GETCOMMEVENT,
         NULL, 0L, 0L, &NewComEvent, 2L, 0L);
   DosDevIOCtl (hFile, IOCTL_ASYNC, ASYNC_GETCOMMSTATUS,
         NULL, 0L, 0L, &NewComStatus, 1L, 0L);
   DosDevIOCtl (hFile, IOCTL_ASYNC, ASYNC_GETINQUECOUNT,
         NULL, 0L, 0L, &NewReceiveQueue, sizeof(RXQUEUE),
         0L);
   DosDevIOCtl (hFile, IOCTL_ASYNC, ASYNC_GETOUTQUECOUNT,
         NULL, 0L, 0L, &NewTransmitQueue,
         sizeof(RXQUEUE), 0L);
   DosDevIOCtl (hFile, IOCTL_ASYNC, ASYNC_GETMODEMINPUT,
         NULL, 0L, 0L, &NewModemInput, 1L, 0L);
   DosDevIOCtl (hFile, IOCTL_ASYNC, ASYNC_GETMODEMOUTPUT,
         NULL, 0L, 0L, &NewModemOutput,
         sizeof(MODEMSTATUS), 0L);
   DosDevIOCtl (hFile, IOCTL_ASYNC, ASYNC_GETLINESTATUS,
         NULL, 0L, 0L, &NewTransmitStatus, 1L, 0L);
   DosDevIOCtl (hFile, IOCTL_ASYNC, ASYNC_GETCOMMERROR,
         NULL, 0L, 0L, &NewComError, 2L, 0L);

   DosExitCritSec ();

   /* Determine if any values have changed - if so then
      post message */
   if (NewReceiveQueue.cch != ReceiveQueue.cch)
   {
      ReceiveQueue = NewReceiveQueue;
      WinPostMsg (hWndStatus, WM_USER_RECEIVEQUEUE, 0L,
            0L);
   }
   if (NewTransmitQueue.cch != TransmitQueue.cch)
   {
      TransmitQueue = NewTransmitQueue;
      WinPostMsg (hWndStatus, WM_USER_TRANSMITQUEUE, 0L,
            0L);
   }
   if (NewComStatus != ComStatus)
   {
      ComStatus = NewComStatus;
      WinPostMsg (hWndStatus, WM_USER_COMSTATUS, 0L, 0L);
   }
   if (NewTransmitStatus != TransmitStatus)
   {
      TransmitStatus = NewTransmitStatus;
      WinPostMsg (hWndStatus, WM_USER_TRANSMITSTATUS, 0L,
            0L);
   }
   if (NewComEvent != ComEvent)
```

```
      {
         ComEvent = NewComEvent;
         WinPostMsg (hWndStatus, WM_USER_COMEVENT, 0L, 0L);
      }
      if (NewComError != ComError)
      {
         ComError = NewComError;
         WinPostMsg (hWndStatus, WM_USER_COMERROR, 0L, 0L);
      }
      if (NewModemInput != ModemInput)
      {
         ModemInput = NewModemInput;
         WinPostMsg (hWndStatus, WM_USER_MODEMINPUT, 0L,
               0L);
      }
      if (NewModemOutput.fbModemOn != ModemOutput.fbModemOn)
      {
         ModemOutput = NewModemOutput;
         WinPostMsg (hWndStatus, WM_USER_MODEMOUTPUT, 0L,
               0L);
      }

      /* Go to sleep for 0.2 seconds */
      DosSleep(200);
   } while (TRUE);
}

/* ------ ReceiveData Thread Function -------- */

/*
The ReceiveData thread is responsible for reading the data from
the communications port and placing the bytes into the Receive
Buffer.  When a carriage return character (0x0D) is received, a
message is posted to the main message queue thread so that it
can insert the line into the Remote listbox. If all data has
been processed from the communications port and it has not
received the carriage return character, then a message is posted
to the main message queue thread so that it can update the
Remote text window.

Access to the communication port file handle (hFile) is protected
within a critical section. In order to protect the receive queue
buffer from being updated before the main message queue thread
can process the posted message, an event semaphore is used. The
event semaphore is reset prior to posting the message and this
thread will wait for the main message queue thread to post the
event semaphore before continuing.

This is a Non-Message queue thread, so it cannot send messages to
a message queue thread.
*/

VOID ReceiveDataThread (ULONG ulThreadParam)
{
   CHAR   szBuffer[255];
   ULONG  ulBytesRead;
```

```
      /* Set the priority of the CommStatus thread to idle
         time */
      DosSetPriority (PRTYS_THREAD, PRTYC_IDLETIME, 0,
         StatusThreadID);
   }

   if (bConnected)
   {
      WinEnableControl (hWnd, IDC_CONNECT, FALSE);
      WinEnableControl (hWnd, IDC_HANGUP, TRUE);
      WinEnableWindow (hWndLocalEdit, TRUE);
      WinSetFocus (HWND_DESKTOP, hWndLocalEdit);
   }
   else
      WinMessageBox (HWND_DESKTOP, hWnd,
            "Unable to connect", "Phone Application",
            0, MB_ERROR ¦ MB_OK);

   return;
}

VOID DeInitializeControls (HWND hWnd)
{
   CHAR  szTxt[2];
   ULONG ulValue;

   /* Query values */
   PortInfo[ulPort].BaudIndex =
      (ULONG)WinSendDlgItemMsg (hWnd, IDC_BAUDRATE,
      SLM_QUERYSLIDERINFO,
      MPFROM2SHORT (SMA_SLIDERARMPOSITION,
      SMA_INCREMENTVALUE),
      0L);
   PortInfo[ulPort].BaudRate =
      BaudRates[PortInfo[ulPort].BaudIndex].ulValue;
   if (WinQueryButtonCheckstate (hWnd, IDC_DATABITS_5))
      PortInfo[ulPort].LineControl.bDataBits = 5;
   else if (WinQueryButtonCheckstate (hWnd, IDC_DATABITS_6))
      PortInfo[ulPort].LineControl.bDataBits = 6;
   else if (WinQueryButtonCheckstate (hWnd, IDC_DATABITS_7))
      PortInfo[ulPort].LineControl.bDataBits = 7;
   else if (WinQueryButtonCheckstate (hWnd, IDC_DATABITS_8))
      PortInfo[ulPort].LineControl.bDataBits = 8;
   if (WinQueryButtonCheckstate (hWnd, IDC_STOPBITS_1))
      PortInfo[ulPort].LineControl.bStopBits = 0;
   else if (WinQueryButtonCheckstate (hWnd,IDC_STOPBITS_15))
      PortInfo[ulPort].LineControl.bStopBits = 1;
   else if (WinQueryButtonCheckstate (hWnd, IDC_STOPBITS_2))
      PortInfo[ulPort].LineControl.bStopBits = 2;

   if (WinQueryButtonCheckstate (hWnd, IDC_PARITY_NONE))
      PortInfo[ulPort].LineControl.bParity = 0;
   else if (WinQueryButtonCheckstate (hWnd, IDC_PARITY_ODD))
      PortInfo[ulPort].LineControl.bParity = 1;
   else if (WinQueryButtonCheckstate (hWnd,IDC_PARITY_EVEN))
      PortInfo[ulPort].LineControl.bParity = 2;
```

```
else if (WinQueryButtonCheckstate (hWnd,IDC_PARITY_MARK))
   PortInfo[ulPort].LineControl.bParity = 3;
else if (WinQueryButtonCheckstate(hWnd,IDC_PARITY_SPACE))
   PortInfo[ulPort].LineControl.bParity = 4;

PortInfo[ulPort].DCBInfo.fbCtlHndShake = 0;
PortInfo[ulPort].DCBInfo.fbFlowReplace = 0;
if (WinQueryButtonCheckstate (hWnd,IDC_HANDSHAKING_DTRC))
   PortInfo[ulPort].DCBInfo.fbCtlHndShake |=
      MODE_DTR_CONTROL;
if (WinQueryButtonCheckstate (hWnd,IDC_HANDSHAKING_DTRI))
   PortInfo[ulPort].DCBInfo.fbCtlHndShake |=
      MODE_DTR_HANDSHAKE;
if (WinQueryButtonCheckstate (hWnd,IDC_HANDSHAKING_CTSO))
   PortInfo[ulPort].DCBInfo.fbCtlHndShake |=
      MODE_CTS_HANDSHAKE;
if (WinQueryButtonCheckstate (hWnd,IDC_HANDSHAKING_DSRO))
   PortInfo[ulPort].DCBInfo.fbCtlHndShake |=
      MODE_DSR_HANDSHAKE;
if (WinQueryButtonCheckstate (hWnd,IDC_HANDSHAKING_DCDO))
   PortInfo[ulPort].DCBInfo.fbCtlHndShake |=
      MODE_DCD_HANDSHAKE;
if (WinQueryButtonCheckstate (hWnd,IDC_HANDSHAKING_DSRI))
   PortInfo[ulPort].DCBInfo.fbCtlHndShake |=
      MODE_DSR_SENSITIVITY;

if (WinQueryButtonCheckstate (hWnd,IDC_HANDSHAKING_RTSI))
   PortInfo[ulPort].DCBInfo.fbFlowReplace |=
      MODE_RTS_HANDSHAKE;
if (WinQueryButtonCheckstate (hWnd,
      IDC_FLOWCONTROL_XONXOFFT))
   PortInfo[ulPort].DCBInfo.fbFlowReplace |=
      MODE_AUTO_TRANSMIT;
if (WinQueryButtonCheckstate (hWnd,
      IDC_FLOWCONTROL_XONXOFFR))
   PortInfo[ulPort].DCBInfo.fbFlowReplace |=
      MODE_AUTO_RECEIVE;
if (WinQueryButtonCheckstate (hWnd,
      IDC_FLOWCONTROL_ERRORREP))
   PortInfo[ulPort].DCBInfo.fbFlowReplace |=
      MODE_ERROR_CHAR;
if (WinQueryButtonCheckstate (hWnd,
      IDC_FLOWCONTROL_NULLSTRIP))
   PortInfo[ulPort].DCBInfo.fbFlowReplace |=
      MODE_NULL_STRIPPING;
if (WinQueryButtonCheckstate (hWnd,
      IDC_FLOWCONTROL_BREAKREP))
   PortInfo[ulPort].DCBInfo.fbFlowReplace |=
      MODE_BREAK_CHAR;
if (WinQueryButtonCheckstate (hWnd,
      IDC_FLOWCONTROL_RTSC))
   PortInfo[ulPort].DCBInfo.fbFlowReplace |=
      MODE_RTS_CONTROL;
if (WinQueryButtonCheckstate (hWnd,
      IDC_FLOWCONTROL_TOGGLING))
   PortInfo[ulPort].DCBInfo.fbFlowReplace |=
      MODE_TRANSMIT_TOGGLE;
```

```
   WinQueryDlgItemText (hWnd, IDC_XONCHAR, 2, szTxt);
   PortInfo[ulPort].DCBInfo.bXONChar = szTxt[0];
   WinQueryDlgItemText (hWnd, IDC_XOFFCHAR, 2, szTxt);
   PortInfo[ulPort].DCBInfo.bXOFFChar = szTxt[0];
   WinQueryDlgItemText (hWnd, IDC_ERRORREPCHAR, 2, szTxt);
   PortInfo[ulPort].DCBInfo.bErrorReplacementChar =
         szTxt[0];
   WinQueryDlgItemText (hWnd, IDC_BREAKREPCHAR, 2, szTxt);
   PortInfo[ulPort].DCBInfo.bBreakReplacementChar =
         szTxt[0];

   WinSendDlgItemMsg (hWnd, IDC_TIMEOUT_WRITE,
         SPBM_QUERYVALUE, (MPARAM)&ulValue, (MPARAM)0L);
   PortInfo[ulPort].DCBInfo.usWriteTimeout =(USHORT)ulValue;
   WinSendDlgItemMsg (hWnd, IDC_TIMEOUT_READ,
         SPBM_QUERYVALUE, (MPARAM)&ulValue, (MPARAM)0L);
   PortInfo[ulPort].DCBInfo.usReadTimeout = (USHORT)ulValue;

   PortInfo[ulPort].DCBInfo.fbTimeout =
      (BYTE)(PortInfo[ulPort].DCBInfo.fbTimeout & 0x0F8);
   if (PortInfo[ulPort].DCBInfo.usWriteTimeout == 0)
      PortInfo[ulPort].DCBInfo.fbTimeout |=
         MODE_NO_WRITE_TIMEOUT;
   if (PortInfo[ulPort].DCBInfo.usReadTimeout == 0)
      PortInfo[ulPort].DCBInfo.fbTimeout |=
      MODE_NOWAIT_READ_TIMEOUT;
   else
      PortInfo[ulPort].DCBInfo.fbTimeout |=
         MODE_READ_TIMEOUT;

   return;
}

VOID HangUpFromPort (HWND hWnd)
{
   BYTE Cmd;

   /* Flush the input and output buffers */
   DosDevIOCtl (hFile, IOCTL_GENERAL, DEV_FLUSHOUTPUT,
         (PVOID)&Cmd, 1L, NULL, NULL, 0L, NULL);
   DosDevIOCtl (hFile, IOCTL_GENERAL, DEV_FLUSHINPUT,
         (PVOID)&Cmd, 1L, NULL, NULL, 0L, NULL);

   if (!DosClose (hFile))
   {
      WinEnableControl (hWnd, IDC_CONNECT, TRUE);
      WinEnableControl (hWnd, IDC_HANGUP,  FALSE);
      WinEnableWindow (hWndLocalEdit, FALSE);

      /* Stop the CommStatus and ReceiveData threads */
      DosKillThread (StatusThreadID);
      DosKillThread (ReadThreadID);

      /* Close the receive data event semaphore */
      DosCloseEventSem (hevRcvQueue);
```

```
      bConnected = FALSE;
   }
   else
      WinMessageBox (HWND_DESKTOP, hWnd,
            "Unable to hangup", "Phone Application",
            0, MB_ERROR | MB_OK);

   return;
}

VOID InitializeAppWindow (HWND hWnd)
{
   LONG lColor;

   RegisterLEDClass (hab);

   /* Local Connections Windows */

   hWndLocalTitle  = WinCreateWindow (hWnd, WC_STATIC,
         "Local Connection", WS_VISIBLE | SS_TEXT |
         DT_BOTTOM, 0L, 0L, 140L, 16L, hWnd, HWND_BOTTOM, 1,
         NULL, NULL);

   hWndLocalEdit   = WinCreateWindow (hWnd, WC_ENTRYFIELD,
         "", WS_VISIBLE | ES_AUTOSCROLL | WS_GROUP |
         WS_TABSTOP | WS_DISABLED, 0L, 0L, 0L, 0L, hWnd,
         HWND_BOTTOM, 2, NULL, NULL);

   hWndLocalBevel1 = WinCreateWindow (hWnd, BEVELCLASS, "",
         WS_VISIBLE | BVS_PREVWINDOW, 0L, 0L, 0L, 0L, hWnd,
         HWND_BOTTOM, 0, NULL, NULL);
   WinSendMsg (hWndLocalBevel1, BVM_SETTHICKNESS,
         MPFROMSHORT(2), 0L);

   hWndLocalList   = WinCreateWindow (hWnd, WC_LISTBOX, "",
         WS_VISIBLE | LS_NOADJUSTPOS | LS_HORZSCROLL |
         WS_TABSTOP, 0L, 0L, 0L, 0L, hWnd, HWND_BOTTOM, 3,
         NULL, NULL);

   hWndLocalBevel2 = WinCreateWindow (hWnd, BEVELCLASS, "",
         WS_VISIBLE | BVS_PREVWINDOW, 0L, 0L, 0L, 0L, hWnd,
         HWND_BOTTOM, 0, NULL, NULL);
   WinSendMsg (hWndLocalBevel2, BVM_SETTHICKNESS,
         MPFROMSHORT(2), 0L);


   /* Remote Connections Windows */

   hWndRemoteTitle  = WinCreateWindow (hWnd, WC_STATIC,
         "Remote Connection", WS_VISIBLE | SS_TEXT |
         DT_BOTTOM, 0L, 0L, 140L, 16L, hWnd, HWND_BOTTOM, 4,
         NULL, NULL);

   hWndRemoteText   = WinCreateWindow (hWnd, WC_STATIC, "",
         WS_VISIBLE | SS_TEXT | DT_LEFT | DT_VCENTER, 0L,
         0L, 0L, 0L, hWnd, HWND_BOTTOM, 5, NULL, NULL);
```

```
   hWndRemoteBevel1 = WinCreateWindow (hWnd, BEVELCLASS, "",
         WS_VISIBLE ¦ BVS_PREVWINDOW, 0L, 0L, 0L, 0L, hWnd,
         HWND_BOTTOM, 0, NULL, NULL);
   WinSendMsg (hWndRemoteBevel1, BVM_SETTHICKNESS,
         MPFROMSHORT(2), 0L);

   hWndRemoteList  = WinCreateWindow (hWnd, WC_LISTBOX, "",
         WS_VISIBLE ¦ LS_NOADJUSTPOS ¦ LS_HORZSCROLL,
         0L, 0L, 0L, 0L, hWnd, HWND_BOTTOM, 6, NULL, NULL);

   hWndRemoteBevel2 = WinCreateWindow (hWnd, BEVELCLASS, "",
         WS_VISIBLE ¦ BVS_PREVWINDOW, 0L, 0L, 0L, 0L, hWnd,
         HWND_BOTTOM, 0, NULL, NULL);
   WinSendMsg (hWndRemoteBevel2, BVM_SETTHICKNESS,
         MPFROMSHORT(2), 0L);


   /* Load the dialog windows */

   hWndButtons = WinLoadDlg (hWnd, hWnd, StatusDlgProc, 0L,
         IDD_BUTTONS, NULL);
   hWndStatus  = WinLoadDlg (hWnd, hWnd, StatusDlgProc, 0L,
         IDD_STATUS, NULL);


   /* Initialize settings of certain control windows */

   WinSendMsg (hWndLocalEdit, EM_SETTEXTLIMIT,
         MPFROMSHORT(254), 0L);

   lColor = CLR_DARKCYAN;
   WinSetPresParam (hWndLocalList, PP_BACKGROUNDCOLORINDEX,
         sizeof(lColor), &lColor);

   lColor = CLR_DARKRED;
   WinSetPresParam (hWndRemoteList, PP_BACKGROUNDCOLORINDEX,
         sizeof(lColor), &lColor);

   return;
}

VOID InitializeControls (HWND hWnd, BOOL bInit)
{
   ULONG ulInx;
   CHAR  szTxt[2] = " ";

   /* Set limits and attributes */
   if (bInit)
   {
      for (ulInx = 0; ulInx < 13; ulInx++)
      {
         WinSendDlgItemMsg (hWnd, IDC_BAUDRATE,
               SLM_SETTICKSIZE,
               MPFROM2SHORT (SMA_SETALLTICKS, 5), 0L);
         WinSendDlgItemMsg (hWnd, IDC_BAUDRATE,
               SLM_SETSCALETEXT,MPFROMSHORT(ulInx),
               MPFROMP(BaudRates[ulInx].szTxt));
```

```
    }
    WinSendDlgItemMsg (hWnd, IDC_TIMEOUT_WRITE,
          SPBM_SETTEXTLIMIT, (MPARAM)4, (MPARAM)0);
    WinSendDlgItemMsg (hWnd, IDC_TIMEOUT_WRITE,
          SPBM_SETLIMITS, (MPARAM)9999L, (MPARAM)0L);
    WinSendDlgItemMsg (hWnd, IDC_TIMEOUT_READ,
          SPBM_SETTEXTLIMIT,(MPARAM)4, (MPARAM)0);
    WinSendDlgItemMsg (hWnd, IDC_TIMEOUT_READ,
          SPBM_SETLIMITS, (MPARAM)9999L, (MPARAM)0L);
    WinSendDlgItemMsg (hWnd, IDC_XONCHAR, EM_SETTEXTLIMIT,
          MPFROMSHORT(1), 0L);
    WinSendDlgItemMsg (hWnd, IDC_XOFFCHAR,
          EM_SETTEXTLIMIT, MPFROMSHORT(1), 0L);
    WinSendDlgItemMsg (hWnd, IDC_ERRORREPCHAR,
          EM_SETTEXTLIMIT, MPFROMSHORT(1), 0L);
    WinSendDlgItemMsg (hWnd, IDC_BREAKREPCHAR,
          EM_SETTEXTLIMIT, MPFROMSHORT(1), 0L);

    for (ulInx = 0; ulInx < ulNumPorts; ulInx++)
    {
       szCom[3] = (CHAR)('1' + ulInx);
       WinSendDlgItemMsg (hWnd, IDC_PORT, LM_INSERTITEM,
          (MPARAM)LIT_END, szCom);
    }
    WinSendDlgItemMsg (hWnd, IDC_PORT, LM_SELECTITEM,
       (MPARAM)ulPort, (MPARAM)TRUE);
}

/* Set values */
WinSendDlgItemMsg (hWnd, IDC_BAUDRATE, SLM_SETSLIDERINFO,
      MPFROM2SHORT (SMA_SLIDERARMPOSITION,
      SMA_INCREMENTVALUE),
      MPFROMSHORT(PortInfo[ulPort].BaudIndex));
WinCheckButton (hWnd,
 IDC_DATABITS_5+PortInfo[ulPort].LineControl.bDataBits-5,
   TRUE);
WinCheckButton (hWnd,
   IDC_STOPBITS_1+PortInfo[ulPort].LineControl.bStopBits,
      TRUE);
WinCheckButton (hWnd,
   IDC_PARITY_NONE+PortInfo[ulPort].LineControl.bParity,
      TRUE);
WinCheckButton (hWnd, IDC_HANDSHAKING_DTRC,
   PortInfo[ulPort].DCBInfo.fbCtlHndShake &
      MODE_DTR_CONTROL ? TRUE : FALSE);
WinCheckButton (hWnd, IDC_HANDSHAKING_DTRI,
   PortInfo[ulPort].DCBInfo.fbCtlHndShake &
      MODE_DTR_HANDSHAKE ? TRUE : FALSE);
WinCheckButton (hWnd, IDC_HANDSHAKING_CTSO,
   PortInfo[ulPort].DCBInfo.fbCtlHndShake &
      MODE_CTS_HANDSHAKE ? TRUE : FALSE);
WinCheckButton (hWnd, IDC_HANDSHAKING_DSRO,
   PortInfo[ulPort].DCBInfo.fbCtlHndShake &
      MODE_DSR_HANDSHAKE ? TRUE : FALSE);
WinCheckButton (hWnd, IDC_HANDSHAKING_DCDO,
   PortInfo[ulPort].DCBInfo.fbCtlHndShake &
      MODE_DCD_HANDSHAKE ? TRUE : FALSE);
```

```
    WinCheckButton (hWnd, IDC_HANDSHAKING_DSRI,
       PortInfo[ulPort].DCBInfo.fbCtlHndShake &
          MODE_DSR_SENSITIVITY ? TRUE : FALSE);
    WinCheckButton (hWnd, IDC_HANDSHAKING_RTSI,
       PortInfo[ulPort].DCBInfo.fbFlowReplace &
          MODE_RTS_HANDSHAKE ? TRUE : FALSE);
    WinCheckButton (hWnd, IDC_FLOWCONTROL_XONXOFFT,
       PortInfo[ulPort].DCBInfo.fbFlowReplace &
          MODE_AUTO_TRANSMIT ? TRUE : FALSE);
    WinCheckButton (hWnd, IDC_FLOWCONTROL_XONXOFFR,
       PortInfo[ulPort].DCBInfo.fbFlowReplace &
          MODE_AUTO_RECEIVE ? TRUE : FALSE);
    WinCheckButton (hWnd, IDC_FLOWCONTROL_ERRORREP,
       PortInfo[ulPort].DCBInfo.fbFlowReplace &
          MODE_ERROR_CHAR ? TRUE : FALSE);
    WinCheckButton (hWnd, IDC_FLOWCONTROL_NULLSTRIP,
       PortInfo[ulPort].DCBInfo.fbFlowReplace &
          MODE_NULL_STRIPPING ? TRUE : FALSE);
    WinCheckButton (hWnd, IDC_FLOWCONTROL_BREAKREP,
       PortInfo[ulPort].DCBInfo.fbFlowReplace &
          MODE_BREAK_CHAR ? TRUE : FALSE);
    WinCheckButton (hWnd, IDC_FLOWCONTROL_RTSC,
       PortInfo[ulPort].DCBInfo.fbFlowReplace &
          MODE_RTS_CONTROL ? TRUE : FALSE);
    WinCheckButton (hWnd, IDC_FLOWCONTROL_TOGGLING,
       PortInfo[ulPort].DCBInfo.fbFlowReplace &
          MODE_TRANSMIT_TOGGLE ? TRUE : FALSE);
    szTxt[0] = PortInfo[ulPort].DCBInfo.bXONChar;
    WinSetDlgItemText (hWnd, IDC_XONCHAR, szTxt);
    szTxt[0] = PortInfo[ulPort].DCBInfo.bXOFFChar;
    WinSetDlgItemText (hWnd, IDC_XOFFCHAR, szTxt);
    szTxt[0]=PortInfo[ulPort].DCBInfo.bErrorReplacementChar;
    WinSetDlgItemText (hWnd, IDC_ERRORREPCHAR, szTxt);
    szTxt[0]=PortInfo[ulPort].DCBInfo.bBreakReplacementChar;
    WinSetDlgItemText (hWnd, IDC_BREAKREPCHAR, szTxt);
    WinSendDlgItemMsg (hWnd, IDC_TIMEOUT_WRITE,
          SPBM_SETCURRENTVALUE,
          (MPARAM)PortInfo[ulPort].DCBInfo.usWriteTimeout,
          (MPARAM)0L);
    WinSendDlgItemMsg (hWnd, IDC_TIMEOUT_READ,
          SPBM_SETCURRENTVALUE,
          (MPARAM)PortInfo[ulPort].DCBInfo.usReadTimeout,
          (MPARAM)0L);

    return;
}

VOID PositionWindows (ULONG ulWidth, ULONG ulHeight)
{
    PSWP  pSwp;
    RECTL Rectl;

    /* Allocate memory to hold the SWP structures */
    if (!DosAllocMem ((PPVOID)&pSwp, sizeof(SWP) * 8L,
             fALLOC))
    {
```

```
/* Position buttons window */
WinQueryWindowRect (hWndButtons, &Rectl);
pSwp[0].fl    = SWP_MOVE;
pSwp[0].x     = ulWidth - Rectl.xRight - 5;
pSwp[0].y     = ulHeight - Rectl.yTop - 20;
pSwp[0].hwnd = hWndButtons;

/* Position status window */
WinQueryWindowRect (hWndStatus, &Rectl);
pSwp[1].fl    = SWP_MOVE;
pSwp[1].x     = 0;
pSwp[1].y     = 0;
pSwp[1].hwnd = hWndStatus;

ulWidth       = pSwp[0].x - 5;
ulHeight      = (ulHeight - Rectl.yTop) >> 1;

/* Position the local title window */
pSwp[2].fl    = SWP_MOVE;
pSwp[2].x     = 5;
pSwp[2].y     = Rectl.yTop + (ulHeight << 1) - 16;
pSwp[2].hwnd = hWndLocalTitle;

/* Size and position local edit window */
pSwp[3].fl    = SWP_MOVE ¦ SWP_SIZE;
pSwp[3].x     = 8;
pSwp[3].y     = pSwp[2].y - 20;
pSwp[3].cx    = ulWidth - 16;
pSwp[3].cy    = 16;
pSwp[3].hwnd = hWndLocalEdit;

/* Size and position local list window */
pSwp[4].fl    = SWP_MOVE ¦ SWP_SIZE;
pSwp[4].x     = 8;
pSwp[4].y     = Rectl.yTop + ulHeight + 8;
pSwp[4].cx    = ulWidth - 16;
pSwp[4].cy    = ulHeight - 50;
pSwp[4].hwnd = hWndLocalList;

/* Position the remote title window */
pSwp[5].fl    = SWP_MOVE;
pSwp[5].x     = 5;
pSwp[5].y     = Rectl.yTop + ulHeight - 16;
pSwp[5].hwnd = hWndRemoteTitle;

/* Size and position remote text window */
pSwp[6].fl    = SWP_MOVE ¦ SWP_SIZE;
pSwp[6].x     = 8;
pSwp[6].y     = pSwp[5].y - 20;
pSwp[6].cx    = ulWidth - 16;
pSwp[6].cy    = 16;
pSwp[6].hwnd = hWndRemoteText;

/* Size and position remote list window */
pSwp[7].fl    = SWP_MOVE ¦ SWP_SIZE;
pSwp[7].x     = 8;
```

```
        pSwp[7].y     = Rectl.yTop + 8;
        pSwp[7].cx    = ulWidth - 16;
        pSwp[7].cy    = ulHeight - 50;
        pSwp[7].hwnd = hWndRemoteList;

        /* Arrange the windows */
        WinSetMultWindowPos (hab, pSwp, 8L);

        /* Tell the bevel windows to resize themselves since
           the window they were sized around has changed its
           size */
        WinSendMsg (hWndLocalBevel1,  BVM_RESIZE,
              MPFROM2SHORT(2,2), 0L);
        WinSendMsg (hWndLocalBevel2,  BVM_RESIZE,
              MPFROM2SHORT(2,2), 0L);
        WinSendMsg (hWndRemoteBevel1, BVM_RESIZE,
              MPFROM2SHORT(2,2), 0L);
        WinSendMsg (hWndRemoteBevel2, BVM_RESIZE,
              MPFROM2SHORT(2,2), 0L);

        /* Free the allocated memory    */
        DosFreeMem ((PVOID)pSwp);

     }

     return;
  }

  VOID QueryBaudRate (ULONG ulPort)
  {
     DosDevIOCtl (hFile, IOCTL_ASYNC, ASYNC_GETBAUDRATE,
           NULL, 0L, 0L, (PVOID)&PortInfo[ulPort].BaudRate,
           2L, 0L);
     PortInfo[ulPort].BaudIndex = 12;
     while ((PortInfo[ulPort].BaudIndex > 0) &&
           (PortInfo[ulPort].BaudRate <
           BaudRates[PortInfo[ulPort].BaudIndex].ulValue))
        PortInfo[ulPort].BaudIndex--;

     return;
  }

  VOID QueryDCBInfo (ULONG ulPort)
  {
     DosDevIOCtl (hFile, IOCTL_ASYNC, ASYNC_GETDCBINFO,
           NULL, 0L, 0L, (PVOID)&PortInfo[ulPort].DCBInfo,
           sizeof(DCBINFO), 0L);

     return;
  }

  VOID QueryLineCtrl (ULONG ulPort)
  {
     DosDevIOCtl (hFile, IOCTL_ASYNC, ASYNC_GETLINECTRL,
           NULL, 0L, 0L, (PVOID)&PortInfo[ulPort].LineControl,
           sizeof(LINECONTROL), 0L);
```

```
   return;
}

VOID QueryValidCommPorts ()
{
   ULONG ulInx;
   ULONG ulAction;
   BYTE  cCommPorts;

   /* Determine the number of communication ports on the
      system */
   DosDevConfig (&cCommPorts, DEVINFO_RS232);
   ulNumPorts = (ULONG)cCommPorts;

   /* Attempt to query current com port settings */
   for (ulInx = 0; ulInx < ulNumPorts; ulInx++)
   {
      szCom[3] = (CHAR)('1' + ulInx);
      if (!DosOpen (szCom, &hFile, &ulAction, 0L,
            FILE_NORMAL, FILE_OPEN, OPEN_ACCESS_READWRITE ¦
            OPEN_SHARE_DENYNONE, 0L))
      {
         QueryBaudRate (ulInx);
         QueryDCBInfo (ulInx);
         QueryLineCtrl (ulInx);
         DosClose (hFile);
         PortInfo[ulInx].DCBInfo.usWriteTimeout        = 0;
         PortInfo[ulInx].DCBInfo.usReadTimeout         = 0;
      }
      else
      {
         /* Set to default values */
         PortInfo[ulInx].BaudIndex                = 11;
         PortInfo[ulInx].BaudRate                 = 9600;
         PortInfo[ulInx].LineControl.bDataBits    = 5;
         PortInfo[ulInx].LineControl.bStopBits    = 0;
         PortInfo[ulInx].LineControl.bParity      = 0;
         PortInfo[ulInx].DCBInfo.fbCtlHndShake    = 0;
         PortInfo[ulInx].DCBInfo.fbFlowReplace    = 0;
         PortInfo[ulInx].DCBInfo.bXONChar      = 0x11;
         PortInfo[ulInx].DCBInfo.bXOFFChar     = 0x13;
         PortInfo[ulInx].DCBInfo.bErrorReplacementChar=' ';
         PortInfo[ulInx].DCBInfo.bBreakReplacementChar=' ';
         PortInfo[ulInx].DCBInfo.usWriteTimeout        = 0;
         PortInfo[ulInx].DCBInfo.usReadTimeout         = 0;
      }
   }

   return;
}

BOOL SetPortSettings (HWND hWnd)
{
  BOOL bSet =
   !DosDevIOCtl (hFile, IOCTL_ASYNC, ASYNC_SETBAUDRATE,
      &PortInfo[ulPort].BaudRate,2L,NULL,NULL,0L,NULL) &&
```

```
   !DosDevIOCtl (hFile, IOCTL_ASYNC,
      ASYNC_SETLINECTRL, &PortInfo[ulPort].LineControl, 3L,
         NULL, NULL, 0L, NULL) &&
   !DosDevIOCtl (hFile, IOCTL_ASYNC, ASYNC_SETDCBINFO,
      &PortInfo[ulPort].DCBInfo,sizeof(DCBINFO),0L,NULL,0L,
         NULL);

   if (!bSet)
      WinMessageBox (HWND_DESKTOP, hWnd,
         "Unable to set port settings", "Phone Application",
         0, MB_ERROR ¦ MB_OK);

   return (bSet);
}

VOID ToggleTransmit (HWND hWnd)
{
   /* Toggle the data transmission state */

   if (bTransmitting)
   {
      if (!DosDevIOCtl (hFile, IOCTL_ASYNC,
            ASYNC_STOPTRANSMIT,
            NULL, 0L, NULL, NULL, 0L, NULL))
      {
         bTransmitting = FALSE;
         WinSetDlgItemText (hWnd, IDC_TRANSMIT, "Start");
      }
   }
   else
   {
      if (!DosDevIOCtl (hFile, IOCTL_ASYNC,
            ASYNC_STARTTRANSMIT,
            NULL, 0L, NULL, NULL, 0L, NULL))
      {
         bTransmitting = TRUE;
         WinSetDlgItemText (hWnd, IDC_TRANSMIT, "Stop");
      }
   }

   return;
}

VOID TransmitLine ()
{
   CHAR  szBuffer[255];
   ULONG ulLen;
   ULONG ulBytesWritten;

   WinSendDlgItemMsg (hWndStatus, IDC_LINESTATUS_WRT,
         WM_ENABLE, MPFROMSHORT(TRUE), 0L);

   /* If data transmission is turned off then beep - can't
      send the data */
   if (!bTransmitting)
   {
```

```
      DosBeep (500, 50);
      return;
   }

   /* Limit the number of lines in the listbox */
   if (ulNumLocalLines == 100)
   {
      WinSendMsg (hWndLocalList, LM_DELETEITEM, (MPARAM)99L,
            0L);
      ulNumLocalLines--;
   }
   ulLen = WinQueryWindowText (hWndLocalEdit,
            sizeof(szBuffer)-2, szBuffer);
   szBuffer[ulLen++] = 0x0D;
   szBuffer[ulLen++] = 0x0A;

   /* Write data to the communications port */
   DosEnterCritSec ();

   if (!DosWrite (hFile, szBuffer, ulLen, &ulBytesWritten))
   {
      szBuffer[ulLen-2] = '\0';
      WinSendMsg (hWndLocalList, LM_INSERTITEM, 0L,
            (MPARAM)szBuffer);
      WinSetWindowText (hWndLocalEdit, "");
      ulNumLocalLines++;
   }

   DosExitCritSec ();

   WinSendDlgItemMsg (hWndStatus, IDC_LINESTATUS_WRT,
         WM_ENABLE, MPFROMSHORT(FALSE), 0L);

   return;
}

/* -------- Window and Dialog Functions -------- */

MRESULT EXPENTRY ClientWndProc (HWND hWnd, ULONG msg,
      MPARAM mp1, MPARAM mp2)
{
   BOOL    bHandled = TRUE;
   MRESULT mReturn  = 0;
   RECTL   Rectl;
   HPS     hps;

   switch (msg)
   {
      case WM_CREATE:
         {
            LONG RGBBack = 0x00CCCCCCL;
            LONG RGBText = 0x00000000L;
            WinSetPresParam (hWnd, PP_FONTNAMESIZE,
                  FONTNAMELEN, HELV8FONT);
            WinSetPresParam (hWnd, PP_BACKGROUNDCOLOR,
                  sizeof(RGBBack), &RGBBack);
```

```
         WinSetPresParam (hWnd, PP_FOREGROUNDCOLOR,
            sizeof(RGBText), &RGBText);
         QueryValidCommPorts ();
      }
      break;

   case WM_USER_RCVLIST:
      /* Data in the receive buffer is a complete line -
         insert it into the Remote listbox. */

      WinSendDlgItemMsg (hWndStatus, IDC_LINESTATUS_RED,
            WM_ENABLE, MPFROMSHORT(TRUE), 0L);

      /* Limit the number of lines in the listbox */
      if (ulNumRemoteLines == 100)
      {
         WinSendMsg (hWndRemoteList, LM_DELETEITEM,
               (MPARAM)99L, 0L);
         ulNumRemoteLines--;
      }
      WinSendMsg (hWndRemoteList, LM_INSERTITEM, 0L,
            (MPARAM)szReceiveBuffer);
      ulNumRemoteLines--+;

      /* Post the receive data event semaphore to notify
         the ReceiveData thread that we are done with
         szReceiveBuffer */
      DosPostEventSem (hevRcvQueue);

      WinSendDlgItemMsg (hWndStatus, IDC_LINESTATUS_RED,
            WM_ENABLE, MPFROMSHORT(FALSE), 0L);
      break;

   case WM_USER_RCVTEXT:
      /* Data in the receive buffer is an incomplete line
         - update the Remote text window */

      WinSendDlgItemMsg (hWndStatus, IDC_LINESTATUS_RED,
            WM_ENABLE, MPFROMSHORT(TRUE), 0L);

      WinSetWindowText (hWndRemoteText, szReceiveBuffer);

      /* Post the receive data event semaphore to notify
         the ReceiveData thread that we are done with
         szReceiveBuffer */
      DosPostEventSem (hevRcvQueue);

      WinSendDlgItemMsg (hWndStatus, IDC_LINESTATUS_RED,
            WM_ENABLE, MPFROMSHORT(FALSE), 0L);
      break;

   case WM_PAINT:
      hps = WinBeginPaint (hWnd,0,0);
      WinQueryWindowRect (hWnd, &Rectl);
      WinFillRect (hps, &Rectl, CLR_PALEGRAY);
      WinEndPaint (hps);
      break;
```

```
      case WM_CONTROL:
         /* If we get a doubleclick or enter from the Local
            listbox then copy the text from the listbox to
            the Local edit window */

         if ( bConnected &&
               (SHORT2FROMMP(mp1) == LN_ENTER) &&
               ((HWND)mp2 == hWndLocalList) )
         {
            SHORT sIndex;
            CHAR  szTxt[255];

            sIndex = (SHORT)WinSendMsg (hWndLocalList,
                  LM_QUERYSELECTION, (MPARAM)LIT_FIRST, 0L);
            if (sIndex != LIT_NONE)
            {
               WinSendMsg (hWndLocalList, LM_QUERYITEMTEXT,
                     MPFROM2SHORT(sIndex,255), szTxt);
               WinSetWindowText (hWndLocalEdit, szTxt);
               WinSetFocus (HWND_DESKTOP, hWndLocalEdit);
            }
         }
         break;

      case WM_CHAR:
         /* If the enter key is pressed in either the Local
            edit or Local listbox then transmit the data */

         if ( bConnected &&
               (WinQueryFocus(HWND_DESKTOP)==hWndLocalEdit) &&
               !(SHORT1FROMMP(mp1) & KC_KEYUP) &&
               (SHORT1FROMMP(mp1) & KC_VIRTUALKEY) &&
               ( (SHORT2FROMMP(mp2) == VK_ENTER) ||
               (SHORT2FROMMP(mp2) == VK_NEWLINE) ) )
            TransmitLine ();
         break;

      case WM_SIZE:
         PositionWindows ((ULONG)SHORT1FROMMP(mp2),
         (ULONG)SHORT2FROMMP(mp2));
         break;

      default:
         bHandled = FALSE;
         break;
   }

   if (!bHandled)
      mReturn = WinDefWindowProc (hWnd,msg,mp1,mp2);

   return (mReturn);
}

MRESULT EXPENTRY StatusDlgProc (HWND hWnd, ULONG msg,
      MPARAM mp1, MPARAM mp2)
{
```

```
         WinSendDlgItemMsg (hWnd, IDC_MODEM_DCD, WM_ENABLE,
               MPFROMSHORT(ModemInput & DCD_ON), 0L);
         break;

      case WM_USER_MODEMOUTPUT:
         WinSendDlgItemMsg (hWnd, IDC_MODEM_DTR, WM_ENABLE,
               MPFROMSHORT(ModemOutput.fbModemOn & DTR_ON),
               0L);
         WinSendDlgItemMsg (hWnd, IDC_MODEM_RTS, WM_ENABLE,
               MPFROMSHORT(ModemOutput.fbModemOn & RTS_ON),
               0L);
         break;

      case WM_COMMAND:
         switch (LOUSHORT(mp1))
         {
            case IDC_CONNECT:
               ConnectToPort (hWnd);
               break;

            case IDC_HANGUP:
               HangUpFromPort (hWnd);
               break;

            case IDC_SETTINGS:
               WinDlgBox (HWND_DESKTOP, hWnd,
                  SettingsDlgProc, 0L, IDD_SETTINGS, NULL);
               break;

            case IDC_TRANSMIT:
               ToggleTransmit (hWnd);
               break;

            case IDC_ABOUT:
               DisplayAbout (hWnd, szTitle);
               break;
         }
         if (bConnected)
            WinSetFocus (HWND_DESKTOP, hWndLocalEdit);
         break;

      case WM_DESTROY:
         if (bConnected)
            HangUpFromPort (hWndButtons);
         break;

      default:
         bHandled = FALSE;
         break;
   }

   if (!bHandled)
      mReturn = WinDefDlgProc (hWnd, msg, mp1, mp2);

   return (mReturn);
}
```

```
MRESULT EXPENTRY SettingsDlgProc (HWND hWnd, ULONG msg,
            MPARAM mp1, MPARAM mp2)
{
   MRESULT mReturn  = 0;
   BOOL    bHandled = TRUE;

   switch (msg)
   {
      case WM_INITDLG:
         CenterWindow (hWnd);
         InitializeControls (hWnd, TRUE);
         if (bConnected)
            WinEnableControl (hWnd, IDC_PORT, FALSE);
         break;

      case WM_CONTROL:
         switch (LOUSHORT(mp1))
         {
            case IDC_PORT:
               if (HIUSHORT(mp1) == CBN_EFCHANGE)
               {
                  ulPort = (ULONG)WinSendDlgItemMsg (hWnd,
                           IDC_PORT, LM_QUERYSELECTION,
                           (MPARAM)LIT_FIRST, 0L);
                  InitializeControls (hWnd, FALSE);
               }
               break;
         }
         break;

      case WM_COMMAND:
         switch (LOUSHORT(mp1))
         {
            case DID_OK:
               DeInitializeControls (hWnd);
               if (bConnected)
                  SetPortSettings (hWnd);

               /* FALL THROUGH */

            case DID_CANCEL:
               WinDismissDlg (hWnd, DID_OK);
               break;
         }
         break;

      default:
         bHandled = FALSE;
         break;
   }

   if (!bHandled)
      mReturn = WinDefDlgProc (hWnd, msg, mp1, mp2);

   return (mReturn);
}
```

PHONE.H

```
/* --------------------------------
          Phone Header File
     Real-World Programming for OS/2
Copyright (c) 1994 Blain, Delimon, and English
-------------------------------- */

#define FONTNAMELEN 7         /* length + 1 */
#define HELV8FONT   "8.Helv"


/* Dialog and Control Identifiers     */

#define ID_APPNAME                      1

#define IDD_SETTINGS                   10
#define IDD_STATUS                     20
#define IDD_BUTTONS                    30

#define IDB_LED                        50

#define IDC_PORT                      100
#define IDC_BAUDRATE                  101
#define IDC_DATABITS_5                103
#define IDC_DATABITS_6                104
#define IDC_DATABITS_7                105
#define IDC_DATABITS_8                106
#define IDC_STOPBITS_1                107
#define IDC_STOPBITS_15               108
#define IDC_STOPBITS_2                109
#define IDC_PARITY_NONE               110
#define IDC_PARITY_ODD                111
#define IDC_PARITY_EVEN               112
#define IDC_PARITY_MARK               113
#define IDC_PARITY_SPACE              114
#define IDC_HANDSHAKING_DTRC          115
#define IDC_HANDSHAKING_DTRI          116
#define IDC_HANDSHAKING_CTSO          117
#define IDC_HANDSHAKING_DSRO          118
#define IDC_HANDSHAKING_DCDO          119
#define IDC_HANDSHAKING_DSRI          120
#define IDC_HANDSHAKING_RTSI          121
#define IDC_FLOWCONTROL_XONXOFFT      122
#define IDC_XONCHAR                   123
#define IDC_XOFFCHAR                  124
#define IDC_FLOWCONTROL_XONXOFFR      125
#define IDC_FLOWCONTROL_ERRORREP      126
#define IDC_FLOWCONTROL_NULLSTRIP     127
#define IDC_FLOWCONTROL_BREAKREP      128
#define IDC_FLOWCONTROL_RTSC          129
#define IDC_FLOWCONTROL_TOGGLING      130
#define IDC_ERRORREPCHAR              131
#define IDC_BREAKREPCHAR              132
#define IDC_TIMEOUT_WRITE             133
#define IDC_TIMEOUT_READ              134
```

```
#define IDC_COMMEVENT_CTS              200
#define IDC_COMMEVENT_DSR              201
#define IDC_COMMEVENT_DCD              202
#define IDC_COMMEVENT_BRK              203
#define IDC_COMMEVENT_ERR              204
#define IDC_COMMEVENT_RI               205
#define IDC_COMMSTATUS_CTS             206
#define IDC_COMMSTATUS_DST             207
#define IDC_COMMSTATUS_DCD             208
#define IDC_COMMSTATUS_XON             209
#define IDC_COMMSTATUS_XOF             210
#define IDC_COMMSTATUS_BRK             211
#define IDC_COMMSTATUS_IMM             212
#define IDC_COMMSTATUS_DSR             213
#define IDC_QUEUE_IN                   214
#define IDC_QUEUE_OUT                  215
#define IDC_MODEM_CTS                  216
#define IDC_MODEM_DSR                  218
#define IDC_MODEM_RI                   219
#define IDC_MODEM_DCD                  220
#define IDC_MODEM_DTR                  221
#define IDC_MODEM_RTS                  222
#define IDC_LINESTATUS_WRQ             223
#define IDC_LINESTATUS_DTQ             224
#define IDC_LINESTATUS_HTX             225
#define IDC_LINESTATUS_CRS             226
#define IDC_LINESTATUS_XON             227
#define IDC_LINESTATUS_XOF             228
#define IDC_LINESTATUS_RED             229
#define IDC_LINESTATUS_WRT             230
#define IDC_COMMERROR_QOV              231
#define IDC_COMMERROR_HOV              232
#define IDC_COMMERROR_PAR              233
#define IDC_COMMERROR_FRM              234

#define IDC_CONNECT                    300
#define IDC_HANGUP                     301
#define IDC_SETTINGS                   302
#define IDC_TRANSMIT                   303
#define IDC_ABOUT                      304
```

PHONE.RC

```
/* ------------------------------
        Phone Resource File
     Real-World Programming for OS/2
Copyright (c) 1994 Blain, Delimon, and English
   ------------------------------ */

#include <os2.h>
#include "phone.h"
#include "led.h"

ICON ID_APPNAME PHONE.ICO
```

```
      AUTOCHECKBOX "Error Replacement",
                    IDC_FLOWCONTROL_ERRORREP,
                    218,  82, 73, 10
      AUTOCHECKBOX "Null Stripping",
                    IDC_FLOWCONTROL_NULLSTRIP,
                    218,  72, 73, 10
      AUTOCHECKBOX "Break Replacement",
                    IDC_FLOWCONTROL_BREAKREP,
                    218,  62, 73, 10
      AUTOCHECKBOX "RTS Control",
                    IDC_FLOWCONTROL_RTSC,
                    218,  52, 73, 10
      AUTOCHECKBOX "Toggling",
                    IDC_FLOWCONTROL_TOGGLING,
                    218,  42, 73, 10
      ENTRYFIELD    "", IDC_ERRORREPCHAR, 295, 82, 6, 8,
                    ES_CENTER ¦ NOT ES_AUTOSCROLL ¦ ES_MARGIN

      ENTRYFIELD    "", IDC_BREAKREPCHAR, 295, 62, 6, 8,
                   ES_CENTER ¦ NOT ES_AUTOSCROLL ¦ ES_MARGIN
      GROUPBOX      "Timeouts", -1, 54, 8, 128, 23
      LTEXT         "Write", -1, 59, 14, 20, 8
      CONTROL       "", IDC_TIMEOUT_WRITE, 83, 12, 32, 12,
                    WC_SPINBUTTON, SPBS_ALLCHARACTERS ¦
                   SPBS_NUMERICONLY ¦ SPBS_MASTER ¦
                   SPBS_SERVANT ¦ SPBS_JUSTRIGHT ¦
                   SPBS_FASTSPIN ¦ WS_GROUP ¦ WS_TABSTOP ¦
                   WS_VISIBLE
      LTEXT         "Read", -1, 119, 14, 20, 8
      CONTROL       "", IDC_TIMEOUT_READ, 143, 12, 32, 12,
                   WC_SPINBUTTON, SPBS_ALLCHARACTERS ¦
                   SPBS_NUMERICONLY ¦ SPBS_MASTER ¦
                   SPBS_SERVANT ¦ SPBS_JUSTRIGHT ¦
                   SPBS_FASTSPIN ¦ WS_GROUP ¦ WS_TABSTOP ¦
                   WS_VISIBLE
      PUSHBUTTON    "OK",     DID_OK,     229, 11, 40, 14
      PUSHBUTTON    "Cancel", DID_CANCEL, 279, 11, 40, 14
   END
END
```

STATUS.DLG

```
/* -------------------------------
           Status Dialog
     Real-World Programming for OS/2
Copyright (c) 1994 Blain, Delimon, and English
--------------------------------*/

DLGTEMPLATE IDD_STATUS LOADONCALL MOVEABLE DISCARDABLE
BEGIN
   DIALOG  "", IDD_STATUS, 41, 184, 373, 43, NOT
           FS_DLGBORDER ¦

WS_VISIBLE, FCF_NOBYTEALIGN
   PRESPARAMS PP_FONTNAMESIZE, "8.Helv"
   BEGIN
```

```
GROUPBOX "Comm Event", -1,           2, 24, 119, 19
CONTROL  "CTS", IDC_COMMEVENT_CTS,    5, 26,  17, 11,
         LEDCLASS, WS_VISIBLE
CONTROL  "DSR", IDC_COMMEVENT_DSR,   24, 26,  17, 11,
         LEDCLASS, WS_VISIBLE
CONTROL  "DCD", IDC_COMMEVENT_DCD,   43, 26,  17, 11,
         LEDCLASS, WS_VISIBLE
CONTROL  "BRK", IDC_COMMEVENT_BRK,   62, 26,  17, 11,
         LEDCLASS, WS_VISIBLE
CONTROL  "ERR", IDC_COMMEVENT_ERR,   81, 26,  17, 11,
         LEDCLASS, WS_VISIBLE
CONTROL  "RI",  IDC_COMMEVENT_RI,   100, 26,  17, 11,
         LEDCLASS, WS_VISIBLE
GROUPBOX "Comm Status", -1,         127, 24, 156, 19
CONTROL  "CTS", IDC_COMMSTATUS_CTS, 130, 26,  17, 11,
         LEDCLASS, WS_VISIBLE
CONTROL  "DSR", IDC_COMMSTATUS_DST, 149, 26,  17, 11,
         LEDCLASS, WS_VISIBLE
CONTROL  "DCD", IDC_COMMSTATUS_DCD, 168, 26,  17, 11,
         LEDCLASS, WS_VISIBLE
CONTROL  "XOF", IDC_COMMSTATUS_XON, 187, 26,  17, 11,
         LEDCLASS, WS_VISIBLE
CONTROL  "XON", IDC_COMMSTATUS_XOF, 206, 26,  17, 11,
         LEDCLASS, WS_VISIBLE
CONTROL  "BRK", IDC_COMMSTATUS_BRK, 225, 26,  17, 11,
         LEDCLASS, WS_VISIBLE
CONTROL  "IMM", IDC_COMMSTATUS_IMM, 244, 26,  17, 11,
         LEDCLASS, WS_VISIBLE
CONTROL  "DSR", IDC_COMMSTATUS_DSR, 263, 26,  17, 11,
         LEDCLASS, WS_VISIBLE
GROUPBOX "Queue", -1,               292, 24,  80, 19
LTEXT    "Rcv",    -1,              295, 27,  15,  8
LTEXT    "0000", IDC_QUEUE_IN,      311, 27,  18,  8
LTEXT    "Xmt",    -1,              334, 27,  15,  8
LTEXT    "0000", IDC_QUEUE_OUT,     350, 27,  18,  8
GROUPBOX "Modem", -1,                 2,  3, 119, 19
CONTROL  "CTS", IDC_MODEM_CTS,        5,  5,  17, 11,
         LEDCLASS, WS_VISIBLE
CONTROL  "DSR", IDC_MODEM_DSR,       24,  5,  17, 11,
         LEDCLASS, WS_VISIBLE
CONTROL  "RI",  IDC_MODEM_RI,        43,  5,  17, 11,
         LEDCLASS, WS_VISIBLE
CONTROL  "DCD", IDC_MODEM_DCD,       62,  5,  17, 11,
         LEDCLASS, WS_VISIBLE
CONTROL  "DTR", IDC_MODEM_DTR,       81,  5,  17, 11,
         LEDCLASS, WS_VISIBLE
CONTROL  "RTS", IDC_MODEM_RTS,      100,  5,  17, 11,
         LEDCLASS, WS_VISIBLE
GROUPBOX "Line Status", -1,         127,  3, 156, 19
CONTROL  "WRQ", IDC_LINESTATUS_WRQ, 130,  5,  17, 11,
         LEDCLASS, WS_VISIBLE
CONTROL  "DTQ", IDC_LINESTATUS_DTQ, 149,  5,  17, 11,
         LEDCLASS, WS_VISIBLE
CONTROL  "HTX", IDC_LINESTATUS_HTX, 168,  5,  17, 11,
         LEDCLASS, WS_VISIBLE
```

```
      CONTROL  "CRS", IDC_LINESTATUS_CRS, 187,  5,  17, 11,
               LEDCLASS, WS_VISIBLE
      CONTROL  "XON", IDC_LINESTATUS_XON, 206,  5,  17, 11,
               LEDCLASS, WS_VISIBLE
      CONTROL  "XOF", IDC_LINESTATUS_XOF, 225,  5,  17, 11,
               LEDCLASS, WS_VISIBLE
      CONTROL  "RED", IDC_LINESTATUS_RED, 244,  5,  17, 11,
               LEDCLASS, WS_VISIBLE
      CONTROL  "WRT", IDC_LINESTATUS_WRT, 263,  5,  17, 11,
               LEDCLASS, WS_VISIBLE
      GROUPBOX "Comm Error", -1,          292,  3,  80, 19
      CONTROL  "QOV", IDC_COMMERROR_QOV,  295,  5,  17, 11,
               LEDCLASS, WS_VISIBLE
      CONTROL  "HOV", IDC_COMMERROR_HOV,  314,  5,  17, 11,
               LEDCLASS, WS_VISIBLE
      CONTROL  "PAR", IDC_COMMERROR_PAR,  333,  5,  17, 11,
               LEDCLASS, WS_VISIBLE
      CONTROL  "FRM", IDC_COMMERROR_FRM,  352,  5,  17, 11,
               LEDCLASS, WS_VISIBLE
   END
END
```

BUTTONS.DLG

```
/* ------------------------------
           Settings Dialog
     Real-World Programming for OS/2
Copyright (c) 1994 Blain, Delimon, and English
-------------------------------- */

DLGTEMPLATE IDD_BUTTONS LOADONCALL MOVEABLE DISCARDABLE
BEGIN
   DIALOG  "Communications Settings", IDD_SETTINGS, 41, 104,
           327, 125, WS_VISIBLE,
           FCF_SYSMENU | FCF_TITLEBAR | FCF_NOBYTEALIGN
           PRESPARAMS PP_FONTNAMESIZE, "8.Helv"
   BEGIN
      LTEXT          "Port", -1, 3, 112, 20, 8
      CONTROL        "", IDC_PORT, 3, 77, 35, 35,
                 WC_COMBOBOX,
                 CBS_DROPDOWNLIST | WS_GROUP | WS_TABSTOP |
                 WS_VISIBLE
      LTEXT          "Baud Rate", -1 , 3,  92, 37,  8
      CONTROL        "", IDC_BAUDRATE, 7, 1, 44, 91,
                 WC_SLIDER,
                 SLS_VERTICAL | SLS_LEFT |
                 SLS_SNAPTOINCREMENT |
                 SLS_BUTTONSBOTTOM | SLS_HOMETOP |
                 SLS_PRIMARYSCALE1 | WS_GROUP|WS_TABSTOP |
                 WS_VISIBLE
      CTLDATA 12, 0, 13, 0, 0, 0
      GROUPBOX       "Data Bits", -1, 55, 100, 79, 20
      AUTORADIOBUTTON "5", IDC_DATABITS_5,   59, 102, 18,
                 10, WS_TABSTOP
      AUTORADIOBUTTON "6", IDC_DATABITS_6,   78, 102, 18,
                 10, WS_TABSTOP
```

```
AUTORADIOBUTTON "7", IDC_DATABITS_7,   95, 102, 18,
            10, WS_TABSTOP
AUTORADIOBUTTON "8", IDC_DATABITS_8,  113, 102, 18,
            10, WS_TABSTOP
GROUPBOX        "Stop Bits", -1, 55, 75, 79, 22
AUTORADIOBUTTON "1",  IDC_STOPBITS_1,  60, 78, 18, 10,
            WS_TABSTOP
AUTORADIOBUTTON "1.5",IDC_STOPBITS_15, 84, 78, 24, 10,
            WS_TABSTOP
AUTORADIOBUTTON "2",  IDC_STOPBITS_2, 114, 78, 18, 10,
            WS_TABSTOP
GROUPBOX        "Parity", -1, 54, 33, 80, 38
AUTORADIOBUTTON "None",  IDC_PARITY_NONE,  58, 52, 33,
            10, WS_TABSTOP
AUTORADIOBUTTON "Odd",   IDC_PARITY_ODD,   58, 43, 33,
            10, WS_TABSTOP
AUTORADIOBUTTON "Even",  IDC_PARITY_EVEN,  58, 35, 33,
            10, WS_TABSTOP
AUTORADIOBUTTON "Mark",  IDC_PARITY_MARK,  96, 52, 33,
            10, WS_TABSTOP
AUTORADIOBUTTON "Space", IDC_PARITY_SPACE, 96, 43, 33,
            10, WS_TABSTOP
GROUPBOX        "Handshaking", -1, 139, 33, 70, 87
AUTOCHECKBOX "DTR Control", IDC_HANDSHAKING_DTRC, 144,
            102, 50, 10
AUTOCHECKBOX "DTR Input",   IDC_HANDSHAKING_DTRI, 144,
            92, 50, 10
AUTOCHECKBOX "CTS Output",  IDC_HANDSHAKING_CTSO, 144,
            82, 50, 10
AUTOCHECKBOX "DSR Output",  IDC_HANDSHAKING_DSRO, 144,
            72, 50, 10
AUTOCHECKBOX "DCD Output",  IDC_HANDSHAKING_DCDO, 144,
            62, 50, 10
AUTOCHECKBOX "DSR Input",   IDC_HANDSHAKING_DSRI, 144,
            52, 50, 10
AUTOCHECKBOX "RTS Input",   IDC_HANDSHAKING_RTSI, 144,
            42, 50, 10
GROUPBOX     "Flow Control", -1, 214, 33, 105, 87
AUTOCHECKBOX "XON/XOFF Transmit",
            IDC_FLOWCONTROL_XONXOFFT,
            218, 102, 73, 10
ENTRYFIELD   "", IDC_XONCHAR,  295, 102, 6, 8,
            ES_CENTER ¦ NOT ES_AUTOSCROLL ¦
            ES_MARGIN
ENTRYFIELD   "", IDC_XOFFCHAR, 305, 102, 6, 8,
            ES_CENTER ¦ NOT ES_AUTOSCROLL ¦
            ES_MARGIN
AUTOCHECKBOX "XON/XOFF Receive",
            IDC_FLOWCONTROL_XONXOFFR,
            218,  92, 73, 10
AUTOCHECKBOX "Error Replacement",
            IDC_FLOWCONTROL_ERRORREP,
            218,  82, 73, 10
AUTOCHECKBOX "Null Stripping",
            IDC_FLOWCONTROL_NULLSTRIP,
            218,  72, 73, 10
```

```
BOOL bSet =
   !DosDevIOCtl (hFile, IOCTL_ASYNC, ASYNC_SETBAUDRATE,
     &PortInfo[ulPort].BaudRate, 2L, NULL, NULL, 0L, NULL) &&
   !DosDevIOCtl (hFile, IOCTL_ASYNC, ASYNC_SETLINECTRL,
     &PortInfo[ulPort].LineControl,3L,NULL,NULL,0L, NULL)    &&
   !DosDevIOCtl (hFile, IOCTL_ASYNC, ASYNC_SETDCBINFO,
      &PortInfo[ulPort].DCBInfo,sizeof(DCBINFO),0L,NULL, 0L,

      NULL);
```

When the data is ready to be transmitted, `TransmitLine` is called. In addition to adding the line to the local history list, it calls `DosWrite` to transmit the data. Notice that we surround the call to `DosWrite` with calls to `DosEnterCritSec` and `DosExitCritSec` so that we protect the port file handle from being used by the other threads at the same time:

```
/* Write data to the communications port */
DosEnterCritSec ();

if (!DosWrite (hFile, szBuffer, ulLen, &ulBytesWritten))
{
   szBuffer[ulLen-2] = '\0';
   WinSendMsg (hWndLocalList, LM_INSERTITEM, 0L,
         (MPARAM)szBuffer);
   WinSetWindowText (hWndLocalEdit, "");
   ulNumLocalLines++;
}

DosExitCritSec ();
```

When we are ready to hang up the session, we call `HangUpFromPort`. The first thing to be done is flush both the input and output queues. This is done, not by an `IOCTL_ASYNC` call, but by using an `IOCTL_GENERAL` call:

```
/* Flush the input and output buffers */
DosDevIOCtl (hFile, IOCTL_GENERAL, DEV_FLUSHOUTPUT,
      (PVOID)&Cmd, 1L, NULL, NULL, 0L, NULL);
DosDevIOCtl (hFile, IOCTL_GENERAL, DEV_FLUSHINPUT,
      (PVOID)&Cmd, 1L, NULL, NULL, 0L, NULL);
```

We then call `DosClose` to close the connection, kill the other two threads, and close the event semaphore:

```
if (!DosClose (hFile))
{
   WinEnableControl (hWnd, IDC_CONNECT, TRUE);
   WinEnableControl (hWnd, IDC_HANGUP,  FALSE);
   WinEnableWindow (hWndLocalEdit, FALSE);

   /* Stop the CommStatus and ReceiveData threads */
   DosKillThread (StatusThreadID);
   DosKillThread (ReadThreadID);

   /* Close the receive data event semaphore */
   DosCloseEventSem (hevRcvQueue);
```

```
   bConnected = FALSE;
}
```

The ReceiveData thread is a continuous loop calling DosRead to receive data from the receive queue. Again, we make the call to DosRead within a critical section:

```
DosEnterCritSec ();

DosRead (hFile, szBuffer, (ULONG)sizeof(szBuffer), &ulBytesRead);

DosExitCritSec ();
```

When the carriage return character is detected, signalling that characters are ready to be written out to the port, the line can be added to the remote history list. We call DosResetEventSem to clear the event semaphore and post a message to the main thread telling it that the data in szReceiveBuffer contains a complete line of text.

After posting the message, we wait for the event semaphore to be set by the main thread before continuing:

```
/* Clear the event semaphore */
DosResetEventSem (hevRcvQueue, &ulEventCnt);

WinPostMsg (hWndClient, WM_USER_RCVLIST, 0L, 0L);

/* Wait for main message queue thread to process message */
DosWaitEventSem (hevRcvQueue, 1000);
```

When all the data from the last DosRead has been processed, we notify the main thread that the data in szReceiveBuffer contains an incomplete line of text. This is done similarly to the previous state:

```
/* Clear the event semaphore */
DosResetEventSem (hevRcvQueue, &ulEventCnt);

szReceiveBuffer[usNextPos] = '\0';
WinPostMsg (hWndClient, WM_USER_RCVTEXT, 0L, 0L);

/* Wait for main message queue thread to process message */
DosWaitEventSem (hevRcvQueue, 1000);
```

Finally, before repeating the loop, we put the thread to sleep for 0.10 seconds.

The CommStatusThread is a continuous loop calling DosDevIOCtl to query the current state of the various communication flags. Like the other two threads, the use of the file handle is enclosed in a critical section:

```
DosEnterCritSec ();

DosDevIOCtl (hFile, IOCTL_ASYNC, ASYNC_GETCOMMEVENT,
   NULL, 0L, 0L, &NewComEvent, 2L, 0L);
DosDevIOCtl (hFile, IOCTL_ASYNC, ASYNC_GETCOMMSTATUS,
   NULL, 0L, 0L, &NewComStatus, 1L, 0L);
DosDevIOCtl (hFile, IOCTL_ASYNC, ASYNC_GETINQUECOUNT,
   NULL, 0L, 0L, &NewReceiveQueue, sizeof(RXQUEUE), 0L);
```

```
DosDevIOCtl (hFile, IOCTL_ASYNC, ASYNC_GETOUTQUECOUNT,
   NULL, 0L, 0L, &NewTransmitQueue, sizeof(RXQUEUE), 0L);
DosDevIOCtl (hFile, IOCTL_ASYNC, ASYNC_GETMODEMINPUT,
   NULL, 0L, 0L, &NewModemInput, 1L, 0L);
DosDevIOCtl (hFile, IOCTL_ASYNC, ASYNC_GETMODEMOUTPUT,
   NULL, 0L, 0L, &NewModemOutput, sizeof(MODEMSTATUS), 0L);
DosDevIOCtl (hFile, IOCTL_ASYNC, ASYNC_GETLINESTATUS,
   NULL, 0L, 0L, &NewTransmitStatus, 1L, 0L);
DosDevIOCtl (hFile, IOCTL_ASYNC, ASYNC_GETCOMMERROR,
   NULL, 0L, 0L, &NewComError, 2L, 0L);

DosExitCritSec ();
```

Each set of flags is compared with the previous values, and a message is posted to the main thread indicating which set of flags has changed. The main thread then enables or disables the various LED windows to indicate the current state of the flags. Finally, before repeating the loop, we put the thread to sleep for 0.20 seconds.

When the main thread receives the `WM_USER_RCVLIST` message posted from the `ReceiveDataThread`, it adds the text in the `szReceiveBuffer` to the remote history list and posts the event semaphore so that the `ReceiveDataThread` can continue processing the data:

```
/* Post the receive data event semaphore to notify the
   ReceiveData thread that we are done with szReceiveBuffer */
DosPostEventSem (hevRcvQueue);
```

Likewise, the `WM_USER_RCVTEXT` is posted from the `ReceiveDataThread` and when this message is received, the text in the `szReceiveBuffer` is set in the remote display window. Again, the event semaphore is posted to allow the `ReceiveDataThread` to continue.

The remaining portions of the code are involved with creating and positioning the windows and setting and querying the various controls contained in those windows. This application is not meant to be a complete communications program, but is meant to show how to use the `DosDevIOCtl` function for OS/2 communications and how to utilize threads to perform all the asynchronous activities involved with communications. However, it is an excellent foundation on which to build a number of useful apps.

Chapter 16

Miscellaneous Topics

Miscellaneous Application

We have covered a lot of topics at this point. There are several areas of OS/2 programming that can be useful in your applications development, although they do not neatly fall into any particular subject area. This chapter will cover some of these additional areas of interest.

A single application will be used for demonstrating some of the topics in this chapter. The "MISC" application will simply display a window with menu options for each of the topics being demonstrated. Each topic will discuss its menu options and a description of the portion of code involved. The code to display the miscellaneous application and issue the calls to perform the menu options is contained in the files MISC.C, MISC.H, MISC.RC, and MISC.DEF. The application window is shown in Figure 16.1.

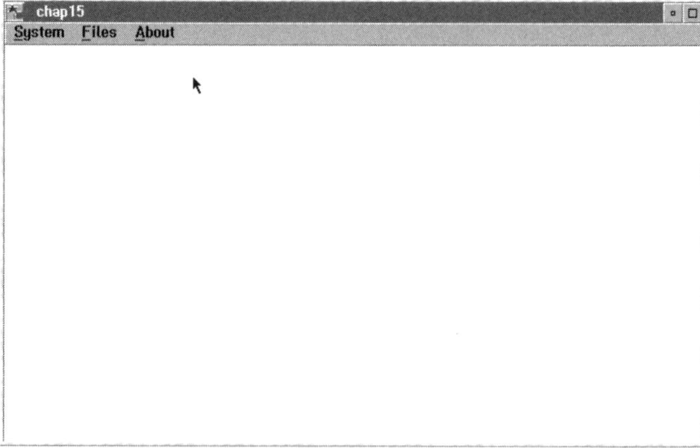

Figure 16.1.
Main application window.

MISC.C

```
/* ------------------------------
         Miscellaneous Program
     Real-World Programming for OS/2
Copyright (c) 1994 Blain, Delimon, and English
------------------------------ */

#define INCL_WIN
#define INCL_GPI

#include <os2.h>
#include "misc.h"
#include "pibtib.h"
#include "drives.h"
#include "filesrch.h"
#include "sysinfo.h"
#include "..\common\about.h"

/* Window and Dialog Functions      */
MRESULT EXPENTRY ClientWndProc  (HWND,ULONG,MPARAM,MPARAM);

/* Global Variables                 */
HAB      hab;
HWND     hWndFrame,
         hWndClient;
CHAR     szTitle[64];

int main()
{
   HMQ   hmq;
   QMSG  qmsg;
   ULONG flFrameFlags    = FCF_TITLEBAR ¦ FCF_SYSMENU ¦
                           FCF_ICON ¦ FCF_SIZEBORDER ¦
                           FCF_MINMAX ¦ FCF_MENU ¦
                           FCF_SHELLPOSITION ¦ FCF_TASKLIST;
```

```
   CHAR  szClientClass[] = "CLIENT";

   hab = WinInitialize (0);
   hmq = WinCreateMsgQueue (hab, 0);

   WinRegisterClass (hab, szClientClass, ClientWndProc, 0,
            0);
   WinLoadString (hab, 0, ID_APPNAME, sizeof(szTitle),
         szTitle);

   /* Create the main application window */
   hWndFrame = WinCreateStdWindow (HWND_DESKTOP, WS_VISIBLE,
      &flFrameFlags, szClientClass, szTitle, 0, 0,
      ID_APPNAME, &hWndClient);

   while (WinGetMsg (hab, &qmsg, 0, 0, 0))
      WinDispatchMsg (hab, &qmsg);

   WinDestroyWindow (hWndFrame);
   WinDestroyMsgQueue (hmq);
   WinTerminate (hab);
   return (0);
}

/* ---------- Window Function --------- */

MRESULT EXPENTRY ClientWndProc (HWND hWnd, ULONG msg,
      MPARAM mp1, MPARAM mp2)
{
   BOOL    bHandled = TRUE;
   MRESULT mReturn  = 0;

   switch (msg)
   {
      case WM_ERASEBACKGROUND:
         mReturn = MRFROMLONG(1L);
         break;

      case WM_COMMAND:
         switch (LOUSHORT(mp1))
         {
            case IDM_PIBTIB:
               WinDlgBox (HWND_DESKTOP, hWnd, PIBTIBDlgProc,
                     0L, IDD_PIBTIB, NULL);
               break;

            case IDM_DRIVES:
               WinDlgBox (HWND_DESKTOP, hWnd, DrivesDlgProc,
                     0L, IDD_DRIVES, NULL);
               break;

            case IDM_FILESEARCH:
               DoFileSearch (hWnd);
               break;

            case IDM_SYSINFO:
```

```
               WinDlgBox (HWND_DESKTOP, hWnd,
                  SysInfoDlgProc, 0L, IDD_SYSINFO, NULL);
               break;

            case IDM_ABOUT:
               DisplayAbout (hWnd, szTitle);
               break;
         }
         break;

      default:
         bHandled = FALSE;
         break;
   }

   if (!bHandled)
      mReturn = WinDefWindowProc (hWnd,msg,mp1,mp2);

   return (mReturn);
}
```

MISC.H

```
/* --------------------------------
       Miscellaneous Header File
     Real-World Programming for OS/2
Copyright (c) 1994 Blain, Delimon, and English
-------------------------------- */

/* Dialog and Control Identifiers     */

#define ID_APPNAME                     1
#define IDD_PIBTIB                     2
#define IDD_DRIVES                     3
#define IDD_FILESEARCH                 4
#define IDD_SYSINFO                    5

#define IDM_SYSTEM                   100
#define IDM_PIBTIB                   101
#define IDM_SYSINFO                  102

#define IDM_FILES                    110
#define IDM_DRIVES                   111
#define IDM_FILESEARCH               112

#define IDM_ABOUT                    120
```

MISC.RC

```
/* --------------------------------
Miscellaneous Resource File
Real-World Programming for OS/2
Copyright (c) 1994 Blain, Delimon, and English
-------------------------------- */
```

```
#include <os2.h>
#include "misc.h"
#include "pibtib.h"
#include "drives.h"
#include "filesrch.h"
#include "sysinfo.h"

ICON ID_APPNAME MISC.ICO

STRINGTABLE LOADONCALL MOVEABLE
BEGIN
   ID_APPNAME      "Miscellaneous Topics Application"
END

MENU ID_APPNAME
{
   SUBMENU  "~System",             IDM_SYSTEM
   {
      MENUITEM "~ThreadInfo",     IDM_PIBTIB
      MENUITEM "~SysInfo",        IDM_SYSINFO
      MENUITEM "",               -1,  MIS_SEPARATOR
      MENUITEM "~About...",       IDM_ABOUT
   }
   SUBMENU  "~Files",              IDM_FILES
   {
      MENUITEM "~Drives",         IDM_DRIVES
      MENUITEM "~File Search",    IDM_FILESEARCH
   }
}

rcinclude pibtib.dlg
rcinclude drives.dlg
rcinclude filesrch.dlg
rcinclude sysinfo.dlg
rcinclude ..\common\about.dlg
```

MISC.DEF

```
NAME        MISC   WINDOWAPI
DESCRIPTION 'Miscellaneous Topics  1994 Blain, Delimon, & English'
PROTMODE

HEAPSIZE    4096
STACKSIZE   16384

EXPORTS
      ClientWndProc      @1
      PIBTIBDlgProc      @2
      DrivesDlgProc      @3
      FileSearchDlgProc  @4
      AboutDlgProc       @5
```

continues

```
#define INCL_DOS
#define INCL_WIN

#include <os2.h>
#include <string.h>
#include <stdio.h>
#include "pibtib.h"

/* External variables */
extern HAB      hab;         /* Handle to anchor block   */

/* Local Functions    */
VOID ParseEnvironment (HWND,PCHAR,USHORT);
VOID SetNumberField   (HWND,ULONG,USHORT);

char szProcType[4][18] =
{
   "Unknown",
   "Not Window Compat",
   "Window Compat",
   "Window API"
};

/* ---------- Local Functions ---------- */

VOID ParseEnvironment (HWND hWnd, PCHAR pEnv,
      USHORT usCtlID)
{
   /* Parse the environment buffer. Each line is terminated
      by a NULL byte and the last line in the buffer
      includes an additional NULL byte */
   while (*pEnv)
   {
      WinSendDlgItemMsg (hWnd, usCtlID, LM_INSERTITEM,
         (MPARAM)LIT_END, pEnv);
      pEnv += strlen(pEnv) + 1;
   }

   return;
}

VOID SetNumberField (HWND hWnd, ULONG ulNumber, USHORT usCtlID)
{
CHAR    szNumber[9];

/* Convert number to hexadecimal string */
sprintf (szNumber, "%8lX", ulNumber);
/* Set the text of the control */
WinSetDlgItemText (hWnd, usCtlID, szNumber);

return;
}

/* ---------  Dialog Function ---------- */
```

```
MRESULT EXPENTRY PIBTIBDlgProc (HWND hWnd, ULONG msg,
         MPARAM mp1, MPARAM mp2)
{
   BOOL     bHandled = TRUE;
   MRESULT mReturn  = 0;
   PPIB     ppib;
   PTIB     ptib;


   switch (msg)
   {
      case WM_INITDLG:
         /* Query the thread information */
         DosGetInfoBlocks (&ptib, &ppib);

         SetNumberField (hWnd, ppib->pib_ulpid, IDC_PID);
         SetNumberField (hWnd, ppib->pib_ulppid, IDC_PPID);
         SetNumberField (hWnd, ppib->pib_hmte,
            IDC_MODULEHANDLE);
         SetNumberField (hWnd, ppib->pib_flstatus,
            IDC_STATUS);
         WinSetDlgItemText (hWnd, IDC_TYPE,
            szProcType[ppib->pib_ultype & 0x03]);
         SetNumberField (hWnd,
            (ptib->tib_ptib2)->tib2_ultid, IDC_TID);
         SetNumberField (hWnd,
            (ptib->tib_ptib2)->tib2_ulpri, IDC_PRIORITY);

         /* The OS/2 2.0 Toolkit defines this field as
            tib_arbpointer */
         /* The OS/2 2.1 Toolkit defines this field as
            tib_ordinal     */
         SetNumberField (hWnd, (ULONG)ptib->tib_ordinal,
            IDC_SLOT);

         SetNumberField (hWnd, (ULONG)ptib->tib_pstack,
            IDC_STACKBASE);
         SetNumberField (hWnd, (ULONG)ptib->tib_pstacklimit,
            IDC_STACKEND);
         WinSendDlgItemMsg (hWnd, IDC_COMMANDLINE,
            EM_SETTEXTLIMIT, MPFROMSHORT(255), 0L);
         WinSetDlgItemText (hWnd, IDC_COMMANDLINE,
            ppib->pib_pchcmd);
         ParseEnvironment (hWnd, ppib->pib pchenv,
            IDC_ENVIRONMENT);
         break;

      case WM_SYSCOMMAND:
         switch (SHORT1FROMMP(mp1))
         {
            case SC_CLOSE:
               WinDismissDlg (hWnd, FALSE);
               bHandled = TRUE;
               break;
         }
         break;
```

continues

```
      default:
         bHandled = FALSE;
         break;
   }

   if (!bHandled)
      mReturn = WinDefDlgProc (hWnd, msg, mp1, mp2);

   return (mReturn);
}
```

PIBTIB.H

```
/* -------------------------------
      Thread Information Header File
      Real-World Programming for OS/2
Copyright (c) 1994 Blain, Delimon, and English
-------------------------------w */

/* Exported Function */
MRESULT EXPENTRY PIBTIBDlgProc  (HWND,ULONG,MPARAM,MPARAM);

/* PIBTIB Dialog Controls            */

#define IDC_PID                     200
#define IDC_PPID                    201
#define IDC_MODULEHANDLE            202
#define IDC_STATUS                  203
#define IDC_TYPE                    204
#define IDC_COMMANDLINE             205
#define IDC_ENVIRONMENT             206
#define IDC_TID                     207
#define IDC_PRIORITY                208
#define IDC_SLOT                    209
#define IDC_STACKBASE               210
#define IDC_STACKEND                211
```

PIBTIB.DLG

```
/* -------------------------------
       Thread Information Dialog
      Real-World Programming for OS/2
Copyright (c) 1994 Blain, Delimon, and English
------------------------------- */

DLGTEMPLATE IDD_PIBTIB LOADONCALL MOVEABLE DISCARDABLE
BEGIN
   DIALOG  "PIBTIB - DosGetInfoBlocks", IDD_PIBTIB, 17, 13,
            318, 119,
            WS_VISIBLE ¦ NOT WS_SAVEBITS, FCF_SYSMENU ¦
            FCF_TITLEBAR ¦ FCF_NOBYTEALIGN
```

```
BEGIN
   GROUPBOX   "Process Information (PIB)", -1,   3, 64,
         188, 51
   LTEXT      "Process ID",                -1,   7, 98,
         51,  8
   LTEXT      "Parent Process ID",         -1,   7, 90,
         78,  8
   LTEXT      "Module Handle",             -1,   7, 82,
         66,  8
   LTEXT      "Status",                    -1,   7, 74,
         31,  8
   LTEXT      "Type",                      -1,   7, 66,
         23,  8
   RTEXT      "", IDC_PID,                     130, 98,
         50,  8
   RTEXT      "", IDC_PPID,                    130, 90,
         50,  8
   RTEXT      "", IDC_MODULEHANDLE,            130, 82,
         50,  8
   RTEXT      "", IDC_STATUS,                  130, 74,
         50,  8
   RTEXT      "", IDC_TYPE,                     30, 66,
         150,  8
   GROUPBOX   "Thread Info (TIB)",         -1, 198, 64,
         115, 51
   LTEXT      "Thread ID",                 -1, 203, 98,
         42,  8
   LTEXT      "Priority",                  -1, 203, 90,
         34,  8
   LTEXT      "Slot",                      -1, 203, 82,
         20,  8
   LTEXT      "Stack Base",                -1, 203, 74,
         54,  8
   LTEXT      "Stack End",                 -1, 203, 66,
         48,  8
   RTEXT      "", IDC_TID,                     254, 98,
         50,  8
   RTEXT      "", IDC_PRIORITY,                254, 90,
         50,  8
   RTEXT      "", IDC_SLOT,                    254, 82,
         50,  8
   RTEXT      "", IDC_STACKBASE,               254, 74,
         50,  8
   RTEXT      "", IDC_STACKEND,                254, 66,
         50,  8
   LTEXT      "Command Line",              -1,   7, 55,
         66,  8
   ENTRYFIELD "", IDC_COMMANDLINE,  3, 45, 308,  8,
         ES_MARGIN ¦ ES_READONLY
   LTEXT      "Environment",               -1,   7, 35,
         66,  8
   LISTBOX    IDC_ENVIRONMENT,  3,  3, 308, 31,
               LS_HORZSCROLL
  END
END
```

SYSINFO.C

```
/* ------------------------------
          System Information
      Real-World Programming for OS/2
Copyright (c) 1994 Blain, Delimon, and English
   ------------------------------ */

#define INCL_DOS
#define INCL_WIN
#define INCL_ERRORS

#include <os2.h>
#include <stdio.h>
#include "sysinfo.h"

/* Local Functions    */
VOID QueryAllValues (HWND);

/* External variables */
extern HAB       hab;       /* Handle to anchor block  */

CHAR szSysValues[QSV_MAX][18] =
{
   "MAX_PATH_LENGTH  ",
   "MAX_TEXT_SESSIONS",
   "MAX_PM_SESSIONS  ",
   "MAX_VDM_SESSIONS ",
   "BOOT_DRIVE       ",
   "DYN_PRI_VARIATION",
   "MAX_WAIT         ",
   "MIN_SLICE        ",
   "MAX_SLICE        ",
   "PAGE_SIZE        ",
   "VERSION_MAJOR    ",
   "VERSION_MINOR    ",
   "VERSION_REVISION ",
   "MS_COUNT         ",
   "TIME_LOW         ",
   "TIME_HIGH        ",
   "TOTPHYSMEM       ",
   "TOTRESMEM        ",
   "TOTAVAILMEM      ",
   "MAXPRMEM         ",
   "MAXSHMEM         ",
   "TIMER_INTERVAL   ",
   "MAX_COMP_LENGTH  "
};

/* ---------- Local Functions ---------- */

VOID QueryAllValues (HWND hWnd)
{
   ULONG ulValues[QSV_MAX];
   CHAR  szText[31];
   ULONG ulInx;
```

```
    DosQuerySysInfo (QSV_MAX_PATH_LENGTH, QSV_MAX, &ulValues,
          sizeof(ulValues));

    for (ulInx = 0; ulInx < QSV_MAX; ulInx++)
    {
       sprintf (szText, "%17s   0x%08lx", szSysValues[ulInx],
             ulValues[ulInx]);
       WinUpper (hab, 0, 0, szText);
       szText[21] = 'x';
       WinSendDlgItemMsg (hWnd, IDC_SYSINFOLIST,
          LM_INSERTITEM, (MPARAM)LIT_END, szText);
    }
    return;
}

/* ----------  Dialog Function ---------- */

MRESULT EXPENTRY SysInfoDlgProc (HWND hWnd, ULONG msg,
      MPARAM mp1, MPARAM mp2)
{
   BOOL     bHandled = TRUE;
   MRESULT  mReturn  = 0;
   HWND     hWndListBox;
   SWP      Swp;

   switch (msg)
   {
      case WM_INITDLG:
         QueryAllValues (hWnd);
         break;

      case WM_WINDOWPOSCHANGED:
         if (((PSWP)mp1)->fl & SWP_SHOW)
         {
            /* Center the listbox horizontally in the
               window */
            hWndListBox = WinWindowFromID (hWnd,
               IDC_SYSINFOLIST);
            WinQueryWindowPos (hWndListBox, &Swp);
            WinSetWindowPos (hWndListBox, 0L,
               (((PSWP)mp1)->cx - Swp.cx) >> 1, Swp.y, 0L,
               0L, SWP_MOVE);
         }
         bHandled = FALSE;
         break;

      default:
         bHandled = FALSE;
         break;
   }

   if (!bHandled)
      mReturn = WinDefDlgProc (hWnd, msg, mp1, mp2);

   return (mReturn);
}
```

SYSINFO.H

```
/* --------------------------------
     System Information Header File
     Real-World Programming for OS/2
Copyright (c) 1994 Blain, Delimon, and English
-------------------------------- */

/* Exported Function */
MRESULT EXPENTRY SysInfoDlgProc  (HWND,ULONG,MPARAM,MPARAM);

/* SysInfo Dialog Controls             */

#define IDC_SYSINFOLIST        500
```

SYSINFO.DLG

```
/* --------------------------------
       System Information Dialog
    Real-World Programming for OS/2
Copyright (c) 1994 Blain, Delimon, and English
-------------------------------- */

DLGTEMPLATE IDD_SYSINFO LOADONCALL MOVEABLE DISCARDABLE
BEGIN
   DIALOG  "System Information - DosQuerySysInfo",
            IDD_SYSINFO, 23, 42, 213, 86,
            WS_VISIBLE, FCF_SYSMENU | FCF_TITLEBAR |
            FCF_NOBYTEALIGN
   BEGIN
      LISTBOX IDC_SYSINFOLIST, 4, 3, 195, 80
         PRESPARAMS PP_FONTNAMESIZE, "10.System Monospaced"
   END
END
```

We query all the system values with a single call to `DosQuerySysInfo`:

```
ULONG ulValues[QSV_MAX];

DosQuerySysInfo (QSV_MAX_PATH_LENGTH, QSV_MAX, &ulValues,
                 sizeof(ulValues));
```

`QSV_MAX` is defined to be the number of predefined system value identifiers.

Determining Drive Types

Many applications need to know what drives are available and if the drive is removable, fixed, or remote. There is no single call in PM to retrieve this information. Several calls must be made.

The `DosDevConfig` API is used to retrieve information about the number of printers, communication ports, diskette drives, and so on. This function was used in Chapter 15, "Communications Basics," to retrieve the number of communication ports available:

```
APIRET APIENTRY DosDevConfig(PVOID pdevinfo, ULONG item);
```

PVOID	pdevinfo	Address to return data.
ULONG	item	Requested item:

DEVINFO_PRINTER	Number of printers attached.
DEVINFO_RS232	Number of communication ports.
DEVINFO_FLOPPY	Number of diskette drives.
DEVINFO_COPROCESSOR	Coprocess present.
DEVINFO_SUBMODEL	Submodel type of computer.
DEVINFO_MODEL	Model type of computer.
DEVINFO_ADAPTER	Display adapter.

All items return a BYTE value. To determine the number of diskette drives installed on the system, the following call could be used:

```
BYTE cDisketteDrives;
DosDevConfig (&cDisketteDrives, DEVINFO_FLOPPY);
```

The DosQueryFSAttach API is used to retrieve information about the attached file system used for each drive. To retrieve the file system type for each drive based on its drive letter, the following options are used:

```
APIRET APIENTRY DosQueryFSAttach(PSZ pszDeviceName,
   ULONG ulOrdinal, ULONG ulFSAInfoLevel, PFSQBUFFER2 pfsqb,

   PULONG pcbBuffLength );
```

PSZ	pszDeviceName	Drive letter followed by colon (for example, "A:").
ULONG	ulOrdinal	0L.
ULONG	ulFSAInfoLevel	FSAIL_QUERYNAME.
PFSQBUFFER2	pfsqb	Pointer to FSQBUFFER2 buffer to receive data.
PULONG	pcbBuffLength	Size of buffer pointed to by pfsqb.

If the drive does not exist, ERROR_INVALID_DRIVE will be returned. ERROR_BUFFER_OVERFLOW is returned if the buffer is not large enough to contain all the returned data. If the drive is a diskette drive and there is no media in the drive, ERROR_DRIVE_NOT_READY will be returned. The buffer pointed to by pfsqb must at least be as large as the FSQBUFFER2 structure plus enough space for the three names and data fields returned. The FSQBUFFER2 contains the information about the attached file system.

```
typedef struct
{
   USHORT  iType;
           FSAT_CHARDEV   - Resident character device
           FSAT_PSEUDODEV - Pseudo-character device
           FSAT_LOCALDRV  - Local drive
```

```
          FSAT_REMOTEDRV - Remote drive
   USHORT  cbName;
           String length of name in szName field
   USHORT  cbFSDName;
           String length of name in szFSDName field
   USHORT  cbFSAData;
           Length of file system attached data
   UCHAR   szName[1];
           Drive name
   UCHAR   szFSDName[1];
           Name of the file system driver (FAT, HPFS, CDFS,
           etc.)
   UCHAR   rgFSAData[1];
           Data for the attached file system driver
} FSQBUFFER2;
```

The DosQueryFSAttach function call will help determine if the drive is a local or remote drive. It will not, however, tell you if the local drive is a fixed disk. To determine if the drive is removable or fixed, we must open the drive and issue either a DSK_BLOCKREMOVABLE or DSK_GETDEVICEPARAMS DosDevIOCtl request. The DosDevIOCtl API was first discussed in Chapter 15. The same API can be used to issue requests to the drive.

```
APIRET APIENTRY DosDevIOCtl(HFILE hDevice, ULONG category,
   ULONG function, PVOID pParams, ULONG cbParmLenMax,
   PULONG pcbParmLen, PVOID pData, ULONG cbDataLenMax,

   PULONG pcbDataLen)
```

hDevice	File handle returned from DosOpen.
category	Device category. IOCTL_DISK—Logical Disk Support.
function	Device function.
pParams	Input parameter list for function.
cbParmLenMax	Maximum length of data in pParams.
pcbParmLen	Pointer to variable to receive length of return parameters in pParams.
pData	Output data area.
cbDataLenMax	Maximum length of data in pData.
pcbDataLen	Pointer to variable to receive length of return parameters in pData.

The device functions we are interested in are DSK_BLOCKREMOVABLE and DSK_GETDEVICEPARAMS. For the IOCTL_DSK device category, it is important to note that the fields pcbParmLen and pcbDataLen are required because the current CD drivers do not allow NULL to be used for these fields.

DSK_BLOCKREMOVABLE—Is block device removable?

Input data:

BYTEReserved byte with value of 0.

Output data:

```
USHORT  Drive type
0  Removable
1  Fixed
```

Example:

```
BYTE   cCmd      = 0;
USHORT usType    = 0;
ULONG  ulParmLen = sizeof(BYTE);
ULONG  ulDataLen = sizeof(USHORT);
DosDevIOCtl (hFile, IOCTL_DISK, DSK_BLOCKREMOVABLE,
      (PVOID)&cCmd, ulParmLen, &ulParmLen,
      (PVOID)&usType, ulDataLen, &ulDataLen, NULL);
```

`DSK_GETDEVICEPARAMS`—Query device parameters for a drive.

Input data:

`BYTE`	Specifies which parameter block to query.
`0`	Recommended parameter block for the drive.
`1`	Parameter block for current medium in the drive.

Output data:

`BIOSPARAMETERBLOCK`—Parameter block for the drive.

```
typedef struct
{
   USHORT usBytesPerSector;
   BYTE   bSectorsPerCluster;
   USHORT usReservedSectors;
   BYTE   cFATs;
   USHORT cRootEntries;
   USHORT cSectors;
   BYTE   bMedia;
   USHORT usSectorsPerFAT;
   USHORT usSectorsPerTrack;
   USHORT cHeads;
   ULONG  cHiddenSectors;
   ULONG  cLargeSectors;
   BYTE   abReserved[6];
   USHORT cCylinders;
   BYTE   bDeviceType;
         DEVTYPE_48TPI   - Low density floppy
         DEVTYPE_96TPI   - High density floppy
         DEVTYPE_35      - 3 1/2" floppy
         DEVTYPE_8SD     - 8" single density floppy
         DEVTYPE_8DD     - 8" double density floopy
         DEVTYPE_FIXED   - Fixed disk
         DEVTYPE_TAPE    - Tape drive
         DEVTYPE_UNKNOWN - Other
         0x0008          - R/W optical disk
         0x0009          - 3 1/2" 4.0MB floppy
```

```
   WinSetDlgItemText (hWnd, IDC_LOCATION,
      DriveInfo[ulInx].szLocation);
   WinSetDlgItemText (hWnd, IDC_REMOVABLE,
      DriveInfo[ulInx].szRemovable);
   WinSetDlgItemText (hWnd, IDC_FILESYSTEM,
      DriveInfo[ulInx].szFileSystem);
   WinSetDlgItemText (hWnd, IDC_DESCRIPTION,
   szDriveDescription[DriveInfo[ulInx].ulDescriptionIndex]);

   WinSetPointer (HWND_DESKTOP,
      WinQuerySysPointer (HWND_DESKTOP,SPTR_WAIT,FALSE));

   QueryVolumeLabel (DriveInfo[ulInx].szDrive[0] - 'A' + 1,
      szVolumeLabel);
   WinSetDlgItemText (hWnd, IDC_VOLUMELABEL, szVolumeLabel);

   QueryDiskSpace (DriveInfo[ulInx].szDrive[0] - 'A' + 1,
      &ulTotalSpace, &ulAllocated, &ulAvailable);

   FormatNumberField (hWnd, IDC_TOTALSPACE, ulTotalSpace);
   FormatNumberField (hWnd, IDC_ALLOCATED,  ulAllocated);
   FormatNumberField (hWnd, IDC_AVAILABLE,  ulAvailable);

   WinSetPointer (HWND_DESKTOP,
      WinQuerySysPointer (HWND_DESKTOP,SPTR_ARROW,FALSE));

   return;
}

VOID FormatNumberField (HWND hWnd, USHORT usCtlID,
   ULONG ulNumber)
{
   CHAR  szNumber[13];
   sprintf (szNumber, "%12lu", ulNumber);

   WinSetDlgItemText (hWnd, usCtlID, szNumber);

   return;
}

VOID QueryDiskSpace (ULONG ulDriveNumber,
   PULONG pulTotalSpace, PULONG pulAllocated,
   PULONG pulAvailable)
{
   FSALLOCATE fsAllocate;

   DosError (FERR_DISABLEHARDERR);

   if (!DosQueryFSInfo (ulDriveNumber, FSIL_ALLOC,
         &fsAllocate, sizeof(FSALLOCATE)))
   {
      *pulTotalSpace =
         fsAllocate.cSectorUnit * fsAllocate.cUnit *
         fsAllocate.cbSector;
      *pulAvailable  =
         fsAllocate.cSectorUnit * fsAllocate.cUnitAvail *
```

```
          fsAllocate.cbSector;
      *pulAllocated  = *pulTotalSpace - *pulAvailable;
   }
   else
      *pulTotalSpace = *pulAllocated = *pulAvailable  = 0L;

   DosError (FERR_ENABLEHARDERR);

   return;
}

VOID QueryVolumeLabel (ULONG ulDriveNumber,
   PSZ pszVolumeLabel)
{
   FSINFO fsInfo;

   DosError (FERR_DISABLEHARDERR);

   if (!DosQueryFSInfo (ulDriveNumber, FSIL_VOLSER, &fsInfo,
         sizeof(FSINFO)))
      strcpy (pszVolumeLabel, fsInfo.vol.szVolLabel);
   else
      pszVolumeLabel[0] = '\0';

   DosError (FERR_ENABLEHARDERR);

   return;
}

VOID QueryDrives (HWND hWnd)
{
   PFSQBUFFER2       pfsq2;
   ULONG             ulLen,
                     ulInx,
                     ulAction,
                     ulParmLen,
                     ulDataLen;
   APIRET            RetCode;
   HFILE             hFile;
   BIOSPARAMETERBLOCK bpb;
   CHAR               szDrive[3] = " :";
   BYTE               cBlock     = 0;

   WinSetPointer (HWND_DESKTOP,
   WinQuerySysPointer (HWND_DESKTOP,SPTR_WAIT,FALSE));

   /* Allocate buffer */
   DosAllocMem ((PPVOID)&pfsq2, 1024L, fALLOC);

   DosError (FERR_DISABLEHARDERR);

   ulNumDrives = 0L;

   for (ulInx = 0; ulInx < 26; ulInx++)
   {
      szDrive[0] = (CHAR)('A' + ulInx);
```

```
ulLen = 1024L;
RetCode = DosQueryFSAttach (szDrive, 0L,
      FSAIL_QUERYNAME, pfsq2, &ulLen);

DriveInfo[ulNumDrives].szDrive[0] = szDrive[0];
DriveInfo[ulNumDrives].szDrive[1]         = '\0';

if (RetCode == ERROR_NOT_READY)
{
   /* Assume local, removable, and FAT file system */
   strcpy (DriveInfo[ulNumDrives].szLocation,
         "Local");
   strcpy (DriveInfo[ulNumDrives].szRemovable,
         "Yes");
   strcpy (DriveInfo[ulNumDrives].szFileSystem,
         "FAT");
   DriveInfo[ulNumDrives].ulDescriptionIndex = 10L;
   ulNumDrives++;
}
else if (RetCode != ERROR_INVALID_DRIVE)
{
   bpb.fsDeviceAttr = 0;

   /* Attempt to open the device */
   if (!DosOpen (szDrive, &hFile, &ulAction, 0L,
         FILE_NORMAL, FILE_OPEN,
         OPEN_FLAGS_DASD ¦ OPEN_SHARE_DENYNONE, 0L))
   {
      ulParmLen = sizeof(BYTE);
      ulDataLen = sizeof(BIOSPARAMETERBLOCK);
      DosDevIOCtl (hFile, IOCTL_DISK,
            DSK_GETDEVICEPARAMS,
            (PVOID)&cBlock, ulParmLen, &ulParmLen,
            (PVOID)&bpb, ulDataLen, &ulDataLen);
      DosClose (hFile);
   }
   else
   {
      /* Remote drives may not allow themselves to be
         opened with the OPEN_FLAGS_DASD access flag.
         Default to not removable and description of
         unknown. */
      bpb.fsDeviceAttr = 0x0001;
      bpb.bDeviceType  = 7;
   }

   /* Is the drive remote?      */
   if (pfsq2->iType == FSAT_REMOTEDRV)
      strcpy (DriveInfo[ulNumDrives].szLocation,
         "Remote");
   else
      strcpy (DriveInfo[ulNumDrives].szLocation,
         "Local");

   /* Is the drive removable?   */
```

```
         if (bpb.fsDeviceAttr & 0x0001)
            strcpy (DriveInfo[ulNumDrives].szRemovable,
               "No");
         else
            strcpy (DriveInfo[ulNumDrives].szRemovable,
               "Yes");

         /* Set the description index */
         if (bpb.bDeviceType < 10)
            DriveInfo[ulNumDrives].ulDescriptionIndex =
               (LONG)bpb.bDeviceType;
         else
            DriveInfo[ulNumDrives].ulDescriptionIndex = 7L;

         /* Set the file system name  */
         strncpy (DriveInfo[ulNumDrives].szFileSystem,
            (PSZ)(pfsq2->szName + 1 + pfsq2->cbName), 15);

         ulNumDrives++;
      }
   }

   DosError (FERR_ENABLEHARDERR);

   DosFreeMem (pfsq2);

   /* Add items to the drive listbox */
   for (ulInx = 0; ulInx < ulNumDrives; ulInx++)
      WinSendDlgItemMsg (hWnd, IDC_DRIVELIST, LM_INSERTITEM,
         (MPARAM)LIT_END, DriveInfo[ulInx].szDrive);
   WinSendDlgItemMsg (hWnd, IDC_DRIVELIST, LM_SELECTITEM,
         0L, (MPARAM)TRUE);

   WinSetPointer (HWND_DESKTOP,
      WinQuerySysPointer (HWND_DESKTOP,SPTR_ARROW,FALSE));
   return;
}

/* ----------  Dialog Function ---------- */

MRESULT EXPENTRY DrivesDlgProc (HWND hWnd, ULONG msg,
   MPARAM mp1, MPARAM mp2)
{
   BOOL     bHandled = TRUE;
   MRESULT mReturn  = 0;

   switch (msg)
   {
      case WM_INITDLG:
         QueryDrives (hWnd);
         break;

      case WM_CONTROL:
         switch (LOUSHORT(mp1))
         {
            case IDC_DRIVELIST:
```

```
            if (HIUSHORT(mp1) == CBN_EFCHANGE)
            {
               DisplayDriveInfo (hWnd,
                  (ULONG)WinSendDlgItemMsg (hWnd,
                  IDC_DRIVELIST, LM_QUERYSELECTION,
                  (MPARAM)LIT_FIRST, 0L));
            }
            break;
         }
         break;

      case WM_SYSCOMMAND:
         switch (SHORT1FROMMP(mp1))
         {
            case SC_CLOSE:
               WinDismissDlg (hWnd, FALSE);
               bHandled = TRUE;
               break;
         }
         break;

      default:
         bHandled = FALSE;
         break;
   }

   if (!bHandled)
      mReturn = WinDefDlgProc (hWnd, msg, mp1, mp2);

   return (mReturn);
}
```

DRIVES.H

```
/* --------------------------------
              Drives Header File
       Real-World Programming for OS/2
Copyright (c) 1994 Blain, Delimon, and English
-------------------------------- */

/* Exported Function */
MRESULT EXPENTRY DrivesDlgProc  (HWND,ULONG,MPARAM,MPARAM);

VOID QueryDrives (HWND);

typedef struct
{
   CHAR  szDrive[2];
   CHAR  szLocation[7];
   CHAR  szRemovable[4];
   CHAR  szFileSystem[16];
   ULONG ulDescriptionIndex;
} DRIVEINFO;

/* Drives Dialog Controls             */
```

```
#define IDC_DRIVELIST                300
#define IDC_LOCATION                 301
#define IDC_REMOVABLE                302
#define IDC_FILESYSTEM               303
#define IDC_DESCRIPTION              304
#define IDC_VOLUMELABEL              305
#define IDC_TOTALSPACE               306
#define IDC_ALLOCATED                307
#define IDC_AVAILABLE                308
```

DRIVES.DLG

```
/* --------------------------------
              Drives Dialog
      Real-World Programming for OS/2
Copyright (c) 1994 Blain, Delimon, and English
-------------------------------- */

DLGTEMPLATE IDD_DRIVES LOADONCALL MOVEABLE DISCARDABLE
BEGIN
   DIALOG  "Drive List", IDD_DRIVES, 39, 74, 186, 82,
           WS_VISIBLE,
           FCF_SYSMENU | FCF_TITLEBAR | FCF_NOBYTEALIGN
   BEGIN
      LTEXT       "Drive",         -1,  3, 68, 22, 8
      CONTROL     "", IDC_DRIVELIST, 4, 4, 22, 63,
            WC_COMBOBOX, CBS_DROPDOWNLIST | WS_GROUP |
            WS_TABSTOP | WS_VISIBLE
      LTEXT       "Location:",     -1, 36, 68, 43, 8
      LTEXT       "Removable?",    -1, 36, 60, 58, 8
      LTEXT       "File System:",  -1, 36, 52, 58, 8
      LTEXT       "Description:",  -1, 36, 44, 54, 8
      LTEXT       "Volume Label:", -1, 36, 36, 62, 8
      ENTRYFIELD "", IDC_LOCATION,    99, 68, 81, 8,
            ES_RIGHT | ES_READONLY | NOT WS_TABSTOP
      ENTRYFIELD "", IDC_REMOVABLE,   99, 60, 81, 8,
            ES_RIGHT | ES_READONLY | NOT WS_TABSTOP
      ENTRYFIELD "", IDC_FILESYSTEM,  99, 52, 81, 8,
            ES_RIGHT | ES_READONLY | NOT WS_TABSTOP
      ENTRYFIELD "", IDC_DESCRIPTION, 99, 44, 81, 8,
            ES_RIGHT | ES_READONLY | NOT WS_TABSTOP
      ENTRYFIELD "", IDC_VOLUMELABEL, 99, 36, 81, 8,
            ES_RIGHT | ES_READONLY | NOT WS_TABSTOP

      LTEXT       "Total Space:",  -1, 36, 24, 58, 8
      LTEXT       "Allocated:",    -1, 36, 16, 46, 8
      LTEXT       "Available:",    -1, 36,  8, 45, 8
      ENTRYFIELD "", IDC_TOTALSPACE,  99, 24, 81, 8,
            ES_RIGHT | ES_READONLY | NOT WS_TABSTOP
      ENTRYFIELD "", IDC_ALLOCATED,   99, 16, 81, 8,
            ES_RIGHT | ES_READONLY | NOT WS_TABSTOP
      ENTRYFIELD "", IDC_AVAILABLE,   99,  8, 81, 8,
            ES_RIGHT | ES_READONLY | NOT WS_TABSTOP
   END
END
```

The `QueryDrives` function is responsible for determining all the valid drive letters and querying the type of file system installed on each. It begins by allocating a buffer to contain the file system data and disabling the system error handling.

```
/* Allocate buffer */
ulLen = 1024L;
DosAllocMem ((PPVOID)&pfsq2, ulLen, fALLOC);

DosError (FERR_DISABLEHARDERR);
```

Following these calls, the code attempts to query the file system data for each possible drive letter, as follows:

```
szDrive[0] = (CHAR)('A' + ulInx);

RetCode = DosQueryFSAttach (szDrive, 0L, FSAIL_QUERYNAME,

      pfsq2, &ulLen);
```

If no error code is returned from this call, you then need to query the drive. In order to make the call to `DosDevIOCtl`, you need to have a file handle. However, you are querying the drive, not a file. How do you get a file handle for a drive? You use the `OPEN_FLAGS_DASD` flag of the `DosOpen` API. This flag enables you to open a drive and treat it as an open file. After the drive has been opened and you have the file handle, you call `DosDevIOCtl` to query the device parameters for the drive:

```
if (!DosOpen (szDrive, &hFile, &ulAction, 0L,
      FILE_NORMAL, FILE_OPEN, OPEN_FLAGS_DASD |
      OPEN_SHARE_DENYNONE, 0L))
{
   ulParmLen = sizeof(BYTE);
   ulDataLen = sizeof(BIOSPARAMETERBLOCK);
   DosDevIOCtl (hFile, IOCTL_DISK, DSK_GETDEVICEPARAMS,
      (PVOID)&cBlock, ulParmLen, &ulParmLen,
      (PVOID)&bpb, ulDataLen, &ulDataLen);
   DosClose (hFile);
}
else
{
   /* Remote drives may not allow themselves to be opened
      with the OPEN_FLAGS_DASD access flag. Default to
      not removable and description of unknown. */
   bpb.fsDeviceAttr = 0x0001;
   bpb.bDeviceType  = 7;
}
```

The `DosOpen` call may fail when attempting to open remote drives using the `OPEN_FLAGS_DASD` flag. If the open fails, you simply assume that the drive is not removable and set the drive description to "unknown." After all drives have been queried, the system error handling is enabled and the temporary buffer is freed:

```
DosError (FERR_ENABLEHARDERR);

DosFreeMem (pfsq2);
```

When you know the valid drive letters and the type of file system installed for each drive, you might also want to know the volume label and disk space utilization for a drive. Both types of information can be retrieved by using the `DosQueryFSInfo` API:

```
APIRET APIENTRY DosQueryFSInfo(ULONG disknum,
   ULONG infolevel, PVOID pBuf,ULONG cbBuf);

ULONG disknum   - Logical drive number to query (0=current
                  drive, 1=A, 2=B, etc)
ULONG infolevel - Type of drive informatino to retrieve
                  FSIL_ALLOC  - Level 1 (disk utilization)
                  FSIL_VOLSER - Level 2 (volume information)
PVOID pBuf      - Pointer to buffer to return requested
                  information
ULONG cbBuf     - Size of buffer pointed to by pBuf
```

For `FSIL_ALLOC` requests, the buffer pointed to by `pBuf` is an `FSALLOCATE` structure:

```
typedef struct _FSALLOCATE
{
   ULONG  idFileSystem;
          File System identifier
   ULONG  cSectorUnit;
          Number of sectors per allocation unit
   ULONG  cUnit;
          Number of allocation units
   ULONG  cUnitAvail;
          Number of available allocation units
   USHORT cbSector;
          Number of bytes per sector
} FSALLOCATE;
```

The `QueryDiskSpace` function in DRIVES.C demonstrates how to query the disk utilization and calculate the total amount of disk space allocated, the amount of disk space available, and the amount of disk space in use:

```
VOID QueryDiskSpace (ULONG ulDriveNumber,
      PULONG pulTotalSpace, PULONG pulAllocated,
      PULONG pulAvailable)
{
   FSALLOCATE fsAllocate;

   DosError (FERR_DISABLEHARDERR);

   if (!DosQueryFSInfo (ulDriveNumber, FSIL_ALLOC,
            &fsAllocate, sizeof(FSALLOCATE)))
   {
      *pulTotalSpace =
         fsAllocate.cSectorUnit * fsAllocate.cUnit *
         fsAllocate.cbSector;
      *pulAvailable  =
         fsAllocate.cSectorUnit * fsAllocate.cUnitAvail *
         fsAllocate.cbSector;
      *pulAllocated  = *pulTotalSpace - *pulAvailable;
   }
```

```
   else
      *pulTotalSpace = *pulAllocated = *pulAvailable  = 0L;

   DosError (FERR_ENABLEHARDERR);

   return;
}
```

For FSIL_VOLSER requests, the buffer pointed to by pBuf is an FSINFO structure:

```
typedef struct
{
   BYTE cch;
         String length of volume label
   CHAR szVolLabel[12];
         Volume label
} VOLUMELABEL;

typedef struct
{
   ULONG ulVSN;
         Volume serial number
   VOLUMELABEL vol;
         Volume label structure
} FSINFO;
```

The QueryVolumeLabel function in DRIVES.C demonstrates how to query the volume label for a drive:

```
VOID QueryVolumeLabel (ULONG ulDriveNumber,
      PSZ pszVolumeLabel)
{
   FSINFO fsInfo;

   DosError (FERR_DISABLEHARDERR);

   if (!DosQueryFSInfo (ulDriveNumber, FSIL_VOLSER, &fsInfo,
         sizeof(FSINFO)))
      strcpy (pszVolumeLabel, fsInfo.vol.szVolLabel);
   else
      pszVolumeLabel[0] = '\0';

   DosError (FERR_ENABLEHARDERR);

   return;
}
```

File Searching

Searching for files can be done in many ways. Perhaps the easiest way is to utilize a set of PM functions specifically designed for this purpose. Three functions, DosFindFirst, DosFindNext, and DosFindClose are used to search a specific directory for any and all files matching a specified search criteria. Two nice features of these functions are that the file specification need only be specified once, and support is provided for recursively searching subdirectories.

To begin a search, the DosFindFirst API is used. In this call, the file specification is provided and a "snapshot" of the directory is taken. This "snapshot" is a list of all files in the specified directory that match the file specification. Although this API can be used to search not only for filenames but also for extended attributes, we are only concerned with filenames now. The DosFindFirst API has the following format when used to search only for files:

```
APIRET APIENTRY DosFindFirst(PSZ pszFileSpec, PHDIR phdir,
   ULONG flAttribute,PVOID pfindbuf, ULONG cbBuf,
   PULONG pcFileNames, ULONG ulInfoLevel );
```

PSZ	pszFileSpec	File path or filename to search (may contain wild cards).
PHDIR	phdir	Address or handle associated with this search request. On input, the values for this handle may be: HDIR_SYSTEM Reusable handle for any search. HDIR_CREATE Unique handle created for this search (used for nested or recursive searches).
ULONG	flAttribute	File attributes to search for: FILE_NORMAL File with no attribute bits set. FILE_READONLY Include readonly files. FILE_HIDDEN Include hidden files. FILE_SYSTEM Include system files. FILE_DIRECTORY Include directory files. FILE_ARCHIVED Include archived files. MUST_HAVE_READONLY Must have read only attribute. MUST_HAVE_HIDDEN Must have hidden attribute. MUST_HAVE_SYSTEM Must have system attribute. MUST_HAVE_DIRECTORY Must be a directory. MUST_HAVE_ARCHIVED Must have archived attribute.
PVOID	pfindbuf	Address of buffer to receive file list entries.
ULONG	cbBuf	Size of buffer pointed to by pfindbuf.
PULONG	pcFileNames	On input, number of file entries to return in buffer. On output, number of file entries placed in buffer.
ULONG	ulInfoLevel	Requested file information level. FIL_STANDARD File information only (no extended attribute data).

If you do not need to perform a recursive or nested search (that is, search another directory while a search of a directory is currently in progress); then you can set the search request handle to HDIR_SYSTEM. Otherwise, you must use the HDIR_CREATE handle. Each call to DosFindFirst

using the HDIR_CREATE handle will create a unique handle for that search. The returned data in the buffer referenced by pfindbuf is in the form of a FILEFINDBUF3 structure:

```
typedef struct
{
   ULONG oNextEntryOffset;
            Reserved for system use
   FDATE fdateCreation;
            Date of file creation
   FTIME ftimeCreation;
            Time of file creation
   FDATE fdateLastAccess;
            Date file was last accessed
   FTIME ftimeLastAccess;
            Time file was last accessed
   FDATE fdateLastWrite;
            Date file was last written
   FTIME ftimeLastWrite;
            Time file was last written
   ULONG cbFile;
            Size of file
   ULONG cbFileAlloc;
            Allocated size of file
   ULONG attrFile;
            File attributes
   UCHAR cchName;
            String length of the file name
   CHAR  achName[CCHMAXPATHCOMP];
            File name
} FILEFINDBUF3;
```

The achName field contains the file's name as it exists in the directory. It is not a complete pathname of the file. Normally, file searching is performed one file at a time. However, it is possible to retrieve multiple FILEFINDBUF3 structures with each call. By setting the cbBuf field to the number of entries to retrieve on input and defining the buffer to be large enough to contain those entries, the call will attempt to return that many entries in the buffer. The cbBuf field will be updated with the actual number of entries placed in the buffer.

To begin a search for files that must have the readonly attribute, the following call could be used:

```
FILEFINDBUF3 FindBuf3;
HDIR         hDir        = HDIR_CREATE;
ULONG        ulFileCount = 1L;

if (!DosFindFirst (szFullPath, &hDir,
      FILE_MUST_HAVE_READONLY, &FindBuf3,

      sizeof(FILEFINDBUF3), &ulFileCount, FIL_STANDARD))
```

After the file search has begun, DosFindNext is used to repeatedly return the next file from the search "snapshot":

```
APIRET APIENTRY DosFindNext(HDIR hdir, PVOID pfindbuf,
   ULONG cbfindbuf, PULONG pcFilenames );
```

HDIR	hDir	Search handle from DosFindFirst call.
PVOID	pfindbuf	Address of buffer to receive file list entries.
ULONG	cbfindbuf	Size of buffer pointed to by pfindbuf.
PULONG	pcFileNames	On input, number of file entries to return in buffer. On output, number of file entries placed in buffer.

Like the DosFindFirst call, it is possible to request multiple files to be retrieved with each call. The hDir parameter must be the matching search handle for the DosFindFirst call.

When the directory search is complete, it is necessary to call DosFindClose to terminate the search and release any resources being used by the system to maintain the search handle:

```
APIRET APIENTRY DosFindClose(HDIR hDir);
```

HDIR hDir—Search handle from DosFindFirst call.

Performing a file search is demonstrated by selecting the menu options Files and then File Search in the Miscellaneous application. Figure 16.5 shows how this might appear on a typical system.

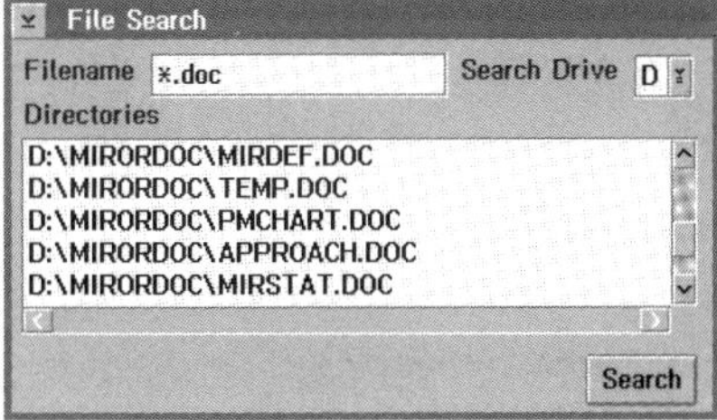

Figure 16.5.
File Search dialog.

Our file search will simply search for a file, or files matching a wild card specification on a specific drive. It will recursively search subdirectories finding all occurrences. This implementation will also make use of multithreading to perform the search in a separate thread. Because searching may be a time-consuming process, it is a good idea to put that processing in a separate thread so that the user can continue performing other tasks in the application while the search is proceeding. The code to perform the file searching and to display the dialog is contained in the files FILESRCH.C, FILESRCH.H, and FILESRCH.DLG.

FILESRCH.C

```
/* ------------------------------
              File Search
    Real-World Programming for OS/2
Copyright (c) 1994 Blain, Delimon, and English
------------------------------*/
```

```
#define INCL_DOS
#define INCL_DOSFILEMGR
#define INCL_WIN
#define INCL_ERRORS

#include <os2.h>
#include <string.h>
#include "misc.h"
#include "drives.h"
#include "filesrch.h"

/* Thread Function */
VOID SearchThread (HWND);

/* Local Functions    */
VOID SearchForFile (HWND);
VOID SetControlStates (HWND);
VOID StartSearch (HWND);
VOID StopSearch (VOID);

/* External variables */
extern HAB       hab;       /* Handle to anchor block    */
extern DRIVEINFO DriveInfo[];
extern ULONG     ulNumDrives;

/* Global variables */
TID  SearchThreadID;         /* Thread ID of Search thread*/
CHAR szFileName[CCHMAXPATHCOMP]; /* Filename to search  */
CHAR szFullPath[CCHMAXPATH] = " :\\"; /* File path buffer */
HWND hWndFileSearch  = 0;  /* File search dialog window */
BOOL bSearching  = FALSE;   /* Search in progress flag  */

/* ---------- Search Thread Function ---------- */

/*
The Search thread is responsible for searching the selected disk
for the specified filename. This function will search all
subdirectories starting with the directory in szFullPath.
The field IDC_CURRENTDIR is updated with the name of each
directory that is being searched. Each matching filename is
added to the IDC_DIRLIST listbox.

Since this thread will be directly updating the dialog box control
windows, it must create a message queue. Thus, it will be a
Message queue thread.

The thread is automatically terminated when all subdirectories
have been search or when the bSearching flag is reset.
*/

#ifdef __IBMC__#pragma linkage(SearchThread, system)
#endif

VOID SearchThread (HWND hWnd)
{
```

```
    HMQ hmqThread;
    HAB habThread;

    /* Create message queue for this thread */
    habThread = WinInitialize (0);
    hmqThread = WinCreateMsgQueue (hab, 0);

    bSearching = TRUE;

    SetControlStates (hWnd);

    /* Perform the search */
    SearchForFile (hWnd);

    bSearching = FALSE;

    SetControlStates (hWnd);

    /* Destroy the message queue for this thread */
    WinDestroyMsgQueue (hmqThread);
    WinTerminate (habThread);

    DosExit (EXIT_THREAD, 0L);
}

/* ---------- Local Functions ---------- */

VOID SearchForFile (HWND hWnd)
{
    HDIR          hDir        = HDIR_CREATE;
    ULONG         ulDirPos    = strlen (szFullPath);
    ULONG         ulFileCount = 1L;
    FILEFINDBUF3 FindBuf3;

    /* Check for filename length overflow */
    if ((ulDirPos + strlen(szFileName)) > CCHMAXPATH)
       return;

    WinSetDlgItemText (hWnd, IDC_CURRENTDIR, szFullPath);

    /* Search for all files in directory matching the
       filename */
    strcat (szFullPath, szFileName);
    if (!DosFindFirst (szFullPath, &hDir, FILE_NORMAL,
          &FindBuf3,
          sizeof(FILEFINDBUF3), &ulFileCount, FIL_STANDARD))
    {
       do
       {
          szFullPath[ulDirPos] = '\0';
          strncat (szFullPath, FindBuf3.achName, CCHMAXPATH);
          WinSendDlgItemMsg (hWnd, IDC_DIRLIST,
                LM_INSERTITEM, (MPARAM)LIT_END, szFullPath);
          ulFileCount = 1L;
       } while (bSearching &&
             !DosFindNext (hDir, &FindBuf3,
```

```
            sizeof(FILEFINDBUF3), &ulFileCount));
        DosFindClose (hDir);
    }

    /* Has the user cancelled the searching? */
    if (!bSearching)
        return;

    /* For each subdirectory in this directory call
        SearchForFile */
    szFullPath[ulDirPos] = '\0';
    strcat (szFullPath, "*.*");
    ulFileCount = 1L;
    hDir        = HDIR_CREATE;
    if (!DosFindFirst (szFullPath, &hDir,
            MUST_HAVE_DIRECTORY,
            &FindBuf3, sizeof(FILEFINDBUF3), &ulFileCount,
            FIL_STANDARD))
    {
        do
        {
            if (!strcmp(FindBuf3.achName, ".") ||
                    !strcmp(FindBuf3.achName, ".."))
                continue;

            /* Check for path name length overflow */
            if ((ulDirPos + FindBuf3.cchName + 1) >=
                    CCHMAXPATH)
                continue;

            szFullPath[ulDirPos] = '\0';
            strcat (szFullPath, FindBuf3.achName);
            strcat (szFullPath, "\\");
            SearchForFile (hWnd);
            ulFileCount = 1L;
        }
            while (bSearching &&
                !DosFindNext (hDir, &FindBuf3,
                sizeof(FILEFINDBUF3), &ulFileCount));
        DosFindClose (hDir);
    }

    return;
}

VOID SetControlStates (HWND hWnd)
{
    /* Show the searching fields */
    WinShowWindow (WinWindowFromID (hWnd, IDC_SEARCHING),
            bSearching);
    WinShowWindow (WinWindowFromID (hWnd, IDC_CURRENTDIR),
            bSearching);

    /* Disable filename and drivelist input controls */
    WinEnableControl (hWnd, IDC_FILENAME, !bSearching);
```

```
   WinEnableControl (hWnd, IDC_DRIVELIST, !bSearching);

   /* Change button text */
   WinSetDlgItemText (hWnd, IDC_SEARCH,
         bSearching ? "Stop" : "Search");

   return;
}

VOID StartSearch (HWND hWnd)
{
   ULONG ulInx;

   /* Get file spec to search */
   WinQueryDlgItemText (hWnd, IDC_FILENAME,
         sizeof(szFileName), szFileName);
   if (!szFileName[0])
   {
      DosBeep (750, 200);
      return;
   }

   /* Get drive selection and start at the root directory */
   ulInx = (ULONG)WinSendDlgItemMsg (hWnd, IDC_DRIVELIST,
         LM_QUERYSELECTION, (MPARAM)LIT_FIRST, 0L);
   szFullPath[0] = DriveInfo[ulInx].szDrive[0];
   szFullPath[3] = '\0';

   /* Clear the directory listbox */
   WinSendDlgItemMsg (hWnd, IDC_DIRLIST, LM_DELETEALL, 0L,
            0L);

   /* Start the search thread */
   DosCreateThread (&SearchThreadID,
         (PFNTHREAD)SearchThread, (ULONG)hWnd, 0, 0x10000);

   return;
}

VOID StopSearch ()
{
   /* Signal search thread to stop */
   bSearching = FALSE;

   /* Don't attempt to call DosWaitThread here. Doing so
      will hang the process because when the search thread
      returns from the initial call to SearchForFile, it
      will call SetControlStates. The call to WinShowWindow,
      for example, will attempt to send a message to
      the control window's owner and since the main thread
      would be blocked waiting for the search thread, the
      message could not be sent and the search thread would
      block.

      The thread will terminate as soon as it sees the
      bSearching flag has been set to FALSE. */
```

```
   return;
}

/* ---------- Dialog Function ---------- */

VOID DoFileSearch (HWND hWnd)
{
   if (!hWndFileSearch)
      hWndFileSearch = WinLoadDlg (HWND_DESKTOP, hWnd,
         FileSearchDlgProc, 0L, IDD_FILESEARCH, NULL);
   else
      WinSetActiveWindow (HWND_DESKTOP, hWndFileSearch);

   return;
}

MRESULT EXPENTRY FileSearchDlgProc (HWND hWnd, ULONG msg,
   MPARAM mp1, MPARAM mp2)
{
   BOOL    bHandled = TRUE;
   MRESULT mReturn  = 0;
   switch (msg)
   {
      case WM_INITDLG:
         QueryDrives (hWnd);
         WinShowWindow (WinWindowFromID (hWnd,
            IDC_SEARCHING), FALSE);
         WinShowWindow (WinWindowFromID (hWnd,
            IDC_CURRENTDIR), FALSE);
         WinSendDlgItemMsg (hWnd, IDC_FILENAME,
            EM_SETTEXTLIMIT, MPFROMSHORT(CCHMAXPATHCOMP),
            0L);
         break;

      case WM_COMMAND:
      case WM_SYSCOMMAND:
         switch (SHORT1FROMMP(mp1))
         {
            case IDC_SEARCH:
               if (bSearching)
                  StopSearch ();
               else
                  StartSearch (hWnd);
               break;

            case SC_CLOSE:
               if (bSearching)
                  StopSearch ();
               WinDestroyWindow (hWnd);
               bHandled = TRUE;
               break;

            default:
               bHandled = (msg == WM_COMMAND);
         }
```

```
         break;

      case WM_DESTROY:
         hWndFileSearch = 0;
         break;

      default:
         bHandled = FALSE;
         break;
   }

   if (!bHandled)
      mReturn = WinDefDlgProc (hWnd, msg, mp1, mp2);

   return (mReturn);
}
```

FILESRCH.H

```
/* -------------------------------
        File Search Header File
     Real-World Programming for OS/2
Copyright (c) 1994 Blain, Delimon, and English
------------------------------- */

/* Exported Function */
MRESULT EXPENTRY FileSearchDlgProc(HWND,ULONG,
   MPARAM,MPARAM);

VOID DoFileSearch (HWND);

/* FileSearch Dialog Controls              */

#define IDC_DRIVELIST           300

#define IDC_FILENAME            400
#define IDC_DIRLIST             401
#define IDC_CURRENTDIR          402
#define IDC_SEARCHING           403
#define IDC_SEARCH              404
```

FILESRCH.DLG

```
/* -------------------------------
             File Search Dialog
        Real-World Programming for OS/2
Copyright (c) 1994 Blain, Delimon, and English
------------------------------- */

DLGTEMPLATE IDD_FILESEARCH LOADONCALL MOVEABLE DISCARDABLE
BEGIN
   DIALOG  "File Search", IDD_FILESEARCH, 57, 35, 239, 93,
           WS_VISIBLE,
           FCF_SYSMENU | FCF_TITLEBAR | FCF_NOBYTEALIGN
```

```
    BEGIN
        LTEXT             "Filename",      -1,      4, 81,  44,  8
        ENTRYFIELD        "", IDC_FILENAME,        49, 80,  97,
              8, ES_MARGIN
        LTEXT             "Search Drive", -1,    152, 80,  58,  9
        CONTROL           "", IDC_DRIVELIST,     211, 46,  21,
              43, WC_COMBOBOX, CBS_DROPDOWNLIST ¦ WS_GROUP ¦
              WS_TABSTOP ¦ WS_VISIBLE
        LTEXT             "Directories",  -1,      4, 70,  48,  8
        LISTBOX           IDC_DIRLIST,             4, 20, 227,
              50, LS_HORZSCROLL ¦ NOT WS_TABSTOP
        LTEXT             "Searching", IDC_SEARCHING, 3, 10,
              44,  8
        LTEXT             "", IDC_CURRENTDIR,      4,  2, 189,  8
        PUSHBUTTON        "Search", IDC_SEARCH, 194,  1,  40, 14
    END
END
```

The main application code will call `DoFileSearch` when the File Search menu option is selected. Because the file search dialog will be a modeless dialog, this function will ensure that only one file search dialog is present. During the `WM_INITDLG` processing, we call the `QueryDrives` function from the previous section to enumerate the available drives and insert the entries into the drive list combo box. In the filename entry field, the filename to search is entered. For example, to search for all executable files on the drive, you would enter *.EXE. Notice that we have not added any code to remove leading spaces, so your entry must not include any leading spaces when searching for files on a FAT file system.

The variable `bSearching` is used to indicate if a search is presently underway. The text of the Search button will be changed to read "Stop" while a search is being performed. When the Search button is pressed, the `StartSearch` function is called to start the search thread:

```
VOID StartSearch (HWND hWnd)
{
   ULONG ulInx;

   /* Get file spec to search */
   WinQueryDlgItemText (hWnd, IDC_FILENAME,
         sizeof(szFileName), szFileName);
   if (!szFileName[0])
   {
      DosBeep (750, 200);
      return;
   }

   /* Get drive selection and start at the root directory */
   ulInx = (ULONG)WinSendDlgItemMsg (hWnd, IDC_DRIVELIST,
         LM_QUERYSELECTION, (MPARAM)LIT_FIRST, 0L);
         szFullPath[0] = DriveInfo[ulInx].szDrive[0];
         szFullPath[3] = '\0';

   /* Clear the directory listbox */
   WinSendDlgItemMsg (hWnd, IDC_DIRLIST, LM_DELETEALL, 0L,
         0L);
```

```
    /* Start the search thread */
    DosCreateThread (&SearchThreadID,
         (PFNTHREAD)SearchThread, (ULONG)hWnd, 0, 0x10000);

    return;
}
```

This function simply retrieves the input filename, sets the starting drive path specification, clears the list box, and creates the search thread. When the Stop search button is pressed, the function `StopSearch` is called. This function simply sets the `bSearching` flag to `FALSE`. The search thread will recognize this flag change and stop the search process. Taking a look at the search thread, we see that we need to create a message queue thread because this thread will be sending messages to the main thread.

```
/* Create message queue for this thread */
habThread = WinInitialize (NULL);
hmqThread = WinCreateMsgQueue (hab, NULL);
```

It then calls the `SearchForFile` function, which actually performs the file search. Upon return from `SearchForFile`, the message queue is destroyed and the thread terminated:

```
/* Perform the search */
SearchForFile (hWnd);

/* Destroy the message queue for this thread */
WinDestroyMsgQueue (hmqThread);
WinTerminate (habThread);

DosExit (EXIT_THREAD, 0L);
```

All the real work is performed in the `SearchForFile` function. The search handle, `hDir`, is declared locally so that recursive calls to `SearchForFile` for each subdirectory will create its own unique search handle. The current path and file specification are built by concatenating the filename to the current directory path:

```
strcat (szFullPath, szFileName);
```

The search is then performed on that directory, and each entry is added to the dialog's list box:

```
if (!DosFindFirst (szFullPath, &hDir, FILE_NORMAL,
       &FindBuf3, sizeof(FILEFINDBUF3), &ulFileCount,
       FIL_STANDARD))
{
   do
   {
      szFullPath[ulDirPos] = '\0';
      strncat (szFullPath, FindBuf3.achName, CCHMAXPATH);
      WinSendDlgItemMsg (hWnd, IDC_DIRLIST, LM_INSERTITEM,
         (MPARAM)LIT_END, szFullPath);
      ulFileCount = 1L;
   }
   while (bSearching &&
         !DosFindNext (hDir, &FindBuf3,
```

```
        sizeof(FILEFINDBUF3), &ulFileCount));
   DosFindClose (hDir);
}
```

Notice that our loop termination also includes a check of the `bSearching` flag because the user may have cancelled the search operation. This would be our signal to terminate early. After all files have been found in this directory, we must then repeat the process for each subdirectory found in this directory. To do this, we begin another search, but this time we use the `MUST_HAVE_DIRECTORY` file attribute so that we retrieve only directory entries:

```
/* For each subdirectory in this directory call
   SearchForFile */
szFullPath[ulDirPos] = '\0';
strcat (szFullPath, "*.*");
ulFileCount = 1L;
hDir        = HDIR_CREATE;
if (!DosFindFirst (szFullPath, &hDir, MUST_HAVE_DIRECTORY,
      &FindBuf3, sizeof(FILEFINDBUF3), &ulFileCount,
      FIL_STANDARD))
{
   do
   {
      if (!strcmp(FindBuf3.achName, ".") ||
            !strcmp(FindBuf3.achName, ".."))
         continue;

      /* Check for path name length overflow */
      if ((ulDirPos + FindBuf3.cchName + 1) >= CCHMAXPATH)
         continue;

      szFullPath[ulDirPos] = '\0';
      strcat (szFullPath, FindBuf3.achName);
      strcat (szFullPath, "\\");
      SearchForFile (hWnd);
      ulFileCount = 1L;
   }
   while (bSearching &&
      !DosFindNext (hDir, &FindBuf3, sizeof(FILEFINDBUF3),
      &ulFileCount));
   DosFindClose (hDir);
}
```

For each entry found, we rebuild the path of the directory and call `SearchForFile`, again checking the `bSearching` flag after each directory search.

Dialog Directory Listing

If you are familiar with Windows programming then you have probably used the `DlgDirList` and `DlgDirSelect` functions. The `DlgDirList` function fills a specified listbox with files, subdirectories, and drive letters. The `DlgDirSelect` function retrieves the current selection from a listbox that was filled using `DlgDirList`. Both functions perform the tedious tasks of parsing and directory searching required for providing an easy to use interface to the user.

While it is possible to create a custom file open dialog template which displays drives, directories, and files you may wish to have a single listbox which displays all three items. The implementation of these two functions is fairly simple and uses the `DosFindFirst`, `DosFindNext`, and `DosFindClose` APIs discussed in the previous section.

Displaying the dialog directory listing is demonstrated by selecting Files and then `DlgDir` in the MISC application. (See Figure 16.6.)

The code to implement the `DlgDirList` and `DlgDirSelect` functions along with a sample dialog using these functions to fill a listbox is contained in the files DLGDIR.C, DLGDIR.H, and DLGDIR.DLG.

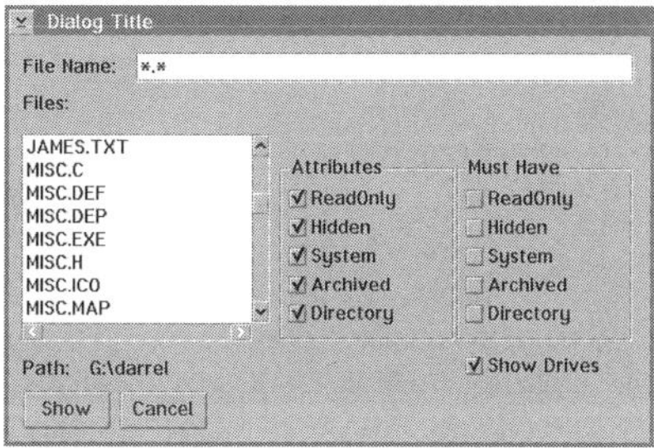

Figure 16.6
`DlgDirList` dialog.

DLGDIR.C

```
/* ----------------------------------------------------------------
                              DlgDir
                  Real World Programming for OS/2
          Copyright (c) 1994, 1994 Blain, Delimon, and English
---------------------------------------------------------------- */

#define INCL_DOS
#define INCL_WIN

#include <os2.h>
#include "dlgdir.h"

/* Local Functions    */
VOID  DrawPathWithEllipses (HWND hWndCtl);
VOID  FillDlgDirListBox (HWND hWndCtl, PSZ pszPathSpec,
                         ULONG ulFileType, BOOL bListDrives);
ULONG GetFileAttributes (HWND hWnd);
BOOL  DlgDirList (HWND hWnd, PSZ pszPathSpec, LONG lIDListBox,
                  LONG lIDStaticPath, ULONG ulFileType,
                  BOOL bListDrives);
BOOL  DlgDirSelect (HWND hWnd, PSZ pszPathSpec, LONG lIDListBox);

/* External variables */
extern HAB      hab;  /* Handle to anchor block  */
```

```
/* Global variables   */
CHAR szFullPathSpec[CCHMAXPATH];

/* --------------------- Local Functions --------------------- */

/* --------------------------------------------------------------
   DrawPathWithEllipses:

   Format the current path in szFullPathSpec so that it fits
   within the static control window. If the string is too long
   then ellipses (...) will replace interior components of the
   path.
   -------------------------------------------------------------- */

VOID DrawPathWithEllipses (HWND hWndCtl)
{
  PSZ   pszSlash;
  BOOL  fInsert;
  RECTL Rectl;
  HPS   hPS;
  LONG  lWidthStatic;
  CHAR  szInsert[7];

  /* Make sure the path will fit in the static windows */
  if (strlen (szFullPathSpec) > 6)
  {
    pszSlash      = &szFullPathSpec[3];
    fInsert       = FALSE;
    hPS           = WinGetPS (hWndCtl);

    /* Get the width of the static window */
    WinQueryWindowRect (hWndCtl, &Rectl);
    lWidthStatic  = Rectl.xRight - Rectl.xLeft;

    /* Get the width of the "C:\\..." string */
    strcpy (szInsert, " :\\...");
    szInsert[0]  = szFullPathSpec[0];
    WinDrawText (hPS, 6, szInsert, &Rectl, 0, 0, DT_QUERYEXTENT);

    /* Shrink available width */
    lWidthStatic -= (Rectl.xRight - Rectl.xLeft);

    /* While space is available and there are characters left */
    if (lWidthStatic > 0)
    {
      /* Query the extent of the text string */
      WinDrawText (hPS, -1, pszSlash, &Rectl, 0, 0, DT_QUERYEXTENT);
      while (*pszSlash &&
             (lWidthStatic < (Rectl.xRight - Rectl.xLeft)))
      {
        /* Advance to the next backslash */
        while (*pszSlash && (*pszSlash++ != '\\'))
        {}
        fInsert = TRUE;
        /* Query the extent of the text string */
```

```
        WinDrawText (hPS, -1, pszSlash, &Rectl, 0, 0, DT_QUERYEXTENT);
      }
    }
    WinReleasePS (hPS);

    /* If we need to insert ellipses then do so */
    if (fInsert)
    {
      memmove (&szFullPathSpec[7], pszSlash, strlen (pszSlash) + 1);
      memmove (&szFullPathSpec[3], "...\\", 4);
    }
  }

  /* Set the window text of the static control window */
  WinSetWindowText (hWndCtl, szFullPathSpec);

  return;
}

/* -------------------------------------------------------------
   FillDlgDirListBox:

   Fill the listbox control with the list of files, directories,
   and/or drives.
   ------------------------------------------------------------- */

VOID FillDlgDirListBox (HWND hWndCtl, PSZ pszPathSpec,
                        ULONG ulFileType, BOOL bListDrives)
{
  HPOINTER      hPtr;
  ULONG         ulFileFlags;
  HDIR          hDir;
  ULONG         ulFileCount;
  ULONG         ulBit;
  FILEFINDBUF3 FindBuf3;
  ULONG         ulCurrentDrive;
  ULONG         ulDriveMap;
  CHAR          cDrive;
  CHAR          szDrive[] = "[- -]";

  /* Change the pointer to the wait pointer */
  hPtr = WinQueryPointer (HWND_DESKTOP);
  WinSetPointer (HWND_DESKTOP,
    WinQuerySysPointer (HWND_DESKTOP, SPTR_WAIT, FALSE));

  /* Turn off redrawing of the listbox and delete all of
     its entries */
  WinEnableWindowUpdate (hWndCtl, FALSE);
  WinSendMsg (hWndCtl, LM_DELETEALL, MPVOID, MPVOID);

  /* If any file flags are specified or the MUST_HAVE_DIRECTORY bit
     is not turned on then list the files matching the attribute. */

  ulFileFlags = ulFileType & ~MUST_HAVE_DIRECTORY;
  if (ulFileFlags ||
      ((ulFileType & (FILE_DIRECTORY << 8)) == 0))
```

```
{
  hDir          = HDIR_CREATE;
  ulFileCount   = 1;
  if (!DosFindFirst (pszPathSpec, &hDir, ulFileFlags,
          &FindBuf3, sizeof(FILEFINDBUF3), &ulFileCount,
          FIL_STANDARD))
  {
    do
    {
      WinInsertLboxItem (hWndCtl, LIT_SORTASCENDING,
        FindBuf3.achName);
      ulFileCount = 1;
    } while (!DosFindNext (hDir, &FindBuf3,
              sizeof(FILEFINDBUF3), &ulFileCount));
    DosFindClose (hDir);
  }
}

/* List directories if they were requested */
if (ulFileType & FILE_DIRECTORY)
{
  hDir          = HDIR_CREATE;
  ulFileCount   = 1;
  szFullPathSpec[0] = '[';
  if (!DosFindFirst ("*.*", &hDir, MUST_HAVE_DIRECTORY,
          &FindBuf3, sizeof(FILEFINDBUF3), &ulFileCount,
          FIL_STANDARD))
  {
    do
    {
      /* Ignore the current directory */
      if (strcmp (FindBuf3.achName, "."))
      {
        strcpy (&szFullPathSpec[1], FindBuf3.achName);
        strcat (szFullPathSpec, "]");
        WinInsertLboxItem (hWndCtl, LIT_SORTASCENDING,
          szFullPathSpec);
      }
      ulFileCount = 1;
    } while (!DosFindNext (hDir, &FindBuf3,
              sizeof(FILEFINDBUF3), &ulFileCount));
    DosFindClose (hDir);
  }
}

/* List drives if they were requested */
if (bListDrives)
{
  DosQueryCurrentDisk (&ulCurrentDrive, &ulDriveMap);
  cDrive = 'A';

  for (ulBit = 1; ulBit < 0x04000000; ulBit *= 2)
  {
    if (ulDriveMap & ulBit)
    {
      szDrive[2] = cDrive;
```

```
        WinInsertLboxItem (hWndCtl, LIT_END, szDrive);
      }
      cDrive++;
    }
  }

  /* Turn on redrawing of the listbox and invalidate it */
  WinEnableWindowUpdate (hWndCtl, TRUE);
  WinInvalidateRect (hWndCtl, NULL, FALSE);

  /* Reset the pointer */
  WinSetPointer (HWND_DESKTOP, hPtr);

  return;
}

/* --------------------------------------------------------------
   GetFileAttributes:

   Build the file attribute flags based on the current settings of
   the checkboxes in the dialog windows.
   -------------------------------------------------------------- */

ULONG GetFileAttributes (HWND hWnd)
{
  ULONG ulFileAttr = FILE_NORMAL;

  if (WinQueryButtonCheckstate (hWnd, IDC_READONLY))
    ulFileAttr |= FILE_READONLY;
  if (WinQueryButtonCheckstate (hWnd, IDC_HIDDEN))
    ulFileAttr |= FILE_HIDDEN;
  if (WinQueryButtonCheckstate (hWnd, IDC_SYSTEM))
    ulFileAttr |= FILE_SYSTEM;
  if (WinQueryButtonCheckstate (hWnd, IDC_DIRECTORY))
    ulFileAttr |= FILE_DIRECTORY;
  if (WinQueryButtonCheckstate (hWnd, IDC_ARCHIVED))
    ulFileAttr |= FILE_ARCHIVED;
  if (WinQueryButtonCheckstate (hWnd, IDC_MUSTHAVE_READONLY))
    ulFileAttr |= MUST_HAVE_READONLY;
  if (WinQueryButtonCheckstate (hWnd, IDC_MUSTHAVE_HIDDEN))
    ulFileAttr |= MUST_HAVE_HIDDEN;
  if (WinQueryButtonCheckstate (hWnd, IDC_MUSTHAVE_SYSTEM))
    ulFileAttr |= MUST_HAVE_SYSTEM;
  if (WinQueryButtonCheckstate (hWnd, IDC_MUSTHAVE_DIRECTORY))
    ulFileAttr |= MUST_HAVE_DIRECTORY;
  if (WinQueryButtonCheckstate (hWnd, IDC_MUSTHAVE_ARCHIVED))
    ulFileAttr |= MUST_HAVE_ARCHIVED;

  return (ulFileAttr);
}
```

```
/* -----------------------------------------------------------
   DlgDirList:

   Fill a listbox control with the list of files, directories,
   and/or drives based on the specified file flags. Update the
   static control with the path specification for the list of
   files.
   ----------------------------------------------------------- */

BOOL DlgDirList (HWND hWnd, PSZ pszPathSpec, LONG lIDListBox,
                 LONG lIDStaticPath, ULONG ulFileType,
                 BOOL bListDrives)
{
  HWND         hWndCtl;
  PSZ          pszCur;
  PSZ          pszSlash    = NULL;
  CHAR         cTempChar;
  BOOL         bWildCard   = FALSE;
  ULONG        ulCurrentDrive;
  ULONG        ulDriveMap;
  ULONG        ulSize;

  /* Build the fully qualified path specification for the directory
     and/or filename. If no path is specified then use the current
     drive and directory.  */

  if (pszPathSpec)
  {
    if (*pszPathSpec)
    {
      /* Build requested path with wildcard characters */

      strcpy (szFullPathSpec, pszPathSpec);
      pszSlash = szFullPathSpec + strlen(szFullPathSpec);

      /* If the last character is a colon or backslash then just
         append "*.*" */

      cTempChar = *(pszSlash - 1);
      if ((cTempChar == ':') || (cTempChar == '\\'))
        strcat (szFullPathSpec, "*.*");
      else
      {
        /* Search backwards for the first occurrence of a
           wildcard or a backslash or colon */

        while (pszSlash != szFullPathSpec)
        {
          pszSlash--;
          if ((*pszSlash == '*') || (*pszSlash == '?'))
          {
            bWildCard = TRUE;
            break;
          }
          else if ((*pszSlash == '\\') || (*pszSlash == ':'))
            break;
```

```
      }

      /* If a wildcard was not found then append "\\*.*" */
      if (!bWildCard)
        strcat (szFullPathSpec, "\\*.*");
    }
  }
  else
      strcpy (szFullPathSpec, "*.*");

  /* Query the full path specification */
  if (DosQueryPathInfo (szFullPathSpec, FIL_QUERYFULLNAME,
        szFullPathSpec, sizeof(szFullPathSpec)))
  {
    WinAlarm (HWND_DESKTOP, WA_WARNING);
    return (FALSE);
  }

  /* Locate the last slash in the fully qualified pathname. We
     are guaranteed that a backslash exists. */

  pszSlash = szFullPathSpec + strlen(szFullPathSpec) - 1;
  while (*pszSlash != '\\')
    pszSlash—;

  /* Copy the filename portion of the path to pszPathSpec  */
  strcpy (pszPathSpec, pszSlash + 1);

  /* Set the current drive and directory */
  if (*(pszSlash - 1) == ':')
    *(pszSlash + 1) = '\0';
  else
    *pszSlash = '\0';
  if (DosSetDefaultDisk (szFullPathSpec[0] - 'A' + 1) ¦¦
      DosSetCurrentDir (&szFullPathSpec[2]))
  {
    WinAlarm (HWND_DESKTOP, WA_WARNING);
    return (FALSE);
  }
}
else
{
  /* As a default us the current drive and directory */
  strcpy (szFullPathSpec, " :\\");
  DosQueryCurrentDisk (&ulCurrentDrive, &ulDriveMap);
  szFullPathSpec[0] = 'A' + ulCurrentDrive - 1;
  ulSize = sizeof(szFullPathSpec) - 3;
  DosQueryCurrentDir (0, &szFullPathSpec[3], &ulSize);
  strcat (szFullPathSpec, "\\*.*");
  pszPathSpec = "*.*";
}

/* If there is a static control window then display path */
if (lIDStaticPath &&
    (hWndCtl = WinWindowFromID (hWnd, lIDStaticPath)))
  DrawPathWithEllipses (hWndCtl);
```

```
  if (lIDListBox &&
      (hWndCtl = WinWindowFromID (hWnd, lIDListBox)))
    FillDlgDirListBox (hWndCtl, pszPathSpec, ulFileType, bListDrives);

  return (TRUE);
}

/* ------------------------------------------------------------
   DlgDirSelect:

   Retrieve the current selection from a listbox that was filled
   using DlgDirList. Format the returned string appropriately.
   ------------------------------------------------------------ */

BOOL DlgDirSelect (HWND hWnd, PSZ pszPathSpec, LONG lIDListBox)
{
  SHORT sSel;
  HWND  hWndCtl = WinWindowFromID (hWnd, lIDListBox);

  /* Get the currently selected item */
  if ((sSel = WinQueryLboxSelectedItem (hWndCtl)) == LIT_NONE)
    return (FALSE);

  /* Get the text for the selected item */
  WinQueryLboxItemText (hWndCtl, sSel, szFullPathSpec,
    sizeof(szFullPathSpec));

  /* If it was a drive then return the drive letter followed by
     a colon. If it was a directory then return the directory
     followed by a backslash. Otherwise, just return the
     filename. */
  if (szFullPathSpec[0] == '[')
  {
    if (szFullPathSpec[1] == '-')
    {
      *pszPathSpec       = szFullPathSpec[2];
      *(pszPathSpec + 1) = ':';
      *(pszPathSpec + 2) = '\0';
    }
    else
    {
      strcpy (pszPathSpec, &szFullPathSpec[1]);
      pszPathSpec[strlen(pszPathSpec) - 1] = '\\';
    }

    return (TRUE);
  }
  else
    strcpy (pszPathSpec, szFullPathSpec);

  return (FALSE);
}

/* --------------------- Dialog Function --------------------- */

MRESULT EXPENTRY DlgDirDlgProc (HWND hWnd, ULONG msg, MPARAM mp1,
```

```
                                  MPARAM mp2)
{
  BOOL    bHandled = TRUE;
  MRESULT mReturn  = 0;
  ULONG   ulFileAttrs;
  BOOL    bIncludeDrives;
  CHAR    szPathBuffer[CCHMAXPATH];
  CHAR    szFileBuffer[CCHMAXPATH];

  switch (msg)
  {
    case WM_INITDLG:
      /* Initialize check button states for all files */
      WinCheckButton (hWnd, IDC_READONLY,  TRUE);
      WinCheckButton (hWnd, IDC_HIDDEN,    TRUE);
      WinCheckButton (hWnd, IDC_SYSTEM,    TRUE);
      WinCheckButton (hWnd, IDC_ARCHIVED,  TRUE);
      WinCheckButton (hWnd, IDC_DIRECTORY, TRUE);
      WinCheckButton (hWnd, IDC_DRIVES,    TRUE);
      WinSendDlgItemMsg (hWnd, IDC_FILESPEC, EM_SETTEXTLIMIT,
        MPFROMSHORT(CCHMAXPATHCOMP), MPVOID);
      WinSetDlgItemText (hWnd, IDC_FILESPEC, "*.*");

      /* Fill the listbox with the files and directories */
      szFileBuffer[0] = '\0';
      DlgDirList (hWnd, szFileBuffer, IDC_FILELIST, IDC_PATH,
        FILES_ONLY | FILE_DIRECTORY, TRUE);
      break;

    case WM_COMMAND:
      switch (SHORT1FROMMP(mp1))
      {
        case DID_OK:
          /* Retrieve the file specification and file
             attributes */
          WinQueryDlgItemText (hWnd, IDC_FILESPEC,
              sizeof(szFileBuffer), szFileBuffer);
          ulFileAttrs    = GetFileAttributes (hWnd);
          bIncludeDrives = WinQueryButtonCheckstate (hWnd,
                             IDC_DRIVES);

          /* Fill the listbox with files and directories */
          DlgDirList (hWnd, szFileBuffer, IDC_FILELIST,
            IDC_PATH, ulFileAttrs, bIncludeDrives);
          break;

        case DID_CANCEL:
          WinDismissDlg (hWnd, 0);
          break;
      }
      break;

    case WM_CONTROL:
      if ((SHORT1FROMMP(mp1) == IDC_FILELIST) &&
          (SHORT2FROMMP(mp1) == LN_ENTER))
      {
```

```
        /* Double-click or enter in the listbox. Retrieve
           the selected item and refresh the listbox if the
           selected item is a directory or drive. */

        if (DlgDirSelect (hWnd, szPathBuffer, IDC_FILELIST))
        {
          /* Retrieve the file specification and file
             attributes */
          WinQueryDlgItemText (hWnd, IDC_FILESPEC,
            sizeof(szFileBuffer), szFileBuffer);
          if ((strlen (szPathBuffer) + strlen (szFileBuffer)) <
              sizeof(szPathBuffer))
            strcat (szPathBuffer, szFileBuffer);

          ulFileAttrs    = GetFileAttributes (hWnd);
          bIncludeDrives = WinQueryButtonCheckstate (hWnd,
                             IDC_DRIVES);

          /* Fill the listbox with files and directories */
          DlgDirList (hWnd, szPathBuffer, IDC_FILELIST,
            IDC_PATH, ulFileAttrs, bIncludeDrives);
        }
      }
      break;

    default:
      bHandled = FALSE;
      break;
  }

  if (!bHandled)
    mReturn = WinDefDlgProc (hWnd, msg, mp1, mp2);

  return (mReturn);
}
```

DLGDIR.H

```
/* -----------------------------------------------------------------
                        DlgDir Header File
                 Real World Programming for OS/2
          Copyright (c) 1994, 1994 Blain, Delimon, and English
---------------------------------------------------------------- */

#define FILES_ONLY (FILE_READONLY ¦ FILE_HIDDEN ¦ FILE_SYSTEM ¦ \
                    FILE_ARCHIVED)

/* Exported Function */
MRESULT EXPENTRY DlgDirDlgProc  (HWND,ULONG,MPARAM,MPARAM);

/* DlgDir Dialog Controls */

#define IDC_FILESPEC            600
#define IDC_PATH                601
#define IDC_FILELIST            602
```

```
#define IDC_READONLY            603
#define IDC_HIDDEN              604
#define IDC_SYSTEM              605
#define IDC_DIRECTORY           606
#define IDC_ARCHIVED            607
#define IDC_DRIVES              608
#define IDC_MUSTHAVE_READONLY   609
#define IDC_MUSTHAVE_HIDDEN     610
#define IDC_MUSTHAVE_SYSTEM     611
#define IDC_MUSTHAVE_DIRECTORY  612
#define IDC_MUSTHAVE_ARCHIVED   613
```

DLGDIR.DLG

```
/* -----------------------------------------------------------------
                        DlgDir Dialog
                Real World Programming for OS/2
         Copyright (c) 1994, 1994 Blain, Delimon, and English
----------------------------------------------------------------- */

DLGTEMPLATE IDD_DLGDIR LOADONCALL MOVEABLE DISCARDABLE
BEGIN
  DIALOG  "Dialog Title", IDD_DLGDIR, 20, -4, 288, 141, WS_VISIBLE,
          FCF_SYSMENU ¦ FCF_TITLEBAR ¦ FCF_NOBYTEALIGN
  BEGIN
    LTEXT           "File Name:", -1,  6, 126,  50,  8
    ENTRYFIELD      "", IDC_FILESPEC, 58, 126, 221,  8, ES_MARGIN
    LTEXT           "Files:",     -1,  6, 113,  20,  8
    LISTBOX             IDC_FILELIST,  6,  35, 109, 76, LS_HORZSCROLL
    LTEXT           "Path:",      -1,  6,  21,  24,  8
    LTEXT           "", IDC_PATH,     36,  21, 164,  8
    AUTOCHECKBOX    "Show Drives", IDC_DRIVES,  205, 21, 71, 10
    GROUPBOX        "Attributes", -1, 121, 35, 79, 64
    AUTOCHECKBOX    "ReadOnly",    IDC_READONLY,  125, 79, 58, 10
    AUTOCHECKBOX    "Hidden",      IDC_HIDDEN,    125, 69, 64, 10
    AUTOCHECKBOX    "System",      IDC_SYSTEM,    125, 59, 64, 10
    AUTOCHECKBOX    "Archived",    IDC_ARCHIVED,  125, 49, 64, 10
    AUTOCHECKBOX    "Directory",   IDC_DIRECTORY, 125, 39, 64, 10
    GROUPBOX        "Must Have",  -1, 201, 35, 79, 64
    AUTOCHECKBOX    "ReadOnly",    IDC_MUSTHAVE_READONLY,
                                   205, 79, 58, 10
    AUTOCHECKBOX    "Hidden",      IDC_MUSTHAVE_HIDDEN,
                                   205, 69, 64, 10
    AUTOCHECKBOX    "System",      IDC_MUSTHAVE_SYSTEM,
                                   205, 59, 64, 10
    AUTOCHECKBOX    "Archived",    IDC_MUSTHAVE_ARCHIVED,
                                   205, 49, 64, 10
    AUTOCHECKBOX    "Directory",   IDC_MUSTHAVE_DIRECTORY,
                                   205, 39, 64, 10
    PUSHBUTTON      "Show",        DID_OK, 6, 4, 40, 14
    PUSHBUTTON      "Cancel",      DID_CANCEL, 49, 4, 40, 14
  END
END
```

The listbox is initialized with the files from the current directory. This is accomplished with a call to DlgDirList in the WM_INITDLG message processing:

```
/* Fill the listbox with the files and directories */
szFileBuffer[0] = '\0';
DlgDirList (hWnd, szFileBuffer, IDC_FILELIST, IDC_PATH,
  FILES_ONLY ¦ FILE_DIRECTORY, TRUE);
```

The DlgDirList function has six parameters.

hWnd	Dialog window handle.
pszPathSpec	Path or file specification used for file searching. Upon return from DlgDirList the buffer referenced by this pointer is updated to contain the filename portion of the path specification.
lIDListBox	Identifier of the listbox control in the dialog to be filled.
lIDStaticPath	Identifier of the static control in the dialog to display the drive and directory of the listed files.
ulFileType	Attributes of the files to display. Any of the FILE_... attributes can be combined.
bListDrives	Indicates if the file listing should include a list of the available drive letters.

Note that if the pszPathSpec is NULL or a pointer to a null-string the current drive and directory are used and the file specification will be "*.*". The DlgDirList function begins by parsing the specified path to locate the file name. A call is made to DosQueryPathInfo using the FIL_QUERYFULLNAME option to determine if the name is valid:

```
if (DosQueryPathInfo (szFullPathSpec, FIL_QUERYFULLNAME,
      szFullPathSpec, sizeof(szFullPathSpec)))
{
  WinAlarm (HWND_DESKTOP, WA_WARNING);
  return (FALSE);
}
```

If a static control window identifier was specified, then the function DrawPathWithEllipses is called. This function will attempt to display the full path in the static control window. If the length of the text to display is too long to fit within the static control window, ellipses will replace interior components of the path. The function WinDrawText is used with the DT_QUERYEXTENT option to determine the length of the text that will be displayed.

If a listbox control window identifier was specified then the function FillDlgDirListBox is called. This function first finds all files matching the specified file flags. As long as at least one file attribute flag is specified or the MUST_HAVE_DIRECTORY flag is not specified the files will be enumerated. Next it enumerates the directories, if the FILE_DIRECTORY flag was specified. Finally, if the bListDrives parameter was set to TRUE the drives are added to the list. Note that directories are formatted within square brackets and drives are formatted within square brackets and hyphens. After returning from the DlgDirList function, the current drive and directory are changed to the drive and directory specified.

The file specification can be changed in the edit field at the top of the listbox. Clicking on the "Show" button will refresh the display. You can also double-click on any of the directory or drive entries in the listbox. Doing so will cause the `DlgDirSelect` function to be called to retrieve the currently selected entry. The `DlgDirSelect` function is necessary also, since the directory and drive entries have been formatted with brackets. The `DlgDirSelect` function has three parameters:

`hWnd`	Dialog window handle
`pszPathSpec`	Buffer to receive the selected path and file.
`lIDListBox`	Identifier of the listbox control in the dialog that was filled using `DlgDirList`.

If the currently selected entry is a directory or drive, `DlgDirSelect` will return the unformatted name in the buffer referenced by `pszPathSpec`. The return code is `TRUE` if the selected entry is a directory or drive, otherwise the return code is `FALSE`. In the `DlgDir` dialog, if the return code is `TRUE` then `DlgDirList` is called again to fill the listbox with the entries from the selected directory or drive.

Index

Symbols

A

B

C

T

U

V-W-X-Y-Z

Book ISBN 0-672-30563-1

What's on the Disk

- Complete source code for all sample programs in the book
- Executable versions of the programs
- Makefile for Borland C++, IBM C/Set2, Zortech C++, Watcom C/386, and CL386 compilers.

Installing the Disk

To copy the software to your hard drive, run the INSTALL.EXE program on the floppy disk. The INSTALL program is a Presentation Manager program.

You'll be able to select several options on the opening screen of the install program:

- Where the software will be installed on your hard drive. The default location is C:\RWPOS2.
- Which software components to install. All components will be installed unless you choose otherwise.
- Creation of a folder by the install program.

When you are ready, select *Install*. The program will notify you when the installation is complete. To install all the files on the disk, you'll need at least 2.5MB of free space on your hard drive.

Note: If you choose to install only some of the software during the installation, and you choose to create a folder, do not select *Create folder* when you run the install program again. Otherwise, a duplicate folder will be created on your desktop.